KU-602-704

Colonial America in an Atlantic World

A Story of Creative Interaction

T. H. Breen
Northwestern University

Timothy Hall
Central Michigan University

PEARSON
Longman

New York Boston San Francisco
London Toronto Sydney Tokyo Singapore Madrid
Mexico City Munich Paris Cape Town Hong Kong Montreal

Vice President and Publisher: Priscilla McGeehon
Acquisitions Editor: Ashley Dodge
Development Manager: Betty Slack
Executive Marketing Manager: Sue Westmoreland
Production Manager: Ellen MacElree
Project Coordination, Text Design, and Electronic Page Makeup: Nesbitt Graphics, Inc.
Cover Design Manager: Wendy Ann Fredericks
Cover Designer: Maria Illardi
Art Studio: Mapping Specialists Limited
Photo Researcher: Photosearch, Inc.
Manufacturing Buyer: Dennis J. Para
Printer and Binder: Hamilton Printing Company
Cover Printer: Phoenix Color Corps.

Library of Congress Cataloging-in-Publication Data

Breen, T. H.
    Colonial America in an Atlantic World : a story of creative interaction / T. H. Breen,
Timothy Hall.
        p. cm.
    Includes bibliographical references and index.
    ISBN 0-321-06181-0
    1. United States—History—Colonial period, ca. 1600-1775. 2. United States—Ethnic
relations. 3. Acculturation—United States—History. 4. United States—Social conditions—
To 1865. 5. North America—Colonization. I. Hall, Timothy D., 1955- II. Title.
E188.B79 2003
973.2—dc21   2003044489

Copyright © 2004 by Pearson Education, Inc.

All rights reserved. No part of this publication may be reproduced, stored in a retrieval system,
or transmitted, in any form or by any means, electronic, mechanical, photocopying, recording,
or otherwise, without the prior written permission of the publisher. Printed in the United States.

Please visit our website at http://www.ablongman.com

ISBN 0-321-061810

    3 4 5 6 7 8 9 10—HT—06 05 04

Contents

Part III   Provinces in a Contested Empire: The Eighteenth Century   243

Chapter 10   *Empires of Guns and Goods*
North America at the Opening of the Eighteenth Century   **245**

Chapter 11   *Shifting Borderlands*
Population Growth, Immigration, and the Movement of Peoples in Eighteenth-Century America   **272**

Chapter 12   *The Anglicization of Provincial America*   **298**

Chapter 13   *Slavery and African American Cultures in the Colonial British Atlantic*   *324*

Chapter 14   *Contesting Rule in a Commercial Empire*   *351*

Maps

Preface

Colonial America in an Atlantic World approaches the history of colonial America as a story of dynamic interaction among the peoples of four continents and a multiplicity of nations scattered across the Atlantic world of the fifteenth to the eighteenth centuries. The narrative centers on the development of the North American region that became the United States. Yet we have sought to capture the drama of colonial cultural and social development as it unfolded in a persistent context of transatlantic imperial conflict, complex interactions among Europeans and indigenous peoples of North and South America, the tragic enslavement and transport of African peoples to the New World, and the creation of resilient African American cultures within diverse colonial contexts. In this way we have sought to capture the fresh picture of colonial American development that has been emerging from a quarter-century of historical scholarship and have set it within a narrative that will engage readers with a vivid sense of the past. We hope that the organization and length will make the text especially useful for providing students of history a comprehensive overview of colonial development which they can deepen through further investigation of specialized works like those included in each chapter's bibliographic essay.

APPROACH AND THEMES

Colonial America in an Atlantic World explores the creative adaptation of various European, American Indian, and African peoples to the unprecedented presence of one another and to the variety of social, political, environmental, and cultural processes set in motion by European exploration and settlement. We have sought to maintain a balance of emphasis among social, cultural, economic, and political dimensions of early American experience, since each comprises a field of creative human endeavor and adaptation. The narrative expresses our view of history as a distinctly human process rather than an impersonal unfolding of inexorable forces. We believe that the history of colonial North America, like all other history, was made by the everyday choices of human beings in anticipation of or in response to the specific circumstances in which they found themselves.

In recounting the story of the colonial American past, we see worlds in flux. Early Africans, Europeans, and American Indians first encountered one another in a variety of contexts often centered on exchange. Contact often provided the various groups fresh opportunities to explore mutual benefits such as trade or military alliance. To be sure, such exchanges often embroiled the participants in conflict, but European conquest and exploitation were by no means inevitable. Diverse patterns of exchange and exploitation developed in ways powerfully shaped by differing local circumstances and schemes of value. American Indians and Africans alike selectively appropriated European goods or practices, adapting them to uses often very different from what European makers intended. Enslaved Africans found themselves forced to draw on disparate languages, rituals, traditions, and musical forms of their scattered coastal African homes. By combining these with selected European and American Indian elements, they created distinctive African American cultures that enabled them to survive the brutal experience of slavery. European colonists also adapted traditional customs, modes of rural life, legal and political forms to a New World of apparently abundant land and few of the centralizing institutions that had shaped political and social life at home.

As colonization proceeded into the eighteenth century, the patterns of interaction increasingly came to be structured by a contest among powerful European rivals for control of New World territory and resources. The growth of transatlantic communication and commerce drew successive generations of colonists more tightly into competing imperial systems. England's mainland North American colonies grew in population and economic power, attracting a fresh wave of migrants from the British Isles and German lands who steadily pushed into backcountry regions occupied by native peoples and counterclaimed by the French. Profits from mainland and Caribbean plantations anchored a burgeoning Atlantic traffic in colonial staples, English manufactured goods, and African slaves. Yet Africans and American Indians remained active, influential participants throughout this period. Indian peoples such as the Iroquois and African states such as Dahomey retained a robust capacity for economic and military action which colonial authorities could not afford either to take for granted or ignore. Even as slaves or conquered peoples, Indians and Africans remained active participants in the creation and development of a colonial Atlantic world.

STRUCTURE AND FEATURES

The structure and features of *Colonial America in an Atlantic World* are intended to stimulate student interest and to reinforce learning. The book traces the theme of creative interaction and adaptations within a three-part structure organized chronologically. The first three chapters of the book comprise Part I, "Three Worlds Meet." The first chapter of this section reviews the pre-Columbian background of Europe, Africa, and the Americas. The next two chapters survey sixteenth-century Iberian colonization of the Caribbean and North America and the contest among other European powers for entry into this lucrative Atlantic system. Together, these chapters provide an indispensable historical context for understanding the specific shape taken by English, Dutch, and French colonization of North America during the following century. The six chapters of Part II, "The Contest for Seventeenth-Century Settlement," focus more closely on English and Dutch colonization of the Caribbean and North America while continuing to trace Spanish and French development on the North American continent. The varieties of adaptation that took place in each colonial region help explain both the striking diversity that appeared—even among colonies established by the same European nation—and the course of imperial conflict that emerged among various European and native rivals for North America. Part III, "Provinces in a Contested Empire: The Eighteenth Century," which comprises the final five chapters of the book, surveys the maturation of Anglo-American colonies through the continuing process of adaptation. It sets this process within a context of an accelerating struggle among the British and French for control of the North Atlantic world as Spanish influence in the region waned.

Each chapter of *Colonial America in an Atlantic World* opens with an account of human experience designed to engage the reader, raise one or more significant questions about the chapter topics, and provide a concrete example of how inhabitants of the period experienced the historical changes of their era. Chapters are organized chronologically and by colonial region, incorporating the main theme of the text in the appropriate context. Each chapter includes a brief chronology and a bibliographic essay that includes works consulted in preparation of the chapter and offers additional suggestions for further investigation.

ACKNOWLEDGMENTS

We acknowledge with gratitude the contributions of the conscientious historians who served as reviewers of the manuscript. Their thoughtful comments and valuable suggestions have greatly strengthened the final product.

Chris Beneke
The Citadel

James Bratt
Calvin College

Patricia Cleary
California State University

Martin Cohen
Los Angeles Mission College

Chris Daniels
Michigan State University

Thomas Gage
Lincoln University

H. Warren Gardner
University of Texas of the Permian Basin

John V. Jezierski
Saginaw Valley State University

John T. Juricek
Emory University

Jessica Kross
University of South Carolina

Johanna Miller Lewis
University of Arkansas at Little Rock

Cathy Matson
University of Delaware

Timothy E. Morgan
Christopher Newport University

Rick Pointer
Westmont College

Louis Potts
University of Missouri at Kansas City

Tom Ray
Wayland Baptist University

James B. M. Schick
Pittsburgh State University

Brenda T. Schoolfield
Bob Jones University

Rebecca Shoemaker
Indiana State University

Edward H. Tebbenhoff
Luther College

Eldon R. Turner
University of Florida

T. H. Breen
Timothy Hall

Part I

Three Worlds Meet

"I have found a continent more densely peopled and abounding in animals than our Europe or Asia or Africa," the explorer Amerigo Vespucci reported to his Florentine sponsors in 1503. "These we may rightly call a new world, because our ancestors had no knowledge of them, and it will be a matter wholly new to all those who hear about them."

The "new world" that Vespucci saw soon came to bear his name as word of America spread throughout Europe. The news stimulated a rush of exploration across the Atlantic: adventurers in search of treasure for themselves and empire for their sovereigns, as well as missionaries seeking converts to Christianity. Opportunities for enterprise seemed boundless. Within a few decades after Columbus first set foot on the island of Hispaniola, the Americas were undergoing a cataclysmic change that shattered the old world of the native Indian peoples who had inhabited the landmass for thousands of years before European encounter. The transformation quickly swept Africa into its wake as America's new overlords brought Africans in chains to replenish a native labor supply unexpectedly decimated by the introduction of epidemic disease to the Americas.

Iberian adventurers and missionaries dominated the New World in the sixteenth century. Spain took possession of vast territories rich in precious metals, which enriched the entire European economy as they entered circulation through the port of Seville. Spanish rulers initially hoped to secure all lands discovered in the western Atlantic through the Treaty of Tordesillas in 1494. Yet the subsequent discovery that the Brazilian coast lay east of the treaty line allowed Portugal to stake its own claim to New World territory that was rich in dyewood and soil suitable for sugar cultivation.

Ambitious European rivals viewed the burgeoning Iberian empires with a mixture of envy and fear. By the 1560s both England and France were mounting vigorous challenges to Iberian hegemony in the New World. Soon Spain's rebellious northern provinces in the Netherlands entered the fray. The ensuing contest for treasure and territory brought a fresh wave of contact and exchange as northern Europeans raided Spanish and Portuguese possessions and probed for resources and trading partners not yet exploited by the Iberians.

Spanish authorities found themselves increasingly pressed. They strengthened the armed escorts of their treasure fleet. They seized foreign vessels in American waters and enslaved the crews in galleys or on plantations. They patrolled the North American coastline, searching out rival settlements, razing the buildings, and enslaving or killing the inhabitants. They sent out missionaries to win converts, establish missions, and strengthen ties with native peoples in hopes of shutting their rivals out. Yet English, French, and Dutch raiders kept striking at the edges of Spain's mighty but increasingly brittle empire, exploiting every weakness they could find and growing more effective with every success. By the end of the sixteenth century, the widening cracks in Iberian hegemony were creating new opportunities for rivals to gain permanent colonial footholds in the New World.

Chapter 1

On the Eve of Conquest
Worlds Old and New

In 1519, the conquistador Bernal Díaz del Castillo caught his first glimpse of the great Aztec city of Tenochtitlán. Nothing in his own experience had prepared him for such a moment. The people who constructed such a civilization were obviously not inferior beings. Indeed, their architectural achievements rivaled those of contemporary Europeans. The grandeur and sophistication of the Aztec city on Lake Texcoco—the "Venice of America," as one historian has called it—overwhelmed the Spanish soldier who described "the great towers and temple pyramids and buildings rising from the water, all built of masonry." Aztec leaders invited the Spanish to stay in spacious palaces constructed of "beautiful stone work and cedar wood, and the wood of other sweet-scented trees, with great rooms and courts, wonderful to behold, covered with awnings of cotton cloth." Outside their chambers lay orchards and gardens so wonderful that Díaz "never tired of looking at the diversity of the trees, and noting the scent which each one had, and the paths full of roses and flowers, and the many fruit trees and native roses, and the pond of fresh water."

Such physical splendor raised for the Europeans hard questions about the histories of the peoples they encountered in the New World. After all, these groups could not convincingly be classified as primitive. Díaz concluded on the basis of his own observations that the great temple pyramid at Tenochtitlán had been built "more than a thousand years ago." Although the conquistador missed his guess—in 1519 the temple was not much more than 100 years old—Díaz was right about the antiquity of the larger native cultural traditions that produced such architectural marvels. Other Europeans speculated that Aztec and other American civilizations must have originated in biblical times, when lost Hebrew tribes somehow traveled to America. The Europeans reasoned that it must have required at least a millennium to develop sophisticated law codes, advanced methods of record-keeping, and innovative mathematics, producing by the year 1492 a rich fund of shared knowledge capable of sustaining vast and populous empires.

Like so much that the Indian peoples of North America lost during the period of the conquest, they forfeited their past. Contagious disease and chronic warfare decimated indigenous populations so quickly and so thoroughly that the Europeans treated Indians as men and women without a real history. The newcomers established settlements on the ruins of ancient America, ignoring as they colonized the significance of the physical evidence they could see with their own eyes. It was as if the Indians had been frozen in time, simply waiting for the dynamic Europeans to arrive. Modern historians have sometimes replicated the interpretive errors of the earliest colonists by treating the experience of the Native Americans before Columbus as part of an insignificant and timeless past, thus discounting what we now know were a multiplicity of long and complex Indian histories that had been unfolding for thousands of years before Díaz and the other conquistadores reached Mexico. Far from being passive victims of the conquest, the Indians brought sophisticated cultural traditions to their exchanges with Europeans and Africans, influencing powerfully the character of the interracial societies that developed in the New World.

In much the same manner, modern historians have undervalued the complex and separate histories of West African peoples on the eve of American conquest. The focus of this literature has been on slavery and the effects of racism in the New World—important topics to be sure—but a perspective that has inadvertently served to deflect our attention away from different, often competing ethnic identities within West Africa. We are left with a homogenized African past that bears no more relation to reality than does the notion of an unchanging pre-Columbian America.

A recent outpouring of scholarship reminds us that none of the three worlds—European, African, or American—were either new or united when they came into sustained contact in the sixteenth century. Each world was divided into a multiplicity of nations and peoples embroiled in intense and constantly shifting conflicts and alliances. Each participant brought to the New World encounter conflicting cultural beliefs, assumptions, aspirations, customs, and practices that had been shaped by long historical development. The diverse perspectives that each world brought to the encounter sometimes overlapped, allowing them to find common ground for cooperation. On other occasions conflicting agendas sparked deadly clashes, which engulfed neighboring peoples as well. Whatever the outcome, the processes of conflict, adaptation, resistance, and accommodation that marked colonial American history were conditioned by histories that had been shaping each world long before Columbus plotted his westward course in 1492.

NATIVE AMERICANS BEFORE CONQUEST

By 1492, thousands of years of development had produced tremendous linguistic and cultural diversity among the original inhabitants of North America. Hundreds of distinct nomadic hunting bands traversed the northern woods and plains in search of game. Groups of traders often served as middlemen between the hunter-gatherers and the more settled farming bands of the Great Lakes and Eastern Woodlands. Great civilizations had risen and declined along the Mississippi and Ohio River systems. Populations in well-developed agricultural regions like the Valley of Mexico probably rivaled that of similar regions in Europe, Asia, and Africa. The origins of this dynamic world remain obscure, but scholars have begun to tease the broad outline of its development from a sketchy archaeological record.

In 1798, the revered Miami chief Little Turtle traveled on a diplomatic mission to the U.S. capital at Philadelphia, where he met a fellow visitor, the French aristocrat Constantin-François de Chasseboeuf. Like many contemporaries, this French man of letters was fascinated by the history of America, and he decided to test his theories concerning the Asian origins of Native Americans on the eminent Miami leader. Chasseboeuf noted the facial similarities between American Indian and Asian Tartars and used a map to point out the narrow gap between Asia and North America across the Bering Sea. Little Turtle offered a different interpretation of the evidence. "Isn't it possible," he replied, "that the Tartars, who resemble us so closely, came from America? Is there evidence to the contrary? Why shouldn't we have been born here?"

America's First Immigrants

Although archaeologists have discovered much new evidence since Little Turtle's retort to Chasseboeuf, debate persists today over most aspects of American Indian history prior to Columbus's arrival in America in 1492. Many Indian groups insist that their ancestors were truly indigenous North Americans rather than ancient migrants from the Eastern Hemisphere. Experts continue to debate such issues as the timing of migration, the patterns of interaction among various cultures, and the trajectories of expansion, exchange, and cultural diffusion prior to the arrival of Europeans. Much remains to be learned. Nevertheless, the painstaking archaeological, linguistic, and anthropological research of the past several decades provides good basic insights into the experiences of American peoples before Columbus.

Archaeologists are uncertain when the first migrants entered North America. Most now believe that people were inhabiting the continent at least 30,000 years ago. All agree that at the time of the initial migration, the earth's climate was considerably colder than it is today. Huge glaciers, often more than a mile thick, pushed as far south as the present states of Illinois and Ohio. Much of the world's moisture was transformed into ice, and the oceans dropped hundreds of feet below their current level. The receding waters created the subcontinent of Beringia, spanning the distance between Asia and North America now covered by the Bering Sea.

The northern region of Beringia was most likely an area of low, marshy land that was free of glacial ice for several long periods. Temperate climatic cycles during those times opened the way for small bands of spear-throwing Siberian hunters to chase giant mammals—woolly mammoths and mastodons, all now extinct—into North America. Other bands probably arrived in North America from fishing communities established along the Beringian coast and an Aleutian island chain made much longer than the present one by the low sea level. These hunters and fishermen were the first human beings to set foot on a vast, uninhabited continent. The migrations continued for thousands of years, interrupted only by the ebb and flow of the ocean and glaciers that periodically blocked passage.

Because these migrations took place over a long period of time and involved small, independent bands of nomadic people, the groups never developed a sense of themselves as representing a single ethnic or racial group. The isolated bands distributed themselves across two continents, each pursuing its own interests as it adjusted to various microenvironments. Some peoples, presumably those who had first crossed the land bridge, migrated the longest distances, settling South and Central America. The more recent arrivals probably remained in North America.

The migration experience had a significant role in shaping Native American cultures. The extended, small-scale, and highly opportunistic character of this human transfer may explain the obvious and profound differences distinguishing various Indian groups to this day. Over the centuries, relatively isolated lineage groups—in other words, people claiming a common ancestry—developed distinct languages. At the time of European conquest the Native Americans who settled north of Mexico spoke between 300 and 350 separate languages and comprised over a thousand different cultural groups and societies.

The Agricultural Revolution

Native hunter-gatherer cultures changed substantially during the long period before European colonization. The early Indians developed many of the same technologies that appeared in other parts of the world. Their single-most significant contribution was the introduction of agriculture. No one knows precisely when people first cultivated plants for food in North America, but archaeologists working in the Southwest have uncovered evidence suggesting that some groups were farming as early as 2000 B.C. These early cultivators depended on maize (corn), beans, and squash. Knowledge of the domestication of these crops spread slowly north and east, and by 800 B.C., cultivation of squash had reached present-day Michigan.

The agricultural revolution transformed Indian societies wherever cultivation developed. The availability of a more reliable food source helped liberate men and women from the insecurities of a nomadic existence based on hunting and gathering. A hunter consumed many calories constantly pursuing wild game. The vegetable harvest made it possible to establish permanent villages, and as the supply of food increased, the Native American population expanded. Population estimates for the precontact Americas are highly speculative and much contested. Historical demographers believe that sophisticated agricultural techniques had boosted the population of central Mexico to as much as 30 million by A.D. 1500. North of Mexico many societies continued to rely heavily on hunting and gathering, yet there too agriculture gradually boosted the population to anywhere from 4 to 10 million Indians by the time of first encounter with Europeans.

The practice of agriculture profoundly changed communal living in the Americas. As the population grew, the structure of Indian society changed. Urban centers began to emerge, making possible the development of specialized occupations, a growing complexity in the social structure, and a concentration of labor that produced impressive roads and architectural structures. The temple complexes at Cahokia on the Mississippi River, Teotihuacán in central Mexico, and Tikal in present-day Guatemala attest to an advanced society. By A.D. 1000 a number of sophisticated urban centers had sprung up in several parts of North America, served as nodes of far-flung exchange systems linking culture groups across half a continent.

Classical American Civilizations

In what is now the southwestern United States, Anasazi farmers, brick makers, and stonemasons built a network of towns stretching from Montezuma Canyon in present-day southern Colorado to Chaco Canyon in northwestern New Mexico. Dubbed by archaeologists the "Chaco phenomenon," this network encompassed more than 25,000 square miles. Straight, well-made roads up to 40 feet wide connected central towns with outlying villages and supply posts as far as 60 miles away. A complex settlement at Chaco Canyon served as the center of Anasazi society until approximately A.D. 1150. Chaco Canyon towns supported a population of at least 15,000 people. Another center at Mesa Verde sustained a population of at least 2,500 in dwellings dramatically situated among almost inaccessible cliffs, while a cluster of settlements in nearby Montezuma Canyon was home to as many as 30,000. The Indians of these sophisticated communities excelled in construction and craftsmanship as well as agriculture, and they almost certainly carried on extensive trade far beyond their frontiers. Exchanges took place between these core settlements and a neighboring center on the site of present-day Santa Fe. One historian has recently argued that Chaco Canyon lay on a long-distance trade route that extended south through Casas Grandes in northwestern Chihuahua and further into central Mexico.

The Chaco Phenomenon

Anasazi achievements are evident in the remains of their towns as well as in the surprising emergence of an agricultural society in a region as arid as the San

Chaco Canyon's Pueblo Bonito ruins, located in New Mexico's San Juan River basin, display the sophistication of twelfth-century A.D. Anasazi culture. This semicircular Great House originally consisted of multiple stories containing many apartment-like dwellings. At its peak, this central Anasazi town was home to over 1,000 people.

Photo by David Muench

Juan Basin. Semicircular Chacoan great houses such as the one at Pueblo Bonito were located at points where major drainage systems converged to maximize the use of floodwaters. Large logs required to support the roofs of Anasazi kivas were transported from forests as far as 60 miles away. The construction of cliff dwellings at Mesa Verde required considerable engineering skill as well as large-scale organization of labor. Mesa Verde farmers also built an ingenious system of irrigation ditches and reservoirs capable of storing up to half a million gallons of water. Anasazi water conservation supported a flourishing civilization throughout the region until about A.D. 1300, when experts believe that a dry climatic cycle made it impractical to maintain such population densities. The ultimate fate of these extraordinary people remains a mystery. The Anasazi probably dispersed into smaller villages where they were exposed to attacks by Indian enemies. Most seem to have been absorbed into later Native American groups that the Spaniards collectively termed the "Pueblos."

Societies of Mesoamerica

Hundreds of miles to the south of Chaco Canyon lay the great city-states of Mesoamerica. The cultivation of maize and other staple crops enabled the Indians of Mexico and Central America to begin organizing into sedentary farming communities as early as 3000 B.C. By the first centuries A.D., inhabitants were constructing the sophisticated Mayan centers of the Yucatán, the highland city of Monte Albán, and the great Mesoamerican metropolis of Teotihuacán. Like the Incas who lived in present-day Peru, Mayan and Toltec peoples ruled their great city-states through government bureaucracies that controlled large tributary populations. The Mayans developed hieroglyphic writing as well as a solar calendar that predicted eclipses as accurately as any Old World systems. In size and population, Mesoamerican cities often exceeded those of medieval and early modern Europe. It is no wonder that when the Spanish conquistadores first saw Aztec "towns and villages built in the water," they asked "whether it was not all a dream."

The rise and fall of some Mesoamerican civilizations predated the European conquest. The Toltec and Mayan civilizations had faded to distant memory by A.D. 1250, when the Mexica migrated into the Valley of Mexico to begin their rapid rise to dominance. An aggressive, warlike people, this group of late Aztec arrivals established themselves in the region by occupying swampy, snake-infested territory no one else wanted. In 1325 the Mexica founded Tenochtitlán on an island in the center of marshy Lake Texcoco, and began transforming the swamps into a system of dikes, canals, and productive raised fields. Tenochtitlán's nobles extended the city-state's wealth and territorial influence by forging shrewd alliances with neighboring city-states, which they supplied with mercenary soldiers. By 1400, Lake Texcoco's swamps had become a ring of lush raised fields surrounding a beautiful lake, in the center of which rose the splendid capital city of Tenochtitlán. The city attracted migrants from all over the Valley of Mexico, and its population eventually reached 250,000. Aztec princes and nobles secured alliances with neighboring city-states through diplomacy and intermarriage, while Aztec warriors extended Tenochtitlán's dominance through conquest.

The Aztecs ruled by force, reducing defeated rivals to tributary status. When Hernán Cortés arrived in 1519, Aztec rule extended outward from Tenochtitlán to the Pacific coast as well as the Gulf of Mexico. Elaborate human sacrifice associated with Huitzilopochtli, the Aztec sun god, horrified Europeans, who seldom questioned the savagery of their own civilization. These Aztec ritual killings were connected to the agricultural cycle. The Indians believed the blood of their victims possessed extraordinary fertility powers and that daily human sacrifice ensured the return of the sun each morning. A fragment of an Aztec song-poem captures the fiercely self-confident spirit that once pervaded this militant culture:

> Proud of itself
> is the city of Mexico-Tenochtitlán. Here no one fears to die in war.
> This is our glory. . . .
> Who could conquer Tenochtitlán?
> Who could shake the foundation of heaven?

Far to the north and east, the extensive tributary systems that emptied into the great Mississippi River basin and the Gulf of Mexico supported a succession of highly developed societies, some of whose trade and influence extended over an

Empires of Exchange in North America

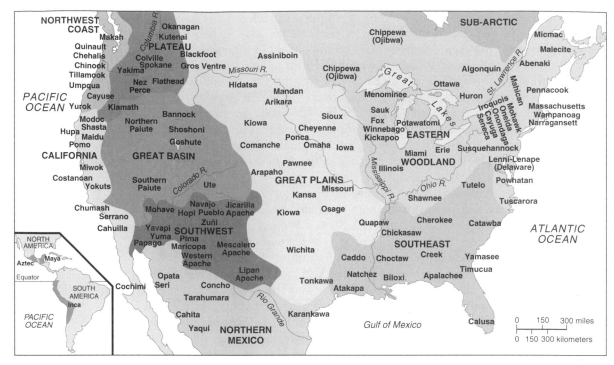

North American Amerindian Groups and Culture Areas in the Era of Contact

Great linguistic and cultural diversity characterized Native American peoples of the sixteenth and seventeenth centuries. Groups possessed complex social and religious systems, and many pursued a well-developed agricultural technology.

area as large as modern India. The mound-building Adena and Hopewell cultures flourished in the Ohio River Valley and its tributaries from 1000 B.C. to A.D. 400. They constructed impressive burial and ceremonial mounds of dirt laboriously piled one basketful at a time by members of large kin groups. Artifacts buried with the Hopewell dead—items containing Lake Superior copper and silver, quartz objects from southern Appalachia, trade goods and materials from Florida, seashells from the Gulf of Mexico, and obsidian from Yellowstone—testify to the vast extent of the Hopewell trading system at the height of their influence in the third and fourth centuries A.D.

Mississippian culture groups who inhabited the southeast and the Mississippi Valley around A.D. 1100 constructed large moundlike ceremonial centers and lived in well-populated towns. The greatest, Cahokia near present-day St. Louis, was dominated by flat-topped, pyramid-shaped earthen mounds, the largest of which was over 100 feet tall. A surrounding palisade separated the great mound, its plaza, and a 200-acre complex of mounds and dwellings from the rest of the city. The entire site supported a population of between 20 and 40 thousand, nearly as large as that of medieval London. Various local Mississippian communities extended along the Mississippi Valley as far north as southern Wisconsin and south and east to Florida and made their influence felt through a trade as far-flung as the earlier Hopewell culture. Cahokia itself went into decline and was largely abandoned by A.D. 1400, permitting Mississippian cultures elsewhere to expand. Rival provinces or chiefdoms vied for preeminence in the Southeast throughout the following century, producing nations such as the Natchez, Choctaw, and Cherokee that endure to the present day. The Mississippian chiefdom of Coosa, centered on the site now known as Little Egypt in northwest Georgia, had achieved regional supremacy by the time Hernando de Soto arrived in 1540.

Europeans who seized what became known as New England and Virginia encountered an entirely different Indian world. There were no great cities along the North Atlantic coast. Indeed, the historian Colin Calloway has observed that the Europeans who laid claim to eastern North America arrived at the back door of an Indian America whose major exchange networks had been centered on the Mississippi Valley and the Gulf coast for much of the previous millennium. By 1500, however, Atlantic coastal Indians lived on the fringes of a system that was in severe decline. The causes of this decline remain unknown, but the collapse of the great Mississippian trading network threw much of eastern North America into flux as various groups competed for territory and influence. Indians of the Northeast did not practice the type of intensive agriculture common among inhabitants of the Gulf coast and Southwest; generally they supplemented mixed farming with seasonal hunting and gathering. Conservative estimates put the total population at less than a million before the arrival of Europeans, and most belonged to what ethnographers term the Eastern Woodland cultures. Small bands formed villages during the warm summer months. The women cultivated maize and other crops while the men hunted and fished. During the winter, difficulties associated with feeding so many people forced these communities to disperse. Each family lived off the land as best it could.

Eastern Woodland Cultures

The northeastern woodlands were nevertheless home to a number of nations and confederacies that were coming to exert considerable influence in their own right. A vast exchange network stretched from western Lake Superior to the St. Lawrence River Valley. Indian traders such as the western Ojibway bartered meat and skins in exchange for maize produced by Iroquoian-speaking Huron farmers of southern Ontario.

To the south of Lake Ontario lay the settlements of the Hurons' powerful enemies, the Hodenosaunee, or People of the Long House. More than a century before their first contact with Europeans, the Five Nations of this people—the Mohawks, Oneidas, Onondagas, Cayugas, and Senecas—formed what European observers termed the Iroquois League. According to oral traditions, the league originated during a time of constant feuding among the Five Nations and surrounding groups. This state continued until an Onondaga chieftain remembered as Hayenwatha or Hiawatha lost three of his daughters in a conflict, or, in some versions of the tradition, through the malevolent powers of a twisted Onondaga shaman. Rather than seeking blood vengeance as the Iroquois "mourning war" tradition demanded, Hiawatha determined to break the cycle of violence. A stranger named Deganawidah met Hiawatha in the forest and assuaged his grief with comforting words and wampum beads. Together Hiawatha and Deganawidah, who became known as the Peacemaker, traveled from village to village, persuading the Five Nations to adopt laws and teachings of peace, each of which they had woven onto a string of wampum for posterity to remember. The nations agreed to unite in a Great League of Peace and Power for common defense. The Seneca became Keepers of the Western Door; the Mohawk, Keepers of the Eastern Door; and the Onondaga, Keepers of the Council Fire. The Cayuga and Oneida comprised the league's younger moiety.

Confederation generated strength. The League of Peace made the Iroquois a powerful military force capable of holding its own against other Indian groups as well as Europeans. Although the Five Nations apparently did not establish sustained diplomatic or trade relations with surrounding groups, they did view their league as a great shelter for other peoples. They could extend protection to client groups through treaty, and they augmented their own population and increased the league's ethnic diversity by taking in refugees and adopting captives.

To the east of the Iroquois League lived many bands of Algonquian-speaking peoples, the Indians whom most seventeenth-century English settlers first encountered as they explored and settled the Atlantic coast from North Carolina to Maine. Included in this large linguistic family were the Powhatans of tidewater Virginia, the Narragansetts of Rhode Island, and the Abenakis of northern New England.

Despite common linguistic roots, however, these scattered Algonquian communities would have found communication with each other extremely difficult. In their separate, often isolated environments, they had developed very different dialects. A sixteenth-century Narragansett, for example, could not have understood a Powhatan. Linguistic ties, moreover, had little effect on Indian politics. Algonquian groups who lived in different regions, exploited different resources, and spoke different dialects did not develop strong ties of mutual identity. When their own interests were involved, Algonquian leaders were more than willing to ally themselves with Europeans or "foreign" Indians against other Algonquians. This is an important point. These Indians did not see themselves as representatives of a single racial group, but as Narragansetts or Powhatans. Divisions among Indian groups would in time facilitate European conquest. Local Native American peoples greatly outnumbered the first settlers, and had the Europeans not forged alliances with the Indians, they could not so easily have gained a foothold on the continent.

However divided the Indians of eastern North America may have been, they shared many cultural values and assumptions. Most Native Americans, for example, defined their place in society through kinship. These personal bonds determined the character of economic and political relations. As historian James Axtell explains, "The basic unit of social membership in all tribes was the exogamous clan, a lineal descent group determined through one parent." The farming bands living in areas eventually claimed by England were often matrilineal, which meant in effect that the women owned the planting fields and houses, maintained tribal customs, and had a role in tribal government. Among the native communities of Canada and the northern Great Lakes, patrilineal forms were much more common. In these groups, the men owned the hunting grounds that the family needed to survive.

Eastern Woodland communities organized diplomacy, trade, and war around reciprocal relationships that impressed Europeans as being extraordinarily egalitarian, even democratic. Chains of authority were loosely structured. Native leaders were renowned public speakers because persuasive rhetoric was often their only effective source of power. It required considerable oratorical skills for an Indian leader to persuade independent-minded warriors to support a certain policy.

Before the arrival of the white settlers, wars among Eastern Woodland peoples took place on a small scale and were seldom very lethal. Young warriors attacked neighboring bands largely to exact revenge for a previous insult or the murder of a relative. Avengers tortured some captives to death, sparking cycles of revenge. Other captives they adopted into the community as replacements for fallen relatives.

AFRICA: DIVERSE PEOPLES AND COMPLEX HISTORIES

During the era of the European slave trade, a number of enduring myths arose about sub-Saharan Africa. Even today, some historians claim that the people who inhabited West and Central Africa 400 years ago were isolated from the rest of the world and possessed a simple, self-sufficient economy. Indeed, some scholars still depict this vast region stretching from the Senegal River south to modern Angola as a single cultural unit, the inhabitants of which shared common political, religious, and social values.

Sub-Saharan Africa defies such easy generalizations. The first Portuguese who explored the African coast during the fifteenth century encountered a great variety of political and religious cultures with long and distinguished histories. As with American Indians before Columbus, the work of archaeologists, ethnographers, and anthropologists over the past hundred years has done much to uncover the rich complexity of sub-Saharan Africa's ancient past. Written Arabic accounts of sub-Saharan Africa began appearing in the centuries after the Prophet Muhammad (A.D. 570–632) founded the religion of Islam. These accounts reveal how Islam became increasingly entwined with the history of sub-Saharan Africa even as they provide historians with a detailed record that supplements and enriches knowledge obtained through archaeological evidence. Around 1030 the King of Takrur, a small state in the Senegal Valley, converted to the Muslim religion. The new faith slowly spread to other kingdoms of the western Sudan, the Savannah region south of the Sahara called in Arabic *Bilād-es-Sudan*, the "Country of the Blacks." The advance of Islam helped to foster a growing exchange of goods, culture, and knowledge across the Sahara as Muslim scholars came south to teach the Koran, the sacred text of Islam, and as West African Muslims began making pilgrimages to Mecca on the Arabian peninsula. A French priest marveled in 1686 that African pilgrims were able to travel to "Mecca to visit Mahomet's tomb, although they are eleven or twelve hundred leagues distance from it." Other West Africans, such as those in ancient Ghana, prospered by participating in this expanding world of knowledge and commerce while resisting Islam in favor of various traditional religions.

Trade and Empire

In these complex societies, trade provided a powerful incentive for expansion. Muslim Berbers from North Africa and Tuaregs from the Sahara oases pressed southward in search of valuable commodities such as gold, spices, cloth, and slaves. In exchange they brought salt, a scarce and valuable commodity in West Africa. The salt trade stimulated the emergence of sophisticated, prosperous exchange networks that linked the villagers of Senegambia with the urban centers of Morocco, Tunisia, and Cyrenaica in northwest Africa. Great camel caravans regularly crossed the Sahara carrying trade goods that were exchanged for West African commodities. Some West African goods ultimately made their way into Europe through the Mediterranean trade route.

The growing trans-Sahara commerce stimulated the establishment of a succession of populous states, sometimes termed empires, which vied for control of lucrative trade routes and the prosperous cities that sprang up along them. The authority exercised by these states varied in extent and intensity: rulers rose through the influence of kinship groups as well as by personal ambition. The leaders of these kingdoms supplemented traditional, kin-based forms of leadership with a variety of formal structures, including Islamic law in those states whose leaders embraced Islam. Ancient African empires such as Ghana were vulnerable to external attack as well as internal rebellion. The oral and written histories of the region record the rise and fall of several large kingdoms.

Although ancient Ghana itself was only a memory when European traders arrived, other large kingdoms still dominated important nodes of African exchange. The empire of Mali reached its peak of development in the fourteenth century. Under Mali's greatest king, Mansa ("Lord") Kankan Mūsā, the empire extended over most of the western Sudan, including most of its prosperous trading centers. In 1324 Mansa Mūsā began a pilgrimage to Mecca, which became legendary for its magnificence and opulence. The Mali lord's generosity reportedly caused runaway inflation in Cairo by flooding the market with gold. Mali had lost much of its influence by the sixteenth century, but the kingdom continued to control the headwaters of the Senegal, Gambia, and Niger Rivers as well as the lucrative portage routes between them. Dyula and Wangara traders strategically located in towns between these great river systems could divert exports to the Atlantic from one river to the other depending on which route promised the best returns at a given point in time.

East of Mali on the great bend of the Niger River, the rival kingdom of Songhay grew steadily in power and influence through the sixteenth century. It began its rise when its chief city, Gao, gained independence from Mali's control in 1375. Songhay eventually came to incorporate the former Mali trade centers of Timbuktu and Jenné. To the southwest of Songhay and Mali, the Jolof state dominated the downriver region between the Senegal and Gambia Rivers to the coast, where this "mother state" controlled a number of lesser states also ruled by the Wolof people. The Yoruba kingdom of Oyo was similarly organized to control client states of the upper Niger delta. The kingdom of Benin, famed for its fine textiles and brass sculptures, also used such a system to control much of the lower Niger delta. Benin held the stretch of coastline still possessed by the modern state of that name as well as a large territory in what is now western Nigeria, including the important slave-trading port of Lagos. Further south near the mouth of the Congo River, the large and complex kingdoms of Loango and Kongo each commanded influence that extended over scores of smaller states nearby. Loango spanned an interconnected system of waterways to the north of the Congo that facilitated movement of goods on a large scale and was renowned for its production of fine cloth. Kongo's location along the south bank of the Congo River permitted its merchants to extend trade networks deep into Central Africa drawing wealth to the kingdom in the form of trade goods and slaves. The small powerful kingdom of Ndongo vied directly with Kongo for influence over neighboring states.

These and other West and Central African states wielded great power, often fielding formidable armies and cavalries to extend their borders and beat back rivals. Yet other West Africans such as the populous Igbo people preferred to live in what anthropologists call "stateless societies," largely autonomous communities organized around lineage structures or clans. Visitors and Igbo writers themselves described village government as democracies in which every man, and in some cases women, had a voice in decision making. The eighteenth-century Igbo author and abolitionist Olaudah Equiano—one of the earliest witnesses to the character of these societies—described his people as possessing and laboring to improve an "uncommonly rich and fruitful" land that blessed its inhabitants with benefits in the form of "the general healthiness of the people, and in their vigour and activity."

The complex of self-sufficient communities and states along the West and Central African coast supported significant coastal trade in addition to transporting goods northward along rivers and overland for trade with trans-Sahara merchants. Although Africans never developed long-distance oceangoing craft comparable to those of Europeans, the crews of large, sturdy African boats were highly skilled at managing the dangerous coastal surf. Indeed, European vessels commonly had to anchor far offshore and rely on African boatmen to transfer their cargos to land, and captains learned to avoid certain stretches of coast inhabited by fearsome African pirates who ambushed ships from open boats. This boatmanship enabled Africans to maintain control of much of the coastline well after contact with Europeans. Before then, such boats traveled from port to port, carrying valuable cargo such as iron bars and implements, a rich variety of cloth, gold, silver, kola, gum, and slaves. This early African maritime tradition helps explain why so many slaves in the Carolinas and Georgia were valued for their skill in handling small river craft.

The multiplicity of African states and societies obscured some important overarching unities among the peoples of various regions. Scholars now identify three broad cultural zones in West and Central Africa. The Upper Guinea cultural zone encompassed the region from the Senegal River to modern Liberia and incorporated the dialects of two great linguistic families, the Wolof and the Mande. Trade along the Senegal and Gambia Rivers brought these groups into routine contact,

African Societies and Cultures

producing extensive cultural exchange. Most people of the region spoke several languages, and Mandiga emerged as a common language of trade and diplomacy. The widespread interaction also facilitated the spread of Islam, which provided a shared set of beliefs that enabled the region's peoples to understand and communicate with each other. Islamic literacy strengthened these links further as Muslim scholars and missionaries traveled along the rivers and set up centers of learning in important towns. Even those groups who did not convert to Islam shared with the Muslims the belief in a supreme being. The Muslims, in turn, accepted many elements of local worldviews such as the practice of divination and the veneration of ancestors.

The Lower Guinea cultural zone stretched from the Ivory Coast to modern-day Cameroon. Little interaction took place between Lower and Upper Guinea; however, trade and travel flourished among the two major cultural and linguistic groups of Lower Guinea, the Akan of the west, many of whom mined gold, and the Aja farmers, fishermen, and salt traders of the east. A complex of lagoons and river systems linked the region's diverse states and societies, while linguistic similarities often made it possible for people from widely separated areas in the region to learn each other's language within a few weeks. By the seventeenth century, Yoruba emerged as the region's lingua franca. Islam was widespread along this zone's northern edge, whereas traditional religion dominated along the coast.

The third cultural zone, the Angola Coast of Central Africa, extended north and south from the mouth of the Congo River and stretched hundreds of miles inland throughout the Congo's vast network of tributaries. Most coastal peoples spoke either Kikongo or Kimbundu, two western Bantu languages as similar as Spanish and Portuguese. One or the other of these tongues served as the lingua franca among the linguistically diverse interior groups. Like the peoples of the two culture zones to the north, these peoples shared many religious concepts, artistic forms, social customs, and religious beliefs. In political life, however, sharp rivalries marked relations between the elite leaders of the many states, especially the powerful Kongo and Ndongo kingdoms. Yet ordinary people cared little for their rulers' stance toward other states, and they interacted readily with one another during war as well as peace.

In all three culture zones, women and men found their primary social identity within well-defined lineage groups. Everyone in a group claimed descent from a common ancestor, often traced through the mother's line. Clan elders usually settled disputes among members of their lineage groups. The elders also allocated the society's economic and human resources. In large, organized states the elders might comprise a group of electors who served as stakeholders for the state and chose successive rulers, often along hereditary lines. The elders or their chosen ruler often determined which inhabitants of a village or state received use of the land and even who might take a wife—critical decisions in the villages of West and Central Africa, because women and children cultivated the fields.

Despite the shared elements of culture within each of the three zones, differences in local linguistic, religious, artistic, and social customs persisted. People clung to local modes of expression. Most believed that spiritual beings could communicate with the physical world through revelation, and in most regions religious and political power went hand in hand. Yet different local groups employed diverse procedures to make sense of revelations, and the local deities that one group worshiped might go unacknowledged by neighboring peoples. In some states, religious and political leadership resided in a single individual or group, whereas other societies distinguished between priests and political leaders. Even in regions where a high percentage of the population embraced Islam, local differences persisted. Rulers of some West African states sought to organize their kingdoms and rule by Islamic law, whereas others, though Muslims themselves, chose to accommodate local traditions.

African Slavery

The practice of slavery was widespread in precontact Africa, though the institution functioned differently in Africa than it did in the plantation economies of the Americas. In African societies where all land was corporately owned, slaves "were the only form of private, revenue-producing property recognized in African law," according to the historian John Thornton. Because of the slaves' role within the African economy, ruling elites prized them highly, and rival states often went to war over slaves for the same reason that European powers battled over territory. Indeed, the quest for slaves made conflict among African states endemic long before Europeans entered the scene.

African slavery was much more diverse than the backbreaking production of export staples that characterized American plantation slavery. Some slaves in Africa did labor in the fields for masters, but many of these unfree people led lives similar to European peasants, working the land at their own direction and giving a small percentage of the crop to their masters as a sort of rent. Others performed domestic service. In the eyes of local law, wives and concubines were often slaves. Warrior slaves bore arms in military service, sometimes commanding a king's armies. Other slaves exercised great authority as deputies of a royal master or served in the court as scribes and scholars. The laws of some states extended ownership by ruling families or clans over all inhabitants of their dominions. Most laws also distinguished between "settled" and "trade" slavery. Trade slaves were enslaved through capture and held by right of conquest in lieu of death. Their captors often transported them long distances to be sold in faraway regions that made escape or rescue more difficult. Those who arrived at a final West African destination might often be assimilated into the local society. Slaves who accepted their lot might gain the protection of local law and be incorporated into their masters' kinship networks. Other trade slaves found themselves carried north across the Sahara and, after European contact, to plantations in the Atlantic islands and the Americas.

No matter where they found themselves, Africans experienced slavery as loss and injustice. Olaudah Equiano no doubt spoke for millions of earlier slaves whose memories went unrecorded when he described spending his first months of slavery in Africa "oppressed and weighed down by grief after my mother and friends." Though the apparent kindness of some African masters sometimes tempted him to "forget I was a slave," Equiano regarded the loss of his freedom as slavery's defining characteristic in Africa and America alike. In Africa, he remained vulnerable to the caprice of masters who might treat him as an adopted son one day and sell him into "hardship and cruelty" the next. Slavery among the Europeans sometimes reduced him to "grieving and pining, and wishing for death rather than anything else." Yet Equiano's "love of liberty" empowered him and other slaves to join in creating resilient African American cultures that sustained them through the harsh experience of slavery, providing strategies of survival, resistance, and sometimes escape from bondage.

EUROPE ON THE EVE OF CONQUEST

Fifteenth-century Europe entered a period of unprecedented expansion fueled by population growth, the opening of new trade, and a new curiosity about the world beyond European shores. Stories brought from distant lands by traders and explorers such as Marco Polo captivated Europeans, prompting them to see their societies as isolated, backward, and severely divided when compared with the impressive learning, technological achievements, and superior craftsmanship of Islamic society or the vastness of the Chinese empire. Much of the classical West's extensive knowledge of the world, lost to medieval Europeans, was preserved and cherished by Muslim scholars. Medieval Europe's loosely organized kingdoms had been vexed by fierce provincial loyalties. Dreadful plagues such as the Black Death discouraged people from thinking expansively about the world beyond their own immediate communities.

After 1400, however, conditions began to change. Europe became more prosperous, political authority became more centralized, and the overlapping movements of the Renaissance and the Reformation fostered an extraordinary intellectual ferment, religious reform, and political change. A major element in this shift was the slow but steady growth of the population after 1450. Historians are uncertain about the cause of this increase—after all, neither the quality of medicine nor personal sanitation improved much—but the result was a substantial rise in the price of land. Landlords profited from these trends, and as their income expanded, they demanded more consumer goods, often luxury items such as spices, silks, and jewels, that came from distant ports. Economic prosperity created powerful new incentives for exploration and trade even as new political and religious developments presented new opportunities to ambitious, talented persons of ordinary birth.

European Nation-States

The political centralization of the fifteenth and sixteenth centuries took place under a group of rulers sometimes referred to collectively as the New Monarchs. Before the mid-fifteenth century, powerful, highly independent men dominated small territories throughout Europe. Conceding only nominal allegiance to a king, these local barons—whom one historian called "overmighty subjects"—taxed the peasants and waged war against rivals. They also dispensed what passed for justice. The New Monarchs challenged the nobles' autonomy. The changes that accompanied this restructuring of national authority came slowly, and in many areas violently, but the results radically altered traditional political relationships between the nobility and the crown, and between the citizen and the state. The New

Monarchs of Europe hired armies and supported these largely mercenary troops with revenues generated by new, often bitterly hated taxes. They created more effective national courts of law. Although these monarchs were often despotic, they personified the emergent nation-states of Europe and brought a measure of peace to local communities weary of chronic feudal war.

Far-reaching political consolidation spread through most of western Europe. In England the Tudor monarch Henry VII (r. 1485–1509) defeated rival barons in 1485, bringing to an end a long period of civil uncertainty known as the Wars of the Roses. Louis XI, the French monarch (r. 1461–1483), strengthened royal authority by reorganizing state finances. The political unification of Spain began in 1469 with the marriage of Ferdinand of Aragon and Isabella of Castile.

These strong-willed monarchs forged nations out of groups of independent kingdoms. If political centralization had not occurred, the major European countries could not possibly have generated the financial and military resources necessary for worldwide exploration. As the New Monarchs competed among themselves for even greater wealth and power, the New World seemed a particularly inviting field of activity. Their ambitions brought the peoples of these continents into contact for the first time.

European Renaissance and Reformation: Expanding Imaginative Horizons

Worldwide exploration was not the primary goal of centralization of state authority. It was the unanticipated consequence of the restructuring of state power. Centralization as well as exploration were enormously complicated by contemporary intellectual and religious developments as much as by the dynastic disputes that sparked military clashes. The revival of classical learning and culture known as the Renaissance began in Italy during the fourteenth century as merchants and nobles made rich by the Mediterranean trade used their wealth to patronize scholarship and art. Renaissance scholars extended the process of rediscovering the lost knowledge of Greek and Roman learning that medieval scholastic churchmen had already begun, often through their contact with Arab scholars who had come to appreciate the value of classical texts, especially in the fields of mathematics and philosophy. This "new" learning helped to generate great intellectual curiosity about the world of humankind not only in Europe and the Mediterranean, but also in areas of the globe beyond. Renaissance poets introduced new literary forms, painters and sculptors drew on classical models to give dramatic expression to human aspiration, political thinkers generated fresh reflection on what constituted effective political rule, and innovators opened new fields of investigation and discovery in science and technology.

A revolution in communications technology facilitated the social change brought on by the Renaissance. The invention of printing from movable type by Johann Gutenberg in the 1440s stimulated an unprecedented exchange of these new ideas among a growing long-distance community of educated Europeans. Renaissance humanists engaged in spirited printed discussions on an ever-expanding list of topics ranging from arcane matters of theology to the glut of English wool on the Antwerp market. Seafaring and geography were popular topics of inquiry, and sea captains published their findings as quickly as they could engage a printer. By the beginning of the sixteenth century, a small, though growing, number of educated readers throughout Europe were well informed about the exploration of the New World. The printing press opened the European mind to exciting prospects that could hardly have been perceived when the Vikings sailed the North Atlantic five hundred years before.

Renaissance humanism and the printing press also exerted an incalculable influence on the spread of the great popular religious movement known as the Reformation. Northern humanists such as Erasmus of Rotterdam (1466?–1536) and England's John Colet (1467?–1519) were drawn to the ancient Hebrew and Greek texts of the Bible, much as their counterparts in southern Europe had been attracted to the texts of Greek and Roman antiquity. Immersion in these foundational texts of Christianity led an obscure German monk, Martin Luther, to begin criticizing what he saw as the corrupt teachings and practices of the Roman Catholic Church, the Christian faith that had long enjoyed a virtual religious monopoly throughout western Europe. In 1517, Luther's challenge to Roman Catholicism riveted international attention when his Ninety-Five Theses attacking church practice were printed and distributed across Europe. Within four years, Luther's prolific writings had caused such a bitter controversy that the Hápsburg emperor Charles V (1500–1558) summoned him to an Imperial Diet in the city of Worms to answer serious charges of heresy. Declaring his personal conscience "captive to the Word of God," Luther refused to recant his criticism. By the end of the 1520s the Catholic unity of Europe had been destroyed. The Reformation divided kingdoms, sparked bloody religious wars, and unleashed an extraordinary flood of theological publication, printed not only in scholarly Latin but in English, German, and French, the languages of humble believers.

Luther's message was easy for ordinary people to comprehend. God spoke through the Bible, Luther maintained, not through a pope or priests. Scripture taught that women and men were saved by faith alone. Indeed, the human predicament was so dire, and God's demands so great, that traditional Catholic ritual and observance—its sacraments, pilgrimages, fasts, alms, and indulgences—seemed utterly inadequate to rescue humankind from eternal damnation. Yet those who in faith threw themselves on God's mercy would find forgiveness. Luther's radical ideas challenged the traditional structure of Catholicism as they spread rapidly across northern Germany and Scandinavia.

In Luther's wake, other Protestant theologians—religious thinkers who would determine the course of Christian reform in France, England, Scotland, Holland, and the early American colonies—mounted an even more strident attack on Catholicism. The most influential of these was John Calvin, an austere French lawyer turned theologian, who lived most of his adult life in the Swiss city of Geneva. Calvin held a theological perspective similar to other Swiss and Rhenish Reformers and gave definitive expression to Reformed theology through his *Institutes of the Christian Religion* (1536). In this and other writings Calvin developed Luther's ideas on sin, divine grace, and salvation within a framework that stressed God's omnipotence over human affairs. The Lord, he maintained, chose or "elected" some persons to receive the gift of salvation rather than eternal punishment, the penalty for human sin. Calvin taught that God carried out this process of election in a way that humans experienced as a genuine, heartfelt response to God. Yet ultimately, a man or woman could do nothing to alter God's decision.

Common sense suggests that such a bleak doctrine—known as predestination—might lead to fatalism or hedonism. After all, why not enjoy the world's pleasures to the fullest if such actions have no effect on God's judgment? But many sixteenth-century Europeans did not share modern notions of what constitutes common sense. Indeed, Calvinists were constantly "up and doing," searching for signs that they had received God's gift of grace. The uncertainty of their eternal state proved a powerful psychological spur, for as long as people did not know whether they were scheduled for heaven or hell, they worked diligently to demonstrate that they possessed at least the seeds of grace. From centers in Geneva, Zurich, and Strasbourg, Reformed leaders carried their teachings throughout northern Europe. In France, the reformed Protestants became known as Huguenots. The Protestants of the Netherlands embraced Reformed principles. In Scotland, people of Calvinist persuasion founded the Presbyterian Church. And in seventeenth-century England and America, most of those who put Calvin's teachings into practice were called Puritans.

Roman Catholics, from the pope in Rome to parish clergy and laity throughout Europe, responded vigorously to the Protestant challenge. By 1540, a Catholic Counter-Reformation was moving on many fronts to correct abuses within the Church, to shore up Church teaching and ritual, and to regain territory that had been lost to the Protestants. The Counter-Reformation gave rise to a new religious order, the Society of Jesus or Jesuits, founded by the Spanish military veteran Ignatius Loyola. The Jesuits became effective foot soldiers in the campaign to reform the Church and restore people to the Catholic fold. The Jesuit "Black Robes"—along with the Dominicans and other religious orders—spurred a powerful new thrust of missionary outreach to the Americas, Africa, and Asia.

The clash between Protestantism and Catholicism profoundly shaped the course of sixteenth-century history, a period one scholar has aptly termed "the Age of Religious Wars." Catholicism and Protestantism influenced how ordinary men and women across the continent interpreted the everyday experiences of life. Religion set expectations for political and economic activities. Protestant leaders, for example, purged the English calendar of the many saints' days—even Christmas—that had punctuated the agricultural year in Catholic countries. Indeed, it is helpful to view Protestantism and Catholicism as warring ideologies much like those that divided the United States and the Soviet Union for much of the twentieth century. These bundles of deeply held beliefs divided countries as well as families.

The Reformation certainly had a profound impact on the economic development of Calvinist countries. The brilliant German sociologist Max Weber argued in his *Protestant Ethic and Spirit of Capitalism* that a gnawing sense of self-doubt created by the doctrine of predestination drove Calvinists to extraordinary diligence. They generated large profits not because they wanted to become rich, but because they wanted to be doing the Lord's work in their "callings" or "vocations," which for Protestants incorporated not only religious service but every honest occupation. Protestant work values also demanded habits of thrift, humility, and a productive use of resources that stimulated saving and accumulation of capital rather profligate, ostentatious spending. Although the cultivation of such habits could not secure salvation, they might, on Weber's reading of Calvinism, provide some evidence that their practitioners were among God's elect.

God, Gold, and Glory: The Iberian Peninsula in the Age of Conquest

In the early fifteenth century, the Iberian Peninsula consisted of several autonomous kingdoms. It lacked rich natural resources and possessed few good seaports. In fact, little about this land suggested its people—loyal Catholics whose descendants hated the Protestant Reformation—would take the lead in conquering and colonizing the New World.

The kingdom of Portugal proved an exception, however. In 1253, this small realm on the western coast of the Iberian Peninsula wrested authority from the Moors, Muslim rulers of North African origin who had controlled much of the region for hundreds of years. Like other Iberian kingdoms, Portugal possessed sparse natural resources beyond agriculture. Indeed, even after the Black Death decimated the population, the kingdom still had to rely on supplements of imported Moorish grain to feed its people. Yet Portugal managed to develop an extensive seaborne trade by placing much of its cultivable coastal plains into production of goods for European markets and providing shipping among Europe's Atlantic and Mediterranean ports. The kingdom also pressed its conflict with the Muslims southward along the Moroccan coast. Their military operations in Atlantic waters led the Portuguese to settle the islands of Madeira (1420) and the Azores (1430s). These settlements, valuable for wine and sugar, gave Portugal experience in the logistics of colonization as well as an excellent position from which to launch and supply further expeditions.

By the end of the fifteenth century, neighboring Spain also exploded with new creative energy. The marriage of Ferdinand and Isabella sparked a drive for political consolidation that, because of the monarchs' militant Catholicism, took on the characteristics of a religious crusade. Spurred by the driving faith of their monarchs, the armies of Castile and Aragon waged holy war—known as the Reconquista—against the independent states in southern Spain that had long been held under Muslim rule. In 1492, the Moorish kingdom of Granada fell, and, for the first time in centuries, the entire Iberian Peninsula came under Christian rule. Spanish authorities showed no tolerance for people who rejected the Catholic faith, an inauspicious development for the Indians who would confront them in the New World.

During the Reconquista, thousands of Jews and Moors were driven from the country. Indeed, Christopher Columbus undoubtedly encountered such refugees as he was preparing for his famous voyage. From this volatile social and political environment came the conquistadores, men eager for personal glory and material gain, uncompromising in matters of religion, and unswerving in their loyalty to the crown. They were prepared to employ fire and sword in any cause sanctioned by God and king, and these adventurers carried European culture to the most populous regions of the New World.

Long before the Portuguese rounded the Cape of Good Hope or Spaniards reached the West Indies, both nations colonized strategic and economically valuable archipelagos in the eastern Atlantic. The Portuguese settled Madeira and the Azores, which first served as important stations for reprovisioning merchant vessels, as well as providing timber, dyes, and grain for Portuguese consumption. Portuguese planters eventually introduced sugar to their colonies, an intensive plantation crop requiring a large labor force. The workers came from Africa, where they were captured in raids or obtained through trade. Well before 1500 this valuable slave-produced Madeira luxury was sweetening the palates of the wealthy throughout Europe.

In the fifteenth century Spain conquered the indigenous peoples of the Canary Islands, an archipelago to the north of the Portuguese Azores. These expeditions, leading eventually to colonization, provided a kind of unplanned rehearsal for the invasion of the New World. The harsh labor systems the Spanish developed in the Canaries served as models of subjugation in America. Indeed, the Spanish experience paralleled that of the English in Ireland. An early fifteenth-century Spanish chronicle described the Canary natives as "miscreants . . . [who] do not acknowledge their creator and live in part like beasts." Many islanders died of disease; others were killed in battle or enslaved. The new Spanish landholders followed the Portuguese in introducing sugar cultivated by a large slave labor force. In this sense, the Spanish Canaries and the Portuguese Azores may truly have constituted the first American frontiers.

In 1500, England was not prepared to compete with Spain and Portugal for the riches of the Orient. Although Henry VII, the first Tudor monarch, brought peace to England after a bitter civil war, the country still contained too many "overmighty subjects," powerful local magistrates who maintained armed retainers and who often paid little attention to royal authority. Henry possessed no standing army; his small navy intimidated no one. The Tudors gave nominal allegiance to the pope in Rome, but unlike the rulers of Spain, they were not crusaders for Catholicism. Religion did not provide England's impetus for exploration.

The English Moment

A complex web of international diplomacy worked against England in the early sixteenth century. In 1509, to preserve what seemed a promising alliance between Spain and England, the future Henry VIII married Catherine of Aragon, the widow of his deceased brother Arthur. As a result of this marital arrangement, English merchants enjoyed limited rights to trade in Spain's American colonies, but any attempt by England at independent colonization would have threatened those rights and would have jeopardized the alliance.

By the end of the sixteenth century, however, conditions within England had changed dramatically, in part as a result of the Protestant Reformation. Religion transformed diplomacy. The English began to view their former ally, Spain, as the greatest threat to England's independence. Tudor monarchs, especially Henry

VIII (r. 1509–1547) and his daughter Elizabeth I (r. 1558–1603), developed a strong central administration, while England became more and more a Protestant society. This merger of English Protestantism and English nationalism affected all aspects of public life. It helped propel England into a pivotal role in European affairs and was crucial in creating a powerful sense of English identity among all classes of people.

Popular anti-Catholicism helped spark religious reformation in England. The English people had long resented paying revenues to a pope who lived in far-off Rome. Early in the sixteenth century, criticism of the Catholic clergy grew increasingly vocal. Cardinal Thomas Wolsey, the most powerful prelate in England, flaunted his immense wealth and unwittingly became a symbol of spiritual corruption. Parish priests were objects of ridicule. Poorly educated men for the most part, they seemed theologically ignorant and perpetually grasping. Anticlericalism did not run as deep in England as it had in Martin Luther's Germany, but by the late 1520s, the Catholic Church had lost the allegiance of the great mass of the population. The people's pent-up anger is central to an understanding of the English Reformation. If ordinary men and women throughout the kingdom had not supported separation from Rome, then Henry VIII could not have forced them to take the Protestant road.

The catalyst for Protestant Reformation in England was the king's desire to rid himself of his wife, Catherine of Aragon, who happened to be the daughter of the former king of Spain. Their marriage had produced a daughter, Mary, but, as the years passed, no son. The need for a male heir obsessed Henry and his counselors. They assumed that a female ruler could not maintain domestic peace and England would fall once again into civil war. The answer seemed to be remarriage. Henry convinced himself that God had denied him a male heir as punishment for marrying his deceased brother's wife, a violation of Old Testament law. On these grounds he petitioned Pope Clement VII for a divorce (technically, an annulment). The Spanish, however, were unwilling to play along. Smarting over the public humiliation of Catherine, they forced the pope to procrastinate. In 1527, time ran out. The passionate Henry fell in love with Anne Boleyn, who later bore him a daughter, Elizabeth. The king decided to divorce Catherine with or without papal consent.

The final break with Rome came swiftly. Between 1529 and 1536, the king, acting through Parliament, severed all ties with the pope, seized church properties, and dissolved many of the monasteries. In March 1534, the Act of Supremacy announced, "The King's Majesty justly and rightfully is supreme head of the Church of England." The entire process, which one historian termed a "state reformation," was conducted with impressive efficiency. Land formerly owned by the Catholic Church passed quickly into private hands, and within a short period, property holders throughout England had acquired a vested interest in Protestantism. Beyond breaking with the papacy, Henry showed little enthusiasm for radical theological change. Most Catholic ceremonies survived, as did the office of bishop.

Despite the king's doctrinal conservatism, the split with Rome did open the door to increasingly bold religious reform. The year 1539 saw the publication of an

English language Bible. Before then the Scripture had been available only in Latin, the tongue of an educated elite. For the first time in English history, ordinary people could read the Word of God in the vernacular. It was a liberating experience that persuaded some men and women that Henry had not yet fully purified the English church of all Catholic influence. During Henry's lifetime, however, those who pressed too aggressively for reform placed their lives in as much danger as those who supported Catholicism.

With Henry's death in 1547, England entered a period of acute political and religious instability. Edward VI, Henry's young son by a third wife, Jane Seymour, came to the throne. He was still a child and sickly besides. Militant Protestants took advantage of the political uncertainty, insisting that the Church of England remove every trace of its Catholic origins. With the death of young Edward in 1553, these ambitious efforts came to a sudden halt. Henry's eldest daughter, Mary, next ascended the throne. Fiercely loyal to the Catholic faith of her mother, Catherine of Aragon, Mary I—known to her enemies as Bloody Mary—vowed to return England to the pope.

However misguided were the queen's plans, she possessed her father's stubborn will. Hundreds of English Protestants were executed; others scurried off to the safety of Geneva and Frankfurt, where they absorbed the most radical Reformed doctrines of the day. When Mary died in 1558 and was succeeded by Elizabeth, these "Marian exiles" flocked back to England, more eager than ever to rid the Tudor church of Catholicism. Mary had inadvertently advanced the cause of Calvinism by creating so many Protestant martyrs, reformers who burned for their faith and now were celebrated in the woodcuts of the most popular book of the period, John Foxe's *Acts and Monuments*, commonly known as the *Book of Martyrs* (1563). Once again, new print technologies empowered large-scale mobilization. The Marian exiles served as the leaders of the Elizabethan church, an institution that remained fundamentally Calvinist until the end of the sixteenth century.

The Protestant Queen

Elizabeth demonstrated that Henry and his advisers had been mistaken about the capabilities of female rulers. She was a woman of such talent that modern biographers find little to criticize in her decisions. She governed the English people from 1558 to 1603, an intellectually exciting period during which some of her subjects took the first halting steps toward colonizing the New World.

Elizabeth recognized that her most urgent duty as queen was to end the religious turmoil that had divided England for a generation. She had no desire to restore Catholicism. After all, the pope openly declared her a woman of illegitimate birth. Nor did she want to recreate the church exactly as it had been in the final years of Henry's reign. Rather, Elizabeth established a unique religious institution, Catholic in much of its ceremony and government but clearly Protestant in doctrine. Under her so-called Elizabethan settlement, the queen assumed the title "Supreme Head of the Church." Some churchmen who had studied with Calvin in Geneva urged her to drop immediately all Catholic rituals, but she ignored these strident reformers. The young queen understood that she could not rule effectively without the full support of her people, and as the examples of Edward and Mary before her demonstrated, neither radical change nor widespread persecution gained a monarch lasting popularity.

The confrontations between Protestantism and Catholicism affected Elizabeth's entire reign. Soon after she became queen, Pope Pius V excommunicated her, and in his papal bull *Regnans in Exelsis* (1570), he stripped Elizabeth of her "pretended title to the kingdom." Philip II of Spain, the most fervently Catholic state in Europe, vowed to restore England to the "true" faith, and Catholic militants constantly plotted to overthrow the Tudor monarchy.

Philip's vow to overthrow Elizabeth infused a religious fervor into the emerging competition between England and Spain, fusing English Protestantism with English national identity. A loyal English subject in the late sixteenth century loved the queen, supported the Church of England, and hated Catholics, especially those who happened to live in Spain. Elizabeth herself came to symbolize this militant new chauvinism for her subjects, who adored their Virgin Queen. As the English people began spinning visions of a New World empire in the 1570s, it became obvious that they were driven by ideological forces similar to those that had inspired the Spanish subjects of Isabella and Ferdinand almost a century earlier.

CONVERGING HORIZONS

Nothing in their ancient pasts could prepare Europeans, Africans, or American Indians for the moment of first contact with one another. Yet their diverse histories did provide each a fund of analogies, metaphors, assumptions, and interests that shaped their response to the American encounter that began in the fifteenth century. Each was predisposed to situate the other within specific horizons of local interest, viewing the other as an ally or instrument for achieving particular aims. Europeans sought control over the flow of Asian wealth, which would buy power for their princes over European rivals and riches and glory for the adventurers themselves. They also hoped that these advantages would enable them to win converts for their God. Africans readily welcomed opportunities to increase their access to a wider variety of goods and markets at more competitive rates, which might in turn strengthen their advantage over rival powers. Various American Indian groups also sought alternatively to extend or escape the dominance of rivals as well as the opportunity to acquire those goods and resources they could incorporate within their particular cultural worlds.

The alien interests that motivated inhabitants of each world ensured that conflict would certainly follow the moment of first encounter. But with equal certainty, the diversity of interests and perspectives that divided each world's peoples ensured that encounter would not be marked by conflict alone. A Bristol fisherman might compete with a Breton for Micmac furs; an Akan miner might offer a Portuguese trader gold for a Yoruba slave; a Tlaxcalan noble might join forces with the Spanish to throw off the cruel Aztec yoke. On the eve of contact, many outcomes were possible. Only specific human choices, made within particular historical circumstances of time, contingency, and cultural setting, would tell the tale.

CHRONOLOGY

30,000–12,000 B.C.	Migrants cross the Bering Strait from Asia into North America.
2000–1500 B.C.	Agricultural revolution transforms Native American life.
1000 B.C.–A.D. *400*	Adena and Hopewell cultures flourish in North America.
A.D. *1001*	Norsemen establish a small settlement in Vinland (Newfoundland).
1030	Death of War Jaabi (King of Takrur), first Muslim ruler in West Africa.
1100	Mississippian society flourishes.
1150	Anasazi center at Chaco Canyon begins to decline.
1324	Mali ruler Mansa Mūsā, takes pilgrimage to Mecca.
1325	Tenochtitlán founded by Aztecs.
1375	Gao, capital of kingdom of Songhay, gains independence from Mali.
1420–1440	Portuguese settle Madeira and Azores.
1450	Gutenberg perfects movable type.
1469	Marriage of Isabella and Ferdinand leads to unification of Spain.
ca. 1480	Iroquois Great League of Peace established.
1481	Portuguese build castle at Elmina on the Gold Coast of Africa
1492	Columbus lands at San Salvador.
1517	Luther's Ninety-Five Theses spark Protestant Reformation.
1534	Act of Supremacy begins Reformation in England.
1536	John Calvin publishes *Institutes of the Christian Religion*.
1558	Ascension of Elizabeth I consolidates English Protestantism.

RECOMMENDED READING

For a general overview of African history prior to Portuguese arrival see Basil Davidson, *West Africa Before the Colonial Era: A History to 1850* (New York, 1998). J. H. Elliott provides a helpful overview of Spanish expansion in his *Imperial Spain, 1469–1716* (New York, 1963), while G. R. Elton, *England Under the Tudors* (London, 1974) surveys English history during the same period. For early European exploration see Felipe Fernández-Armesto, *Before Columbus: Exploration and Colonisation from the Mediterranean to the Atlantic, 1229–1492* (Philadelphia, 1987). Ralph Davis, *The Rise of the Atlantic Economies* (Ithaca, 1973) explores the expansion of trade in the Atlantic world from the fifteenth century forward. Alvin M. Josephy, Jr., ed., *America in 1492:*

The World of the Indian Peoples Before the Arrival of Columbus (New York, 1992) gives an account of the diverse Indian groups in the pre-encounter Americas. For a sweeping synthetic account of the North American environment from distant prehistory to the present, see Tim Flannery, *The Eternal Frontier: An Ecological History of North America and Its Peoples* (New York, 2001).

The demand for dependent labor in America beginning in the early sixteenth century brought dramatic changes to African society and economy. Paul H. Lovejoy, *Transformations in Slavery: A History of Slavery in Africa* (Cambridge, 1983), provides a helpful overview. Philip Curtin explores the dimensions of that change in West Africa in his *Economic Change in Precolonial Africa: Senegambia in the Era of the Slave Trade* (Madison, 1975), as does Ray A. Kea, *Settlements, Trade, and Politics in the Seventeenth-Century Gold Coast* (Baltimore, 1982). Joseph C. Miller examines the slave trade's impact on southwest Africa in *Way of Death: Merchant Capitalism and the Angolan Slave Trade, 1730–1830* (Madison, 1988).

North American history before Columbus is attracting a growing body of sophisticated scholarship. For a fascinating overview, see Brian M. Fagan, *Ancient North America: The Archaeology of a Continent* (New York, 1991). Joseph H. Greenberg, *Language in the Americas* (Stanford, 1987) reviews linguistic patterns in the New World and what they reveal about the movement of peoples and development of culture in the era before European contact. Francis Jennings, *Founders of America: How the Indians Discovered the Land, Pioneered in It, and Created Great Classical Civilization; How They Were Plunged into a Dark Age by Invasion and Conquest; and How They Are Reviving* (New York, 1993), advances a provocative thesis concerning the Mesoamerican origins of North American Indian cultures. Inga Clendinnen explores the rise of the Aztecs in her *Aztecs: An Interpretation* (Cambridge, 1991). Lynda Norene Shaffer explores the Mississippian origins of many Eastern Woodland groups in her *Native Americans before 1492: The Moundbuilding Centers of the Eastern Woodlands* (Armonk, 1992), while Bruce G. Trigger explores the archaeological and documentary history of an important Great Lakes nation in *The Children of Aataentsic: A History of the Huron People to 1660* (Kingston, 1976).

Historical scholarship on the European background of exploration and colonization is vast. A good overview of popular responses to the Protestant Reformation is available in Robert W. Scribner, *Popular Culture and Popular Movements in Reformation Germany* (London, 1988). John Calvin exerted enormous influence on Protestantism on the Continent and the British Isles, and a good biographical treatment is available in William J. Bouwsma, *John Calvin: A Sixteenth-Century Portrait* (New York, 1988). The rise of Protestantism in England after Elizabeth I's ascension is the subject of Patrick Collinson, *The Religion of the Protestants: The Church in English Society, 1559–1625* (Oxford, 1982). Richard Helgerson, *Forms of Nationhood: The Elizabethan Writing of England* (Chicago, 1992) explores the beginnings of an English Protestant national identity. David B. Quinn's *The Elizabethans and the Irish* (Ithaca, 1966) remains a valuable study of English policy in Ireland during the reign of Elizabeth I, while Nicholas P. Canny, *Kingdom and Colony: Ireland in the Atlantic World, 1560–1800* (Baltimore, 1988) explores Ireland's role in the development of English methods of colonization. Keith Wrightson, *English Society, 1580–1680* (London, 1979) provides a helpful overview of the social origins of colonization, while Lawrence Stone's *The Crisis of the Aristocracy, 1558–1641* (Oxford, 1965) offers a classic account of sweeping changes in English society from the reign of Elizabeth to the English civil wars.

Chapter 2

Many Voices
Patterns of New World Encounter

On August 7, 1498, inhabitants of the Paría Peninsula on the northern coast of South America welcomed Admiral Christopher Columbus to their shores with presents of "bread and maize and things to eat and pitchers of a beverage." According to his custom, the Spanish admiral brought the Native Americans on board his ship and laid out samples of trade goods for their inspection. His guests proved discriminating customers, giving "nothing for the beads, but all they had for hawks' bells. . . . They esteemed brass very highly." In return the Indians offered him "parrots of two or three species" and "kerchiefs of cotton carefully embroidered and woven in colors and workmanship exactly like those . . . from the rivers of Sierra Leone [West Africa]." The Indians left Columbus's vessel before nightfall, thwarting his desire to take "half a dozen" New World souvenirs with him.

The account of this brief exchange during Columbus's third voyage reminds us that the story of cultural encounter involved much more than simply discovery and conquest. Yet the native voice in this exchange was quickly drowned out by a familiar European narrative in which intrepid explorers brought glory to the Christian faith, to the Spanish monarchs, and not least, to the conquerors themselves. In a letter circulated throughout Europe at the end of his first voyage—the new print technology spread knowledge of the New World to an eager public—Columbus announced, "As I know that you will be pleased at the great victory with which Our Lord has crowned my voyage, I write this to you, from which you will learn how in thirty-three days, I passed from the Canary Islands to the Indies. . . . And there I found very many islands filled with people innumerable, and of them all I have taken possession for their highnesses [King Ferdinand and Queen Isabella]."

Columbus and the adventurers who sailed in his wake wove a tale of discovery that survived in Western memory long after many of the Indians he encountered had become extinct. The story recounted first in Europe and later in the United States depicted visionary captains, selfless missionaries, and intrepid settlers carrying civilization to the peoples of the New World and opening a vast virgin land to economic progress. This tale celebrated the inevitable spread of European values and the pushing back of frontiers. It was a history populated by the victors—usually opportunistic males—and by the children of the victors to explain how they had come to dominate the world we know today.

Since the 1960s an explosion of interdisciplinary inquiry into early American history has exposed the inadequacy of this traditional explanation of European conquest and colonization. It is not so much wrong, as partisan and incomplete. History written from the perspective of the conquistador or joint-stock company inevitably silenced the voices of the victims, the native peoples who, in this view, resisted economic and technological progress. Heroic tales of the advance of Western civilization failed to acknowledge the millions of Native Americans who died following conquest or the huge numbers of Africans carried to America as slaves. Although some authors tried to erase pain and exploitation from the record, nevertheless, a huge body of evidence remains, and it is possible from these rich yet underused sources to reconstruct much more balanced accounts of early encounters among Europeans, Indians, and Africans.

By placing these complex, often unsettling events within a framework of encounters—rather than exploration, colonization, or settlement—we can begin to recapture the full human dimensions of accommodation and resistance. At the same time, we must recognize that the manifold settings of encounter, which historians have variously described as "cultural frontiers," "zones of exchange," or "middle grounds," were extremely precarious. Like environmental ecotones—the border areas between two ecological systems—New World settings of encounter were fraught with opportunity and danger. Too often, the New World was the scene of tragic violence and systematic exploitation. Yet it also presented ordinary people with opportunities to exercise extraordinary creativity in shaping their own lives; neither Native Americans nor Africans were passive victims of European colonization. Nor, for that matter, were the poor whites who took their chances on the New World.

Within their own families and communities, these obscure men and women made choices, sometimes rebelling, sometimes accommodating. They always labored to make sense of what was happening to them, taking advantages and minimizing costs as they were able. Although they sometimes failed to preserve dignity and often lost independence, their efforts poignantly reveal that the history of the New World—be it from the per-

spective of the Native American, the African American, or the European—
is above all else a story of human agency.

FIRST VENTURES ACROSS THE ATLANTIC

In ancient times, the West possessed mythical appeal to people living along the
shores of the Mediterranean Sea. Classical writers speculated about the fate of
Atlantis, a fabled civilization that was said to have sunk beneath the ocean. Fallen
Greek warriors allegedly spent eternity in an uncharted western paradise. But be-
cause the ships of Greece and Rome were ill-designed to navigate the open
Atlantic, the lands to the west remained the stuff of legend. In the fifth century
A.D. the inventive Irish monk St. Brendan reported visiting enchanted islands far
out in the Atlantic. He even claimed to have met a talking whale named
Jasconius, who showed amazing cross-species generosity by allowing the famished
voyager to cook a meal on his back.

In the tenth century, Scandinavian seafarers known as Norsemen or Vikings actually established settlements in the New World. In part because they had no printing presses to carry the news, almost a thousand years passed before they received
credit for their accomplishment. In the year 984, a band of Vikings led by Erik the
Red sailed west from Iceland to a large island in the North Atlantic. Eric, a master of
public relations, named the island Greenland, reasoning that others would more
willingly colonize this icebound region "if the country had a good name." A few
years later, Erik's son Leif founded a small settlement called Vinland at a location in
northern Newfoundland now known as L'Anse aux Meadows. At the time, the
Norse voyages went unnoticed by other Europeans. The hostility of Native
Americans, poor lines of communication, and political upheavals in Scandinavia
made maintenance of these tenuous outposts impossible. The Vikings abandoned
the settlements, though Greenland's inhabitants maintained sporadic contact with
North America into the fourteenth century. At the time of his first voyage in 1492,
Columbus seemed to have been unaware that other Europeans had preceded him.

The inhabitants of Europe's Iberian Peninsula led the way to permanent
European contact with the Americas. The Iberians' seafaring impulse sprang from
a potent combination of religious and economic motives bound up with their long
struggle to reclaim territory long ruled by Muslims from North Africa and unify it
under the rule of Catholic monarchs (see Chapter 1). This *reconquista* shaped not
only the internal cultures of Spain and Portugal, but their efforts at exploration
and colonization as well.

The Atlantic Route to Gold, Slaves, and Spices

The Iberian path to America took a circuitous route along the coast of West
Africa, where the Portuguese invented the sailing technology that eventually carried Columbus to Hispaniola. Strong winds and currents along the Atlantic coast
moved southward, which meant a ship could sail with the wind from Portugal to
West Africa without difficulty. The problem was returning. Not surprisingly,
Portuguese sailors were reluctant to venture too far south. Yet the lure of African
riches, coupled with a passion to press Portugal's anti-Islamic crusade southward,

prompted Portuguese rulers and merchants to push further down the African coast.

Backed by the steady funding and encouragement of Prince Henry the Navigator (1394–1460), Portuguese seafarers solved the problems of Atlantic navigation as they encountered them. Their experimentation culminated in the caravel, a vessel that combined a northern European hull design with lateen (triangular) sails and rigging borrowed from North African shipwrights. The caravel's sturdy hull could withstand heavy seas, while the lateen sails allowed seamen to tack much closer to contrary winds than traditional European ships. During the fifteenth century, Portuguese sailors also discovered that by sailing far to the west, often as far as the Azores, they could, on the return trip to Europe, catch a reliable westerly wind. Columbus was evidently familiar with this technique. Before attempting to cross the Atlantic Ocean, he sailed to the Gold Coast, and on the way, he undoubtedly studied the wind patterns that would carry his famed caravels to the New World and back again.

Decades of Portuguese investment and experimentation began paying off in 1443 when Nuno Tristão returned to Portugal with a cargo of slaves from the Bay of Arguin. In the following years the flow of trade increased dramatically as seamen pressed further along the African coast. Early Portuguese traders initiated commerce by a combination of coastal trading and raids, but African military might soon put an end to the raids and forced the Portuguese to abide by African trade regulations. Under these terms, officials of West African states such as Mali and Joloff became willing partners in trade, integrating the Portuguese into already existing coastal trade networks. Africans required the Europeans to pay tolls and other fees and restricted the foreign traders to conducting their business in small "factories," which were forts or castles located at the mouths of the major rivers. Local merchants acquired slaves and gold in the interior and transported them to the coastal traders in exchange for European manufactures. Merchants calculated transactions in terms of local African currencies: a slave, for example, would be offered to a European trader for so many bars of iron or ounces of gold.

The Portuguese were only too ready to leave the control of interior trade to Africans on a continent where the virulence of local diseases commonly condemned six out of ten Europeans to die within a single year's stay in Africa. There is tragic irony in this exchange, for when the Portuguese and other Europeans carried Africans to the New World, the captives died at rates that paralleled those of Europeans in Africa. Portuguese agents remained at their factories on the coast, where they cultivated the favor of local rulers and traders to build networks of mutual obligation and exchange. Some who survived the initial onslaught of disease sought to strengthen their ties by adopting African customs, settling in African villages, and taking African wives. Those who adopted African ways of life completely became known as *lançados* or *tangos-maos*, and the mulatto families they established often served for generations as powerful intermediaries between Europeans and Africans. Their position gave *lançados* leverage against the Portuguese crown's efforts to regulate and levy taxes on trade.

Even with African regulations, the coastal trade gave the Portuguese an advantage in commerce. North African traders charged Portugal's European competitors a much higher price for sub-Saharan goods. By the 1480s, Portuguese traders were diverting so much African gold from the trans-Sahara trade that their Genoese rivals, who continued to obtain African gold from Moorish traders, were beginning to suffer. The center of international commerce was making a crucial shift from the Mediterranean to the Atlantic. The flow of gold to the coast increased even more when in 1482, the Portuguese obtained permission from Akan authorities to build a castle at Elmina on the coast of modern Ghana. This fort further strengthened their position, giving them a reliable supply of African gold which they obtained in exchange for European iron and slaves brought from other places along the coast.

Portuguese mariners pressed further south along the African coast during the next decade, establishing factories along the way. In 1487, Bartholomeu Dias rounded the Cape of Good Hope, and in 1498 Vasco da Gama returned from India with a fortune in spices and other luxury goods. Da Gama secured a Portuguese monopoly on trade with Africa and the Far East, which endured into the seventeenth century.

These exploratory efforts in reconquista infused in the Portugese a religious as well as commercial purpose that persisted throughout the period of discovery and encounter. Portuguese Catholics regarded Muslims as infidels and potential enemies wherever they encountered them along the African coast and on the islands of the Indian Ocean as well. Catholic missionaries traveled with the mariners to provide them spiritual guidance and to propagate Christianity among the peoples they encountered. Most Africans resisted, especially the Muslims, who had experienced a long history of antagonism with Portuguese Catholics. Missionaries did manage to establish a few enclaves of Catholic believers near trading posts in West and Central Africa. In the 1490s, a series of revelations prompted Kongo's King Nzinga Nkuwu to lead his people to convert to Christianity. The new religion flourished in Kongo throughout the sixteenth century as priests trained native catechists to propagate the faith. Moreover, several of Kongo's princes and children of royal officials sailed to Portugal, where they resided in the royal court while studying theology and the arts.

The combined efforts of Portuguese mariners, *lançados*, and missionaries provided increasing access to the African trade in slaves, which quickly became an indispensable link in the Portuguese commercial system. Even before Europeans colonized the New World, the Portuguese were purchasing almost a thousand slaves a year on the West African coast. The slaves consisted mainly of men and women taken captive during wars, but others fell victim to judicial practices designed specifically to supply the growing Atlantic market. The Portuguese traded many slaves to African buyers further along the coast for goods desired in Europe. Indeed, the historian Robin Blackburn has argued that African demand for European commodities was not sufficient to make the gold trade profitable; the Portuguese could ensure profits only by participating in the African coastal slave trade. The Portuguese also forced African captives to work on the sugar plantations of Madeira (Portuguese) and the Canaries (Spanish), Atlantic islands on which Europeans experimented with forms of slave labor that would later be more fully and more ruthlessly established in the American colonies (see Chapter 3).

Portuguese colonists also established lucrative sugar plantations on the islands of São Tomé and Principe in the Bight of Biafra.

Spain's "Admiral of the Ocean Sea"

If it had not been for Christopher Columbus (Cristoforo Colombo), Spain might never have gained an American empire. Little is known about his early life. Born in Genoa in 1451 of humble parentage, Columbus devoured the Renaissance learning that had so recently become available in printed form. Like other humanists, he combined the study of classical texts with the latest scientific and spiritual developments of his age. He mastered geography, and—perhaps while exploring the coast of West Africa—he seems to have convinced himself that God had called him to sail west across the Atlantic Ocean to reach Cathay, as China was then known.

In 1484, Columbus presented an ambitious plan to King John II of Portugal. However, while the Portuguese were just as eager as Columbus to reach Cathay, their discoveries had already convinced them that the way to the riches of the East lay around the continent of Africa rather than across the Atlantic Ocean, as Columbus suggested. They rightly suspected that Columbus's enthusiasm had outrun his mathematical ability. He had substantially underestimated the circumference of the earth. As the expert Portuguese navigators reminded Columbus, no ship then known could carry enough food and water for such a long voyage. Columbus was clever, but his sailors would surely starve. The Portuguese alternative route around the Cape of Good Hope seemed much more promising even before da Gama reached India; thus John II declined to sponsor Columbus.

Like a modern inventor looking for capital, Columbus turned to European monarchs for financial backing. Henry VII of England rebuffed him in 1489, as did the French regent, Anne de Beaujeu. Undaunted by rejection, Columbus ventured to the court of Isabella and Ferdinand. The Spanish were initially no more interested in his grand design than other European monarchs had been. But time was on Columbus's side. Spain's aggressive new monarchs envied Portugal's recent success in oceangoing trade. Columbus boldly played on the competition between these countries, talking constantly of wealth and empire. Indeed, for a person with so few contacts with those in power, he seemed brazenly confident. One contemporary reported that when Columbus "made up his mind, he was as sure he would discover what he did discover, and find what he did find, as if he held it in a chamber under lock and key."

Columbus's stubborn lobbying on behalf of his "Enterprise of the Indies" gradually wore down opposition in the Spanish court. The two sovereigns provided him with a small fleet containing two of the most famous caravels ever constructed, the *Niña* and the *Pinta*, as well as the square-rigger, the *Santa María*. Without the slightest knowledge that America stood between Spain and China, Columbus demanded that Isabella and Ferdinand grant him grand titles and broad authority over any new islands or mainland territories he might discover. The indomitable admiral set sail for Cathay in August 1492, the year of Spain's unification.

Contrary to popular modern myth, educated Europeans of the fifteenth century knew the world was round. No one seriously believed that Columbus and his crew would tumble off the edge of the earth. The concern was with size, not shape. Columbus estimated the distance to the mainland of Asia to be about 3,000 nautical miles, a voyage his small ships would have little difficulty completing. The estimates of the navigators and church scholars who had challenged him in his pleas before the king of Portugal came much closer to the actual distance of 10,600 nautical miles. These experts, however, could not shake Columbus's confidence in his own calculations. Had the New World not been in his way, he and his crew would have run out of food and water long before they reached China, as the Portuguese had predicted.

After putting in at the Canary Islands to refit the ships, Columbus continued his westward voyage in early September. When the tiny Spanish fleet sighted an island in the Bahamas after only thirty-three days at sea, the admiral announced he had reached Asia. Because his mathematical calculations had apparently been correct, he began looking for the Chinese. It never occurred to Columbus that he had stumbled upon a world hitherto unknown to Europeans. He assured his men, his patrons, and perhaps himself that these islands were indeed part of the fabled "Indies." Or if not the Indies themselves, then they were surely an extension of the great Asian landmass. He searched for the splendid cities Marco Polo had described, but instead of meeting wealthy Chinese, Columbus encountered Native Americans, whom he called "Indians," a triumph of theory over fact.

After his first voyage of discovery, Columbus returned to the New World three more times. But despite his stubborn courage, he could never find the treasure his financial supporters in Spain demanded with ever increasing impatience. Columbus had oversold his dream. Indeed, his third voyage of 1498 was brought to an abrupt end when a royal commissioner charged Columbus and his brothers with maladministration of Spanish claims and sent them to Madrid in chains. His influence at court plummeted. Columbus died in 1506 a frustrated but wealthy visionary, unaware to the very end of his life that he had reached a previously unknown continent separating Asia from Europe. The final disgrace came in December 1500 when an ambitious falsifier, Amerigo Vespucci, fabricated a sensational account of his travels across the Atlantic, convincing German mapmakers that he, not Columbus, had discovered a completely new continent. Before Amerigo's claim could be corrected, his name had spread throughout Europe on the latest published maps.

Only two years after Columbus's first voyage, Spain and Portugal almost went to war over the treasure anticipated from Asia. Pope Alexander VI negotiated a settlement that pleased both kingdoms. Portugal wanted to exclude the Spanish from the west coast of Africa and, what was more important, from Columbus's new route to "India." Spain insisted on maintaining complete control over lands discovered by Columbus, which were still regarded as an extension of China. In 1493 Alexander had initially supported the Spanish effort by issuing two bulls, *Inter Caetera* and *Dudum Siquidem*. Both seemed to threaten Portuguese interests in Africa by dividing the entire world along an imaginary line starting only 100 leagues west of the Azores. The Treaty of Tordesillas (1494) averted conflict by moving the demarcation line another 170 leagues west. Any new lands discovered

The World Divided in Two

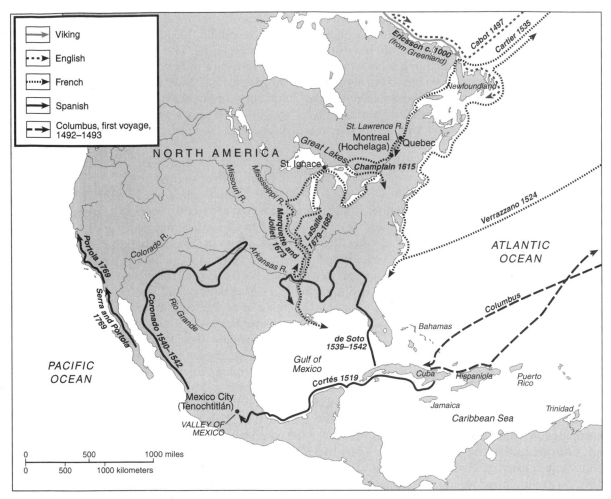

Voyages of Exploration

The early explorers who followed these routes established land claims for the European nations.

west of the line belonged to Spain. At the time, no European had ever seen Brazil, which turned out to be on Portugal's side of the line (a fact which explains why, to this day, Brazilians speak Portuguese). The treaty prohibited any other European power from trying their luck in the New World, at least in theory.

CONQUISTADORES: A MIXED LEGEND

Spain's new discoveries unleashed a horde of entrepreneurial conquistadores on the Caribbean. History once depicted these ambitious figures as brave explorers, in other words, as men worthy of modern admiration. But the conquistadores merit only tepid regard. Even by the values of their own time, they brought violence and suffering wherever they went.

As a result of laws developed during the reconquista, the conquistadores received a license to extend Spanish dominions in the pursuit of their own interests. These *adelantados*, or independent proprietors, were not interested in creating a permanent society in the New World. Rather, they risked their own resources to pursue instant wealth, power, and honor. They preferred to take their profits in gold and were not squeamish about the means they used to obtain it. Bernal Díaz del Castillo, one of the first Spaniards to migrate to this region, explained he had traveled to America "to serve God and His Majesty, to give light to those who were in darkness, and to grow rich, as all men desire to do."

The Caribbean

For a quarter century after first encounter, the conquistadores concentrated their actions on the major Caribbean islands. For the first seven years Columbus himself oversaw Spanish exploration and settlement, but he proved utterly incompetent to wield the unprecedented administrative powers the Spanish monarchs had granted him. In 1499, Francisco de Bobadilla superceded him and reorganized Spanish colonial rule. From the port of Santo Domingo, which served as the capital of Spain's American dominions for half a century, officials of the crown continued exploration of the Caribbean islands. In 1501, settlement began in earnest with the arrival of a new governor, Frey Nicolás de Ovando, and 2,500 colonists.

Spanish dominion expanded steadily throughout the West Indian archipelago, led by ruthless adventurers in search of gold. Expeditionary forces took each new Caribbean island by storm, terrorizing native inhabitants and brutally crushing any attempts at rebellion. Puerto Rico fell to Spain in 1508, Jamaica in 1509, and Cuba in 1511.

Once they had captured a Caribbean island, Spanish conquistadores quickly enslaved its Indian inhabitants and distributed them among the adventurers. "One got thirty, another forty, a third as many as a hundred or twice that number," the Spanish observer Bartolomé de Las Casas reported; "everything depended on how far one was in the good books of the despot who went by the title of governor." Colonists put their Indian slaves to work panning for gold in island streams or pasturing herds of pigs and cattle. When the gold ran out on the smaller islands, the colonists abandoned them to the surviving livestock, which quickly overran them. On larger islands such as Cuba and Hispaniola, the Spanish put the Indians to work on sugar plantations. In less than two decades, most of the Arawaks and Caribs who originally inhabited the Caribbean islands had been exterminated, victims of exploitation and disease. The Spanish planters sought to meet the consequent labor shortage with African slaves (see Chapter 3).

The Conquest of Mexico

As the Caribbean settlements expanded, rumors of fabulous wealth in Mexico stirred the avarice of many Spaniards, including Hernán Cortés, a minor government functionary in Cuba. Like so many members of his class, he dreamed of glory, military adventure, and riches that would transform him from an ambitious court clerk into a preeminent *adelantado*. On November 18, 1518, Cortés and a small army left Cuba to verify the stories of Mexico's treasure. Events soon demonstrated that Cortés possessed extraordinary ability as a leader.

His adversary was the legendary Aztec emperor, Montezuma. The confrontation between these two powerful personalities is one of the more dramatic of early American history. A fear of competition from rival conquistadores coupled with a burning desire to conquer a vast new empire drove Cortés forward. Determined to push his men to their imagined rendezvous with glory, he scuttled the ships that had carried them to Mexico, preventing them from retreating in the face of danger. Cortés led his band of six hundred followers across rugged mountains and on the way gathered allies from among the Tlaxcalans, a tributary people eager to free themselves from Aztec domination.

In matters of war, Cortés possessed obvious technological superiority over the Aztecs. The sound of gunfire frightened the Indians. Moreover, Aztec troops had never seen horses, much less armored ones carrying sword-wielding Spaniards. But these elements would have counted for little had Cortés not also gained a psychological advantage. For some reason, the emperor hesitated. Early accounts state that Montezuma first believed that the Spaniards were gods, representatives of the fearful plumed serpent, Quetzalcoatl. Many scholars now believe that Aztec survivors invented this explanation after the fact, and that the emperor simply needed time to assess the strength of his alien adversary. When Montezuma's resolve finally hardened, it was too late. Cortés seized the Aztec ruler as a hostage, setting in motion a chain of tragic and bloody events that culminated in the utter destruction of Tenochtitlán. Cortés shrewdly retained the symbolic power of the site by building the colonial capital of Mexico City on the ruins of the Aztec metropolis. Spanish victory in the Valley of Mexico, coupled with other conquests in South America, made Spain the wealthiest state in Europe.

The conquest of Tenochtitlán became a model for Spanish conquest elsewhere in the Americas. Later conquistadores such as Hernando de Soto sought to replicate Cortés' methods. When Spanish governors extended authority over the Pueblos and other Indians who had once maintained diplomatic relations with the Aztecs, they communicated their intentions through symbolic plays portraying Spanish destruction of the great city. Indians who watched the plays soon came to understand that a similar fate awaited all who refused to submit to the Spanish conquerors.

Spanish Exploration in Florida and the Southwest

Inspired by Cortés's conquests, other ambitious and now jealous conquistadores ventured to mainland North America in search of fabled wealth and glory. In 1513 Juan Ponce de León led the first Spanish expedition to Florida. No surviving first-hand evidence supports the idea that he hoped to find a fabled Fountain of Youth, but he certainly hoped to bring gold and slaves back to his home base on Puerto Rico. Ponce's initial voyage netted him little, but Cortés's exploits in Mexico prompted him to try again in 1521. Ponce met his death during a fierce battle with Calusa Indians. Later explorers pressed Spanish dominion over Florida. In 1565 Pedro Menéndez de Avilés established the municipality of St. Augustine on Florida's Atlantic coast. The town's impressive fortress discouraged European rivals from entering the region until 1763.

From Mexico the Spanish directed further explorations of North America by land and sea. Two of Cortés's men, Fortún Jiménez and Francisco de Ulloa, sailed

Mexican-built vessels north from the port of Zacatula to explore the peninsula of Lower California in 1532. Cortés's rival, Viceroy Antonio de Mendoza, sent his protégé, Juan Rodríguez Cabrillo, with a small expeditionary force which pressed north to Santa Catalina Island before Cabrillo died there of infection in 1541. His chief pilot, Bartolomé Ferrer, sailed further up the California coast to the California-Oregon boundary before turning back. These voyages were important in forming the basis of Spanish claims to the Pacific coast. Sustained efforts to colonize the Pacific coastline did not occur until the eighteenth century.

Mixed results or outright failure did little to cool the European lust for gold. In 1538, two years before Cortés departed Mexico never to return, his rival Antonio Mendoza quietly sent Fray Marcos de Niza to reconnoiter New Mexico, a region rumored to harbor a civilization greater than that of the Aztecs. Within a year the friar returned with such promising reports that Mendoza commissioned Francisco Vásquez de Coronado to lead an elaborate expedition into the North American interior. Fray Marcos's fabled city of Cibola turned out to be a small pueblo of about one hundred families, and Coronado sent the imaginative friar home to Mexico. Nevertheless, the conquistador captured the Zuñi city, the center of sixteenth-century Pueblo power, and made Cibola his headquarters for further exploration. Coronado spent the next three years in a fruitless quest for wealth and empire that carried him all the way to the Arkansas River at the site of present-day Lyons in central Kansas. Coronado returned to Mexico City empty-handed in 1542. Spanish settlement proceeded slowly northward over the next six decades, culminating in the submission of the Pueblos to Juan de Oñate in 1598 and the establishment of Santa Fe as the capital of New Mexico.

At the same time that Coronado was exploring the Southwest, another even less appealing conquistador, Hernando de Soto, was wreaking havoc among the Mississippian peoples of the Southeast. From his starting point near Tampa Bay, de Soto led a force of more than six hundred adventurers on a sanguinary quest for gold and slaves. His route took him north into what is now North Carolina, across the Appalachians into Tennessee, down the Tennessee River Valley into Alabama, overland to the Mississippi River and across the great river into present-day Arkansas. The Spanish reputation for cruelty preceded de Soto, sparking fierce Indian resistance to his progress. The conquistador, whom one observer described as "much given to the sport of hunting Indians on horseback," exceeded the Indian's worst fears. He slaughtered his Indian foes mercilessly, plundered Indian crops to feed his troops and livestock, and mounted vicious attacks on peaceful Indian towns with little or no provocation. Indian enemies slowly whittled down his forces, and in May 1542, de Soto himself took ill and died. The three hundred survivors of his expedition wandered another year traveling from the Mississippi River to Texas and back before making their way down the Mississippi and along the Gulf coast to a small Spanish settlement at the mouth of the Pánuco River.

From the earliest days of New World colonization, the Spanish crown confronted a difficult problem. Ambitious *adelantados*, semi-independent entrepreneurs interested chiefly in their own wealth and glory, had to be brought effectively under royal authority, a task easier imagined than accomplished. Adventurers such as

Managing an Empire

Cortés were stubbornly independent, quick to take offense, and thousands of miles away from the seat of imperial government. Their brutality toward indigenous populations provoked endemic conflict, making government of the colonies even more difficult and costly.

The crown found a partial solution in the *encomienda* system, an adaptation of the *repartimiento* system that the Spanish had developed to govern the Canary Islands. Like earlier conquering peoples such as the Normans of medieval England, Spanish rulers treated the New World's native inhabitants as a valuable source of tribute labor, and rewarded the leaders of the conquest with Indian villages. The people who lived in these settlements provided the *encomenderos* with labor tribute in exchange for legal protection and religious guidance. In Mexico the system combined Spanish methods with older Aztec mechanisms for levying labor tribute. Wherever it was imposed, the *encomienda* subjected Indians to cruel exploitation. The first generation of *encomenderos* in Mexico treated Spanish authority as an unlimited opportunity to enrich themselves. Cortés alone was granted the services of more than twenty-three thousand Indian workers. The *encomienda* system made the colonizers more dependent on the king, for it was he who legitimized their title. In the words of one scholar, the new economic structure helped to transform "a frontier of plunder into a frontier of settlement." The rapid decline of the native population eventually gave rise to a modified *repartimiento*, in which scarce Indian labor was allocated to wage-paying employers for limited periods on the basis of need.

Spain's rulers attempted to maintain tight personal control over their American possessions. The volume of correspondence between the two continents, much of it concerning mundane matters, was staggering. All documents were duplicated several times by hand. Because the trip to Madrid took many months, more than a year often passed before receipt of an answer came to a simple request. But the cumbersome system took on a momentum of its own. In Mexico, officials appointed in Spain established a rigid hierarchical order, directing the affairs of the countryside from urban centers. The practice of building such cities on the sites of former centers of native administration helped governors such as Cortés to transfer Indian obedience from indigenous overlords to Spanish ones. Spanish and Indian populations of these cities mingled, producing the rich admixture of European and native cultures that remains characteristic of Mexico and other Latin American nations.

The Spanish also brought Catholicism to the New World. The Dominicans and Franciscans, the two largest monastic orders of Catholic clergy, established Indian missions throughout New Spain. Some barefoot friars tried to protect the Native Americans from the worst forms of exploitation. One Dominican, Fray Bartolomé de Las Casas, published an eloquent defense of Indian rights, *Historia de las Indias*, which among other things questioned the legitimacy of European conquest of the New World. Las Casas deplored "the violence, the oppression, the despotism, the killing, the plunder, the depopulation, the outrages, the agonies, and the calamities" that Spanish conquistadores had inflicted on the Indians of the Americas. He suggested sweeping reforms in the crown's policy toward native peoples, including the replacement of Indian laborers with African slaves. Las

Casas's work provoked heated debate in Spain, and while the king had no intention of repudiating his vast American empire, he did initiate certain measures designed to bring greater "love and moderation" to Spanish-Indian relations.

To ascertain how many converts these friars made is impossible. Some conversions, especially in the early years of settlement, took place at the point of a sword. Many early Spanish governors were also priests who authorized their missionaries to build churches and shrines on sites held sacred by indigenous peoples. In Puerto Rico, for example, settlers carved a chapel for celebrating Mass into the trunk of an enormous sacred tree. In Mexico, Cortés built the cathedral in Mexico City on the site of the principal Aztec temple, refashioning the temple treasures into Christian icons and artifacts. Elsewhere in Mexico, Catholic churches also sprang up on Aztec temple sites. Such practices gained at least the external conformity of many Indians. Indigenous converts throughout New Spain also began making Catholicism an Indian religion. In other words, accommodation did not signal the eradication of traditional Indian cultures. The Native Americans made compromises when compelled to do so, then resisted domination through half measures. In 1531, a newly converted Christian reported a vision of the Virgin, a dark-skinned woman of obvious Indian ancestry, who became known throughout the region as the Virgin of Guadalupe. This figure—the result of a creative blending of Indian and European cultures—served as a powerful symbol of Mexican nationalism in the wars for independence fought against Spain almost three centuries later.

The New World attracted hundreds of thousands of Spanish colonists in the first hundred years after conquest. About 250,000 Spaniards migrated to the New World during the sixteenth century. Another 200,000 made the journey between 1600 and 1650. Most colonists were impoverished single males in their late twenties seeking economic opportunities. They generally came from the poorest agricultural regions of southern Spain, almost 40 percent migrating from Andalusia alone. Because so few Spanish women migrated, especially in the sixteenth century, the men often married Indians and blacks, unions which produced mestizos and mulattos. The frequency of interracial marriage indicated that, among other things, the people of New Spain tolerated racial differences more readily than the English who settled in North America. Economic worth affected the people of New Spain's social standing as much as, or more than, color. The Spanish regarded persons born in the New World, even those of Spanish parentage (*criollos*), as socially inferior to those born in the mother country (*peninsulares*).

EARLY NORTHERN EUROPEAN EXPLORATION

Ferdinand and Isabella's sponsorship of Columbus gave Spain an early lead in exploring and colonizing the Americas. Rulers of other nations, however, were reluctant to accept a Spanish monopoly over what Europeans at first believed was an unimpeded route to Asia, even if a papal treaty had granted it. Critics pointed out that the pope who had negotiated the treaty was himself Spanish-born. Even after recognizing that Spain had claimed a pair of continents hitherto unknown to Europeans, rival powers persisted in the belief that they could find a route through those lands to Asia. Northern European powers persisted in their search for a Northwest Passage to the Pacific Ocean well into the seventeenth century.

English Reconnaissance in North America

The first English visit to North America remains shrouded in mystery. Fishermen working out of Bristol and other western English ports began sailing across the Atlantic in search of new cod fisheries in the fourteenth century, and were fishing off the coast of Iceland by 1400. English merchantmen soon struck a prosperous trade with Icelanders while the fishermen pressed even further west. The knowledge they gained of navigating North Atlantic winds and currents may have enabled them to land in Nova Scotia and Newfoundland as early as the 1480s. There they began fishing regularly for codfish along the Grand Banks, and during the summer months some sailors probably dried and salted their catches on Canada's convenient shores.

The Bristol fishermen's knowledge of North Atlantic navigation proved valuable to John Cabot (Giovanni Caboto), a Venetian sea captain commissioned by Henry VII to search out a new trade route to Asia in 1497. Cabot's main contribution on this voyage was to publicize the location of the Grand Banks fisheries. Soon ships of other nations such as France, Portugal, and Spain began appearing annually to cast their nets in North American waters alongside the veteran Bristol fishermen. Cabot died during a second attempt to find a direct route to Cathay in 1498, but the English fishermen continued venturing further into the Gulf of St. Lawrence. English merchantmen also explored the coast between Labrador and New England between 1498 and 1505, but their failure to establish profitable trade brought formal efforts to a halt. Sebastian Cabot continued his father's exploration in the Hudson Bay region in 1508–1509, after which English interest in such ventures subsided.

The Newfoundland cod fishery, however, attracted the growing attention of English investors from Bristol, Plymouth, and even London itself throughout the sixteenth century. By mid-century it became one of the largest multinational European business ventures in the New World, attracting investors across national boundaries and annually drawing to the Grand Banks ships from all over Europe. Each year between March and May, fleets of vessels would depart from England's western ports for the coast of Newfoundland, where they arrived in early June just about the time the cod began to come inshore. While one portion of the crew fished, another set up operations on shore for gutting and drying the cod. Once dried, the cod was carefully packed in the holds. English vessels commonly rendezvoused in St. John's harbor or Placentia harbor to return in convoy to Europe, often joining ships of other nations there to trade for commodities and surplus fish. Fishermen also engaged in casual trade for furs with coastal Indians.

For the next half-century, the English people were preoccupied with more pressing domestic and religious concerns, and the crown sponsored only a few minor ventures into the Atlantic. When interest in the New World revived, however (see Chapter 3), Cabot's voyages established England's belated legal and diplomatic claim to American territory, and the valuable Grand Banks fishery excited Elizabethan greed to monopolize that claim.

Official French interest in the New World developed more slowly than in England, although individual French mariners were quick to recognize the potential of the North American fisheries. Indeed, soon after the Portuguese explorers Gaspar and Miguel Côrte-Real publicized their discoveries of Labrador and Newfoundland, Norman and Breton fishermen began flocking to the Grand Banks each summer. In 1506 the French navigator Jean Denys of Honfleur explored the eastern coast of Newfoundland. In 1508 another Frenchman, Thomas Aubert of Dieppe retraced Denys's route, returning to Rouen, France with seven Indians he had captured from the region. Only in 1524, however, did King Francis I commit French royal backing to a voyage of exploration by sponsoring Giovanni da Verrazano's quest for a short water route to China.

Initial French Ventures

Verrazano's quest initiated a series of sixteenth-century French exploratory efforts along the North American coast. He concluded that North America blocked the route to China and that it held no treasures comparable to those of Mexico. Nevertheless, Verrazano claimed the coast from present-day South Carolina to Maine for the King of France. Despite their apparent lack of value, these claims proved useful to Francis in persuading Pope Clement VII that an earlier papal division of the world between Spain and Portugal applied only to lands known in 1493, not to those discovered later by other nations.

In 1534, Francis I attempted to build on this diplomatic triumph by commissioning the French explorer Jacques Cartier to renew the quest for a route to China. Cartier's first voyage led him to the Gulf of St. Lawrence, where he found the rocky, barren coast of Labrador depressing. "I am rather inclined to believe that this is the land God gave to Cain," he grumbled. Yet Cartier reported to the king promising signs both in the eagerness of local Indians to trade and in the discovery of a large, promising waterway to the interior. The next year he returned to reconnoiter the St. Lawrence, traveling up the magnificent river as far as modern Montreal. Despite his high expectations, Cartier got no closer to China. He did, however, bring back to France several captive Indians who assured Francis I that a kingdom of fabulous wealth lay within reach of the St. Lawrence. In 1541 the king sent Cartier and the French nobleman Jean-François de la Rocque de Roberval to establish a settlement that would secure France's exclusive title to the hoped-for wealth of Canada. The explorers failed to find any treasure, however, and the harsh Canadian winter made the land seem uninhabitable. In 1542, Cartier gave up the effort to establish a permanent settlement and returned to the comforts of France.

Despite these early failures, French fishermen carried on sporadic trade with North American coastal peoples throughout the sixteenth century. Indeed, Cartier discovered during his first voyage that this trade was already going on when he encountered a French merchant vessel in the Gulf of St. Lawrence. Cartier's voyages helped to ensure the gradual increase of such trade by enabling Francis I to win trade concessions in the New World from Spain and Portugal. By 1550, both kingdoms grudgingly accepted the right of French subjects to trade peaceably in territories such as Canada, which remained unoccupied by Europeans. The unofficial French presence on the St. Lawrence grew as a result. By the 1570s traders were establishing small, permanent settlements along the riverbanks to secure a share of the growing market for beaver pelts.

THE INDIANS' NEW WORLD

The Indians were not passive spectators to the process of European discovery and colonization. The arrival of white men and women on the North American continent confronted Native Americans with a world which was, as historian James Merrell has reminded us, just as "new" as the one that greeted European invaders. Indian-white encounters presented unprecedented opportunities and dangers while profoundly altering Native American cultures. Change did not occur at the same rates in all places. Indian villages located on the Atlantic coast came under severe pressure almost immediately; inland groups had more time to adjust. Wherever they lived, however, Indians discovered that conquest strained traditional ways of life, and as daily patterns of experience changed almost beyond recognition, native peoples had to devise new answers, new responses, new ways to survive in physical and social environments that eroded tradition.

Native Americans were not hapless victims of geopolitical forces beyond their control. So long as they remained healthy, they held their own in the early cultural exchanges. They eagerly accepted certain trade goods but generally resisted other aspects of European intrusion. The earliest recorded contacts between Indians and explorers suggest curiosity and surprise rather than hostility. A southeastern Indian who encountered Hernando de Soto in 1540 expressed awe: "The things that seldom happen bring astonishment. Think, then, what must be the effect on me and mine, the sight of you and your people, whom we have at no time seen . . . things so altogether new, as to strike awe and terror to our hearts."

When relations turned hostile, as they did very quickly in de Soto's case, Indians could exact a terrible price for European aggression. No conquistador, not even Cortés, found them pushovers in battle. Europeans may have possessed tremendous firepower with cannons and cumbersome matchlock firearms, but Indians wielded their own weapons with deadly effect. The Mississippians of the Southeast deployed expert longbowmen against de Soto's forces—marksmen who could sink an arrow 6 inches into a poplar trunk and shoot more accurately than any European archer. Longbows gave the ability to strike with stealth; an archer could hit a distant target without revealing his position. A matchlock's report inevitably gave away the marksman's location. Longbows could also be reloaded faster than matchlock guns, were more reliable, more accurate, less cumbersome, required far less maintenance, and still worked after the powder ran out. Indians knew the terrain much better than Europeans, and they initially enjoyed a significant—sometimes overwhelming—numerical advantage over the small groups of European explorers, traders, and settlers.

Trade and Cultural Exchange

What Indians desired most was peaceful trade, and conditions in many areas enabled them to conduct exchanges on terms they regarded as highly favorable. The earliest French explorers reported that natives waved from shore, urging the Europeans to exchange metal items for beaver skins. The Indians did not perceive themselves at a disadvantage in these dealings. They could readily see the technological advantage of guns, metal blades, and metal arrow points over their own weaponry. Metal knives made daily tasks much easier. And to acquire these goods they gave up pelts, which to them seemed in abundant supply. "The English have

This illustration produced by Jacques Le Moyne in 1564 depicts Native Americans of coastal Florida depositing gifts of food at the foot of a column erected by French explorers who had established a short-lived settlement in the region.

Print Collection, Miriam and Ira D. Wallach Division of Art, Prints and Photography, New York Public Library, Astor, Lenox and Tilden Foundation

no sense," one Indian informed a seventeenth-century French priest. "They give us twenty knives like this for one Beaver skin." Another native announced that "the Beaver does everything perfectly well: it makes kettles, hatchets, swords, knives, bread . . . in short, it makes everything." The man who recorded these observations reminded French readers—in case they had missed the point—that the Indian was "making sport of us Europeans." Trading sessions along the eastern frontier were really cultural seminars. The Europeans tried to make sense out of Indian customs, and although they may have called the natives "savages," they quickly discovered that the Indians drove hard bargains. They demanded gifts; they set the time and place of trade.

The Indians used these occasions to study the newcomers. They formed opinions about the Europeans, some flattering, some less so, but no Indian group concluded from these observations that Indian culture was inferior to that of the colonizers. Many regarded the beards worn by European men as particularly revolting. An eighteenth-century Englishman said of the Iroquois, "They seem always to have Looked upon themselves as far Superior to the rest of Mankind and accordingly Call themselves Ongwehoenwe, i.e., Men Surpassing all other Men."

Europeans always found communicating with the Indians an ordeal. The invaders reported having gained deep insight into Native American cultures through sign languages. How much accurate information explorers and traders took from these crude improvised exchanges is a matter of conjecture. In a letter written in 1493, Columbus expressed frustration: "I did not understand those people nor they me, except for what common sense dictated, although they were saddened and I much more so, because I wanted to have good information concerning everything."

In the absence of meaningful conversation, Europeans often concluded that the Indians held them in high regard, perhaps seeing the newcomers as gods. Such one-sided encounters involved a good deal of projection, a mental process of translating alien sounds and gestures into messages that Europeans wanted to hear. Sometimes the adventurers did not even try to communicate, assuming from superficial observation—as did the sixteenth-century explorer Giovanni da Verrazano—"that they have no religion, and that they live in absolute freedom, and that everything they do proceeds from Ignorance."

Ethnocentric Europeans tried repeatedly to "civilize" the Indians. That meant persuading natives to dress like the colonists, attend European-style schools, live in permanent structures, and, most important, accept Christianity. The Indians listened more or less patiently, but in the end, most rejected European values so long as they remained independent of European control and unscathed by epidemic disease. Some Indians were sincerely attracted to Christianity during early encounters, but most paid it lip service or found it irrelevant to their needs. As one Huron told a French priest, "It would be useless for me to repent having sinned, seeing that I never have sinned." Another Huron announced that he did not fear punishment after death since "we cannot tell whether everything that appears faulty to Men, is so in the Eyes of God."

Among some Indian groups, gender figured significantly in a person's willingness to convert to Christianity. Native men who traded animal skins for European goods had more frequent contact with the whites, and they proved more receptive to the arguments of missionaries. Native women, however, jealously guarded traditional culture, a system that often sanctioned polygamy—a husband having several wives—and gave women substantial authority over the distribution of food within the village. French Jesuits quickly recognized the independence of Native American women and seemed especially eager to undermine it. Among other demands, missionaries insisted on monogamous marriage, an institution based on Christian values that made little sense in Indian societies where constant warfare killed off large numbers of young males and increasingly left native women without sufficient marriage partners.

Varieties of Encounter

The opportunities and threats Indians encountered in their contact with Europeans varied widely according to timing, circumstance, location, and ethnicity as well as the intentions and assumptions of each party. Spain's widespread application of the techniques of the *reconquista* in their early colonial ventures often cut short any period of peaceful cooperation between Indians and Spanish conquerors. Indeed, conflict erupted quickly between the native inhabitants of Hispaniola and the ruthless young adventurers that accompanied Columbus on his first voyages. As in later encounters, the Caribbean Indians initially hoped for trade, willingly accepting the European goods they valued in exchange for Indian products, including the food supplies on which the small bands of early Spanish settlers relied for survival. Yet most Indians quickly found themselves driven to resistance by Spanish aggression.

In Mexico, native groups subordinate to the Aztecs welcomed Cortés's arrival as a chance to throw off the rule of their oppressors. Cortés could not have hoped to conquer the Aztec empire without the cooperation of the Aztecs' own rebellious subject peoples, who paid a heavy price in wartime casualties for their actions. In a culture in which subject peoples commonly paid tribute to their overlords in labor, goods, and even human sacrifice, many of these groups may well have understood that their alliance with Cortés only replaced Aztec with Spanish overlords. That was certainly what all but the Tlaxcalans received with the *encomienda* system. Whatever their initial arrangement, the outbreak of hostilities committed tributary groups to fight to victory with the Spanish or face the gruesome vengeance of their former Aztec rulers. By allying with Cortés, the Indians of central Mexico ensured that they would make their way in their new world from a position of dependence.

Despite their subordination, the Indian peoples of central Mexico were not completely powerless in negotiating with the Spanish. The *encomienda* system permitted them to continue the annual cycle of planting and harvest, though they had to pay a portion of their crop in tribute to the *encomendero* and often found their own work interrupted by their masters' demands. The Indians of Mesoamerica converted in droves to the Christianity of their conquerors—one observer placed the total at 9,000,000 baptisms by 1536—but infused it with many native elements. They fashioned statues of Mary with native features and dress and adapted themes from their traditional agricultural cycles and native pantheon to the new religion. Statues of native gods sometimes assumed a place in processions beside those of Catholic saints, and the saints were eventually made to absorb the characteristics of various local deities. The gods of war had proved impotent and were abandoned, but the priest Bernardino de Sahagún found that when his Indian informants knelt in a church built on ancient temple ruins, many secretly venerated the old gods of that site.

In frontier areas where the Spanish were fewer, Indians could sometimes exercise more leverage in negotiating the terms of encounter even when the Europeans insisted on holding the reins of power. Rather than suffer the high cost of armed resistance, many sixteenth-century Pueblos of the Southwest cautiously accepted the terms of Spanish rule, which the conquerors communicated through a commemorative dramatization of the conquest of Tenochtitlán. Some Pueblo chiefs embraced Christianity as charismatic Franciscan missionaries convinced them of its spiritual power, sparking factionalism as others resisted the new ways. Inhabitants of the pueblos selectively appropriated Spanish goods and Spanish became the lingua franca among Zuñis, Hopis, Acomas, and other Pueblo groups. Pueblos offered varying degrees of outward conformity to Catholicism, but traditional religion remained strong. Many of the baptized embraced Catholic words and rituals as new names for traditional beliefs and new ways to access traditional sacred powers. Worship in the circular kivas continued, often secretly when Franciscan missionaries attempted to stamp it out.

In the Southeast, repeated depredations by conquistadors such as Ponce de León and Hernando de Soto taught the Indians to keep the Spanish at arm's length whenever possible. Throughout the sixteenth century, St. Augustine and other Spanish garrisons encountered resistance from groups such as the Calusas, who resented the Spanish presence and attempts to extend its authority over them. Yet the outposts did present enticing opportunities to barter for European goods, eventually persuading southeastern groups to forge trading partnerships with the Spanish. Here too, some Indians embraced Catholicism. Other groups favored the Spanish missionaries who sought the grisly gift of martyrdom, highly prized by the Catholic clergy—in theory at least—for the glory and divine favor its victims could anticipate when they died for their faith.

When the French and English began establishing official trading partnerships with North American Indians in the later sixteenth century, native peoples could often draw on a long history of contact with Europeans that had taught them how volatile encounter could be. Some acted on this knowledge in ways similar to a group of Chesapeake Indians who paddled out to a French trading vessel in "over thirty canoes, in each of which were fifteen or twenty persons with bows and arrows." The Indians would not permit "more than two to come on board," but struck a deal satisfying to both sides. The French went home with "a thousand marten skins" for which they gave "knives, fishhooks and shirts."

Like other coastal groups during the early years of contact, these Indians bargained with European traders from positions of strength. French trappers relied heavily on their Native American trading partners, which allowed the Indians to set many terms of cultural as well as economic exchange. By the 1580s, the benefits of European trade were beginning to entice Indian groups to concede the French *Père* preeminence within a long-existing system of trade alliances. Yet native acknowledgment of French authority remained little more than a formality well into the seventeenth century. Micmac, Abenaki, and Huron allies still held the balance of power in exchange. To secure their position within trade alliances, Frenchmen often married native wives and went to live in native villages, adopting many Indian ways in the process. Early French governors often found they could only preserve a commercial alliance by joining their trading partners in battle against traditional enemies.

Benign though it was in comparison with Spanish rule, French trade and settlement introduced its own set of cultural upheavals. Jacques Cartier described the St. Lawrence of his 1534 visit as a lush river lined with populous towns and fertile fields. Decades of intermittent contact brought about the abandonment of those fields and villages as various groups competed for European trade and as epidemic disease, inadvertently introduced by French traders, ravaged local populations.

The Columbian Exchange and Cultural Transformation

Epidemic disease was the most devastating result of the contact sixteenth-century Europeans initiated among previously separate biological environments. The Columbian exchange of plants, animals, and microbes continues even today, and the contagious diseases that it introduced destroyed the cultural integrity of many sixteenth-century North American tribes. European adventurers exposed the Indians to bacteria and viruses, which spread like wildfire in "virgin soil epidemics" among populations with no natural immunity. Smallpox, measles, and influenza decimated the Native American population. Other diseases such as alcoholism took a terrible toll.

Within a generation of initial contact with Europeans, the Caribs, who gave the Caribbean its name, had become virtually extinct on the larger islands. Neighboring Arawak populations were also decimated. The population of central Mexico fell from as many as 25 million in 1519 to around 1.3 million by 1600. Algonquian communities of New England experienced appalling rates of death. One Massachusetts colonist reported in 1630 that the Indian peoples of his region "above twelve years since were swept away by a great & grievous Plague . . . so that there are verie few left to inhabite the Country." Since the earliest settlers possessed no knowledge of germ theory, they speculated that a Christian God had providentially cleared the wilderness of heathens.

Historical demographers now estimate that some tribes suffered a 90 to 95 percent population loss within the first century of European contact. The death of so many Indians decreased the supply of indigenous laborers, who were needed by the Europeans to work the mines and to grow staple crops such as sugar and tobacco. The decimation of native populations helped persuade colonists throughout the New World to seek a substitute labor force in Africa. Indeed, the enslavement of African blacks has been described as an effort by Europeans to "repopulate" the New World, one that ironically brought with it African strains of virulent diseases such as yellow fever and malaria.

Indians who survived the epidemics often found that the fabric of traditional culture had come unraveled. Whole villages, bands, and even nations could be wiped out in a single epidemic, obliterating all memory of a people's customs, beliefs, and way of life. The enormity of the death toll and the agony that accompanied it called traditional religious beliefs and practices into question. The living remnant lost not only members of their families, but also elders who might have told them how properly to bury the dead and give spiritual comfort to the living.

Nevertheless, survivors struggled to reconstitute tribal groups and customs and, when that failed, to create new communities made up of people from different tribes who supported one another by pooling resources and cultural traditions. The biological devastation that followed in the wake of de Soto's rampage through the Southeast gave rise to the groups eighteenth-century colonists knew as Catawbas, Cherokees, and Natchez. Such groups often combined a variety of dialects into distinctive new tongues and drew upon various traditions to shape the beliefs, rituals, and customs that bound them together as a people.

Inland native peoples often withstood the crisis better than did the coastal Indians who first confronted Europeans and Africans. The distance of Iroquois lands from the northeastern Atlantic coast gave them more time to respond to the challenge, as did the situation of the Chickasaws and Choctaws of the Southeast. Refugee Indians from the hardest-hit eastern communities were absorbed into healthier western groups. Nonetheless, the cultural and physical shock that the dwindling Native American population experienced is beyond the historian's power ever fully to comprehend.

On balance, sixteenth-century Europeans benefited from the Columbian exchange. Native American populations hosted few diseases deadly to Europeans, with the likely exception of syphilis. However, native crops such as beans, squash, potatoes, tomatoes, and maize supplemented European as well as African diets and helped fuel the rapid growth of the European population and economy. Europeans also brought crops such as sugarcane and bananas, which flourished in the fertile American soil, as did European weeds such as dandelions. European livestock also thrived. Pigs escaped into the surrounding forests from the herds that accompanied de Soto's southeastern expedition, multiplying into herds of dangerous razorbacks that supplemented native supplies of game.

No European introduction transformed native life more than the horse, which Spanish explorers reintroduced to a land where it had been extinct for thousands of years. Indians acquired horses by capturing them directly from Spanish troops, rounding up strays from expeditions or supply trains, or capturing animals from the wild herds that multiplied from stray Spanish stock. Horses permanently changed the cultures of those groups that employed them by making possible long-distance travel. Plains Indians could now track buffalo herds much more effectively over their entire range. They also gained the speed needed to kill buffalo in large numbers, and the increased food supply permitted large mobile villages to supplant the small roving bands of earlier times. Pawnees, Wichitas, and Comanches rose to dominate the plains north of Texas and New Mexico, far from the effective reach of Spanish military might. Groups such as the Apache found themselves caught in a deadly three-way struggle as Comanches swept south from the Rockies, Wichitas moved west from the Arkansas River, and Spanish pushed north from the pueblos.

Trade and Dependence

At the center of every cultural clash was a struggle to preserve, augment, or acquire access to resources such as land, game, and trade goods. The Europeans found it almost impossible to understand the Indians' relation to the land and other natural resources. Spanish settlers prospected ceaselessly for new laborers for their silver mines, whereas Franciscan missionaries pursued native converts that could bejewel their martyrs' crowns. French traders trekked deeper into North American forests in search of furs. English planters cleared the forests and fenced the fields and, in the process, radically altered the ecological systems on which the Indians depended. The European system of land use inevitably reduced the supply of deer and other animals essential to traditional native cultures.

The Indians resisted European aggression, but they welcomed the transatlantic commerce that brought them so many useful goods. Over time, groups lost the knowledge of how to make traditional products replaced by European items such as knives, hatchets, and woolen blankets. European firearms brought Indians buyers back to the trader repeatedly for fresh powder, shot, and repairs. Like so many consumers throughout recorded history, the Indians discovered that the objects they most coveted inevitably dragged them into debt. To pay for the trade goods, the Indians hunted more aggressively, further reducing the population of fur-bearing mammals and sparking conflicts with neighboring groups as they transgressed territorial boundaries in search of new trapping grounds.

Commerce eroded Indian independence in other ways. After disastrous wars—the Yamasee War in South Carolina (1715), for example—the natives learned that demonstrations of force usually resulted in the suspension of normal trade, on which the Indians had grown quite dependent for guns and ammunition, among other things. A hardened English businessman made the point quite bluntly. When asked if the Catawbas would harm his traders, he responded that "the danger would be . . . little from them, because they are too fond of our trade to lose it for the pleasure of shedding a little English blood."

A WORLD TRANSFORMED

By the time the first Virginia Company colonists left port for the Chesapeake Bay in 1607, the wrenching processes of encounter had already transformed much of the North American landscape. Disease had wiped out whole peoples who once boasted a long and glorious past. Yet Native Americans had displayed a remarkable tenacity and resilience, a fierce determination to survive. New groups had arisen from the ashes of conquest, weaving together elements of ancient and disparate traditions into new cultures adapted to the world after encounter. Experience had taught all the participants how to survive in unfavorable circumstances and sometimes to prosper beyond expectations. American Indians proved themselves resourceful participants along with Africans and Europeans in the creation of the Atlantic world that emerged from the sixteenth-century process of encounter, trade, and conquest.

CHRONOLOGY

984	Erik the Red leads transatlantic Viking voyage.
1443	Nuno Tristão brings first cargo of slaves to Portugal from Arguin.
1481	Portuguese build Elmina castle on Gold Coast of Africa.
1492	Columbus lands at San Salvador.
1494	Treaty of Tordesillas establishes dividing line 270 leagues west of the Azores separating Spanish and Portuguese claims.
1497	Cabot leads first English exploration of North America.
1498	Vasco da Gama of Portugal reaches India by sailing around Africa.
1500	Pedro Cabral discovers Brazilian coast.
1502	Montezuma becomes emperor of the Aztecs.
1506	Columbus dies in Spain after four voyages to America.
1513	Juan Ponce de León leads first expedition to Florida.
1521	Cortés defeats the Aztecs at Tenochtitlán.
1531	Vision of Virgin of Guadalupe reported by Indian convert.
1534	Cartier claims Canada for France.

1536	Pedro Menéndez de Avilés establishes St. Augustine on Florida's Atlantic coast.
1540	Coronado explores the Southwest for Spain.
1600	Population of Mexico declines to 1.3 million.

RECOMMENDED READING

The early modern encounter of Atlantic peoples from Europe, Africa, and the Americas has become the subject of some of the most exciting and provocative scholarship of the past twenty years. For a succinct overview see A. W. Crosby *The Columbian Voyages, the Columbian Exchange, and Their Historians* (Washington, D.C., 1987). A good introduction to more than three centuries of encounter among Atlantic people groups may be found in Anthony Pagden, *European Encounters with the New World: From Renaissance to Romanticism* (New Haven, 1993). Stephen Greenblatt analyzes how early European visitors to the New World attempted to make sense of what they saw in his *Marvelous Possessions: The Wonder of the New World* (Oxford, 1991). Kirkpatrick Sale offers a provocative interpretation of encounter in his *Conquest of Paradise: Christopher Columbus and the Columbian Legacy* (New York, 1990). See also Tzvetan Todorov, *The Conquest of America: The Question of the Other* (New York, 1984).

A good overview of early Portuguese–West African exchange may be found in Ivana Elbl, "Cross-Cultural Trade and Diplomacy: Portuguese Relations with West Africa, 1441–1521," *Journal of World History* 3 (1992): 165-204. John Thornton explores the African impact on Atlantic trade and colonization in his *Africa and Africans in the Making of the Atlantic World, 1400–1800*, rev. ed. (Cambridge, 1998). For the beginnings of the slave trade, see Hugh Thomas, *The Slave Trade: The Story of the Atlantic Slave Trade, 1440-1870* (New York, 1997).

The process of encounter, conquest, and colonization between Spanish and Indians in the Caribbean and Mexico is treated in many recent studies. James Lockhart and Stuart B. Schwartz provide an excellent overview in *Early Latin America: A History of Colonial Spanish America and Brazil* (Cambridge, 1983). Inga Clendinnen analyzes the clash between Mayas and Spaniards in her *Ambivalent Conquests: Maya and Spaniard in the Yucatan, 1517–1570* (Cambridge, 1987). Good investigations of native peoples after the Spanish conquest may be found in James Lockhart, *The Nahuas After the Conquest: A Social and Cultural History of the Indians of Central Mexico, Sixteenth Through Eighteenth Centuries* (Stanford, 1992), and Stuart B. Schwartz, *Victors and the Vanquished: Spanish and Nahua Views of the Conquest of Mexico* (Boston, 1999).

An excellent starting point for reading about the European exploration of North America is Kirstin A. Seaver, *The Frozen Echo: Greenland and the Exploration of North America, ca.* A.D. *1000–1500* (Stanford, 1996). Mark Kurlasky, *Cod: The Biography of the Fish That Changed the World* (New York, 1998), surveys the long history of codfishing, beginning with an excellent account of its role in European exploration and colonization of North America. David J. Weber's *The Spanish Frontier in North America* (New Haven, 1992) offers a thorough and fascinating account of early explorers from

Ponce de León to Coronado and de Soto. W. J. Eccles, *The French in North America, 1500–1783* (East Lansing, 1998) treats early French exploration, while Neal Salisbury, *Manitou and Providence: Indians, Europeans, and the Making of New England* (Oxford, 1982) analyzes some of the earliest English encounters with North American peoples. For the Dutch in North America, see Oliver A. Rink, *Holland on the Hudson: An Economic and Social History of the Dutch in New York* (Ithaca, 1986).

The variety of encounter among North American Indians and Europeans has been the subject of some of the most exciting and creative scholarship of the past thirty years. Francis Jennings's intentionally provocative *The Invasion of America: Indians, Colonialism, and the Cant of Conquest* (Chapel Hill, 1975) stimulated a fresh effort to write the history of encounter from the native point of view. Even before Jennings's book appeared, however, the Canadian historian Bruce Trigger was employing the insights of archaeology and anthropology to reconstruct a carefully nuanced, culturally sensitive description of specific North American peoples in works such as his *Natives and Newcomers: Canada's "Heroic Age" Reconsidered* (Kingston, 1987). James Axtell's *The European and the Indian: Essays in the Ethnohistory of Colonial North America* (Oxford, 1981) offers similar analyses of North American peoples in contact with the English, while his *The Invasion Within: The Contest of Cultures in Colonial North America* (Oxford, 1986) offers a comparative analysis of Franco-native and Anglo-native patterns of contact and exchange. James H. Merrell, *The Indians' New World: Catawbas and Their Neighbors from European Contact Through the Era of Removal* (Chapel Hill, 1989) explores how one southern native group responded to an environment transformed by European colonization. Richard White, *The Roots of Dependency: Subsistence, Environment, and Social Change Among the Choctaws, Pawnees, and Navajos* (Lincoln, 1983), offers a comparative analysis of adaptation to European colonization in three very different regions of North America.

For the ecological impact of European exploration, see Alfred W. Crosby's path-breaking study, *The Columbian Exchange: Biological and Cultural Consequences of 1492* (Westport, Conn., 1972), as well as his *Ecological Imperialism: The Biological Expansion of Europe, 900–1900* (Cambridge, 1986). For ecological change in New England, see William Cronon, *Changes in the Land: Indians, Colonists, and the Ecology of New England* (New York, 1983), and for the Southeast, see Timothy Silver, *A New Face on the Countryside: Indians, Colonists, and Slaves in South Atlantic Forests, 1500–1800* (Cambridge, 1990). For a comprehensive study of North America's historical geography, see D. W. Meinig's *The Shaping of America: A Geographical Perspective on 500 Years of History*, Vol. 1, *Atlantic America, 1492–1800* (New Haven, 1986).

Chapter 3

Creating A Militant Atlantic World, 1500–1625

Anthony Knivet was a survivor in a harsh seafaring world. In 1591 he sailed with the English navigator Thomas Cavendish on an ill-fated attempt to circumnavigate the globe in search of plunder and glory. Knivet fell into Portuguese hands during a raid on the Brazilian coast, and his captors put him to work as a slave on the governor's sugar plantation. His varied tasks brought the Englishman into contact with a diverse range of fellow slaves from Africa, Brazil, and Europe. Knivet oversaw gangs of African and Native American fishermen who plied the coasts in dugout canoes to catch fish for the plantation labor force. He beat paths into the interior as a member of several slave-trading expeditions, gaining knowledge of native Brazilian customs from allied bands and surviving deadly skirmishes with enemy groups targeted for raids.

Knivet remained alert for any opportunity to escape, listening eagerly to the rumors that flew among fellow slaves about the comings and goings of ships from England, Holland, and France as well as Spain and Portugal. On one occasion, Knivet heard that the famous English seafarer Sir John Hawkins had anchored at a nearby island. Knivet stole a rowboat and tried to slip away to Hawkins's vessel, but he crashed on some rocks and was recaptured. Another time, Knivet managed to board undetected a Portuguese vessel bound for Angola, where he hoped to get away to an African port open to English or Dutch vessels that might take him home. In Angola, however, a Portuguese captain recognized Knivet and reported him to the governor, who clapped him in chains and sent him back to Brazil. Knivet worked there several more years before his master eventually brought him to Portugal. There his skill as an interpreter enabled Knivet to make connections with influential English patrons who finally helped him get home nearly a decade after he had departed.

Anthony Knivet was an English Protestant casualty in an ongoing struggle for religious and political control of a new Atlantic world, one that embroiled peoples from Africa, Europe, and the Americas in a series of brutal, far-flung conflicts over the Atlantic world for trade and plunder. This world began to emerge within a decade after Columbus's first voyage to America as Spanish adventures sailed west to exploit their monarchs' New World possessions, while other nations launched their own efforts to find westward routes to Asia. By 1510, Spanish vessels were plying regular trade routes from the Caribbean to Seville. The Portuguese likewise began developing trade along the Brazilian coastline they first discovered in 1500.

Not until Spain's conquests of Mexico and Peru, however, did America begin producing the fabulous wealth that sparked the vicious competition for control of this emerging Atlantic world. The conquests not only prompted Spain to develop an orderly system for securing its American riches but also fired the imaginations of competing nations, which mounted stiff challenges to Iberian dominance as the century wore on. By 1570, the Spanish and the Portuguese found themselves increasingly pressed by English, French, and Dutch competitors who sought alternative sources of New World wealth even as they tried to siphon off a share of Iberian colonial wealth through unofficial warfare and piracy. The rivals found ready cooperation among American Indian and African traders for whom increased competition meant leverage for negotiating more favorable terms of exchange. These efforts did not immediately displace the Iberians, but English, French, and Dutch challengers did manage by 1600 to gain a toehold in Atlantic commerce. In the process, they helped create a volatile, exploitative world that held great dangers for the powerless and unwary but promised fabulous returns for those who possessed sufficient resources, daring, and good fortune to risk their lives in New World ventures.

THE IBERIAN ATLANTIC

Spain and Portugal entered the sixteenth century with pretensions to exclusive control of the Atlantic world, but they soon found themselves waging a doomed defensive struggle to preserve their tenuous monopoly. The Treaty of Tordesillas in 1494 granted Spain control of all non-Christian lands discovered south and west of an imaginary line of demarcation drawn approximately 1,100 miles west of the Azores. Portugal gained rights to non-Christian lands east of that line. Other European nations refused to acknowledge the treaty's terms, but the Iberian powers remained best positioned during the early 1500s to turn their paper claims into the reality of transatlantic empires. Spain's energetic exploration of the Americas (see Chapter 2) made it the great territorial power of the age, while Portugal was able to build on its valuable African and East Indian trade to become the century's great maritime commercial power. It took several decades for European rivals to overcome the Iberians' head start. When they began to do so by the mid-sixteenth century, the cumbersome Atlantic system that the Spanish had constructed proved vulnerable indeed.

La Carrera de Indias

From the very beginning of transatlantic navigation, Spain's dominance rested on precious metals extracted from New World sources. Caribbean islands such as Cuba and Hispaniola contained significant gold deposits. By 1510 Spanish seafarers were averaging over 50 voyages per year on its east-west "Indies Run," carrying grain, supplies, missionaries, and colonists to the Caribbean and bringing precious metals and colonial products back to Seville. Despite this steady traffic, the yield from the first quarter-century of Spanish commerce in the New World seemed disappointing in comparison with Spain's own trade with European partners, let alone Portugal's enormously profitable African and East Indian routes.

Cortés's conquest of Tenochtitlán in 1519 marked a dramatic shift toward Spain in the balance of Atlantic commerce as ships laden with Mexican gold plied annual routes from Veracruz to Seville. Francisco Pizarro's conquest of Peru in the 1530s and the opening in 1545 of colonial Peru's rich Potosí silver mines (located

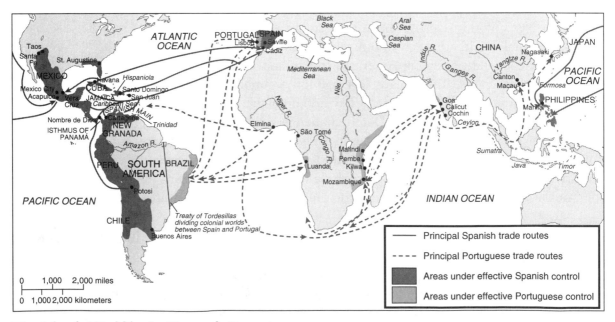

The Atlantic World in the Sixteenth Century

By 1600, European competition for New World wealth made the Atlantic basin a scene of protracted conflict among the rivals.

in what is now Bolivia) extended Spain's lead even further. Peruvian silver, like Mexican gold, passed through the Caribbean after being transported up the Pacific coast of South America and across the Isthmus of Panama to the region's Caribbean port of Nombre de Dios. Once loaded, the ships left the swampy, exposed coastline of Nombre de Dios for the well-defended harbor of Cartagena on the coast of Colombia, where they waited for favorable winds that would carry them back across the Atlantic. Through the remainder of the sixteenth century, precious metals flowed in torrents from Veracruz and Nombre de Dios to Seville. By 1610, Spain was importing nearly fourteen times as much New World treasure annually as it had a century before.

As the artery of Spain's New World wealth, the *Carrera de Indias* enriched several important ports through which it passed on its way to Seville. Chief among these were San Juan, Puerto Rico, the first Caribbean port of call for convoys from Seville, and Havana, Cuba, where treasure-laden ships from both Veracruz and Cartagena would regroup into convoys for the return voyage to Spain. Havana's harbor could hold up to a thousand vessels at once, and a chain of fortifications kept the treasure fleets formidably secure. In Havana's superior shipyards, Spanish vessels were repaired for the return voyage to Seville; they also produced Creole ships whose quality rivaled that of vessels made in the best Spanish yards. The French explorer Samuel de Champlain admired Havana in 1599 as the "warehouse where all the riches of America are held."

This great current of New World wealth flowed into the cosmopolitan port of Seville, stimulating the city's rapid growth as people from the surrounding countryside came to Seville to take advantage of new commercial opportunities. Merchants from other European commercial centers established residence in Seville to sell items such as English wool, Flemish textiles, German iron, and French trade goods for Spanish gold and silver. Banking families from the Italian city of Genoa helped make Seville a center of European finance. The transactions made by these merchants and bankers channeled Spanish wealth through powerful mercantile networks to stimulate production and commerce in many other parts of Europe.

New World gold made Spain a military as well as a commercial threat to other maritime powers. It enabled Spanish monarchs to buy the navy, artillery, and armaments needed to make their dominion the most powerful in Europe. After the Spanish Crown passed to the Hapsburg Emperor Charles V, he used its wealth and power aggressively to extend his influence over continental Europe. Charles's successor, Philip II of Spain continued his father's expansive policies. The English promoter Richard Hakluyt the Younger warned that "the contynuall commynge of . . . threasure" from Spanish America to Philip II would enable the monarch to finance international "mischief" that could destroy England.

Spanish Treasure and Indian Labor

Spanish colonists depended heavily on Native American workers to keep the treasure flowing into Seville. The *repartimiento* system established in the first decades of conquest harnessed Indian labor to produce profits for the Spanish colonists (see Chapter 2). In the earliest years of colonization, Columbus sanctioned the enslavement of Carib and Arawak Indians, many of whom panned gold for Spanish masters from the rivers and streams of the Caribbean islands of Hispaniola, Cuba, and Puerto Rico. The Crown soon halted indiscriminate enslavement of Indians, permitting colonists to enslave only hostile "cannibals" on whom they had declared war. Colonists often circumvented this restriction by declaring as "cannibals" whichever Indians they wanted to enslave. Nevertheless, the restriction ensured that they had to obtain most native workers by exacting various forms of labor tribute.

In Mexico, Cortés and his successors initially extended a form of *encomienda* that gave the new Spanish lords almost absolute control over the Indians within their borders. *Encomenderos* often enslaved, branded, rented, and sold their native laborers or put them to work on estates to produce goods or mine ore for export. Soon after the discovery of rich silver lodes at Zacatecas in 1546, the Spanish Crown introduced to Mexico a reformed *repartimiento* system of labor tribute. The new laws prohibited enslavement of Indians except captives of war, and they adapted the old Aztec method of exacting labor from the resident population on a rotating basis. In distant mining zones like Zacatecas, however, the owners and managers had to rely primarily on free wage labor to attract sedentary Indian workers from populated centers of Spanish dominion. The Spanish supplemented the wage labor force with Indian slaves captured in the endemic frontier warfare as well as smaller numbers of slaves transported from Africa.

Indians also comprised the bulk of the mine workers in early Peru. As in Mexico, the Spanish adapted a previously existing system of labor tribute to supply the earliest Peruvian mining operations with forced workers. The discovery of silver in the high Andean region of Potosí in 1545, however, brought about a shift to free contract labor as Quechua-speaking Indians flocked to the mines in search of opportunity. The Spanish depended on Indians not only to mine the ore, but also to refine it using smelting technology that Inca craftsmen had developed for oxygen-poor high altitudes. For 20 years, Spanish and Indian alike profited from mining and refining the abundant, high-quality ore. After 1570, Indian contract laborers began to drift away as depletion of the purest ore made the task of mining and processing much less profitable. Spanish officials responded by instituting the *mita* system of forced tribute labor once again to sustain production in the Potosí mines.

The various forms of forced labor that the Spanish imposed on their conquered peoples enriched colonists and Crown alike. Yet the catastrophic decline in Spanish America's native population soon produced a chronic labor shortage, precipitating a search for new sources of workers. The Spanish turned increasingly to African slaves during the sixteenth century, augmenting the economic power of the Portuguese who controlled the transatlantic slave trade.

The Portuguese Atlantic

Although the Spanish were busy using the wealth of the *Carrera de Indias* to expand their economic and political might, the Portuguese were building a worldwide commercial empire that profoundly shaped the Atlantic world. Although the English promoter Sir Thomas Peckham regarded Portugal as "scarce comparable to some three shires of Englande," he marveled at its leaders' resourcefulness in "fortifying, peopling, and planting" the coasts of "the West, the South, and the East partes of Africa, and also at Calicute (Calcutta) and in the East Indies, and in America." Until Portuguese planters began settling Brazil after 1530, however, their far-flung empire consisted mainly of fortified trading depots strategically located where their European commodities would command favorable returns in spices, textiles, gold, and slaves. Until 1530, Portugal imported more gold through its Africa trade than Spain imported from the Caribbean and Mexico combined. Portugal's control of the lucrative Asian spice routes continued to make it the envy of Spain and other European nations even after imports of New World gold began outpacing imports from Africa.

Portugal began extending its trading empire to the New World shortly after Pedro Cabral discovered the Brazilian coast in 1500. Cabral was not primarily interested in discovering New World territory, but in finding a way to avoid sailing into the teeth of the southeast trade winds that made navigation to the Cape of Good Hope so difficult. In this he succeeded, and Brazil soon became a stop for Portuguese vessels to take on fresh fruit and water en route to the Indian Ocean. Brazil's location east of the demarcation line gave Portugal the exclusive right to exploit its resources, and the Portuguese Crown claimed a monopoly on coastal trade in brazilwood, a source of valuable dye.

For three decades Portuguese merchants remained content to use Brazil's coast primarily as a provisioning stop on the route to more profitable ports. The minor trade in dyewood did bring the Portuguese into contact with indigenous peoples who bartered their labor for European commodities, cutting the wood that grew wild in the forest and piling it on the shore for loading. During this period, French merchants also traded regularly with Brazilian Indians for dyewood with little opposition from the Portuguese. Only in 1530 did the Portuguese begin to view its American territory as a place for permanent settlement of traders. The Crown organized existing trading forts into a system of hereditary captaincies to secure the monopoly on brazilwood and begin developing other resources.

The Portuguese colonization of Brazil proceeded slowly until the 1550s, when settlers began shifting attention from the dyewood trade to sugar planting. The change proved fateful both for their relations with their native neighbors and for the larger history of the Atlantic world. Early planters obtained financing from Antwerp's traditional sugar investors to purchase sugarcane and expensive mills. They brought sugar-producing supplies and technology from the well-established Portuguese sugar islands of Madeira off the coast of Morocco and São Tomé in the Gulf of Guinea. More importantly, Brazilian planters transferred from those islands the plantation system based on slave labor. While the east Atlantic sugar planters had long relied on the labor of African slaves, Brazilian planters initially enslaved neighboring Indians to work their cane fields and mills. As in other parts of America, however, epidemic diseases soon began taking their toll on Brazil's indigenous population. As the Indian labor supply declined, planters increasingly turned to slaves shipped from Africa.

Brazil's sugar plantations proved highly successful, stimulating rapid expansion of transatlantic Portuguese shipping between Europe, Africa, and America. The abundance of prime land near the coast made it possible to produce sugar on a much larger scale than ever before. While a Madeira sugar mill could produce a yearly average of around 15 metric tons of sugar, the average mill in Brazil was producing better than double that amount only two decades after large-scale planting began. By 1600, the average Brazilian sugar mill was producing 130 metric tons per year. The wealth that circulated the Atlantic from Brazilian sugar and African slaves stirred European rivals to envy Portugal as much as they did Spain. Indeed, mid-sixteenth-century English promoters commonly referred to the wealth of the "King of Spaine and the King of Portingal" in the same breath.

Shrewd exploitation of their New World possessions enabled Spain and Portugal to transform the sixteenth-century Atlantic into a greater Iberian world. Spanish ships dominated the central east-west route from southern Europe to the Caribbean and Spanish Main, while a growing stream of Portuguese vessels dominated the triangular route between Africa, Brazil, and Europe. Other European seafarers navigated on the fringes of this great Atlantic world, gleaning what profits they could at the sufferance of Spain and Portugal or from pockets of trade and plunder neglected by the Iberian lords of the sea. By 1580, when King Philip II of Spain seized the Portuguese Crown, the combined wealth of the United Kingdoms made Iberian might seem truly invincible.

Spain's apparent might masked deep flaws in its imperial system, however. The sudden acquisition of so much American wealth stimulated an enormous inflation that hurt ordinary Spaniards who had no desire to emigrate to America. They were hurt further by long, debilitating European wars funded by American gold and silver. Moreover, instead of developing its own industry, Spain became dependent on the annual shipment of bullion from America. In 1603, one insightful Spaniard declared, "The New World conquered by you, has conquered you in its turn."

AFRICANS IN THE SIXTEENTH-CENTURY ATLANTIC

The ability of the Portuguese to extend African slavery to the Americas flowed out of nearly a century of well-developed trade relations with powerful African commercial interests (see Chapter 2). Too often, historians have given short shrift to Africa in their haste to tell the story of colonial American development. Yet we should not allow the enormity of the slave trade to obscure either the diversity of Africa's transatlantic commerce or the active role that African leaders themselves took in developing the Atlantic economy. The expansion of slavery represented a continuous process of change in Africa as new slavers carried the trade to new recruitment areas. Europeans did not simply dictate the terms of exchange to hapless, benighted primitives. Coastal African rulers and merchant communities brought sophisticated bargaining skills and discriminating preferences to the Atlantic market. In most ports, African law governed the terms of trade. Europeans had to trade using African weights and measures. European rulers often had to lubricate the wheels of commerce with generous gifts to local African rulers. Europeans who balked at or tried to circumvent these constraints often ran afoul of African laws backed by formidable military force. European merchants depended on their African partners to develop the sustained supply and demand—in goods as well as slaves—that made Africa a vital link in the emerging Atlantic world economy. The story of New World slavery remains incomplete until we understand how it set in motion an ongoing complex of transformative factors operating on both sides of the Atlantic.

Africa's entry into the Atlantic market did not come about because Europeans arrived on the African coast with goods superior to those that Africans could produce for themselves. Indeed, the reverse often proved true, as early Portuguese traders on the Gold Coast discovered when their Akan partners demanded African slaves rather than European goods as the price for their gold. African ironworkers possessed the technology to produce what was arguably the best steel in the sixteenth-century world. African weavers could produce cloth as fine as any available in Europe.

> **Competition and Conspicuous Consumption**

To break into this sophisticated African market, European traders had to identify and meet specific market demands as well as create new demand by appealing to their customers' instinct for a bargain and taste for variety. Europeans managed this in several ways. Sometimes they supplied the African demand for products from distant ports on the African coast by using their sailing vessels to transport the goods more cheaply, quickly, and in greater volume than could African traders. In the case of iron, Europeans found a market niche in supplying poorer grades at prices far cheaper than those of African producers. African craftsmen could use inferior European iron selectively to produce everyday utensils for which it was adequate, while preferring higher-grade African steel for stronger, more durable items such as metalworking tools and swords. European textiles eventually found a market as well, even among the Akan of the Gold Coast who were already well-supplied with beautiful cloth of African manufacture. European fabrics offered a greater range of texture, beauty, and design, and large collections of cloth became a mark of wealth and status for their African owners.

African merchants also offered a wide variety of goods that Europeans valued, besides the gold that served as the basis of Portugal's fifteenth and early-sixteenth-century African trade. Sixteenth-century Spanish and Portuguese traders regularly purchased grain from several parts of West Africa for shipment to their plantation colonies. Exquisitely crafted items made from native African materials such as ivory fetched high prices in Europe, as did raw ivory itself. Senegambian mats covered European beds. Some types of African cloth enjoyed a significant European demand. Weavers in the West African region of Allada produced their highly prized fabrics by unraveling the threads from cloth imported from Europe, which they rewove in distinctive patterns for sale to markets as distant as the Caribbean island of Barbados.

Whatever the European market was for African minerals and manufactured goods, it always existed alongside a demand for slaves. The demand rose steadily even before 1492 as the Portuguese and Spanish sought workers for the sugar plantations on their Atlantic islands (see Chapter 2). The introduction of sugar planting in Brazil after 1550, coupled with the decimation of the native population throughout the sixteenth-century in the Caribbean islands and Latin America, brought a dramatic increase in the trade in African slaves. Between 1550 and 1600, the number of Atlantic slave exports from West Africa rose to over 200,000, at least

> **Africans and the Atlantic Slave Trade**

30,000 more slaves than were exported during the previous one hundred years. During the seventeenth century, nearly 2 million Africans were carried to the New World, and the number soared to over 6 million in the eighteenth century. By the time Brazil became the last Atlantic nation to abolish slavery in 1880, over 11 million Africans had crossed the Atlantic in chains. The vast majority of those who survived the Atlantic crossing—around 80 percent—wound up on plantations in Brazil and the Caribbean.

European demand alone cannot account for the rapid growth of the Atlantic slave trade, for no early modern European state wielded the military or economic power sufficient to coerce African rulers into supplying slaves. Indeed, the Portuguese concluded as early as the 1450s that it was far more practical to trade for slaves than to risk war with powerful West African coastal states by attempting to capture them in raids. African authorities remained firmly in control over all but a few regions such as the Portuguese colony of Angola, and even there European traders depended heavily on African suppliers who readily exchanged slaves for the commodities they desired. Europeans tapped into systems of slavery that had existed for centuries among these African states (see Chapter 1). The slaves in most cases were captured prisoners of war—casualties in the endemic conflict that raged constantly among Africa's many fractious states. Captives were taken in a variety of ways: some during pitched battles, others during lightning raids on villages or fields, still others as tribute from defeated territories. Captors did not regard their slaves as members of a common racial group, but as alien peoples who had forfeited their freedom by right of conquest and thus could be put to work or sold as circumstances demanded.

Captives of wars or raids often traveled long distances overland, chained or yoked together and marched in single file so they could be easily guarded. Marching distances increased as the coastal supply of slaves dwindled, prompting traders to offer higher prices that made it worthwhile for inland rulers to bear the cost of transport. Slaves might change hands between traders several times during transit. A buyer might put a newly acquired slave to work for a while before re-selling him, as the eighteenth-century slave Olaudah Equiano experienced on his long march to the West African coast. African masters living in port towns often put newly arrived slaves to work in fields or on projects for several months while waiting for a European slave trader to arrive.

Over time, the slave trade shifted to different centers along the African coast as states responded to new internal demands and pressures as well as new commercial opportunities. During the fifteenth and early sixteenth centuries, for example, Portuguese merchants purchased many slaves from the coast of Benin for resale on the Gold Coast or for transport to their sugar islands of Madeira and São Tomé. By 1550, however, Benin's rulers cut off the supply, possibly because they needed slave laborers themselves to support the brisk export trade they had developed in cloth and pepper. The kingdom of Kongo, on the other hand, continued to deal in slaves until the early seventeenth century, when war with neighboring states disrupted the trade. As some states pulled out of the trade, others entered, enticed by rising prices or the desire for specific goods. Still other regions, such as the Portuguese colony of Angola with its many links to the continent's interior, continued supplying slaves to the Atlantic market from the late sixteenth through the seventeenth centuries.

The European demand for slaves produced a dramatic shift in the direction of the long-distance African trade. Before the sixteenth century, many slaves remained in the region where they were captured. Others were transported to more distant regions along the coast, and a large number were carried north across the Sahara to the Mediterranean and Middle East, where most masters purchased them as domestic servants and concubines. The growing demand for laborers in America, however, redirected the trade to the Atlantic during the seventeenth century.

The Atlantic trade also produced a shift in the demographic impact of slavery in Africa. Not only did it draw off many more slaves than had the trans-Sahara trade, it also demanded a much higher proportion of males. The earlier long-distance trade had drawn a higher proportion of female slaves to satisfy the demand for concubines. European buyers, by contrast, preferred male slaves for heavy plantation labor, although they also put slave women to work in the fields. The sexual imbalance in the Atlantic trade contributed to the ongoing demand for new slaves from Africa by making it difficult in most areas for the New World slave population to sustain itself through natural increase. The African population may also have suffered from siphoning off so many males, but the widespread practice of polygamy partially compensated for the loss.

Portuguese dominance of the sixteenth-century African coast ensured that their vessels carried the vast majority of slaves to the New World until the 1620s, when the Dutch finally began to break their monopoly. Portuguese ships could make the trip from West Africa to Brazil in approximately six weeks, making large-scale transport of Africans to their American colony practical and cost-effective. Portuguese vessels also carried Africans to the Spanish American mainland ports of Cartagena and Veracruz as well as Spanish Caribbean ports such as Havana and San Juan, where the much longer voyages took a heavy toll in mortality, disease, and profits.

The Middle Passage

The voyage across the Atlantic united the slaves that endured it in a shared experience of trauma and deprivation. Mortality during the middle passage was high, the ordeal often taking a third of a ship's slaves during the voyage. Long chains often bound slaves together in groups of six or more, and many captains took the additional precaution of shackling two captives together at the ankles to prevent escape. Slaves spent much of the voyage locked below decks, where the stifling heat and poor circulation made the air so bad that a candle would not remain lit. The stench of vomit, urine, and feces soon became intolerable, even on vessels whose crews periodically cleaned the holds. A port's inhabitants often knew when a slave ship had arrived by the foul smell near the harbor. On some vessels, the captains gave the sufferers temporary relief from these horrible conditions by bringing them on deck for a short period each day in small, closely watched groups.

Slaves on the middle passage also endured malnourishment, dehydration, and illness that only worsened as the voyage grew longer. After 1520, the Portuguese

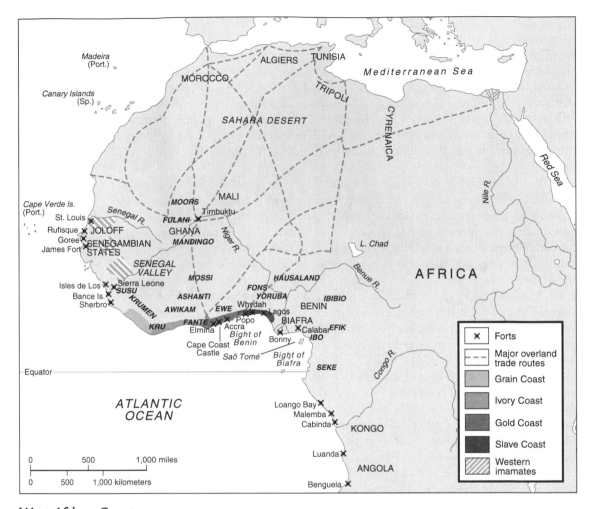

West African Coast

The arrival of European trading vessels along the coast of West Africa supplemented existing Trans-Saharan trade networks and eventually produced a shift to Atlantic trade. African rulers and merchants competed with each other for European trade, offering sites for European "factories" such as those shown on this map.

Crown required crews to load royal vessels with adequate food and water supplies. The regulations did not bind private traders, however, who commonly overloaded their vessels with slaves and skimped on supplies in an effort to make as much profit as possible. Alonso de Sandoval, an early-seventeenth-century observer of the Portuguese trade, reported that slaves usually received only a "small jar of water" and one meal of millet gruel per day. Sandoval wrote that slaves arriving at the end of the long voyages to Cartagena or Veracruz were typically "reduced to skeletons." Poor nutrition made the captives especially susceptible to epidemic diseases such as typhoid fever, measles, yellow fever, and smallpox. These diseases sometimes claimed entire shiploads of slaves along with their crews, and infected ships sometimes spread their epidemics to the ports where they anchored.

The middle passage marked its survivors with enduring scars of unspeakable psychological and physical trauma. Yet contrary to the assertions of some modern historians, it neither stripped Africans of their cultural memory nor reduced them to a state of fawning dependence on their European masters. Abundant evidence testifies that the middle passage began the process of forging new African communities bound together by a common experience on which they could build coherent cultural traditions. In doing so, African slaves drew on their past for the resources to cope with their experience in the New World and to create communities that could provide support and nurture in the midst of a harsh experience. They also exhibited a persistent determination to resist bondage when opportunity arose, and some escaped to forge independent maroon societies in areas beyond the control of Latin American authorities.

THE AFRICAN DIASPORA: SIXTEENTH-CENTURY BEGINNINGS

African slaves participated in the colonization of the New World from Columbus's first voyage onward. African slaves served as seamen on the early voyages of discovery as well as servants in the households and estates of early Spanish conquistadores and royal officials. Spanish colonists soon came to rely on African labor for mining and agricultural enterprises as well, especially after epidemic disease deprived them of their Native American workers. Portuguese colonists in Brazil likewise turned to African labor almost instinctively to supplement indigenous labor on the colony's sugar plantations. As the number of African slaves in Spanish and Portuguese America grew, so did their power to contribute distinctive African elements to the emerging Atlantic world.

African slaves filled an important niche in the Spanish American labor system even before the devastating declines in the native population. The limitations that the Crown placed on Indian slavery, coupled with the *repartimiento* system's restrictions on the use of Indian labor, created a need for a permanent labor force to sustain and coordinate crucial operations. *Encomenderos* used African slaves to fill the gaps. Throughout Spanish America, African workers provided the domestic labor force as permanent members of colonial households. Africans occupied supervisory and administrative roles in Spanish mining operations both in the Caribbean and on the Mexican and Peruvian mainland. Slaves from Senegambia, who brought to the Americas cattle-herding skills unknown among the Indians, tended herds on Spanish American *haciendas*. Expert divers from the Gold Coast fished pearls for Spanish masters off the coasts of Venezuela and Trinidad. Skilled African craftsmen worked as blacksmiths, barrel makers, carpenters, and cabinetmakers. African slaves worked in the cane fields and sugar mills of the Spanish Caribbean. In many of these operations, they worked alongside or supervised Native American slaves, tribute laborers, and wage earners. As disease decimated the supply of native laborers, Spanish masters replaced them wherever possible with African slaves.

In Portuguese Brazil, enslaved Tupinambá Indians provided most of the labor on the early sugar plantations. Even so, Portuguese masters preferred to employ African slaves in domestic service and skilled tasks. The rapid expansion of the plantation economy soon created a demand for African slaves in the fields and mills as well, one that was only exacerbated as epidemic disease began to take its toll on the Tupinambá population. By the early 1600s, African slaves almost completely replaced the Tupinambá in all aspects of plantation labor.

The experience of Africans in colonial Latin America varied widely according to the type of labor they performed and the conditions in which they lived. Most African slaves in the Spanish mining regions, for instance, were male. Though they enjoyed some privileges associated with their supervisory and skilled positions, they usually could not marry African women or create the families and stable communities that could nurture their cultural traditions. The slave populations of plantation regions also suffered from an imbalanced sex ratio of two or more men for every woman. Nevertheless, the greater presence of African women on some plantations did make it possible for African slaves to marry, have children, and form communities. Africans also forged a variety of relationships with Indian co-workers as well as Europeans. Both Spanish-American and Brazilian colonists tolerated sexual unions among Europeans, Africans, and Indians. The resulting mulatto (offspring of African-European unions) and mustee (African-Indian offspring) populations were incorporated along with mestizos (European-Indian offspring) into colonial Latin American societies.

The African slave communities of colonial Latin America rarely reproduced the culture of any specific ethnic group. Although the ethnic makeup of individual slave cargos was often homogeneous, the slaves arrived into port only to be dispersed onto plantations where they encountered people from very different cultural backgrounds. Slaves living in the cities of Spanish and Portuguese America often overcame this separation by seeking out fellow countrymen with whom they formed ethnic secret societies. Slave communities on the plantations, however, combined features of diverse native African cultures with European and Native American elements, producing new cultural forms. The resulting innovations in music, dress, language, religion, and customs of marriage and family life sustained the members of slave communities and eventually linked slaves of entire regions to one another through a shared cultural system. African seamen traveling from port to port on European vessels may have tapped into several of these regional cultural systems to provide even wider links among maritime Atlantic slave communities.

Not all Africans who came to Spanish and Portuguese America as slaves remained so throughout their lives. A master could manumit a slave in reward for particular services performed or as a show of magnanimity, or he might allow a slave to purchase his freedom through additional labor. Over time, significant communities of free blacks emerged in colonial Latin America. Other slaves simply escaped, running away to remote areas where they formed maroon communities that resisted capture while they lived by preying on Spanish and Portuguese settlements and shipping. Maroons on Caribbean islands often pursued the time-honored coastal African tradition of piracy, ambushing unsuspecting vessels from canoes and open boats. Maroon communities in Brazil formed powerful, well-armed states that could effectively repel colonial militia units periodically dis-

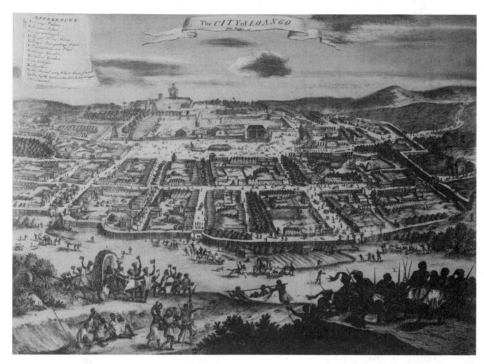

The well-designed streets of Loango 100 miles north of the Congo River (see the map of the West African Coast on p. 64), display the wealth and sophistication of its rulers and merchants. In the mid-eighteenth century when this engraving was made, Loango was a free port, open to trade from all European nations. At its peak, nearly 15,000 Africans were taken in chains from Loango to the Caribbean and North America each year, making the city one of the most important sources of slaves in that period.

The Granger Collection, New York

patched to suppress them. Maroons of Central America, whom the Spanish called *cimarrónes*, staged periodic raids from their well-hidden jungle villages, harassing coastal communities and attacking the treasure convoys that carried Peruvian silver across the Isthmus of Panama.

In thinking about the long history of the New World, we tend to focus on European migrations. But this is a tale told by the winners, by those who profited from unfree black labor. In fact, during every single year between 1650 and 1831, more Africans than Europeans came to the Americas. As historian Davis Eltis writes, "In terms of immigration alone. . . America was an extension of Africa rather than Europe until late in the nineteenth century."

THE NORTHERN EUROPEAN CHALLENGE

By the mid-sixteenth century, the African demand for European commodities had combined with its supply of slaves to make the continent an indispensable part of the Iberian Atlantic system. African slave labor increasingly sustained the flow of precious metals from the Spanish Main as well as the growth in Brazilian sugar production. The transatlantic circulation of wealth excited the envy of Spain's and Portugal's rivals to the north, while growing Spanish military power aroused their fears.

As the century wore on, these challengers moved ever more boldly to wrest the Atlantic economy from Iberian control. Privateers raided colonial ports and seized vulnerable galleons. Traders intruded into African and New World networks of exchange. Explorers sought alternative routes to the riches of the East and laid claim to stretches of coast unoccupied by Spanish or Portuguese colonists. In most instances, they ignored the prior claims of native peoples, although a few such as the Dutch adventurer Peter Minuit sought to gain legal advantage by purchasing claims from the original inhabitants. The boundaries of the Atlantic world steadily expanded as northern Europeans secured new American beachheads to find new sources of wealth and "cutt off the common mischefes that commes to all Europe by the peculiar aboundance" of the Spanish king's "Indian treasure."

The French

Spain and Portugal no sooner began consolidating their control of Atlantic shipping lanes between Africa, the New World, and Europe than the French monarch Francis I began challenging them. France and Spain were locked in almost perpetual warfare from 1521 to 1559, and King Francis viewed New World enterprise as a means of gaining advantage over his rival Charles V. This motive had driven the French Crown's sponsorship of Verrazano's and Cartier's quests for a Northwest Passage to Asia (see Chapter 2). It also prompted several direct challenges to Spanish and Portuguese claims in the Caribbean, the Gulf of Mexico, and the coast of Brazil. Although most of their early attempts to wrest a toehold in the New World ended in failure, explorers in the service of the French Crown nevertheless established a persistent French presence in America in the sixteenth century and laid the foundations for successful seventeenth-century colonial ventures.

Early French Ventures in the Caribbean and Brazil

France and Spain had barely been at war a year when in 1522 French squadrons belonging to the Norman nobleman Jean Ango captured four galleons returning to Spain laden with treasure from newly conquered Mexico. The richness of these prizes, which were taken near the Azores, soon emboldened French captains to seek letters of marque from the French Crown authorizing them to invade the Caribbean itself in search of Spanish plunder. By 1550, these French corsairs had established a fearsome reputation through their yearly raids on the coastal towns of Puerto Rico, Cuba, and Hispaniola. In 1655, the privateer Jacques de Sores captured and burned Havana, the fortress of the Spanish Caribbean itself. The conclusion of peace between Spain and France in 1559 did little to diminish the French presence in the Caribbean, where corsairs continued raiding and smuggling operations into the seventeenth century.

The corsairs wasted little time in extending their activities to the coast of Brazil, where they competed with Portuguese merchants for dyewood. The Portuguese initially tolerated the trade out of fear that the French Crown would issue letters of marque against their ships. As the tide of war turned against France in Europe, however, Portugal's King John III sent a fleet to round up French traders and execute them as pirates. In spite of this action, the French refused to surrender the contest for Brazil. By 1550 the corsairs controlled a significant stretch of the Brazilian coast, where they traded for dyewood and staged raids on Portuguese settlements. French traders established amicable relations with their Indian trading partners, often settling in native villages and intermarrying to cement alliances in a manner that became characteristic of French–Native American interaction throughout the Americas. These alliances helped the French hold out against Portuguese efforts to dislodge them from Brazil until 1603.

French adventurers also made sporadic attempts during the sixteenth century to compete with Spain for a foothold in southeastern North America near Florida. In 1562, a group of French Protestants established a settlement on what is now Parris Island in South Carolina's Port Royal Sound. This new colony of Charlesfort was the first European settlement in what would become Britain's thirteen mainland colonies. Its founders hoped it would become a Huguenot refuge, a center for exploiting new discoveries of American wealth, and a base for preying on Spanish shipping. Internal strife soon tore the colony apart, however, and Spanish forces from Havana burned Charlesfort's abandoned buildings in 1564. That same year the Huguenots attempted to found a second colony at Fort Caroline near the mouth of the St. Johns River on the Atlantic coast of Florida. It lasted less than a year. In 1565 the Spanish governor Pedro Menéndez de Avilés surprised the settlement, sparing women and children but systematically executing more than 130 male defenders of the "evil Lutheran sect."

Challenging Spanish Florida

France's sixteenth-century efforts along the Florida coast succeeded mainly in spurring the Spanish Crown to pour more funds into American defenses. During the 1560s Florida's Governor Menéndez established St. Augustine along with six other Spanish forts to secure the coast of Florida and the Bahama Channel. He also devised a scheme to bypass Caribbean routes by transporting silver overland from the Zacatecas mines in Mexico to the new fort of Santa Elena on Parris Island near the former site of the Huguenot's ill-fated Charlesfort. Menéndez's idea, though impractical, testified to Spain's growing fear of the French corsairs who infested Caribbean waters and to the rising costs of defending Spain's New World empire.

While intrepid corsairs contended in the sixteenth-century Caribbean for a share of Spanish treasure, French merchants and fishermen were quietly pursuing a more peaceful and increasingly lucrative enterprise in the Gulf of St. Lawrence. By the 1550s, the Grand Banks were attracting large squadrons of French fishing vessels to supply a huge demand for fish during France's Lenten season, when consumption of meat and poultry was prohibited by church tradition. In addition, the growing popularity in Europe of wide-brimmed hats was boosting the demand for American beaver pelts, the soft underfur of which made excellent felt. Each year, the abundant supply of pelts and fish enticed more Frenchmen to establish permanent outposts in the region, belying earlier Spanish predictions that Canada's frigid climate would soon force the French to abandon any colony they attempted there. Wherever they settled, the traders soon began farming their own crops and cultivating good relations with nearby native bands.

New France on the St. Lawrence

By the 1570s, these unofficial fishing and trading communities were producing healthy profits for French merchants, who pressed the Crown to protect their American investments. Religious turmoil, however, diverted royal attention and resources from North America for another 30 years. Only in 1598 was King Henry IV able to begin securing the French foothold in Canada by appointing officials to organize government and supervise trade. During the next decade, these men made several abortive efforts to establish a seat of royal government in the region. Finally, in 1608, Samuel de Champlain succeeded in founding the city of Quebec on the banks of the St. Lawrence River.

Quebec proved an excellent strategic choice. From its site at a point where the St. Lawrence River narrowed, French artillery could command both riverbanks and control all traffic to the interior. Its location near Huron population centers also enabled the French to forge an alliance with an important nation whose networks of exchange extended throughout the Great Lakes. The Hurons and other northern nations were eager to trade for European goods and readily accepted Champlain's new settlement as a center of commerce with France. To consolidate the native trade network, Champlain reciprocated by cementing an alliance with Hurons against their enemies, the Iroquois. The alliance secured France reliable trading partners, while Quebec's strategic location insulated it from European competitors.

As was the case with other colonial powers, the French declared they had migrated to the New World in search of wealth as well as in hopes of converting the Indians to Christianity. As it turned out, these economic and spiritual goals required full cooperation between the French and the Native Americans. In contrast to the English settlers, who established independent farms and who regarded the Indians at best as obstacles to proper cultivation of the land, the French viewed the natives as necessary economic partners. Furs constituted Canada's most valuable export, and to obtain the pelts of beaver and other animals, the French depended completely on Indian hunters and trappers. French traders continued to live among the Indians throughout the colonial period, often taking native wives and studying local cultures.

Catholic missionaries also depended on Indian cooperation. Canadian priests came from two orders, the Jesuits and the Récollets. In 1618, Récollet missionaries laid out a plan to populate New France with settlers who could familiarize the natives with European ways of life to facilitate their conversion. Récollets and Jesuits also traveled far inland with their message, living among the Indians and learning to speak their languages as the fur traders did. Jesuit missionaries distinguished themselves by a careful study of native customs and beliefs in an effort to frame Christian teachings in terms intelligible to Indian cultures. Despite their unavoidable cultural bias, Jesuit accounts remain valuable sources of information on seventeenth-century native culture. This culturally sensitive approach appears to have helped French Catholic missionaries convert more Indians to Christianity than did their English Protestant counterparts to the south.

The establishment of Quebec secured France a permanent outpost in the Atlantic world, albeit one far removed from the great arteries of coveted Iberian wealth. Moreover, the French dream of expanding its northern claims into a vast

American empire suffered from serious flaws. Political turmoil in France and Europe prevented the Crown from giving much attention to Canadian affairs until late in the seventeenth century. Royal officials stationed in New France received limited and sporadic support from Paris. An even greater problem was the decision to settle what seemed to many rural peasants and urban artisans a cold, inhospitable land. Canada's European population throughout the period of French rule, which came to an end in 1763, was small. A census of 1663 recorded a mere 3,035 French residents. By 1700, the figure had reached only 15,000. Moreover, because of the colony's geography, all exports and imports had to go through Quebec. It was relatively easy, therefore, for Crown officials to control that traffic, usually by awarding fur-trading monopolies to court favorites. Such practices created political tensions and hindered economic growth.

The Dutch entered the competition for Atlantic wealth as an act of rebellion against the Spanish Crown. King Philip II had sparked unrest in the seventeen provinces of the Netherlands soon after his accession to the throne when he began revoking their ancient privileges, imposing a Spanish garrison, and instituting the Spanish Inquisition to stamp out the Calvinistic Protestantism that had taken root in the seven northern provinces called Holland. The war that broke out in 1572 wore on by fits and starts for eighty years, although it was interrupted in the early seventeenth century by the Twelve Years' Truce. The Catholic southern provinces of Belgium bore the brunt of war and were exhausted into complete submission by the early 1590s. The seven Protestant northern provinces, however, concluded the Union of Utrecht in 1579 and proclaimed their independence from Spain.

The Rise of the Dutch

Despite warfare with Spain, the United Provinces enjoyed a security and fund of resources that enabled them to capture a significant share of transatlantic commerce very quickly. Holland's treacherous coastline was a curse to potential Spanish invaders, but a blessing to the Dutch navigators who knew the waters well and could take advantage of their strategic location near the center of northern European sea-lanes. During the fifteenth century, Dutch navigators had captured the bulk of the carrying trade between the Baltic and southern Europe, while Dutch artisans had developed a burgeoning trade in export goods. The provinces also experienced a great influx of wealth and talent as refugees poured in from the war-torn south. By the 1590s, the merchants, financiers, and artisans that had once made Antwerp the economic center of northern Europe were poised to capture world markets from Amsterdam.

Amsterdam investors began moving to capture Portuguese markets around the world during the last two decades of the sixteenth century. The sea battles of that period had disrupted the Portuguese trade with Africa and the Indian Ocean, creating an opportunity for the Dutch to move in. By 1602, the newly created Dutch East India Company controlled a large share of the spice trade. Many of the company's investors financed voyages to the coast of Africa as well, where they quickly undercut Portuguese traders by offering cheaper, better cloth from Europe and India as well as superior iron ingots from Sweden. Out of this trade the Guinea

Challenging the Portuguese

Company emerged to contend with Portugal for the African slave trade. The company built forts at strategic points in Senegambia and the Gold Coast to double as trading posts and bases of operation against Portuguese slaving vessels.

The Dutch conquest of world markets would be incomplete without a rich American possession, and investors first set their sights on Portuguese Brazil. By the end of the sixteenth century, Dutch shippers regularly carried a large share of Brazilian sugar to European markets. Not content with this, the Dutch launched a struggle for possession of the territory itself. In 1621, the newly created Dutch West India Company began pouring its resources into a protracted effort to capture Brazil while continuing the now-defunct Guinea Company's contest for key Portuguese possessions in Africa. The company eventually captured Portugal's West African forts at Elmina and Axim (see Chapter 7), but failed in Brazil. The long struggle diverted resources away from Dutch colonization efforts in the Caribbean, where they gained possession of only a few islands in the Lesser Antilles including Curaçao and St. Eustatia.

New Netherland on the Hudson

The Dutch, like the French before them, ultimately found it most practical to establish a foothold on the North American periphery of the Iberian Atlantic. And like the French, they happened on the site of their North American colony while searching for the elusive Northwest Passage. In 1609, Henry Hudson, an English explorer employed by the Dutch East India Company, sailed up the river that now bears his name in search of a shorter and safer route to the Indian Ocean. Further voyages led to the establishment of trading posts in New Netherland, the most important of which was Fort Nassau on Castle Island near present-day Albany. The area also seemed an excellent staging ground for attacks on Spanish American ports and shipping.

Fort Nassau provided a base from which early Dutch traders fanned out into the surrounding countryside to search for mineral deposits and forge trade alliances with neighboring Indians. This proved difficult along the Hudson, where fierce rivalries among Mohawks, Mahicans, and Munsees threatened to divide Dutch interests. Conflict among the traders was frequent, and relations with one Indian nation could jeopardize trade with another. On one occasion, for instance, a group of traders risked a potentially devastating war with the powerful Iroquois Confederacy by joining Mahican allies in an attack on Mohawk villages. Dutch officials soon established the New Netherland Company in 1614 to quell cutthroat trading practices and to impose a policy of strict neutrality in military affairs. In 1621, the Dutch West India Company assumed a monopoly over the Hudson River trade.

The directors of the Dutch West India Company sponsored the establishment of two permanent outposts on the Hudson in 1624. Fort Orange (Albany) replaced Fort Nassau, which a spring flood had washed away in 1618. New Amsterdam (New York City) on Manhattan Island provided an excellent harbor that remained free of ice year round. The company populated these settlements with salaried employees, and their superiors in Holland expected them to spend most of their time gathering animal furs. They did not receive land for their troubles. Needless to say, this arrangement attracted relatively few Dutch immigrants.

New Netherland remained a small, struggling colony neglected by Dutch West India Company officials in their vain quest to conquer Brazil. It nevertheless secured the Dutch an important foothold in the New World, a base for staging forays into the Spanish Caribbean and the Brazilian coast, and a steady flow of profits from the fur trade. New Amsterdam soon became an integral port in the Dutch carrying trade, which dominated the Atlantic by the mid-seventeenth century (see Chapter 7). The colony's Iroquois, Mahican, and Munsee trading partners also provided an eager transatlantic market for Dutch manufactured goods. Indeed, Dutch trade linked the Iroquois Five Nations to a transatlantic supply of arms, which they used to extend their influence in all directions.

THE EMERGING ENGLISH ATLANTIC

As French corsairs preyed on Spanish gold shipments and revolt brewed in the Netherlands, English interest in the New World began to rebound after lying dormant for nearly half a century. In the 1560s, the realm emerged from decades of religious conflict and reformation to become a leader of Protestant Europe and one of Spain's most implacable foes. A rising group of English adventurers pointed out that the Spanish monarch owed the "mighty and marvelous" increase of his "territories and dominions" to his American possessions. They argued that England could best respond by challenging Spain's monopoly on New World treasure. Under the effective guidance of Elizabeth I and her councilors, English seafarers began carving out a niche for their nation in the Atlantic later in the sixteenth century. They interloped in Iberian trade, raided Spanish treasure shipments, made the first efforts to plant English colonies in America, and eventually launched an all-out war with Spain.

The Sea Dogs

Elizabethan mariners became the shock troops of English Protestant militancy. They plunged into the contest for New World wealth at a time when the lucrative trade in slaves to Brazil and the Caribbean was beginning to offer an attractive alternative to risky raids on Spanish gold shipments. English shipowners began interloping into the Portuguese-controlled slave trade as early as 1551. In 1662 the English captain John Hawkins made hefty profits for himself and his investors by capturing 300 slaves from Portuguese ships in Sierra Leone and carrying them to the Spanish Caribbean. Hawkins's piracy attracted the attention of wealthy Englishmen, including members of the English court, who readily financed a second slaving voyage in 1564. This excursion, which included one of the queen's own ships, netted Hawkins and his investors a 60 percent profit and helped win Hawkins a knighthood. A third expedition for gold and slaves ended in disaster for Hawkins when the Spanish viceroy captured him at San Juan, Puerto Rico, but the Sea Dog succeeded in making himself a *cause célèbre* by blaming the loss on Spanish treachery.

In the aftermath of Hawkins's disastrous third voyage, Queen Elizabeth herself challenged Spain's New World and Asian monopolies with increasing boldness, authorizing pirate raids against Spanish shipping. Soon royal sponsorship of daring Caribbean raiders such as Francis Drake became an open secret. When Drake led a force of Englishmen and *cimarrónes* to capture a shipment of Spanish gold at Panama in 1673, King Philip II fumed at Elizabeth but did nothing. The next year the Treaty of Bristol brought a temporary moratorium on English freebooting. Yet the expansionists had tasted opportunities for wealth in Spain's vulnerable empire, and the scheming, information gathering, and sorties into New World waters persisted.

The adventurers who directed Elizabeth's expeditions remembered Cabot's voyages only vaguely, and their only experience in settling distant outposts was in Ireland. During the last three decades of the sixteenth century, English adventurers made almost every mistake one could imagine. They did, however, acquire valuable information about winds and currents, supplies, and finance.

Religion, War, and Nationalism

In the mid-1580s, King Philip II, who had united the empires of Spain and Portugal in 1580, decided that he could tolerate England's arrogantly Protestant queen no longer. He ordered the construction of a mighty fleet, hundreds of transport vessels designed to carry Spain's finest infantry across the English Channel. When one of Philip's lieutenants viewed the Armada at Lisbon in May 1588, he described it as *la felicissima armada*, the invincible fleet. The king believed that with the support of England's oppressed Catholics, Spanish troops would sweep Elizabeth from power, restore England to the Catholic fold, and halt English depredations against Spain's Atlantic empire.

It was a grand scheme; it was an even grander failure. In 1588, a smaller, more maneuverable English navy dispersed Philip's Armada, and severe storms finished it off. Spanish hopes for Catholic England lay wrecked along the rocky coasts of Scotland and Ireland. Not surprisingly, English Protestants interpreted victory in providential terms: "God breathed and they were scattered."

However spectacular their defeat of the Spanish Armada, the English did not yet possess the sea power necessary to capitalize on the victory. Over the next few years, English naval officers made several large-scale attempts to strangle Iberian commerce by capturing Lisbon and Seville as well as the Azores, which were indispensable to Spanish treasure fleets. Spanish forces repelled each effort. By 1591 Spain rebuilt much of the naval fleet lost in the Armada, forcing the English to reduce the scale of their naval offensives. The English again reverted to hit-and-run privateering operations, which inflicted heavy losses on Iberian trade in the Atlantic and the Caribbean.

Irish Rehearsal for American Colonization

During Elizabeth's reign, England's designs for a transatlantic empire became entwined with a renewed policy of colonizing the nearby island of Ireland. The experience of colonizing Ireland paralleled the Iberian conquest of the Canaries and Azores (see Chapter 1), powerfully shaping how later emigrants would view the New World. It was not a happy precedent, for it was in Ireland that ambitious Englishmen first learned to subdue a foreign population and to seize its lands. When Elizabeth assumed the throne, Ireland's one million inhabitants were scattered across the countryside. There were few villages, most of which were located along the coast. To the English eye, the Irish people seemed wild and barbaric. They were also fiercely independent and difficult to control. The English dominated a small region around Dublin by force of arms, but much of Ireland's terri-

During the reign of the powerful and resourceful Elizabeth I (r. 1558–1603), English adventurers such as the famous sea captain Sir Francis Drake began challenging Spain's control over New World wealth and territory.

By kind permission of the Marquess of Tavistock and Trustees of the Bedford Estate

tory remained in the hands of Gaelic-speaking Catholics who presumably managed to survive without English culture.

During the 1560s and 1570s, English adventurers—curious parallels to the Spanish conquistadores they claimed to hate—decided that considerable fortune could be made in Ireland. There were substantial risks, of course, not the least of which was the resistance of the Irish. Nevertheless, private "projectors"—a number of whom were also deeply involved in various schemes for raiding or colonizing in the New World—sponsored English settlements. In turn, these colonists forced the Irish either into tenancy or off the land altogether. During this period, the English planted semimilitary colonies in Ulster and Munster.

Colonization was a disaster for the Irish. The English settlers, however humble their origins, felt superior to the Catholic Irish. After all, the English people had championed the Protestant religion. They had constructed a complex market economy and created a powerful nation-state. They saw the conquest of Ireland as part of one vast effort to humble the forces of Catholic Europe on both sides of the Atlantic. To the English settlers, the Irish appeared lazy, licentious, superstitious, even stupid—characteristics that they would project onto subjected peoples throughout the British empire for centuries to come. English settlers ridiculed unfamiliar local customs, and it is not surprising that even educated representatives of the two cultures found communication almost impossible. English colonists, for example, criticized pastoral farming methods prevalent in sixteenth-century Ireland.

It seemed perversely wasteful for the Irish to be forever moving about, because as any English person could see, such practices retarded the development of towns. Sir John Davies, a leading English colonizer, declared that if the Irish were left to themselves, they would "never (to the end of the world) build houses, make townships or villas or manure or improve the land as it ought to be." Such stubborn inefficiency—surely (the English reasoned) the Irish must have known better—became the standard English justification for the seizure of large tracts of land wherever they established colonies.

English ethnocentrism remained relatively benign so long as the Irish accepted the subservient roles the colonizers assigned them. But when the indigenous population rebelled against the invaders, something it did with great frequency, English condescension turned to violence. The brutality of Sir Humphrey Gilbert in Ireland resembled that of the more unsavory Spanish conquistadores. Gilbert wrote treatises on geography, explored the coast of North America, and entertained Queen Elizabeth with witty conversation. As a colonizer, in a strange land, however—in what some historians now call England's "permissive frontier"—he became a military autocrat. In 1569, he was appointed military governor of Munster, and when the Irish in his district rose up, he executed everyone he could catch, "mane, woman and childe."

The Irish experiments served as models for English colonies in the New World. Indeed, one modern Irish scholar argues that "English colonization in Virginia was a logical continuation of the Elizabethan conquest of Ireland." Indeed, Gilbert himself projected a detailed scheme to colonize Newfoundland, but he was lost at sea in 1583 while attempting to carry it out. English adventurers to the New World commonly compared Native Americans with the "wild" Irish, a kind of ethnocentric shorthand that equated all alien races. This mental process was a central element in the transfer of English culture to America. The English, like the Spanish before them, did not perceive America in objective terms. Instead, they saw an America they had already constructed in their imaginations, and the people and objects that greeted them on the other side of the Atlantic were forced into Old World categories. Preconceived notions about strangers hardened into stereotypes, hurtful images that have sometimes survived into our own modern age.

Raleigh and Roanoke

Like Spain's French and Dutch challengers, English adventurers regarded it most practical to found a permanent American beachhead sufficiently distant from Spanish settlements to remain undetected but near enough to prey on Spanish galleons. To Sir Walter Raleigh, the coast of North Carolina seemed a likely spot. In 1584 he obtained from Queen Elizabeth a grant for the region and dispatched two English captains to search out a likely site for a settlement. The men returned with glowing reports aimed at opening the pockets of financial backers. "The soile," declared Captain Arthur Barlowe, "is the most plentifull, sweete, fruitfull, and wholesome of all the world."

Raleigh diplomatically renamed this marvelous region Virginia, in honor of his patron, the Virgin Queen. Indeed, one should note the highly gendered vocabulary that figured prominently in the European contest for an Atlantic empire. As historian Kathleen M. Brown explains, "Associations of the land with virgin innocence reinforced the notion that Virginia had been saved from the Spaniard's lust to be conquered by the chaste English." Elizabeth encouraged Raleigh in private conversation but rejected his persistent requests for money. With rumors of war in the air, she did not want to alienate Philip II unnecessarily by sponsoring a colony on land long ago claimed by Spain.

Raleigh finally raised the funds for his adventure, but his enterprise seemed ill-fated from the start. The colonists landed on Roanoke Island in August 1585. Despite careful planning, everything went wrong. The settlement was poorly situated. Located inside the Outer Banks—perhaps to avoid detection by the Spanish—the Roanoke colony proved extremely difficult to reach. Even experienced navigators feared the treacherous currents and storms off Cape Hatteras. Sir Richard Grenville, the leader of the expedition, added to the colonists' troubles by destroying an entire Roanoke Indian village in retaliation for the suspected theft of a silver cup. The incident bred the ill-will of the Roanokes. Tension between Indians and colonists only compounded the settlements difficulties.

Grenville hurried back to England in the autumn of 1585 for additional settlers and supplies, leaving the colonists to fend for themselves. Although they coped quite well, a peculiar series of accidents transformed Raleigh's settlement into a ghost town. In the spring of 1586, Sir Francis Drake was returning from a Caribbean voyage and decided to visit Roanoke. The colonists, tired of waiting for an overdue shipment of supplies, climbed aboard Drake's ships and went home.

In 1587, Raleigh launched a second colony. This time he placed in charge John White, a veteran administrator and talented artist, who a few years earlier had produced a magnificent sketchbook of the Algonquian Indians who lived near Roanoke. For modern anthropologists, White's drawings remain a key source about early Native American culture. Once again, Raleigh's luck turned sour. The Spanish Armada severed communication between England and America. Every available English vessel was pressed into military service, and between 1587 and 1590, no ship visited the Roanoke colonists. When rescuers eventually reached the island, they found the village deserted. The fate of the "lost" colonists remains a mystery to this day. The best guess is that they were absorbed by neighboring groups of natives, some from as far away as the James River in Virginia.

Selling a Transatlantic Empire

Had it not been for Richard Hakluyt, the Younger, who publicized the Sea Dogs' Atlantic adventures, the dream of American colonization might have died in England. After all, North Carolina yielded no gold. Hakluyt, a supremely industrious man, never saw America. Nevertheless, his vision of the New World powerfully shaped English public opinion. He interviewed captains and sailors upon their return from distant voyages and carefully collected their stories in a massive book titled *The Principall Navigations, Voyages, and Discoveries of the English Nation* (1589). The work's strength lay in the fact that it seemed a straightforward description of what these sailors had seen across the sea. In reality, Hakluyt edited each piece so it would drive home the book's central point: England's freedom and prosperity depended on America. So did that of American Indians, who languished everywhere under the Spaniard's cruel yoke. In Hakluyt's America, there would be no losers. The Indians would bask in the light of Protestant Christianity, and English colonists would live by simply plucking fruit from the trees. "The earth bringeth fourth all things in aboundance, as in the first creations without toil or labour," he wrote of Virginia. Hakluyt's blend of piety, patriotism, and self-interest proved immensely popular, as evidenced by the frequent reprinting of his *Voyages*.

A BRAVE NEW WORLD

By the opening of the seventeenth century, the principal European contenders for New World wealth had created an Atlantic system of commerce, colonization, and plunder. The united kingdoms of Spain and Portugal still controlled the core of this vast oceangoing network, but their hold was beginning to slip under increasing pressure from French, Dutch, and English challengers. Iberian influence declined steadily in the following decades, transforming the Atlantic into a field of open competition as rival nations raced to capture trade and develop new American enterprises that could enrich European coffers and enhance national glory.

Nevertheless, the Atlantic world emerged through cooperation as well as by conflict, as colonists and seafarers of rival powers discovered ways to profit from overlapping interests. Spanish colonists benefited from northern European smugglers who skirted Spain's stifling navigation laws to bring desired goods at better prices. Portuguese, French, and English colonists eventually came to depend on Dutch vessels to carry their plantation goods to European markets. Spanish doubloons and "pieces of eight" circulated throughout the New World, lubricating the wheels of commerce in England, France, and the Netherlands as well as in Latin America. This cooperation helped to make the Atlantic basin a place of great opportunity for those resourceful and lucky enough to become winners in the scramble for fortune. Yet most of those caught in its vast swirl—European as well as African and Native American—experienced the seventeenth-century Atlantic world as a place of continuous human suffering and ecological disaster.

CHRONOLOGY

1530	Portuguese begin exporting dyewood from Brazil.
1545	Potosí (Peru) silver mining begins.
1546	Zacatecas (Mexico) silver mining begins.
1550	Portuguese begin planting sugar in Brazil.
1555	French privateer Jacques de Sores burns Havana.
1562	Captain John Hawkins captures 300 slaves from Portuguese.
1564	Spanish burn newly established French settlement at Charlesport in South Carolina.

1565	Spanish establish St. Augustine.
1573	Sir Francis Drake captures Spanish gold at Panama.
1579	Dutch proclaim independence from Spain.
1585	First Roanoke settlement established on coast of South Carolina.
1588	English defeat Spanish Armada.
1602	Dutch East India Company established.
1608	Samuel de Champlain founds city of Quebec.
1614	New Netherland Company established to license Hudson River traders.
1624	Founding of New Amsterdam and Fort Orange (Albany) on the Hudson.

RECOMMENDED READING

Over the past decade, historians have increasingly come to view the sixteenth-century Atlantic basin as a single vast theater of economic, military, and cultural interaction among the peoples who inhabited its rim. Two comprehensive treatments of the Atlantic world to date may be found in Paul Butel's *The Atlantic* (London, 1999) and Roger Morris's *Atlantic Seafaring: Ten Centuries of Exploration and Trade in the North Atlantic* (Aukland, 1992). Philip D. Curtin explores one of the most important institutions in the creation of the Atlantic economies in his *Rise and Fall of the Plantation Complex: Essays in Atlantic History* (Cambridge, 1990). Ralph Davis's *The Rise of the Atlantic Economies* (Ithaca, 1973) remains a valuable analysis of the ways in which transatlantic economic development transformed the various economic systems of European nation-states and the larger European market.

The determination to view the Atlantic world as an arena of multiple initiative and interaction among its peoples has prompted recent historians to reexamine the role of Africans in the shaping of that world. John Thornton's *Africa and Africans in the Making of the Atlantic World, 1400–1800* (Cambridge, 1998) treats the various coastal peoples of sub-Saharan Africa as active participants in the shaping of that world through their control of commerce with Europeans. Basil Davidson's *West Africa Before the Colonial Era: A History to 1850* (London, 1998) provides a rich account of West African cultures, states, and stateless societies through the period of the slave trade.

The history of the slave trade itself continues to attract much scholarly attention and generate a great deal of debate. Two excellent syntheses of recent scholarship are available in Herbert S. Klein, *The Atlantic Slave Trade* (Cambridge, 1999) and Hugh Thomas, *The Slave Trade: The Story of the Atlantic Slave Trade: 1440–1870* (New York, 1997). David Eltis argues that the slave trade developed as a result of African strength rather than African weakness in his *Rise of African Slavery in the Americas* (Cambridge,

2000). Michael L. Conniff and Thomas J. Davis trace the expansion of African peoples and cultures to the New World in their *Africans in the Americas: A History of the Black Diaspora* (New York, 1994).

James D. Tracy, ed., *The Rise of Merchant Empires: Long-Distance Trade in the Early Modern World, 1350–1750* (Cambridge, 1990) contains excellent essays examining the overall structure of Atlantic trade as well as the efforts of various European nations to develop transatlantic empires in the sixteenth and seventeenth centuries. Henry Kamen's *Empire: How Spain Became a World Power, 1493–1763* (New York: Harper-Collins, 2003) sets the development of Spain's New World empire within a context of international European enterprise and investment. For the development of Spanish treasure shipments and the international contest over them, see Timothy R. Walton, *The Spanish Treasure Fleets* (Sarasota, 1994). For the Portuguese empire see James Lang, *Portuguese Brazil: The King's Plantation* (New York, 1979). W. J. Eccles, *The French in North America, 1500–1783* (East Lansing, 1998) includes excellent chapters on France's sixteenth-century contest for a toehold in the New World. For England's efforts to establish a presence in the Americas, see David B. Quinn and A. N. Ryan, *England's Sea Empire, 1550–1642* (London, 1983). Garrett Mattingly's *The Armada* (Boston, 1959) is a classic study of that decisive clash between England and Spain from an English perspective, while Felipe Fernández-Armesto's *The Spanish Armada: The Experience of War in 1588* (Oxford, 1988) attempts to balance Mattingly's largely pro-English narrative with an analysis more sympathetic to the Spanish. For Dutch activity in the New World, see Pieter Emmer, *The Dutch in the Atlantic Economy, 1580–1880: Trade, Slavery, and Emancipation* (Aldershot, 1998).

Part II

The Contest for Seventeenth-Century Settlement

In 1584, Richard Hakluyt presented to Queen Elizabeth I his *Discourse on Western Planting*, a work urging "her Majestie . . . to take a hande in the westerne voyadge and plantinge" of "Norumbega." English maps of the period located this fabled land of wealth and natural resources near present-day New York and New England. Hakluyt argued that by planting a colony in Norumbega, the English could gain multiple advantages against their rivals. Such a colony would "staye the spanish kinge from flowinge over all the face of . . . America." It would generate new markets for English woolen goods. It would stimulate production of a "new navie of mightie new stronge shippes" for trade, defense, and conquest. A North American colony would allow English Protestants to "plant sincere religion" and provide a haven for Protestant refugees "from all partes of the worlde that are forced to flee for the truth of gods word." It would offer asylum to the native slaves of Spanish "pride and tyranie." And it would provide a second chance for English victims of poverty and debt. In short, Norumbega "offered the remedie" for a wide range of English economic, political, and military ills.

Hindsight gives a prophetic ring to Hakluyt's words, but they must have struck many of his contemporaries as crackbrained dreams. In a world seemingly dominated by Iberian gold and military might, risky colonization schemes threatened to divert scarce resources and manpower from the important tasks of securing a Protestant England against the forces of Catholic Europe.

Early colonial ventures only confirmed the difficulty of establishing even the most tenuous English presence overseas. Sir Walter Raleigh's Roanoke venture disappeared with scarcely a trace during the 1580s while the ships that might have saved it were occupied instead with repelling Spain's "invincible Armada" from the English coast. Colonists perished by the thousands during Virginia's early decades through their own folly in alienating potential native allies and in underestimating the arduous demands of establishing a viable settlement. Well into the last third of the seventeenth century, English, Dutch, and French remained locked in an uncertain struggle for influence with the Iroquois League and control of territory in northeastern America.

Only by recovering this sense of precarious contingency can we begin to understand a seventeenth-century Atlantic world created through the vicious conflict, unexpected alliance, resourceful adaptation, and amazing resilience of its varied native and colonizing peoples. The nascent English Atlantic empire of the 1690s, far from a straightforward outcome of Richard Hakluyt's dream of colonizing "Norumbega," would emerge through a contest whose outcome remained uncertain well into the eighteenth century.

Chapter 4

Smoke and Greed on the Tobacco Coast, 1607–1660

George Yeardley succeeded in Virginia beyond his wildest dreams. He was clever and ambitious, lucky and self-absorbed. Indeed, after only a few years in the New World, Yeardley amassed an impressive fortune and gained the governorship. In 1617 Yeardley returned to London, an obscure soldier who had taken a chance on Virginia and become a celebrity. During his visit, Yeardley spent almost £3,000 in an ostentatious show of wealth. His display commanded enough public acclaim to win him a knighthood from the king. Sir George, as he was now called, strutted the streets of London, followed by fifteen fawning servants.

Yeardley's braggadocio masked the sorry state of the colony of Virginia. From the moment English adventurers had first sailed up the James River almost everything had gone wrong. During the so-called "starving time" of 1609–1610 the population of Jamestown dropped from over 500 to about 60 within a few months. Despite massive assistance from England, the colonists seemed incapable of producing enough grain to feed themselves. They certainly made no progress in paying back English investors who had purchased shares of stock in the Virginia Company. Disease killed thousands. So too did local Indians who had been provoked by English intruders into almost perpetual hostilities. By 1618 Virginia appeared an experiment gone sour.

Through it all, Yeardley prospered. He and a few cronies figured out how to line their pockets, even though their callous greed brought death to ordinary migrants and bankruptcy to English investors. Theirs was an extraordinary tale, one repeated many times in Virginia and Maryland. As governor, Yeardley persuaded the London officers of the Virginia Company to give him over 3,000 acres of prime land as well as 100 servants. He looked out for himself. During his term of office, 3,570 colonists poured into Jamestown—ordinary men and women dreaming of a better life—but within a few years almost 3,000 of these people had needlessly perished, victims of gross mismanagement. Their misfortune hardly affected Yeardley. The company sent him 30 new servants to replace others who had died. His self-serving policies invited massive Indian attack, and in 1622 the local Native Americans killed another 347 colonists. The stench of corruption finally reached the king. In 1624 he revoked the company's charter. Still Yeardley turned a profit. By the time of his death in 1627, he owned a huge estate that he successfully passed on to his wife and children.

In the scramble for wealth, Sir George knew how to be "a right worthie statesman, for his owne profit." In fact, as one historian observed, Virginians did not develop a meaningful sense of community, since everyone was so busy "looking out for number one." In this world, Yeardley was a winner. But for every Yeardley, thousands of cruelly disappointed settlers faced death and oppression. In their ignominy they may have been more fortunate than those other losers, Indians and the Africans whose lives were forever transformed by the returns from the "stinking weed" known as tobacco.

A NATIVE AMERICAN EMPIRE

The Chesapeake Bay region for which English colonists set sail in December of 1606 was firmly in control of the Powhatan chiefdom, one of coastal North America's most powerful Algonquian-speaking peoples. Early colonial writers reported that the Powhatan tribes had moved into the region some 300 years before the Jamestown settlers, but archaeological evidence suggests that people with a similar culture had been living in the region much longer. Sometime during the early years of Elizabeth I's reign, an enterprising leader named Wahunsaunacock inherited authority over six Chesapeake tribes. He ruled as Powhatan, or paramount chief, until 1618, more than a decade beyond Elizabeth (r. 1558–1603). A capable and aggressive leader, Powhatan expanded his rule throughout the Chesapeake region. By 1600 he controlled a loose association of some thirty tribes that may well have constituted the largest Native American empire east of the Mississippi River. Powhatan's influence extended over a region he called Tsenacommacah, probably meaning "densely inhabited territory." The core of Tsenacommacah included the coastal plain between the James and Mattapony Rivers, while the fringes of Powhatan's influence extended across the bay to Virginia's Eastern Shore and as far north as the Potomac River. Powhatan governed a population of around 14,000 people, of whom 3,200 were warriors.

Powhatan's inherited authority and military conquests made him overlord to a cluster of lesser tribal chiefs called *werowances*. Werowances inherited rule from the mother's line. Inheritance passed first to the brothers of the chief who had died and then to his eldest sister and her sons. Some werowances such as

Wowinchopunck, the chief of the Paspahegh tribe of the lower James River, had been born or elevated to power within their own tribes but acknowledged Powhatan's dominion in exchange for peace and security. Other werowances were Powhatan's own kinsmen. The Pamunkey chief Opechancanough, for example, was either brother or cousin to Powhatan and eventually assumed the paramount chief's mantle of leadership, while the werowance of the Kecoughtan tribe at the mouth of the James River was one of Powhatan's sons. Each of Powhatan's werowances held sway over lesser werowances who owed them allegiance, tribute, and obedience.

Werowances enjoyed great advantages in Powhatan society. In theory, anyone could achieve status and wealth by great deeds in war or shrewd dealings in trade. The werowances' status, however, was assured by the tribute in corn, game, trade goods, and labor they received to support their families. Werowances usually held trade monopolies and channeled the profits to their own families. Powhatan himself, for example, held a monopoly on copper goods, which before Europeans arrived were available only from Native American trading partners far inland. Women could wield authority as *werowansquas* equal or even superior to their male counterparts. Ruling families regulated social mobility, rewarding achievement with wealth and status. Werowances shared power with advisers (*cockarouses, cronoccoes*) and priests (*quiyoughcosucks*), all of whom were men and enjoyed membership among Powhatan ruling families.

Like other Eastern Woodland peoples, the tribes of the Powhatan chiefdom based their economy on a mixture of hunting and agriculture centering on the production of corn. The people lived in riverfront villages of semipermanent dwellings during the summer months, fishing and cultivating fields planted simultaneously with corn, beans, and squash. A portion of the cultivated crops went to Powhatan in tribute, but people paid no taxes on certain edible plants and herbs gathered from the wild such as the tuber-producing tuckahoe. The Powhatans' mixed agriculture kept nutrients in the soil from depleting as quickly as they would have with a single crop. When a field became less productive, the cultivators would move to a new one which the men of the village cleared by girdling the trees and burning off the brush.

Women controlled agricultural production, giving them great economic power and occupying their days with a variety of tasks. In the autumn, the men hunted as the communities prepared to disperse into small parties for the winter to reduce competition for foraging. Hunts were communal operations in which groups of men worked to surround game within a particular area, then set fire to the brush and shoot the animals as they ran from hiding to escape the flames. Later European colonists adopted this practice to supplement their own diets.

Maize cultivation formed the basis of wealth among Powhatan ruling families. Powhatan prized maize above all other commodities. His subjects cultivated the paramount chief's maize in special fields set aside for the purpose, while subordinate tribes paid much of their annual tribute in maize. Powhatan and his werowances stored their maize in raised scaffolds or "treasure houses" along with quantities of dried meat, fish, and oysters. These stored surpluses became valuable trade commodities for products of inland tribes and indirectly for European goods from Spanish Florida. Maize and other food products were never mere economic goods, however; when exchanged they also held profound social significance that bound the giver and receiver together in a relationship of mutual obligation. When the English arrived in the Chesapeake, the Powhatan wealth in agricultural commodities gave the great chief a powerful initial advantage in trade and diplomacy.

The Powhatan tribes gained firsthand experience of European ways when in 1560 a Spanish expedition kidnapped the son of a chief in the Chesapeake Bay area and carried him to Havana to learn Spanish and Christianity. There he received the Spanish name Don Luis de Velasco. He traveled to Spain, where he was presented to King Philip II and received instruction at the royal court. In 1570 Don Luis returned to the Chesapeake with several Jesuit missionaries who hoped to establish a permanent presence in the region and convert the local tribes to Roman Catholicism. Instead, Don Luis returned to his father's people and led a war party that wiped out the Jesuit mission in 1571. The Spanish partially avenged the Jesuits' martyrdom later that year in a punitive raid that claimed the lives of thirty Powhatan, but they did not make another attempt to settle the Chesapeake.

This episode of Spanish contact in the Chesapeake may have contributed in at least two ways to Powhatan's position of strength in subsequent dealings with the English. In the first place, a wave of epidemic disease that accompanied Spanish contact may have weakened many tribes' ability to resist Powhatan's efforts to consolidate power in the Chesapeake. When the English arrived in 1607, however, the Powhatan population had rebounded. The Powhatan continued to outnumber the English until the 1630s. The history of contact with the Spanish, and possibly with English survivors of Roanoke (see Chapter 3), may also have given Powhatan some knowledge of European cultures. He grasped very quickly the distinction between the English and the Spanish and exploited differences for his own advantage.

THE ILL-FATED SETTLEMENT AT JAMESTOWN

After the Roanoke debacle in 1590, English interest in American settlement declined, and only a few propagandists such as Richard Hakluyt kept alive the dream of English colonies in the New World. These advocates argued that the North American mainland contained resources of incalculable value. An innovative group, they insisted, might reap great profits while supplying England with items that it would otherwise be forced to purchase from their European rivals, Holland, France, and Spain.

Moreover, any English enterprise that annoyed Catholic Spain or revealed its weakness in America seemed a desirable end in itself to patriotic English Protestants. Anti-Catholicism and hatred of Spain became an integral part of English national identity during this period, and unless one appreciates just how deeply these sentiments ran in the English popular mind, one cannot fully understand why ordinary people who had no direct stake in the New World so generously supported English efforts to colonize America. Soon after James I ascended to the throne in 1603, adventurers were given an opportunity to put their theories into practice in the colonies of Virginia and Maryland, an area known as the Chesapeake.

During Elizabeth's reign, the major obstacle to successful colonization of the New World had been raising capital. No single person, no matter how rich or well connected, could underwrite the vast expenses a New World settlement required. And the English government had no interest in footing the bill. The solution to this financial problem was the joint-stock company, a new business organization in which scores of people could participate in a major project. A merchant or landowner could purchase a share of stock at a stated price, and at the end of several years the investor could anticipate recovering the initial amount plus a portion of whatever profits the company had made. Joint-stock ventures sprang up like mushrooms. Affluent English citizens, and even some of more modest incomes, rushed to invest. As a result, the London Company was formed, and it amassed enough capital to launch a new colony in Virginia.

On April 10, 1606, King James I issued the first Virginia charter. This document authorized the London Company to establish plantations in Virginia. The London Company was an ambitious business venture. Its leader, Sir Thomas Smith, was reputedly London's wealthiest merchant. Smith and his partners gained possession of the territory lying between Cape Fear and the Hudson River. These generous but vague boundaries reflected ignorance about the details of American geography. The Virginia Company—as the London Company soon called itself—set out immediately to find the natural resources Hakluyt had promised.

In December 1606, the *Susan Constant*, the *Godspeed*, and the *Discovery* sailed for America. The ships carried 104 men and boys, who had been instructed to establish a fortified outpost some hundred miles up a large navigable river. The natural beauty and economic potential of the region was apparent to everyone. A voyager on this expedition reported seeing "faire meaddowes and goodly tall trees, with such fresh waters running through the woods, as almost ravished [us] at first sight."

The leaders of the colony selected—without consulting resident Powhatans— what the Europeans considered a promising location more than 30 miles from the mouth of the James River. A marshy peninsula jutting out into the river became the site for one of America's most unsuccessful villages, Jamestown. Modern historians have criticized this choice, for the low-lying ground proved to be a disease-ridden death trap; even the drinking water was contaminated with salt. But the first Virginians were neither stupid nor suicidal. Jamestown seemed the ideal place to build a fort, since surprise attack by the Spaniards rather than sickness appeared the more serious threat in the early months of settlement.

Early contacts with Powhatan tribes gave the settlers additional reason for apprehension, although not because native inhabitants seemed inherently hostile. Mistaken cultural assumptions on the part of both groups led to missteps, which prompted each to remain wary of the other. Nearby tribes, for example, found it impossible to understand the English disregard for the social dimensions of gift-giving and exchange; moreover, the English misunderstood Indian conceptions of land use. A series of misadventures resulted as the English traveled up the James

Dreamers and Schemers: The Virginia Project

River during the first few weeks after their arrival, making contact with subordinate tribes and asking pointed questions about the region and its resources. On May 26, only thirteen days after the founding of Jamestown, a large force of warriors representing four Powhatan tribes attacked the settlement while Captain Christopher Newport was away exploring and laying claim to Powhatan territory further up the James. Powhatan observed from a distance as raids and sniping continued over the next three weeks. Finally, on June 15, the paramount chief himself intervened to restore peace and establish trade relations.

Almost immediately, greed and self-interest began dividing the Jamestown colonists in ways that gave the more unified Powhatans an enormous early advantage in trade and diplomacy. The adventurers were not prepared for the challenges that confronted them in America. Some men may have been depressed by conditions in Virginia; others may have assumed that lower class people performed physical labor. But part of the problem was surely cultural.

Most colonists had grown up in a depressed agricultural economy that could not provide full-time employment for all who wanted it. In England, laborers shared what little work was available. One man, for example, might perform a certain chore while others simply watched. Later, the men who had been idle were given an opportunity to work for an hour or two. This labor system may have been appropriate for England, but in Virginia it nearly destroyed the colony. Adventurers sat around Jamestown while the other colonists performed crucial agricultural tasks. There was more than enough work to go around in their new environment. In fact, people were starving because too little labor was being expended on the planting and harvesting of crops. Some modern historians branded the early Virginians as lazy, irresponsible beings who preferred to play while others labored. In fact, however, these first settlers were attempting to replicate a traditional work experience.

Avarice exacerbated these problems. The adventurers had traveled to the New World in search of the sort of instant wealth they imagined the Spaniards to have found in Mexico and Peru. Tales of rubies and diamonds lying on the beach probably inflated their expectations. Even when it must have been apparent that these expectations were unfounded, the first settlers often behaved in Virginia as if they fully expected to become rich. Instead of cooperating for the common good—guarding the settlement or farming, for example—many of the men pursued personal interests. They searched for gold when they might have helped plant maize. No one was willing to take orders, and those who were supposed to govern the colony looked after their private welfare while disease, war, and starvation ravaged the settlement.

The unified Powhatans capitalized on the colonists' self-interest and factionalism. The Jamestown settlers' reluctance to plant maize resulted in chronic food shortages that made Powhatan maize extremely valuable. When colonial leaders attempted to impose price controls on maize, colonists simply ignored them by paying their Indian neighbors as much as four times the official price. Colonists pilfered from each other and from common stores to obtain the goods needed for barter, exacerbating disunity within the colony. Jamestown's leadership changed hands three times in the first eighteen months, placing each new leader at a disadvantage in dealing with the stable leadership of Powhatan and his werowances. Indeed, members of the Jamestown council vied for Powhatan's favor and sought to undercut each other by offering the great chief gifts and trade concessions more generous than those of their rivals'.

Captain John Smith: Saving the Colonists from Greed

Virginia might have gone the way of Roanoke had it not been for Captain John Smith. By any standard, he was a resourceful man. Before coming to Jamestown, he had traveled throughout Europe and fought with the Hungarian army against the Turks—and, if Smith is to be believed, he was saved repeatedly from certain death by various beautiful women. Because of his reputation for boasting, historians have discounted Smith's account of his experience in early Virginia. Recent scholarship, however, has affirmed the essential truthfulness of his curious story. In Virginia, Smith brought order out of anarchy.

While members of the council in Jamestown debated petty politics, Smith negotiated with the local Indians for food and mapped the Chesapeake Bay as the colony's "cape merchant" in charge of trade. During the fall and winter of 1607, his efforts kept the colonists alive. At one point, Smith was taken captive by Powhatan's kinsman, Opechancanough. The experience gave Smith the opportunity to observe Powhatan culture closely as Opechancanough escorted him through the central region of the chiefdom. Smith eventually met Powhatan face to face in a series of ritual encounters and feasting lasting for three days. Historians still debate the truth of Smith's claim that he was in danger of execution during

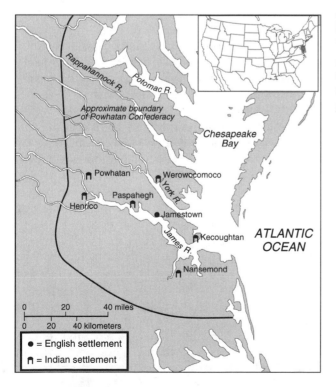

Powhatan's Chesapeake Bay

When the first English vessels sailed up the James River, they encountered in Powhatan a powerful and ambitious native sovereign who exercised great influence over the peoples inhabiting the banks of the deep rivers that flowed into the Chesapeake Bay.

this encounter or that Powhatan's 12-year-old daughter, Pocahontas, rescued him. Those who accept the account regard Pocahontas's action as part of an elaborate ritual by which Powhatan adopted Smith and the English into his chiefdom. In the end, Smith did promise that the English would become Powhatan's vassals in exchange for sustenance throughout the winter.

Smith's pragmatic promise helped the English survive the winter of 1608–1609. The next fall, however, he joined Captain Christopher Newport in an attempt to turn the tables by conducting a coronation ceremony to make Powhatan a vassal of King James. Powhatan recognized what the English were attempting. He accepted his coronation crown but refused submission to a foreign ruler.

Through encounters such as these, Powhatan and John Smith took each other's measure, developing an increasingly sophisticated understanding of the other's cultural assumptions, political aims, and terms of exchange. In his later accounts of these years, Smith declared that the Spanish had the right idea in forcing "the treacherous and rebellious infidels to doe all manner of drudgery worke and slavery for them, themselves living like souldiers upon the fruits of their labours." He did not hesitate to browbeat or coerce Powhatan tribes into trading their maize when negotiation failed. Yet even with firearms, Smith's contingent of a few hundred colonists posed no serious threat to Powhatan's 3,000-man force in the early years. The colony's survival depended far more on negotiation than on English military might.

Besides his trade dealings with the Powhatans, Smith moved to impose order on the colony itself. In the fall of 1608, he seized control of the ruling council and instituted a tough military discipline. Convinced that the colonists would "starve and eat one another" if the council's reckless policies continued, Smith organized the settlers into work gangs and marched them out to labor in the maize fields. Under Smith, no one enjoyed special privilege. He warned colonists that "every one that gathereth not every day as much as I doe, the next daie shall be set beyond the river, and for ever be banished from the fort, and live there or starve." To prevent a mass exodus from Jamestown to the surrounding tribal villages, he persuaded neighboring werowances to enforce the same discipline on any runaway settlers they found. The colonists grew to hate him, but he managed to keep them alive, no small achievement in such a deadly environment.

Leaders of the Virginia Company in London recognized the need to reform the entire enterprise. They had spent considerable sums and had received nothing in return. In 1609, the company directors obtained a new charter from the king, which completely reorganized the Virginia government. Henceforth all commercial and political decisions affecting the colonists rested with the company, who ruled directly through the governor. The company stripped the colonial council of any other than a strictly advisory role and gave the governor absolute civil and military power. Moreover, in an effort to raise scarce capital, the original partners opened the "joint stock" to the general public. For a little more than £12–approximately one year's wages for an unskilled English laborer—a person or group of persons could purchase a stake in Virginia. Company officials anticipated that in 1616 the profits from the colony would be distributed among the shareholders.

The company sponsored a publicity campaign; pamphlets and sermons extolled the colony's potential and exhorted patriotic English citizens to invest.

This burst of energy came to nothing. Bad luck, poor planning, and ongoing conflict with Powhatan plagued the Virginia Company. A vessel carrying additional settlers and supplies went aground in Bermuda, and while this misadventure did little to help the people at Jamestown, it provided Shakespeare with the idea for *The Tempest*. The new governor, Thomas West, Lord De la Warr, added to the confusion by postponing his departure for America. To make matters worse, English-Powhatan relations soured in the summer of 1609. Powhatan refused to trade any more maize to the colonists and ordered his subordinates to put Captain John Smith to death. Smith retaliated, using armed intimidation to extort tribal maize, surviving at least one attempt to poison him in the process. In the fall of 1609 the indomitable captain suffered a gunpowder accident that forced him to return to England.

Between 1609 and 1611, the remaining Virginia settlers suffered from lack of capable leadership. A poor harvest in the fall of 1609 combined with the cessation of the maize trade resulted in a severe food shortage. The terrible winter of 1609–1610 became known as the "starving time." A few desperate settlers engaged in cannibalism, an ironic behavior because Europeans had assumed that only savages would eat human flesh. In England, Smith heard that one colonist had killed his wife, powdered [salted] her, and "had eaten part of her before it was known; for which he was executed." The captain, who possessed a curious sense of humor, observed, "Now, whether she was better roasted, broiled, or carbonadoed, I know not, but such a dish as powdered wife I never heard of." Other people simply lost the will to live.

In June 1610, the surviving settlers decided on their own to abandon Virginia. Through a stroke of luck, however, they encountered Lord De la Warr just as they commenced their voyage down the James River. The new governor and the deputy governors who succeeded him, Sir Thomas Dale and Sir Thomas Gates, veterans of England's wars against the Spanish, ruled by the *Lawes Divine, Morall and Martial*. This code of mainly martial law was proclaimed by Thomas Dale in 1611 to maintain civil order by threat of force. The new colonists, many of them male and female servants employed by the company, were marched to work by the beat of a drum. Gates and Dale also moved to expand English settlement in the region and to bring neighboring tribal peoples under English rule by military force. Guerrilla raids between colonists and Powhatan tribes became increasingly vicious. Such methods saved the colony but could not make it flourish. In 1616, company shareholders received no profits. Their only reward was the right to a piece of unsurveyed land located 3,000 miles from London.

The solution to Virginia's economic problems grew in the vacant lots of Jamestown. Only the Powhatan tribes bothered to cultivate tobacco in the Chesapeake region until John Rolfe, a settler who arrived in 1610, realized this local weed might be a valuable export. Rolfe experimented with the crop, eventually growing in Virginia a milder variety that had been developed in the West Indies and was more appealing to European smokers.

The Tobacco Road to Riches and Slavery

Virginians suddenly possessed a means to make money. Tobacco proved relatively easy to grow, and settlers who had avoided work now threw themselves into its production with single-minded diligence. In 1617, one observer found that Jamestown's "streets and all other spare places [are] planted with tobacco . . . the Colony dispersed all about planting tobacco." Although King James I originally considered smoking immoral and unhealthy, he changed his mind when the taxes he collected on tobacco imports began to mount. He was neither the first nor the last ruler who decided a vice that generates revenue is not really so bad.

Tobacco cultivation eventually introduced a new source of tension into English-Powhatan relations as settlers spread beyond the negotiated boundaries of the colony to squat on Powhatan land. As tobacco production was first catching on, however, the marriage of John Rolfe to Pocahontas in 1614 helped briefly to foster positive diplomacy and trade. Ironically, Rolfe and Pocahontas fell in love while she was living in Jamestown as a hostage during a period some historians have called "the first Powhatan war" (1610–1613). Pocahontas apparently entered English society and marriage willingly, however. In 1613 she converted to Christianity while living in the household of the Reverend Alexander Whitaker, submitting to baptism and taking the name "Rebecca." Two of her uncles attended the wedding on behalf of Powhatan, who regarded the ceremony an "assurance of [King James's] friendship."

The Rolfes' marriage demonstrates the possibility of English and Powhatan men and women overcoming cultural differences to form lasting unions. In fact, however, surviving records indicate that only two other couples took that road in

This portrait of Powhatan's daughter Pocahontas was painted while visiting London in 1616 with her husband John Rolfe, an early Virginia settler who pioneered tobacco as a cash crop. Shortly before her marriage to Rolfe, she converted to Christianity and took the name of Rebeka.

National Portrait Gallery, Smithsonian Institution/Art Resource, NY

Ætatis suæ 21. Aº. 1616.

seventeenth-century Virginia. A few additional marriages, particularly any sealed by Powhatan authority, may have gone unrecorded, and many colonists engaged in brief sexual liaisons with Indian partners. Yet unlike the French or the Spanish, most English refused to take Indian spouses.

Pocahontas sailed to England in 1616 with Rolfe, their infant son Thomas, and a dozen other Powhatans, where she enjoyed the hospitality of leading Londoners. She died there of a respiratory illness in 1617. Pocahontas's conversion and marriage prompted the English to hope that other Powhatans could be won to Christian faith and English ways. The years after Pocahontas's death, however, witnessed the frustration of those hopes as changes in company policy offered even greater rewards to colonists, thus fueling the competitive drive to plant tobacco on more Powhatan lands.

In 1618 the Virginia Company sponsored another aggressive effort to transform Virginia into a profitable enterprise. Sir Edwin Sandys (pronounced Sands) led a faction of stockholders that began to pump life into the dying organization by instituting a series of sweeping reforms and eventually ousting Virginia Company founder Sir Thomas Smith and his friends. Sandys wanted private investors to develop their own estates in Virginia. Before 1618, company policy had offered little incentive to do so, but by relaxing Dale's martial law and promising a representative assembly called the House of Burgesses, Sandys thought he could make the colony more attractive to wealthy speculators. Even more important was his method for distributing land. Colonists who covered their own transportation costs to America were guaranteed a "headright," a 50-acre lot for which they paid only a small annual rent. Adventurers could gain additional headrights for each servant they brought to the colony. This procedure allowed prosperous planters to build up huge estates at the same time as they acquired dependent laborers. The headright system persisted long after the company's collapse. So too did the notion that the wealth of a few justified the exploitation of many others.

Sandys had only just begun. He also urged the settlers to diversify their economy. Tobacco alone, he argued, was not a sufficient base. He envisioned colonists busily producing iron and tar, silk and glass, sugar and cotton. There was no end to his suggestions. He scoured Europe for skilled artisans and exotic plant cuttings. To finance such a huge project, Sandys relied on a lottery, a game of chance that promised a continuous flow of capital into the company's treasury. The final element in the grand scheme was people. Sandys sent new English settlers by the hundreds to Jamestown, men and women swept up by the same hopes that had carried the colonists of 1607 to the New World.

Deadly Harvest

Between 1619 and 1622, colonists arrived in Virginia in ever larger waves. The Virginia Company's records reveal that during this period, 3,570 individuals embarked for the colony. These people seldom moved to Virginia in families. Although the first women arrived in Jamestown in 1608, most emigrants were single males in their teens or early twenties who came to the New World as indentured servants. In exchange for transportation across the Atlantic, they agreed to serve a master for a stated number of years. The length of service depended in part on the age of the servant. The younger the servant, the longer he or she served. In return, the master promised to give the laborers proper care and, at the conclusion of their contracts, to provide them with tools and clothes according to "the custom of the country." And the master, not the servant, received the headright for 50 more acres of tobacco land.

Whenever possible, planters in Virginia purchased able-bodied workers, in other words, persons capable of performing hard agricultural labor. This preference dramatically skewed the colony's sex ratio. In the early decades, men outnumbered women by as much as six to one. As one historian, Edmund S. Morgan, observed, "Women were scarcer than maize or liquor in Virginia and fetched a higher price." Such gender imbalance meant that even if a male servant lived to the end of his indenture—an unlikely prospect—he could not realistically expect to start a family. Moreover, despite apparent legal safeguards, masters could treat dependent workers as they pleased; after all, these people were legally considered property. Servants were sold, traded, even gambled away in hands of cards. It does not require much imagination to see that a society that tolerated such an exploitative labor system might later embrace slavery.

Most Virginians did not live long enough to worry about marriage. Death was omnipresent in this society. Indeed, extraordinarily high mortality was a major reason the Chesapeake colonies developed so differently from those of New England (see Chapter 5). On the eve of the 1618 reforms, Virginia's population stood at approximately 700. The company sent at least 3,000 more people, but by 1622 only 1,240 were still alive. "It Consequentilie followes," declared one angry shareholder, "that we had then lost 3,000 persons within those 3 yeares." The major killers were contagious diseases. Salt in the water supply also took a toll.

Conflict with the Powhatans exacerbated the insecurity of life in early Virginia. Between 1618 and 1622, colonists seized more and more Powhatan land to plant tobacco. Powhatan had passed the government of his kingdom to his kinsmen Opechancanough and Itoyatan. Opechancanough soon attained the paramount chiefdom. The new ruler grew increasingly concerned as the spread of English settlement threatened his control of the Chesapeake. On Good Friday, March 22, 1622, Opechancanough launched a well-coordinated surprise attack that claimed the lives of 347 Europeans. Most victims inhabited outlying settlements, while Jamestown itself escaped completely. The historian Helen Rountree has recently argued that Opechancanough intended not to exterminate the English, but to drive them back into previously accepted boundaries where the Powhatans could control them more easily while continuing to benefit from English trade. Whatever Opechancanough planned, the English interpreted the attack as an effort to drive them out of the Chesapeake region. Company officials retaliated with a counteroffensive to exterminate the Powhatans, ushering in a "policy of perpetual enmity" that took a horrendous toll on the tribes throughout the following decade.

No one knows for certain what effect such a mortality rate had on the Europeans who survived. At the very least, it must have exacerbated a sense of impermanence, a desire to escape Virginia with a little money before sickness or Indians ended the adventure. The settlers who drank to excess aboard the tavern ships anchored in the James River described the colony "not as a place of Habitacion but only of a short sojourninge."

On both sides of the Atlantic, people wondered who should be blamed for the failure of early Virginia. Why had so many colonists died in such a fertile land? The burden of responsibility lay in large measure with the Virginia Company. Sandys and his supporters were in too great a hurry to make a profit. Settlers were shipped to America, but neither housing nor food awaited them in Jamestown. Weakened by the long sea voyage, they quickly succumbed to contagious disease.

Reinventing Virginia

Company officials in Virginia also bore a share of guilt. Colonial leaders such as George Yeardley were so eager to look out for their own interests that they ignored the common good. Various governors and their councilors grabbed up the indentured servants owned by the company and sent them to their own private plantations to cultivate tobacco. As the 1622 attack demonstrated, officials also ignored the colony's crumbling defenses. Jamestown took on the characteristics of a boomtown, like those more familiar ones in Alaska and California. Colonists shared no sense of purpose, no common ideology, except perhaps unrestrained self-advancement, to keep the society from splintering into highly individualistic, competitive fragments.

The company's scandalous mismanagement embarrassed King James. In 1624, he dissolved the bankrupt enterprise, declaring Virginia a royal colony. The crown appointed a governor and a council. No provision was made, however, for continuing the local elected assembly, an institution the crown heartily opposed. The House of Burgesses had first convened in 1619. Although elections to it were hardly democratic, the assembly did provide wealthy planters with a voice in government. Even without the king's authorization, the representatives gathered annually after 1629, and in 1639, King Charles I recognized the body's existence.

Charles I had no choice. The colonists who served on the council or in the assembly were strong-willed, ambitious survivors. They had no intention of surrendering control over local affairs. Because Charles was having political troubles of his own and lived 3,000 miles from Jamestown, he usually allowed the Virginians to have their own way. In 1634, the assembly divided the colony into eight counties. In each, a group of appointed justices of the peace—the wealthy planters of the area—sat as a court of law as well as a governing body. The "county court" was the most important institution of local government in Virginia, and long after the American Revolution, it served as a center for social, political, and commercial activities.

By the mid-1620s, white society in Virginia was growing somewhat more stable if no less exploitative. The regional balance of power was also shifting against the Powhatans, who found themselves increasingly on the defensive. By the1630s their numbers had declined to perhaps 5,000 while the colonial population was on the rise, reaching 8,000 by 1640. During the 1620s and 1630s the Virginia assembly conducted a sustained offensive, authorizing at least three major military expeditions per year against the Powhatans between 1629 and 1632. As the Indians were killed, made into tributaries, or pushed north and south, Virginians took up large tracts of land along the colony's many navigable rivers.

The Powhatans put up stiff resistance to English expansion, making strategic withdrawals from some regions to avoid attack but fiercely defending crucial territories. In spite of intermittent hostilities throughout the 1630s, Powhatans also found ways to trade furs to the English for the European cloth, metal tools, and even food that they now needed to survive. In the early 1640s, however, the English began contending for control over the strategic headwaters of the York River, the Powhatans' last bastion against English encroachment into the interior. In 1644, Opechancanough sought to push the English back by masterminding a well-coordinated surprise attack in which 500 colonists died. The English responded by conducting retaliatory raids and building forts at the falls of the James, Chickahominy, and Appomattox Rivers.

In 1646, an expeditionary force under Governor William Berkeley captured Opechancanough. The great chief, now nearly 100 years old, was "so decrepit that he was not able to walk alone . . . his eyelids so heavy that he could not see, but as they were lifted up by his servants." Yet he remained defiant, convinced of his moral superiority over his English captors. Berkeley intended to send him to England "hoping to get reputation by presenting his Majesty with a royal captive," but a resentful English soldier "basely shot" Opechancanough in the back. An observer recorded that this "ancient prince" remained "brave to the last minute of his life, and showed not the least dejection at his captivity." Opechancanough's death marked the end of open warfare between the English and Powhatans.

MARYLAND: A CATHOLIC REFUGE

While Virginia authorities extended their hold on the rivers of the lower Chesapeake during the summer of 1632, Charles I inflicted on the colony what the eighteenth-century planter William Byrd II described as its "deepest wound" by "cutting off MARYLAND from it" in a grant to a royal favorite, Sir George Calvert. Byrd surmised that the grant marked "one fatal Instance among many of his Majesty's complaisance to the Queen" and observed that it "provd a Commodious Retreat" for seventeenth-century Roman Catholic refugees from England. By 1700, however, the colony Calvert had hoped to make a feudal haven for persecuted Catholics became a flourishing tobacco colony remarkably similar to Virginia.

Sir George Calvert, later Lord Baltimore, was a talented and well-educated man who enjoyed the patronage of King James I. The king awarded him lucrative positions in the government, the most important being the secretary of state. In 1625, Calvert shocked almost everyone by publicly declaring his Catholicism. The memory of the Gunpowder plot of November 1605, an abortive attempt by Roman Catholic conspirators to assassinate James I, "made England too hot for Papists to live in, without danger of being burnt with the Pope, every 5th of November," as William Byrd later put it. Persons who openly supported the Church of Rome were immediately stripped of civil office. Although forced to resign as secretary of state, Calvert retained the crown's favor.

Before resigning, Calvert sponsored a settlement on the coast of Newfoundland. After visiting the place, however, the proprietor concluded that no English person, whatever his or her religion, would transfer to a place where the "ayre [is] so intolerably cold." He turned his attention to the Chesapeake, and on June 30, 1632, Charles I granted George Calvert's son, Cecilius, a charter for a colony to be located north of Virginia. The boundaries of the settlement, named Maryland in honor of Charles's French queen Mary, were so vaguely defined that they generated legal controversies not fully resolved until the mid-eighteenth century when Charles Mason and Jeremiah Dixon surveyed their famous line between Pennsylvania and Maryland.

Cecilius, the second Lord Baltimore, not only wanted to create a sanctuary for England's persecuted Catholics; he also intended to make money. Without Protestant settlers, it seemed unlikely Maryland would prosper, and Cecilius instructed his brother Leonard, the colony's governor, to do nothing that might frighten off Protestants. The governor was ordered to "cause all Acts of the Roman Catholic Religion to be done as privately as may be and . . . [to] instruct all Roman Catholics to be silent upon all occasions of discourse concerning matters of Religion." On March 25, 1634, the *Ark* and the *Dove*, carrying about 150 settlers, landed safely at the mouth of the Potomac River.

The first Maryland settlers encountered a more complex situation among the Native Americans of the region than the Virginians had nearly three decades before. During the sixteenth century, the Algonquian-speaking Piscataways had ruled much of the northern Chesapeake from their ancient palisaded town of Moyaone on the Potomac River. By 1600, however, a new set of challenges confronted the Piscataways. Their former empire was divided, giving Maryland's Eastern Shore to the Naticokes and the Western Shore and Potomac to the Piscataways. Powhatan soon wrested control of the Potomac's southern bank, while Iroquoian Nacotchtanks pressed down from the upper Potomac onto Piscataway lands. Another Iroquoian tribe, the Susquehannocks, moved down the Susquehanna River to challenge neighboring Yoacomacos. After the founding of Jamestown, English colonists also pushed northward to trade. Virginia-Piscataway relations eventually turned hostile. Thus, when Governor Leonard Calvert requested permission from Wannas, the Piscataway *tayac* or paramount chief, to "set downe in his Countrey," Wannas rebuffed him. Calvert instead purchased an abandoned Yoacomaco village at the mouth of the Potomac that became St. Mary's City, the capital of Maryland.

Within two years of Maryland's founding, however, the Piscataways forged an alliance with the new colonial government after Wannas's brother Kittamaquund murdered him to seize leadership of the tribe. Kittamaquund needed English support to hold on to power, and the whole tribe required the additional security that a military alliance and trading partnership could provide. Maryland also needed the alliance because officials were unsure of the disposition of other tribes and could not count on the support of Virginians, who resented the encroachment of a Roman Catholic colony on land they considered their own. Governor Calvert eventually negotiated the right to select Piscataway tayacs, making the tribe a vassal of the proprietor, Lord Baltimore.

The Calverts also labored to convert the Piscataways to Roman Catholic Christianity by bringing Jesuit missionaries to the colony. Kittamaquund welcomed the Jesuit Andrew White into his own household in 1639 and delighted Maryland colonists by submitting to baptism along with several other Piscataways a year later. During the next three years they baptized another 130 Indians in villages along the Potomac before Susquehannock raids forced them to abandon the mission. Archaeological and textual evidence from the period suggests that the converts likely accepted the new faith without relinquishing their old beliefs, but the conversions nevertheless formed a significant element of an ongoing cultural exchange between the two groups.

Leonard Calvert's success in negotiating Piscataway vassalage suggests how he and his brother, Lord Baltimore, envisioned Native Americans' place within the larger feudal order they hoped to create in Maryland. The colony's charter transformed Lord Baltimore into a "palatine lord," a proprietor with almost royal powers. Settlers swore an oath of allegiance not to the king of England but to Lord Baltimore. In England, such practices had long ago passed into obsolescence. As the proprietor, Lord Baltimore owned outright almost 6 million acres; he possessed absolute authority over anyone living in his domain.

On paper, at least, everyone in the colony of Maryland was assigned a place in an elaborate social hierarchy. Persons who purchased 6,000 acres from Lord Baltimore became members of the colonial ruling class and were styled lords of the manor. These landed aristocrats were permitted to establish local courts of law. People holding less acreage enjoyed fewer privileges, particularly in government. Lord Baltimore figured that land sales and rents would adequately finance the entire venture.

The Calverts probably intended to fit the Piscataways into this feudal system as well. Leonard Calvert's references to the tayac Kittamaquund as his "brother" and Lord Baltimore's "friend and servant" suggest that the governor may have regarded the tayac as one of the lords of the manor, and treaties with the tribe imposed English law on them. In other ways, however, Maryland officials dealt with the Piscataways as a tributary people. Maryland courts, for example, often left them to conduct their internal affairs "according to their owne lawes and customs" so long as no interests of English colonists were at stake.

Lord Baltimore's feudal system never took root in Chesapeake soil. Colonists and Indians alike simply refused to play the social roles the lord proprietor had assigned. These tensions affected the operation of Maryland's government. Lord Baltimore assumed that his brother, acting as his deputy in America, and a small appointed council of local aristocrats would pass necessary laws and carry out routine administration. When an elected assembly first convened in 1635, Lord Baltimore allowed delegates to discuss only those acts he had prepared. The members of the assembly bridled at such restrictions, insisting on exercising traditional parliamentary privileges. Neither side gained a clear victory in the assembly, and for almost twenty-five years, legislative squabbling contributed to the widespread political instability that almost destroyed Maryland.

The colony recruited both Protestants and Catholics. The two groups might have lived in harmony had civil war not broken out in England. When Oliver Cromwell and the Puritan faction executed Charles I, transforming England briefly into a Protestant republic (see Chapter 6), it seemed that Lord Baltimore might lose his colony. To head off such an event and to placate Maryland's restless Protestants, in 1649 the proprietor drafted the famous "Act concerning Religion," extending toleration to all individuals who accepted the deity of Christ. At a time when European rulers regularly persecuted people for their religious beliefs, Lord Baltimore—like Roger Williams in Rhode Island—championed liberty of conscience.

However laudable the act may have been, it did not heal religious divisions in Maryland. When local Puritans seized the colony's government, they promptly repealed the act. For almost two decades, vigilantes roamed the countryside. During the "plundering time" (1644–1646), one armed group temporarily drove Leonard Calvert out of Maryland. In 1655, civil war flared again.

The Piscataways, for their part, used the Calverts' new order for their own ends. Kittamaquund's conversion, for instance, strengthened his ties with the English and made them more willing to support his hold on tribal power. Piscataway converts probably accepted the Roman Catholic faith while continuing to observe traditional beliefs and practices. When the Jesuits fled colonial unrest in 1645, most converts returned to the old ways. After Kittamaquund's death, the tribe simply ignored the Maryland governor's right to appoint a successor and continued to choose their own tayacs. They also obeyed or sought protection of English law when it benefited them and ignored it when it did not. For many years Maryland's need for a native trading and military alliance gave the Piscataways significant bargaining power to retain control of their own affairs.

Tobacco cultivation in this troubled sanctuary rapidly transformed the colony into a reflection of neighboring Virginia. Ordinary planters and their workers cultivated tobacco on plantations dispersed along the Potomac riverfront. In 1678, Lord Baltimore complained that he could not find fifty houses in a space of thirty miles. Tobacco affected almost every aspect of local culture. "In Virginia and Maryland," one Calvert explained, "Tobacco, as our Staple, is our all, and indeed leaves no room for anything Else." A steady stream of indentured servants supplied the plantations with dependent laborers—that is, until they were replaced by African slaves at the end of the seventeenth century.

THE PLANTERS' PERSPECTIVE

Europeans sacrificed much by coming to the Chesapeake Bay region. For most of the century, their standard of living was primitive when compared with that of people of the same social class who had remained in England. The focus of Chesapeake colonists' existence was the isolated plantation, a small cluster of buildings housing the planter's family and dependent workers. Two-thirds of the planters lived in wooden houses of only two rooms, a design associated with the poorest classes in contemporary English society. Not until the eighteenth century did the gentry construct the great Georgian mansions that attract modern tourists. The dispersed pattern of settlement retarded the development of institutions such as schools and churches. Besides Jamestown and St. Mary's, no population centers developed, and as late as 1705, Robert Beverley, a leading planter, reported that Virginia did not have a single place "that may reasonably bear the Name of a Town."

This distinctive pattern of settlement owed much to tobacco cultivation and its associated labor system as contemporaries suggested, but demographic forces also played a role. The crop exhausted the soil quickly, spurring planters to move onto fresh land after only a few years. The many Chesapeake estuaries allowed planters to fan out along the waterfront where they built their own wharves for loading heavy hogsheads. This efficient arrangement saved the cost of transporting goods overland to middlemen in harbor towns. It gave riverfront planters a competitive advantage and a tidy side-business from the loading and storage fees they charged inland planters. The practice also helped to scatter the population across the countryside. Historical demographers have argued, however, that the Chesapeake's death rate constituted the most important reason for the distinctive character of these early southern plantation societies. A frighteningly high mortality tore at the very fabric of traditional family life.

Family Life in a Perilous Environment

Unlike New England settlers, the men and women who emigrated to the Chesapeake region seldom moved in family units. Most traveled to the New World as young unmarried servants, youths cut off from the security of traditional kin relations. Although these immigrants came from a cross section of English society, most had been poor to middling farmers. It is now estimated that 70 to 85 percent of the white colonists who went to Virginia and Maryland during the seventeenth century were not free; that is, they owed four or five years' labor in exchange for the cost of passage to America. If the servant was under the age of 15, he or she had to serve a full seven years. The overwhelming majority of these laborers were males between the ages of 18 and 22. In fact, before 1640, the ratio of males to females stood at 6 to 1. This figure dropped to about $2\frac{1}{2}$ to 1 by the end of the century, but the sex ratio in the Chesapeake was never as balanced as it had been in early Massachusetts.

Most Chesapeake immigrants died soon after arriving. It is difficult to ascertain the exact cause of death in most cases, but malaria and other diseases took a frightful toll. Recent studies also indicate that drinking water contaminated with salt killed many colonists living in low-lying areas. Throughout the entire seventeenth century, high mortality rates had a profound effect on this society. Life expectancy for Chesapeake males was about 43 years, some 10 to 20 years less than for men born in New England. For women, life was even shorter. A full 25 percent of all children died in infancy; another 25 percent did not see their twentieth birthdays. The survivors were often weak or ill, unable to perform hard physical labor.

These demographic conditions retarded normal population increase. Young women who might have become wives and mothers could not do so until they had completed their terms of servitude. They thus lost several reproductive years, and in a society in which so many children died in infancy, late marriage greatly restricted family size. Moreover, because of the unbalanced sex ratio, many adult males simply could not find wives. Migration not only cut them off from their English families but also deprived them of an opportunity to form new ones. Without a constant flow of immigrants, the population of Virginia and Maryland would have actually declined.

High mortality compressed the family life cycle into a few short years. One partner in a marriage usually died within seven years. Only one in three Chesapeake marriages survived as long as a decade. Not only did children not meet grandparents; they often did not even know their own parents. Widows and widowers quickly remarried, bringing children by former unions into their new homes, and it was not uncommon for a child to grow up with persons to whom he or she bore no blood relation.

The psychological effects of such experiences on Chesapeake settlers cannot be measured. People probably learned to cope with a high degree of personal insecurity. However they adjusted, it is clear that family life in this region was vastly more impermanent than it was in either England itself or the New England colonies during the same period.

Women were obviously in great demand in the early southern colonies, a situation made even more acute by the common English refusal to take Indian spouses. Some historians have argued that scarcity heightened the woman's bargaining power in the marriage market. If she was an immigrant, she did not have to worry about obtaining parental consent. She was on her own in the New World and free to select whomever she pleased. If a woman lacked beauty or strength, if she were a person of low moral standards, she could still be confident of finding an American husband. Such negotiations may have provided Chesapeake women with a means of improving their social status.

Nevertheless, liberation from some traditional restraints on seventeenth-century women must not be exaggerated. As servants, women were vulnerable to sexual exploitation by their masters. Moreover, in this unhealthy environment, childbearing was extremely dangerous, and women in the Chesapeake usually died twenty years earlier than their New England counterparts.

Rank and Status in Plantation Society

Colonists who managed somehow to survive grew tobacco—as much tobacco as they possibly could. This crop became the Chesapeake staple, much like sugar in the Caribbean or rice in the Carolinas. Because the plant was relatively easy to cultivate, anyone with a few acres of cleared land could harvest leaves for export.

Cultivation of tobacco did not, however, produce a society roughly equal in wealth and status. To the contrary, tobacco generated striking inequality. Some planters amassed large fortunes; others barely subsisted. Labor made the difference, for to succeed in this staple economy, one had to control the labor of other men and women. More workers in the fields meant larger harvests, and, of course, larger profits. Because free persons showed no interest in growing another man's tobacco, not even for wages, wealthy planters relied on white laborers who were not free, as well as on slaves. The social structure that developed in the seventeenth-century Chesapeake reflected a wild, often unscrupulous scramble to bring men and women of three races—black, white, and Indian—into various degrees of dependence.

Great planters dominated Chesapeake society. The group was small, only a trifling portion of the population of Virginia and Maryland. During the early decades of the seventeenth century, the composition of Chesapeake gentry was continually in flux. Some gentlemen died before they could establish a secure claim to high social status; others returned to England, thankful to have survived. Not until the 1650s did the family names of those who would become famous eighteenth-century gentry appear in the records. The first gentlemen were not—as genealogists sometimes discover to their dismay—dashing cavaliers who had fought in the English civil war for King Charles I. Rather, such Chesapeake gentry as the

Burwells, Byrds, Carters, and Beverleys consisted originally of the younger sons of English merchants and artisans, in other words, ambitious men with fortunes to make.

These favored sons arrived in America with capital. They invested immediately in laborers, and one way or another, they obtained huge tracts of the best tobacco-growing land. The members of this provincial gentry were not technically aristocrats, for they did not possess titles that could be passed from generation to generation. They gave themselves military titles, sat as justices of the peace on the county courts, and directed local (Anglican) church affairs as members of the vestry. Over time, these gentry families intermarried so frequently that they created a vast network of cousins. During the eighteenth century, it was not uncommon to find a half-dozen men with the same surname sitting simultaneously in the Virginia House of Burgesses.

Freemen formed the largest class in white society. Their origins were strikingly different from those of the gentry, or for that matter, from those of New England's yeomen farmers. Chesapeake freemen traveled to the New World as indentured servants. Only by sheer good fortune did they manage to remain alive to the end of their contracts. If they had dreamed of becoming great planters, they were gravely disappointed. Most seventeenth-century freemen lived on the edge of poverty. Some freemen, of course, did better in America than they would have in contemporary England, but in both Virginia and Maryland, historians have found a sharp economic division separating the gentry from the rest of white society.

Below the freemen came indentured servants. Membership in this group was not demeaning; after all, servitude was a temporary status. But servitude in the Chesapeake colonies was not the benign institution it was in New England. Great planters purchased servants to grow tobacco. No one seemed overly concerned whether these laborers received decent food and clothes, much less whether they acquired trade skills. Young people, thousands of them, cut off from family ties, sick often to the point of death, unable to obtain normal sexual release, regarded their servitude as a form of slavery. Not surprisingly, the gentry worried that unhappy servants and impoverished freemen, what the planters called the "giddy multitude," would rebel at the slightest provocation, a fear that turned out to be fully justified.

The character of social mobility—and this observation applies only to the whites—changed considerably during the seventeenth century. Until the 1680s, it was relatively easy for a newcomer who possessed capital to become a member of the planter elite. No one paid much attention to the reputation or social standing of one's English family. Only toward the end of the century did a "creole majority" or indigenous ruling elite begin to emerge as life expectancy rates improved for those who survived childhood in the Chesapeake region. For the first time in the history of Virginia and Maryland, important leadership positions went to men who had actually been born in America. Where earlier immigrant leaders had died without heirs or had returned as quickly as possible to England, the members of the new creole class took a greater interest in local government. Their activities helped give the tobacco colonies the kind of political and cultural stability that had eluded earlier generations of planter-adventurers.

Opportunities for advancement also decreased for the freemen in this region. Studies of mid-seventeenth-century Maryland reveal that some servants managed to become moderately prosperous farmers and small officeholders. But as the gentry consolidated its hold on political and economic institutions, ordinary people discovered it was much harder to rise in Chesapeake society. Those men and women with more ambitious dreams headed for Pennsylvania, North Carolina, or western Virginia.

In 1619, the first immigrants of African descent arrived in the Chesapeake when a Dutch merchant vessel sailed up the James River to sell "20. and odd Negroes" to Virginia planters. Surviving records provide no clear indication of their status, though they may well have been slaves for life. For the next fifty years, the status of the Chesapeake's black people remained unclear. English settlers classified some black laborers as lifetime slaves, chattel to be bought and sold at the master's will. But other Africans became servants, presumably for stated periods of time, and it was even possible for a few blacks to purchase their freedom.

Race and Freedom in the Chesapeake

Early relations between blacks and whites in the Chesapeake were complex. Although colonists certainly took note of differences in skin color and based some decisions on that difference, it remained only one of several factors that shaped black-white interaction. Black and white unfree laborers worked side by side in Chesapeake tobacco fields. They shared a similarly miserable existence on most plantations and often cooperated with one another in efforts to resist poor treatment or escape their bondage. Blacks who gained their freedom also faced challenges and opportunities similar to their white counterparts. They could work for wages or purchase property and set up their own tobacco plantations. Success proved elusive for poor freemen regardless of skin color, and blacks who failed found themselves pushed to the margins of settlement along with whites, where they again had to cooperate to survive.

Several seventeenth-century Africans did beat the odds to become successful planters. Anthony and Mary Johnson, for example, managed to gain their freedom and acquire a respectable estate of 250 acres on Pungoteague Creek on Virginia's Eastern Shore. There the Johnsons supported a family of four children by cultivating tobacco and raising cattle, horses, and hogs. Anthony Johnson's operation was large enough to demand the labor of indentured servants and one black slave, Casor. It also gave him sufficient resources to help his two sons set up their own plantations on adjacent land. Johnson traded with his white neighbors and hauled them into court when they attempted to take advantage of him. He also maintained close ties with other free blacks such as his neighbors Anthony Payne and Emmanuel Driggus. As family patriarch, Johnson led his clan to Somerset County, Maryland in the 1660s, where his grandson carried the Johnson legacy of freedom into its third generation by purchasing his own plantation, which he named "Angola." The plantation name, like the pattern of associations and family arrangements, suggests that the Johnsons managed to incorporate substantial elements of their African cultural heritage into their new lives in America.

The Johnsons likely enjoyed the toleration to pursue their independence in large measure because the Chesapeake's black population remained very small. By

1660, fewer than 1,500 people of African origin lived in the entire colony (compared to a white population of 26,000), and it hardly seemed necessary for the legislature to draw up an elaborate slave code to control so few men and women.

If the planters could have obtained more black laborers they certainly would have done so. There is no evidence that the great planters preferred white indentured servants to black slaves. The problem was supply. During this period, slave traders sold their cargoes on Barbados or the other sugar islands of the West Indies, where they fetched higher prices than Virginians could afford. In fact, before 1680, most blacks who reached England's colonies on the North American mainland came from Barbados or through New Netherland rather than directly from Africa. Only after the Royal Africa Company emerged as a part of a new thrust to develop the British empire (see Chapter 6) did Africans begin to supply the bulk of labor needs in the Chesapeake.

Indians and Colonists Adjust to a New Order

The history of relations among colonists and Indians in both Maryland and Virginia reveals complex patterns of interaction rather than simple conflict and English domination. To be sure, tension and competition characterized relations throughout the seventeenth century as each maneuvered to gain advantage over the other in trade, diplomacy, and territory. Neither Powhatan nor his successors hesitated to use military force when they considered it necessary to defend their interests and keep Virginia colonists within agreed-upon boundaries. The English likewise resorted to armed force to achieve their aims. English planters, always on the lookout for laborers, did not hesitate to enslave Indians captured in combat and put them to work in tobacco fields. Yet colonists and Indians found that they could achieve certain aims more effectively by cooperation.

During Virginia's early years colonists and Powhatans often found themselves living side by side despite the potential for conflict. On various occasions this proved disastrous for both colonists and Indians, most notably during the Powhatan attacks and colonial reprisals in 1622 and 1644. Nevertheless, the pattern persisted as tribal groups continued to live in areas overtaken by English settlement. Some English colonists, especially servants, preferred life among the Indians to the miserable conditions on tobacco plantations. In both Virginia and Maryland, runaway servants caught living among various Chesapeake tribes were punished severely with flogging, branding, and extended terms of service, but this did not always deter others from making the attempt.

Indian and colonial neighbors came to know each other by name as they engaged in a variety of relationships and cooperative ventures. Piscataway leaders in Maryland regularly enjoyed hospitality in English households when they traveled to St. Mary's on business and reciprocated when colonial officials or agents traveled in Piscataway territory. Colonial Virginians learned Powhatan ways of hunting game by traveling with them in joint hunting expeditions. Colonists throughout the Chesapeake hired their Indian neighbors to hunt for them and to kill the wolves that preyed on colonial livestock. Virginians often risked prosecution to lend guns to the Powhatans they hired to hunt for them. After 1646 the colony entered an alliance with the Powhatans and relaxed prohibitions against arming them. Individual colonists and Indians traded with one another, even in regulated or prohibited goods. Planters also tried to control their bound labor force by negotiating agreements with neighboring tribes to control the capture and return of runaways.

As the century progressed, economic and social change among Indian tribes throughout the Northeast prompted both colonists and their nearby Indian neighbors to cooperate in military ventures. Population decline among the Iroquois, for example, prompted them to engage in "mourning wars" to gain captives from neighboring tribes which they could adopt to replace lost clan members. Such actions sparked a chain reaction of conflict that reached the Chesapeake as beleaguered groups pressed into the region to escape conquest elsewhere. Overtrapping also caused clashes as the Iroquois and others ranged far from their traditional lands to find new sources of valuable furs. Chesapeake colonists and tribes benefited from mutual military support against the "new-come" Indians that posed a threat to all.

Over time, the growing English population displaced Indians throughout the Chesapeake, pushing them off ancestral lands or confining them to reservations within English territory. Contemporary observers noted how trade made tribal peoples increasingly dependent on European goods while European disease caused the "numbers of the Indians in these parts [to] decrease very much." Europeans also noticed the toll taken by the Indians' "being so devilishly given to drinking." Tribal people themselves complained that they were "miserable Poor" and "reduced to a small Number." Yet historians such as James Merrell have recently argued that these "supposed signs of decline provide evidence less of cultural disintegration than of cultural persistence." Chesapeake tribes proved remarkably resourceful in resisting cultural change, and their "importance as allies and as suppliers of maize and skins enabled them to retain much of their independence and cultural integrity despite their tributary status."

ESCAPING THE PAST

The pattern of English colonization in the Chesapeake exacted heavy costs on all inhabitants of the region. Life became much harder for the original inhabitants of the land. The ethos of looking out for number one made life hard for the English and African immigrants as well, particularly the great majority who suffered exploitation at the hands of those who came out on top of the scramble for wealth. Even the winners faced a social life in the New World that was severely diminished by Old World standards.

Social institutions associated with stable family and community life were either weak or nonexistent in the Chesapeake colonies. In part, this sluggish development resulted from the continuation of high infant mortality rates. There was little incentive to build grammar schools, for example, if half the children would die before reaching adulthood. The great planters sent their sons to England or Scotland for their education. Even after the founding of Virginia's College of William and Mary in 1693, the gentry continued to patronize English schools. As a result of this practice, higher education in the South languished for much of the colonial period.

Tobacco influenced the spread of other institutions in this region. Planters were scattered along the rivers, often separated from their nearest neighbors by miles of poor roads. Because the major tobacco growers traded directly with English merchants, they had no need for towns. Whatever items they required were either made on the plantation or imported from Europe. Other than the centers of colonial government, Jamestown (and later Williamsburg) and St. Mary's City (and later Annapolis), there were no villages capable of sustaining a rich community life before the late eighteenth century. Seventeenth-century Virginia did not even possess a printing press. In fact, Governor William Berkeley bragged in 1671, "There are no free schools, nor printing in Virginia, for learning has brought disobedience, and heresy . . . into the world, and printing had divulged them . . . God keep us from both!"

Berkeley was making a virtue of necessity, as Virginians would continue to do for the remainder of the colonial period. Colonial Chesapeake chroniclers consistently lamented the colony's woeful history from a vantage point of privilege made possible by the ruthlessly competitive system their fathers created. Still, the planters always hoped for a fresh start. The land was rich and plentiful. Virginians needed only to "rouse . . . out of their lethargy . . . and make the most out of those happy Advantages which Nature had given them."

CHRONOLOGY

1600	Powhatan controls large Native American empire in the Chesapeake.
1605	Gunpowder plot to assassinate James I exposed.
1607	Jamestown established.
1610	Lord De la Warr averts abandonment of Jamestown after "starving time"; establishes *Lawes Divine, Morall and Martial*
1610	John Rolfe introduces West Indian tobacco to Virginia.
1613	Pocahontas weds John Rolfe.
1617	Pocahontas dies in London.
1618	Sir Edwin Sandys initiates reforms leading to establishment of Virginia House of Burgesses.
1619	First blacks arrive in Virginia.
1622	Opechancanough leads surprise attack; 347 Virginia colonists die.
1624	James I dissolves Virginia charter.
1632	Charles I grants Maryland to Sir George Calvert.

1634	First colonists arrive in Maryland.
1640	Colonial population reaches 8,000.
1644–46	"Plundering time" drives Leonard Calvert from Maryland.
1646	Governor William Berkeley's force captures Opechancanough.

RECOMMENDED READING

The best single starting point for understanding the colonization of the Chesapeake and the development of English society there remains Edmund S. Morgan's *American Slavery, American Freedom: The Ordeal of Colonial Virginia* (New York, 1975), while Frederic W. Gleach's *Powhatan's World and Colonial Virginia: A Conflict of Cultures* (Lincoln, Nebr. 1997) provides a well-rounded treatment of Powhatan culture and Powhatan-English relations in the seventeenth century. For a tough-minded account of the ordeal of the first Jamestown colonists, see Captain John Smith, *A Selected Edition of His Writings*, ed. Karen O. Kupperman (Chapel Hill, 1988).

James Horn's *Adapting to a New World: English Society in the Seventeenth-Century Chesapeake* (Chapel Hill, 1994) analyzes how migrants to the Chesapeake adapted English institutions and cultural forms to their new environment. Excellent essays on many aspects of social development in the seventeenth-century Chesapeake may be found in two collections: Thad W. Tate and David L. Ammerman, eds., *The Chesapeake in the Seventeenth Century: Essays on Anglo-American Society* (Chapel Hill, 1979) and Lois Green Carr, Philip D. Morgan, and Jean B. Russo, eds., *Colonial Chesapeake Society* (Chapel Hill, 1988).

A provocative reassessment of social development in Virginia is Kathleen M. Brown's *Good Wives, Nasty Wenches, and Anxious Patriarchs: Gender, Race, and Power in Colonial Virginia* (Chapel Hill, 1996). T. H. Breen's *Puritans and Adventurers: Change and Persistence in Early America* (New York, 1980) contains essays exploring various aspects of cultural values in seventeenth-century Virginia. The fluidity of race relations and the development of a free black community in seventeenth-century Virginia is explored in T. H. Breen and Stephen Innes, *"Myne Owne Ground": Race and Freedom on Virginia's Eastern Shore, 1640–1676* (New York, 1980). For an insightful account of how English law was adapted to the colonial Virginian context, see John Ruston Pagan, *Anne Orthwood's Bastard: Sex and Law in Early Virginia* (New York, 2002).

Insightful analyses of colonial development in early Maryland include Gloria L. Main, *Tobacco Colony: Life in Early Maryland, 1650–1720* (Princeton, 1982), David B. Quinn, *Early Maryland in a Wider World* (Detroit, 1982), and Lois Green Carr, Russell R. Menard, and Lorena S. Walsh, *Robert Cole's World: Agriculture and Society in Early Maryland* (Chapel Hill, 1991).

Helen C. Rountree's *Pocahontas's People: The Powhatan Indians of Virginia through Four Centuries* (Norman, Okla., 1990) provides a good starting point for those interested in the history of native peoples of the Chesapeake before and after the English arrived. Her *Eastern Shore Indians of Virginia and Maryland* (Charlottesville, 1997) draws on archaeology as well as written records to reconstruct native life in that region, while her "Powhatan Indian Women: The People Captain John Smith Barely Saw," *Ethnohistory* 45 (1998): 1–29, analyzes the contributions of native women to Powhatan social life. For early Anglo-native contact in Maryland see James H. Merrell, "Cultural Continuity among the Piscataway Indians of Colonial Maryland," *William and Mary Quarterly*, 3rd Ser., 36 (1979): 548–570.

Chapter 5

Cities on a Hill

Bible Commonwealths in New England, 1620–1660

Governor John Winthrop assured the settlers who traveled with him to Massachusetts Bay that they were on a special mission, sanctioned by God. In the New World, they would emulate the Jews of the Old Testament, creating a "city on a hill" which would stand as a beacon for Protestant reformers throughout Europe. Notwithstanding their mandate, the ordinary men and women who followed Winthrop to America encountered physical conditions that tested their religious resolve.

In March of 1631, one of two brothers named Ponds recounted his experiences as a new colonizer in an unsigned letter to his father in England. The sea voyage had been horrible. The writer's entire family—a wife and two children—suffered from smallpox that scarred the children and killed fourteen passengers. The land itself was not what the young farmer had expected. It was rocky and hilly, the soil shallower than he would have liked, better for livestock than for grain. The struggling colonists lacked the equipment needed for fishing; they found hunting in the dense forests harder than they had imagined. During the first very difficult months, Pond and his neighbors relied on Indian trade and supplies from England. They had crossed the Atlantic Ocean to do God's work, but as Pond confessed to his father, he desperately needed "help with provisions from ould Eingland."

Like most of the families who sailed for Massachusetts Bay during the 1630s, the Ponds discovered that they had seriously underestimated the hardships of settlement. The vast majority of colonists expressed disappointment at what they found in New England. The New England poet Anne Bradstreet wrote that at first her "heart rose" in rebellion against the "new world and new manners" she encountered in Massachusetts, but "after I was convinced it was the way of God, I submitted to it and joined the church at Boston." The deputy governor Thomas Dudley warned prospective settlers that "if any come hither to plant for worldly ends that can live well at home, he commits an error, of which he will soon repent him." Only those who came for "spiritual" reasons would "find here what may well content" them. Yet despite such reports, an estimated 21,000 settlers embarked for New England during the Great Migration of the 1630s. More than 17,000 remained to build a stable communal society that contrasted starkly with England's Chesapeake dominions.

INDIGENOUS PEOPLES

The English who began settling coastal New England in 1620 encountered scattered bands of native peoples whose numbers had been decimated by "a great and grievous plague" that ravaged the region in 1616. Although demoralized, the Indians who survived possessed extensive knowledge of European ways acquired from almost a century of trade and interaction. They remained highly resourceful in using that knowledge to pursue their own interests in an ongoing Anglo-Indian exchange.

Europeans may have begun exploring the northeastern coast of America as early as the late fifteenth century. Many of them were obscure fishermen who came ashore to dry their catches before returning home. These early explorers encountered bands of largely self-sufficient peoples living in a patchwork of territories defined by the region's bays and river valleys. The Massachuset, for example, lived around Massachusetts Bay and its tributaries, while neighboring Algonquian tribes inhabited Cape Cod, southeastern Massachusetts, and the eastern side of Narragansett Bay. Narragansetts inhabited the western side of that bay, Mohegan-Pequots inhabited the region of what is now eastern Connecticut and Long Island, and Quiripi bands inhabited the Connecticut River valley and central Long Island.

Before the arrival of intensive European trade, southern New England native peoples pursued a way of life centered on cycles of farming, hunting, and winter foraging. Almost three-quarters of their diet came from maize, beans and squash, which women farmers planted together in densely tangled fields that "load[ed] the ground with as much as it [would] bear." Men supplemented this nutritious diet through hunting and fishing, risky activities that took them away from home for extended periods. Villages celebrated harvest with feasting, dancing, and gambling combined with rituals in which wealthy individuals gave away most of their possessions to seal reciprocal relations of mutual support and obligation among followers or allies. At the end of harvest feasting, villages moved into fall hunting camps from which the men ranged individually or in groups to track fattened game such as bear and deer. Women hauled the dead animals back to camp where they butchered and processed the meat and hides for later use. December snowfalls drove villagers to sites that offered shelter from the winter elements and provided hunters and fishermen a base of operations for their ongoing expeditions.

Tribal chiefs, usually called *sagamores* from Massachusetts Bay north and *sachems* toward the south, obtained their status through matrilineal inheritance coupled with charismatic leadership. Sagamores further secured their position by generous gift-giving to followers who reciprocated with support and loyalty. Women could also wield authority, as the Pawtuxet "Squaw Sachem" of Massachusetts Bay did during the early 1630s. A loose hierarchy of leadership existed similar to that of the Chesapeake Algonquians, with sagamores of lesser villages often paying tribute to more powerful leaders in exchange for support and protection. Followers supported their sagamores with tribute in fish, corn, furs, game, or hospitality: "a flower in the prince's crown and a royalty paid him," as the Connecticut minister Jared Elliot observed.

The growth of European trade during the sixteenth century stimulated subtle shifts in native economies. The tribes had previously relied on regional exchange networks to supplement their own supplies of food and obtain scarce items such as highly valued purple wampum shells supplied by the Montauks of Long Island. After the French arrived, their northern Micmac fur-trading partners became more dependent on outside sources of food and supplies as their hunters specialized in procuring commodities for trade rather than game for subsistence. The same process began to draw in the Abenakis of Maine in the late sixteenth and early seventeenth century. Abenakis adapted by entering trading partnerships in which they exchanged goods obtained from the French for surplus Massachuset crops. Micmacs responded to the new state of affairs by raiding both Abenaki competitors and native farmers of southern New England for tribute in agricultural goods, transforming the Abenaki–southern New England partnership into a political and military alliance. Dutch fur traders working from the Hudson River were stimulating similar economic and political adjustments among the tribes of Long Island Sound and western Narragansett Bay. By the early seventeenth century, Indians within both the French and Dutch spheres of trade were slipping into dependence on European commerce.

When English adventurers began exploring the region after 1600, groups such as the Abenaki approached them as potential allies who could help their people achieve a competitive advantage in trade. The English, however, repeatedly antagonized native peoples through hostile actions that included kidnapping and taking captives to England, where schemers such as Sir Ferdinando Gorges hoped to transform them into agents for various colonial enterprises. Squanto, the English-speaking Pawtuxet whom schoolchildren remember for assisting the Pilgrims during their first years of settlement, was one such captive. A dozen years of exploration, contact, and occasional trade gained the English extensive knowledge of the region. It also acquainted native inhabitants with prickly English ways, which may explain why no tribe formed a lasting trading partnership with them. In 1614, the indomitable Captain John Smith set out to succeed where his countrymen had hitherto failed, reconnoitering and mapping the region he named New England before returning home to lay plans for a new colony there. Smith planned to use tactics he had practiced on the Powhatans of Virginia to browbeat New England Indians into trading furs and corn, but those plans came to nothing after his expedition fell apart.

Despite the social and economic changes introduced by European trade, New England tribes successfully resisted European domination. They could not, however, resist epidemic disease. From 1616 to 1618 the region's native peoples underwent horrible devastation, succumbing by the tens of thousands to what was probably some strain of plague unwittingly introduced by French traders. Historians estimate that the coastal population dropped as much as 90 percent. Whole tribes, such as that of the famous Pawtuxet, Squanto, disappeared completely, their very memory eventually obliterated as other peoples absorbed their tattered remnants. Where John Smith had seen a land "planted with Gardens and Corne fields, and so well inhabited with a goodly, strong, and well-proportioned people," later visitors found abandoned fields choked with underbrush. When the Englishman Thomas Morton arrived in 1622, the unburied skeletons lying about "made such a spectacle . . . it seemed to me a new found Golgatha (sic)."

The English settlers who began arriving in 1620 found only the remnants of once robust bands struggling to regroup in the wake of unimaginable catastrophe. Surviving sagamores labored to consolidate their people into bands that incorporated the remnants of tribes now too few in number to continue as separate peoples. The Reverend Francis Higginson reported in 1629 that "the greatest sagamores about us cannot make above three hundred men, and other less sagamores have not above fifteen subjects and others near about us but two." Higginson observed that so few people could not "make use of one-fourth part of the land." Under such conditions, the sachems were only too willing to welcome English colonists as allies who could help them repel the advances of interior tribes who had escaped the epidemic. Yet even in this weakened condition, Indian survivors proved adept at using trade and diplomacy to retain a significant degree of self-determination and control over their own affairs.

PILGRIMS AND STRANGERS

The Pilgrims enjoy almost mythic status in American history. These brave refugees crossed the cold Atlantic in search of religious liberty, signed a democratic compact aboard the *Mayflower*, landed at Plymouth Rock, and gave us Thanksgiving Day. As with most legends, this one contains only a core of truth.

The Pilgrims were not crusaders who set out to change the world. Rather, they were humble English farmers. Their story began in the early 1600s in Scrooby Manor, a small community located approximately 150 miles north of London. Many people living in this area believed the Church of England retained too many traces of its Catholic origin. To support such a corrupt institution was like winking at the devil. Its very rituals compromised God's true believers, and so, in the early years of the reign of James I, the Scrooby congregation formally left the established state church. They and the others who followed this logic were called Separatists. Because English statute required citizens to attend

Church of England services, the Scrooby Separatists moved to Holland in 1608–1609 rather than compromise.

The Netherlands provided the Separatists with a good home—too good. The members of the little church feared they were losing their distinct identity; their children were becoming Dutch. In 1617, therefore, a portion of the original Scrooby congregation vowed to sail to America. Included in this group was William Bradford, a wonderfully literate man who wrote *Of Plymouth Plantation*, one of the first and certainly most poignant accounts of an early American settlement.

Poverty presented the major obstacle to their plans. They petitioned for a land patent from the Virginia Company of London. At the same time, they looked for someone willing to underwrite the staggering costs of colonization. These negotiations went well, or so it seemed. Thirty Pilgrims under the leadership of William Brewster embarked in July of 1620, stopping in England long enough to take on supplies and recruit additional voyagers, most of whom were non-Separatist "Strangers." In September, 102 Pilgrims and Strangers set off for America aboard the *Mayflower*, armed with a patent to settle in Virginia and indebted to a group of English investors who were only marginally interested in religious reform.

For reasons not entirely clear, the eight-week voyage brought the Pilgrims to New England instead of Virginia. The patent for which they had worked so diligently had no validity in this region. In fact, the crown had granted New England to another company. Without a patent, the colonists possessed no authorization to form a civil government, a serious matter since the non-Separatist majority threatened mutiny. To preserve the struggling community from anarchy, 41 men agreed on November 21 to "covenant and combine our selves together into a civil body politick."

The Mayflower Compact could not ward off disease and hunger. In early December the settlers selected the abandoned village of Patuxet as their new home, renaming it Plymouth. It was a poor season to begin any settlement. Supplies had run dangerously low and the nearby Pokanoket kept their distance, thwarting hopes of trading for food. Colonists tried to survive by foraging and occasionally pilfering stores of corn from Indian villages. Despite their efforts, death claimed approximately half of the 102 original passengers.

The spring of 1621 brought new hope for the survivors as the Pokanoket relaxed their wariness to enter a pact with the colony which the sachem Massasoit hoped would enhance his tribe's prestige and empower them to resist their Narragansett rivals to the west. Plymouth gained a crucial trading partner as well as the invaluable aid of the Pawtuxet Squanto, who had his own reasons for cooperating with the English. Squanto's services as a guide, interpreter, and diplomat proved at least as valuable to the colonists as his agricultural advice, for Plymouth continued to rely on Indian-produced corn to supplement their own crops during the first three years of settlement.

Early relations between Plymouth colonists and native inhabitants were bedeviled by misunderstandings and conflicting agendas on all sides. The English wanted to extend authority over all tribes in their sphere of influence as subjects "of our Soveraign lord [King James], His Heirs and Successors." They also hoped to gain title to "all the Lands adjacent, to them and their Heirs forever." Massasoit, on the other hand, sought to gain economic and military advantages over his Narragansett rivals. His authority over other Pokanoket sachems, however, rested on prestige and generosity, not coercive force, and any who judged the treaty harmful to their interests could follow a different course. Squanto may have hoped that his favored status with the English would help him reconstitute the Pawtuxets and oust their historic Pokanoket rivals from English favor. In time, Squanto's schemes were exposed and the English came to understand that they could only extend their sphere of influence through separate agreements with each sachem of the region. Under Captain Miles Standish, the colony pursued a militaristic Indian policy to obtain the grudging assistance of their neighbors.

Plymouth colonists extricated themselves from dependence on Pokanoket corn by 1624, cultivating surpluses that not only sustained them through the winters but also gave them a valuable commodity to trade for furs. Corn surpluses enabled the colonists to step into the void left by the demise of native New England farmers to establish a profitable fur-trading partnership with the Abenakis to the north. Plymouth gradually expanded its reach west as well, striking additional trading partnerships that eventually included the Dutch as well as Indians. By 1629 the colony was enjoying modest success as a commercial center.

Even with the fur trade, Plymouth colonists found it difficult to escape the burden of debts contracted in England. The company backing the colony dissolved in 1625, cutting off additional financial support and demanding repayment of funds invested. To their credit, the Pilgrims honored their financial obligations, but it took almost twenty years to satisfy the English investors. Without Bradford, whom they elected as governor, the settlers might have allowed adversity to overwhelm them. Through strength of will and self-sacrifice, however, Bradford persuaded frightened men and women that they could survive in America.

In time, the Pilgrims replicated the humble little farm communities they had once known in England. They formed Separatist congregations to their liking; the population slowly increased. The Abenaki fur trade declined rapidly after 1630, and early experiments with commercial fishing never generated substantial income. Most families relied on mixed husbandry, grain, and livestock. Because Plymouth offered limited economic prospects, it attracted only a trickle of new settlers. In 1691, the colony was absorbed into its larger and more prosperous neighbor, Massachusetts Bay.

A "NEW" ENGLAND IN AMERICA

In the early decades of the seventeenth century, an extraordinary spirit of religious reform burst forth in England. Before it had burned itself out, Puritanism had transformed the face of England and America. Modern historians have difficulty comprehending this powerful force. Some consider the Puritans neurotic individuals who condemned liquor and sex, dressed in drab clothes, and minded their neighbors' business.

The crude caricature is based on a profound misunderstanding of the actual nature of this broad popular movement. Seventeenth-century Puritans were more like today's radical political reformers, men and women committed to far-reaching

institutional change, than like naive do-gooders or narrow Victorian fundamental-
ists. To their enemies, of course, the Puritans were an irritant, always pointing out
civil and ecclesiastical imperfections. Many people, however, shared their vision.
Puritans not only founded several American colonies, but they also sparked the
English Civil Wars, a revolution that generated bold new thinking about republi-
can government and popular sovereignty (see Chapter 6).

The Puritans were products of the Protestant Reformation. They accepted a
Calvinist belief that an omnipotent God chose or "elected" some people to receive
salvation while leaving the rest of sinful humanity to eternal damnation (see
Chapter 1). Instead of waiting passively for Judgment Day, the Puritans examined
themselves for signs of grace, for hints that God had in fact placed them among his
"elect." A member of this select group, they argued, would try to live according to
Scripture, battle sin, and eradicate corruption.

For the Puritans, the logic of everyday life was clear. If the rites of the Church
of England contained unscriptural elements—clerical vestments, for example—
then they must be eliminated. If the pope in Rome was in league with the
Antichrist, then Protestant kings had better not form alliances with Catholic
states. If God condemned licentiousness and intoxication, then local officials
should punish whores and drunks. There was nothing improper about an occasional beer or passionate physical love within marriage, but when sex and drink
became ends in themselves, the Puritans thought England's ministers and magistrates should speak out. Persons of this temperament were more combative than
the Pilgrims had been. They wanted to purify the Church of England from within,
and before the 1630s at least, separatism held little appeal for them.

From the Puritan perspective, the early Stuarts, James I and Charles I, seemed
unconcerned about the spiritual state of the nation. James tolerated corruption
within his own court; he condoned gross public extravagance. His foreign policy
appeased European Catholic powers. At one time, James tried to marry his son to a
Spanish Catholic princess, and Charles I eventually did marry the fervently
Catholic Princess Henrietta Maria of France. Neither king showed interest in puri-
fying the Anglican church. In fact, Charles fanned Puritan suspicions by accommodating his queen's Catholic faith, permitting her to keep a priest at court and to
attend private masses. He also assisted the rapid advance of William Laud, a bishop
who represented everything the Puritans detested. Laud defended "popish" church
ceremonies that they found obnoxious. He persecuted Puritan ministers, forcing
them either to conform to his theology or lose their licenses to preach. As long as
Parliament met, Puritan voters in the various boroughs and counties throughout
England elected men sympathetic to their point of view. These outspoken representatives criticized royal policies and hounded Laud. Because of their defiance,
Charles decided in 1629 to rule England without Parliament and four years later
named Laud, Archbishop of Canterbury, the highest office in the Church of
England. The last doors of reform slammed shut. The corruption remained.

John Winthrop, the future governor of Massachusetts Bay, was caught up in
these events. Little about his background suggested such an auspicious future. He
owned a small manor in Suffolk, one that never produced sufficient income to
support his growing family. He dabbled in law. But the core of Winthrop's life was

his faith in God, a faith so intense his contemporaries immediately identified him as a Puritan. The Lord, he concluded, was displeased with England. Time for reform was running out. In May 1629, he confided to his wife, "I am verily perswaded God will bring some heavye Affliction upon this lande, and that speedy-lye." He was, however, confident that the Lord would "provide a shelter and a hidinge place for us."

Other Puritans, some of them wealthier and politically better connected than Winthrop, reached similar conclusions about England's future. They turned their attention to the possibility of establishing a colony in America, and on March 4, 1629, their Massachusetts Bay Company obtained a charter directly from the king. Charles and his advisers apparently thought the Massachusetts Bay Company was a commercial venture no different from the dozens of other joint-stock companies that had recently sprung into existence.

Winthrop and his associates knew better. On August 26, 1629, twelve of them met secretly and signed the Cambridge Agreement. They pledged to each other to be "ready in our persons and with such of our severall familyes as are to go with us . . . to embark for the said plantation by the first of March next." There was one loophole. The charters of most joint-stock companies designated a specific location where business meetings were to be held. For reasons not entirely clear—a timely bribe is a good guess—the charter of the Massachusetts Bay Company did not contain this standard clause. It could hold meetings anywhere the stockholders, called "freemen," desired, even America. If they met in America, moreover, the king and his archbishop could not easily interfere in their affairs.

A Covenanted People in America

The Winthrop fleet departed England in March 1630. Within a year, almost 2,000 people had arrived in Massachusetts Bay. Throughout the 1630s, thousands more came to carve new English farms and villages from what they regarded as a "howling" American wilderness.

A great deal is known about the background of these particular settlers. A large percentage of them originated in an area northeast of London called East Anglia, a region in which Puritan ideas had taken deep root. London, Kent, and the West Country also contributed to the stream of emigrants. In some instances, entire villages such as Higham were reestablished across the Atlantic. Many Massachusetts colonists had worked as farmers in England, but a surprisingly large number came from commercial centers, such as Norwich, where cloth was manufactured for the export trade.

Whatever their backgrounds, the Puritans moved to Massachusetts as nuclear families, fathers, mothers, and their dependent children, a form of migration strikingly different from the one that peopled Virginia and Maryland. Moreover, because the settlers had already formed families in England, the colony's sex ratio was more balanced than that found in the Chesapeake colonies. Finally, and perhaps more significantly, once they had arrived in Massachusetts, these men and women survived. Indeed, their life expectancy compares favorably to that of modern Americans. Many factors help explain this phenomenon—clean drinking water and a healthy climate, for example. The Reverend Francis Higginson ascribed it to the "extraordinary clear and dry" New England air "that is of a most healing

Colonists elected John Winthrop to serve a total of 13 years as governor and 10 years as deputy governor of Massachusetts. Winthrop proved very effective at translating Puritan values into practical policy.

Courtesy, American Antiquarian Society

nature." While the Puritans could not have planned to live longer than did colonists in other parts of the New World, this remarkable accident reduced the emotional shock of long-distance migration.

The first settlers possessed another source of strength and stability. They were bound together by a common sense of purpose. God, they insisted, had formed a special covenant with the people of Massachusetts Bay. On his part, the Lord expected them to live according to Scripture, to reform the church; in other words, to create a biblical "city on a hill" that would stand as a beacon of righteousness for the rest of the Christian world. If they fulfilled their side of the bargain, the settlers could anticipate peace and prosperity. No one, not even the lowliest servant, was excused from this divine covenant, for as Winthrop stated, "Wee must be knitt together in this worke as one man." Even as the first ships departed England, John Cotton, a popular Puritan minister, urged the emigrants to go forth "with a publicke spirit, looking not on your owne things only, but also on the things of others." Many people throughout the ages have espoused such communal rhetoric, but these particular men and women went about the business of forming a new colony as if they truly intended to transform a religious vision into social reality.

In ecclesiastical affairs, the colonists proceeded by what one founder called "experimental footsteps." They arrived in Massachusetts Bay without a precise plan for their church. Although the rituals and ceremonies enforced by Laud had no place in Massachusetts, the American Puritans refused to separate formally from the Church of England. In this matter, they thought the Pilgrims had made a serious mistake. After all, what was the point of reforming an institution if the reformers were no longer part of it?

Massachusetts bay colonists gradually came to accept a highly innovative form of church government known as Congregationalism. Under this system, each village church was independent of outside interference. The American Puritans, of course, wanted nothing of bishops. "Elect" women and men (the "saints") together with their baptized children were the church, and as a body, they pledged to uphold God's laws. In the Salem church, for example, the members covenanted "with the Lord and with one another and do bind ourselves in the presence of God to walk together in all his ways."

Simply because a person happened to live in a certain community did not mean he or she automatically belonged to the local church. Unlike the parish institutions they knew in England, the churches of Massachusetts were voluntary institutions. To join one, a man or woman had to provide testimony—a personal confession of faith—before neighbors who had already been admitted as full members. It was a demanding process. Whatever the personal strains, however, most men and women in early Massachusetts aspired to full membership. Church membership entitled them to the sacraments—participation in the Lord's supper and baptism for their infants—and gave some of them responsibility for choosing ministers, disciplining backsliders, and determining difficult questions of theology. Although women and blacks could not vote for ministers, they did become members of the Congregational churches. Over the course of the seventeenth century, women made up an increasingly large share of the membership.

Congregational autonomy had limits, to be sure, and civil magistrates sometimes took the lead in ferreting out heretical beliefs. Those who did not become church members were compelled to attend regular religious services. Perhaps because of the homogeneity of the colony's population, however, the loose polity of the Congregational churches held together for the entire colonial period.

In creating a civil government, the colonists faced a particularly difficult challenge. Their charter allowed the investors in a joint-stock company to set up a business organization. When the settlers arrived in America, however, company leaders—men like Winthrop—moved quickly to transform the commercial structure into a colonial government. An early step in this direction took place on May 18, 1631, when the category of "freeman" was extended to all adult males who had become members of a Congregational church. This decision greatly expanded the franchise of Massachusetts Bay, and historians estimate that during the 1630s, at least 40 percent of the colony's adult males could vote in colonywide elections. While this percentage may seem low by modern or even Jacksonian standards, it was higher than anything the emigrants would have known in England. The freemen voted annually for a governor, a group of magistrates called the Court of Assistants, and after 1634, deputies who represented the interests of the individual towns. Even military officers were elected in Massachusetts Bay.

Two popular misconceptions about this government should be dispelled. First, it was neither a democracy nor a theocracy. The magistrates elected in Massachusetts did not believe they represented the voters, much less the whole populace.

They ruled in the name of the electorate, but their responsibility as rulers was to God. In 1638, Winthrop warned against overly democratic forms, since "the best part is always the least, and of that best part the wiser is always the lesser." Second, the Congregational ministers possessed no formal political authority in Massachusetts Bay. They could not even hold civil office, and it was not unusual for the voters to ignore the recommendations of a respected minister such as John Cotton.

In New England, the town became the center of public life. In other regions of British America the county was the focus of local government, and people did not experience the same density of social and institutional interaction. In Massachusetts, groups of men and women voluntarily covenanted together to observe common goals. The community constructed a meetinghouse where religious services and town meetings were held. This powerful sense of shared purpose—something that later Americans have greatly admired—should not obscure the fact that the founders of New England towns also had a keen eye for personal profit. Seventeenth-century records reveal that speculators often made a good deal of money from selling "shares" in village lands. Acquisitiveness, however, never got out of control, and recent studies have shown that entrepreneurial practices rarely disturbed the peace of the Puritan communities. Inhabitants generally received land sufficient to build a house and to support a family. Although villagers escaped the kind of feudal dues collected in other parts of America—quitrents, for example—they were expected to contribute to the minister's salary, pay local and colony taxes, establish schools, and serve in the militia.

Puritan leaders hoped that their Christian commonwealth would become an example not only to Europeans, but also to the New England Indians among whom they would be settling. Indeed, the Massachusetts Bay Company's seal depicted an Indian imploring would-be colonists to "come over and help us." Every Puritan would have recognized this familiar New Testament phrase and understood it as a call to follow St. Paul's missionary example by carrying the gospel of salvation to seventeenth-century "heathen" who had presumably never heard it. During the colony's first years, leaders paid close attention to whether or not their Massachuset and Pawtuxet neighbors spoke "well of our God." Early relations between the two peoples, however, consisted primarily of mundane exchanges associated with establishing a new colony.

"Trucking with the Indians"

The tribes near Massachusetts Bay had only begun recovering from the epidemic of 1616, and Puritans who arrived in 1630 found "but few" native inhabitants. The survivors welcomed the colonists as trading partners and "walls to their bloody enemies," the Micmac of present-day New Brunswick. Indeed, to understand such behavior we must remember that local bands identified themselves as members of specific tribes, not as members of a united racial group. They saw no problem in making alliances with Europeans against other Native Americans.

Although Massachusetts Bay Company officials had instructed colonial leaders to negotiate purchases of any lands settled, the Pawtuxet and Massachuset readily granted colonists the right to occupy the land in exchange for protection.

They also bartered their labor and services, clearing fields, assisting in building, performing domestic tasks, and killing wolves near the settlements.

Like the Plymouth colonists a decade before, Bay Colony leaders assumed that their legal dealings with native peoples included native acceptance of English sovereignty, and they tried to incorporate native peoples into an English framework of hierarchical authority. For example, early colonial magistrates hauled the Pawtuxet "Sagamore John" and the Massachuset sagamore Chicataubut into court when their followers killed English livestock, ordering the sagamores to enforce English judgments against native offenders. Colonial officials tried to replicate this pattern in subsequent negotiations for land and sovereignty as English settlement of the region expanded. Native leaders did not share Puritan conceptions of hierarchy or sovereignty, and they resisted colonial officials' efforts to dominate them whenever they could. Leaders of large groups such as the powerful Narragansetts and Pequots possessed sufficient political and military strength to insist that Bay Colony leaders respect them as equals. Sagamores of small bands could do less, but they sought to buffer English domination while their followers continued to order their lives as much as possible by tribal custom and tradition.

The rapid expansion of Puritan settlements in the 1630s precipitated a dramatic shift in power relations among the region's Indian nations. The nearby Massachuset and Pawtuxet bands suffered yet another epidemic of smallpox in the early 1630s, prompting Governor Winthrop to declare that "God hath hereby cleared our title to this place." For other tribes, however, the expansive English presence in the region presented an unforeseen opportunity. Narragansett leaders seized the moment to break a Dutch monopoly on trade in Narragansett Bay and to launch a military offensive against their former Pequot allies who dominated Connecticut River commerce. Pequot leaders likewise vied for commercial advantage by playing the English off against the Dutch, eventually inviting the English to settle around the mouth of the Connecticut River. By 1636, new English settlements were pressing rapidly up the Connecticut River into Pequot territory, outstripping the capacity of either Bay Colony officials or leading Pequot sachems to control their expansion.

This complex struggle for land, trade, and dominion came to a head in the Pequot War of 1636–1637. Armed conflict erupted after the murder of an English trader named John Oldham was blamed on Pequot tributaries, the eastern Niantics. For nine months, colonists and Pequots periodically raided each others' villages, and Pequot warriors mounted a siege of Fort Saybrook on the Connecticut River. In late May of 1637, Connecticut's Captain John Mason led a combined counterforce from his own colony, Massachusetts Bay, and Plymouth along with Narragansett and Mohegan allies. On the morning of May 26, the force surrounded and set fire to the Pequots' Mystic River stronghold. While the dwellings burned, the English and their allies killed those attempting to flee. Within an hour, all but seven inhabitants lay dead. Appalled Narragansett witnesses protested that the English way of fighting was "too furious, and slays too many men," but Captain Mason exulted that the Lord himself had "judged among the Heathen, filling the Place with Dead Bodies!"

The Pequot War marked the emergence of a pattern of English-Indian relations that persisted until the 1670s. Remaining Pequot villages disappeared as survivors fled or were captured and enslaved, and in 1638 the Treaty of Hartford declared their nation dissolved. Their former allies the Mohegans gained greatly from the war, becoming the major brokers between the English and lesser tribes in the region. For the Narragansetts, however, the victory proved pyrrhic as they found themselves pressed from all sides by increasingly hostile, expansive English settlements in Connecticut, Massachusetts, and Plymouth. Despite this turn in fortune, however, groups such as the Narragansett continued to wield significant power to extract concessions from colonial officials and protect tribal interests.

The 1630s proved as tumultuous for the Massachusetts Bay's internal affairs as it did for diplomatic relations with native neighbors. Colonists managed to resolve most of their disputes within the framework of English law and custom. This was a remarkable achievement considering the chronic instability that plagued other colonies at this time. The colonists disagreed over many issues, sometimes vociferously; whole towns disputed with neighboring villages over common boundaries. But the people inevitably relied on the courts to mediate differences. They believed in a rule of law, and in 1648 the colonial legislature, called the General Court, drew up the *Lawes and Liberties*, the first alphabetized code of law printed in English. This innovative document is of fundamental importance in American constitutional history. In clear prose it explained to the colonists their rights and responsibilities as citizens of the commonwealth. The code engendered public trust in government and discouraged magistrates from the arbitrary exercise of authority.

Dissenting Voices: Diversity and Fragmentation

Some of the sharpest clashes during the first decade arose from differences in religious belief among Massachusetts Bay colonists. The ordered New England society, which seems in hindsight to have emerged so quickly, was actually a product of intense and creative theological debate among leaders of passionate conviction. Subtle variations in Puritan theology, which had seemed unimportant in the face of persecution by the English government, took on fresh significance as ministers and magistrates began implementing their ideas of a pure church and commonwealth. This ferment of opinion compounded the tensions and uncertainty of life in their new environment, while at the same time creating an opening for ideas that the leading magistrates and ministers perceived as heretical.

The most serious challenges to Puritan orthodoxy in Massachusetts Bay came from two remarkable individuals. The first, Roger Williams, arrived in 1631 and immediately attracted a body of loyal followers. Indeed, everyone seems to have liked him as a person. Williams's ideas, however, created controversy. He preached extreme separatism. He declared the Bay colonists impure in the sight of the Lord so long as they remained even nominal members of the Church of England. Moreover, he questioned the validity of Massachusetts Bay Colony's charter, because the king had not first purchased the land from the Indians, a view that threatened the integrity of the entire colonial experiment. Williams also insisted that the civil rulers of Massachusetts had no business punishing settlers for their religious beliefs. God, not men, was responsible for monitoring people's consciences. Bay Colony magistrates were prepared neither to tolerate views they considered heresy nor to accede to Williams's other demands. In 1636, after attempts to reach a compromise had failed, they banished him from the colony.

Williams worked out the logic of his ideas in Providence, a village he founded in what would become Rhode Island. The colony became a haven for dissidents from Old and New England alike. Williams himself was one of the most outspoken. His spiritual pilgrimage as a "Puritan Seeker" ultimately led him to conclude that he could enjoy Christian fellowship with none but his wife. He also became a fierce theological opponent of dissenting groups such as the Quakers whom he nevertheless welcomed as full partners in his colonial enterprise. The colony's location within Narragansett territory gave Williams the opportunity to study native culture closely, and the sympathetic observations recorded in his *Key to the Language of America* remain a valuable source of information on seventeenth-century native cultures. Williams's friendship with the Narragansetts also made him an important figure in early Anglo-Indian relations.

While the magistrates of Massachusetts Bay labored to suppress Roger Williams, an even graver threat to the peace of their commonwealth emerged under the leadership of Anne Hutchinson. This extremely intelligent woman, her husband William, and her children followed John Cotton to the New World in 1634. Even contemporaries found her arcane religious ideas somewhat confusing, but authorities eventually branded them as antinomianism, a heretical position even among Reformed Protestants. Whatever her thoughts, Hutchinson shared them with other Bostonians, many of them women. Her outspoken views scandalized orthodox leaders of church and state. She suggested that all but two ministers in the Bay Colony had lost touch with the Holy Spirit and had begun preaching that people must live a righteous life to be saved, an idea she termed a "covenant of works."

When authorities demanded she explain her assertions, Hutchinson announced that the Holy Spirit had given her a special ability to discern the spiritual condition of other people. She hinted that she could exercise this gift independently of either the Bible or the clergy. Authorities recognized that if Hutchinson really believed in direct revelation, her teachings could not be tested by Scripture, a position that seemed dangerously subjective. Indeed, her theology called the very foundation of Massachusetts Bay into question. Without clear, external standards, one person's truth was as valid as that of anyone else. From Winthrop's perspective, Hutchinson's views invited civil and religious anarchy.

When Hutchinson described Congregational ministers—some of them the leading divines of Boston—as unconverted men, the General Court intervened. For two very tense days in 1637, the ministers and magistrates of Massachusetts Bay cross-examined Hutchinson; in this intense theological debate, she more than held her own. She knew as much about the Bible as did her inquisitors, and no doubt her brilliance at that moment provoked the court's misogyny.

Hutchinson challenged ministers and magistrates to demonstrate exactly where she had erred. Just when it appeared that this gifted woman had outmaneuvered—indeed, thoroughly embarrassed—her opponents, she let down her guard, declaring forcefully that what she knew of God came "by an immediate revelation. . . . By the voice of his own spirit to my soul." Here was what her accusers had suspected all along but could not prove. She had confessed in open court that the Spirit could live without the Moral Law. This Antinomian statement challenged the authority of Bay Colony rulers, and they were relieved to exile Hutchinson and her followers to Rhode Island.

Massachusetts Bay spawned four new colonies, three of which survived to the American Revolution. New Hampshire became a separate colony in 1677. Its population grew very slowly, and for much of the colonial period, New Hampshire remained economically dependent on Massachusetts, its neighbor to the south.

Breaking Away

Far more people were drawn to the fertile lands of the Connecticut River valley. In 1636, settlers founded the villages of Hartford, Windsor, and Wethersfield. No one forced these men and women to leave Massachusetts, and in their new surroundings, they created a society that looked much like the one they had known in the Bay Colony. Through his writings, Thomas Hooker, Connecticut's most prominent minister, helped all New Englanders define Congregational church polity. Puritans on both sides of the Atlantic read Hooker's beautifully crafted works. In 1639, representatives from the Connecticut towns passed the Fundamental Orders, a blueprint for civil government, and in 1662, Charles II awarded the colony a charter of its own, one that recognized annual elections for all civil offices, including governor.

In 1638, another group, led by Theophilus Eaton and the Reverend John Davenport, settled New Haven and several adjoining towns along Long Island Sound. These emigrants, many of whom had come from London, lived briefly in Massachusetts Bay but then insisted on forming a Puritan commonwealth of their own, one that established a closer relationship between church and state than the Bay Colonists had allowed. The New Haven colony never prospered, and in 1662, it was absorbed into Connecticut.

Rhode Island experienced a wholly different history. From the beginning, it was populated by exiles and troublemakers, and according to one Dutch visitor, Rhode Island was "the receptacle of all sorts of riff-raff people. . . . All the cranks of New-England retire thither." This description, of course, was an exaggeration. Roger Williams founded Providence in 1636; two years later, Anne Hutchinson took her followers to Portsmouth. Other groups settled around Narragansett Bay. Not surprisingly, these men and women appreciated the need for toleration. No one was persecuted in Rhode Island for his or her religious beliefs.

One might have thought these separate Rhode Island communities would cooperate for the common good. They did not. Villagers fought over land and schemed with outside speculators to divide the tiny colony into ever smaller pieces. In 1644, Parliament issued a patent for the "Providence Plantations," and in 1663, the Rhode Islanders obtained a remarkably liberal charter that allowed voters to select their own governors. These successes did not calm political turmoil. For most of the seventeenth century, colonywide government existed in

New England Colonies, 1650

The early colonists quickly carved up New England. New Haven flourished briefly before being taken over by Connecticut in 1662. Long Island became part of New York; Plymouth was eventually absorbed by Massachusetts.

name only. Despite their constant bickering, however, the settlers of Rhode Island—many of whom became Quakers or Baptists—established a profitable commerce in agricultural goods.

THE PURITAN ORDER IN NEW ENGLAND

Seventeenth-century New Englanders successfully replicated in America a traditional social order they had known in England. The transfer of a familiar way of life to the New World seemed less difficult for these Puritan migrants than it did for the many English men and women who settled in the Chesapeake colonies. Their contrasting experiences, fundamental to an understanding of the development of both cultures, can be explained, at least in part, by the development of Puritan families.

Longevity, Family, and Society

Early New Englanders believed God ordained the family for human benefit. This biological unit was essential to the maintenance of social order, because outside the family, men and women succumbed to carnal temptation. Such people had no one to sustain them or remind them of Scripture. "Without Family care," declared the Reverend Benjamin Wadsworth, "the labour of Magistrates and Ministers for Reformation and Propagating Religion, is likely to be in great measure unsuccessful."

The godly family, at least in theory, was ruled by a patriarch, father to his children, husband to his wife, the source of authority and object of unquestioned obedience. The wife shared responsibility for the raising of children, but in decisions of importance, especially those related to property, she was expected to defer to her spouse.

The New Englanders' concern about the character of the godly family is not surprising. This institution played a central role in shaping their society. In contrast to those who migrated to the colonies of Virginia and Maryland, New Englanders crossed the Atlantic within nuclear families. That is, they moved within established units consisting of a father, mother, and their dependent children rather than as single youths and adults. People who migrated to America within families preserved local English customs more fully than did the youths who traveled to other parts of the continent as single men and women. The comforting presence of immediate family members reduced the shock of adjusting to a strange environment 3,000 miles from home. Even in the 1630s, the ratio of men to women in New England was fairly well balanced, about three males for every two females. Persons who had not already married in England before coming to the New World could expect to marry and form nuclear families of their own.

The outbreak of the English Civil Wars in 1642 reduced the flood of people moving to Massachusetts Bay to a trickle. Nevertheless, by the end of the century, the population of New England had grown from less than 20,000 to almost 120,000, an amazing increase considering the small number of original immigrants. Historians have been hard-pressed to explain the striking rate of growth. Some have suggested that New Englanders married very young, thus giving couples extra years in which to produce large families. Other scholars have maintained that New England women must have been more fertile than their Old World counterparts.

Neither demographic theory adequately explains how so few emigrants produced such a large population. Early New England marriage patterns, for example, did not differ substantially from those recorded in seventeenth-century England. The average age of first marriage for men was the mid-twenties. Wives were slightly younger than their husbands, the average age being about twenty-two. There is no evidence that New Englanders favored child brides. Nor, for that matter, were Puritan families unusually large by European standards of the period.

The explanation for the region's extraordinary growth turned out to be survival rather than fertility. Put simply, people who, under normal conditions, would have died in contemporary Europe lived in New England. Indeed, the life expectancy of seventeenth-century settlers was not very different from our own. Males who survived infancy could have expected to see their seventieth birthday. Twenty percent of first-generation New England men reached the age of eighty. The figures for women were only slightly lower. Why the early settlers lived so long is not entirely clear. No doubt, pure drinking water, a cool climate that retarded the spread of fatal contagious disease, and a dispersed population promoted general good health.

Longer life altered family relations. New England males lived not only to see their own children reach adulthood but also to witness the birth of grandchildren. One historian has suggested that New Englanders "invented" grandparents. In other words, this society produced real patriarchs. This may have been one of the first societies in recorded history in which a person could reasonably anticipate knowing his or her grandchildren, a demographic surprise that contributed to social stability. The traditions of particular families and communities literally remained alive in the memories of the Bay Colony's oldest citizens.

A Commonwealth of Families

The life cycle of the seventeenth-century New England family began with marriage. Young men and women generally initiated courtships. If parents exercised a voice in such matters, it was to discourage union with a person of unsound moral character. Puritan ministers advised single people to choose godly partners, warning:

> The Wretch that is alone to Mannon Wed,
> May chance to find a Satan in the bed.

In this highly religious society, young people seldom strayed far from shared community values. The overwhelming majority of the region's population married, for in New England, the single life was not only morally suspect but also physically difficult. A couple without land could not support an independent and growing family in these agrarian communities. While men generally brought inherited farmland to the marriage, prospective brides were expected to provide a dowry worth approximately one-half what the bridegroom offered. Women often contributed money or household goods that parents had set aside for them.

The household was primarily a place of work—very demanding work. One historical geographer estimates that a Pennsylvania family of five needed 75 acres of cleared land just to feed itself. Additional cultivation allowed the farmer to produce a surplus that could then be sold or bartered, and because agrarian families required items that could not be manufactured at home—metal tools, for example—they usually grew more than they consumed. Early American farmers were not economically self-sufficient; the belief that they were is a popular misconception.

During the seventeenth century, men and women generally lived in the communities of their parents and grandparents. New Englanders usually managed to fall in love with a neighbor, and most marriages took place between men and women living less than 13 miles apart. Moving to a more fertile region might have increased their earnings, but such thoughts seldom occurred to early New Englanders. Religious values, a sense of common purpose, and the importance of family reinforced traditional communal ties.

Towns, in fact, were collections of families, not individuals. Over time, these families intermarried, so the community became an elaborate kinship network. Social historians have discovered that in many New England towns, the original founders dominated local politics and economic affairs for several generations. Not surprisingly, newcomers who were not absorbed into the family system tended to move away from the village with greater frequency than did the sons and daughters of the established lineage groups.

Congregational churches were also built on a family foundation. During the earliest years of settlement, the churches accepted persons who could demonstrate they were among God's "elect." Members were drawn from a broad social spectrum. Once the excitement of establishing a new society had passed, however, New Englanders began to focus more attention on the spiritual welfare of their own families. This quite normal parental concern precipitated a major ecclesiastical crisis. The problem was the status of the children within a gathered church. Sons and daughters of full church members regularly received baptism, usually as infants, but as these people grew to adulthood, they often failed to provide testimony of their own "election." Moreover, they wanted their own children to be baptized. A church synod—a gathering of Congregational ministers—responded to this generational crisis by adopting the so-called Half-Way Covenant (1662). The compromise allowed the grandchildren of persons in full communion to be baptized even though their parents could not demonstrate conversion. Congregational ministers assumed that "God cast the line of election in the loins of godly parents." Because of the New Englanders' growing obsession with family—termed tribalism by some historians—the Congregational churches by the end of the seventeenth century were increasingly turning inward, addressing the spiritual needs of particular lineage groups rather than reaching out to the larger Christian community.

Colonists regarded education as primarily a family responsibility. Parents were supposed to instruct children in the principles of Christianity, and so it was necessary to teach boys and girls how to read. In 1642, the Massachusetts General Court reminded the colonists of their obligation to catechize their families. Five years later, the legislature ordered towns containing at least fifteen families to open an elementary school supported by local taxes. Villages of a hundred or more families had to maintain more advanced grammar schools, which taught a basic Latin curriculum. At least eleven schools were operating in 1647, and despite their expense, new schools were established throughout the century.

This family-based education system worked. A large majority of the region's adult males could read and write, an accomplishment not achieved in the Chesapeake colonies for another century. The literacy rate for women was somewhat lower, but by the standards of the period, it was still impressive. A printing press operated in Cambridge as early as 1639. The *New-England Primer*, first published in 1690 in Boston by Benjamin Harris, taught children the alphabet as well as the Lord's Prayer. This primer announced:

> He who ne'er learns his ABC,
> forever will a blockhead be.
> But he who to his book's inclined,
> will soon a golden treasure find.

But the best-seller of seventeenth-century New England was the Reverend Michael Wigglesworth's *The Day of Doom* (1662), a poem of 224 stanzas describing in terrifying detail the fate of sinners on Judgment Day. In words that even young readers could comprehend, Wigglesworth wrote of these unfortunate souls:

> They cry, no, no: Alas! and wo!
> Our Courage all is gone:

> Our hardiness (fool hardiness)
> Hath us undone, undone.

Many New Englanders memorized the entire poem.

After 1638, young men could attend Harvard College, the first institution of higher learning founded in England's mainland colonies. The school was originally intended to train ministers, and of the 465 students who graduated during the seventeenth century, over half became Congregational divines. Harvard had a demanding curriculum. The boys read logic, rhetoric, divinity, and several ancient languages, including Hebrew. Yale College followed Harvard's lead, admitting its first students in 1702.

Puritan Women in New England

The role of women in the agrarian societies north of the Chesapeake remains a controversial subject among colonial historians. Some scholars point out that common law as well as English custom treated women as inferior to men. Other historians, however, depict the colonial period as a "golden age" for women. According to this interpretation, wives worked alongside their husbands. They were not divorced from meaningful, productive labor. They certainly were not transformed into the frail, dependent beings much admired by middle-class males of the nineteenth century. Both views provide insights into the lives of early American women, but neither fully recaptures their community experiences.

Certainly, women worked on family farms. They did not, however, necessarily do the same jobs that men performed. Women usually handled separate tasks, including cooking, washing, clothes making, dairying, and gardening. Their production of food was absolutely essential to the survival of most households. Sometimes wives—and the overwhelming majority of adult seventeenth-century women were married—raised poultry, and by selling surplus birds they achieved some economic independence. When people in one New England community chided a man for allowing his wife to peddle her fowl, he responded, "I meddle not with the geese nor turkeys for they are hers." In fact, during this period women were often described as "deputy husbands," a label that drew attention to their dependence on family patriarchs as well as to their roles as decision makers.

Women also joined churches in greater numbers than men. Within a few years of founding, many New England congregations contained two female members for every male, a process historians describe as the "feminization of colonial religion." Contemporaries offered different explanations for this gender shift. Cotton Mather, the leading Congregational minister of Massachusetts Bay, argued that God had created "far more godly Women" than men. Others thought that the life-threatening experience of childbirth gave women a deeper appreciation of religion. The Quakers gave women an even larger role in religious affairs, which may help to explain the popularity of this sect among ordinary women.

In political and legal matters, society sharply curtailed the rights of colonial women. According to English common law, a wife exercised no control over property. She could not, for example, sell land. If her husband decided to dispose of their holdings, he was free to do so without her permission. Divorce was extremely difficult to obtain in any colony before the American Revolution. Indeed, a person married to a cruel or irresponsible spouse had little recourse but to run away or accept the unhappy situation.

Yet most women were neither prosperous entrepreneurs nor abject slaves. Surviving letters indicate that men and women generally accommodated themselves to the gender roles they thought God had ordained. One of early America's most creative poets, Anne Bradstreet, wrote movingly of the fulfillment she had found with her husband. In a piece titled "To my Dear and loving Husband," Bradstreet declared:

> If ever two were one, then surely we.
> If ever man were lov'd by wife, then thee;
> If ever wife was happy in a man,
> Compare with me ye women if you can.

Although Puritan couples worried that the affection they felt for a husband or a wife might turn their thoughts away from God's perfect love, this was a danger they were willing to risk.

Rank and Status in New England Society

During the seventeenth century, the New England colonies attracted neither noblemen nor paupers. The absence of these social groups meant that the American social structure seemed incomplete by contemporary European standards. The settlers were not displeased that the poor remained in the Old World. The lack of very rich persons—and in this period great wealth frequently accompanied noble title—was quite another matter. According to the prevailing hierarchical view of the structure of society, well-placed individuals were natural rulers, people intended by God to exercise political authority over the rank and file. Migration forced the colonists, however, to choose their rulers from men of more modest status. One minister told a Plymouth congregation that because its members were "not furnished with any persons of *special eminency above the rest*, to be chosen by you into office of government," they would have to make do with neighbors, "not beholding in them the ordinariness of their persons."

The colonists gradually sorted themselves out into distinct social groupings. Persons who would never have been "natural rulers" in England became provincial gentry in the various northern colonies. It helped, of course, if an individual possessed wealth and education, but these attributes alone could not guarantee a newcomer's acceptance into the local ruling elite, at least not during the early decades of settlement. In Massachusetts and Connecticut, Puritan voters expected their leaders to join Congregational churches and defend orthodox religion.

The Winthrops, Dudleys, and Pynchons—to cite a few of the more prominent families—fulfilled these expectations, and in public affairs they assumed dominant roles. They took their responsibilities quite seriously and certainly did not look kindly on anyone who spoke of their "ordinariness." A colonist who jokingly called a Puritan magistrate a "just ass" found himself in deep trouble with civil authorities.

The problem was that while most New Englanders accepted a hierarchical view of society, they disagreed over their assigned places. Both Massachusetts Bay and Connecticut passed sumptuary laws—statutes that limited the wearing of fine apparel to the wealthy and prominent—to curb the pretensions of those of lower status. Yet such restraints could not prevent some people from rising and others from falling within the social order.

Governor John Winthrop provided a marvelous description of the unplanned social mobility that occurred in early New England. During the 1640s, he recorded in his diary the story of a master who could not afford to pay a servant's wages. To meet this obligation, the master sold a pair of oxen, but the transaction barely covered the cost of keeping the servant. In desperation, the master asked the employee, a man of lower social status, "How shall I do . . . when all my cattle are gone?" The servant replied, "You shall then serve me, so you may have your cattle again." In the margin of his diary next to this account, Winthrop scribbled "insolent."

Most northern colonists were yeomen (independent farmers) who worked their own land. Although few became rich in America, even fewer fell hopelessly into debt. Their daily lives, especially for those who settled New England, centered on scattered little communities where they participated in village meetings, church-related matters, and militia training. Possession of land gave agrarian families a sense of independence from external authority. As one man bragged to those who had stayed behind in England, "Here are no hard landlords to rack us with high rents or extorting fines. . . . Here every man may be master of his own labour and land . . . and if he have nothing but his hands he may set up his trade, and by industry grow rich."

During the seventeenth century, this independence was balanced by an equally strong feeling of local identity. Not until the late eighteenth century, when many New Englanders left their familial villages in search of new land, did many northern yeomen place personal material ambition above traditional community bonds.

It was not unusual for northern colonists to work as servants at some point in their lives. This system of labor differed greatly from the pattern of servitude that developed in seventeenth-century Virginia and Maryland. New Englanders seldom recruited servants from the Old World. The forms of agriculture practiced in this region, mixed cereal and dairy farming, made employment of large gangs of dependent workers uneconomic. Rather, New England families placed their adolescent children in nearby homes. These young persons contracted for four or five years and seemed more like apprentices than servants. For such persons, servitude was not simply a means by which one group exploited another. It was a form of vocational training program in which the children of the rich as well as the poor participated.

A small minority of seventeenth-century immigrants did come as servants, however, and slavery was not unheard of in early New England. Ships' manifests often listed servants among the members of first-generation households, persons who performed domestic tasks or worked as field hands until they completed their terms of service. Indian or African slaves performed similar tasks for a few prominent individuals such as the Salem minister Samuel Parris. New England commanders occasionally enslaved native captives during conflicts such as the Pequot War, exporting most to plantation colonies in the Caribbean or Chesapeake. The population of servants and slaves rose slowly in seventeenth-century Boston as the city's growing importance as a colonial port increased the demand for sailors and dockworkers. The Rhode Island community of Newport grew notorious by the end of the century as a haven for privateers and slave traders.

A Changing Environment

The extraordinary growth of Puritan society radically altered New England's landscape and embroiled its native peoples in a continuous process of adaptation. As the line of English settlement moved rapidly up river valleys and more slowly into the woodland, forests were transformed into open fields, paths became roads, and English livestock displaced American game. The region's forest floors became choked with brush as English settlers discontinued the native habit of burning the undergrowth each year. Where native women had cultivated multiple crops in small clearings, English men plowed large fields and seeded them with a single crop. Where native peoples had framed their dwellings of slim cord-lashed saplings and sided them with rush mats or bark, colonists sawed great trees into lumber for sturdy English-style houses. Timber was so abundant that settlers were soon using it to roof and side their dwellings, practices that would have seemed wasteful in timber-poor England. As New England towns spread further across the countryside, some native groups moved further away while others found themselves increasingly surrounded as they remained on dwindling patches of ancestral lands.

Varieties of Adaptation

New England Indians adapted to this rapidly changing environment in a variety of ways. Those living beyond the settlement line could scarcely ignore the presence of so many Europeans, and they seldom wanted to. Living nearby white settlements entailed difficulties but it also brought advantages in the form of manufactured goods, resources, and military alliances. Several large tribes such as the Narragansetts, the Pequots, and the Abenakis took early advantage of these opportunities.

The approach of settlements confronted native inhabitants with a fresh set of challenges and opportunities. Settlers bid for native land but also sought diplomatic aid in dealing with tribes further away. They also employed forest-wise Indians for services such as hunting, trapping, pest control, and production of useful goods such as baskets and brooms. It was a very delicate business for Indians to adapt in ways that would preserve their self-determination while accommodating to colonial demands. The Pequots had attempted wholesale armed resistance when English settlers challenged their control of land and trade along the Connecticut River. The outcome of that contest convinced neighboring groups to search for alternative ways to adapt. When the Narragansetts found themselves similarly pressed a few years later, they could convince no other tribe in the region to join them in resisting the English. Indeed, no native leader took the Pequot road to resistance again until Metacom, or King Philip, led his large-scale uprising in 1676 (see Chapter 7).

The Pequots' former allies and kinspeople, the Mohegans, found a different way to deal with the challenge of advancing settlement. As English-Pequot tensions rose, the opportunistic and resourceful Mohegan sachem Uncas (d. 1683) sided with the English. The defeat of the Pequots opened the way for the Mohegans to take their place alongside the English and the Narragansetts as the third great power in the region, a position confirmed by the Treaty of Hartford. Uncas conceded overarching jurisdiction in Anglo-Mohegan relations to the officials of Connecticut, making sachems liable for Mohegan damage to English property and eventually restricting tribal settlement near land ceded to the English. In exchange, he won virtual autonomy for his people in managing their own affairs. As English settlements slowly grew up around them, Mohegan villagers continued to observe traditional beliefs and customs while structuring their lives around annual cycles of migration from summer fields to fall and winter hunting grounds. Through a combination of intrigue and skillful negotiation, Uncas remained an influential broker between Connecticut officials and surrounding New England tribes for the next forty years, and secured for his people an enduring presence in the region.

"Praying Indians"

Conversion to Puritan Christianity presented New England Indians with yet another way to adapt to their changing environment, survive the trauma of disease and loss, or even strengthen their position within their own societies through conversion to Christianity. Colonists made only occasional attempts to evangelize native peoples during the first decade of settlement, although Rhode Island's Roger Williams made a serious effort to master "the language of America" and communicate the light of Puritan Christianity to his native neighbors. Thomas Mayhew, Jr. led the way in Massachusetts missionary endeavors when he began conversing on religious matters with the native inhabitants of Martha's Vineyard in 1642. John Eliot, however, emerged as the colony's leading missionary after 1646, when he began preaching to members of the Natick band near his parish in Roxbury, Massachusetts.

Eliot shared the common Puritan habit of identifying Christianity with English culture while dismissing native culture as irreligious, uncivilized, and at times demonic. He argued that true conversion of Indians to Christianity would require them to reject traditional culture in favor of English ways of dress, dwelling, farming, marriage, child-rearing, and cycles of daily life. To accomplish this enormous cultural transformation, Eliot proposed that the colony establish "praying towns" modeled on English villages, where native converts would learn to order their lives in Christian English ways. He negotiated with the Massachusetts government to set aside 6,000 acres for the first praying town, Natick, and in 1650 he persuaded converts from the nearby Natick band to move there permanently. By 1675, nearly a quarter of the native population of southeastern New England lived in fourteen praying towns.

These native conversions have recently become subjects of sharp historical debate. Why did so many native peoples seem willing to turn their backs on their own traditions to adopt an alien culture? Some historians have argued that the massive dislocation brought about by disease and rapid change left them unusually weak and susceptible to the missionaries' efforts. Others have viewed the Indians' choice as a self-conscious recognition of conversion as a necessary means of survival, a way to preserve their core native identity under a veneer of Christianity. Both perspectives no doubt help to explain many conversions. Yet the fact that large numbers of natives remained able to resist conversion has prompted still other historians to conclude that many converts perceived real advantages in the choices they made.

Indian converts to Puritan Christianity seem to have responded selectively to the Englishmen's gospel and its attendant cultural prescriptions, incorporating features that seemed beneficial while resisting those that seemed harmful. Puritan missionaries scrutinized converts' testimonies for authenticity, and surviving accounts indicate that many praying Indians sincerely believed that Christian faith would save them. Yet conversion held benefits for this life as well. In contests over tribal leadership, for example, conversion could enhance the prestige of one rival by providing access to more power or resources than other contenders. Eliot's first convert, Waban, captured the sachemship of his band by acquiring the missionary's powerful patronage when he accepted the new faith. Eliot's patronage also provided all Natick converts a means of resisting Uncas, who was attempting to bring the band under Mohegan control during the 1640s. Acceptance of the omnipotent God of the English could also enable converts to bypass the influential tribal *powwow* or shaman in their quest for spiritual power.

Life in the praying towns presented inhabitants with even more opportunities for selective appropriation of English culture. Missionaries provided praying Indians a steady supply of English goods such as tools, clothing, cooking utensils, even firearms. Native converts could learn English technologies such as spinning, a craft in which the Natick band expressed particular interest. English literacy enabled native readers and writers to trade and negotiate more effectively with the English. Other aspects of English life held less attraction. Inhabitants of praying towns, for example, often preferred traditional wigwams rather than the English-style houses Eliot had planned. Bands of praying Indians also clung to a variety of traditional lifeways such as hunting and fishing despite English attempts to make sedentary farmers of them.

Praying town life ultimately transformed native converts' culture in spite of their attempts to control the pace and scope of change. The practice of Puritan religious life required converts to order their days much differently, exchanging familiar seasonal patterns of life for weekly cycles of worship and labor. English ideas of gender, marriage, and child-rearing replaced native ones, with mixed consequences for family life and work. Men initially resisted taking on traditional women's tasks such as cultivation and house building, while women embraced those aspects of gender redefinition that discouraged vices such as alcohol abuse and wife beating. English ideas of modesty prompted many praying Indians to adopt English dress and encouraged a growing number to erect partitions in their wigwams to give married couples privacy from other family members.

THE FIRST GENERATION'S LEGACY

By the mid-1660s, a second generation of New England Puritans had begun sketching the outline of a compelling story about their own history in the New World. The founders had been extraordinarily godly men and women, and in a heroic effort to establish a purer form of religion, pious families had passed "over the vast ocean into this vast and howling wilderness." Godly missionaries such as John Eliot and Thomas Mayhew had averted God's wrath for the founders' early neglect by filling praying towns with a growing number of Indian converts. Although the children and grandchildren of the first generation sometimes questioned their own ability to please the Lord, they recognized that the mission to the New World had been a success: they were "as Prosperous as ever, there is Peace & Plenty, & the Country flourisheth."

CHRONOLOGY

1616–18	Native peoples of coastal New England decimated by epidemic disease.
1620	Pilgrims sign Mayflower Compact.
1625	Charles I ascends English throne.
1629	Charles I decides to rule without Parliament.
1630	John Winthrop transfers Massachusetts Bay charter to New England.
1633	William Laud named Archbishop of Canterbury.
1636	Connecticut Valley settlements, Rhode Island founded.
1636–37	Pequot War.
1638	Anne Hutchinson banished to Rhode Island; New Haven founded.
1638	Harvard College founded.
1639	First printing press operating in Cambridge; Connecticut towns accept Fundamental Orders.
1642	Thomas Mayhew establishes mission to native inhabitants of Martha's Vineyard.
1646	John Eliot begins preaching to Natick band near Roxbury.
1648	Cambridge Platform regularizes Congregational order in New England.
1650	Natick, first Indian praying town, established.

RECOMMENDED READING

Two of New England's most capable historians were William Bradford, *Of Plymouth Plantation*, ed. Samuel Eliot Morrison (New York, 1952), and John Winthrop, *Journal of John Winthrop, 1630–1649*, ed. Richard S. Dunn and Laetitia Yeandle (Cambridge, Mass., 1996). The most brilliant exploration of Puritan theology remains Perry Miller, *The New England Mind: From Colony to Province* (Cambridge, Mass., 1956), though more recent studies such as Janice Knight's *Orthodoxies in Massachusetts: Rereading American Puritanism* (Cambridge, Mass., 1994), have questioned whether Puritans were as unified in their theology as Miller suggested. Popular religious belief is examined in such studies as David D. Hall, *Worlds of Wonder, Days of Judgment: Popular Religious Belief in Early New England* (New York, 1989) and Richard Godbeer, *The Devil's Dominion: Magic and Religion in Early New England* (Cambridge, 1992).

Excellent analyses of Puritan migration include Virginia De John Anderson, *New England's Generation: The Great Migration and the Formation of Society and Culture in the Seventeenth Century* (Cambridge, 1991) and David Cressy, *Coming Over: Migration and Communication between England and New England in the Seventeenth Century* (Cambridge, 1987). David Grayson Allen's *In English Ways: The Movement of Societies and the Transferal of English Local Law and Custom* (New York, 1981) discusses the adaptation of English social and cultural institutions to New England.

Puritan political ideals and institutions are discussed in T. H. Breen, *The Character of the Good Ruler: A Study of Puritan Political Ideas in New England, 1630–1730* (New York, 1970). Michael P. Winship offers an insightful analysis of the Antinomian controversy, one of the most explosive events to occur during the first decade of the Massachusetts Bay Colony's existence, in his *Making Heretics: Militant Protestantism and Free Grace in Massachusetts, 1636–1641* (Princeton, 2002). Jane Kamensky offers a provocative analysis of speech, gender, and power in *Governing the Tongue: The Politics of Speech in Early New England* (New York, 1997), while Mary Beth Norton includes extensive consideration of New England in her *Founding Mothers and Fathers: Gender and Power in the Formation of American Society* (New York, 1996). Laurel Thatcher Ulrich examines women's roles more broadly in *Good Wives: Image and Reality in the Lives of Women in Northern New England, 1650–1750* (New York, 1982).

Stephen Innes explores economic development in *Creating the Commonwealth: The Economic Culture of Puritan New England* (New York, 1995). The better New England town studies—and there are many—include Kenneth Lockridge, *The New England Town: The First Hundred Years* (New York, 1970); Philip Greven, Jr., *Four Generations: Population, Land, and Family in Colonial Andover* (Ithaca, 1970); Stephen Innes, *Labor in a New Land: Economy and Society in Seventeenth-Century Springfield* (Princeton, 1983); and John F. Martin, *Profits in the Wilderness: Entrepreneurship and the Founding of New England Towns in the Seventeenth Century* (Chapel Hill, 1991).

The past two decades have witnessed publication of a wealth of studies examining American Indian cultures and Anglo-Indian relations in New England. Neal Salisbury's *Manitou and Providence: Indians, Europeans, and the Making of New England, 1500–1643* (New York, 1982) explores contact from the time English and French fishermen dried their catch on New England shores to the closing years of the great

Puritan migration. William Cronon explores environmental change accompanying colonization in *Changes in the Land: Indians, Colonists, and the Ecology of New England* (New York, 1983). James Axtell's *The Invasion Within: The Contest of Cultures in Colonial North America* (New York, 1985) compares seventeenth-century French-Indian and Anglo-Indian relations. Alfred A. Cave analyzes one of the Puritans' earliest military campaigns against their native neighbors in *The Pequot War* (Amherst, 1995). For Puritan missionary efforts among New England Indians see Dane Morrison, *A Praying People: Massachuset Acculturation and the Failure of the Puritan Mission, 1600–1690* (New York, 1995).

Chapter 6

Sugar, Slaves, and Profits
The Beginnings of the British Caribbean

One evening in 1624, an aged Carib woman made her way quietly to the quarters of Captain Thomas Warner, the leader of England's new tobacco colony on the tiny Caribbean island of St. Christopher. The warriors in her village, she warned the captain, had "made their drinking." They were preparing for battle in a traditional drinking ceremony that would last another three or four days before they attacked Warner's small band of English colonists. The old woman advised the captain that if he and his men did not want to die a gruesome death, they should quickly "gett into his Cannoes and begonn."

The English thought that the Carib woman came to Warner out of "great affecion," but the warriors may possibly have sent her with an advance warning that would frighten the strangers off the island before the conflict came to blows. Either way, her visit disclosed the Caribs' conclusion that these newcomers constituted an unprecedented threat to their existence on this small island. Earlier generations of English privateers had merely used the Indians' homeland as a temporary staging ground for raids on the Caribs' hated Spanish foes. In contrast, Warner's group was constructing a permanent settlement. Indeed, the fort they had begun building near the Carib village alarmed the headman, who became even more suspicious when the English coyly assured him that its defenses would only serve to "looke after those fowles they had about theire houses." The drinking ceremony therefore signaled the headman's decision that the time had come to drive these intruders from his territory.

If the Caribs intended the old woman's visit to warn the English off St. Christopher (also called St. Kitts), they miscalculated badly. Warner had already led one failed expedition to colonize Guiana on the Caribbean coast of South America, and he was determined not to fail again. This tiny island in the Leeward group of the Lesser Antilles held a steady supply of fresh water and sufficient arable land on its 68 square miles for plantations and subsistence farming. It had supported the Carib population; it could support aspiring English tobacco planters equally well. Less than 300 miles from Puerto Rico, it provided ready access to the heart of the Spanish Caribbean while remaining distant enough to help insulate the English settlement from attack. Warner would take any action necessary to secure this island for his investors. Late at night the captain and his men "tooke ye advantage of [the Indians'] being druncke" and attacked the Carib warriors, killing many and driving the survivors off St. Christopher to take refuge among Carib settlements on neighboring islands.

Warner had taken a great risk. Now, in addition to his Spanish foes, he had to worry about the vengeful Caribs. When they returned in force, as Warner knew by their reputation that they would, his handful of gentlemen adventurers could not repel them. Thus, when the crew of a French privateer arrived early in 1625, Warner struck a bargain to occupy the island jointly in exchange for French assistance in arms against Caribs and Spanish. The French took the island's northern and southern ends, while the English remained in the middle. When the Caribs attacked later that year, the combined forces of French and English colonists easily repelled them. They had less success four years later against a concentrated Spanish attack, but survivors of both nations managed to rebuild and live together in an uneasy peace for another three decades.

The tumultuous experience of St. Christopher's early English conquerors was not at all unusual for colonists in the seventeenth-century Caribbean. Yet the harsh and uncertain prospects of Caribbean life did not deter thousands of settlers from embarking for the English West Indies rather than the North American mainland during the first half of the century. Indeed, in 1635, the number of colonists departing London for the Caribbean outnumbered migrants to Massachusetts Bay by more than 500. Only Virginia attracted more. Most arrived as servants, and most fell victim to tropical disease or maltreatment before getting the chance to pursue their dreams of bettering their condition. Most who survived their terms of service saw their hopes cruelly dashed as they found themselves pushed to the hardscrabble margins of life in the island economies. A few ruthless, calculating, and lucky planters eventually managed to strike it rich in sugar production, an enterprise that won them wealth beyond their wildest dreams and turned England's Caribbean possessions into dynamos of economic growth throughout the English Atlantic.

Virtually no leading colonist living anywhere in early America would have relegated the Caribbean to the margins of awareness as subsequent histories of this era have commonly done. To English colonists, the Caribbean was central—the front line in the struggle against Spain, the main market for agricultural staples from the mainland, the source of England's enormously profitable sugar trade, and the primary destination for English and colonial slave ships departing from Africa. Seventeenth- and eighteenth-century colonists understood implicitly how profound an influence the English Caribbean exerted on mainland colonial development. Early mainland colonists understood that their security rested in part on the ability of English privateers to keep Spanish ships occupied in the faraway Caribbean. They knew that the wealthy English sponsors of mainland colonial ventures backed colonizing efforts in the Caribbean as well. Leading mainland colonists such as Massachusetts Governor John Winthrop (a friend and former neighbor of St. Christopher's Captain Thomas Warner) maintained friendships and alliances with English adventurers in the Caribbean, and kept close tabs on developments there. As early as the 1640s, Winthrop began tapping his Caribbean connections to cultivate a market for New England agricultural goods, a trade that expanded dramatically during the following century (see Chapter 7). This budding commerce in turn stimulated the growth of a colonial carrying trade, which soon grew to transatlantic scope as New England sea captains began sailing to the coast of Africa in search of slaves for the Caribbean market.

If English Caribbean history contributed in important ways to the growth of northern mainland colonies, it was absolutely indispensable to the development of the colonial South. Virginia tobacco planters turned to slave labor on a large scale well after Barbadian sugar planters did, and many of the Africans who arrived in colonial Virginia passed through a period of "seasoning" in Barbados en route. Indeed, for much of the colonial period, shipments of slaves to North America constituted a mere side-business for the main enterprise of supplying the Caribbean slave labor market. And South Carolina became a thriving plantation colony primarily through the efforts not of colonists from England, but of slaveholding planters from Barbados (see Chapter 8). By the eighteenth century, the economy of the English West Indies and England's mainland colonies had become so deeply intertwined that either would suffer greatly without the participation of the other. The story of colonial American growth is inseparable from that of the English Caribbean.

"No Peace Beyond the Line"

At the opening of the seventeenth century, the Caribbean was a hornet's nest of privateers from every major seafaring nation in Europe who competed ruthlessly for Spanish silver, Carib slaves, and increasingly for possession of the islands themselves. The sixteenth-century conflict between Spain and other nations over rights to New World territory had resulted in the development of a "line of amity" that marked limits of European treaties. Once an English vessel passed west of the prime meridian in the mid-Atlantic or sailed south past the Tropic of Cancer, it became fair game for Spanish, French, or Dutch vessels, even when peace prevailed among those nations in Europe. Spain reserved the right to drive competing nations out of the Caribbean if they could marshal the strength to do it. Adventurers of other nations reserved the right to trade or raid among Spanish possessions as opportunity arose and to occupy any territory they could seize.

The decision of European rulers to suspend international law in the Caribbean created a scene of anarchy among the region's competing inhabitants. Colonists of rival nations might cooperate as need dictated even if their parent countries were at war. Spanish settlers, for example, readily dealt with English, French, and Dutch smugglers when they could get away with it to circumvent the artificially high prices and sluggish operation of Spain's cumbersome mercantile system. The Spanish held these traders at arms' length, however, well aware that the vessel that this year brought them illicit goods at discount rates might return next year to raid their coasts or capture their ships. Spain's European challengers often cooperated with each other against Iberian enterprise in the Caribbean, but they also readily took advantage of one another when opportunity arose. After the Spanish attacked St. Christopher in 1629, for instance, English survivors joined forces with a fresh group of English colonists who arrived a few weeks later to appropriate abandoned French lands as well as their own. When the French colonists who had fled the invasion returned to the island, they had to fight their way back onto their former possessions.

Despite the chaos that marked the seventeenth-century Caribbean, however, a variety of factors made it increasingly worth the risk for English adventurers to attempt new settlements in the islands. In the first place, Spain entered the seventeenth century a wounded giant, still dangerous near the center of her empire but weakened at its peripheries by decades of war. Spanish officials found it increasingly difficult to police their Caribbean claims, opening the chance for colonists of England and other nations to establish island settlements undetected. Many zealous Puritan gentry thought they detected in this weakness a chance to drive the English Protestant sword into the heart of Spain's popish empire.

Iberian tobacco and sugar planters had also shown their English rivals that a New World colonist could grow rich by means other than capturing a silver mine or finding El Dorado. All one needed was land, seed, and labor—large amounts of each. The sparsely inhabited islands of the Lesser Antilles offered an untapped source of arable land with the proper growing season for plantation staples. Dutch merchants were eager to expand their suppliers of staple goods by providing the seed, equipment, and know-how to launch a plantation. A surplus of young, underemployed English men and women were willing to provide labor in the early years. When the supply of English laborers began to dwindle, the Dutch were ready to step in with African slaves.

As Governor John Winthrop was steering his Massachusetts Bay Colony through its first winter in 1630–1631, the *Seaflower* carried 100 colonists from London to another Puritan colony in the very heart of the Spanish Caribbean. Providence Island had been settled a little more than a year earlier with the backing of a group of England's most powerful Puritan leaders, great lords and gentlemen who were determined to press the cause of godly reform in the face of what they saw as a national decline into civil decay and religious error. They hoped to make the new colony a model of godly society for English leaders to emulate, a profitable enterprise that would shore up English wealth, and a base for advancing the Protestant cause against Catholic Spain in the face of King Charles I's neglect.

A West Indian City on a Hill

Providence Island seemed the perfect spot for achieving all three aims. Visitors reported that the island held rich agricultural potential and could support a large population of godly settlers. Its location a hundred miles from the coast of Nicaragua made it a promising base for launching trading ventures and new colonizing efforts on the mainland. Its strategic position "in the high way of the Spanish fleets" that carried silver from Cartagena and Portobelo (see Chapter 3) would enable Puritan privateers to disrupt the commerce of "popish Spain" for the glory of their Protestant God. The island was a natural fortress, its harbors protected by treacherous sandbars and overlooked by high rock formations from which well-placed artillery could train murderous fire on enemy vessels and landing parties.

Peaceful relations between Spain and England in the 1630s delayed the initiation of Providence Island's privateering enterprise, because Charles I refused to authorize military action against Spain's possessions except in reprisal for prior Spanish aggression. In the meantime, the colony's backers demonstrated their devotion to the cause by pouring vast sums into the project. Providence Island Company founders were determined to avoid the mistakes in planning and governance that had plagued earlier colonial enterprises in Roanoke and Virginia. Men such as the great Parliamentarian John Pym, an avid defender of local government and small property owners' rights during the English Civil War, concluded that the problems of earlier colonies had arisen through too much local control. The backers decided to govern Providence Island from London and retain ownership of all property.

This impractical scheme engendered tension and hampered the island's economic development. The decision makers remained too far distant to respond to urgent problems as they arose. Middling planters who sold out to go to Providence Island soon grew discontent with their status as tenants and company employees. They began to agitate for private ownership of their own plantations, a concession that the London adventurers remained reluctant to grant. The company had promised planters a steady supply of servants, whom they hoped would provide labor for three or four years before assuming a place among the island's free planters.

Recruitment lagged, however, increasing the discontent of planters who needed more labor and servants whose terms were prolonged to compensate for the lack of replacements. Investors made matters even worse by directing colonists to experiment with too many unfamiliar crops at once, an effort that spread the labor too thin and resulted in a string of failures. Eventually, the London grandees had to permit planters to concentrate on tobacco, which grew well on Providence Island and helped stem the investors' losses for a time.

Providence Island's religious life disappointed its pious founders' hopes as well. The settlers shared many religious sensibilities with the founders of Massachusetts Bay Colony, which many of Providence Island's backers also supported. Yet company officials grew increasingly alarmed during the 1630s at the form the Bay Colony religious order was taking. They worried that New England ministers and local congregations wielded too much power over the lives and consciences of the colonists there. The London grandees were determined to follow a different line on Providence Island. They hoped to create parallel civil and religious systems whose leaders would contribute to the common good by devoting themselves wholly to their respective spheres. Ministers would have no civil authority, but "spend their Times and pains in the service of [the colonists'] souls." They were expected to appear before the civil magistrates as humble petitioners, hats in hand, just as every other ordinary colonist on the island. By the same token, civil officials were strictly forbidden from meddling in the colony's religious affairs. Company officials, however, did retain the time-honored right of noble and gentry patrons to handpick ministers for the people under their authority.

The Providence Island plan instituted religious reforms as sweeping in their own way as those of Massachusetts Bay, but New England attracted all the best emigrant ministers. Despite their extensive connections with Puritan clergy, the island's London investors had to content themselves with sending ministers of lesser experience or poorer qualifications, men who ultimately proved unable to unite Puritan colonists. Indeed, ministers such as Lewis Morgan and Hope Sherrard exacerbated tensions among godly colonists who brought with them conflicting ideas of worship and the life of faith. Morgan, for example, antagonized one of the leading colonists, Captain William Rudyerd, by encouraging his congregation to sing psalms in worship. When Rudyerd challenged the practice, Morgan excluded him from participating in communion. In the aftermath of this confrontation, Morgan's colonial followers coalesced into an opposition group and thrust him into the role of spokesperson for their grievances against company policies. The investors recalled Morgan to London in disgrace, but the religious life of the colony remained divided.

In 1635, the colony entered a promising but risky new phase of development after an unsuccessful Spanish assault on the island. The attack gave investors the excuse they needed to ask for letters of reprisal that would authorize English privateers to strike back at Spain. The Crown readily issued the letters, and Providence Island became a central base for staging English raids on Spanish colonial ports and shipping. The colony's London backers hoped that privateering would turn the money-draining settlement into a profitable enterprise, providing a firm fiscal foundation for future development. The island's pious middling planters, however, clashed with the rough seamen who poured into their settlement. They also objected that the turn to privateering would increase the costs and risks of life on the island, a concern that materialized as London investors demanded new defense expenditures in the face of escalating Anglo-Spanish tensions in the region.

By May of 1640, the ongoing depredations of the Providence Island privateers convinced Spanish colonial officials that they could no longer tolerate this English Protestant "den of thieves" living so close to their vital treasure routes. Cartagena's sergeant-major Don Antonio Maldonado de Texeda attacked Providence Island with an amphibious force of 13 Spanish ships carrying more than 700 infantrymen in addition to their crews. The English took excellent advantage of the island's natural defenses, however, and repelled the invasion with a force of around 100 fighting men.

Providence Islanders enjoyed their victory for only one year. In May of 1641, General Francisco Díaz Pimienta organized a second invasion force of 1,400 infantrymen and more than 600 seamen who sailed to the island in 7 large ships and 4 pinnaces. This time, the Spanish captured the island in a well-executed, multi-pronged attack. A few of the island's 350 English captives scattered among remaining English settlements in the Caribbean; the rest returned to London at their own expense. Spanish invaders also captured 381 African slaves, whom they sold in Cartagena. Pimienta turned the island into a Spanish garrison to prevent English or Dutch corsairs from regaining control of a base that had proved so destructive to the colonies and shipping of the Spanish Caribbean. By July of 1641, Pimienta was boasting that more merchant ships had entered Cartagena in the past two months than in the previous two years before the English fell.

The brevity of English Puritan settlement on Providence Island belies the colony's importance in the history of the seventeenth-century English Atlantic. Domestic unrest and civil war demanded all the attention of the colony's great backers during the 1640s, but they did not forsake the hope of making the Caribbean a theater of militant English Protestantism. Indeed, those who survived into Cromwell's Protectorate helped transform their vision into national policy as the Western Design, a renewed effort to capture the Caribbean for England (see Chapter 7). The military dimension of English Caribbean policy persisted throughout the colonial period, as did the Protestant impulse in a less Puritan form. Yet a new road to fabulous wealth was beginning to emerge far off the path of Spain's treasure fleets, among the British sugar islands of the Lesser Antilles.

Barbados: Sugar and Broken Dreams

Sugar was a part of the plan for Barbados at the colony's beginning in 1626, when the Anglo-Dutch merchant Sir William Courteen fetched to the newly founded settlement "32 Indians from the [South American] mayne wth tobacco sugar canes cotton plantaines potatoes cassada pines &c . . . to assist and instruct the English to advance the said plantation." Courteen had chosen an island well-suited to the type of plantation enterprise he had in mind. Barbados' location far away from the Spanish treasure routes afforded it shelter from England's enemies—indeed, throughout the seventeenth century Spain never once attacked the island. English visitors thought Barbados resembled their homeland and was "more healthful than any of hir (Caribbean) neighbors; and better agreeing with the temper of the

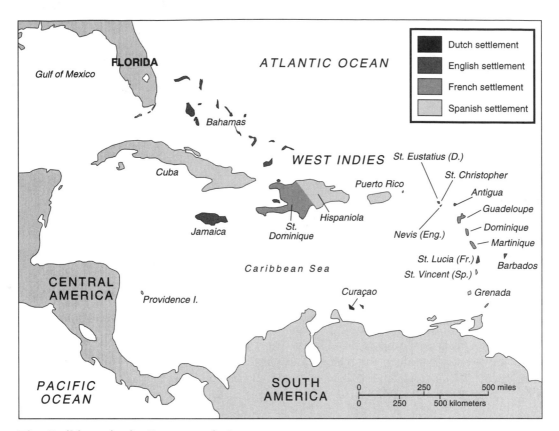

The Caribbean in the Seventeenth Century

The English were latecomers to the Caribbean, but the development of sugar plantations during the seventeenth century made their small West Indian islands the richest colonies in English America.

English nacion," despite the fact that many of its European inhabitants succumbed to tropical disease. The island enjoyed abundant rainfall, and a very high percentage of its 166 square miles consisted of gentle, rolling hills that provided excellent land for planting when cleared.

Despite Barbados' promise, unrest and mismanagement delayed the emergence of sugar as a major crop for over a decade. To be sure, Courteen followed up on his initial preparations quickly enough. By 1627 he obtained a patent for the island and dispatched 74 colonists to begin building, clearing, and planting under the direction of his newly appointed governor, John Powell. Yet within a few months of the colonists' arrival, the Earl of Carlisle, an influential courtier of Charles I, sent his henchman Charles Woolverston with 60 men to challenge Courteen's claim to Barbados. Woolverston soon "seduced the people, imprisoned the Governour &c., and tooke the gouerment upon himselfe for the Earle of Carlile." A two-year power struggle ensued in English courts and on Barbadian soil for control of the island. Carlisle's connections at court eventually enabled him to win a patent for all English possessions in the Lesser Antilles, and Courteen had to forfeit much of his enormous £10,000 investment in Barbados.

Unlike Courteen, who had planned to direct the development of his Barbados plantations from London, Carlisle was interested only in collecting annual quitrents on the land and cared little how the colonists went about generating them. Under his proprietorship, Barbados settlers received grants of land that Carlisle expected them to develop using their own funds and labor. During the 1630s several hundred colonists obtained land from Carlisle and began recruiting servants to the island to help them develop their claims. The grants varied greatly in size, a few as large as 1,000 acres and many parcels no larger than 30 to 50 acres, establishing a pattern of inequality among landholders that would characterize Barbados throughout the colonial period.

The early planters on Barbados followed Virginia in producing tobacco for export, a choice that made the new colony similar to its mainland counterpart in many ways. Like Virginia, Barbados drew thousands of indentured servants to provide labor for the arduous task of clearing rain forest and cultivating tobacco plants among the stumps of the felled trees. During the 1630s, a little less than 9,000 English colonists embarked for the island, most of them single males in their teens or twenties. Though Barbados tobacco compared poorly with that grown in Virginia—Massachusetts governor John Winthrop declared one shipment of it "very ill conditioned, fowle, full of stalkes and evill coloured"—the colony nevertheless attracted young people on the make because it seemed likely to make them moderately prosperous yeoman planters once their terms of service were complete. Not only was the Barbados climate reportedly healthy by Caribbean standards, but crops were said to grow so well in its fertile soil that it quickly became known as "a granary of all the rest of the charybbies Isles."

The island's plantation economy failed to live up to its promise during the 1630s, however, delayed by low prices and the poor quality that kept Barbadian tobacco unprofitable throughout the decade. Planters responded by shifting to cotton for a short time, but it proved no more profitable. Finally, in the early 1640s, they experimented with sugar. The crop grew well—much better than either tobacco or cotton—and the first cargos, though too coarse, dark, and sticky for the finest European tastes, nevertheless reaped a tidy return. During the next few years Barbadian planters learned how to improve production from visiting Dutch merchants or by traveling themselves to Dutch-controlled plantations in South America. By the mid-1640s, the Barbadian sugar boom had arrived in full force.

The turn to sugar cultivation made many Barbadian planters rich within a few years. In 1646, one Barbadian managed to sell his 500-acre plantation for £16,000, more than the value of the entire island a decade before. Some planters sold out and retired to England; others sold off excess lands to increase efficiency—the optimum size of a seventeenth-century sugar plantation proved to be around 200 acres—and a new group of aggressive, well-heeled investors moved onto the island or snapped up plantations from London to reap Barbadian profits as absentee landlords. Real-estate values soared, and planters moved quickly to put as much land as possible into sugar production. By the 1660s, Barbados' rain forests had disappeared, replaced by fields of sugarcane that prompted one visitor to describe the island as a single "beautifully planted green garden" dotted with windmills where the sugar was processed.

Not all Barbadians prospered in the sugar boom, however. Small planters found themselves crowded onto ever-smaller plots of marginal soil, where they scrounged out a meager existence by farming a mixture of sugar, cotton, ginger, and provision crops. Poor nutrition made both hardscrabble farmers and indentured servants more vulnerable to the island's virulent tropical diseases. Those servants who survived their terms in the hope of becoming independent landowners found themselves shut out of the soaring real estate market, shunted into wage-earning jobs on great plantations or forced off the island to seek their fortunes elsewhere. The soaring demand for labor brought additional English servants to Barbados after 1640, but word of the island's dim prospects for landless young men discouraged many others from coming. Planters increasingly had to rely on the labor of transported criminals, prisoners taken during the English Civil War, or hapless victims who had been "barbadosed"—kidnapped—and taken to the island against their will.

The chronic labor shortage made it "fatally easy," as historian Richard S. Dunn has observed, for the English planters on Barbados to take the plunge into African slavery. Sugar cultivation demanded a large workforce. Seventeenth-century planters quickly came to regard as optimum a ratio of one worker for every acre of cane, although only the richest could afford to acquire and maintain such large numbers of slaves. English planters who traveled to Brazil observed firsthand how a handful of European masters and overseers could keep hundreds of Africans on task in the cane fields. They sought to replicate this system on Barbados almost as a matter of course. Dutch merchants were eager to expand their growing market for African slaves by supplying Barbados with as many as the island economy could absorb. The Dutch reaped a dual benefit, profiting not only from the slave trade but also from Barbadian sugar, which they transported to Europe for handsome profits.

The shift to African slavery brought about an explosion in population and prosperity for the planters on Barbados. African slaves multiplied very rapidly on the island after 1640, soaring to 20,000 by 1655. By contrast, the total population of African slaves on all Virginia plantations numbered only 300 in 1650. The European population of the island rose to around 23,000 during the same period, making Barbados the most densely populated colony in English America. Most of the new European arrivals worked as servants alongside African slaves, and their combined labor in sugar production made Barbados one of England's most lucrative New World colonies.

Contested Tobacco Islands

The English who colonized the Leeward Islands—St. Christopher, Nevis, Antigua, and Montserrat—contended with chronic instability in their attempts to establish a viable plantation economy. Unlike Barbados, whose distance from other islands insulated it from conflict, the Leewards' location near the northern end of the

Lesser Antilles placed them much closer to the center of European conflict in the Caribbean. In this region beyond the line, European inhabitants lived by "that common proverb at Sea, Oy por mi, mañana port ti.—To day I have got what tomorrow I may lose again." The earliest settlers had to remain constantly on their guard against raids by Carib Indians and Spanish colonists. Indeed, the Spanish temporarily drove their enemies off both St. Christopher and Nevis in 1629. As the Carib and Spanish threat waned toward the middle of the century, both Anglo-French and Anglo-Dutch tensions began heating up. Between 1650 and 1713, Nevis was sacked once, Montserrat and Antigua twice, and St. Christopher changed hands seven times. They also rode out several devastating hurricanes that destroyed their buildings and wiped out their crops. Yet the English persisted in settling the Leewards despite these repeated losses.

English colonists fanned out to the other Leewards from their initial base on St. Christopher. In 1628, a planter named Anthony Hilton led 150 colonists to Nevis across the 3-mile channel that separated it from St. Christopher. Other colonists ventured to the more distant Antigua and Montserrat in 1632. Colonists found the gentle, rolling terrain of Antigua most suitable to their agricultural purposes, despite the island's shortage of fresh water. The mountainous, volcanic terrain and dramatic coastal cliffs of the other three Leewards, which tourists find so beautiful today, struck the seventeenth-century planters as savage and inhospitable. Nevertheless, they poured great energy into carving fields of tobacco, cotton, and ginger out of the jungle-covered island slopes.

The Earl of Carlisle confirmed Captain Thomas Warner as the governor of St. Christopher when that island and Nevis came into his possession in 1629, making Warner a deputy of the earl's lieutenant governor of Barbados. Each of the other three Leewards received its own deputy governor during the 1630s as well. Each also maintained its own council and assembly. The Leewards' distance from Barbados prevented the Barbadian lieutenant governor from exercising any real influence in their governance. Officials on each of the three islands remained extremely jealous of any outside authority, particularly from their wealthy rivals on Barbados, and they labored to strengthen local control. The restored monarchy of Charles II eventually attempted to unite the four Leewards under a single government distinct from that of Barbados, but the islands remained virtually independent of one another throughout the seventeenth and eighteenth centuries.

In contrast to the relatively high percentage of wealthy planters on Barbados, the early Leeward planters were obscure men who lacked the capital to amass land, purchase slaves, or invest in expensive equipment such as sugar mills. The majority of free English planters on St. Christopher were former indentured servants who had managed to purchase one of the 10- to 12-acre plots that comprised most of the English sector's cultivated land. Prosperity eluded colonists on Antigua through the 1650s as they labored under a chronic burden of debt to the island's governor, Henry Ashton. Montserrat became a refuge for a majority population of Irish Catholics who managed to purchase small plantations after working off their indentures. Like their counterparts on other Leeward Islands, these planters "of an ordinary and low rank" could not establish the credit needed to establish estates or attract investment. Only on Nevis did a sizable group of planters possess sufficient means to establish sugar plantations before 1650. Even there, a shortage of servants and African slaves limited the growth of sugar cultivation.

The Leewards thus remained preserves of mostly small planters with limited prospects and chronically frustrated hopes, yet they attracted a steady stream of immigrants through the 1650s. Tobacco grew better there than on Barbados, though not as well as in Virginia and Maryland. Leeward planters persisted in cultivating it and recruiting additional servants to the island to assist them. Population estimates for the early years are scarce and unreliable, but a traveler to St. Christopher in 1655 reported that the English sector comprising little more than half the island's 68 square miles was "almost worne out by reason of the multitudes that live upon it." In that same year the population of Antigua stood at around 1,200, as did that of Montserrat.

Most who came to the Leewards had to eke out an existence in a rough frontier environment, building flimsy, thatch-roofed huts supported by a frame of forked stakes walled with reeds. Only a few brought with them or earned the capital necessary to build the more substantial plantation dwellings that began appearing on Barbados soon after its planters turned to sugar production. Their reputation for fractious behavior and love of idleness dogged Leeward islanders well after they began turning to sugar cultivation in the 1660s.

The Carib Challenge

Early English settlers in the Caribbean had to contend with the constant presence of Carib Indians, or Karifunas. Sixteenth-century Spanish colonists had all but exterminated the Caribs from the Greater Antilles (Puerto Rico, Hispaniola, Cuba, and Jamaica) through warfare, enslavement, and epidemic disease. Caribs in the Lesser Antilles, however, managed to resist Spanish conquest and maintain an independent existence in a 500-mile chain of island societies that extended from Tobago off the coast of South America to the Leewards. The Caribs living on these islands developed an effective system of communication and cooperation that enabled faraway groups to come to the assistance of any Caribs under pressure from European interlopers. Carib reinforcements might not arrive in time to repel a particular attack, but they could soon amass a force large enough to exact devastating reprisals against any European expedition foolish enough to attack an apparently insignificant, isolated Carib settlement.

The Caribs resisted English attempts to settle the Lesser Antilles as they had resisted the Spanish before them. Captain Thomas Warner's effort to expel Caribs from St. Christopher in 1624 succeeded only temporarily. Although the English and French jointly staved off Carib reprisals against St. Christopher in 1625, small bands of Caribs soon managed to return to the island, where they lived in areas the Europeans found hard to reach. In the later 1620s and early 1630s, the French and English conducted several joint expeditions to search out and destroy persistent Carib settlements on St. Christopher.

English settlers on other Leeward islands faced conflict with the Caribs as well, and the Indians managed to retain complete control of some islands well into the eighteenth century. In 1639, for example, Carib soldiers easily repelled an English effort to capture their stronghold on Saint Lucia. The next year they retaliated with a full-scale attack on Antigua, capturing the governor's wife and children, killing 50 settlers, and destroying English crops and houses. Barbadian governors sought constantly for opportunities to defeat the Caribs on nearby St. Vincent, a common destination for runaway servants and slaves. The Indians always managed to stave off attacks, and governors of other English islands soon began taking a dim view of Barbadian activities that put their own communities at risk of Carib reprisals.

Despite persistent tensions between the Caribs and English, the two groups did find occasions for cooperation as well as conflict. During the earliest years of settlement, the English traded sporadically with Caribs on nearby islands. In 1638, Caribs astounded the English on St. Christopher with their seemingly uncanny ability to forecast a deadly hurricane. Their warning gave the English enough time to prepare, saving both lives and many goods. Carib headmen usually returned to the early planters any runaway servants or slaves they found. English and Caribs occasionally sought each others' assistance against rival European groups as well, though their mutual antagonism made most efforts short-lived. Caribs more often sided with the French or Dutch against the English.

The Carib presence in the Lesser Antilles complicated English efforts to develop sugar plantations there. They resisted settlement when possible and contributed to the instability that delayed sugar planting on the Leewards. As the sugar boom swept across the Caribbean, the Caribs fiercely defended their remaining islands of freedom against a rising sea of slavery. St. Vincent, Saint Lucia, and Dominica emerged as Carib centers of resistance to a system of bondage and commerce that was being built on the foundation of a growing European taste for sweetness.

CULTIVATING SWEETNESS

Sugar rapidly emerged as one of the main engines of economic development in the seventeenth- and eighteenth-century English Atlantic. It transformed Barbados, and eventually the Leewards and Jamaica as well, from struggling tobacco settlements to the richest plantation colonies in English America. The fabulous profits from sugar, even more than those from tobacco, prompted London policymakers to begin enacting the series of laws that gave shape to England's Atlantic commercial empire (see Chapter 7). Sugar transformed the diet of Europe as it made its way from docks to the kitchens and tables of consumers.

Sugar also transformed the lives of Atlantic peoples. Barbadian sugar planters created a society unlike any other in the colonial New World. They ruthlessly exploited the labor of thousands of English servants who embarked from London or Bristol to better their condition, only to see their hopes dashed in the islands. The sugar planters led England's full-scale plunge into African slavery. The Caribbean sugar islands, not the Chesapeake tobacco plantations, first drew the Dutch and English into the circuit linking Africa with the English colonies, carrying hundreds of thousands of Africans in chains to toil and die far from home.

An Appetite for Sweetness

At the opening of the seventeenth century, sugar remained a costly luxury that mainly graced the tables of royalty and nobility, though a growing number of wealthy gentry and merchant elites were also beginning to consume it. Common people satisfied their palates on a diet of grain foods supplemented with meats and dairy products. If they wanted something sweet, they ate honey or fruits, and did so sparingly in the belief that fruit eaten in large quantities posed a danger to health. The gradual introduction of sugar into the everyday diet of ordinary Europeans took place over the course of the seventeenth and eighteenth centuries as a result of the boom in sugar production that took place in that period.

Seventeenth-century Europeans used sugar in many ways that later generations would find peculiar. Wealthy consumers thought of the product as a spice or condiment rather than a sweetener, sprinkling it lightly onto meats, fish, vegetables, or fruit and mixing it into recipes in quantities similar to other spices. Physicians prescribed it as a medicine for treating a variety of maladies such as indigestion, respiratory ailments, and eye infections. Some also sprinkled it onto cuts and scrapes to promote healing; others used it to clean teeth. Monarchs and noblemen used it lavishly to signify their power and status, decorating banqueting halls with large figures of trees, humans, animals, mythical beings, castles or sailing ships armed with working cannons, all sculpted from pure hardened sugar. The powerful regarded sugar as a kind of edible precious stone, and displayed their opulence by lavishing it on their guests on important occasions such as a coronation or wedding.

As the price of sugar gradually dropped within reach of the lesser gentry, the middling sorts, and eventually working people, its uses gradually changed. By the 1680s the extravagant displays were falling out of fashion. Gentry consumers now used sugar to mark status in more subtle ways, most notably in combination with coffee, tea, and chocolate, three exotic tropical beverages that began to appear in Europe about this time. Sugar's growing affordability also stimulated the development of an ever-expanding array of sweet breads, pastries, custards, cakes, and puddings that could complement a hot beverage at teatime or could make a dinner complete. An increasing number of aspiring gentry on mainland North America were also beginning to emulate the European example, spreading the demand for sugar to both sides of the Atlantic.

Sugar Production

It was demanding work to satisfy the growing European taste for sweetness. The complex process of sugar production required a hefty initial investment in workers and equipment; backbreaking, hazardous labor; and painstaking management. Yet sugar offered staggering returns to those willing to expend the necessary capital and to squeeze the maximum labor from their workforce.

Sugar plantations combined agricultural and mechanical procedures into a time-critical process that the historical anthropologist Sidney Mintz has seen as "the closest thing to industry that was typical of the seventeenth century." Sugar planting began with the backbreaking task of clearing and tilling fields, a process accomplished almost exclusively with axes and hoes. Once the field was ready, servants and slaves dug trenches or holes in which they set fresh cuttings of cane, which would quickly sprout new roots. During the sixteen-month period of maturation, workers hoed the fields several times. They also spread manure obtained from large herds of sheep and cattle, which the planters kept mainly for generating fertilizer. When the cane ripened, gangs of workers harvested it with heavy knives called "bills," stripping the leaves and bundling the stalks as they went.

The harvest only began the arduous process of rendering the cane to sugar. Workers had to get the bundled stalks to the mills as quickly as possible to maximize the yield. Mill operators fed the cane into the livestock- or wind-driven rollers, which pressed out the juice into a collecting trough. The cane was light, but the pace so quick and relentless that workers soon became exhausted. All too frequently, the rollers caught the hand of a tired worker and pulled in his arm. The overseer commonly amputated the mangled arm on the spot with a knife kept handy for the purpose, barely slacking the pace as the severed limb passed on through the mill with the cane.

From the mill, the freshly pressed cane juice flowed through a channel or pipe to the boiling house, where it passed through a series of kettles to boil off excess water. Sugar-boiling was an art performed under very difficult and hazardous conditions. The heat was stifling, the stench of smoke and scorching syrup overpowering, and the scalding syrup would "stick like Glew or Birdlime" to a worker who accidentally spilled it on a limb, inflicting serious or even life-threatening injury. Skillful craftsmen tended the sugar through this process, skimming off impurities as the syrup boiled and "striking" or arresting boiling as soon as they judged it ready for cooling.

After cooling, the workers poured the partially granulated sugar into earthenware pots with a hole in the bottom and set the pots in the curing house on ce-

Slaves on West Indian sugar plantations endured arduous labor during harvest, when the cane had to be cut quickly and processed into sugar at mills like the one depicted here.
Lauros, Giraudon/Bridgeman Art Library

ramic trays called "drips." Workers kept the curing houses as hot as possible to promote the draining of molasses and drying of the sugar crystals. After curing, they knocked out the hardened loaves of brown "muscovado" sugar and pressed them into hogsheads for shipping. Some planters followed a somewhat different method to obtain "clayed" sugar, a white, soft product that needed no further processing and fetched a higher price on the English market. Both methods of curing yielded a large amount of molasses which the workers collected for sale or distilling into rum, an English invention that provided yet another source of profit.

The tasks of harvesting, milling, boiling, curing, and distilling kept Caribbean plantation laborers working at a continuous breakneck pace each year from January until May. The staff of the mill and boiling house worked in continuous shifts from dawn until well after sundown and often through the night, resting only on Sundays. A well-run sugar operation demanded careful management to synchronize the various tasks and keep the labor force on a strict production schedule. Few other enterprises required management or time-discipline on such a scale until textile mills began appearing in England during the late eighteenth century.

Sweetness and Profits

Sketchy seventeenth-century records make it difficult to know exactly how much a planter could profit from sugar production, and profit margins fluctuated widely over the seventeenth century as prices fell, costs rose, and war disrupted trade. Nevertheless, historians agree that "only inept and unlucky planters actually lost money, even in the worst of times," while industrious and lucky planters such as the Barbadian Henry Drax did very well indeed. Drax himself was reported to have shipped home around £5,000 worth of sugar annually during the 1680s, a gross income matching that of the wealthiest landed aristocrats in England. While Drax and other planters had to return much of their income into the maintenance and expansion of their plantations and labor forces, the profits they cleared supported lives of extravagant luxury in the islands. Their accumulated wealth also enabled many retiring planters to purchase or build great estates in the English countryside, where they spent their remaining years in leisured opulence.

The sugar trade fueled English commercial expansion throughout the Atlantic during the later seventeenth century, prompting London pamphleteers and policymakers of the period to wax eloquent on its benefits to the nation. Some hoped that England's sugar colonies would soon corner the European sugar market, expanding opportunities for ownership and employment in shipping while bringing an influx of European trade commodities that would increase prosperity and improve the lives of English people. Others pointed out that prosperous sugar colonies themselves could provide significant markets for English manufactured goods. Wealthy planters would want not only luxurious consumer goods such as table service, glassware, textiles, and household furnishings; they would also need great quantities of clothing and tools for their slaves along with supplies of many items such as nails, iron, and cordage used to keep the plantation in good working order.

The sugar colonies stimulated production not only in England, but on the North American mainland as well. Barbados planters found sugar so profitable that they quickly put every available plot of land into cane and began importing the grains needed to feed themselves and their workers. Massachusetts began supplying Barbadian planters with grain and salt pork as early as the 1640s (see Chapter 7). Farmers in coastal New England and the Middle Colonies exported agricultural goods to the Caribbean throughout the colonial period, gleaning modest profits, which many used to purchase cheap English imported goods as they became increasingly available.

The fabulous profits, the transformation of the European diet, the expansion of Atlantic commerce, the gradual emergence of a consumer society—all came at a cost far greater than what bookkeepers could measure in pounds and pence. Sugar production exacted a terrible price in human misery from thousands of European servants and hundreds of thousands of African slaves. Life in the tropics was filled with strain and peril even for the planters themselves. Society on England's Caribbean sugar islands bore the tragic marks of continual, violent exploitation, arduous toil, chronic malnutrition, virulent disease, and death.

SOCIETY IN THE ENGLISH WEST INDIES

Barbados "is divided into three sorts of men, *viz.*, Masters, Servants, and Slaves," the traveler Richard Ligon reported in 1657. Island life presented all three groups with peculiar challenges, but it was especially brutal for servants and slaves. By the time Ligon published his account, African slaves already comprised nearly 50 percent of the island's population. A few aspiring sugar planters on Nevis had begun purchasing slaves by this time as well, but the proportion of African slaves there was much smaller, and it remained negligible on the other Leeward islands until the 1670s. Planters on Providence Island also rapidly turned to slaves to meet their labor demands, but their defeat in 1641 made Barbados the first successful English colony in America to develop a society based on the large-scale employment of African slaves. The social and cultural patterns that resulted there were peculiar to the specific demands of sugar cultivation, the hazards of life in the tropics, and the high percentage of African slaves in the island populations.

Society on the other sugar islands followed the pattern set on Barbados, taking a course distinct from social development on the North American mainland. English West Indian life took on a freewheeling, callous, impermanent quality as planters raced to accumulate the highest possible profits before they died or retired to England. Barbados hosted a diverse, multiethnic population that included, besides English and Africans, significant communities of French, Dutch, and Scots. The largest percentage of servants was Irish, and Bridgetown, the Barbados capital, also hosted a significant community of Portuguese Jews. Barbadians "have that liberty of conscience which we so long have in England fought for," the English visitor Henry Whistler commented in 1655, "but they do abuse it." The unique culture that emerged in the English Caribbean provides an instructive counterpoint to the development of mainland colonial society, as well as an important backdrop for understanding the peculiarities of the Lower South, where transplanted Barbadians exerted a direct influence.

Family and Population in the Tropics

The Barbadian planter gentry "live far better than ours do in England," commented one early visitor. Yet wealth could not buy the sugar barons long lives or stable families. Seventeenth-century Caribbean planters both great and small lived hard, drank even harder, and died like flies. The early English population of the islands was, if anything, more distorted by gender imbalance and high death rates than that of the early Chesapeake. Most first-generation colonists who sailed to the Caribbean were male servants. All founding settlers of Barbados and St. Christopher were men. Almost a decade after its founding, males still constituted more than 90 percent of new arrivals to Barbados. As late as 1680, only one in every four English who arrived in Barbados was a woman. The sex ratio of whites in the islands became more balanced after 1710, but disease and death continued to destabilize family life throughout much of the eighteenth century.

Most English emigrants to the Caribbean succumbed quickly to virulent tropical diseases. Malaria was rampant on every island except Barbados, and dysentery or the "bloody flux" was common everywhere. The turn to slavery brought the introduction of devastating diseases from Africa such as yellow fever, leprosy, and skin-ulcerating yaws, as well as deadly parasites such as hookworm and guineaworm. Chronic deficiencies in nutrition not only lowered resistance to such diseases among servants and slaves but also caused additional maladies such as scurvy and beriberi. Disease reduced the life expectancy of white colonists well below thirty-five years, and death carried off men at a higher rate than women. Masters constantly had to bring new shiploads of laborers to the islands to replace those who had died. Even the wealthiest members of the ruling gentry seldom escaped early death, opening the highest offices of government to unusually young men. Elected leaders typically secured their first seat in the legislature during their twenties and were elevated to the council in their early thirties. Comparable offices in New England seldom went to men under forty years of age.

English colonists found traditional patterns of family life very difficult to sustain in this deadly environment. Many first- and second-generation English males entered into irregular unions with their female slaves. Offspring of such liaisons who survived infancy might sometimes be freed along with their mothers. More often both mother and child remained in bondage, though white fathers extended paternal favors to their mulatto offspring by giving them coveted positions as artisans or domestics.

The unbalanced sex ratio created a great demand for English women in the early years of Caribbean settlement. Planters recruited female servants to increase opportunities for marriage as well as to provide labor. Young women considering this move must have been apprehensive at the prospect of embarking for reputedly sickly tropical islands so far from traditional social supports. Yet surviving evidence suggests that many who accepted the risk had no better option. Indeed, women spirited or press-ganged from London's brothels onto Barbados-bound vessels gained a chance for social betterment unheard of by their sisters who remained in England. One patronizing observer sneered that "a bawd brought over" to Barbados "puts on a demure comportment, and a whore if handsome makes a wife for some rich planter."

Not all English women managed to marry into the Caribbean planter elite, nor did marriage to a planter necessarily translate into other gains for women. West Indian widows rarely gained control of their deceased husband's estate as often happened in the early Chesapeake. Marriage remained a woman's primary means of not only of achieving social advancement, but of maintaining it thereafter. Until the 1680s, the preponderance of males in the white population made this feasible, at least for women who had already managed to marry into elite society. Yet wives of small planters or artisans saw their condition erode as the sex ratio became slowly more balanced and the gap between rich and poor more pronounced. Many poor husbands found themselves squeezed by rising prices and decreasing returns in the later seventeenth century and simply abandoned wives and children to seek their fortunes elsewhere. Destitute white women ended up on parish poor relief, supported by the charitable gifts of great planters so long as their willingness to provide care for orphans or the indigent kept them "deserving."

Marriage and child-rearing increased as the sex ratio among English colonists gradually became more balanced, yet family life remained unstable. Husbands tended to die young, leaving widows and fatherless children to carry on. Death might also spare the husband only to take his wife and children, and many masters poured their short lives into amassing rich estates only to die without legitimate heirs. Families often died out within a generation of their arrival in the islands or retired to England to escape the deadly environment, inhibiting the formation of creole gentry dynasties or kinship networks like those that came to unite the Chesapeake gentry.

Small Fortunes and Great Estates

The relative scarcity of land in the English West Indies limited a colonist's chance of rising from obscurity to great wealth and status. First-generation planters on Barbados tended to be the younger sons of English gentlemen, merchants, and artisans who possessed sufficient capital to secure the largest and choicest grants of land. Moreover, the introduction of sugar cultivation to the islands enabled some of these relatively obscure young men to rise from "small fortunes to great estates" during the 1640s, as Richard Ligon observed. But servants, who were drawn from the lower ranks of English society, found little remaining land to choose from if they managed to survive their terms. Indeed, the rapid inflation of land prices after 1640 squeezed even many middling planters out of the real estate market. Those with good land could sell out at a premium to larger planters or wealthy outside investors, but most who did so had to leave Barbados to find good, productive land at affordable rates. Antigua was a favorite spot for these middling planters to set up new sugar plantations during the later seventeenth century, but many also went on to establish other types of enterprise in England's North American colonies. Leeward colonists enjoyed greater equality until later in the century, when large-scale sugar planting brought about a replication of the Barbados pattern.

Land scarcity combined with sugar prices to create a yawning gulf between the islands' richest and poorest free inhabitants. Small landholders who lacked the capital to move off the islands had to grind out a precarious existence on arid, infertile plots of ground. A fortunate few might be able to secure a modest living with the help of a handful of servants or slaves, but most had to get by on whatever mixed crops they could raise by their own labor. Unlike the majority of the free population elsewhere in English America, the lower half of the property holders in Barbados could not vote.

The great nabobs at the other end of the social scale invested much of their profit first into indentured servants and slaves, and only then into ostentatious displays of wealth. Indeed, first-generation sugar planters put very little into their houses and furnishings. Yet after 1660, these newly rich gentry began building splendid stone great houses, filling them with exquisitely crafted imported furnishings, which they purchased by mortgaging future sugar crops. The sugar barons dined from costly silver plates, quaffed the best imported wines, sweltered under several layers of the finest English fashions, rode in elegant carriages drawn by beautifully matched teams of horses, and kept domestic servants constantly at their elbow. They rapidly achieved a standard of living far higher than that enjoyed anywhere else in English America.

The West Indian sugar barons created versions of English social institutions that advanced the planters' own interests in ways unthinkable for elites elsewhere in British dominions. They created legislative assemblies similar to those of the mainland colonies, but the gentry who filled those legislatures did not answer to a broad electorate as did their counterparts in Virginia and Massachusetts. They replicated the system of courts they had known in England, but the judges set aside the common-law rights of servants and freemen whenever needed to administer the planters' version of justice. They held pews in the Anglican parish churches as well as seats in the vestries that oversaw local church affairs. Although masters allowed the slaves to rest on Sundays, they refused to let the clergy convert Africans to Christianity. They sometimes hired schoolmasters, but made only minimal attempts to promote education among the islands' free inhabitants.

Riotous and Unruly Servants

Richard Ligon thought servants led "the worser lives" of all mid-seventeenth-century Barbados inhabitants, "for they are put to very hard labour, ill lodging, and their diet very slight." The harsh conditions of servitude on Barbados produced sharp tensions between planters and their indentured laborers. Ligon observed that as early as 1647 masters were responding to these tensions by building their houses "in the manner of Fortifications" that could repel the assaults of their bondsmen. They brutally punished the slightest gestures of insubordination, sometimes stringing up servants and lighting matches between their fingers, other times locking them in stocks to roast for hours in the tropical sun or beating them mercilessly over the head until the blood flowed. "Truly," Ligon declared, "I have seen such cruelty there done to Servants, as I did not think one Christian could have done to another."

The Irish origins of many servants only exacerbated tensions. Recruiters began enticing young Irish men and women to the islands as the sugar boom began in the 1640s, and the burgeoning demand for laborers soon prompted English officials to begin deporting large numbers of Irish "undesirables" to Barbados and the Leewards as well. The English planters despised their Irish Catholic servants, whom they considered as fit only for field labor. The Irish, conditioned by English oppression, dispossession, and the ongoing colonization of their homeland, cordially hated their masters. The absence of opportunity on the islands only increased their resentment, and planters fueled further discontent through systematic discrimination against the Irish. Masters shunted Irish servants into the most menial jobs, refused them any chance to learn a craft, meted them especially harsh treatment, and denied due process to any who had the temerity to seek redress for their injuries in a court of law.

These practices yielded only chronic unrest. Planters instituted increasingly harsh measures to keep a lid on the rebellious spirit that simmered constantly among the Irish population. Leeward planters worried that the Catholic convictions of their Irish servants would prompt them to join forces with the French against English rule of the islands, a fear that proved justified in 1667 when Irish servants assisted the French in seizing St. Christopher and Montserrat. Planters on Barbados constantly monitored relations between Irish and African laborers for signs of conspiracy to unite in revolt against their oppressors. Barbados officials eventually passed a strict servant code that restricted Irish movement between plantations and imposed harsh penalties for resistance, absenteeism, or disorderliness. Planters appealed to London to send them no more Irish, but their pleas availed little until late in the seventeenth century.

The turn to sugar in the English West Indies brought a full-scale plunge into African slavery as well. Barbados planters purchased nearly 20,000 slaves in the first decade of sugar production alone. They brought another 51,000 slaves to the island during the next 25 years. Indeed, Africans comprised nearly 75 percent of Barbados' population by 1675. Planters on the Leewards and Jamaica began importing significant numbers of slaves during that period as well. By 1700, the number of enslaved Africans shipped to the English West Indies had soared to more than 260,000, the majority arriving on vessels belonging to the Royal Africa Company or to merchants from New England and New York. It was only the beginning. During the eighteenth century, the English sugar islands would absorb nearly 1.2 million additional slaves, most of whom would die of disease and overwork within a decade of arrival.

Africans in the English West Indies

The horrific death rate of Africans in the West Indies defied English insistence that Africans were better suited than Europeans to tropical heat and disease. Most slaves arrived in the islands debilitated by their ordeal on the Middle Passage (see Chapter 3), making them much more susceptible to the deadly diseases to which they were commonly exposed during the first months of "seasoning." Those who survived seasoning often fell victim to deficiency diseases such as scurvy and beriberi, a bewildering illness stemming from chronic malnutrition, which often stimulates a craving to eat dirt. Planters observed a percentage of dirt-eaters on nearly every Barbados plantation, and beriberi likely caused many of the deaths attributed to "dropsy." Africans who survived seasoning and malnutrition could expect to live between 7 and 17 years after their arrival, their most productive years. Those whose bodies broke down through age or hard labor soon died from neglect and short rations. The annual rate of decline among West Indians of African descent was highest before 1750, but births did not begin exceeding deaths until after the 1790s.

Although men comprised 60 percent of Africans brought to the Caribbean, the sex ratio quickly balanced out as a greater number of women survived seasoning. Birth rates nevertheless remained low for a variety of reasons. Women commonly worked in the field alongside men, and the combination of hard labor and poor nutrition likely reduced fertility. Seventeenth-century planters gave few concessions to pregnant women in either work or discipline, producing a higher rate of miscarriage. Travelers often marveled how African women would stop to give birth beside the row they were hoeing, rarely acknowledging that women entered the field so near the end of their terms because of the master's determination to extract every possible moment of work from each slave. The work regime also contributed to higher infant mortality by forcing new mothers back to the fields within two to three weeks of giving birth, taxing their health and interfering with the care of their newborns. Some African neonatal practices, such as packing the umbilical stump with mud, exacerbated infant mortality by introducing deadly infections. Women may also have resisted bringing children into a life of slavery by practicing contraception or inducing abortion.

Economic considerations governed the planters' turn to slavery as well as their treatment of enslaved Africans, yet English masters seldom justified the practice purely in terms of planter profits. Indeed, they adopted a quite different pattern of rhetoric. English writers associated blacks in Africa with heathen religion, barbarous behavior, sexual promiscuity—in fact, with evil itself. From such a racist perspective, the enslavement of Africans seemed unobjectionable, even defensible. West Indian sugar planters argued that the slaves' dark skin and their "brute natures" best suited them for field work, conveniently ignoring their equal susceptibility to exhaustion as well as their equal facility for acquiring difficult skills in craftsmanship. Masters claimed that even the slaves themselves "prefer their present slavery before their former liberty" in war-torn Africa, "the loss whereof they never afterwards regret."

The rapid expansion of the black population on Barbados frightened the white planters, prompting the passage of stringent laws to control their slaves. In 1661, the Barbadian legislature pulled these laws together into a comprehensive slave code that became the template for later slave codes passed in Jamaica, South Carolina, and Antigua. This code assumed a racial basis for slavery and drew a sharp line between how masters could treat European servants and how they could treat African slaves. Slaves were subject to much harsher penalties than servants, including maiming, castration, and branding. Masters could be prosecuted for manslaughter if they accidentally killed a servant while punishing him or her, but they suffered no penalty for accidental death of a slave. A planter who murdered his slave would incur a fine of £25, far less than the £80 it would cost him if he was caught keeping another planter's runaway slave. Capital offenses for slaves, by contrast, included rebellion, assault, rape, murder, and theft of any item worth more than a shilling.

Despite the severity of their slave codes and the harshness of their racism, Caribbean planters never drew racial lines as sharply as their counterparts on the North American mainland. On no island did the law prohibit sexual liaisons between white masters and black slaves as Virginians attempted to do in the early eighteenth century. To be sure, planters never fully approved "miscegenation," and they actively discouraged sexual relations between black men and white women by refusing poor relief to any white woman who bore a mulatto child. The offspring of slave mothers remained slaves for life no matter who the father was. Yet Caribbean mulattos did occupy a social rank above pure-blooded Africans, gaining access to favored positions in crafts and domestic service. English fathers sometimes freed their mulatto offspring and helped them establish a life in free society. Descendants of such persons could find full acceptance in white society after only three generations, a phenomenon unheard of in mainland society.

Relations between Europeans and Africans in the English West Indies remained tense throughout the period of slavery. Planters maintained tight surveillance over the black majority that emerged on each of the islands, searching their quarters for weapons every other week, requiring Africans to obtain a pass in order to travel, monitoring their movements and associations for any sign of conspiracy, and ruthlessly suppressing any signs of resistance. Masters gave their most despised Irish servants greater privileges in law and custom than their most valued slaves in an effort to drive a wedge between the two groups. Masters sought to divide the slaves against themselves by rewarding those who worked harder, cooperated more fully, or informed on their fellows. Masters also tried to divide slaves by language barriers, according to Richard Ligon, purchasing them from "severall parts of *Africa* . . . some from . . . Guinny and *Binny*, some from *Cutchew*, some from *Angola*, and some from the River of *Gambra*."

Despite harsh slave codes and brutal suppression of dissent, masters could never establish total control over the lives of their slaves. Africans looked for openings to create a culture that could sustain them through the harsh experience of Caribbean slavery. They also found ways to negotiate concessions from their masters that could make their lives more bearable. First-generation slaves on Barbados, for instance, so protested their monotonous diet of the maize-based porridge "loblolly" that their masters provided them plantain instead. During sugar harvest, masters commonly conceded their slaves the right to drink as much as they wanted of the "hot liquor" from the "last copper" in the boiling house. The iron- and vitamin-rich mixture of brown sugar and molasses gave slaves better health during harvest than at any other time of the year. Masters also began importing a higher percentage of slave women during the early years in response to complaints of male slaves who wanted wives.

Slaves drew on elements of their various African traditions, combining them into new cultural forms they could adapt to conditions of life in the West Indian environment. They labored to bridge language barriers by developing a pidgin tongue that combined elements of English and several African dialects. In a similar way, Africans combined various European and African musical forms into unique West Indian patterns of song, instrumental music, and dance. The planters would not permit their slaves to make or play drums because the Africans could use them to communicate across great distances. Instead, slaves shook out rhythms from gourd rattles filled with beans or wrapped with a netting of beads.

Richard Ligon recorded an especially detailed instance of this intercultural creativity after watching an African slave named Macow develop a marimba-like musical instrument. Macow apparently conceived the idea while experimenting with a lute to learn the relationship between the length of the string and the pitch of the sound. He later applied what he had learned to fashion a very different invention, a series of six wooden bars whose progressive lengths produced six different pitches on the scale when struck. When Ligon introduced Macow to the concept of sharps and flats, the African cut additional wooden bars to produce the new pitches. In this way, Macow incorporated European and African features of form and tone into a distinctly new, West Indian instrument capable of producing a new kind of music.

Africans had to create new patterns of marriage and family life within the constraints of West Indian slavery as well. Slaves on Barbados replicated the practice of polygamy even before the sex ratio became balanced, with lower-status slaves conceding to those of higher rank the right to take multiple wives. Marriage patterns, however, varied over time from plantation to plantation and island to island according to the specific conditions of life and labor. Slave marriages were not formalized by law, though Africans respected the unions as long as they endured. The informality of marriage may have given women greater independence from their husbands within the slave community. Child-rearing patterns likewise varied as conditions on the plantations shifted over time. The widespread practice of sending mothers to work in the fields only two or three weeks after giving birth made rearing the children a communal affair. The children's status as property of the master also weakened the parents' power to offer protection and guidance to their children.

Slaves managed to create their own social, religious, and economic institutions within the constraints of plantation society. Slaves as well as masters rested on Sundays, and the slaves spent their discretionary time in dancing, games of skill, and socializing. On these days and at other times slaves also pursued a variety of economic activities. Where land was available, slaves cultivated and sold among one another a variety of provision crops. The scarcity of land on the small sugar islands prevented Africans there from sustaining such a market for long, but a vibrant internal market endured among Jamaican slaves into the nineteenth century. Sundays also gave slaves the opportunity to observe religious rituals and ceremonies adapted from their various African pasts. Slaves invoked supernatural powers for protection from malevolent forces and sought spiritual guidance through divination. They looked to religion for healing from disease or injury as well as for vengeance, all of which could be especially potent when combined with their knowledge of medicinal herbs. Religion also provided solace for the bereaved, and funerals tragically became one of the slaves' most important ritual occasions.

Despite their masters' claims to the contrary, Caribbean slaves were never content in chains. They protested their debasement in many ways: sometimes in passive acts of resistance such as work slowdowns or feigning illness, sometimes in individual acts of violence, sometimes in running away, and sometimes in plotting rebellion. Yet even though slaves comprised a majority on most islands by 1670, only Jamaica and Antigua experienced actual slave rebellions.

To be sure, the Barbadian planter minority experienced a number of scares. In 1675, an islandwide uprising was narrowly averted when a domestic slave named Fortuna alerted her master of the plot. Officials rounded up the ringleaders, burned

6 alive, beheaded 11 others and dragged their bodies through the streets of Speightstown, Barbados as a warning to their comrades. Planters subsequently ferreted out and executed another 17 conspirators to satisfy themselves that they had thwarted the plot. Quick and ruthless suppression also characterized the Barbadian planters' response to four subsequent alarms in 1683, 1686, 1692, and 1702. On Barbados, and on the Leewards too, tight controls, constant surveillance, and the timely warning of a compassionate informer thwarted every attempt at revolt.

Slaves who resisted by flight enjoyed a somewhat higher rate of success, though that avenue proved very difficult as well. The dense settlement on Barbados made leaving the island by boat the only real hope for runaways. Most who attempted this course headed for Carib-controlled Saint Lucia or St. Vincent, where they attempted to enter Indian society. Caribs at first returned most runaways to their masters. As Anglo-Carib tensions increased, however, the Indians provided safe haven for runaway blacks to form maroon communities of "Garifunias" who could help defend Carib territory. Runaways on the Leewards could hide in the forested hills, but the planter militia usually managed to recapture them before long. Only on Antigua did a significant maroon community emerge during the 1680s to foment rebellion among plantation slaves, but in 1687 the planter militia rounded up its members and executed the leaders.

Jamaica's size, its mountainous terrain, and the presence of a Spanish maroon community on the island made control of its slave population a much more difficult matter. Sparser population and a more widely scattered pattern of plantation settlement made it easier for runaways to steal into virtually inaccessible mountainous regions such as the Cockpit country, where large communities of maroons lived undetected for decades. The island experienced six major slave revolts between 1673 and 1694, one of which lasted a year (1685–1686). White authorities dealt ruthlessly with rebels, killing any they captured, but many survivors escaped to the maroons. Jamaica slaves demonstrated by force of arms the love for liberty that their fellows on other English sugar islands could only express by passive resistance.

SUGAR, SLAVES, AND THE ATLANTIC ORDER

By the mid-1650s, the plunge into African slavery had already made Barbados one of the Atlantic world's leading sugar producers. Indeed, the island's output was quickly overtaking that of Brazil, which had dominated world markets in the first half of the century. This development was prompting London officials to think of the Caribbean—indeed, of the New World as a whole—in new ways. The region retained its strategic significance in the clash with Catholic Europe, yet England's Caribbean possessions no longer functioned solely as outposts for raids on Spanish shipping. The islands were beginning to produce a treasure that could rival Spanish American silver, bringing about a fundamental shift in the Atlantic economy. West Indian plantations were providing important new markets for New England farmers. They were attracting a flurry of new London investors. Barbadian sugar was enriching the Dutch merchants whose ships carried it to European markets, even more so than the Chesapeake tobacco trade that Dutch carriers also dominated. Barbadian demand was stimulating a tragic commerce in African slaves. London merchants and policymakers were searching for ways to direct more of the new Caribbean treasure to Bristol and London.

The dim outline of a new Atlantic order was beginning to emerge, thanks in great measure to the growing West Indian traffic in sugar and slaves. It was beginning to transform the international contest for New World dominion as rival powers competed to direct the transatlantic flow of wealth and power. That new impulse was increasingly marking the complex struggle among European and native American rivals over North America as well.

CHRONOLOGY

1624	Captain Thomas Warner establishes English colony on St. Christopher.
1626	Sir William Courteen establishes sugar planting on Barbados.
1628	Anthony Hilton leads colonization of Nevis.
1631	English Puritans establish colony on Providence Island.
1632	English establish plantations on Antigua, Montserrat.
1635	Providence Islanders begin raids on Spanish ports and shipping.
1640	African slave population on Barbados reaches 20,000; European population, 23,000.
1641	General Francisco Díaz Pimienta captures Providence Island.
1661	Barbadian legislature passes race-based slave code.
1667	Irish servants on St. Christopher, Montserrat join French against English masters.
1675	African slaves reach 71,000, 75 percent of Barbados population.

RECOMMENDED READING

The best starting point for further study of English colonization in the Caribbean is Richard S. Dunn, *Sugar and Slaves: The Rise of the Planter Class in the English West Indies, 1624–1713* (New York, 1972). Karen Ordahl Kupperman's *Providence Island, 1630–1641: The Other Puritan Colony* (Cambridge, 1993) provides a fascinating account of this often-forgotten Puritan enterprise. Good general overviews of Caribbean history include Bonham C. Richardson, *The Caribbean in the Wider World, 1492–1992* (Cambridge, 1992), and Jan Rogoziski, *A Brief History of the Caribbean: From the Arawak and the Carib to the Present* (New York, 1992). A sampling of writings by

British colonists in the West Indies is available in Thomas W. Krise, ed., *Caribbeana: An Anthology of English Literature of the West Indies, 1657–1777* (Chicago, 1999).

The elusive histories of Caribbean native peoples are treated in Philip P. Boucher, *Cannibal Encounters: Europeans and the Island Caribs, 1492–1763* (Baltimore, 1992) and Peter Hulme, *Colonial Encounters: Europe and the Native Caribbean, 1492–1797* (London, 1986). Peter Hulme and Neil L. Whitehead, eds., *Wild Majesty: Encounters with the Caribs from Columbus to the Present Day* (Oxford, 1992) provides a revealing collection of firsthand accounts concerning European-native encounter in the Caribbean.

Early English efforts to establish a permanent presence in the seventeenth-century Caribbean are treated in Kenneth R. Andrews, *Ships, Money, and Politics: Seafaring and Naval Enterprises in the Reign of Charles I* (Cambridge, 1991), and Robert Brenner, *Merchants and Revolutionaries: Commercial Change, Political Conflict and London Overseas Traders, 1550–1653* (Cambridge, 1993).

Eric Williams, *Capitalism and Slavery* (Chapel Hill, 1944) remains the classic account of the development of British West Indian slavery. Sidney W. Mintz, *Sweetness and Power: The Place of Sugar in Modern History* (New York, 1985) offers a provocative analysis of the relationship between sugar consumption and the slave trade. A good selection of recent scholarship on slavery throughout the Caribbean is available in Hilary McDonald Beckles and Verene Shepherd, eds., *Caribbean Slave Society and Economy* (New York, 1991). For Barbados, see Hilary McDonald Beckles, *White Servitude and Black Slavery in Barbados, 1627–1715* (Knoxville, 1989).

The development of African culture in the Caribbean has been the subject of innovative scholarship over the past three decades. Sidney W. Mintz and Richard Price, *The Birth of African-American Culture: An Anthropological Perspective* (Boston, 1992) draws from the authors' own work in Caribbean slave culture to provide an excellent introduction to the problems and methods of research into the field. Jerome S. Handler and Frederick W. Lange bring the findings of archaeology to bear in their study of slave culture in Barbados, *Plantation Slavery in Barbados: An Archaeological and Historical Investigation* (Cambridge, Mass., 1978). Ira Berlin and Philip D. Morgan, eds., *Cultivation and Culture: Labor and the Shaping of Slave Life in the Americas* (Charlottesville, Va., 1993) includes essays discussing the role of labor in the development of African American culture among Caribbean slaves. For the experience of African American women in the Caribbean, see essays in David Barry Gaspar and Darlene Clark Hine, eds., *More than Chattel: Black Women and Slavery in the Americas* (Bloomington, Ind., 1996). For slave resistance and the development of maroon communities, see Richard Price, ed., *Maroon Societies: Rebel Slave Communities in the Americas* (Baltimore, 1979); Michael Craton, *Testing the Chains: Resistance to Slavery in the British West Indies* (Ithaca, 1982); and Nancie L. Solien González, *Sojourners of the Caribbean: Ethnogenesis and Ethnohistory of the Garifuna* (Chicago, 1988).

Chapter 7

From Commonwealth to Restoration
The Quest for a Commercial Empire

Iroquois warriors stared across the river in dismay. Their army of 800 Onondaga, Cayuga, and Seneca had expected to score a quick victory that spring day in 1663. Forty years of trade with the Dutch had won the Iroquois wealth and strength of arms sufficient to dominate an already vast territory. They were counting on their muskets to win them another triumph, this time over the powerful Susquehannocks of what is now southern Pennsylvania. They would take the undefended town by surprise and bring home many captives for adoption.

As they came within sight of their target, however, it was the Iroquois' turn for surprise. On the opposite bank of the Susquehanna River lay not an open cluster of dwellings, but a well-defended fort. An amphibious assault across the river would expose the army to murderous fire. Attack by land would prove equally suicidal, for European-style bastions equipped with English-made artillery guarded that approach. A protracted siege was out of the question. The Iroquois had traveled light and were hundreds of miles from home. Indeed, they had expected to return on the strength of food plundered from the town. Clearly, the Dutch-Iroquois fur trade no longer guaranteed military superiority to the Five Nations. The Susquehannock-Maryland trade had more than evened the odds.

Iroquois commanders were not quite ready to give up yet. They had one remaining option—subterfuge. Twenty-five men offered to enter the town, a French Jesuit observer reported, "partly to treat for peace . . . and partly to buy provisions for their return journey." The party hoped that once inside the fort they could capture the big guns and open the gates for their waiting comrades. Instead, the Susquehannocks immediately seized the warriors and made them "mount on scaffolds where, in sight of their own army, they were burned alive."

This gruesome and deeply humiliating experience, coupled with costly clashes that year between Mohawks and English- or French-supplied tribes to the northeast, confronted the Iroquois with the vicious realities of competing for advantage in a confusing commercial environment. Trade had become vital to most Eastern Woodland peoples, sparking trade wars as various groups bid to expand their share of the fur market. Rival European powers readily allied with their native trading partners to protect and increase their own access to pelts.

Moreover, the fur trade constituted only one portion of a rapidly increasing bounty of Caribbean and North American commodities that accelerated competition among merchants from rival colonies and European nations. The English Civil Wars only compounded the challenge for mid-century North American commerce as conflict between supporters of Parliament and those of King Charles I drew attention and resources away from colonial enterprises. Dutch and New England merchants soon stepped into the gap. By 1650 the volume of colonial trade was beginning to attract the notice of London mercantile interests, prompting a search for ways to gain control over Atlantic trade and to channel more of its profits into English pockets. The challenge to do so would have been daunting in the best of times. Complicated as it was by warfare, chronic political instability, and colonial recalcitrance, the task took nearly fifty years.

COLONIAL RESPONSE TO CIVIL WAR

Whatever their reasons for crossing the ocean, seventeenth-century migrants to North America left homelands wracked by recurrent, often violent political and religious controversy. The Thirty Years War embroiled most of the European continent until 1648. For the Netherlands, this war broke a twelve-year truce in a conflict with Spain that had raged since the 1560s. England's first two Stuart monarchs—James I (r. 1603–1625) and his son Charles I (r. 1625–1649)—vied to influence continental affairs while avoiding costly entanglement in war. Yet internal conflict proved more difficult to manage, eventually escalating into a series of bloody civil wars that consumed English lives and resources for much of the 1640s. Despite Dutch military troubles during this period, their maritime trade prospered. Dutch ships dominated Atlantic sea-lanes by the time the dust settled in England.

The English Civil Wars

Conflict between the autocratic James I and the elected members of Parliament began soon after he succeeded Queen Elizabeth to the English throne in 1603, and only intensified when the throne passed to Charles I in 1625. Many royal policies—the granting of lucrative commercial monopolies to court favorites, for example—fueled popular discontent, but the crown's hostility to far-reaching religious reform sparked the most vocal protest. Throughout the kingdom, Puritans became adamant in their demand for radical change.

Tensions grew so severe that in 1629, Charles attempted to rule the country without Parliament's assistance. The strategy backfired. When Charles was finally forced to recall Parliament in 1640 because he was running out of money, Parliament demanded major constitutional reforms. Militant Puritans, supported by many members of Parliament, insisted on restructuring the Church of England. Abolishing the office of bishop was high on their list. In this angry political atmosphere, Charles took up arms against the supporters of Parliament. The confrontation between Royalists and Parliamentarians set off a long and bloody series of civil wars. In 1649, the victorious Parliamentarians beheaded Charles, and for almost a decade, Oliver Cromwell, a skilled general and committed Puritan, governed England.

New England's Response

The recall of Parliament and the outbreak of civil war brought a halt to Puritan migration while provoking great soul-searching among those who had made New England their home. During the early 1640s, over a thousand colonists concluded that the Lord wanted them to return to England and contribute to the great work of reformation that Parliament had begun. Yet over 17,000 remained to pursue the holy mission that they believed God continued to set out for their commonwealth.

The end of the Great Migration also provoked an economic crisis, setting off an intense search for new sources of commerce that could repay English creditors and stockholders of the Massachusetts Bay Company. Throughout the 1630s the New England economy had relied on the steady flow of new immigrants with money to purchase colonial products and services needed to start a new life in America. Without these buyers and the hard currency they brought with them, the price of colonial goods fell precipitously and a massive trade deficit quickly drained New England's money supply. Early experiments in textile manufacturing and ironworks failed. A few merchant families such as the Pynchons of the Connecticut River prospered from the fur trade for a time before the supply reached its limits in the mid-1650s.

New England's economic salvation eventually came from Atlantic fishing and shipping. Their proximity to the great Newfoundland fishing banks gave colonial fishermen an advantage over European competitors, while the abundance of timber provided a cheap source of lumber and naval stores for shipbuilding. New England craftsmen could also fashion native hardwoods into the barrel staves and timber products that proved valuable commodities in Spanish and Portuguese wine islands such as the Azores and Madeira. The east Atlantic islands also provided one ready market for New England fish and agricultural products, while the sugar islands of the Caribbean provided another. Boston seafarers quickly recognized that they could reap even more profits by sailing from the wine islands to the West African coast, where they could purchase slaves for transport to Barbados.

While Civil War raged in their homeland, New England merchants and shippers developed an Atlantic trade along polygon routes that connected their ports with London, the wine islands, West Africa, and the Caribbean. By 1660, they became important contributors to the emerging Atlantic commercial system. Success depended on far more than a shipper's ability to get a vessel into port. In the highly personal world of seventeenth-century commerce, those with transatlantic connections to patrons, clients, merchant "friends," and family stood to profit most. The Hutchinson family of Antinomian fame, for example, built a lucrative transatlantic trade among a network of family members living in Boston, Rhode Island, London, and Barbados. The fortune they began amassing during the 1640s became the foundation of a colonial mercantile dynasty that endured until the American Revolution.

The English Civil Wars provoked less of an economic crisis in England's tobacco and sugar colonies, though it did bring significant political unrest to Maryland (see Chapter 4). Virginia's Governor Berkeley supported Charles I. Most Virginians went along, since a Royalist stance offered such a useful pretext for ignoring Parliament's directives. English neglect of colonial affairs during the 1640s gave Virginia officials opportunity to assert the colony's right to free trade while declaring that "noe lawe should bee established within the Kingdome of England concerninge us without the consent of a grand Assembly here." The Assembly acted on this declaration by inviting Dutch merchants to "trade or traffique for the commodities of the collony in any shipp or shipps of their owne." Dutch merchants happily complied, and tobacco exports climbed steadily over the next two decades.

Civil War, Plantations, and the Dutch

Sugar planters on Barbados initially responded to English events with studied neutrality, declaring that "against the kinge we are resolved never to be, and without the freindshipe of the perliament and free trade of London ships we are not able to subsist." Yet Barbadian Royalist "Cavaliers" and Parliamentarian "Roundheads" clashed in the later 1640s, and the Cavaliers eventually won control of the government. Both sides nevertheless asserted Barbados's right to free trade and welcomed Dutch ships alongside those from England and New England. Until 1660, Dutch merchants carried the lion's share of Barbadian sugar to European markets.

TRADE RIVALRIES

The Civil Wars pushed England's New World colonies to fend largely for themselves in an increasingly competitive Atlantic environment. The mid-seventeenth century witnessed a great expansion of trade throughout the Atlantic as the English, French, and Dutch all pinned their expectations on the development of Caribbean and North American trade. This whirl of new commercial activity left Spain, which had dominated the sixteenth-century Atlantic, struggling to maintain its hold on New World territory as its aggressive rivals overtook it by developing the commercial potential of their American outposts. The growth of trade and competition made the Atlantic a risky environment for all who ventured into it, whether an investor in a European center, a sailor on a merchant vessel, a planter on American soil, or an Indian trapper or hunter. Although the outcome of this mid-century scramble for dominance of New World markets was far from assured, contemporaries believed that the advantage lay with the Dutch.

Dutch *Fluitschips* and American Commerce

In welcoming Dutch vessels, Chesapeake and Caribbean planters were merely recognizing how much seventeenth-century Atlantic trade depended on Dutch shipping. The economical Dutch *fluitschips*, with their long, nearly flat-bottomed hulls, could carry much larger cargoes at cheaper rates than any other ships of European design. Most *fluits* were operated by small joint-stock firms that were flexible, inexpensive, and competitive. In 1601 Dutch ships already outnumbered English in the Port of London by 360 to 207. By 1670, the Dutch merchant fleet outnumbered those of England, France, Spain, Portugal, and Germany combined. English plantation profits, especially in tobacco where prices had fallen steeply during the 1630s, depended on the cheap rates and unparalleled access to European markets which the Dutch provided.

By the mid-seventeenth century, the Dutch had come to concentrate their New World enterprises primarily on shipping rather than colonization. Their settlements were few but strategically located for the carrying trade. New Amsterdam gave the Dutch an excellent harbor with ready access to Iroquois fur trade as well as English plantations, while the islands of Curaçao and St. Eustatius gave them Caribbean harbors in the heart of the lucrative sugar-producing region. The Dutch West India Company waged a long and expensive campaign to establish a colony on the coast of Brazil, but the firm Portuguese hold on the region forced the company to abandon its efforts in 1654. Portuguese planters nevertheless relied on Dutch vessels to get Brazilian sugar to European markets.

After 1640, the majority of enslaved Africans who labored on seventeenth-century Brazilian and Caribbean sugar plantations arrived on Dutch ships. The Dutch captured the Portuguese fort of Elmina in 1637 and another Portuguese outpost at Axim in 1641. From 1641 to 1649 they also occupied Angola. From these African ports, Dutch ships carried hundreds of thousands of slaves on the transatlantic leg of an efficient trading circuit that linked Europe, Africa, Brazil, the Caribbean, and North America. Dutch investors reaped handsome profits from ships, which seldom left an Atlantic port without a cargo in humans or goods.

Even with the sugar trade, New World shipping comprised only a fraction of Dutch commerce during this period. Fully three-fourths of Dutch capital was invested in Baltic trade with Scandinavian and Slavic states as late as the 1670s. Yet the transatlantic carrying trade made many Amsterdam investors rich. Dutch access to mid-century European markets forced Old World merchants to compete for American products, allowing planters of many nations to obtain better prices. Cheap Dutch rates enabled the planters to pocket more of their profits.

The Iroquois and the Competition for Furs

European planters were not the only New World inhabitants whose profits depended on the Dutch carrying trade. The Iroquois, too, had become heavily dependent on Dutch traders along the Hudson, and a trading triangle between New Amsterdam, New England, and the Iroquois benefited Puritan traders as well. The

European economic historian Jan De Vries has pointed out that cheap Dutch shipping opened markets for many new manufactured goods, and the Iroquois proved eager consumers of these European products. The resulting commerce brought a wave of unprecedented prosperity to Dutch and Iroquois alike.

Dutch visitors to mid-seventeenth century Iroquois villages could find ample evidence of the popularity their trade goods enjoyed. Longhouses often sported "interior doors made of split planks furnished with iron hinges." Others contained "iron chains, bolts, harrow teeth, hoops, [and] spikes." Visitors commonly met Iroquois men and women wearing imported linen shirts, which served as excellent rainwear when treated with bear grease. Jewelry of glass, silver, copper, and brass adorned the bodies of women and men alike. Individuals wore in their hair decorative combs carved with intricate new designs made possible by European metal tools. Iroquois women cooked meals in brass and iron kettles instead of ceramic pots. Worn-out kettles furnished metal for arrowheads and jewelry. As European imports displaced traditional items of bone and stone, knowledge of those crafts died out, increasing Iroquois dependence on European goods. Many popular trade items virtually guaranteed a steady market in replacements and supplies. Guns, for example, required an ongoing supply of bullets and powder.

During the first half of the seventeenth century, Hudson River commerce stimulated a trade triangle as Dutch merchants bartered imported goods for highly valued wampum shells in the English and Narragansett communities of Narragansett Bay, then sailed up the Hudson to trade the wampum for beaver pelts. All parties profited from a pattern of exchange in which wampum circulated as currency throughout the Northeast. The beautifully crafted wampum belts that became a trademark of Iroquois culture emerged as a product of this cross-cultural trade.

Successful commerce with the Iroquois rested on the European trader's ability to establish strong personal ties with his contacts. The trader Jacob Eelckens, for example, earned an enduring place in Iroquois memory as "the Governor Called Jacques" by dealing according to native standards of generous reciprocity in his exchanges with the Iroquois. So trusted was Eelckens that when Dutch West India Company officials ousted him in the mid-1620s, he posed a serious threat to company interests by returning as an English agent a decade later to trade with his Iroquois friends. Observers confirmed Eelckens's later claim that during his 1633 expedition "the Indians would not trade with the Dutch" as long as he was among them. Subsequent Dutch traders learned to lubricate the wheels of trade by according at least grudging consideration to Iroquois standards of hospitality and exchange.

By the 1650s, however, Iroquois-Dutch relations were beginning to come unraveled under new political and economic strains. Overproduction of wampum made it much less valuable as currency. Warfare between the Dutch and native peoples on Long Island and Mahicans on the lower Hudson River disrupted Dutch-Iroquois trade. Desperate Dutch merchants began hiring *boslopers* or "woods-runners" who were little better than thugs, often coercing their Iroquois trading partners to accept low prices or stealing goods outright. The repercussions of these actions rippled throughout Iroquoia, sparking war between Iroquois and surrounding tribes as headmen sought to recoup trading losses with new sources of furs and tribute, as well as to acquire captives whom they could adopt to replace kinsmen lost to warfare or disease. Mohawk warriors wrought havoc as far east as the Connecticut River Valley, intensifying the strain between the Dutch and the English as well as the Indian allies of each.

French Missions and Merchandise

Divisions among Iroquois factions also deepened as clans alienated by Dutch abuses sought open alliances with the French of the St. Lawrence River valley. Before 1650 Iroquois resistance had frustrated French traders and Jesuit missionaries, who decried the "perfidy which they have shown toward the Preachers of the Gospel." Indeed, during the 1640s the Iroquois had engaged in a series of sustained offensives against Quebec's Huron allies, culminating in the destruction of the central Huron villages and the French mission of Sainte-Marie in 1649. Iroquois warriors had taken hundreds of Huron captives for adoption, martyred three Jesuit missionaries, and deprived the French of the native commercial and military allies on whom they had hitherto relied to check Iroquois-Dutch ascendancy in the region.

This loss, coupled with the promise of new converts, made the Jesuits eager to exploit mid-century Iroquois-Dutch tensions. They readily accepted the invitation of Seneca, Onondaga, and Mohawk emissaries to establish missions in tribal villages. Iroquois headmen hoped that resident priests would encourage Catholic Huron adoptees to remain in Iroquois villages. The French Jesuits also hoped to establish trade on terms more favorable than those the Dutch *boslopers* had begun offering.

The arrival of French Jesuit missionaries in Iroquois as in Huron villages often signaled the beginning of long-term relationships, which supplemented spiritual benefits with tangible gains in trade, weapons, and military assistance. Since 1639, the Jesuits had acted as agents for the Associates of the Company of New France, displacing the French traders they regarded as a hindrance to their work. This dual role, which had gained toeholds for the missionaries in villages throughout Huronia, now afforded inroads to Iroquoia as eagerness for trade overcame hostility to the Catholic faith. Through such methods the French gradually expanded their influence, diverting Iroquois furs from the Hudson to the St. Lawrence Rivers while rendering the region's political and military stability even more elusive.

In addition to cultivating new friendships among the Iroquois, French missionaries and traders labored to expand their contacts throughout the Great Lakes as colonists consolidated settlements on the St. Lawrence River. By mid-century New France boasted a population of 2,000 colonists, three-fourths of whom supported themselves through traditional European farming. Profits from the fur trade expanded steadily as distant tribes tapped into the French commercial network. Crown officials and French merchants became convinced of New France's commercial promise as fur shipments valued as high as 300,000 livres per year began arriving in French ports on a regular basis.

Iroquois factionalism remained an obstacle to French ambitions for their colony, however. Many headmen remained hostile to French missionaries and traders despite Dutch abuses, and Iroquois proximity to French trade routes made it possible to disrupt their Great Lakes commerce through frequent raids. French colonial officials had to counter Iroquois ascendancy through military action, while traders explored alternative ways of bringing Great Lakes furs to market.

Economic Stagnation on the Spanish Frontier

By the mid-seventeenth century, Spanish hopes of finding the fabled North American cities of gold had begun to fade, and Spanish officials came to regard their colonies in Florida and New Mexico as defensive outposts for nearby shipping and mining operations. Development of Spanish colonies north of the Rio Grande was hindered by restrictive imperial policies and structural weaknesses in the Spanish economy. Ruinous inflation driven by American gold made Spanish manufactures uncompetitive even within Spain itself, producing a massive trade deficit that left the country dependent on foreign goods. Spanish officials discouraged colonial manufacturing and restricted trade largely to Spanish goods carried on Spanish vessels to only a few American ports. Goods bound for Texas and New Mexico, for example, had to pass through the viceroyalty at Vera Cruz on the Mexican coast. Officials refused to open the Texas coast to shipping throughout the colonial period despite its abundance of good harbors. Efforts by New Mexican colonists to link Santa Fe with the Gulf of Mexico also met with bureaucratic resistance.

Within this restrictive environment, Spanish colonists found it difficult to thrive. Nevertheless, they did develop the economic opportunities that were available to them, often by cruel exploitation. Frontier officials in Santa Fe, for example, exacted labor from the region's Pueblos to produce items for export to New Spain such as leather goods, salt, and wagons. New Mexican Spaniards also enslaved nearby native peoples—often enemies of the Pueblos such as the Apaches—for export to the mining regions of New Spain. Spanish traders also fanned out into the Florida and New Mexico countryside in search of more legitimate profits in furs and hides. Deerskins came to serve as currency in the Spanish American Southeast, benefiting the local economy. Yet the fur trade never became an important element of the Spanish Atlantic economy, as it did for the French and English. The supply of furs in Spanish-controlled areas was not as large as the supply further north, and the expense and scarcity of Spanish trade goods made it difficult to compete with English and French traders who could offer a much wider variety at much lower prices.

Spanish Franciscan missionaries continually spoke out against the abuses of the settlers and occasionally managed to persuade Crown authorities to step in. In one instance, the governor of New Mexico, Juan de Eulate (g. 1618–1625) suffered arrest and conviction for slave trading after Franciscans complained about the practice. All too often, however, the Franciscans' complaints masked competition for scarce native labor. Spanish policy allowed the missionaries to make use of native laborers for "things necessary for the church and convenience of the living quarters," a requirement which the Franciscans interpreted very liberally. Colonial governors regularly charged the Franciscans with enriching themselves at Indian expense. Indeed, competition for native labor sometimes led to open conflict between the missionaries and their secular rivals.

Despite abuses by both secular settlers and missionaries, many Pueblos found ways to accommodate to some aspects of Spanish rule while resisting others so long as harvests remained sufficient and enemy tribes were kept at bay. Pueblos incorporated aspects of Spanish culture into their daily lives. Many spoke Spanish in everyday business. Potters incorporated Spanish motifs into their vessels, while farmers planted and tended Spanish-introduced crops and livestock. Pueblos also learned to make woolen textiles, which changed their manner of dress. A significant minority sincerely embraced Catholicism as well.

Spanish borderland colonies stagnated as a result of Spain's seventeenth-century economic problems and imperial policies. While the Anglo-American population rose dramatically, the colonial population of Spanish Florida and New Mexico remained static or declined. While the English, French, and Dutch reaped ever-increasing profits from their North American trade and plantation enterprises, the borderlands became a steady drain on Spanish royal coffers.

CROMWELL'S QUEST FOR DOMINION

Despite growing Atlantic competition, the English Civil Wars prevented Parliament from making any serious initiatives in commercial policy for most of the 1640s. London merchants fretted while Dutch shippers grew richer every year from Chesapeake tobacco and Caribbean sugar. After the execution of Charles I, the Commonwealth Parliament turned its attention to neglected matters of commerce. The great London mercantile companies wanted to strengthen their traditional monopolies over trade at the expense of the Dutch, and they found the Commonwealth Parliament receptive to their interests. Oliver Cromwell, who became Lord Protector in 1653, was less friendly to London merchants, but the chronic lack of funds that bedeviled a succession of English governments during the 1650s did make him alert to potential sources of new customs revenue. Cromwell's New World policy, however, flowed mainly from his quest to secure "godly rule" in England and extend its influence elsewhere.

The First Navigation Act

The long-running tensions between Dutch and English commercial interests reached a breaking point in the early 1650s. For many years their common religious interests and common enemies had held the two countries together despite commercial strife. In 1649, however, the Dutch signed a treaty with Denmark that threatened to widen the commercial gap between England and the Netherlands by giving Dutch ships preferred access to Baltic ports. Dutch diplomats added damage to insult by rebuffing the Commonwealth Parliament's attempts to forge an alliance between England and the Netherlands, Europe's two republics. The commercial stakes were already high and rising every year as the growth of world trade promised unprecedented profits and power to the nations that could control it. English merchants thought the time had come to press their bid for a share of world markets by attempting to channel English plantation profits to London rather than Amsterdam. In 1651 the Commonwealth Parliament obliged by passing the first navigation act.

The Navigation Act of 1651 was expressly designed to drive Dutch ships out of English colonial markets. It prohibited ships of any nation except England or English plantations from importing colonial commodities of Asia, Africa, or America into any English port. It also prohibited merchants of any nation including England from importing any goods except those loaded in the place where they were actually produced or first shipped, and permitted foreign-owned vessels to import only the commodities of their own people. This threatened to cut deeply into the virtual monopoly which the Dutch exercised over European trade, since after 1651 Dutch merchants could no longer import goods to England indirectly through Holland nor carry goods to England from any other European port.

It was one thing for Parliament to pass the act, but quite another to enforce it. Attempts to do so against Dutch ships in European waters sparked a series of incidents that quickly escalated into the full-blown Anglo-Dutch War of 1652–1654. The English suffered early setbacks, but eventually triumphed under the command of Admiral Robert Blake over what was thought to be invincible Dutch sea power. Yet even after striking peace with the Dutch in 1654, the English navy had more than it could do to police the act in European waters. The ships and soldiers that Cromwell sent to enforce the act in colonial ports met success only as long as they remained. Colonists, left largely to themselves, continued to trade when and where they wished.

Oliver Cromwell made his most enduring contribution to England's New World empire almost by accident when he launched a secret, semipiratical expedition to capture a large Spanish island in the Caribbean. Cromwell's "Western Design" arose from a strong religious impulse to strike a crippling blow at the imperial power Puritans regarded as the nation of Antichrist. The "Godly" wanted revenge for all the injuries the Spanish had inflicted on English settlers in the Caribbean. Cromwell and his advisors also hoped to gain an important worldly side-benefit by capturing a Spanish treasure fleet that could pay the costs of the expedition and supplement sagging revenues at home. The memory of the Elizabethan Sea Dogs (see Chapter 3) inspired hope that a Cromwellian force could achieve even greater glory against a foe whose might had now been declining for more than half a century.

The Western Design and Jamaica

Even in decline, however, Spain proved a tenacious adversary. The force that sailed under the combined command of Admiral William Penn and General Robert Venables failed miserably at their attempt to capture their first target, the island of Hispaniola, in the spring of 1655. Tropical heat, poorly disciplined troops, and lack of coordination between the army and naval vessels made them vulnerable to a much smaller Spanish force. Hispaniola's defenders slaughtered troops already half-dead from heat and thirst, "hacking at them fiercely with a clumsy weapon in the shape of a half moon, which they are accustomed to use also to wound wild beasts in the country." English losses totaled 1,000 men, nearly a fifth of the expedition.

Jamaica proved easier prey and contemporaries soon came to the conclusion that it was "far more proper for their purposes." One observer noted that it had "an excellent harbour and is accounted the most healthful and plentiful" of all Spain's

Caribbean possessions. Another gleefully pointed out that it lay "in the very heart of the Spaniard to gall him." The island was poorly defended and its governor, Don Juan Ramirez, surrendered without a fight. Ramirez yielded the island and everything on it—weapons, ships, goods, and estates—to the English. Landowners were allowed to depart with only their clothing, personal effects such as books and writings, and provisions for their voyage. Laborers and artisans who accepted English rule could remain. These terms of surrender echoed those offered English colonists of Providence Island when the Spanish captured it 14 years earlier (see Chapter 6).

Jamaica ultimately fulfilled the expectations of its early promoters, but not in Cromwell's day. Its good soil and relatively temperate climate supported prosperous sugar plantations as well as a diversified economy that could survive the vagaries of the international sugar market better than islands such as Barbados, whose economy depended almost exclusively on sugar production. In the second half of the seventeenth century, Jamaica proved an ideal site for English pirates and privateers to stage raids on Spanish shipping and settlements. The nineteenth-century West Indian writer Michael Scott estimated that Jamaica-based privateers eventually netted "a stream of gold and silver flowing into the Bank of England, to the extent of three millions of pounds sterling annually, in return for British manufactures." For Cromwell, however, "this Jamaica business" proved a constant drain on the treasury. Many of the island's Spanish inhabitants went into hiding in its remote mountain forests, where they organized a stiff guerrilla resistance that terrorized English settlers and frustrated English troops. Hundreds of soldiers succumbed to tropical diseases such as dysentery and yellow fever during the first year of occupation. Spanish resisters did not give up the fight for the island until the Restoration when Charles II proclaimed a cessation of hostilities with Spain in 1660.

RESTORATION AND THE COMMERCIAL IMPULSE

In 1660, following Cromwell's death from natural causes, the Stuarts returned to the English throne. As Charles II (r. 1660–1685) returned to London, tens of thousands of people lined the flower-strewn road, celebrating the Restoration with shouts of "God save King Charles" while women tossed posies of sweet herbs at the royal carriage. The political situation that awaited the king and his Restoration Parliament was less congenial. Two decades of conflict had saddled Charles II with chronic political instability, a heavy burden of debt, and a war with Spain that the country could ill afford. The Dutch continued to expand their share of world commerce at English expense, even trading with impunity in England's own colonial ports.

Neither Charles nor his brother James II (r. 1685–1688) were able to resolve the political or economic problems of the Restoration period, but they began addressing issues of trade in ways that took much greater account of England's colonial possessions. After 1660, intervention in colonial affairs replaced the indifference of the early Stuart monarchs. Englishmen of various sorts—courtiers, merchants, parliamentarians—concluded that the colonists should be brought more tightly under the control of the mother country. The regulatory policies that evolved during this period formed a framework for an empire that survived with only minor adjustment until 1765.

As the newly restored monarchy began establishing rules for the empire, planters of the Chesapeake as well as Puritans of New England discovered that they were not as independent as they imagined. John Norton, a respected Congregational minister, reminded the legislators of Massachusetts Bay in 1661 that "it is not a Gospel-spirit to be against Kings . . . 'tis neither Gospel nor English Spirit for any of us to be against the Government by Kings, Lords and Commons." New England Puritans, Chesapeake tobacco planters, and Barbadian sugar barons shared a duty to submit to royal authority. It would take over thirty years to work out what submission meant.

The famous eighteenth-century Scottish economist Adam Smith coined the term *mercantilist system* to describe Great Britain's commercial regulations, and ever since, his phrase has appeared in history books. Smith's term, however, is misleading. It suggests that English policymakers during the reign of Charles II had developed a well-integrated set of ideas about the nature of international commerce and a carefully planned set of mercantilist government policies to implement them. **Response to Economic Competition**

They did nothing of the sort. Administrators responded to particular problems, usually on an individual basis. In 1668, Charles informed his sister, "The thing which is nearest to the heart of the nation is trade and all that belongs to it." National interest alone, however, did not shape public policy. Instead, the needs of several powerful interest groups gave rise to English commercial regulation.

Each group looked to colonial commerce to solve a different problem. For his part, the king wanted money. English merchants remained eager to exclude Dutch rivals from lucrative American markets. The experience of the Interregnum period showed that English merchants needed government assistance to compete successfully with the Dutch, even in Virginia and Massachusetts Bay. Cromwell's success in the Anglo-Dutch War of 1652–1654 had also demonstrated the value of an effective naval force. The landed gentry who sat in Parliament wanted to strengthen the navy, and that in turn meant expansion of the domestic shipbuilding industry. Almost everyone agreed that England should establish a more favorable balance of trade, that is, increase exports, decrease imports, and grow richer at the expense of other European states. None of these ideas was particularly innovative, but taken together they provided a blueprint for England's first empire.

The Restoration Parliament approached the problem of trade by passing a Navigation Act in 1660 that bore strong similarities to the earlier act of 1651. Also known as the Enumeration Act, this statute was the most important piece of imperial legislation drafted before the American Revolution. Colonists throughout England's possessions paid close attention to the details of this statute, which stated (1) that no ship could trade in the colonies unless it had been constructed in either England or America and carried a crew that was at least 75 percent English (for these purposes colonists counted as Englishmen), and (2) that certain enumerated goods of great value that were not produced in England—tobacco, **An Empire of Trade**

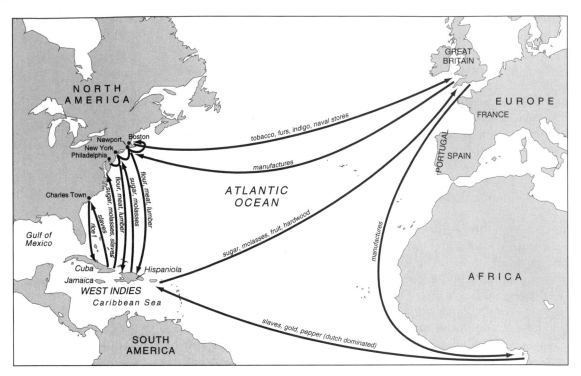

Major Colonial Trade Routes of the Seventeenth Century

The volume of English colonial trade increased steadily throughout the seventeenth century. The trade between New England and the West Indies grew rapidly during the English Civil War and remained important to the mainland economy throughout the colonial period.

sugar, cotton, indigo, dyewoods, ginger—could be transported from the colonies only to England or an English colonial port. In 1704, Parliament added rice and molasses to the enumerated list; in 1705, rosins, tars, and turpentines needed for shipbuilding were included.

The act of 1660 was masterfully conceived. It encouraged the development of domestic shipbuilding and prohibited European rivals from obtaining enumerated goods anywhere except England without restricting English shipping as the act of 1651 had done. Because the Americans had to pay import duties in England on enumerated staples such as sugar and tobacco (for this purpose the colonists did not count as Englishmen), the legislation also provided the crown with another source of income.

In 1663, Parliament supplemented this legislation with a second Navigation Act known as the Staple Act, which stated that, with a few notable exceptions, nothing could be imported into America unless it had first been transshipped through the mother country, a process that greatly added to the price ultimately paid by colonial consumers.

Parliament could not simply legislate the Dutch out of existence, no matter how well-conceived its Navigation Acts. England's principal rival possessed a much larger merchant fleet as well as an excellent North American port at New Amsterdam, which gave them ready access to English colonies. In 1664, the Crown acted to remove this thorn in the side of their budding empire by dispatching a fleet of warships to New Netherland. The commander of this force, Colonel Richard Nicolls, ordered the colonists to surrender. The colony's last director-general, a colorful character named Peter Stuyvesant (g. 1647–1664), rushed wildly about the city urging the settlers to resist the English. But no one obeyed. Even the Dutch remained deaf to Stuyvesant's appeals. They accepted the Articles of Capitulation, a generous agreement that allowed Dutch nationals to remain in the province and to retain their property. New Netherland thus became New York, a chartered English possession that Charles II had already granted his brother James, Duke of York.

Eliminating the Dutch

The capture of New Netherland in 1664 contributed greatly to the outbreak of the second Anglo-Dutch War later that year. Neither this conflict (1664–1667) nor a third war (1672–1674) achieved decisive results for either side. In 1675 an English observer estimated total Dutch shipping at 900,000 tons to England's 500,000, and English pamphleteers fretted about Dutch competition into the eighteenth century. The wars, however, did help to reduce the Dutch presence in English colonial harbors, creating an opportunity for an unanticipated rival. In the aftermath, New England merchant ships sailed out of Boston, Salem, and Newport to become formidable world competitors in maritime commerce.

During the 1660s, the colonists showed little enthusiasm for the new imperial system. Reaction to these regulations varied from region to region. Virginians bitterly protested the Navigation Acts. The collection of English customs on tobacco greatly reduced the colonial planters' profits. Moreover, the exclusion of the Dutch from the trade meant that growers often had to sell their crops at artificially low prices. The Navigation Acts hit the small planters especially hard, for they were least able to absorb increased production costs. Even though the governor of Virginia lobbied on the planters' behalf, the crown turned a deaf ear. By 1670, import duties on tobacco accounted for almost £100,000, a sum the king could scarcely do without.

Colonial Response and English Adjustment

At first, New Englanders simply ignored the commercial regulations. Indeed, one Massachusetts merchant reported in 1664 that Boston entertained "near one hundred sail of ships, this year, of ours and strangers." The strangers, of course, were the Dutch, who had no intention of obeying the Navigation Acts so long as they could reach colonial ports. Some New England merchants found clever ways to circumvent the Navigation Acts. These crafty traders picked up cargoes of enumerated goods such as sugar or tobacco, sailed to another colonial port (thereby technically fulfilling the letter of the law), and then made directly for Holland or France. Along the way they paid no customs.

To plug this loophole, Parliament passed the Navigation Act of 1673. This statute established a plantation duty, a sum of money equal to normal English customs duties to be collected on enumerated products at the various colonial ports.

New Englanders could now sail wherever they pleased within the empire, but they could not escape paying customs. Parliament also extended the jurisdiction of the London Customs Commissioners to America. And in 1675, as part of this new imperial firmness, the Privy Council formed a powerful subcommittee, the Lords of Trade, whose members monitored colonial affairs.

Despite these legal reforms, serious obstacles impeded the execution of imperial policy. The customs service did not have enough effective agents at American ports to enforce the Navigation Acts effectively, and some men sent from the mother country did more harm than good. Edward Randolph, head of the imperial customs service in New England, was such a person. He was dispatched to Boston in 1676 to gather information about the conduct of colonial trade. His behavior was so obnoxious, his reports about New Englanders so condescending, that he became the most hated man in late seventeenth-century Massachusetts. Nevertheless, Randolph's favor with high-ranking London officials enabled him to retain his position. For nearly two decades he conducted a game of imperial cat-and-mouse with New England merchants and magistrates who proved highly adept at finding weaknesses in the new trade regulations. Every new colonial trick for thwarting the Navigation Acts prompted Randolph to fire off another letter to London with a suggestion for closing the loophole. Despite such efforts in New England and other colonial ports, the dream of controlling trade from London proved elusive for much of the century.

Pirates and Privateers

Recalcitrant colonial officials were not the only obstacles to the implementation of the Navigation Acts. England's naval force was also too small to enforce the regulations or protect the nation's far-flung commercial interests. All too often, smugglers escaped detection and English merchants lost whole cargoes to the pirates who plied the Caribbean and the North American coast.

Seventeenth-century Atlantic pirates bore little resemblance to the swash-bucklers of Hollywood legend. From the earliest days of European colonization, the Caribbean attracted adventurers who dreamed of instant wealth and were not particular about the methods used to obtain it (see Chapter 3). The first American pirates arose as some of these sailor-adventurers ended their voyage in shipwreck on Caribbean reefs. The castaways formed small interethnic island communities where people of various European backgrounds often cooperated with surviving Native Americans and escaped or marooned Africans. Inhabitants of such communities soon developed a brisk trade in provisioning passing ships with wild meat smoked and dried on a rack, or *boucan*, over an open fire. The garb of these early buccaneers, as they were called, was a badge of their trade: shoes made from freshly flayed leg skins of calves, wrapped raw around the feet, tied with tendons and allowed to dry; rough jackets and trousers caked with dried blood from animal slaughter. This wild appearance added shock to surprise as the first buccaneer pirates ambushed merchant ships from open boats.

The distinction between pirates and patriots remained as obscure in the seventeenth century as it had been a hundred years before. Buccaneers who made the Spanish the primary target of their piracy became heroes in Restoration England. In wartime, buccaneer captains could obtain official "letters of marque" which made them privateers, that is, privately funded agents authorized to seize enemy vessels in the king's name. After 1660 crown officials frequently issued letters of marque authorizing seizure of smugglers and pirates as well. Crown officials offset the high risks of such expeditions by allowing the owners, captains, and crews of privateer vessels to keep the booty so long as the king received his percentage in duties and fees. The promise of rich rewards attracted English investors as well as Atlantic buccaneers, and the uncertainties of international commerce made it relatively easy to claim even legitimate merchant vessels of one's own nation as prizes.

After 1660, Jamaica's Port Royal became a major base of buccaneer operations, conferring on the city a reputation as the richest and wickedest of many British colonial ports that offered safe haven to pirates. From there Henry Morgan, the most famous buccaneer captain, staged a series of brash, brutal raids on Spanish colonial shipping and settlements that netted a fortune in gold. A 1670 foray into Panama gained Morgan, his men, and his Jamaican investors a total prize worth £70,000. Though that year's signing of the Treaty of Madrid rendered the venture illegal, this technicality neither caused Morgan to forfeit his treasure nor prevented his winning English knighthood and a post as Jamaica's lieutenant governor.

As the volume of Atlantic trade increased, England gradually joined other European trading nations in recognizing that commercial stability was more important than minor pirate victories. Before the 1690s, however, piracy and smuggling proved very difficult to stamp out. Port Royal may have been the richest pirate haven, but mainland colonial ports such as Charleston, New York, and Newport often found pirates an important source of scarce goods and specie. Colonial governors frequently winked at the presence of pirate vessels in their harbors, and friendly colonial judges and juries often legitimated captured prizes on flimsy legal grounds.

War, Rebellion, and the Covenant Chain

The difficulties encountered by London officials in their search for imperial order stemmed not only from the chaotic conditions of seventeenth-century Atlantic trade and diplomacy, but also from internal tensions within the mainland colonies themselves. For colonists, London's intrusion into their commercial affairs only compounded the strains that confronted their governments in the 1660s and 1670s. Virginia officials were struggling to contain a rising and increasingly volatile population of poor yeomen and landless laborers, losers in the scramble for land, wealth, and status who were being pushed to the colony's hardscrabble fringes where they often clashed with the native population. New England enjoyed more social stability, but steady expansion along the region's river valleys and into the hinterland was pressing the native population, sparking tension and resentment. The English had only recently secured New York, and the colony's governors were struggling to find the best means of ruling a substantial non-English population while cultivating an enduring alliance with their powerful Iroquois neighbors. Colonists everywhere continued to perceive their foothold in

North America as tenuous. The bounds of settlement remained narrow, and the settlers seemed surrounded by potentially hostile forces of indigenous peoples and European competitors.

After 1660, native groups grew increasingly conscious both of European vulnerability and of the mixed implications of continued European expansion. In the Chesapeake and New England, friction between expansive colonists and the indigenous peoples whose lands they coveted erupted into war during the 1670s. The Iroquois League, however, faced a more complex situation in which the recent transfer of the Hudson River colony to the English opened promising new avenues for increasing their might. Prior experience with the English had taught them to negotiate with caution, and Francophile factions sought to sway the entire league to ally with New France. This dynamic, coupled with the Iroquois ability to act in both the Chesapeake and New England, gave the Five Nations a pivotal role in the future of England's North American settlements.

Elsewhere in North America tensions were also building between natives and Europeans. Chronic Spanish abuses in New Mexico pushed the Pueblos to open revolt in 1680. A more aggressive French colonial policy after 1660 sparked a renewal of strife with the Iroquois.

The stakes were high everywhere on the continent. The wars severely tested the durability of colonial rule, exposing the weaknesses of provincial government and military power to officials on both sides of the Atlantic. In their aftermath, European rulers began exploring ways to strengthen their hold on New World territory, bringing colonial governments under closer supervision by imperial centers of power. Yet only in New Mexico did native peoples win an outright victory and expel their Spanish enemies from the region. In New England, where colonists faced a similar native challenge that left the economy in shambles, the Europeans ultimately survived. The contrast is instructive, revealing not so much the superiority of English to Spanish colonial might, but the strength of alliance between the English and their powerful Iroquois partners.

Pueblo Revolt

By the summer of 1680, the Spanish had governed New Mexico for more than eighty years. The periodic local revolts that punctuated Spanish rule served mainly to confirm official confidence in the strength of the regime over a fragmented and demoralized native population. A series of droughts began devastating Pueblo communities around 1660, sometimes leaving starving inhabitants to die "along the roads, in the ravines, and in their huts." Navajo and Apache nomads added to the misery by staging repeated raids on scarce Pueblo maize and livestock. Two decades of starvation, disease, and depredation seemed to expose the impotence of the Franciscans' God, prompting Pueblos to return to traditional religious observance. Spanish attempts to suppress Pueblo ceremonies, often through brutal measures, only served to galvanize Pueblo opposition under the charismatic religious leader Popé.

Throughout the summer of 1680, Popé worked from headquarters in Taos to organize a massive revolt of 17,000 Pueblos across hundreds of miles of territory. Runners carried calendars to participating pueblos in the form of knotted ropes that marked off the days until the planned uprising on August 11. Spanish officials discovered the plot two days early, yet Popé had laid his plans so well that he was able to coordinate his forces to strike a day earlier than planned.

The massive uprising overwhelmed Spanish settlements along the Rio Grande and its tributaries. Popé's forces destroyed ranches and villages, plundering Spanish weapons as they went to increase their firepower. They reserved special treatment for captured Franciscan missionaries, humiliating and torturing them before taking their lives. They targeted churches as well, burning or gutting them and desecrating sacred objects. Many survivors of the initial attack fled to Santa Fe, where they soon found themselves surrounded by well-armed rebels. On September 21, the city fell, and its survivors fled to join the remnants of New Mexico's Spanish and Christian Pueblo exiles in El Paso. Pueblos prevented the Spanish from returning to New Mexico for 13 years.

The Pueblo revolt sparked a series of uprisings throughout northern New Spain now remembered as the Great Northern Revolt. Spanish officials in the region found themselves hard-pressed to suppress native outbreaks against missions and settlements, or to find and punish bands who fled from Spanish oppression. Sporadic unrest continued for decades on New Spain's northern frontier.

Over 2,000 miles to the east, another widespread and well-coordinated native uprising broke out against the European inhabitants of New England. Some causes of the Wampanoag-Narragansett outbreak, such as resentment of European religion, overlapped with those of the Pueblos. Others differed. In New England, the primary issue was the loss of native territory to land-hungry farmers.

King Philip's War

The uprising delivered a terrible setback to New England colonists at a time when colonial officials were already facing grave challenges from London to the legitimacy of their regimes. During John Winthrop's lifetime, Massachusetts settlers developed an inflated sense of their independence from the mother country. After 1660, however, it became difficult even to pretend that the Puritan colony was a separate state. Royal officials like Edward Randolph demanded full compliance with the Navigation Acts. Moreover, the growth of commerce attracted new merchants to the Bay Colony, men who were Anglicans rather than Congregationalists and who maintained close business contacts in London. These merchants complained loudly of Puritan intolerance. The Anglican faction was never large, but its presence, coupled with Randolph's unceasing demands, divided the colony's leaders. A few Puritan ministers and magistrates regarded compromise with England as treason, a breaking of the Lord's covenant. Other spokesmen, recognizing the changing political realities within the empire, urged a more moderate course.

Other New England colonies experienced unrest stemming both from London's new assertiveness and from intercolonial rivalries. In the summer of 1675, Connecticut successfully rebuffed an effort by the recently appointed Governor of New York, Edmund Andros, to assert control over the colony. Andros's move represented an opening bid to unite all the squabbling, overly independent New England colonies together with New York under the authority of the Duke of York and the crown. Ill-timed though it proved, the measure seemed justified both by the absolutist ideals that Andros shared with his royal patron and by discord arising from a jealous scramble for territory. Leaders in Rhode Island, Plymouth, Connecticut, and Massachusetts scrambled to expand their settlements by purchasing land from neighboring Narragansetts and Wampanoags.

The purchases exacerbated tensions among the colonies as well as with their Indian neighbors, who resented having to sell so much land to satisfy debts incurred to the English. In depleting the natives' most valuable resource, land transactions served as a painful reminder of how dangerously dependent on European trade the Wampanoags and Narragansetts had become. The Wampanoag sachem Philip, a son of the Pilgrims' old ally Massasoit (see Chapter 5), observed that the English had impoverished his people so that "but a small part of the dominion of my ancestors remains." Early in 1675 he declared to an intercolonial assembly of leaders that he was "determined not to live until I have no country."

Philip, originally named Metacomet, had for several years been laboring to forge alliances of resistance among southern New England tribes. Throughout this time, rumors that he planned to lead an armed assault on English settlements kept

The Wampanoag chief Metacomet, whom the colonists called King Philip, led Native Americans in a war designed to drive the Europeans out of New England.

Shelburne Museum, Shelburne Vermont

nervous colonial officials busy negotiating, cajoling, and attempting to coerce Philip to come to peaceful terms with the English. Whether Philip intended to strike or merely to gain more diplomatic leverage remains unclear. In late June of 1675, however, a band of Wampanoag warriors apparently confirmed the rumors by sacking the Plymouth town of Swansea.

King Philip's War had begun. The powerful Narragansetts joined the Wampanoags, and in little more than a year of fighting, the Indians destroyed scores of frontier villages, killed hundreds of colonists, and disrupted the entire regional economy. The speed and scope of King Philip's offensive caught settlers off balance. He seemed to be everywhere at once. Historic rivalries impeded the colonies' efforts to mount a coordinated defense. The absence of a clear structure of command or rules of engagement gave colonists too much leeway to act, which they sometimes exercised through indiscriminate vengeance against Indian neutrals or allies as well as enemies.

For several months Philip's forces held the upper hand, yet they did not prevail over their European foes as did the Pueblos of New Mexico four years later. Unlike the Pueblos' Spanish foes, who managed to alienate most southwestern tribes, the English retained powerful native friends. The tide turned in the winter of 1675–1676, after Mohawk forces entered the English side and New England troops found effective ways to work together. By August of 1676, when Philip's death in battle brought an end to the conflict, more than one thousand Indians and New Englanders had perished. The cessation of hostilities left New England colonists deeply in debt and more than ever uncertain of their future.

King Philip's War also marked a watershed in New England–Indian relations. Never again would the native peoples of southern New England possess the strength or numbers sufficient to order their own affairs apart from colonial supervision. In the months after the war, colonial officials enslaved hundreds of captured Algonquians and shipped most of them to West Indian sugar plantations. The missionary John Eliot protested this treatment, drawing on biblical texts and the writings of the Spanish missionary Bartolomé de Las Casas to argue that enslavement of the Indians was deeply immoral. His objections fell on deaf ears, and his own life's work lay largely in shambles. The Praying Indians had suffered greatly at the hands of vengeful colonists despite their loyalty to their Puritan coreligionists, who attacked them or forcibly relocated them during the war. After the war the Praying Towns came to function in part as internment camps, their inhabitants placed under the supervision of local officials and forbidden to leave "on paine of death." Over time, inhabitants of these towns along with other native-organized communities found ways to preserve cherished cultural traditions while selectively adopting English forms. The war decisively subjugated New England Indians and pushed them to the margins of white society, etching more sharply the racial line that separated them from the English.

Further north, the war reshaped English-Abenaki relations as well. Although Abenakis and New Englanders had enjoyed a long history of trade in furs and maize, tensions similar to those in southern New England had been building as settlers in Maine and New Hampshire pushed further into traditional native lands. The outbreak of King Philip's War spurred Abenaki leaders into action much as

Pope's revolt sparked sympathetic uprisings in the Southwest. The northern conflict wore on until Edmund Andros, the governor of the New York colony, imposed the Peace of Casco to end hostilities in 1678. Unlike their Algonquian allies to the south, however, the Abenaki remained independent of English control. Indeed, the treaty required each English family in the region to pay Abenaki sachems a quitrent of a peck of maize per year. "As long as one Indian is in the country, we are owners of the country," the Abenakis declared, "and it is wide and full of Indians, and we can drive you out. But our desire is to be quiet." Abenaki sachems sought to ensure their quiet by forging closer relations with New France, a shift that held profound consequences for subsequent imperial conflict.

Civil War in Virginia: Bacon's Rebellion

When Virginia's royal governor Sir William Berkeley learned of Philip's assault on the New England communities, he declared the native forces "Instruments" with which God intended "to destroy the King's enemies." In his view, New England's Puritans shared responsibility for the execution of Charles I, and he was so determined to let divine vengeance run its course that he outlawed the export of Virginia foodstuffs to his embattled northern neighbors. Yet Berkeley was soon to face a crisis of his own, though one that differed greatly from New England's or New Mexico's. Social turmoil within the colony, native unrest on its frontiers, and resentment at the government's cronyism and corruption combined to turn the tables on Berkeley and eventually brought about his recall to England.

Governor Berkeley faced a series of intractable problems in 1676. For sixteen years, the Virginia economy had steadily declined. Returns from tobacco had not been good for some time, and the Navigation Acts reduced profits even further. Into this unhappy environment came thousands of indentured servants, people drawn to Virginia, as the governor explained, "in hope of bettering their condition in a Growing Country."

The reality bore little relation to their dreams. In June of 1667, Dutch warships captured the tobacco fleet just as it was about to sail for England. Only two months later, a hurricane destroyed the entire tobacco crop. Indentured servants complained about lack of food and clothing. No wonder that Berkeley despaired of ever ruling "a People where six parts of seven at least are Poor, indebted, Discontented and Armed." In 1670, he and the House of Burgesses disfranchised all landless freemen, persons they regarded as troublemakers, but the threat of social violence remained.

Enter Nathaniel Bacon. This ambitious young man arrived in Virginia in 1674. He came from a respectable English family and set himself up immediately as a substantial planter. But he wanted more. Bacon envied the government patronage monopolized by Berkeley's cronies, a group known locally as the Green Spring faction. When Bacon attempted to obtain a license to engage in the fur trade, he was rebuffed. This lucrative commerce was reserved for the governor's friends. If Bacon had been willing to wait, he probably would have been accepted into the ruling clique, but as subsequent events would demonstrate, Bacon was not a patient man.

Events beyond Bacon's control thrust him suddenly into the center of Virginia politics. In July of 1675, a minor clash between a Virginia trader and some of his native partners escalated into a frontier conflict between planters and a loose coalition of Piscataway, Doeg, and Susquehannock warriors. The Susquehannocks had only recently moved into the Potomac region following their defeat by Seneca, Onondaga, and Cayuga warriors two years before. They had no quarrel with English colonists—indeed, they had settled on the Potomac at the invitation of the Maryland government—until the Virginia militia colonel George Mason mistakenly killed fourteen Susquehannocks during a punitive raid into Maryland. Throughout the autumn of 1675, Susquehannock bands filtered through Virginia's backcountry forests, exacting vengeance on vulnerable outlying plantations.

Terrified Virginians called on the governor to send an army to retaliate. Instead, early in 1676, Berkeley called for the construction of a line of defensive forts, a plan that seemed to the settlers both expensive and ineffective. Indeed, this strategy raised embarrassing questions. Was Berkeley protecting his own fur monopoly? Was he planning to reward his friends with contracts to build useless forts?

While people speculated about such matters, Bacon stepped forward. He boldly offered to lead a volunteer army against the Indians at no cost to the hard-pressed Virginia taxpayers. All he demanded was an official commission giving him military command and the right to attack other Indians, not just the hostile Susquehannocks. The governor steadfastly refused. With some justification, Berkeley regarded his upstart rival as a fanatic on the subject of Indians. The governor saw no reason to exterminate peaceful tribes simply to avenge the death of a few white settlers.

What followed would have been comic had not so many people died. Bacon thundered against the governor's treachery; Berkeley labeled Bacon a traitor. Both men appealed to the populace for support. On several occasions, Bacon marched his followers to the frontier, but they failed to find the enemy or worse, they massacred friendly Indians. At one point, Bacon burned Jamestown to the ground, forcing the governor to flee to the colony's Eastern Shore. Bacon's bumbling lieutenants chased Berkeley across Chesapeake Bay only to be captured themselves. Thereupon, the governor mounted a new campaign.

As the civil war dragged on, it became increasingly apparent that Bacon and his gentry supporters had only the vaguest notion of what they were trying to achieve. The members of the planter elite never seemed fully to appreciate that the rank-and-file soldiers, often black slaves and poor white servants, had serious, legitimate grievances against Berkeley's corrupt government and were demanding substantial reforms, not just a share in the governor's fur monopoly.

Although women had not been allowed to vote in colony elections, they made their political views clear enough during the rebellion. Some were apparently more violent than others. Sarah Glendon, for example, agitated so aggressively in support of Bacon that Berkeley later refused to grant her a pardon. Another outspoken rebel, Lydia Chiesman, defended her husband before Governor Berkeley, saying that he would not have joined Bacon's forces had she not persuaded him to do so. "Therefore," Chiesman pleaded, ". . . since what her husband had done, was by her meanes, and so, by consequence, she most guilty, that she might be hanged and he pardoned."

When Charles II learned of the fighting in Virginia, he dispatched a thousand regular soldiers to Jamestown. By the time they arrived, Berkeley had regained full control over the colony's government. In October 1676, Bacon died after a brief illness, and within a few months, his band of rebel followers had dispersed. In 1677, the King recalled an old and embittered Berkeley to England.

Virginia's Indian allies suffered as much as their enemies at the hands of Bacon's militia forces. The Pamunkey, whose late werowance Opechancanough had once ruled the entire Powhatan chiefdom, fell victim to an assault by Bacon's forces although "it was well known to the whole country that the Queen of Pamunkey and her People had neere at any time betray'd or injuryed the English." Militiamen chased the unresisting Pamunkey into hiding, killing or capturing those they found and plundering their village. Though Bacon's rebels found few frontier Indians, the conflict proved sufficient to destroy the polity of the already weakened Susquehannocks, who returned north as tributaries of their erstwhile Iroquois enemies.

Forging the Covenant Chain

The fate of the Susquehannocks reveals the extent of Iroquois might during the later seventeenth century. English success in forging an alliance with this powerful northeastern native power may well have constituted the decisive factor in New England's ability to avert a fate similar to that of the Spanish in New Mexico. The Anglo-Iroquois alliance certainly brought an end to the bloodshed earlier than New England could otherwise have done. On the other hand, the alliance permitted the Iroquois to turn the tables completely on the Susquehannocks, absorbing the remnants of a nation that had earlier humiliated them in battle. To be sure, Iroquois tribes remained riven with factionalism, epidemic disease had diminished their numbers, and overhunting had sent their traders in search of new sources of pelts. Yet they remained a formidable power in the Northeast, one that no colonial power could overcome without incurring unacceptable costs.

The French proved very slow to recognize Iroquois influence. In the 1660s, the royal minister Jean-Baptiste Colbert began working to expand France's economy on an imperial basis. He hoped to transform New France into a productive colony that would contribute to the French economy as the English colonies were beginning to do for England. The Five Nations constituted an obstacle to these plans, and Colbert authorized military action against them. In 1665, the 1,000-man Carignan-Salières regiment launched two campaigns into Mohawk country, destroying villages and food supplies. Iroquois delegates negotiated for peace in the aftermath of the French assault, but its memory continued to rankle.

By 1675, many headmen were coming to see in Anglo-Iroquois relations a means of countering French influence while augmenting the league's power. French explorers in the Great Lakes and the Illinois country had begun building a chain of forts that would give their fur traders a direct link to European markets via the Mississippi River. This new route would not only enable the French to bypass Iroquois middlemen in the St. Lawrence trade but would give them a great competitive advantage over Seneca traders in western fur markets. Although Iroquois leaders may not have grasped the full scope of this plan, they experienced its effects in a growing French menace on their western borders and in stiffer competition for western furs.

In this context, a growing number of Iroquois began to see the earlier movement to ally with the French as a bad bargain. It would gain the Iroquois little but conflict with the English who controlled the vital Hudson River trade. Alliance with the English, on the other hand, could ensure not only access to European markets but also military assistance and peace on their long-troubled eastern boundaries, freeing Iroquois forces to defend their vulnerable northern and western flanks. Headmen who had previously opposed alliance with the French now coalesced into identifiable Anglophile factions within Iroquois tribes and villages. Francophile headmen lost influence in tribal councils, and several villages expelled French priests along with tribal members who had converted to Catholicism.

Soon after his appointment in 1674, New York's governor Edmund Andros apparently came to the conclusion that what was good for the Iroquois was good for the English. Access to the lucrative Iroquois fur trade had helped to make the colony an attractive prize for capture in 1664. Moreover, Iroquois ambitions to bring neighboring peoples under their influence meshed with Andros's own desire to simplify Anglo-Indian relations. It would be much easier to deal with a single overarching native authority than a multitude of smaller bands. Ultimately, the Iroquois helped Andros broker an intercolonial settlement that secured New York's preeminence among England's mainland colonies.

During the 1670s, Andros and various Iroquois tribal headmen mediated a series of ad hoc agreements that became the basis for an enduring system of alliances known as the Covenant Chain. One of the chain's central links was an English-brokered end to a long-running Mohawk-Mahican war, which secured safe passage for merchant vessels between Albany and Manhattan. Andros built on this treaty by sponsoring new commercial regulations to prevent abuses that had characterized the earlier Dutch trade. As a result, commerce thrived on the Hudson River. English and Anglo-Dutch merchants prospered, while Anglophile headmen augmented their prestige and influence by acting as brokers between Iroquois villages, Albany merchants, and colonial officials.

King Philip's War represented additional opportunities for both the Mohawks, who wished to extend their influence to the east, and Andros, who hoped to consolidate New England's governments under his control. Mohawk assaults on Philip's villages during the winter of 1675–1676 helped to turn the tide of the war in southern New England, while further raids into northern New England during 1677 helped bring an end to the conflict there. In the aftermath of the war, Andros invited defeated New England tribes to settle on land near Albany as clients under New York's protection as well as "children" under Mohawk patronage. The wartime destruction of Connecticut merchant William Pynchon's fur trading business also permitted Mohawk traders and Albany merchants to extend their control of the fur trade.

In the aftermath of Bacon's Rebellion, Andros and the Iroquois also took a hand in negotiating Anglo-Indian relations in the Chesapeake. Andros persuaded the defeated Susquehannocks to relocate north. Some returned to their original Susquehanna location, where they became known as Conestogas. Others settled among the Delawares, and still others among the Onondaga and Cayuga nations of the Iroquois. Seneca headmen gave assurances for the Susquehannocks' good behavior in a 1677 agreement among Maryland, Virginia, and the Iroquois. In subsequent years, Iroquois bands who had not joined in the 1677 "silver chain" continued to raid Maryland and Virginia frontiers for furs and captives, prompting Andros to broker additional negotiations among Chesapeake and Iroquois leaders. Though the resulting covenants, which the Iroquois termed "handclasps of friendship," were distinct from those with New York, Andros's crucial role nevertheless strengthened his reputation as a man of rare administrative ability.

The Iroquois League emerged from the conflicts of the 1670s with much greater might than they had enjoyed at the opening of the decade. To be sure, full unity proved elusive. Francophile factions sought to recover lost prestige, while emerging neutral factions opposed alliances with either the English or the French. For the moment, however, the Anglo-Iroquois alliance had proven a triumph. It had enabled the Five Nations to absorb once-powerful Mahican and Susquehannock foes as tributaries or adoptees. It had brought in additional clients from the defeated New England tribes. These conquests accomplished traditional wartime aims by replenishing Iroquois numbers, enhancing their spiritual power, and increasing their command of resources in land and furs.

An Unfinished Agenda

By 1680, England's Caribbean and mainland North American colonies had become too important to ignore. The rising volume of colonial exports promised to enrich royal coffers and merchant purses alike. The Iroquois market for manufactured goods now benefited English artisans rather than Dutch. The growing New England merchant fleet was giving English shippers a run for their money. The laws necessary to regulate colonial commerce had been enacted. Yet the unrest in New England and the Chesapeake revealed how much work remained to secure England's hold on its North Atlantic possessions. Officials in London and the colonies alike worried that they still remained vulnerable to capture by a hostile foreign power such as France or Spain, perhaps with the support of the powerful Iroquois nations. The challenge was to make any attempted conquest of the colonies more costly than control "of the country could compensate."

Sir Edmund Andros thought he knew the solution to the problem of colonial administration, at least in the Northeast: union "as one people and country." The conflicts of the 1670s had provided him opportunity to lay the groundwork for that project. Yet the inhabitants of each New England colony continued to defend the independence of their "popular governments" despite the fatal weaknesses Andros believed the "late Indian wars" had exposed. "Knoweing noe other governmt then their owne," he observed, they "think it best, and are wedded to and opnionate for it." Only by "his Majesty's asserting, & regulating the militia or force of ye severall colonies," Andros believed, could union, and with it the security of England's emerging empire, be assured.

CHRONOLOGY

1637	Dutch capture Portuguese slave-trading post at Elmina.
1639	French Jesuit trader-missionaries challenge Dutch monopoly on Iroquois trade.
1641	Dutch capture slave-trading posts at Axim, Angola.
1642	English Civil War breaks out.
1648	Peace of Westphalia ends Thirty Years War in Europe.
1649	Charles I beheaded.
1651	Commonwealth Parliament passes first Navigation Act.
1652	First Anglo-Dutch War breaks out.
1653	Oliver Cromwell becomes Lord Protector of England.
1655	English forces capture Jamaica.
1660	English monarchy restored under Charles II.
1660	Enumeration Act passed.
1663	Staple Act passed.
1664	Colonel Richard Nicolls captures New Netherland for Duke of York.
1673	Plantation duty imposed to close loopholes in commercial regulations.
1675	King Philip's War breaks out in New England.
1676	Bacon's Rebellion breaks out in Virginia.
1677	Anglo-Iroquois alliance secured with "Covenant Chain" agreements.
1680	Pueblo Revolt against the Spanish.

RECOMMENDED READING

Jan De Vries, *The Economy of Europe in an Age of Crisis, 1600–1750* (Cambridge, 1976) provides an excellent starting point for understanding the European context of the contest for Atlantic commercial empire in the later seventeenth century. For French imperial concerns, see Philip Boucher, *Les Nouvelles Frances: France in America, 1500–1815: An Imperial Perspective* (Providence, R.I., 1989). For the Spanish, see relevant essays in Richard L. Kagan and Geoffrey Parker, eds., *Spain, Europe, and the Atlantic World: Essays in Honour of J. H. Elliott* (Cambridge, 1995). For the Dutch, see Jonathan I. Israel, *Dutch Primacy in World Trade, 1585–1740* (Oxford, 1989). For developments in England in the later Stuart period, see Mark Kishlansky, A

Monarchy Transformed: Britain 1603–1714 (London, 1996), and Steven C. A. Pincus, *Protestantism and Patriotism: Ideologies and the Making of English Foreign Policy, 1650–1668* (Cambridge, 1996). For Anglo-Dutch conflict, see J. R. Jones, *The Anglo-Dutch Wars of the Seventeenth Century* (London, 1996).

The development of England's Atlantic commercial and colonial policy in the later seventeenth century is detailed in Charles M. Andrews, *The Colonial Period of American History*, vol. 4, *England's Commercial and Colonial Policy* (New Haven, 1938). The early entry of New England merchants and shippers into Atlantic commerce is detailed in Bernard Bailyn, *The New England Merchants in the Seventeenth Century* (Cambridge, Mass., 1955). J. M. Sossin examines the changing nature of Anglo-American relations during the Restoration in *English America and the Restoration Monarchy of Charles II: Transatlantic Politics, Commerce, and Kinship* (Lincoln, Nebr., 1981). Michael Garibaldi Hall examines the development of English colonial policy through one of its most persistent and irascible agents in his *Edward Randolph and the American Colonies, 1676–1703* (Chapel Hill, 1960). Thomas C. Barrow provides a broader overview in his *Trade and Empire: The British Customs Service in Colonial America, 1660–1775* (Cambridge, Mass., 1967). Ian K. Steele, *The English Atlantic, 1675–1740: An Exploration of Communication and Community* (Oxford, 1986) provides a broader analysis of the cultural impact of improvements in transatlantic commerce. For an example of one buccaneer who profited handsomely in the vacuum of seventeenth-century commercial policy, see Dudley Pope, *Harry Morgan's Way: The Biography of Sir Henry Morgan* (London, 1977).

Daniel K Richter's *The Ordeal of the Longhouse: The Peoples of the Iroquois League in the Era of European Colonization* (Chapel Hill, 1992) offers a brilliant analysis of the Iroquois' strategic engagement in the imperial conflicts of the late seventeenth century. For a cultural interpretation of King Philip's War, see Jill Lepore, *The Name of War: King Philip's War and the Origins of American Identity* (New York, 1998). For Bacon's rebellion, see Ian K. Steele, *Warpaths: Invasions of North America* (New York, 1994) and Wilcomb E. Washburn, *The Governor and the Rebel: A History of Bacon's Rebellion in Virginia* (Chapel Hill, 1957). Excellent analyses of the growing role of Ohio and Great Lakes peoples in the late seventeenth-century contest for territory may be found in Richard White's *The Middle Ground: Indians, Empires, and Republics in the Great Lakes Region, 1650–1815* (New York, 1991), and Eric Hinderaker, *Elusive Empires: Constructing Colonialism in the Ohio Valley, 1673–1800* (New York, 1997). For an analysis of Anglo-native relations in the aftermath of 1676, see Daniel K. Richter and James H. Merrell, eds., *Beyond the Covenant Chain: The Iroquois and their Neighbors in Indian North America, 1600–1800* (Syracuse, 1987). For Popé's revolt see Andrew L Knaut, *The Pueblo Revolt of 1680: Conquest and Resistance in Seventeenth-Century New Mexico* (Norman, Okla., 1995).

Chapter 8

Toleration, Commerce, and Settlement

The Restoration Colonies

For Arnoldus de la Grange, the narrow road to salvation and prosperity ran from New York City through New Castle in the newly established colony of Pennsylvania. Indeed, by 1686 this former New York shopkeeper and recent convert to the teachings of the French mystic Jean de Labadie had become one of New Castle's leading citizens. In England, la Grange's extreme convictions would have disqualified him for office, because they required him to separate from the Established Church and live simply among a strict community of self-denying fellow-believers. In Pennsylvania, however, Proprietor William Penn had appointed the Labadist to the important local office of Justice of the Court. In England, thousands of Dissenters from the Established Church had been fined into bankruptcy, jailed, or deprived of their estates for persisting in their religious convictions. But in New Castle, the Labadist farmer and his Quaker neighbors were enjoying bountiful harvests on the fertile land they had obtained from the Lenni-Lenape Indians.

La Grange himself harvested 1,000 bushels of wheat in 1686, far more than he needed for himself. Neighboring farmers reaped similar results. The enterprising Labadist processed this surplus grain at a mill he shared with two Swedes. He then sold the flour for export to the West Indies, which now depended on imported grain to feed their burgeoning slave populations. The profits from his share of the business enabled la Grange to help purchase a 3,000-acre estate in neighboring Maryland. His path to heaven eventually led him there to live out his days in simple community with other Labadists, supported in part by profits from the West Indian trade.

La Grange's career might have afforded excellent practical support for an argument that was appearing ever more frequently in Restoration-era pamphlets: religious toleration was good for trade. Contemporary English policymakers such as Anthony Ashley Cooper, the first Earl of Shaftesbury and a patron of the philosopher John Locke, urged fellow policymakers to follow the Dutch example in this matter. Shaftesbury maintained a keen interest in Atlantic trade and colonial expansion throughout his life. He owned a Barbadian sugar plantation during the 1650s, became one of the leading Lords Proprietors of Carolina, invested heavily in the Royal Africa Company, and provided direction to the crown's Committee for Trade. Shaftesbury resented Dutch dominance in colonial trade but tried his best to learn from the success of England's greatest seventeenth-century rival. Religious toleration, he concluded, had enabled the Dutch not only to retain their own best artisans and merchants, but also to attract those from other nations who fled persecution "to enjoy the liberty of their mistaken consciences." As a result, the Dutch had managed to enrich their nation by dominating world commerce, while the Restoration-era demand for religious conformity was forcing out some of England's best and brightest to flee elsewhere and exerting a continual drain on national wealth.

These two tensions—internal conflict over conformity to the Established Church and external competition for an empire of trade—revitalized English efforts to colonize North America during the reign of Charles II. The realm expanded to include four new mainland colonies during this period, two acquired through conquest and two obtained by charter and settlement. Colonists and London officials alike expected that each colony would enhance the trade and wealth of the English nation. The realities of colonial life soon forced officials to concede that the settlements could best realize their economic potential by tolerating a wide array of religious opinion among their colonial inhabitants.

DIVERSITY IN THE MIDDLE COLONIES

New York, New Jersey, Pennsylvania, and Delaware were settled for quite different reasons. William Penn, for example, envisioned a Quaker sanctuary; the duke of York worried chiefly about his own income. Despite the founders' intentions, however, some common characteristics emerged. Each colony developed a strikingly heterogeneous population, men and women of different ethnic and religious backgrounds. This cultural diversity became a major influence on the economic, political, and ecclesiastical institutions of the Middle Colonies. The raucous, partisan public life of the Middle Colonies foreshadowed later American society.

The English capture of New Netherland in 1664 (see Chapter 7) could scarcely eliminate Dutch influence in the Middle Colonies. The Dutch had pioneered settlement on the Hudson River in the 1620s through the Dutch West India Company (see Chapter 3). At the time of English conquest the company also possessed extensive claims on the Delaware, which they had acquired by asserting control over the rival colony of New Sweden in 1655. The Dutch population of these regions had languished in the early years because the company treated prospective settlers as salaried employees and refused to grant them land. During the 1640s, however, the company shifted its policies to attract new settlers from the Netherlands and other European nations as well. As a result, the Duke of York's new dominions contained an extraordinary ethnic mix. One visitor to New Amsterdam in 1644 maintained he had heard "eighteen different languages" spoken in the city. Even if this report was exaggerated, there is no doubt the Dutch colony also drew English, Finns, Germans, and Swedes.

The Dutch and Swedish Legacy

Further up the Hudson, Fort Orange and the nearby town of Beverwyck (which the English renamed Albany) hosted an equally diverse population of "Flemings, Scandinavians, Frenchmen, Portuguese, Croats, Irishmen, Englishmen, Scotsmen, Germans, Spaniards, blacks from Africa and the West Indies, Indians and people of mixed blood." A core population of Dutch families held this polyglot trading settlement together and fashioned the townscape into a replica of a low-country community. They constructed Dutch-style townhouses on narrow frontages, cramming the buildings tightly together. The families who occupied the houses gained their living by trade, and used their profits to build strong networks of wealth and kinship that enabled people of Dutch descent to dominate the region's politics and social life for generations. Dutch remained the most commonly spoken language, and the Dutch Reformed Church dominated the town's religious life.

The "Swedish nation" that had been established on the Delaware in 1638 still existed at the time of English conquest as a cluster of distinct communities under Dutch control. The population consisted of only a few hundred Swedes and Finns who obtained their living by trading for furs, planting tobacco, and farming grain. The Swedes sought to preserve a strong ethnic identity in their insular communities, and nursed for many years the forlorn hope that their king would send a fleet of warships to rescue their colony from foreign domination. In the meantime, they submitted grudgingly to the succession of Dutch and English governors and cooperated with their non-Swedish neighbors in common ventures.

The Dutch West India Company's heavy involvement in the slave trade made New Amsterdam a destination for many African slaves as well. During the colony's early years the company had sought to compensate for its shortage of European laborers by introducing African slaves, many of whom remained company property. Slaves took advantage of their uncertain status in seventeenth-century Dutch law to sue for expansion of their rights as well as for outright freedom. By the 1640s, the company had manumitted a sizable number of its slaves, and these formed the nucleus of a free black community that persisted throughout the colonial period. Many won only "half freedom," a status usually open only to older slaves on an individual basis. The children of the half-free remained enslaved, and those manumitted remained employees of the Dutch West India Company. The company assigned them plots of land on which they could grow their own crops and livestock. The black workers had to pay an annual percentage of their produce to the company or face re-enslavement. Other blacks managed to obtain rights as freeholders from Dutch authorities and pursue independent livelihoods as artisans or farmers. They created stable families and participated in the religious life of the Dutch Reformed Church, taking communion and baptizing their children alongside Dutch families. Still others remained in slavery, and the company brought additional slaves every year to augment its own labor force or to sell to free colonists. By 1664, blacks—free, half-free, and enslaved—comprised between 20 and 25 percent of New Amsterdam's population.

New England Puritans who left Massachusetts and Connecticut to stake out farms on Long Island and along the east bank of the Hudson further fragmented New Netherland's culture. The English brought with them their strong traditions of local government and legal rights which they sought to assert in relations with their new Dutch rulers, especially in predominantly English settlements such as Flushing. English living further east within the Dutch jurisdiction of Long Island acted more as extensions of New England than of New Netherland, ignoring Dutch rule as much as possible and dealing far more with Boston and New Haven than with New Amsterdam. The communities on the far eastern end of the island—Easthampton, Southold, and Southampton—remained under Connecticut's jurisdiction until 1664.

The Duke's Dominions

Despite its fractious diversity under the Dutch, James, Duke of York and brother of King Charles II, viewed New Netherland as a very handsome prize. As Lord High Admiral of England, York was pressing for action against the Dutch, and their poorly defended North American colony seemed ripe for the taking. He was keenly aware of the colony's strategic significance in Dutch Atlantic navigation, both as an important commercial port and a potential military base that could threaten the surrounding English colonies if the Dutch began strengthening it. York's circle included other high-ranking officials who were deeply involved in trade and colonization, including John, Lord Berkeley and Sir George Carteret. These men urged York to act, knowing that they too stood to gain from the favors of appointive offices and trade monopolies that a new colony would place in his hands. Seizure of the established colony also presented the opportunity to reap its financial benefits without the heavy outlays of cash that it commonly took to establish a new colony. New Netherland already hosted a large population, enjoyed a well-developed fur trade, and exported more tobacco and agricultural crops every year. York's advisors assured him that the colony would generate £10,000 annually, a tidy supplement to York's cash-starved income.

Despite York's high hopes, the colony's history under Dutch rule ensured that New York's first English governor, Colonel Richard Nicolls, would face a daunting challenge in his effort to assert authority over the fractious population. The vast size of the territory included in the charter that Charles II granted his royal brother further complicated Nicolls's task. The king made York absolute proprietor over Maine, Martha's Vineyard, Nantucket, Long Island, and the rest of New York all the way to Delaware Bay. Perhaps Charles wanted to encircle New England's potentially disloyal Puritan population, but whatever his aims may have been, he created a bureaucratic nightmare.

During the English Civil War, the duke had acquired a thorough aversion to representative assemblies. After all, Parliament had executed the duke's father, Charles I, and raised up Oliver Cromwell. York had no intention of letting participatory government take root in New York. "I cannot but suspect," he announced, that an assembly "would be of dangerous consequence." The Long Islanders felt betrayed. They had expected that the advent of English rule would include representative assemblies like those in New England. The disappointed colonists protested bitterly. In part to appease these outspoken critics, Governor Nicolls—one of the few competent administrators to serve in the Middle Colonies—drew up in March 1665 a legal code known as the Duke's Laws. It guaranteed religious toleration and created local governments.

There were no provisions, however, for an elected assembly or for democratic town meetings. The legal code disappointed the Puritan migrants on Long Island, and when the duke's officers attempted to collect taxes, these people grumbled that they were "inslav'd under an Arbitrary Power." Long Island's easternmost communities protested especially vigorously, even petitioning Charles II to restore them to Connecticut's jurisdiction. The king ignored their petition, leaving the towns to chafe under the duke's iron hand.

The Dutch made the transition to English rule with apparent resignation. Governor Nicolls knew that the colony's commercial value depended on securing Dutch cooperation. He moved cautiously in his dealings with them, respecting Dutch property rights and asserting his authority only gradually. English authorities did not apply the Duke's Laws to Dutch areas between Manhattan and Albany until Nicolls's successor, Francis Lovelace, implemented them in 1670. Both governors worked to meld Dutch and English legal forms. Early English governors encouraged additional Dutch immigration to the colony to augment the population and kept trade flowing by allowing Dutch West India Company ships to trade in New York in violation of the Navigation Acts. Nevertheless, many Dutch officeholders lost their posts to English aspirants during Nicolls's term as governor, and the Dutch settlers remained keenly sensitive to their status as a conquered people. Altercations between Dutch and English were not uncommon, and prominent Dutch merchants nursed the hope of regaining control of the colony.

Dutch hopes came true for a time in 1672 when a fleet of warships from the Netherlands recaptured the colony during the third Anglo-Dutch War. The Dutch embraced the opportunity to throw off the hated English yoke, seizing English property, rounding up English officials and shipping them back to England. The invaders restored Dutch names to the colony, Dutch officials to their posts, and Dutch commerce to the merchants. The restoration of Dutch rule proved short-lived. In 1674, the Netherlands gave up all rights to the area in the Treaty of Westminster, leaving the Dutch colonists to fend for themselves against vengeful Englishmen.

The return of New York to the English accelerated the effort to Anglicize the government and commerce of the colony. The new governor, Edmund Andros, moved rapidly to dispossess the Dutch of most political offices and to require that all records be kept in English. He also imposed on all residents an oath of fidelity and allegiance to the King's government, prohibiting any who refused the oath to engage in any commerce. A group of eight leading Dutch merchants refused to submit unless Andros would guarantee that the oath did not compromise their religious liberties, their inheritance customs, their freedom from impressment into English military service, and their right not to take up arms against their own nation. When Andros remained unmoved, one merchant submitted. The other seven ended up in a court packed with hostile English judges, who convicted them of promoting rebellion and threatened to confiscate their entire estates if they did not submit. The outraged merchants protested, and one of them, Nicholas Bayard, let loose such a torrent of abuse that he was thrown into solitary confinement for three days. In the end, the merchants were allowed to keep two thirds of their estates in exchange for taking the oath, but the trial left deep scars on the Dutch community in New York.

For several decades the Dutch remained a large, unassimilated ethnic group. They continued to speak their own language, worship in their own churches (Dutch Reformed Church), and eye their English neighbors with suspicion. Dutch merchant families in Manhattan and Albany held the reins of commerce tightly, often extending their monopolies over furs and other exports with the assistance of English governors. A few leading Dutch families did accommodate to English rule, cultivating mercantile contacts among the English, marrying into English families, and rising to high office. Anglo-Dutch leaders such as Stephanus Van Cortlandt and Frederick Philpse became some of Andros's most trusted advisors. Many other Dutch families kept their distance, however, and eventually formed an opposition "Dutch party" or faction in New York's political life.

Despite the early Dutch hold on New York's economic life, the English did manage to make inroads. In 1676, fully a third of New York City's wealthiest merchants and artisans were English, and two of the colony's leading English families had begun their rise to prominence. Richard Morris, a captain in Cromwell's army, arrived in New York in the 1660s and managed to acquire estates on both sides of the Hudson River. Morris died when his son Lewis was less than a year old, but an uncle, Lewis Morris of Barbados, secured the family's place in New York political and social life while serving as guardian for the boy. The young Scotsman Robert Livingston arrived in New York in 1674 and made his way quickly up the social ladder by marrying into the wealthy Schuyler family of Albany. Even before his marriage, Livingston caught the attention of Governor Andros, who appointed him to important offices in Albany to secure English rule there. Andros's successor, Governor Thomas Dongan, granted Livingston a princely estate of 160,000 acres on the Hudson, as well as a one-seventh share of another 180,000-acre tract near Saratoga. Livingston Manor on the Hudson became the cornerstone of the family's far-flung commercial enterprises. The Livingstons and the Morrises remained leading families of New York's "landed interest" throughout the colonial period.

Even with the increasing English numbers, New York remained a diverse mix of ethnic and religious communities that included Jews, Scots, Irish, French, and Germans as well as English and Dutch. People of African descent also remained a large minority population—as much as 18 percent in 1700. Slaves continued to arrive in New York to satisfy a brisk internal demand. The steady growth of slavery made the status of free blacks increasingly precarious as white masters began viewing them as a threat to security. Nevertheless, slaves themselves continued to enjoy many traditional privileges that set New York apart from the emerging slave societies of the Caribbean and southern mainland colonies. Slaves could hold their own property and raise their own crops for sale. Slaves could often negotiate terms of bondage which permitted them to be hired out, and to keep a portion of their wages. Traders sometimes permitted slaves to choose their own masters, which allowed them to move nearer to kin or escape an unsatisfactory situation. Masters sometimes expressed frustration with this comparatively lax system, but slaves exploited it wherever possible to increase their autonomy.

The concentration of blacks in New York City fostered strong communal ties centered on distinct cultural forms. Black women and men congregated on Sundays and holidays to celebrate through dance, song, and physical competition. New York blacks developed their own distinctive forms for marriage and funerals and interred their dead in separate graveyards that historian Ira Berlin has called "the first truly African-American institution in the northern colonies."

The English and the Iroquois

The importance of New York's fur trade prompted the first English governor, Richard Nicolls, to secure a treaty with the Iroquois as soon as his agents assumed control of Albany. In it, the English promised to continue trade with the Iroquois on the same terms as the Dutch and to support the Iroquois with English arms and soldiers in case of attack. Internal struggles among the Iroquois as well as the Anglo-Dutch tensions of the 1660s and early 1670s made the early Anglo-Iroquois alliance tenuous. Only after the English secured their hold in 1674 were Governors Andros and Dongan able to forge lasting ties in a series of alliances known as the Covenant Chain. Arising as it did out of the Anglo-Iroquois response to King Philip's War (see Chapter 7), the Covenant Chain positioned New York and the Five Nations to claim roles as principal mediators in Anglo-Indian relations from New England to Virginia.

New York's dependence on the fur trade helped keep Anglo-Iroquois relations stable and peaceful well into the eighteenth century. For much of this period the colony's population remained small and clustered along the Hudson River and Long Island. New York farmers remained content to farm lands in those regions, reducing the pressure of agricultural expansion that had generated conflict in New England and the Chesapeake. The Five Nations' importance also prompted the Crown to appoint officials directly over Indian affairs rather than entrusting Anglo-Indian relations to governors who might allow their own provincial aims to obscure larger British interests on the continent. The Iroquois shared the desire to keep trade flowing, and their strategic location along the Mohawk and upper Hudson River valleys allowed them to dominate the region's trade. English New

York provided an important alternative to commerce with the French as well as a vital military ally against the Five Nations' French and Indian rivals.

Confusion in New Jersey

New Netherland originally encompassed the region between the Hudson and Delaware Rivers as well as the lands to the north, and Charles II had accordingly included this region in the charter issued to his brother. New York's Governor Nicolls regarded the land between the two rivers as the "most improveable" for agriculture and believed it vital for his officials to control both banks of the Hudson River. Yet only three months after receiving the charter, the Duke of York made a terrible blunder—something this stubborn, humorless man was prone to do. As a gift to two courtiers who had served Charles during the English Civil War, the duke awarded the land lying between the Hudson and Delaware Rivers to John, Lord Berkeley, and Sir George Carteret. This colony was named New Jersey in honor of Carteret's birthplace, the Isle of Jersey in the English Channel. When Nicolls heard what the duke had done, he exploded. In his estimation, the decision to give away so casually this fertile region seemed the height of folly.

The duke's impulsive act bred confusion. Soon it was not clear who owned what in New Jersey. Before he had learned of York's decision, Nicholls had allowed migrants from New England to take up farms west of the Hudson River. He promised these settlers an opportunity to establish an elected assembly, a headright system, and liberty of conscience. In exchange for these privileges, Nicolls asked only that they pay a small annual quitrent to the duke. The new proprietors, Berkeley and Carteret, recruited colonists on similar terms, codifying them in a document entitled the "Concessions and Agreement." They assumed, of course, that they would receive the rent money.

The result was chaos. The testy New England colonists, who were used to owning their property outright, objected to the quitrents. Some colonists insisted that Nicolls had authorized their assembly. Others, equally insistent, claimed that Berkeley and Carteret had done so. Both sides were wrong. Neither the proprietors nor Nicolls possessed any legal right whatsoever to set up a colonial government. James could transfer land to favorite courtiers, but no matter how many times the land changed hands, the government remained his personal responsibility. Knowledge of the law failed to settle the controversy. Through it all, the duke showed not the slightest interest in the peace and welfare of the people of New Jersey.

Berkeley grew tired of the venture. It generated headaches rather than quitrents, and in 1674, he sold his proprietary rights to a group of surprisingly quarrelsome Quakers. The sale necessitated the division of the colony into two separate governments known as East and West Jersey. Neither half prospered.

Carteret and his heirs tried unsuccessfully to turn a profit in East Jersey. He continued to encourage small farmers to emigrate, granting them 100- to 200-acre plots of ground. At the same time, he attempted to stimulate the development of tobacco plantations by issuing large grants of up to 10,000 acres of land to Barbadian émigrés in an area that became known as "New Barbados." The planters

who claimed these grants brought with them slaves to clear fields and begin planting tobacco as well as grain crops for export. In addition, the elder Lewis Morris of
New York brought a force of nearly seventy African slaves to the "Monmouth
grant" near the Atlantic coast where he established the region's first iron plantation, Tinton Manor ironworks. Despite these efforts, the East Jersey economy remained predominantly focused on family farms, generating little in either
quitrents or customs for its proprietor. When Carteret died in 1681, the trustees of
his estate sold the disappointing proprietorship to a group of 24 investors that included William Penn.

Penn and his partners hoped to secure the entire territory of both Jerseys as
well as Pennsylvania for their Quaker coreligionists. The management of East
Jersey soon fell to the colony's new governor, the Scottish Quaker Robert Barclay.
Barclay promoted East Jersey vigorously in his homeland, even persuading the
powerful Earls of Perth and Melfort to purchase shares in the proprietorship.
Nearly 500 Scots, most of them Presbyterians who were experiencing severe persecution under Charles II, responded to Barclay's enticing advertisements. After
1685, persecution declined, and with it the influx of Scots to East Jersey. Most of
the earlier immigrants to Scotland's first American colony remained, and they
soon came to exercise influence out of all proportion to their numbers.

The Quaker proprietors of neighboring West Jersey issued in 1677 a remarkable democratic plan of government—the Laws, Concessions, and Agreements.
The plan envisioned a unicameral, or one-house, legislature of one hundred
elected representatives that would enact all laws and a ten-member "Commission
of State" that would manage provincial affairs when the legislature was not in ses-
sion. The legislature was limited only by the requirement that all laws be conso-
nant with the laws of England and the Concessions themselves. The document
provided elaborate safeguards for the people's religious rights, declaring that "no
man, nor number of men on earth, hath power or authority to rule over men's consciences in religious matters."

West Jersey's visionary constitution was never fully implemented. Shifting
royal policies and internal bickering buffeted the colony for the next two decades.
Indeed, the Quakers fought among themselves with such intensity that not even
William Penn could bring tranquility to their affairs. Penn wisely turned his attention to the unclaimed territory across the Delaware River.

Despite the colony's political instability, the Quaker population did manage to
establish a number of prosperous farming communities along a 20-mile-wide strip
stretching from Trenton to Delaware Bay. Farmers raised mixed crops of grain, flax,
and hemp as well as livestock. Interspersed among the family farms were several
larger operations where African slaves and English indentured servants worked
cash crops of tobacco and foodstuffs. West Jersey soon developed a brisk export
trade in agricultural goods to the British West Indies, as well as a trade with
England in tobacco, furs, and naval stores such as pitch, tar, resin, and hemp.

The prosperity of individual landholders in East and West Jersey could not
save the proprietors of either colony from bankruptcy. In 1702, both sets of proprietors surrendered their powers to Queen Anne, who reunited the two Jerseys into

a single royal colony. At that time the population of New Jersey stood at approximately fourteen thousand. Largely because it lacked a good deepwater harbor, the colony never developed a commercial center to rival New York City or Philadelphia. Most residents lived on scattered family farms, and the large landowners often left much of their property undeveloped or gradually sold it off in smaller plots.

Visitors often commented on the diversity of New Jersey's settlers. There were colonists from almost every European nation as well as a significant population of Africans. Most were slaves who worked as field hands on family farms, but some formed a significant labor force for larger farm operations and mining, while a few others worked as free laborers or farmed land of their own. The ethnic diversity of the Jerseys coupled with the policy of religious toleration produced a wide range of religious opinion in the colony. Congregationalists, Presbyterians, Quakers, Baptists, Anabaptists, Dutch Reformed, and Anglicans somehow managed to live together peacefully in New Jersey.

QUAKERS IN AMERICA

The founding of Pennsylvania cannot be separated from the history of the Quaker movement. This radical religious sect, a product of the social upheaval in England during the Civil War, gained its name from the derogatory term that English authorities sometimes used to describe those who "tremble at the word of the Lord." The name persisted even though Quakers preferred being called Professors of the Light or, more commonly, Friends.

By the time the Stuarts regained the throne in 1660, the Quakers had developed a strong following throughout England. One person responsible for their remarkable success was George Fox (1624–1691), a poor shoemaker whose spiritual anxieties sparked a powerful new religious message that pushed beyond traditional reformed Protestantism. According to Fox, he experienced despair "so that I had nothing outwardly to help me . . . [but] then, I heard a voice which said, 'There is one, even Christ Jesus, that can speak to thy condition.'" Throughout his life, Fox and his growing number of followers testified to the working of the Holy Spirit. They informed ordinary men and women that if they would only look, they too would discover they possessed an "Inner Light." This message was a wonderfully liberating invitation, especially for persons of lower-class origin. With the Lord's personal assistance, anyone could attain greater spiritual perfection on earth. Gone was the stigma of original sin; discarded was the notion of eternal predestination. Everyone could be saved. Likewise, everyone could preach or prophesy, an activity the Quakers termed "bearing witness to the Truth." Quakers saw no need for a learned ministry, because the Spirit's Inner Light could guide each person alike to a valid interpretation of Scripture.

Quakers practiced humility in their daily lives. They wore simple clothes and employed old-fashioned forms of address that set them apart from their neighbors. Friends refused to honor worldly position and accomplishment. They would not doff their hats, bow, curtsy, or use deferential terms of address, even when appearing before royalty. Quakers declined to swear oaths in courts of law, a refusal that landed many of them in jail for contempt of court. They were also pacifists. According to Fox, all persons were equal in the sight of the Lord, a belief that generally annoyed people of rank and achievement.

Moreover, the Quakers never kept their thoughts to themselves. They preached conversion constantly, spreading the "Truth" throughout England, Ireland, and America. The Friends played important roles in the early history of New Jersey, Rhode Island, and North Carolina, as well as Pennsylvania. In some places, the "publishers of Truth" wore out their welcome. English authorities harassed the Quakers. Thousands, including Fox himself, were jailed, and in Massachusetts Bay between 1659 and 1661, Puritan magistrates ordered several Friends put to death. Such measures proved counterproductive, for persecution only inspired the Quakers to redouble their efforts.

This drawing, The Quakers Unmasked *(1691), satirizes the mystical sect and its leaders. William Penn and other Quakers believed that an "Inner Light" of Christ resided within every person, making all men and women equal before the Lord. In meetings such as the one depicted here, members sat in silence until the spirit prompted an individual to speak.*

Library Company of Philadelphia

Penn's "Holy Experiment"

William Penn lived according to the Inner Light, a commitment that led eventually to the founding of Pennsylvania. Penn possessed a curiously complex personality. He was an athletic person who threw himself into intellectual pursuits. He was a bold visionary capable of making pragmatic decisions. He came from an aristocratic family and yet spent his entire adult life involved with a religious movement associated with the lower class.

Penn's father had served with some distinction in the English navy. Through luck and skill, he acquired a considerable estate in Ireland, and as a wealthy landowner, he naturally hoped his son would be a favorite at the Stuart court. He befriended the king, the Duke of York, and several other powerful Restoration figures. But William disappointed his father. He was expelled from Oxford University for holding unorthodox religious views. Not even a grand tour through Europe could dissuade the young man from joining the Society of Friends. His political connections and driving intellect quickly propelled him to a position of prominence within the struggling sect. Penn wrote at least forty-two books testifying to his deep attachment to Quaker principles. Even two years in an English jail could not weaken his faith.

Precisely when Penn's thoughts turned to America is not known. He was briefly involved with the West Jersey proprietorship. This venture may have suggested the possibility of an even larger enterprise. In any case, Penn negotiated in 1681 one of the more impressive land deals in the history of American real estate. Charles II awarded Penn a charter making him the sole proprietor of a vast area called Pennsylvania (literally, "Penn's woods"). The name embarrassed the modest Penn, but he knew better than to look the royal gift horse in the mouth.

Why the king bestowed such generosity on a leading Quaker who had recently been released from prison remains a mystery. Perhaps Charles wanted to repay an old debt to Penn's father. The monarch may have regarded the colony as a means of ridding England of its troublesome Quaker population, or, quite simply, he may have liked Penn. In 1682, the new proprietor purchased from the Duke of York the so-called Three Lower Counties that eventually became Delaware. This astute move guaranteed that Pennsylvania would have access to the Atlantic and determined even before Philadelphia had been established that it would become a commercial center.

Penn lost no time in launching his Holy Experiment. In 1682, he set forth his ideas in an unusual document known as the Frame of Government. The charter gave Penn the right to create any form of government he desired, and his imagination ran wild. His plan blended traditional notions about the privileges of a landed aristocracy with radical concepts of personal liberty. Penn guaranteed that settlers would enjoy liberty of conscience, freedom from persecution, no taxation without representation, and due process of law.

In designing his government, Penn drew heavily on the writings of James Harrington (1611–1677). This English political philosopher argued that no government could ever be stable unless it reflected the actual distribution of landed property within society. Both the rich and poor had to have a voice in political affairs; neither should be able to overrule the legitimate interests of the other class. Penn's Frame of Government envisioned a governor appointed by the proprietor, a

72-member Provincial Council responsible for initiating legislation, and a 200-person Assembly that could accept or reject the bills presented to it. Penn apparently thought the Council would be filled by the colony's richest landholders, or in the words of the Frame of Government, "persons of most note for their wisdom, virtue and ability." The governor and Council were charged with the routine administration of justice. Smaller landowners spoke through the Assembly. It was a clumsy structure, and the entire edifice crumbled under its own weight.

Penn promoted his colony aggressively throughout England, Ireland, and Germany. He had no choice. His only source of revenue was the sale of land and the collection of quitrents. Penn commissioned pamphlets in several languages extolling the quality of Pennsylvania's rich farmland. The response was overwhelming. People poured into Philadelphia and the surrounding area. In 1685 alone, 8,000 immigrants arrived. Most of these settlers were Irish, Welsh, and English Quakers, and they generally moved to America as families. But Penn opened the door to men and women of all nations. He asserted that the people of Pennsylvania "are a collection of divers nations in Europe, as French, Dutch, Germans, Swedes, Danes, Finns, Scotch, Irish, and English."

The settlers were by no means all Quakers. The founder of Germantown, Francis Daniel Pastorius, called the vessel that brought him to the New World a "Noah's Ark" of religions, and within his own household, there were servants who subscribed "to the Roman [Catholic], to the Lutheran, to the Calvinistic, to the Anabaptist, and to the Anglican church, and only one Quaker." Ethnic and religious diversity were crucial in the development of Pennsylvania's public institutions, and its politics took on a quarrelsome quality absent in more homogeneous colonies such as Virginia and Massachusetts.

Penn himself emigrated to America in 1682. His stay, however, was unexpectedly short and unhappy. The Council and Assembly—reduced now to more manageable size—fought over the right to initiate legislation. Wealthy Quaker merchants, most of them residents of Philadelphia, dominated the Council. By contrast, the Assembly included men from rural settlements and the Three Lower Counties who showed no concern for Penn's Holy Experiment. Indeed, Penn's control over the lower counties was very precarious, and in 1684 he had to return to England to defend his ownership against a challenge by Lord Baltimore, who claimed them as part of Maryland. Penn sailed from Philadelphia discouraged over the infighting among colonial leaders.

A string of misfortunes in England prevented Penn from seeing his colony again until 1699. During his absence, much had changed. His religiously tolerant experiment had become a booming commercial success. Pennsylvania's agricultural products, especially its excellent wheat, were in demand throughout the Atlantic world. The English West Indies by this time provided one of the most lucrative markets for the colony's grain and meat to feed the large slave population there. Despite this economic prosperity, however, Pennsylvania's population remained deeply divided. Even the Quakers had briefly split into hostile factions. Penn's handpicked governors had failed to win general support for the proprietor's policies, and one of them exclaimed in anger that each Quaker "prays for his neighbor on First Days and then preys on him the other six." As the seventeenth century closed, few colonists still shared Penn's desire to create a godly, paternalistic society.

In 1701, legal challenges in England again forced Penn to depart for the mother country. Just before he sailed, Penn signed the Charter of Liberties, a new frame of government that established a unicameral or one-house legislature (the only one in colonial America) and gave the representatives the right to initiate bills. Penn also allowed the Assembly to conduct its business without proprietary interference. The charter provided for the political separation of the Three Lower Counties (Delaware) from Pennsylvania, something people living in this area had demanded for years. This hastily drafted document served as Pennsylvania's constitution until the American Revolution.

Quakers and Indians

The Friends' principles of equality, brotherhood, and pacifism made the early history of Pennsylvania's Anglo-Indian relations an exception to the usually conflict-ridden story of English colonization. William Penn was determined to live in friendship and peace with the Lenni-Lenape Indians who had inhabited the Delaware River valley for centuries. Even before coming to the new colony, Penn sent a letter to the chief of these people whom the English called Delawares, informing him that "The king of the Countrey where I live, hath given unto me a great Province therein, but I desire to enjoy it with your Love and Consent, that we may always live together as Neighbours and friends." Penn instructed his first deputy governor, William Markham, to "buy land of the true owners" before selling it to prospective settlers. He assured the Delawares that he would put a stop to the injustices they had suffered in previous dealings with Europeans by imposing strict regulations on trade. He also promised to adjudicate any Anglo-Indian disputes through a body composed of "an equal number of honest men on both sides."

The Delawares had heard bland assurances of European friendship before, but a variety of factors disposed them to accept Penn's overtures. Nearly a half century of trade with Swedes, Dutch, and English had taught them the benefits as well as the perils of contact. Like other native groups, the Delawares had suffered devastating epidemics that reduced their numbers to half the strength they had enjoyed in 1620. Many of their fields lay abandoned, and their 1,000 warriors seemed too few to resist their powerful Iroquois rivals to the north. Delaware leaders had witnessed how readily the Iroquois, with the blessing of the English, had subjugated the neighboring Susquehannocks and relocated them to New York (see Chapter 7). They saw an opportunity to balance the odds by forging a friendship with this powerful Englishman they called "Brother Onas" (meaning "Quill," a play on Penn's surname). The Delawares were also attracted by the rich variety of goods Penn offered them as "presents and tokens" of his goodwill. They had never seen such quantities of wampum, cloth, clothing, kettles, firearms, tobacco, and rum, to name only a few of the items Penn offered them in exchange for title to their lands. There was enough to distribute among all members of the band, and Penn's initial generosity promised very favorable terms of trade for the future.

Penn hoped that his overture to the Indians would secure not only peace and clear title to the lands, but also a prosperous share of the fur trade. Indeed, he initially believed that the Indians with whom he was dealing were the Susquehannocks, who had gained a reputation as resourceful suppliers of valuable furs to earlier generations of Dutch and Swedish traders. The Delawares also kept a number of Pennsylvania and New Jersey fur traders well supplied, but the Susquehannocks' removal to Iroquois country during the 1670s left the colonists with a shortage of native trading partners west of the Delaware Valley. Penn attempted to compensate by diverting Iroquois trade from the Hudson to the Susquehanna River, but New York's Governor Dongan moved quickly to thwart this effort.

The dearth of native trading partners in the region probably contributed to good relations between the Delawares and first-generation Quaker settlers by removing significant sources of frontier conflict. Misunderstandings and disputes over trade were rare between Indians and settlers. Indeed, for most Quakers and Delawares, Penn's ideal of living together in peace meant living separate lives with only occasional interaction. Rivalry between the Delawares and other native suppliers remained minimal during the first decades of settlement, enabling Pennsylvanians to avoid becoming caught up with the Indians in the beaver wars that raged periodically between the Iroquois and southern tribes. Penn and his deputies succeeded only partially in their efforts to discourage Delaware participation in Iroquois war parties. Nevertheless, they managed to preserve peace in the colony so well that hard-pressed bands of Indians who had become victims of conflicts with Europeans or other Indians elsewhere began migrating to Pennsylvania's Susquehanna River valley for refuge. In fact, the removal of the Susquehannocks left a vacuum in their former territories which not only attracted refugee Indians from other colonial regions, but also drew bands of western Shawnee and Miami to hunt and plant crops.

Even with the influx of new native bands such as the Naticokes and Conoys of Maryland, Pennsylvania seemed to offer plenty of land for everyone during the first generation. William Penn offered the Delawares generous prices for their ancestral lands as he negotiated his way through the colony between 1682 and 1684. Penn took great pains to make certain the Indians understood that the treaties they signed permanently conveyed the ownership of the land to him. However, he also made clear to his Commissioners of Property that he did not intend to dispossess or remove the Indians from the lands he had purchased. The commissioners were not to sell the lands to white settlers as long as the original inhabitants continued to live there. When a band did decide to move, the virtually empty lands along the Susquehanna provided them plenty of room for resettlement. In two instances, Penn oversaw the resettlement of specific groups of Indian families from their original lands to reservations further removed from white settlement, but he did not do so without securing full approval from the families involved.

Penn's efforts to win the Indians' "love and friendship by a kind, just, and peaceable life" earned him great respect among the Delaware, a respect that he returned in the interest he took in their language and culture. The Quaker leader remarked that he did not know a "Language spoken in Europe that hath words of more sweetness in Accent and Emphasis, than theirs." He also regarded them skillful, eloquent partners in negotiation, declaring that "In treaties about land, or traffic [trade], I find them deliberate in council, and as designing as I have ever observed among the politest of our Europeans." Penn himself possessed great skills at negotiation, however, and was determined to enforce his land purchases with severity if he thought it necessary. His insistence on permanently alienating Indians from their ancestral lands also suggests that, for all his professions of regard for them, he envisioned a future Pennsylvania without Indians. Nevertheless, as long as Brother Onas continued to wield influence in Pennsylvania affairs, Anglo-Indian relations remained not only peaceful but also relatively equitable.

During the first generation of settlement, Penn's coreligionists followed the proprietor's lead in Indian relations, but not all settlers shared the Friends' humane convictions. Quaker family farmers were no less land-hungry than New Englanders, especially after the opening of markets to the West Indies, but the proprietor's policy of land purchase and disposition provided them all the acreage they needed. Yet Penn's effort to recruit among the oppressed religious minorities of continental Europe and the British Isles eventually brought an influx of other colonists who wished only to build a new life and practice their faith freely. These settlers viewed the Indians as obstacles to their goals. Back in England, Penn was imprisoned in 1707 for debts incurred by dishonest colonial agents. After 1710, the rising influence of expansionists colonists in Pennsylvania coincided with a series of debilitating strokes that left Penn unable to direct his colony's Indian affairs, and tensions with the Indians escalated rapidly. His experience in America must have depressed Penn, now both old and sick. In 1718, Pennsylvania's founder died a broken man, his vision of Pennsylvania as an experiment in interracial harmony dying with him.

PLANTING THE CAROLINAS

In some ways, Carolina society looked much like the one that had developed in Virginia and Maryland. In both areas, white planters forced African slaves to produce staple crops for a world market. But such superficial similarities masked substantial regional differences. In fact, "the South"—certainly the fabled solid South of the early nineteenth century—did not exist during the colonial period. The Carolinas, joined much later by Georgia, stood apart from their northern neighbors. As a historian of colonial Carolina explained, "the southern colonies were never a cohesive section in the same way that New England was. The great diversity of population groups . . . discouraged southern sectionalism."

Proprietors of the Carolinas

Carolina was a product of the Restoration of the Stuarts to the English throne. Court favorites who had followed the Stuarts into exile during the Civil War demanded tangible rewards for their loyalty. New York and New Jersey were obvious plums. So too was Carolina. Sir John Colleton, a successful English planter returned from Barbados, organized a group of eight powerful courtiers who styled themselves the True and Absolute Lords Proprietors of Carolina. On March 24, 1663, Charles II granted these proprietors a charter to the vast territory between Virginia and Florida and running west as far as the "South Seas."

The failure of similar ventures in the New World taught the Carolina proprietors valuable lessons. Unlike the first Virginians, for example, this group did not expect instant wealth. Rather, the proprietors reasoned that they would obtain a steady source of income from rents. What they needed, of course, were settlers. Recruitment turned out to be no easy task. Economic and social conditions in

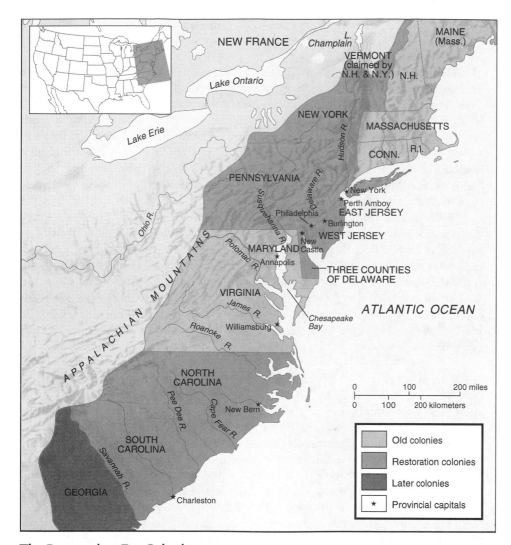

The Restoration-Era Colonies

The reign of Charles II (r. 1660-1685) was a period of renewed English interest in New World colonization. The Crown captured New Netherland from the Dutch, renaming it New York, and granted charters for the Jerseys, Pennsylvania, and the Carolinas.

England improved considerably after its civil war, and people were no longer so willing to transfer to the New World. Even if they had shown interest, the cost of transporting settlers across the Atlantic seemed prohibitively expensive. The proprietors concluded, therefore, that with the proper incentives—a generous land policy, for example—they could attract men and women from established American colonies and thereby save themselves a great deal of money. Unfortunately for the proprietors, such people were not easily persuaded.

Colonists had begun to take for granted certain rights and privileges, and as the price of settlement, they demanded a representative assembly, liberty of conscience, and a liberal headright system.

The Carolina proprietors divided their grant into three distinct jurisdictions, anticipating no doubt that these areas would become the centers of settlement. The first region, called Albemarle, abutted Virginia. As the earlier ill-fated Roanoke colonists had discovered, the region lacked a good deepwater port. Nevertheless, it attracted a number of dissatisfied Virginians who drifted south in search of fresh land. Farther south, the mouth of the Cape Fear River seemed a second likely site for development. And third, within the present state of South Carolina, the Port Royal region contained a maze of fertile islands and meandering tidal streams.

Colleton and his associates waited for the money to roll in, but to their dismay, no one seemed particularly interested in moving to the Carolina frontier. A tiny settlement at Port Royal failed. One group of New Englanders briefly considered taking up land in the Cape Fear area in 1665 but these people were so disappointed by what they saw that they departed, leaving behind only a sign that "tended not only to the disparagement of the Land . . . but also to the great discouragement of all those that should hereafter come into these parts to settle." By 1667, Colleton had died, two others had withdrawn, and four more had simply given up on Carolina.

The Barbadian Connection

Anthony Ashley Cooper, later Earl of Shaftesbury, was the exception. In 1669, he persuaded the remaining Carolinian proprietors to invest their own capital in the colony. Without such financial support, Ashley recognized, the project would surely fail. Once he received sufficient funds, this energetic organizer dispatched three hundred English colonists to Port Royal under the command of Joseph West. The fleet put in briefly at Barbados to pick up additional recruits, and in March 1670, after being punished by Atlantic gales that destroyed one ship, the expedition arrived at its destination. Only one hundred people were still alive. The unhappy settlers did not remain long at Port Royal, an unappealing, low-lying place vulnerable to Spanish attack. They moved northward, locating eventually along the more secure Ashley River. Later the colony's administrative center, Charles Town (it did not become Charleston until 1783) was established at the junction of the Ashley and Cooper Rivers.

Ashley wanted to bring order to the new society. With assistance from the English political philosopher John Locke (1632–1704), Ashley devised the Fundamental Constitutions of Carolina. Like Penn, Ashley had been influenced by the writings of James Harrington. The Constitutions created a local aristocracy consisting of proprietors and lesser nobles called landgraves and cassiques, terms as inappropriate to the realities of the New World as was the idea of creating a hereditary landed elite. Persons who purchased vast tracts of land automatically received a title and the right to sit in the Council of Nobles, a body designed to administer justice, oversee civil affairs, and initiate legislation. A parliament in which smaller landowners had a voice could accept or reject bills drafted by the Council. The very poor were excluded from political life altogether. Ashley thought his scheme maintained the proper "Balance of Government" between aristocracy and democracy, a concept central to Harrington's philosophy. Not surprisingly, the Constitutions had little impact on the actual structure of government.

Before 1680, almost half the men and women who settled in the Port Royal area came from Barbados. By the third quarter of the seventeenth century, Barbados had become overpopulated. Wealthy families could not provide their sons and daughters with sufficient land to maintain social status, and as the crisis intensified, Barbadians looked to the North American mainland for relief.

These migrants, many of whom were quite rich, traveled to Carolina both as individuals and family groups. Some brought gangs of slaves with them to the American mainland. The Barbadians carved out plantations on the tributaries of the Cooper River and established themselves immediately as the colony's most powerful political faction. "So it was," writes historian Richard Dunn, "that these Caribbean pioneers helped to create on the North American coast a slave-based plantation society closer in temper to the islands they fled from than to any other mainland English settlement."

Much of the planters' time was taken up with the search for a profitable crop. The early settlers experimented with a number of plants: tobacco, cotton, silk, and grapes. The most successful items turned out to be beef, skins, and naval stores (especially tar used to maintain ocean vessels). By the 1680s, some Carolinians had built up great herds of cattle—seven or eight hundred head in some cases—many of which they slaughtered, salted, and shipped to Barbados to supply food for the overpopulated island. Traders who dealt with Indians brought back thousands of deerskins from the interior, and they often returned with Indian slaves as well. Tar and turpentine also enjoyed a good market. Only in the 1690s did the planters come to appreciate fully the value of rice, but once they had done so, it quickly became the colony's main staple.

Proprietary Carolina was in a constant political uproar. Factions vied for special privilege. The Barbadian settlers, known locally as the Goose Creek Men, resisted the proprietors' policies at every turn. A large community of French Huguenots located in Craven County distrusted the Barbadians. The proprietors—an ineffectual group following the death of Shaftesbury—appointed a series of utterly incompetent governors who only made things worse. One visitor observed that "the Inhabitants of Carolina should be as free from oppression as any [people] in the Universe . . . if their own Differences amongst themselves do not occasion the contrary." By the end of the century, the Commons House of Assembly had assumed the right to initiate legislation. In 1719, the colonists overthrew the last proprietary governor, and in 1729, the king created separate royal governments for North and South Carolina.

Black Carolinians

African slaves were indispensable to the settlement of Carolina. From the earliest years of settlement, one of every three to four newcomers was a black slave. The decision to employ slave labor in the colony was not a difficult one for the Barbadians who brought to the colony long experience in a slave society. The difficulty of recruiting white servants made the decision that much easier. Even the Irish would no longer risk servitude in the New World. The memory of being shipped to the Caribbean islands "where they were sold as slaves" so terrified them that they would "hardly give credence to any other usage."

The effort to maintain slavery in an early frontier environment presented the Carolinians with some unique challenges. In Barbados the planters had developed laws and institutions for controlling their slaves. The population density coupled with the boundaries of ocean on every side made running away difficult. By contrast, the Carolina settlement rested on the edge of a seemingly boundless frontier filled with Indians who might assist runaway slaves on their journey to freedom. Slave owners had to establish good relations with neighboring Indian bands to ensure that runaways would be returned. Colonists likewise had to devise legal codes and practical systems of control that could prevent rebellion and keep their slaves at work on their assigned tasks. Over time, Carolinians found ways to address each of these issues, but some slaves still managed to escape their chains and disappear into the western forest.

During the earliest years of settlement, most slaves arrived in Carolina from other ports in the Western Hemisphere, though not all of them English. Caribbean pirates raided coastlines in search of captives, slavers "salvaged" slaves who had escaped or been marooned in shipwrecks, and English or colonial traders purchased a few slaves in various ports they visited for resale in Carolina. Some of the slaves had been born in the New World, whereas others were first-generation slaves with sharp memories of life and work in various parts of Africa. The slave population thus comprised a polyglot of diverse European and African languages and a wide array of cultural traditions. Many slaves also brought to Carolina special knowledge and skills that would prove very useful in the search for a viable economy.

Africans supplied nearly every type of labor in Carolina. Black craftsmen quickly came to dominate the coopers' trade, supplying barrels for packing the various export crops as well as for use around shops and plantations. Many became expert woodsmen, cutting trees to clear fields or scoring pines to collect pitch and turpentine for the colony's trade in naval stores. African cattle herders tended the great herds of their early Carolina masters using methods similar to those employed in the savannahs of their homeland. Skilled African boatmen constructed dugout canoes for use in the early Carolina fishing industry, which they dominated. Anglo-Carolinians relied on their slaves' expert knowledge of canoe travel and river navigation for transportation as well. African boatmen became indispensable to the fur trade along the Savannah River, which formed "the ordinary thorowfare to the Westward Indians."

African know-how may have been most valuable to Carolinians in the production of rice. English settlers had experimented with the crop in the first years of the settlement, but their unfamiliarity with its methods of cultivation led them to discard it for a time. In contrast, slaves from several parts of Africa, especially those from West Africa's Gambia River and the Windward Coast, which stretched from modern-day Sierra Leone to the Ivory Coast, possessed thorough knowledge of rice cultivation. Africans had been growing rice in those regions for centuries before European contact, and they readily adapted their methods to the new varieties introduced by the Portuguese and French during the 1500s. Although not all slaves who came to Carolina understood rice cultivation, a significant minority did come from African regions where rice was grown. Historian Daniel Littlefield has shown that as rice grew in importance as a staple after 1690, Carolinians preferred to purchase slaves from rice-growing regions. Slaves planted, hoed, and threshed the crop using methods similar to those employed in African rice fields.

Relations between English and Africans were relatively fluid in early Carolina due to the colony's rugged character and its location on the exposed southern flank of English settlements, closest to hostile Spanish Florida. Slaves and masters often worked side by side clearing fields, formed common hunting parties to search for the game that fed both groups, and fought together in skirmishes against the Spanish or hostile Indians. They also suffered debilitating bouts of disease together in Carolina's humid subtropical climate. Although never free from the threat of the whip, slaves enjoyed significant latitude to participate in the frontier economy. They were often allowed to keep their own gardens or hire themselves out after finishing their assigned tasks, and many took advantage of this latitude to carve out for themselves a degree of economic autonomy. A few slaves managed to save enough of their own earnings to purchase their freedom, while a few others achieved manumission by performing special acts of service or winning unusual favor from their masters.

Africans frequently engaged in sexual relations with both English and Indians in Carolina's early years, sometimes entering unofficial unions that endured for years. White men most commonly took African or Indian female partners, but white women were not punished for joining in sexual relationships with black men until 1717. The offspring of these interracial unions born to slave mothers became slaves themselves unless a white father claimed them, but those whose mother was a white servant or freewoman often became free. Some of these free persons of color managed to become members of white society, but most occupied a tenuous status on the lowest rungs of the social ladder and faced a lifelong struggle to retain their freedom.

Black Carolinians interacted constantly with Indians as well as whites. First-generation colonists often put enslaved Indians into the fields to supplement their workforce, bringing them into daily contact with Africans. Such contact encouraged cultural exchange between the two groups. Africans learned much from the Indians concerning the new environment in which they found themselves, the geography of the land, the climate, and the use of medicinal plants. A few such as Colonel Alexander Mackey's slave Timboe mastered native languages and put to use their knowledge of Indian lore as highly valued interpreters. Many others took advantage of early Carolina's fluid environment and entered the fur trade as semi-independent agents—so many, in fact, that colonial authorities eventually prohibited slaves from participating except as agents of their masters.

The first Carolina settlers arrived in an area already transformed by more than a century of contact with Europeans. The Guale, Timucua, and Apalachee tribes to the south of the new English colony had been substantially incorporated into the Spanish empire and the Roman Catholic Church (see Chapter 2). Many of these Indians lived in villages either transformed or in some cases established by Franciscan missionaries. Their hereditary leaders had in many ways become Spanish dons, adopting Spanish dress, receiving Spanish horses, and enjoying the

Traders, Raiders, and Indian Slaves on the Carolina Frontier

exemptions from corporal punishment, manual labor, and taxation that were due their rank. Each year they received rich gifts of goods from the governor in the name of the King of Spain as their reward for loyal service. In return, they governed the villages, even exercising considerable authority over the Spanish friars and soldiers themselves. They also oversaw the supply of native tribute labor that the Spanish demanded from those under their control. The heavy toll this labor exacted in Indian life and health had provoked several rebellions in the two decades before the English settled Carolina, yet the Spanish were still managing to keep their frayed empire intact.

Indians to the west and north of Charles Town had long enjoyed a steady commerce with traders from Virginia. Until the 1670s, most English trade to the region passed through Occaneechi middlemen, whose territory straddled the route to the southern Piedmont Indians such as the Cherokees and Creeks. When followers of Nathaniel Bacon decimated the Occaneechis in 1676, they cleared the way for Virginia merchants to trade directly with the southern tribes.

Trade and contact with Europeans, whether Spanish or English, had produced its familiar effects on the Indians who engaged in it. The inadvertent introduction of epidemic disease destroyed local populations. Villages contracted, moved, or disappeared, and the remnants of affected ethnic groups combined to form new tribes such as the Catawbas of North Carolina. The intentional introduction of products such as firearms, metal utensils, and cloth displaced items made with traditional materials and technologies of the forest. As traditional skills were lost, dependence on European trade increased.

Thus Carolina settlers arrived in the 1670s to find a ready market for their goods among the region's native peoples, who already understood the use of these items and were looking only for greater advantages in trade. The Barbadian settlers were also especially quick to recognize that the region's intertribal rivalries presented them an opportunity to increase their own security and clear title to the land by setting the Indians against one another. Captives taken as a by-product of this intertribal warfare could generate substantial profits when sold as slaves on an Atlantic market. The proprietors opposed these practices, asserting a monopoly on Indian trade and prohibiting the enslavement of Indians within 400 miles of Charles Town. The colonists, however, did not find it difficult to circumvent regulations imposed from a distance of over 3,000 miles.

Between 1670 and 1700, Charles Town colonists pursued their Indian policy by establishing a series of alliances with tribal peoples who proved useful to their ends, shifting loyalties whenever a given alliance had outlived its purpose. In the early years the Westoes of the Savannah River readily aided their new Charles Town allies in decimating the small coastal tribes who stood in the way of English settlement. The Westoes received a rich supply of arms and trade goods for their friendship until 1680, when they found themselves in the way of Carolina's expansion. Ambitious traders then enticed the Lower Creeks of Carolina and the Savannah band of Shawnees to push eastward, eliminate their Westoe rivals, and enjoy the bounties of English trade.

The Creek and Savannah alliance proved a virtual gold mine for Carolina traders, bringing a steady supply of furs, deerskins, and Indian slaves to Charles Town over the next three decades. The alliance gave traders access deep into the interior, so that by the turn of the century the French of Louisiana reported encountering a constant stream of English in search of commodities for trade. Chief among those commodities was the traffic in human laborers, "each person being traded for one gun." Carolina's Lower Creek and Yamassee trading partners also invaded Florida to enslave Catholic Indians. By 1685 they had pushed all the Guale villages to within 50 miles of St. Augustine. Over the next two decades they trained their sights on the Apalachee, raiding their villages repeatedly until 1704, when a combined English and Indian force under the leadership of Colonel James Moore struck the final blow. Moore's campaign netted over 1,000 Christian Indian slaves for sale to Carolina planters, West Indian sugar barons, and mainland colonial customers as far north as New England. St. Augustine was left to preside over a colony in ruins, its villages deserted and its missions destroyed. Florida's governor estimated in 1708 that the Carolina trade in Indian slaves had claimed between 10,000 and 12,000 of the Spanish crown's Indian subjects.

AN EMPIRE OF CONTRADICTIONS

The tragic contrast between the Carolina settlers' actions and the proprietors' ideals was only the most glaring of many ironies that marked those colonies established or seized during the Restoration era. The Long Island towns welcomed the Duke of York's capture of New Netherland only to chafe under his autocratic rule. The Quakers hoped to make Pennsylvania and the two Jerseys into models of racial, ethnic, and religious harmony, only to clash with each other over how to govern their holy experiments. Virtually no Restoration-era colonist, not even Quakers, detected any conflict between their demand for freedom of conscience and their ready reliance on the labor of African slaves.

The contradictions of life in England's Restoration-era colonies mirrored the conflict and tensions of later Stuart England itself. Yet overarching all was the determination of English merchants and officials to make their nation preeminent in Atlantic trade. By the time of Charles II's death in 1685, the budding success of the newest colonies suggested how far the English had gone toward achieving their goal. The colonial enterprise of the Restoration era had emerged little less haphazardly than had that under Charles II's father and grandfather. Yet investors and colonists had learned from earlier failures and successes. The new ventures took hold alongside well-established older colonies, which could not only provide resources but also settlers from their own surplus populations. Moreover, the British West Indies provided most of the new colonies with a steady demand for their agricultural goods.

Out of this haphazard mixture of colonial ventures was emerging the outline of an English Atlantic commercial system. The legal groundwork for that system had been laid in the Navigation Acts of the 1660s, but the political framework of Anglo-American relations remained strongly contested as Charles's absolutist brother James II ascended the English throne. The coming years would witness a transatlantic constitutional struggle over the shape of England's new empire, one whose outcome would establish the terms of an international rivalry for control of North America.

CHRONOLOGY

1663	Charles II grants charter to True and Absolute Lords Proprietors of Carolina.
1664	Duke of York grants the Jerseys to John, Lord Berkeley, Sir George Carteret.
1665	Duke's Laws establish English royal government in New York.
1670	Barbadian emigrants begin colonizing South Carolina.
1672	Dutch recapture New York and hold it for two years.
1674	Sir Edmund Andros Anglicizes New York government and commerce.
1681	William Penn receives charter for Pennsylvania.
1682	Robert Barclay promotes Scottish emigration to East Jersey.
1682	Penn purchases Three Lower Counties (Delaware).
1685	Carolina-Yamasee alliance devastates Guale of northern Florida.
1696	First slave code passed in South Carolina.
1701	Penn's Charter of Liberties establishes unicameral legislature for Pennsylvania.

RECOMMENDED READING

A good overview of the development of colonial New York after its capture by the English is available in Robert C. Ritchie, *The Duke's Province: A Study of New York Politics and Society, 1664–1691* (Chapel Hill, 1977). For South Carolina, see Robert M. Weir, *Colonial South Carolina: A History* (Millwood, NY, 1983) and M. Eugene Sirmans, *Colonial South Carolina: A Political History, 1663–1763* (Chapel Hill, 1966). The standard account of Pennsylvania's early development remains Gary B. Nash, *Quakers and Politics: Pennsylvania, 1681–1726* (Princeton, 1968), while a good overview of the development of New Jersey is Richard P. McCormick, *New Jersey: From Colony to State 1609–1789*, rev. ed. (Newark, 1981). Brendan McConville, *These Daring Disturbers of the Peace: The Struggle for Property and Power in Early New Jersey* (Ithaca, 1999) offers a fresh examination of New Jersey's turbulent early history. A good biography of William Penn is Mary M. Dunn's *William Penn: Politics and Conscience* (Princeton, 1967).

The ethnic diversity of the Middle Colonies has become the subject of many excellent and innovative studies in recent years. Oliver A. Rink, *Holland on the Hudson: An Economic and Social History of Dutch New York* (Ithaca, 1986) explores the establishment and persistence of Dutch settlement in New York, while Donna Merwick's *Death of a Notary: Conquest and Change in Colonial New York* (Ithaca, 1999) offers a fascinating and unsettling case study of the impact of English occupation on the original Dutch inhabitants of New York. Cynthia A. Kerner's *Traders and Gentlefolk: The Livingstons of New York, 1675–1790* (Ithaca, 1992) explores the opportunities New York opened to one enterprising English family. Barry Levy explores the transfer of northern English culture and patterns of family life to Pennsylvania in *Quakers and the American Family: British Settlement in the Delaware Valley* (New York, 1988). Richard and Mary M. Dunn, eds., *The World of William Penn* (Philadelphia, 1986) contains essays on the diversity of early Pennsylvania settlement. For early Scottish settlement in New Jersey, see Ned C. Landsman, *Scotland and Its First American Colony, 1683–1765* (Princeton, 1985).

For a splendid analysis of the development of slavery and slave culture in South Carolina, see Peter H. Wood, *Black Majority: Negroes in Colonial South Carolina from 1670 through the Stono Rebellion* (New York, 1974). Daniel C. Littlefield explores the impact of African ethnicity on South Carolina slavery in *Rice and Slaves: Ethnicity and the Slave Trade in Colonial South Carolina* (Urbana, 1981). Alan Gallay discusses early Carolinian efforts to establish an American slave coast in his *Indian Slave Trade: The Rise of the English Empire in the American South, 1670-1717* (New Haven, 2002). Judith A. Carney, *Black Rice: The African Origins of Rice Cultivation in the Americas* (Cambridge, Mass., 2002) sets Carolina rice cultivation in a broader Atlantic context.

Several of the essays in Daniel K. Richter and James H. Merrell, eds., *Beyond the Covenant Chain: The Iroquois and Their Neighbors in Indian North America, 1600–1800* (Syracuse, 1987) treat Anglo-Indian relations in the Middle Colonies during this period. Richter's *Ordeal of the Longhouse: The Peoples of the Iroquois League in the Era of European Colonization* (Chapel Hill, 1992) includes an extensive analysis of New York-Iroquois relations after the arrival of the English. For the Delawares, see C. A. Weslager, *The Delaware Indians: A History* (New Brunswick, 1972). A number of innovative recent studies have added greatly to our knowledge of native peoples of the colonial Southeast. For an excellent overview, see James Axtell, *The Indians' New South: Cultural Change in the Colonial Southeast* (Baton Rouge, 1997). For the Cherokees see Tom Hatley, *The Dividing Paths: Cherokees and South Carolinians through the Era of Revolution* (New York, 1993). For the Choctaws see Patricia Galloway's *Choctaw Genesis, 1500–1700* (Lincoln, 1995). James H. Merrell's pathbreaking *The Indians' New World: Catawbas and Their Neighbors from European Contact Through the Era of Removal* (Chapel Hill, 1989) explores the emergence of this group and the history of their dealings with Carolina settlers.

Chapter 9

Glorious Revolution and International Realignment

A heavy snowstorm brought nightfall to Schenectady, New York even earlier than usual on February 8, 1690. By 11 P.M. the snow was "above Knee Deep" and the English, Dutch, and Mohawk inhabitants fast asleep. No one heard as two hundred French and Algonquian raiders silently encircled the village and slipped past the unguarded gates. At a signal, the entire force rushed at once. So complete was the surprise, the French commander reported, that "few houses made any resistance." Those who awoke in time fired "severall gunns" to raise the alarm to farmers in the surrounding countryside, but the deep snow muffled the shots. No one came to Schenectady's aid. For two hours the Canadian force swarmed the village, putting "everyone who defended the place to the sword" and setting afire every house but one. The raiders took twenty-seven surviving inhabitants as prisoners and spared "some twenty Mohawks . . . to show them that it was the English and not they against whom the grudge was entertained."

Although Schenectady's unfortunate inhabitants lived an ocean away from European centers of power, the attack reveals the frontier community's significance as a strategic outpost of a larger Atlantic world. Schenectady's English, Dutch, and Mohawk inhabitants fell victim that night to transatlantic aftershocks of England's so-called Glorious Revolution, in which English leaders ousted the Catholic King James II in favor of James's Protestant daughter Mary and her husband, the Dutch ruler William of Orange, who became William III of England. The action rekindled Anglo-French conflict throughout the Atlantic world, a circumstance that gave the beleaguered Iroquois new hope for English assistance in their wars against New France's Algonquian allies. Indeed, the gesture of sparing

Mohawk warriors at Schenectady had only confirmed the Iroquois' determination to "regard *Yonondio* [the French governor] as our Enemy, for he is a Cheat." Yet the ouster of James also sparked an uprising in New York that divided the colonists themselves into warring factions too busy quarreling with each other to offer effective assistance to their Iroquois allies or to respond to the renewed French threat.

News of the "Sack of Schenectady" generated a torrent of finger-pointing by factions divided over Dutch colonist Jacob Leisler's effort to stage his own Glorious Revolution in New York. As early as November 1689, Leislerians and anti-Leislerians had both heard of plans by the enterprising Canadian governor, Comte Louis de Buade de Frontenac, to capitalize on Anglo-French hostilities by leading a military force to capture New York. Yet even with ample advance warning, the colonists failed to respond in time to avert disaster.

In its aftermath, each side sought to exonerate its own behavior and shift responsibility to the other. Leisler charged that without the "treachery cowardice and carelessness" of his opponents at Albany, New Yorkers "would have discovered the enemy & prevented that disaster" at Schenectady. Albany's Robert Livingston countered that Leisler had "so bygotted" Schenectady's inhabitants with "seditious letters" that the "poor people" refused reinforcements sent from Albany in the king's name. Leisler's blood-soaked letters themselves had survived the attack as proof of the rebels' culpability. "We want nothing but a Governor," Livingston declared, "to call [Leisler] to account."

The blame-shifting efforts of the two factions revealed the terms of a constitutional struggle that engulfed most English colonies in the late 1680s, even as the sack of Schenectady exposed the transatlantic peril posed by England's Glorious Revolution and subsequent war with France. Throughout his American dominions, James II's absolutist policies had sparked conflict over the role English settlers should exercise in their own governments. The dramatic coup by William and his English supporters gave aggrieved colonists a chance to overturn many of James's reforms, as Leisler's letters to Schenectady promised. Colonists throughout America seized that chance in various ways, helping to define a new imperial order in which they would share a significant measure of control over their own affairs.

Yet such efforts proved hazardous in an atmosphere of heightened imperial rivalry, as Schenectady's inhabitants learned too late. The Sack of Schenectady reminds us that as early as the 1690s, the American colonies— in the Caribbean as well as on the mainland—were being drawn into an elaborate world system, where decisions made in distant places and markets affected warfare on the colonial frontier. We cannot consider European-Indian relations or life along the frontier as somehow removed from this context, for it was in this period that the major European powers—France and England especially—were experiencing military and fiscal changes that would transform the world. The Anglo-American Revolution of 1688–1689 not only made possible a new transatlantic constitutional order; it also plunged the French, Algonquian, Iroquois, and English into a seventy-year contest for a North American empire.

JAMES II AND THE AMERICAN COLONIES

James II ascended the throne of England in 1685 amid a climate of grave domestic unrest and diplomatic uncertainty. As England's first Catholic monarch in more than 130 years, James aroused Protestant fears of a renewal of the anti-Protestant persecution carried out under his ancestor "Bloody Mary" Tudor. Supporters of Parliament feared that James would intensify the efforts of his late brother Charles II to strengthen the Crown's prerogative and centralize authority at the expense of the Houses of Lords and Commons, and the localities. Dutch authorities feared that James might betray them in the Netherlands' impending conflict with France. So acute were these misgivings that James's accession sparked a revolt led by Charles II's illegitimate son, James Scott, Duke of Monmouth, and supported by many influential gentry and nobility as well as the philosopher John Locke. James commanded enough loyalty at the beginning of his reign to suppress the uprising, but his Catholicizing and authoritarian policies in Church and state increased English and Dutch apprehensions about the new monarch's rule. These fears extended to the American colonies as James stepped up efforts begun under his late brother Charles II to bring the colonies under more effective royal control.

Edmund Andros and the Dominion of New England

The government of Massachusetts had been under siege by royal officials for at least ten years by the time of James II's accession. In 1676, an officious royal agent named Edward Randolph had paid a brief visit to the Bay Colony to investigate its compliance with England's Navigation Acts (see Chapter 7). On Randolph's return to England, he submitted two reports charging that Massachusetts ignored the Navigation Acts. He also complained that Massachusetts authorities put English subjects to death for religious views, denied accused Englishmen the right of appeal from colonial courts to the Privy Council, and refused the oath of allegiance to the English Crown.

Randolph's dutiful service won him an appointment as collector and surveyor of customs for Massachusetts. In 1678 he brought his new wife to the colony and settled in to bring the recalcitrant Puritans to heel. New England merchants, judges, and juries repeatedly thwarted Randolph's zealous efforts to collect the king's customs. Determined to make the Bay Colony submit, Randolph fired off a series of hostile reports urging London authorities to revoke the charter of 1629. His letters helped set in motion a series of actions in England that culminated in the charter's annulment in 1684, clearing the way for the Crown to impose a new government on Massachusetts Bay.

Two years passed before Sir Edmund Andros, former governor of New York and architect of England's Covenant Chain with the Iroquois, arrived in Boston with instructions to establish a consolidated royal government over all colonies from Connecticut to Maine. Andros's instructions authorized him to appoint and rule through a new council without an elected assembly. The new royal governor possessed full authority "by and with the advise and consent of our said Councill, or the major part of them," to tax, to appoint all judges and officers of the peace, and to muster and command the militia "for the resisting and withstanding all enemies pyrats and rebells."

Andros moved quickly to extend royal authority over this new Dominion of New England, as his consolidated government was called. An experienced military commander, the governor expected his handpicked council to carry out his orders with the same alacrity he demanded of his military subordinates. The day after his arrival in Boston he ordered that he and other communicants in the Established Church be given space in the Old South meetinghouse to observe Anglican services. Three months later he converted the building to an Anglican church. Andros also imposed new taxes on the colonists. When the Reverend John Wise of Ipswich led the town meeting in resisting the new rates, Andros ordered him arrested, tried, and fined £10. The governor dealt similarly with other such attempts to defy his authority and eventually moved to minimize further obstruction by restricting town meetings to one annually.

None of Andros's actions galled colonists so sharply as his declaration that the revocation of the original Massachusetts charter had voided all their land titles. The governor warned that families who had inherited and farmed their land for the past sixty years were now considered intruders on the King's possessions. Landholders would have to petition the Crown for new royal patents that would legitimate their ownership but make them liable to the Crown for new fees and quitrents. Andros added injury to insult by issuing choice grants of common land and land not yet granted to his friends, including the colonists' old nemesis Edward Randolph.

Without their elected assemblies, and with the Dominion courts now packed against them by Andros's appointments, New England colonists possessed few legal means to resist the Dominion government. Connecticut and Rhode Island enjoyed a brief reprieve from Andros's rule because the Crown had temporarily left their charters intact, but by November 1687 both colonies submitted. By then Massachusetts colonists had concluded that they could gain relief from Andros's rule only by petitioning James II himself. In April 1688, Harvard College's president, the Reverend Increase Mather, boarded a ship bound for London to carry the colonists' grievances against Andros to the King.

The Middle Colonies and the Dominion

During the first year of Andros's governorship in New England, New York and the Jerseys remained separate colonies. Indeed, James II had appointed a fellow Catholic, Colonel Thomas Dongan as governor of New York to advance the King's interests in the colony. Dongan served the King faithfully by competing with Andros for rule over Connecticut, hoping to persuade its leaders to petition James

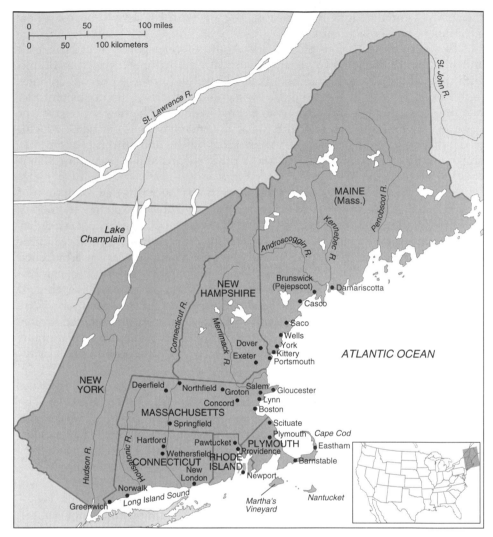

The Dominion of New England, 1688

During the late 1680s, Governor Edmund Andros implemented Royal efforts to consolidate the various governments of New England and New York under a single imperial authority.

to annex the colony to New York. Instead, James issued Andros a new commission in the spring of 1688 that extended the Dominion to New York and the Jerseys as well as Connecticut and Rhode Island. The commission may have relieved Dongan of his authority, but it also relieved him of the administrative headache of trying to govern a colony chronically short on funds.

As proprietary colonies, East and West Jersey presented the King and Andros with a more complicated problem. The people of West Jersey submitted to Andros quickly, but colonists in East Jersey remembered earlier conflict with the imperious governor when he had tried to impose customs and meddle in their affairs from his seat in New York. The colony's mostly Scottish proprietors also insisted on submitting to Andros's rule only the government of East Jersey while retaining full ownership and rights to the land. In the end, the proprietors and Andros both got most of what they wanted.

As a favorite of the Stuarts, William Penn managed to remain proprietor of Pennsylvania throughout James II's reign. Penn was residing in England at the time of James's succession and became intimately involved in the monarch's efforts to extend religious tolerance to all non-Anglican Christians, Catholics included. Penn served James not only out of gratitude that "the King was always his Friend, & his Father's Friend," but also because James was "a Friend to those of his Persuasion." He hoped by his service to secure permanent liberty of conscience not only for Quakers in America but for those in England as well.

James II's governors attempted to apply the king's absolutist policies to Anglo-Iroquois relations, but their presumption crashed against the Five Nations' power to assert their independence as a "free people" who could make war and peace as they chose. When Andros arrived in Boston in December 1686, the Iroquois were facing renewed hostilities from the French and their Algonquian allies. In London, however, royal instructions were being dispatched to Andros and New York's governor Dongan to observe a new Treaty of American Neutrality with France, which had been signed only in November. The treaty angered even some of James's closest supporters in England because it settled none of the territorial disputes between England and France over North America. The treaty's ink had scarcely dried when word reached English officials of new French aggression in America, suggesting that the French had no intention of honoring the terms of neutrality. James's English subjects could only fume as their sovereign insisted on implementing the treaty.

The Dominion and the Covenant Chain

The Five Nations, however, refused to act as English subjects or parties to a treaty made 3,000 miles away. Open war erupted in Iroquois lands in the summer of 1687 when Jacques-René de Brisay de Denonville led an invasion of French and Algonquian forces into the Seneca country. On his way to sacking and burning a broad swath of Seneca countryside, Denonville captured and enslaved a party of Iroquois diplomats. Denonville's treachery toward the diplomats alienated even those Iroquois families and leaders who had earlier favored the French.

Governor Dongan recognized that his Covenant Chain obligations to the Five Nations demanded more action than his absolutist sovereign would permit. The governor could not "ingage the French" himself and pled ineffectually for his Iroquois "Brethren" to "have a little patience." Nevertheless, American realities prompted Dongan to "put off" his native allies "by giving them Powder, Lead, Arms, and other things fitting and necessary for them," turning a blind eye to how the arms would be used.

Throughout the winter and spring of 1687–88, Iroquois warriors used Dongan's gifts to prosecute mourning war against French settlements along the St. Lawrence River. By summer the experience of having "women and children . . . daily carried off" persuaded Denonville to begin negotiations for peace. Governor

Dongan employed whatever meager stratagems he possessed to prevent his Iroquois "children" from engaging in independent negotiations without English participation. The Five Nations ignored Dongan. Negotiations continued throughout the summer of 1688, only to break down when Wyandot allies of New France ambushed an Iroquois delegation and falsely blamed their action on orders from Denonville.

The Wyandots' treachery united the Five Nations to renew their campaign against the French and Algonquians. By autumn of 1688, when Andros arrived in Albany to proclaim the incorporation of New York under his authority, Iroquois warriors had forced the French to abandon western strongholds including Forts Frontenac and Niagara. They had captured the Jesuit priest Pierre Millet as revenge for Denonville's earlier capture of the Iroquois diplomats. One war party had penetrated as far north as Lachine on Montreal Island, where they killed 24 French and took between 70 and 90 prisoners. Andros could only bluster at his Five Nations "children" to cease their hostilities and abide by the Treaty of American Neutrality.

By the time Andros addressed the Iroquois in Albany, the failure of the Anglo-French treaty had become clear to all. In the fall and winter of 1688–89, Andros levied a force of 709 Massachusetts militia and led them to Maine, where he hoped to secure the province against Abenaki and French Acadian foes. Andros spent the winter employing a combination of paternalism and military discipline to contain his resentful New England force while he negotiated for peace with the Abenaki through exchanges of words and gifts. Thus Anglo-Indian diplomacy, in which the governor possessed significant skill, occupied him far from Boston in March 1689 when word reached the capital that James had fled for France.

James II and the Plantation Colonies

Beyond the Dominion of New England's boundaries, James II was also acting to bring the southern plantation colonies under the royal thumb. In Maryland, a long-running power struggle between the Catholic proprietor Cecilius Calvert, the second Lord Baltimore, and aggressive Protestant planters gave James a pretext to begin action against Baltimore's charter. Maryland planters had been agitating for such measures since the 1660s under the leadership of the fiery Anglican assemblyman John Coode. They believed that the proprietor's determination to exercise his prerogative prevented Marylanders from enjoying the full "rights of Englishmen." They hoped that dissolution of the Calvert family's charter and imposition of direct royal government would usher in a more stable government secured by English law and Parliamentary precedent, one in which their own assembly would play a more reliable role in protecting English rights.

James's well-known antipathy to elective assemblies should have made the Maryland planters wary, as should his efforts to consolidate governments and enlarge the governors' prerogatives elsewhere. So opposed were the colonists to proprietary rule, however, that one of Coode's cronies, Nehemiah Blackiston, accepted appointment as the king's collector of customs. In that post Blackiston could further undermine Lord Baltimore's precarious position with the Crown by filing damaging official reports that exposed the proprietor's attempts to evade the Navigation Acts. Yet even as opponents in Maryland and London chipped away at Baltimore's charter, Virginia's royal governor, Francis, Lord Howard of Effingham, campaigned for the Crown to consolidate Maryland within his own government. Doing so, Effingham argued, would increase Crown revenues on to-bacco as well as augment the Virginia governor's own perquisites.

In the British West Indies, James made a series of appointments designed to bring to heel each island's overmighty planter class. As chief stockholder and pres-ident of the Royal Africa Company, James also wanted to make sure that his Caribbean governors and customs agents would protect the company's monopoly on the slave trade by suppressing all interlopers.

One of James II's earliest acts, however, was to increase the supply of bound la-bor on the islands by transporting between 800 and 1,200 prisoners who had par-ticipated in Monmouth's abortive rebellion of 1685. Around 100 of the best arti-sans among them went to Virginia, where Effingham sold them and split the profits with William Blathwayte, James's secretary of war and plantations. The rest went to Jamaica, Barbados, and the Leewards, where most labored on the estates of James's appointees to royal office in those colonies.

James II's governors in all the sugar islands allied themselves with discontented small planters to overthrow the sugar barons. In the Leewards, Sir Nathaniel Johnson raised taxes and challenged all titles. He made landholders petition for new patents requiring payment of a quitrent to the King, just as Sir Edmund Andros was doing in New England. In Barbados, Edwin Stede vigorously sup-pressed interlopers to the slave trade, packed the ruling council with appointments drawn from outside the great planter class, and rigorously enforced a newly dou-bled tax on sugar.

Jamaica's new royal governor Christopher Monck, the second duke of Albemarle, sided with the island's buccaneers as well as its small planters to wrest control from the planter class. A profligate, drunken wastrel who had squandered the family fortune in England, Albemarle was only too ready to escape to the Caribbean where he hoped to prey on Spanish treasure. In 1684 he had sponsored the successful expedition of Boston's Sir William Phips to recover twenty-six tons of Spanish silver treasure from the wreck of the *Almiranta*. The operation had net-ted Albemarle £50,000, whetting his appetite for even more booty. The bucca-neers and small planters helped Albemarle turn the great planters out of most of-fices and cheerfully supported his treasure-hunting efforts. Many big planters, meanwhile, followed their Barbadian and Leeward counterparts to England. There some joined the opposition to James's colonial policy, while others retired to enjoy their wealth.

THE GLORIOUS REVOLUTION IN ENGLAND AND AMERICA

Throughout England's emerging Atlantic empire, James II and his councilors were working to strengthen royal authority and undercut rival claims to a share in gov-ernment, whether a Parliament at home or a planter-elected assembly in Barbados. The King's opponents everywhere saw his unfolding policies through anti-Catholic and anti-French lenses. Members of the English ruling elite watched with increas-ing alarm as James turned Protestants out of office to install his Catholic favorites.

The joint monarchs William III and Mary II ruled England after the Glorious Revolution of 1688, which deposed Mary's father, James II. The European political realignment that attended their ascension to the throne helped to intensify the eighteenth-century Anglo-French contest for North American empire.

left: By Courtesy of the National Portrait Gallery, London (NPG 1902); right: By courtesy of the National Portrait Gallery, London (NPG 197)

Alarm turned to widespread popular unrest in 1688 when the King imprisoned seven Anglican bishops for refusing to read from the pulpits his Declaration of Indulgence, which extended toleration to Catholics and dissenting Protestants alike. Against James's expectations, leading Dissenters stood with the bishops against "letting Papists into the Government."

American colonists thought they detected similar patterns in the policies of James's colonial governors. New Englanders rapidly convinced themselves that Andros's efforts to enforce the Treaty of American Neutrality, along with his negotiations with the Iroquois, Abenaki, and French Canadians, cloaked a "Popish Plot" to "serve the French Interest" and "Ruine New England." In New York, Dutch Calvinists joined English Anglicans and Puritans in worrying that the Catholic Governor Dongan was hatching a similar plot.

By autumn of 1688, support for James's rule in England was rapidly melting away. Even some of his closest advisors joined a plot to support a Protestant invasion of England led by James's nephew, the Dutch ruler, William of Orange, husband of the King's Protestant daughter Mary. In November 1688, William crossed the English Channel with an invasion force of over 15,000 men in 250 ships. A "Protestant Wind" swept the Dutch flotilla around the English Channel Fleet to

Torbay in southern England. There William landed his troops and began a march toward London, gathering strength as he went. James soon lost his nerve and fled to France with his wife, Mary of Modena, and their new baby son. With the help of a newly elected Convention Parliament (so called because it was summoned without an official order from the King), William and Mary quickly consolidated their power and were crowned joint rulers in February 1689.

This Glorious Revolution altered the course of English political history, transformed the diplomatic landscape of Europe, and reshaped American colonial affairs. As a part of the Settlement of 1689, William and Mary accepted a Bill of Rights, a document stipulating the rights of all Englishmen. In doing so, they surrendered some of the prerogative powers that had destabilized English politics for almost a century. The crown remained a potent force in the political life of the nation, but never again would an English king or queen attempt to govern without Parliament.

The Bill of Rights also aligned England with the Protestant forces of Europe by securing Protestantism firmly within the English Church and state. The bill excluded all Catholic heirs of the royal family "forever" from inheriting "the crown and government of this realm." It also required monarchs to swear at their coronation that they would not appoint known Papists to office. The Toleration Act of 1689 rounded out the safeguards to Protestantism by extending religious toleration to dissenting Protestants while denying it to Catholics.

In America, the Glorious Revolution initiated a process of political re-Anglicization. After this time the colonies, which had begun as separate, experimental enterprises, became more integrated into an English imperial system. Colonists came increasingly to think of themselves as inhabitants of provinces, self-conscious extensions of English culture in America.

The Glorious Revolution in Massachusetts

In March 1689, rumors of the Glorious Revolution in England stirred the colonists of Boston into action. Sir Edmund Andros hastened to the capital from the outpost in Maine where he had been attempting to secure peace with the Abenakis. Within weeks after he left, the provincial troops he had brought with him revolted and began making their own way back to Boston. On April 18, Boston townspeople turned out in the streets, with many of the Maine deserters joining in. They quickly formed themselves into companies, arrested Andros's military officers and royal officials, including the colonists' old nemesis, Edward Randolph, and bottled up the governor in the town fort along with a company of regular troops. Sometime during the day, leaders assembled the companies before the Boston Town House to hear a declaration justifying the rebellion in secular terms of the rights of English subjects. Colonists knew that such a declaration would win far more sympathy in England than one that appealed to traditional Puritan ideas of a divine covenant. That afternoon, the local gentry persuaded Andros to leave the fort and meet them in the Town House, where the sheriff arrested him. The next day the former governor ordered the evacuation of the town's fort and the castle in Boston harbor. New England's version of the Glorious Revolution was complete.

The coup in Boston was so popular that no one came to Andros's defense. The governor was jailed without a single shot having been fired. According to Increase Mather's son Cotton, who was also a leading Congregational minister, the colonists were united by the "most Unanimous Resolution perhaps that was ever known to have Inspir'd any people."

However united they may have been, the Massachusetts colonists could not take the crown's support for granted. William III, the new English monarch, believed that a strong colonial administration would help him achieve his strategic aims. Indeed, Sir Edmund Andros had fully expected the King to confirm Dominion policies, which enjoyed substantial support among administrators of colonial policy in England. William could have declared the New Englanders rebels and summarily reinstated Andros, as some of the King's councilors hoped he would do.

Thanks largely to the tireless efforts of Reverend Increase Mather, William instead abandoned the Dominion of New England. Mather had gone to London to petition James II for relief from Andros's abuses, but by the time he arrived events were rapidly moving toward William's invasion. Mather did receive multiple audiences with James during the summer of 1688, but spent most days cultivating the influential connections that could help him gain a favorable settlement for Massachusetts. After William and Mary came to the throne, Mather spent two years laboring incessantly to thread a middle course between the demands of colonial leaders for a full reinstatement of the 1629 charter and the determination of London officials to strengthen the Crown's power over the colony.

Finally in 1691, Massachusetts received a new royal charter. Reinstatement of the company patent of 1629 had proved politically impossible, because it had conceded far too much autonomy to the colonists. In the charter of 1691, the freemen no longer selected their governor. That choice now belonged to the king. Membership in the General Court was determined by annual election, and these representatives from the various towns in turn chose the men who sat in the council or upper house, subject always to the governor's veto. Moreover, the franchise, restricted here as in other colonies to adult males, was determined on the basis of personal property rather than church membership, a change that brought Massachusetts into conformity with general English practice. On the local level, town government remained much as it had been in Winthrop's time.

The Glorious Revolution and the charter of 1691 produced a significant shift in the political culture of Massachusetts Bay. The colonists had recovered a significant amount of self-determination, but at the price of shifting the theoretical basis of their government from an explicitly religious to a more secular foundation. Ministers and many magistrates continued to speak as if the colony was in covenant with God. Most, however, argued that government's primary purpose was to uphold the rights of Englishmen, especially the property rights that Andros had challenged. Any Protestant could perform that function. Indeed, the new charter required that Massachusetts government remain open to non-Puritans. England's Toleration Act of 1689 reinforced this requirement. This meant that magistrates must now permit the Church of England's "*Common Prayer*" books and "unwarrantable *ceremonies*" as well as the worship of other dissenting groups such as Baptists and Quakers.

In granting Massachusetts a new charter, William III also reversed much of the Dominion's consolidation of New England territory. Connecticut resumed government under its charter of 1662, which had never been formally annulled after its government submitted to Andros. Rhode Island likewise resumed government under its charter of 1663, which William III eventually restored. Both charters gave freemen of the two colonies a right to elect governors from their own ranks, a practice that continued until the American Revolution. New Hampshire received its own royal governor and elected assembly. Tiny Plymouth Colony, however, was absorbed into Massachusetts's jurisdiction, as were the settlements of Maine.

The instability of the Massachusetts government following Andros's arrest—what Reverend Samuel Willard described as "the short Anarchy accompanying our late Revolution"—allowed what under normal political conditions would have been an isolated, though ugly, local incident to expand into a major colonial crisis. Hysterical men and women living in Salem Village, a small, unprosperous farming community, nearly overwhelmed the new rulers of Massachusetts Bay. Accusations of witchcraft were not uncommon in seventeenth-century New England. Puritans believed that an individual might make a compact with the devil, but during the first decades of settlement, authorities executed only about fifteen alleged witches. Sometimes villagers simply left suspected witches alone. Never before had fears of witchcraft plunged an entire community into panic.

Contagion of Witchcraft

The terror in Salem Village began in late 1691, when several adolescent girls began to behave in strange ways. They cried out for no apparent reason; they twitched on the ground. When concerned neighbors asked what caused their suffering, the girls announced that they were victims of witches, seemingly innocent persons who lived in the community. The arrest of several alleged witches did not relieve the girls' "fits," nor did prayer solve the problem. Additional accusations were made, and at least one person confessed, providing a frightening description of the devil as "a thing all over hairy, all the face hairy, and a long nose." In June 1692, a special court convened and began to send men and women to the gallows. By the end of the summer, the court had hanged nineteen people; another was pressed to death. Many more suspects awaited trial.

Then suddenly, the storm was over. Led by Increase Mather, a group of prominent Congregational ministers belatedly urged leniency and restraint. Especially troubling to the clergymen was the court's decision to accept "spectral evidence," that is, reports of dreams and visions in which the accused appeared as the devil's agent. Worried about convicting people on such dubious testimony, Mather declared, "It were better that ten suspected witches should escape, than that one innocent person should be condemned." The colonial government accepted the ministers' advice and convened a new court, which promptly acquitted, pardoned, or released the remaining suspects. After the Salem nightmare, witchcraft ceased to be a capital offense.

No one knows exactly what sparked the terror in Salem Village. The community had a history of religious discord, and during the 1680s, the people split into angry factions over the choice of a minister. Economic tensions played a part as well. Poorer, more traditional farmers accused members of prosperous, commercially oriented families of being witches. The underlying misogyny of the entire culture meant the accused were more often women than men. Some historians have suggested that the symptoms of torment described by the victims bore striking similarities to the hallucinations, nausea, and prickling sensations characteristic of poisoning from ergot, a mold sometimes found in rye which the colonists cultivated. Other historians have noted that many of the accused had ties with the war-torn Maine frontier, and it is possible that fear of Indian attack fueled the panic.

Whatever the ultimate physical, social, and psychological sources of this event may have been, jealousy and bitterness apparently festered to the point that adolescent girls who normally would have been disciplined were allowed to incite judicial murder. As so often happens in incidents like this one—the McCarthy hearings of the 1950s, for example—the accusers later came to their senses and apologized to the survivors for the needless suffering they had inflicted on the community.

Leisler's Rebellion in New York

The Glorious Revolution in New York was more violent than it had been in Massachusetts Bay. Divisions within New York's ruling class ran deep and involved ethnic as well as religious differences. English newcomers and powerful Anglo-Dutch families who had recently risen to commercial prominence in New York City and Albany opposed the older Dutch elite.

The leader of New York's uprising, Jacob Leisler, was a man entangled in events beyond his control. The son of a German minister, Leisler emigrated to New York in 1660 and through marriage aligned himself with the Dutch elite. While he achieved moderate prosperity as a merchant, Leisler resented the success of rising Anglo-Dutch families such as the Schuylers, the Van Cortlandts, and the Livingstons.

When news of the Glorious Revolution reached New York City in May 1689, Leisler raised a group of militiamen and seized the local fort in the name of William and Mary. Leisler maintained a tenuous hold over the fort and the city for the next few weeks and eventually managed to organize the election of a Committee of Safety. The committee affirmed his leadership early in June, an action which prompted Andros's lieutenant governor in New York, Captain Francis Nicholson, to give up the struggle for control of the government and sail for England.

Although Leisler expected an outpouring of popular support, it was not forthcoming. His rivals waited, watching while "the hott brain'd Capt Leisler" desperately attempted to legitimize his actions. Through bluff and badgering, Leisler managed to hold the colony together, especially after French forces burned Schenectady in February 1690. The French threat prodded Leislerians and anti-Leislerians into grudging cooperation for the colony's defense throughout the following year, but Leisler never established a secure political base.

In March 1691, a new royal governor, Henry Sloughter, reached New York. He ordered Leisler to surrender his authority, but when Sloughter refused to prove he had been sent by William rather than by the deposed James, Leisler hesitated. The pause cost Leisler his life. Sloughter declared Leisler a rebel, and in a hasty trial, a court sentenced him and his chief lieutenant, Jacob Milbourne, to be hanged "by the Neck and being Alive their bodyes be Cutt downe to Earth and

Their Bowells to be taken out and they being Alive, burnt before their faces. . . ." In 1695, Parliament officially pardoned Leisler, but he not being "Alive," the decision arrived a bit late.

Unlike the New England colonies, New York never received a charter as part of its settlement. Instead, Governor Sloughter convened a council and assembly to pass a declaratory law that would ensure New Yorkers a measure of self-determination for which many had been struggling since the 1660s. In a preamble, the act thanked William and Mary for restoring the rights of Englishmen to New Yorkers. It then moved to secure those rights by placing the colony's supreme legislative power in the hands of a royally appointed governor, a council, and the "people" through an assembly of representatives elected annually by male heads of households who possessed "fourty shillings per Annum in freehold." The governor could veto colonial legislation, as could the Crown, but all laws remained effective until the King disapproved them. William's official approval of this law the next year made New York's framework of government permanent.

The settlement of New York's government in 1691 did not bring an end to the colony's fractious political life. Long after Leisler's death, factions calling themselves Leislerians and Anti-Leislerians struggled to dominate New York government. Indeed, in no other eighteenth-century colony was the level of bitter political rivalry so high.

The Glorious Revolution in Maryland

When the first rumors of James's overthrow reached Maryland early in 1689, pent-up antiproprietary and anti-Catholic sentiment exploded. During the spring and early summer wild rumors flew about the countryside that the Catholics had hired the Senecas to butcher the Protestants, that Protestants awaited a fleet of reinforcements to aid them in butchering Catholics, that the English had captured and beheaded James II. The scarcity of reliable news from England only compounded the problem. Especially troubling was the proprietary government's delay in proclaiming the new monarchs.

When the government of neighboring Virginia proclaimed William and Mary as the new English monarchs in late April, John Coode's patience ran out. The leader of Maryland's antiproprietary faction formed a group called the Protestant Association. Coode waited more than two months before leading the association's members in a march against the capital at St. Mary's. No one would fight for the proprietor's side. Proprietary officials fled to Mattapany, Lord Baltimore's estate, where Governor William Joseph lay sick. Coode's forces borrowed several cannons from a London vessel in St. Mary's harbor and laid siege to the mansion, whereupon its inhabitants capitulated "to prevent Effusion of blood."

Coode avoided Leisler's fatal mistakes. The Protestant Association, citing many wrongs suffered at the hands of local Catholics, petitioned the crown to transform Maryland into a royal colony. After reviewing the case, William accepted Coode's explanation, and in 1691, the king dispatched a royal governor to Maryland. A new assembly dominated by Protestants declared Anglicanism the established religion. Catholics were excluded from public office on the grounds that they might be in league with French Catholics in Canada. Lord Baltimore lost control of the colony's government, but he and his family did retain title to

Maryland's undistributed lands. In 1715, the crown restored to full proprietorship the fourth Lord Baltimore, who had been raised a member of the Church of England, and Maryland remained in the hands of the Calvert family until 1776.

A Framework for Political Order

England's Glorious Revolution exerted similar political effects throughout mainland North America, establishing a framework for imperial politics that remained in place until 1763. In most colonies, Crown-appointed governors and imperial officials looked after London's interests, usually aided by a council which colonists eventually came to view as a functional equivalent of England's House of Lords.

Crown officials also engaged in a decade-long struggle to eliminate all proprietary charters and bring those governments under direct royal control. The New Jersey proprietors capitulated in 1701, and the two colonies became united under a single royal government. William Penn, however, survived the cloud of suspicion that hung about him during the early years of William and Mary's reign to become the leading defender of proprietary charters. Penn briefly lost his charter rights over Pennsylvania in 1692 when he and his Quaker assembly refused on pacifist principles to support the English war effort. Yet William III restored them in 1694 after Penn promised to support Crown policies, including the laws on trade. During the next decade Penn sought to enforce imperial policy in Pennsylvania while defending charter rights before the Board of Trade and in Parliament. He lost a battle over the Three Lower Counties of Delaware, which became a Crown colony in 1701. He ultimately won the war for Pennsylvania, however, which remained in the Penn family until the American Revolution.

In every colony, elected houses of assembly exerted a potent check on Crown or proprietary appointees. The assemblies retained the power of initiating money bills, levying taxes, and even paying the governor's salary. Widespread ownership of land meant that a majority of free male inhabitants in every colony possessed the forty-shilling freehold required to vote, lending the lower houses a degree of popular representation unheard of in England and insulating them from manipulation by royal officials. Though London officials still wielded great power in colonial affairs, the various colonial settlements of the 1690s prevented them from dictating policy as James II's administration had attempted to do. Colonists regained significant power to shape colonial policy in ways favorable to their own interests.

In the following decades, colonial assemblies worked tirelessly to expand their powers still further. They increasingly came to see themselves as little Parliaments. The irony is that, as colonial assemblymen made their representative bodies more English in form, they began to defend more fervently against the home government their political rights as Englishmen.

AN AGE OF ATLANTIC WARS

William's invasion of England not only transformed English and colonial politics, but also produced a major shift in the balance of power in Europe. Charles II had pursued a pro-French policy throughout his reign while waging intermittent warfare on the Dutch. James II had not followed his brother's active pro-French policies, but he attempted to secure English neutrality in European affairs while concentrating on his absolutist and Catholicizing policies at home. William had watched these developments with increasing alarm as his troops fought to defend Dutch territory and commerce against the ambitions of Louis XIV of France. Indeed, the Dutch need for English military support in the face of imminent war with France helped drive William's decision to make a bid for James's crown. It also persuaded Dutch leaders to support their prince's risky enterprise.

The Glorious Revolution thus thrust England into an almost unprecedented role in European affairs after 1689. William's invasion sparked a series of hot and cold wars between England and France that would not finally subside until Wellington's defeat of Napoleon in 1815. The conflict began with Louis XIV's declaration of war against the United Provinces of the Netherlands almost immediately after William set foot on English soil. In March 1689, the Sun King sent aid to James II's supporters in Ireland, an act which permitted William III to cast his own English declaration of war against France as a measure "not so properly an act of choice as an inevitable necessity in our own defence." The ensuing War of the League of Augsburg—known in America as King William's War—lasted until 1697, when the Treaty of Ryswick brought a brief peace. The fevered religious atmosphere in England prompted William's supporters to describe the conflict in stark apocalyptic terms that pitted the forces of an English Protestant constitutional monarchy against Popish French tyranny. The theme played well in America, where the Anglo-French contest spread within a matter of months.

This new role in large-scale European military conflict stimulated the development of what the historian John Brewer has called England's "fiscal-military state." As the English army and navy began growing steadily larger under William III, Parliament increased taxes while the Crown instituted administrative reforms to streamline revenue collection. Heavy borrowing to supplement taxes contributed to a national debt whose growth helped to prompt establishment of the Bank of England in 1694. The debt rose steadily over the next century, eventually making the government the chief force in the English economy. Yet after 1696, the determination of many in the ruling class to preserve their hard-won limits on royal authority led them to obstruct royal adventurism on the Continent. Instead, opposition leaders in Parliament managed to steer the fiscal-military state toward developing a great naval power that could extend England's commercial and colonial interests throughout the world.

News of William's invasion and the subsequent French declaration of war sent shock waves throughout England's Caribbean sugar islands. Sir Nathaniel Johnson, governor of the Leewards, wrote William in May 1689 that he could not accept the revolution even as the French on neighboring islands prepared for war. Within a month of Johnson's letter to William, 130 Irish servants sacked English plantations on St. Christopher. An invasion force from the French half of the island soon followed to oust the English completely. English planters on Nevis, Antigua, and Montserrat feared a similar fate when a letter, intercepted in transit from Johnson to the French Governor Blenac, appeared to indicate that the Jacobite Johnson would betray all the Leewards to France. They persuaded Johnson to resign and appoint the wealthy West Indian planter Christopher Codrington in his place.

Anglo-French Conflict in the West Indies

Under Codrington, English planters launched a contest with the French for control of the Lesser Antilles, a costly string of assaults and reprisals that continued with only brief respite for the next fifteen years. Codrington's huge estates on both Barbados and Antigua generated profits from which the governor could draw to subsidize English military efforts in the Caribbean. His investment seemed to pay off in 1690, when Codrington led the English in a successful campaign to retake all of St. Christopher. The governor carved himself yet another vast plantation from some of the island's best French holdings and staffed it with a workforce of plundered slaves. Codrington eventually lost his St. Christopher estate, however, when the Treaty of Ryswick restored the French half of the island to its former owners in 1697.

The insecurity of captured West Indian estates did not prevent either the French or the English from attempting to seize each others' lands and slaves. Neither side managed to deal a knockout blow to the interests of the other, and the conflict eventually settled into mutual looting and plundering that resulted in enormous property damage. When the French commander, the Comte de Chavagnac led still another invasion of St. Christopher in 1706, for instance, the English holed up in Fort Charles to watch as the French seized their slaves and burned their plantations. Chavagnac did not bother laying siege to the fort, nor did the English trouble to put up a fight except to fire on the few French companies that strayed within range. When supplies ran low, Chavagnac abruptly departed, leaving the English to petition the home government for compensation of a staggering £145,000 in losses.

Jamaica endured similar conflict throughout the 1690s, but became more stable after 1700. King William's governor of the colony, Sir William Beeston, led islanders in resisting a string of French raids as well as a major invasion of the colony in 1694. The Treaty of Ryswick brought a peace to Jamaica that continued throughout the next decade, thanks to a large garrison of English troops who discouraged French attack.

Equally significant for Jamaica's future was the final defeat of the buccaneering interest during the reign of William and Mary. Spurred by Albemarle's abuses of power in Jamaica, the great planters formed an effective lobby in London to argue that their own interest in profits and the Crown's interest in customs revenues were united. The King, persuaded both by arguments and falling revenues, restored to planters the offices Albemarle had taken away. The defeated buccaneers moved to new bases on St. Domingue and the Bahamas.

Distance insulated Barbados from the depredations that stalked the Leewards during the reigns of William III and his successor, Queen Anne. Nevertheless, the era's Anglo-French conflict helped transform the dynamics of island life by establishing a pattern of absentee ownership that endured through the next century. Warfare discouraged the return of the great Barbadian planters who had left the island after James II's appointment of Edwin Stede. Repeated delays eventually persuaded them to remain in England permanently, where they found they could guard their interests more effectively than by occupying seats in a distant Barbadian assembly. Barbados's leading planter families became a powerful interest group that quickly learned how to obtain favorable policies by lobbying the Crown and Parliament. Great planters in the Leewards and Jamaica formed similar lobbies, making the sugar interests a potent force in the development of imperial commercial policy.

English-leaning leaders within the Five Nations welcomed the news of war between France and England when it arrived in June 1689. Mohawk headmen swore on behalf of their Iroquois confederates that "as they are one hand and Soul with the English, they will take Up the Ax with pleasure against the French." During the following decade, deepening involvement in the Anglo-French conflict transformed a complex of internal alliances among autonomous Iroquois village leaders into a coherent political confederacy. The new Iroquois Confederacy paralleled the older Iroquois League, whose sachems continued to preserve Iroquois culture and traditions above the fray of Confederacy factionalism. The political Confederacy incorporated old tensions among its Anglophile and Francophile leaders without resolving them. Indeed, tensions only increased as English reluctance to hold up their end of the Covenant Chain exposed the Iroquois to repeated defeats by the French and the western Algonquians.

Native Americans and European Wars

The conflict of the 1690s pitted the Iroquois allies of England against not only the French, but also their Canadian Iroquois cousins and a strengthening alliance of western Algonquians. Earlier in the century, the Iroquois had pressed these groups hard by battling west and north to expand access to beaver pelts. Western Indians such as the Wyandots, Ojibwas, Potawatomis, and Ottawas responded by forging ties with the French through trade, intermarriage, and military alliance. Efforts by La Salle and other French explorers to link the Great Lakes–St. Lawrence and the Mississippi trade networks (see Chapter 7) began paying off in the 1690s. A painfully won complex of reciprocal friendships, trade, and kinship among French colonists and members of these Algonquian groups—one that historian Richard White has termed the "middle ground"—permitted them to coalesce against their common Iroquois enemy.

Aided by the aggressive military leadership of Governor Louis de Buade de Frontenac and commander Antoine Laumet de La Mothe, Sieur de Cadillac, the western Algonquians hit the Iroquois hard. At the same time, Frontenac made diplomatic overtures to woo the Five Nations away from the English, thereby monopolizing the fur trade and forging an alliance that could ultimately push the English out of North America. This carrot-and-stick approach confirmed to many Iroquois their assessment of the French as treacherous double-dealers. Yet persistent losses prompted them to engage in two years of peace talks with the French after 1694.

New York's Governor Benjamin Fletcher, who replaced the deceased Sloughter in 1691, took a dim view of Iroquois peace efforts. Negotiation with the French smacked of an independence inappropriate for a people Fletcher saw as subjects of the English Crown. At worst, the governor feared that such talks could swing the Iroquois to the French. In 1694, a delegation of Five Nations leaders presented Fletcher with a carefully negotiated plan that included concessions from Frontenac and proposed a peace "not only between all the Indians but between all their relations," including the governors of Canada and New York. Fletcher refused to "treat of Peace with the Governour of Canada," something he was not authorized to do. This refusal and an accompanying denunciation of the Five Nations' "shame and dishonour" left the Iroquois peace plans in tatters.

Iroquois leaders also conducted separate peace talks with Wyandots and Ottawas during the mid-1690s. The two sides discovered mutual mistrust of the French, whom the western Indians suspected of attempting to forge a secret deal that would elevate Iroquois interests above those of the west. By summer's end in 1695, the Wyandots and Ottawas had convinced their western neighbors to join a truce with the Iroquois, which both sides hoped would lead to full peace. Yet new French plans for an invasion of Iroquois country ultimately thwarted these efforts as well.

The failure of Iroquois peace efforts spelled suffering in the years ahead. In the summer of 1696, Frontenac himself led a force of two thousand French and native allies into the heart of Iroquoia. The force destroyed the main Onondaga town, burned a neighboring Oneida village to the ground, and wiped out the region's ripening crops. Meanwhile, Cadillac persuaded the western Algonquians to break the hard-won truce of 1695 and step up their raids against the Five Nations. Even the 1697 Treaty of Ryswick between England and France brought no relief to the Iroquois. The French governors of Canada vowed to continue war until the Confederacy negotiated a separate peace that would strengthen French pretensions to Iroquois lands.

Thus, hostilities ground on through the turn of the century between the weakened Five Nations and a strengthening alliance of French and western Algonquians. By century's end, the Indians of the Ohio Valley and the western Great Lakes controlled the region's fur trade and exchanged pelts for trade goods, which bound them ever more tightly with their French partners. These ties enabled them not only to threaten the Iroquois, but also to augment Algonquin strength by extending French influence to groups even further west.

Finally, in 1701, the exhausted Five Nations managed to conclude a peace in the Grand Settlement of that year. The Confederacy agreed to remain neutral between the French and English in exchange for French cessation of hostilities and an English commitment to protect their western hunting grounds. The English, probably contrary to Iroquois intentions, understood their part of the bargain as securing a Crown title to western Iroquois territory. In fact, the Grand Settlement of 1701 represented a reassertion of the Five Nations' status as an equal party in mutual covenant with the English. In so doing, it altered the Covenant Chain forged in the 1670s that had formally allied the Five Nations under English sovereignty.

The Grand Settlement also gave various Iroquois factions the flexibility to negotiate semi-independent agreements that would advance their own interests. One faction of neutralists led by Teganissorens forged a covenant chain with western nations that siphoned more furs to Albany. Later groups negotiated similar arrangements with Indian nations and even rival English colonial governments.

The settlement of 1701 forced the Iroquois to recognize the western limits of their power. Losses from the wars of the 1690s soon prompted them to replenish their diminished numbers by renewing the tradition of mourning war to the south, where they had earlier cowed native peoples with their superior military might (see Chapter 7). After 1700, however, they began encountering stiffer resistance from nations to the west of Virginia and the Carolinas. A flood of European traders and goods into the Piedmont and backcountry had enabled groups such as the Catawbas and Cherokees to even the odds in warfare by purchasing firearms, which they used effectively to repel Iroquois raiders and their native allies. At times, Catawba parties retaliated by carrying the fight into Iroquois territory.

The Grand Settlement of 1701 complemented the great European realignments of the 1690s by establishing a new North American framework of commerce, diplomacy, and warfare. Although the Anglo-French contest for empire imposed limits on Iroquois autonomy, the settlement nevertheless demonstrated the Five Nations' resilience and skill in adapting to changing circumstances to achieve their own ends. Though severely pressed and divided by the conflicts of the 1690s, the Iroquois managed to gain a new flexibility in trade and diplomatic affairs. The ambiguity of the Grand Settlement made the Five Nations something less than the third imperial force some older historians have made them. Yet the Iroquois Confederacy emerged from the first round of Anglo-French conflict with substantial power to guard their own interests against French and English pretensions.

A COMMERCIAL EMPIRE TAKES SHAPE

Iroquoia and the Caribbean bore the brunt of King William's War in America, but trade throughout the colonies also suffered. During the war's early years, the French conducted a successful campaign to disrupt English shipping throughout the Atlantic. In Europe, French naval vessels lay in wait for English merchant vessels entering the English Channel, and the French Crown issued letters of marque, which authorized private seizure of a hostile nation's ships, to hundreds of French privateers who fanned out into American, Caribbean, African, and East Indian waters in search of lucrative prey. English commerce remained chronically underprotected through the war because the navy could never spare enough "ships of the line"—battle vessels large enough to sail in a line exchanging broadsides with enemy ships. William's commanders periodically disrupted trade even further by hiring private vessels away from merchant shipping to supplement the royal navy in large operations.

London merchants and their colonial trading partners suffered enormous losses. In 1695 and 1696 alone, the Royal Africa Company lost over £57,000 while the Barbados merchants lost a princely £387,000. The trade between the Anglo-American mainland and the Caribbean suffered nearly as much during the same period, with New England, Jamaican, and Leeward Island merchants losing £320,000. "The losses from the plantations are double for the nation," the Barbadian planters lamented to Parliament. Without taxes from the re-export of sugar and tobacco to Europe, many English troops would go unpaid and "foreigners will have our silver to be sure, for the exchange is governed by the balance of trade."

The enormous financial losses measured only a part of the total cost of conflict on the high seas. Privateers usually tried to capture rather than sink merchant vessels with their valuable cargoes. Nevertheless, many merchant sailors lost their lives attempting to defend their vessels, and many others drowned as their battle-damaged ships sank. Harassment by privateers often prevented Caribbean vessels from leaving port until the height of the hurricane season, resulting in additional loss of life when the ships went down in storms. Warfare at sea made the Middle Passage even more miserable for slaves, who often found themselves caught in the crossfire between their captors and enemy privateers who attempted to seize them for profit.

Warfare did not bring unmitigated disaster to colonial producers, merchants, and shippers, however. The need to provision the English army and navy increased demand for colonial agricultural products. French disruption of Anglo-Swedish trade—a crucial source of naval stores such as pitch, tar, masts, and rope—prompted shipbuilders to look to America for alternate supplies. Crown bounties on naval stores prompted South Carolina planters to head for the woods with their slaves where they collected pine resin for rendering into pitch and tar. New England further bolstered its reputation as a source of valuable white pine masts, and vessels from New England shipyards replaced many losses in the Anglo-American mercantile fleet.

Colonists and London merchants alike exploited the disruptions of King William's War. War exacerbated colonial evasion of the Navigation Acts by forcing the Crown to relax enforcement. Even more vexing were English privateers who abused their commissions to prey on legitimate English shipping. After 1695, Parliament set out to put a stop to these practices by plugging the loopholes in English maritime law. In doing so, Parliament extended London's effective reach ever further, drawing the American colonies into a global commercial system.

Enforcing the Marketplace: 1696

Parliament passed its last major piece of imperial commercial legislation with the Navigation Act of 1696. Among other things, the statute tightened enforcement procedures, putting pressure specifically on the colonial governors to keep England's competitors out of American ports. The Navigation Act also expanded the American customs service and for the first time set up vice-admiralty courts in the colonies. This decision rankled the colonists. Established to settle disputes that occurred at sea, vice-admiralty courts required neither juries nor oral cross-examination, both traditional elements of common law. They were effective and sometimes even popular, however, for resolving maritime questions quickly enough to send the ships to sea again with little delay.

The year 1696 witnessed one other significant change in the imperial system. William III replaced the ineffective Lords of Trade with a body of policy advisers that came to be known as the Board of Trade. This group was expected to monitor colonial affairs closely and to provide government officials with the best available advice on commercial and other problems. For several decades, at least, it energetically carried out its responsibilities.

The members of Parliament believed these reforms would belatedly compel the colonists to accept the Navigation Acts, and in large measure they were correct. By 1700, American goods transshipped through England accounted for a quarter of all English exports, an indication that the colonists found it profitable to obey the commercial regulations. In fact, during the eighteenth century, smuggling from Europe to America dried up almost completely.

The new enforcement procedures of the 1696 Navigation Act also represented Parliament's fresh determination to stamp out piracy. Many Anglo-American ports had acquired a reputation for harboring buccaneers who used letters of marque as a cover for preying indiscriminately on commercial shipping. Inadequate enforcement coupled with lax rules for legitimating seized cargoes often enabled privateers and their merchant backers to profit handsomely even when the vessels they seized belonged to fellow English subjects. By the 1690s, however, the steady growth of English shipping had made colonial commerce too valuable to tolerate these shady practices.

Policing Commerce: The War on Piracy

Royal officials in London began pressing their counterparts throughout the colonies to round up pirates or drive them out of colonial ports. Jamaica planters were actually ahead of the game, having driven buccaneers off the island in the early 1690s. Royal officials in Pennsylvania sent damaging reports to London that Philadelphia merchants were harboring crew members of the notorious buccaneer, Henry Avery. This blot on his reputation prompted William Penn to launch a vigorous campaign to suppress piracy when he returned to govern the colony in 1699.

The most notorious pirate of the era, Captain William Kidd, inadvertently intensified the campaign against piracy by blundering into a hornets' nest of East Indian and English commercial and political interests. Had Kidd not chosen this period to embark on his most enterprising voyage, he would probably have ended his days as another of colonial New York's many obscure privateers. In 1695 the lure of East Indian gold led this buccaneer to London, where he acquired the backing of the Earl of Bellomont, an ambitious politician who had just been appointed Royal governor of New York. In 1696 Kidd and his crew set sail in the thirty-four-gun *Adventure Galley*, armed with a royal commission to capture pirate booty for the profit of himself, his crew, and his investors.

Once in the Indian Ocean, however, Kidd assured the Madagascar pirates that "he was as bad as they," and hoisted the blood-red pirate flag in pursuit of merchant vessels. He invoked the British flag to gain his one valuable prize, the Indian-owned *Quedah Merchant*, after tricking the ship's captain into presenting French papers. Kidd then began a circuitous return voyage to New York in hope that his patron Bellomont, now governor of the colony, would declare the seizure a legal prize of war.

In Kidd's absence, the Navigation Act of 1696 had made such seizures much more difficult to legitimate, while a diplomatic uproar over the *Quedah Merchant's* seizure made the captain himself too hot to handle. The circumstances of Bellomont's appointment to New York had forced him to side with the colony's Leislerian faction and to shore up his reputation in England by suppressing pirates sponsored by his anti-Leislerian enemies. In this position, the governor could scarcely afford exposure as a patron of pirates himself, especially one as notorious as Kidd had become. News of the *Quedah Merchant's* capture had circulated from Madagascar throughout the Atlantic ports and into the court of William III. It had also provoked the members of the Indian ruling class to suspend trade with the

British East India Company until London took firmer measures to suppress piracy. When Kidd finally returned to Long Island Sound in the fall of 1698, Bellomont had him arrested.

Ultimately, Captain Kidd's criminal adventure hastened the passage of Parliament's first meaningful antipiracy law, the Act for the More Effectual Suppression of Piracy of 1700. Word of Kidd's capture arrived in Parliament during a committee report on the bill, prompting members to order Kidd's trial delayed until they could pass the act. The Piracy Act imposed the death penalty on anyone convicted of piracy as well as those found guilty of aiding and abetting pirates. On May 13, 1701, William Kidd and three accomplices died on a gallows by the Thames as the first victims of the Piracy Act.

The unambiguous criminalization of piracy after 1700 contributed to imperial stability even as it drove a wedge between pirates and the merchants and officials who had earlier sponsored them. The threat of prosecution encouraged colonial officials to uphold order, refusing to harbor pirates as they had once done in exchange for a share of the booty. The rising value of colonial exports steadily united the Anglo-American merchant community to secure the sea-lanes and profits against buccaneers who exploits had once injected cash into the local economy.

Pirates themselves reflected this alienation in a growing hostility to the "base Merchants, and cruel commanders of ships." Pirates spurned family, society, and religion to join ostensibly egalitarian crews governed by written ship's agreements, though members nevertheless often found themselves exposed to the treachery and capricious violence of their fellows. The "bloody flag" of seventeenth-century piracy gave way to flags symbolizing time and death, including the skull and crossbones. The choice to engage in piracy increasingly expressed not a quest for instant wealth, but a desperate attempt to escape low wages, unemployment, or a captain's brutal treatment.

COMMON EXPERIENCES, SEPARATE CULTURES

"It is no little Blessing of God," Cotton Mather announced proudly in 1700, "that we are part of the English nation." A half-century earlier, John Winthrop would not have spoken these words, at least not with such enthusiasm. The two men were, of course, products of different political cultures. It was not so much that the character of Massachusetts society had changed. In fact, the Puritan families of 1700 were much like those of the founding generation. Rather, the difference was in England's attitude toward the colonies. Rulers living more than 3,000 miles away now made political and economic demands that Mather's contemporaries could not ignore.

Yet the various settlements of 1688–1689 had given the inhabitants of English America significant power to determine how they would meet royal demands. Colonial legislatures protected property rights and guarded the interests of local merchants and producers. Crown officials steadily drew back from the overweening authoritarianism of James II's appointees to concern themselves primarily with regulating imperial commerce. The Iroquois and other native leaders managed to preserve their status as free peoples, staving off royal governors' efforts to extend authority over their persons and lands. Even the strengthening of the imperial commercial system worked to the ultimate advantage of Indians and colonists as well as English merchants, providing an increasingly secure framework in which transatlantic trade could flourish.

The creation of a new imperial system did not erase profound sectional differences. By 1700, for example, the Chesapeake colonies were more, not less, committed to the cultivation of tobacco and slave labor. Although the separate regions were being pulled slowly into England's commercial orbit, they did not have much to do with each other. The elements that sparked a powerful sense of nationalism among colonists dispersed over a huge territory would not be evident for a very long time.

CHRONOLOGY

1677	New Hampshire becomes a royal colony.
1684	Charter of Massachusetts Bay Company revoked.
1685	Duke of York becomes James II.
1686	Dominion of New England established.
1687	Connecticut, Rhode Island submit to Dominion government; Iroquois launch war against French outposts.
1688	James II driven into exile during Glorious Revolution.
1689	William and Mary crowned joint monarchs in England; rebellions break out in Massachusetts, New York, and Maryland; War of the League of Augsburg (King William's War) commences.
1690	Sir William Codrington launches English campaign for control of Lesser Antilles.
1691	Jacob Leisler executed.
1692	Salem Village wracked by witch trials.
1694	Bank of England established.
1696	Parliament establishes Board of Trade; passes Navigation Act of 1696.
1697	Treaty of Ryswick ends War of the League of Augsburg.
1701	Grand Settlement among Iroquois, French, and English.
1702	East Jersey and West Jersey unite to become single colony under royal authority.

RECOMMENDED READING

The most detailed discussion of the Glorious Revolution in America remains David S. Lovejoy, *The Glorious Revolution in America* (New York, 1972). A good collection of documents illustrating the event may be found in Michael G. Hall, Lawrence H. Leder, and Michael G. Kammen, eds., *The Glorious Revolution in America: Documents in the Colonial Crisis of 1689* (Chapel Hill, 1964). Michael Garibaldi Hall's *Edward Randolph and the American Colonies, 1676–1703* (Chapel Hill, 1960) explores the importance of the royal customs official's role in the formation of England's late-seventeenth-century colonial policy. Stephen Saunders Webb provides a provocative transatlantic perspective on the events of 1688–1689 in his *Lord Churchill's Coup: The Anglo-American Empire and the Glorious Revolution Reconsidered* (New York, 1995). For additional English and European background, see W. A. Speck, *Reluctant Revolutionaries: Englishmen and the Revolution of 1688* (Oxford, 1988); Dale Hoak and Mordechai Feingold, eds., *The World of William and Mary: Anglo-Dutch Perspectives on the Revolution of 1688–89* (Stanford, 1996); and Craig Rose, *England in the 1690s: Revolution, Religion and War* (Oxford, 1999).

On imperial developments after 1789, John Brewer's *The Sinews of Power: War, Money and the English State, 1688–1783* (New York, 1989) provides a crucial starting point in his analysis of the development of England's "fiscal-military state" stimulated by the Glorious Revolution and international realignment. See also Ian K. Steele, *The English Atlantic, 1675–1740* (Oxford, 1986), and Thomas C. Barrow, *Trade and Empire: The British Customs Service in Colonial America, 1660–1775* (Cambridge, Mass., 1967). On piracy, see Robert C. Ritchie, *Captain Kidd and the War against the Pirates* (Cambridge, Mass., 1986), and Marcus Rediker, *Between the Devil and the Deep Blue Sea: Merchant Seamen, Pirates, and the Anglo-American Maritime World, 1700–1750* (Cambridge, 1987).

Treatments of the Glorious Revolution's impact on Anglo-Indian relations may be found in Kenneth M. Morrison, *The Embattled Northeast: The Elusive Ideal of Alliance in Abenaki-Euramerican Relations* (Berkeley, 1984); Daniel K. Richter, *The Ordeal of the Longhouse: The Peoples of the Iroquois League in the Era of European Colonization* (Chapel Hill, 1992); Richard White, *The Middle Ground: Indians, Empires, and Republics in the Great Lakes Region, 1650–1815* (Cambridge, 1991); and Daniel K. Richter and James H. Merrell, eds., *Beyond the Covenant Chain: The Iroquois and Their Neighbors in Indian North America, 1600–1800* (Syracuse, 1987).

There is no shortage of literature on witchcraft in colonial America. Richard Godbeer's *The Devil's Dominion: Magic and Religion in Early New England* (Cambridge, 1992) explores witchcraft within the context of a struggle between folk belief and formal Puritan religion in seventeenth-century New England. John Demos explores the part played by beliefs about witchcraft within community life in his *Entertaining Satan: Witchcraft and the Culture of Early New England* (New York, 1982). Carol Karlsen, *The Devil in the Shape of a Woman: Witchcraft in Colonial New England* (New York, 1987), argues that witchcraft accusations and convictions reveal a systematic pattern of gender bias and underlying conflicts over gender roles in New England society. Mary Beth Norton's *In the Devil's Snare: The Salem Witchcraft Trials of 1692* (New York, 2002) treats the trials at Salem as an outcome of fears concerning political instability and imperial conflict as well as traditional beliefs about witchcraft. Paul Boyer and Stephen

Nissenbaum's *Salem Possessed: The Social Origins of Witchcraft* (Cambridge, Mass., 1974) takes a more localistic approach interpreting the trials and convictions at Salem as expressions of deep social divisions in the community. Good collections of readings and primary documents include Boyer and Nissenbaum, eds., *The Salem Witchcraft Papers: Verbatim Transcripts of the Legal Documents of the Salem Witchcraft Outbreak*, 3 vols. (New York, 1977), and Elaine G. Breslaw, ed., *Witches of the Atlantic World: A Historical Reader and Primary Sourcebook* (New York, 2001).

Part III

Provinces in a Contested Empire: The Eighteenth Century

In April 1710, four warriors, billed by their promoters as "kings" of the Iroquois League, rode to Queen Anne's Court of St. James in two royal coaches. Only one was truly a sachem, but that did not matter to the English royal officials who hoped this display of strategic transatlantic alliance would bolster their own influence with the Queen. Her Royal Highness received the emissaries graciously and heard their petition for a new English assault on Canada that would bring an end to "our long and tedious War . . . against her enemies the *French*." The warriors reminded the Queen that as allies they had provided a "strong wall" for English colonial security, "even to the loss of our best Men." They also promised "a most hearty Welcome" for any Anglican missionaries she might send to counter the "Insinuations" of French priests.

The voyage of the "Indian kings" to England revealed how much had changed over the past hundred years. The arduous process of establishing colonies in America was paying off for England and France alike. The two now boasted extensive empires and vied primarily with each other for control of North American trade and resources. Spain, which had dominated the Western Hemisphere a century before, had seen its southeastern chain of Apalachee missions decimated by English raiders. Spain now retained only St. Augustine and Pensacola in Florida and a few forts along the Texas coast. Queen Anne's willingness not only to entertain the Iroquois emissaries at court, but to "make a shew" of them on a month-long circuit of official appearances, demonstrated the importance of its North American empire to England's strategic and commercial goals.

The visit of the "Indian kings" also reveals to historians a glimpse of native peoples' shifting fortunes in this European contest for empire. Three of the warriors represented only one faction of a League torn by pro-English, pro-French, and neutralist advocates. One was not Iroquois at all. Colonization and trade had drawn native peoples into growing dependence on European goods and exposed them to the ravages of European conflict over land and commerce. American Indians retained control over the North American interior, and their strength in arms forced imperial strategists to seek wartime alliances and deterred most settlers from venturing too far from colonial defenses. Nevertheless, native peoples found themselves increasingly pressed by advancing colonization, forced to react to European initiatives rather than setting the terms of contact and exchange themselves.

Over the next fifty years, the contest between Great Britain and France for North Atlantic empire would intensify along commercial as well as military lines. The success of England's seventeenth-century ventures would breed eighteenth-century growth. The promise of cheap western land attracted second- and third-generation settlers from the coast and drew fresh waves of immigrants from northern Ireland, Scotland, and Germany. Transatlantic commerce also fueled the growth of African slave labor—indeed, the trade in human cargo was becoming one of the most lucrative of the era. The growth in Anglo-American population and commerce was laying a foundation for British dominion, but it would come only through a long and costly struggle.

Chapter 10

Empires of Guns and Goods

North America at the Opening of the Eighteenth Century

Francisco Romo de Uriza scrutinized his surroundings as he entered Charles Town in the colony of South Carolina; it was the summer of 1698. Romo had come from St. Augustine in Florida to pay for African slaves recently acquired from the English, but he also hoped to pick up some information concerning English activities near Florida and the Gulf of Mexico. He had departed a colony abuzz with rumors that the English were reconnoitering the Gulf Coast for trade and possible settlement. Reported sightings of English vessels alarmed Spanish officials, who were already waging a futile struggle to dislodge French interlopers from toeholds they had recently gained in Louisiana and at Biloxi in present-day Mississippi. French traders were fanning out from those posts to entice Southeastern Indians with a wider range of cheaper goods than the Spanish could offer. English intrusion into the area would only exacerbate the problem, because English traders could offer goods that were better-made and even cheaper than those of the French. Spanish officials felt their grip on the Gulf Coast slipping despite Spain's historical New World claims.

Romo's suspicions about his English hosts intensified when he spied a group of Indians at the residence of the Carolina governor, Joseph Blake, while paying a visit. He asked Governor Blake where they came from. Blake walked over to a large map on the wall and pointed out their home near a bay marked "Espíritu Santo," which the Spanish had renamed "Pensacola" in their recent effort to reassert possession of the Gulf Coast against French interlopers. Romo protested that the King of Spain owned the region, and these Indians had no right to trade with the English. The

Carolina governor only shook his head and declared that, according to his calculations, Pensacola lay within the King of England's domain. In any case, the governor told Romo, he had read in a recent gazette that the kings of France and England had agreed to concede ownership of the bay to whomever settled it first. The governor himself planned on entering the race for settlement the next spring.

When Romo reported back to St. Augustine, the Spanish governor did not pause to wonder about the plausibility of a gentleman's agreement over territory between two such ambitious empire-builders as William III and Louis XIV. He knew already that the French were especially well positioned to expand their presence in the Gulf of Mexico if he did not act quickly. He hastily assembled an expedition and dispatched it to Pensacola Bay. By mid-November 1698, the Spanish flag was flying over the construction site of a new presidio (fort) at the bay's entrance.

Romo's visit to Charles Town provides a glimpse into the contradictions of turn-of-the-century life in the borderlands of three great European imperial powers and dozens of Indian nations. The Spanish army officer and the English governor represented rival interests in an often bitter contest for New World trade and resources. Yet they also found mutual advantages in their proximity to each other, with the Carolinians supplying a desperate Spanish need for labor in exchange for hard currency that could lubricate the wheels of Anglo-American commerce. The Treaty of Ryswick secured in Europe in 1697 made the transaction easier, but eighteenth-century colonists of rival nations seldom allowed even the fiercest conflict to stand in the way of a chance to trade for mutual profit.

The Indians at the governor's residence, probably Creeks, knew well how to play these European rivals against one another to gain the greatest advantage in trade. Charles Town represented a special danger for Indian nations not allied with the Carolina colony of brutal slave catchers, but it also extended the opportunity to acquire an abundance of cheap manufactured goods for those willing to take the risk.

By 1700, cartographers could map out North American centers of colonial territory such as Charles Town, St. Augustine, and Louisiana. Mapmakers, colonial officials, and backcountry interpreters could even approximate with some confidence the territorial range and identity of many native groups such as the Creeks. Yet the maps they left behind afford only static glimpses of an extraordinarily dynamic world. Representatives of rival nations often read on the maps opportunities to expand their holdings, as Carolina's governor did. Cartographers for competing nations gave rival names to contested sites and drew rival boundaries around coveted territory.

On printed maps they sometimes deliberately omitted or obscured especially sensitive or prized possessions.

Each European colonial people sensed an insecurity in its grip on New World possessions. The feeling of uncertainty pressed colonists on all sides to cling more tightly, compete more keenly, and fight more desperately to retain and extend their hold on land, commerce, and power. Native peoples often found themselves caught in the crossfire. But just as often, they found chances to exploit the fierce contest among European rivals to achieve a variety of Indian goals. The blank spaces separating rival imperial possessions on a map obscured highly charged zones of opportunity and danger.

FRENCH AMERICA AFTER 1700

During the last quarter of the seventeenth century, intrepid French explorers such as René-Robert Cavelier, Sieur de La Salle, and Father Jacques Marquette pressed steadily further west and south into the Great Lakes basin and the Mississippi River valley (see Chapter 7). At the same time, aggressive governors and military leaders such as Louis de Buade, Comte de Frontenac and Antoine Laumet de La Mothe, Sieur de Cadillac sought to secure and extend the Canadian possessions of Louis XIV (see Chapter 9). By 1701, the French had gained an enormous ring of territory that split Spain's North American possessions in two and threatened to confine Anglo-America to the Atlantic seaboard.

As explorers and governors extended France's North American territorial claims, Louis XIV's ambitious minister Jean-Baptiste Colbert tried to encourage emigration to New France and to strengthen the colony's economic viability. Colbert sent soldiers to secure the colony and provided incentives for them to remain as colonists. He continued to encourage the dispensing of seigneuries, or grants of land, to landholders and helped them recruit the *engagés* or hired men needed to work the grants. These *engagés* typically contracted for three-year terms to work on the seigneuries. They received pay during that time as well as free passage back to France should they wish to return. Colbert's policy predictably resulted in an overbalance of males, so between 1663 and 1673 the minister recruited and sent to New France over seven hundred *filles du roi*, female orphans without other prospects. The marriages and families that resulted from Colbert's policies brought stability to French American society and contributed to a steady growth in the population.

Despite these enterprising efforts, only around 15,000 colonists populated New France in 1700, less than one-sixth the combined population of neighboring New York and New England. Expanding opportunities in France itself kept most people at home. Indeed, more than half the *engagés* and soldiers returned to prospects in France once their contracts or terms of enlistment had expired. Those who remained exerted a transforming impact that belied their comparatively small numbers.

**Whalers,
Traders, and
Farmers in the
Gulf of St.
Lawrence**

In 1700, visitors to New France might receive their first introduction to the colony at one of the four royal trading posts at the mouth of the St. Lawrence River or Baye Phélypeaux at the Strait of Belle Isle. These harsh Atlantic outposts remained largely transient throughout the French colonial period. Traders and fishermen at the four King's Posts worked as employees of the Crown or its agents, who reserved most of the profits from trade and fishing for themselves. South of the King's Posts lay Anicosti Island, where French and Basque whalers rendered oil from their yearly catches. The rugged coast of Labrador north of Belle Isle hosted over a thousand French fishermen annually to dry cod netted off the Grand Banks for sale in Europe. A commandant oversaw these operations, enforcing royal regulations and collecting a generous share of valuable fish, fur, and oil.

To the south lay Acadia, the territory encompassing much of present-day Canada's Maritime Provinces. In 1701, Acadia supported just over 1,100 settlers clustered in a few small farming and trading communities near Port Royal, now Annapolis Royal in Nova Scotia. The Acadians forged a tightly knit, homogenous family and community life much like that of France's Poitou region, where many of them originated. They carved out small family farms from marshland in the valley of the Rivière Dauphin (now the Annapolis River), building broad dikes of sod reinforced with branches and logs.

The Acadians' Micmac neighbors cared little for the marshlands and welcomed the manufactured goods the French brought to the region. They quickly incorporated the Acadians into their extensive hunting and trading network. To maintain the flow of trade goods, the Acadians sold furs obtained through the Micmac network and produced small crop surpluses for clandestine sale in New England. After 1718, when Fort Louisbourg was built on Île Royale (now Cape Breton Island), the Acadians carried on a brisk trade supplying the fort with grain and meat.

**"A Village
Beginning at
Montreal and
Ending at
Quebec"**

Canada, the heart of New France, stretched along three main centers of trade and administration on the St. Lawrence: Quebec, Trois-Rivières, and Montreal. A 1699 engraving of Quebec, the seat of government, reveals a small city with several impressive government buildings, a formidable citadel, and at least five beautiful spires arising from the churches, the convents, the hospice, and the hospital. All three towns boasted planned streets, although the terrain on which they stood thwarted any effort to lay them out on the rectangular grid structure so popular in late seventeenth- and eighteenth-century planning. High stone walls encircled each town, protecting the dwellings within and offering refuge to outlying residents in case of attack. Trade in furs and lumber underpinned the economy of all three towns, providing the flow of cash needed to sustain trades and services characteristic of city life.

Most Canadian settlers, or *habitants*, lived on farms rather than in the cities. Each family wanted river access, and colonial officials obliged by laying out lots or *rotures* perpendicular to the river in long narrow strips about 165 yards wide. In 1700, a single strip of farms lay along each bank of the St. Lawrence except near the cities. There greater demand for land prompted officials to build roads behind the original fields, laying out a second and eventually third and fourth tiers of lots for settlement and cultivation. This pattern persisted throughout the colonial period, presenting the Swedish traveler Peter Kalm in 1749 with the "exceedingly beautiful" prospect of houses lining the river for 180 miles. "It could really be called a village," Kalm remarked, "beginning at Montreal and ending at Quebec."

Families farmed primarily wheat for their own consumption and other cereal crops such as oats and corn for their sheep, hogs, cattle, and horses. Men cleared timber, drained marshes, and tilled the fields while women kept vegetable gardens, tended poultry and swine, reared children, and managed the household. Women often carded wool, spun thread, knit, and wove. Most families produced modest surpluses of grain, meat, and wool for sale in the towns or trade with neighboring Indians.

Canada's pattern of settlement proved a mixed blessing. The long strips of farms made it hard for *habitants* to muster for defense in case of attack and provided much less protection than the clustered houses of a village. The layout also made more difficult the official tasks of policing and regulating as well as the priests' tasks of caring for souls. People adapted, organizing the *habitants* by parishes and creating a series of riverfront communities called *côtes* to deal with common problems and meet local needs for trades such as blacksmithing and carpentry.

For Canadians, the advantages of riverfront settlement far outweighed its drawbacks. The river gave *habitants* access to vital hunting and fishing. It provided easy transportation to the towns. The difficulties of policing made it easy for young men to slip into boats or canoes and head upstream to the *pays d'en haut*, the high country of the Great Lakes. There they evaded French licensing laws to trade among the Indians as *coureurs de bois*, illegal "forest runners" who turned tidy profits exchanging French manufactured goods for beaver pelts.

By 1701, New France's governors had consolidated their hold on the vast fur trading territory beyond Montreal through a series of firm alliances among Great Lakes native peoples. They had secured key trade routes against Iroquois and English incursions by building Fort Frontenac on Lake Ontario and Fort Detroit on the St. Clair River. They had also won an Iroquois commitment to neutrality in the Grand Settlement of 1701.

**Forest Life in the
*Pays d'en Haut***

Though the French officially claimed the Great Lakes in the great European imperial contest, they actually occupied very little of the region. Soldiers garrisoned at Frontenac and Detroit formed the nucleus of the posts' small communities. Traders, craftsmen, and a few farming *habitants* also clustered at these posts, accompanied by a priest and often a missionary. From there, French *coureurs de bois*, also called *voyageurs*, fanned across the countryside, establishing other minor trading posts or living among the Indians exchanging goods. By 1700 these traders had overtaken the Jesuit missionaries, who struggled to maintain a dwindling number of missions along Great Lakes shores.

A *voyageur* labored hard for his profits in furs. Many set out from Montreal in early spring, paddling up rivers and along the lake shores in long canoes laden with European goods. Others wintered at various trading posts or among their native partners, accumulating furs in exchange for goods obtained the previous summer. In late spring or early summer these too set out to rendezvous at Detroit or

Michilimackinac with traders from Montreal. Indian hunters and trappers also joined the rendezvous, which became annual cross-cultural occasions of feasting, conviviality, brawling, and wantonness. At the rendezvous traders exchanged the pelts they had brought for fresh stocks of goods needed to carry on the next year's trade. Those who had come from Montreal loaded their canoes with pelts and headed downstream on the thousand-mile return trip.

Voyageurs forged ties with native trading partners that extended far beyond a mere commercial relationship. Though the Great Lakes Algonquians wanted trade goods, they did not see themselves as mere dependents of the French. Indeed, the Frenchman Nicolas Perrot complained of their "arrogant notion that the French cannot get along without . . . the assistance they give us." Western Indians saw the transaction of furs for goods as an exchange of gifts that imposed mutual obligations of fair dealing, peace, friendship, and political or military alliance. French traders thus found their commerce embedded within systems of implicit understandings which they ignored at great peril. A Frenchman who made the mistake of dealing with an enemy of his previous trading partners risked hostile capture or death as a traitor. On the other hand, a trader could confirm and strengthen ties that an exchange of goods had already established by marrying a native woman. Many Frenchmen in the *pays d'en haut* did so not only to benefit from a woman's companionship but also to gain access to her labor and to cement relations with his wife's kin and community.

By the early eighteenth century, hundreds of marriages or more temporary unions between French *coureurs de bois* and native women had produced a significant population of mixed-blood offspring or *métis*. Many *métis* participated as full members of their own kinship groups and bands, but many others formed separate communities. The *métis* of these communities came to regard themselves as French, but they could also draw on native kinship ties to become important mediators, interpreters, and brokers between the French and various native groups.

Colonial officials and European visitors believed that the *voyageurs'* experience transformed them into a breed apart both from French at home and from other colonial Europeans. The late-seventeenth-century governor, the Marquis de Denonville, complained of the "attraction that this Indian way of life has for all these youths." They freely associated with Indians, ate and dressed like them, copulated with native women, and lived in the forest for months or even years at a time, far beyond the effective reach of French law and Roman Catholic sacraments. Nevertheless, observers and others praised the Canadian backwoodsmen's strength and prowess. Denonville observed they were "big, well-built, and firmly planted on their legs, accustomed when necessary to live on very little, robust and vigorous . . . witty and vivacious." The Swedish traveler Peter Kalm remarked that he met "scarcely one of them who was not a clever marksman and who did not own a rifle." Kalm believed that their experience in the forest made them formidable in warfare: "they become such brave soldiers, and so inured to fatigue that none of them fears danger or hardships." One French officer boasted that his Canadian troops "almost always" enjoyed success in battle with the English, "who are not as vigorous nor as adroit in the use of fire arms as they, nor as practiced in forest warfare."

Whether or not their experience made French colonists better warriors than their Anglo-American neighbors, their access to the Great Lakes, mastery of the forest, and extensive alliances with native peoples enabled the French to press far into the North American west. Indeed, by the early 1730s, Pierre Gaultier de Varennes et de La Vérendrye was pressing westward from Lake Superior's Thunder Bay to extend New France's reach to the foothills of the Rocky Mountains. Vérendrye carved out a new region, the *Mer de l'Ouest* (Western Sea), centered on posts in the basin of Lakes Winnipeg and Manitoba. From there *hommes du nord* carried French manufactured goods up the Assiniboine, Saskatchewan, and Souris Rivers to native partners. Peoples such as the Mandan and Hidatsa, who lived on the Big Bend of the Missouri River in what is now west-central North Dakota, maintained far-flung networks of exchange that carried French manufactured goods to many Plains Indian groups. The *hommes du nord* lived most of their lives among native peoples just as had Frenchmen in the Great Lakes, marrying native women and adopting native ways of life.

France entered the eighteenth century with yet another North American treasure on its imperial map: the mouth of the Mississippi River. Early in 1699, Pierre Le Moyne, Sieur d'Iberville, led an expedition of three French naval vessels along the Gulf Coast to the Mississippi Delta. He had set out to establish a fort at Pensacola Bay, but moved on after finding a newly built Spanish stockade there. Iberville became the first European to enter the Mississippi from the sea after stumbling upon its channel when a storm drove him to shore. To secure his prize, Iberville established Fort Maurepas on the shores of Biloxi Bay, leaving behind his brother Jean-Baptiste Le Moyne, Sieur de Bienville with a small garrison. Only a few months later, Bienville encountered an English ship which had also managed to find its way up the Mississippi and was scouting a suitable site for a proposed colony under the proprietorship of the London physician Daniel Coxe. Bienville warned the English off, and reported the incident when his brother returned. Iberville quickly established Fort Mississippi approximately 30 miles south of present-day New Orleans to prevent any further incursions by foreign vessels. By 1700, the new French colony of Louisiana had become a reality.

France on the Mississippi

The French had established a claim with tremendous economic and military potential. The founding of Louisiana broke Spain's hold on the Gulf of Mexico and gave the French access to a vast natural transportation system stretching from the western slopes of the Appalachians to the high plains and the Rockies. Within months of Fort Mississippi's founding, Iberville established trade agreements with nearby native groups of Chickasaws, Choctaws, Mobilians, Alibamons, and Tohomés. During the following decades, French traders made their way up the Mississippi River and its tributaries to establish trading partnerships with native groups along the Arkansas, Missouri, and Ohio River systems. Traders found ready markets for manufactured goods, especially guns, which enabled southeastern groups beleaguered by English-supplied rivals to hold their own and gave Plains Indians such as the Comanches a great advantage over rivals in hunting and warfare.

Louisiana, however, never lived up to its promise. Policymakers and merchants in France invested little in the colony during its early years. For more than a decade after 1713, owners of a succession of monopoly ventures attempted to people the region with immigrants and African slaves who could provide labor for various enterprises. By 1731, 2,000 French colonists and 4,000 slaves inhabited the colony, many on narrow strips of property fronting the river as in Canada. Company agents sought to extract profits from the inhabitants by imposing rigid trade restrictions and pricing schemes that had failed elsewhere in French America.

French mercantilist policies fared poorly in Louisiana as well. *Habitants* simply skirted the regulations to carry on an illegal trade aimed not to fill company coffers, but, as one official complained, to gain "what they need day by day like the Indians who find their happiness in an idle and lazy life." In fact, neither settlers,

This map of New Orleans parish in 1723 shows long, narrow plots of land fronting the Mississippi River, a pattern of settlement common to French colonies throughout North America.
The Newberry Library, Chicago

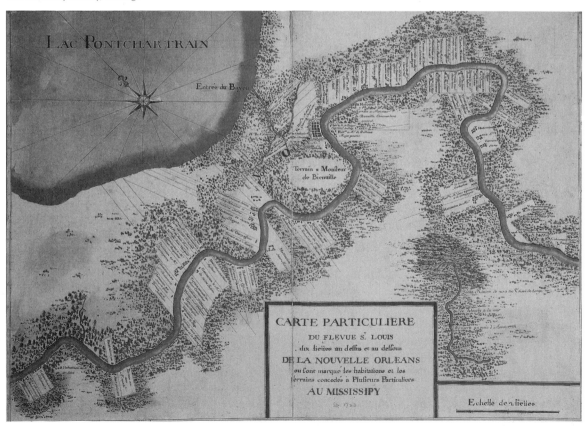

nor slaves, nor Indians were lazy. All worked hard to obtain their livelihoods through a mixture of farming, herding, fishing, hunting, and trade. These activities brought the region's inhabitants into frequent contact, giving rise to an intercultural system which historian Daniel Usner has called a "frontier exchange economy." Slaves, settlers, and Indians "pieced subsistence and commercial endeavors together" by participating flexibly in exchange, with members of each group taking on a variety of economic roles as specific circumstances demanded. Slaves, for instance, hoed tobacco fields and also worked as boatmen, soldiers, and peddlers. Indian farmers and herdsmen supplied French settlers with daily food as well as profitable pelts in exchange for manufactured goods. This intercultural economic system made few French investors rich, yet it came to support the region's inhabitants fairly well while supplying modest surpluses in furs and agricultural products.

The founding of Louisiana stimulated the development of yet another French colony hundreds of miles up the Mississippi: the *pays des Illinois*. This cluster of six small farming villages along the river in what is now Illinois formed when *coureurs de bois* from Canada found themselves stranded by the sudden collapse and temporary closing of the French fur trade during the 1690s. French control of the river's mouth permitted farmers from this region to begin cultivating small surpluses of grain for sale to the French sugar islands. The opportunity to set up as independent farming families on good prairie land attracted a small stream of migrants from Canada and France during the eighteenth century. The *pays des Illinois* never grew large, however; by 1750 only about 3,000 people lived in the colony, one-third of them slaves.

Spanish Borderlands of the Eighteenth Century

In 1700, Spanish authorities were feeling increasing pressure on their vast northern frontier from resistant native peoples and determined European competitors. Spain had only recently reasserted control over the Pueblos of New Mexico after a thirteen-year interruption precipitated by Popé's revolt of 1680 (see Chapter 7). Colonial officials had begun strengthening settlements along the Texas coast to prevent the French from gaining a foothold there. The Spanish governor of St. Augustine hoped that a new fort at Pensacola would dampen English and French competition in the region, but control of such a colonial backwater scarcely compensated for severe losses to neighboring South Carolina and the French occupation of the Mississippi.

Yet Spain continued to hold an unsteady grasp on far-flung communities from Santa Fe to St. Augustine. In these borderland communities, European colonists mixed with peoples of other races and backgrounds, forming multicultural societies. According to historian Ramón A. Gutiérrez, the Spanish provinces present a story of "the complex web of interactions between men and women, young and old, rich and poor, slave and free, Spaniard and Indian, all of whom fundamentally depended on the other for their own self-definition."

Securing the Northern Frontier

Spain's position in Florida had become very precarious by 1700. Despite the existence of an impressive fort at St. Augustine, the colony had never managed to attract many Spanish migrants. "It is hard to get anyone to go to St. Augustine because of the horror with which Florida is painted," the governor of Cuba complained in 1673. "Only hoodlums and the mischievous go there from Cuba." In the absence of sufficient colonists, Spain had attempted to consolidate control over the region through the missions and trade. Yet since 1680, Carolina raiders and their Indian allies had devastated the Spanish missions and client Apalachee communities (see Chapter 8). Indeed, by 1706, officials in St. Augustine were writing that in all of Florida's "extensive dominions and provinces, the law of God and the preaching of the Holy Gospel have now ceased."

The missions never recovered. Throughout the eighteenth century, Spain's presence in Florida remained confined to three coastal outposts: St. Augustine, Fort San Marcos de Apalachee on the Gulf Coast some 30 miles south of present-day Tallahassee, and the presidio of San Carlos de Austria at the mouth of Pensacola Bay. Ongoing imperial competition with the French and the English prevented Spain from abandoning its Florida posts, but officials came to regard them as money-losing garrisons useful mainly for securing Spanish interests farther south and west.

Native hostility and the failure to find precious metal had cooled Spain's enthusiasm for Texas and New Mexico as well, yet Spanish officials continued to view these regions as strategically important. Interest in reasserting Spanish control heightened in the face of new French intrusions during the last two decades of the seventeenth century. In 1686, rumors reached Mexico that the French explorer, René-Robert Cavelier, Sieur de La Salle, had established a secret fort on the Texas coast. Authorities there sent out several expeditions to find and destroy the settlement. They feared that such a toehold would enable the French to "settle as far as New Mexico and make themselves Lords of many Kingdoms and Provinces." After three years of searching, the veteran frontier soldier and explorer Sargento Mayor Alonso de León found an abandoned Fort St. Louis on the shore of Matagorda Bay. Most of La Salle's men lay dead, but some had murdered the commander himself and fled to live among the neighboring Indians.

The new French forts at the mouth of the Mississippi intensified the threat to Spain's northern frontier. Soon aggressive French traders were making their way westward along the Gulf Coast enticing native peoples with comparatively inexpensive manufactured goods. León had urged Spanish authorities to respond to these incursions by establishing a line of forts, but the strapped colonial government opted instead to encourage Franciscan missions. Although the missions cost the government almost nothing to operate, they depended on the cooperation of their Indian hosts to remain in existence. Franciscan missionaries had not established a good record of maintaining such cooperation for long, and their attempts to win converts in Texas were no exception. The prosperous Caddo farmers of what is now east Texas initially welcomed one such missionary, Father Damián Mazanet. Yet within a few years the friars wore out their welcome among the Caddos or Hasinai, who called themselves "Tejas" or "friends." When a smallpox epidemic ravaged the Caddo, Mazanet declared it was "God's holy will." The

Caddo warned him to leave or they would kill him, and for decades afterward they refused baptism in the belief that it would kill them. Other missionary efforts also struggled and failed, some ending with the martyrdom of hapless friars.

The failure of early Texas missions and the persistent intrusion of French traders eventually persuaded Spanish officials to spend money on garrisons. In 1718 the Texas governor Martín de Alarcón founded a *villa* and mission at San Antonio and strengthened other missions and garrisons in east Texas. Three years later another governor, the Marqués de San Miguel de Aguayo, established Los Adaes only 12 miles from French Natchitoches. It remained the capital of Texas until 1763.

Farther west, concern over French ambitions prompted the Spanish nobleman Diego de Vargas to attempt the reconquest of New Mexico in 1693. A preliminary campaign the year before from his base at El Paso had won token submission of twenty-three Pueblo communities. Vargas found it far more difficult to reassert full Spanish rule. He stormed Santa Fe with the aid of Indian allies and appeals to *Nuestra Señora de la Conquista*, a wooden image of the Virgin Mary which surviving Spanish had carried away after Popé's revolt in 1680. From his headquarters in Santa Fe, Vargas campaigned throughout 1694 to subdue the remaining Pueblos. The Franciscans followed up with an attempt to rebuild their missions, encountering stiff Pueblo resistance that exploded into a second revolt in 1696.

The second Pueblo rebellion did not achieve independence, but it ultimately forced the Spanish to reach some accommodation with the surviving Indians. Vargas suppressed the revolt with a costly war of attrition, destroying food supplies and striking hard at rebel positions. Yet after regaining control over all but the Hopi community farthest to the west, Spanish officials took greater care to avoid provoking further rebellions. Eighteenth-century friars, too, learned to overlook persistent Pueblo religious practices that their predecessors had tried to stamp out. The image popularly called *La Conquistadora* became the ethnic symbol of a New Mexico marked by peaceful coexistence between Spanish and Pueblos.

California never figured prominently in Spain's plans for the New World. Early explorers had reported finding only impoverished Indians living along the Pacific coast. Adventurers saw no natural resources worth mentioning, and since the area proved extremely difficult to reach from Mexico City—the overland trip could take months—California received little attention. Fear that the Russians might seize the entire region belatedly sparked Spanish activity, however, and after 1769, two indomitable servants of the empire, Fra Junipero Serra and Don Gaspar de Portolá, organized permanent missions and forts at San Diego, Monterey, San Francisco, and Santa Barbara.

In sharp contrast to the English frontier settlements of the eighteenth century, the Spanish outposts in North America grew very slowly. A few Catholic priests and imperial administrators traveled to the northern provinces, but the danger of Indian attack as well as a harsh physical environment discouraged ordinary colonists. The European migrants were overwhelmingly male, most of them soldiers in the pay of the empire. Although some colonists came directly from Spain,

Peoples of the Spanish Borderlands

most had been born in other Spanish colonies such as Minorca, the Canaries, or New Spain. Because European women rarely appeared on the frontier, Spanish males formed relationships with Indian women, fathering large numbers of *mestizos*, children of mixed race.

As in other European frontiers of the eighteenth century, encounters with Spanish soldiers, priests, and traders altered Native American cultures. The experience in Spanish North America was quite different from that of the whites and Indians in the British backcountry. The Spanish exploited Native American labor, reducing entire Indian villages to servitude. Many Indians moved to the Spanish towns, and although they lived in close proximity to the Europeans—a rare occurrence in British America—they were consigned to the lowest social class, objects of European contempt. Yet, no matter how much their material conditions changed, the Indians of the Southwest resisted strenuous efforts to convert them to Catholicism. The Pueblos maintained their own religious forms—often at great personal risk—and they sometimes murdered priests who became too intrusive. Angry Pueblos at Taos reportedly fed the hated Spanish friars corn tortillas containing urine and mouse meat.

The Spanish empire never had the resources necessary to secure fully the northern frontier. The small military posts were intended primarily to discourage other European powers such as France, Great Britain, and Russia from taking possession of territory claimed by Spain. It would be misleading, however, to stress the fragility of Spanish colonization. The urban design and public architecture of many southwestern cities still reflect the vision of the early Spanish settlers, and to a large extent, the old borderlands remain Spanish speaking to this day.

Anglo-America on the Move

France and Spain each claimed control of vast North American territories as the eighteenth century opened, yet both were coming to regard Anglo-America as the gravest threat to their imperial ambitions. Indeed, as war loomed over Europe in 1701, the French minister Louis Phélypeaux, Comte de Pontchartrain, did his best to persuade Spanish officials that the new French forts on the Mississippi would actually protect New Spain from English encroachment. With a population estimated at "more than 60,000 families," Pontchartrain warned, the English might soon overrun the continent. Only by uniting with France against Anglo-American expansion could the Spanish crown—recently inherited by Louis XIV's grandson, the Duc d'Anjou—ensure protection of its Mexican silver mines.

Pontchartrain may have exaggerated for effect, but England's North American colonies were indeed expanding in 1700. Most Anglo-American settlement remained concentrated along rivers and inlets of the Atlantic coastal plain. Inhabitants of each colonial region often maintained stronger ties with London than with people in neighboring colonies. Yet the Anglo-American population was growing rapidly and colonists were moving west, some of them quite far. Carolinians were regularly trading and raiding for pelts and slaves as far west as the Mississippi. English traders farther north were also pressing westward into the Appalachian Mountains in search of furs and skins. Anglo-American farmers and planters were following the trails to take possession of fresh land, pressing the line of settlement gradually closer to the Appalachians and the French claims beyond. At over 260,000 people, the population of British America dwarfed that of New France, with only 15,000, and the Spanish borderlands, with just over 4,000.

Families and Farms in New England

By 1700, the third generation of New Englanders had rebuilt frontier communities destroyed during King Philip's War (see Chapter 7) and pressed well beyond. Driven by a rate of increase that doubled the population every twenty-seven years, these heirs of the great Puritan migration of the 1630s had extended the line of settlement 50 miles inland from the coast and more than 100 miles up the Connecticut River. The towns and farms they carved out of the forest bore strong resemblance to their communities of origin further east (see Chapter 5). Town councils governed local affairs from a meetinghouse that often also housed Sunday worship. Dissent from the established Congregational order was rare, though visitors to some communities might find a few Quaker or Baptist families living on the outskirts of town. Ties of kinship, friendship, and faith knit the people of the frontier settlements together with those along the coast, further strengthening the homogeneity of New England society while setting it apart from both England and more diverse English colonies to the south.

Early-eighteenth-century New England was well on its way to becoming a thriving Anglo-American province, but it had fallen short of its Puritan founders' hopes. As the Boston minister Cotton Mather wrote, a candid observer "must not be called, A *Calumniator*" who admitted that European visitors "will not find *New-England* a New Jerusalem." The region's culture had come to revolve around local cycles of farm, family, and community life, punctuated by seasons of planting, harvest, birth, marriage, and death. Parochial though it had become, New England culture remained highly literate. Most adults could follow in their own Bibles as the minister read Scripture from the pulpit, and they were not afraid to challenge their pastor's interpretation of a passage based on their own judgment of its meaning. Many farmers consulted almanacs for advice on planting and tending their crops, sometimes jotting crabbed notes on the weather or local matters into the margins of a page. They also read almanacs for astrological insights into life and love, for pithy wisdom, and for knowledge of distant or exotic events and places.

Third-generation Puritans neither neglected their lofty past nor severed their transatlantic ties. On the Connecticut Valley frontier, the Northampton, Massachusetts, minister Solomon Stoddard sparked successions of local revival with fiery sermons that called his parishioners to the repentance and conversion that had formed the core of their grandparents' religious experience. Similar revivals became a regular feature of religious life elsewhere in New England. A literate elite of ministers and magistrates sustained links between past and present, New England and Old, by various means. Cotton Mather wrote massive tomes expounding the wonders of the invisible world and tracing God's providential guidance in New England's history. He published literally hundreds of works in England as well as America and contributed well-received letters to the Royal Society of London on popular scientific topics of his day, including astronomy, botany, zoology, geology, and meteorology. Mather also maintained a voluminous correspondence with friends in England, Scotland, Germany, Holland, India,

France, and the West Indies. Royal administrators strengthened these transatlantic ties even further by serving as visible representatives of England's government and by enforcing colonial compliance with English commercial regulations. Boston merchants imported British manufactured goods on a modest scale for sale to colonial customers.

As New England settlers pushed the frontier line further inland, native inhabitants of coastal regions such as the Narragansetts and Mohegans found themselves occupying increasingly marginal positions in their ancestral land. As postcolonial peoples, they eked out a living in praying towns or on small fractions of their former territories. They exchanged goods and services with their Anglo-American neighbors, selectively adopting whatever European practices and beliefs they found useful for preserving their own identity. They also participated with white neighbors in military expeditions against hostile Indians and French beyond the line of English settlement. The Abenaki, whose villages and hunting grounds occupied the gradually narrowing territory between New England and New France, constituted a daunting obstacle to Anglo-American expansion. Many Abenakis had allied with the French and adopted Roman Catholicism. Their resentment of English colonization generated tension even in times of peace and made the New England frontier deadly in times of war.

Trade and Diversity in the Middle Colonies

The ethnically diverse Middle Colonies, especially New York, held far more strategic significance for England's imperial ambitions than did homogenous New England. New York's powerful English and Anglo-Dutch merchant families controlled the commerce of the Hudson River valley, a highway not only for the lucrative fur trade with the Iroquois but also for recurring military conflicts with French Canada. The colony hosted Anglo-America's only permanent garrison of British regular troops to protect the crucial Hudson River–Lake Champlain corridor. A relatively small but diverse population of Dutch, English, Huguenot, and German farmers cultivated land as tenants on princely Hudson River estates owned by families such as the Livingstons and the Rensselaers or maintained their own small farms near the river or on Long Island. New York, the port city of 5,000 on Manhattan Island, boasted even greater ethnic and religious diversity. Along with the Dutch, Germans, English, and French, New York City supported a small Jewish community. In addition, enslaved Africans comprised as much as 15 percent of the population.

New Jersey, Pennsylvania, and Delaware boasted similar diversity. The Delaware and Susquehanna Rivers gave some inhabitants of this region access to trade with the Iroquois as well, but most obtained their living by farming the fertile lands of the Delaware Valley. Philadelphia's Quaker merchants cultivated connections throughout the Atlantic, finding ready markets for the region's furs, iron, and agricultural products in exchange for European manufactures and West Indian sugar. The Delaware Valley's cheap, plentiful land attracted English, German, Welsh, Scottish, Irish, and French Huguenot colonists to settle among the remaining Dutch and Swedes. By 1700, over 21,000 settlers had arrived in Pennsylvania, making it the fastest growing colony in North America.

In the Middle Colonies, members of churches long established in Europe lived at peace with neighbors who had fled persecution by those very religious establishments. In England, the Quakers remained a small minority whose persecution had only recently ceased, but Pennsylvania Quakers outnumbered all other groups and controlled the colony's government. Quakers also comprised a large minority of New Jersey's population. On Sundays in New York Dutch Reformed worshipers made their way to churches in one part of the city, while Anglicans met in another. German Lutheran and Reformed groups remained suspicious of one another in New York as they had in Europe, but many cooperated to share a building for worship, meeting at different times of day. German Anabaptists seized on William Penn's promise of religious freedom to settle on fertile land in southeastern Pennsylvania, where their Mennonite and Amish descendants remain to this day. So also did more exotic groups such as that of the learned mystic Johannes Kelpius, founder in 1694 of The Woman in the Wilderness, a community of forty ascetics who lived in tiny cells contemplating magic numbers, esoteric symbols, and alchemical formulas.

The Lenni-Lenape of the Delaware Valley did not fare so well. Although William Penn insisted on paying for Lenni-Lenape lands before deeding them to European colonists, he nevertheless understood the transaction as permanently removing the Indians from the soil, a pattern of land use not shared by native peoples (see Chapter 8). As Pennsylvania settlers flooded west, the Lenni-Lenape, whom colonists called the Delaware, withdrew. By 1700, many Delaware were vying for space along the Susquehanna River along with migrating Shawnee, Conoy, Susquehannock, and Iroquois groups. To protect the Delaware from European American squatters, the Pennsylvania government set aside "manors" where the Indians could pursue their traditional way of life. Yet the white settlements that soon surrounded these manors restricted native access to hunting and fishing, prompting the Lenni-Lenape to withdraw once more to the Alleghenies and further westward.

In the Chesapeake, a momentous transformation from indentured servitude to slave labor was well under way even as the majority of Virginia and Maryland inhabitants eked out a precarious living on small western tracts. Since the 1680s, the supply of English indentured servants had been declining by about 3 percent annually while the demand rose about the same amount. The resulting turn to African slaves had by 1700 boosted the black population to around 20 percent of Virginia's 60,000 inhabitants. Most African slaves labored singly alongside their masters or with one or two other slaves or indentured servants. The relative wealth of those few masters who could afford ten or more slaves was making families such as the Wormeleys, Carters, Byrds, Beverleys, and Lees the core of a rising Chesapeake gentry.

"Venturing Backwards" in Virginia

Few of the great brick houses that now adorn the banks of the Potomac, Rappahannock, York, and James Rivers were standing in 1700. Residents themselves reported that the colony "looks all like a wild desart; the high-lands overgrown with trees, and the low-lands sunk with water, marsh, and swamp." Yet wealthy Virginians aspired for their children a place among a transatlantic elite, graced by a liberal education and supported by the patronage of powerful and well-connected "friends" in England. Such men plowed their surpluses into more slaves and more land, gradually squeezing the smaller planters away from the Tidewater region onto less desirable western soil. In sharp contrast to the settled town life of New England, most Chesapeake planters lived in small wooden houses a mile or more apart, "dribbled over the landscape without apparent design," as one wry observer reported.

By 1700, the rising Virginia gentry were also busily pressing their own land claims westward along the rivers into the Piedmont, pushing out white squatters and incorporating the remnants of Virginia's once-great Powhatan chiefdom into a postcolonial order. Virginia's Indian population had fallen a disastrous 87 percent to only 1,900, most of whom lived well to the west of their ancestral homes on land increasingly claimed by white elites. They paid meager tribute or rent from crops raised on marginal lands and found themselves subjected to English laws and customs. They exchanged furs and deerskins for European goods, often serving as brokers as well as buffers between Virginia traders and more robust western nations such as the Shawnees, Tuscaroras, and Cherokees. The skins they sold helped make the fortunes of traders such as William Byrd I, who operated a lucrative fur-trading network from a base at the frontier post of Fort Charles near the site of present-day Richmond. In 1710, newly arrived Lieutenant Governor Alexander Spotswood initiated a flurry of negotiations with western Indians to strengthen the fur trade and ensure security for migrating colonists. Spotswood also encouraged colonists to "venture backwards" to the west. In 1716, he personally led an expedition beyond the Blue Ridge Mountains into the Shenandoah Valley. By 1720, settlements were springing up along the Shenandoah River and its tributaries.

Carolina Planters and Traders

Less than 30 miles south of Virginia, a scattering of meager farms and villages along Albemarle and Pamlico Sounds formed the core of what was becoming the colony of North Carolina. Still a formal part of the vast territory that Charles II had granted to the Carolina proprietors in 1665, Albemarle lagged far behind Charles Town in population and commerce. In the first decade of the eighteenth century, however, the region was beginning to attract Huguenot and Palatine immigrants despite a ring of coastal sand reefs that impeded access to the ocean and Atlantic trade. Religious and ethnic strife dogged Albemarle's inhabitants as they scratched out a living by raising tobacco, cereal crops, and cattle on the sandy soil. The coves along the Outer Banks and the inlets of the sounds provided excellent hideouts for smugglers and pirates such as Edward Teach, the notorious Blackbeard. Local settlers and the deputy governor himself often sheltered these freebooters, who sold goods more cheaply than established merchants and who injected scarce cash into the economy by purchasing provisions and spending in the taverns.

To the south, Charles Town was becoming the center of a thriving, if brutal, colony of planters, traders, and slaves. White indentured servants and African and Indian slaves comprised nearly half of its 7,000 inhabitants in 1703, with slaves rapidly displacing indentured servants in the labor force. These unfree laborers worked side by side with masters to clear fields, herd cattle, plant experimental crops, and extract naval stores from the pine forests. Yet the sharing of common tasks hardly put slaves on an equal footing with their masters. One colonist observed that anyone who could "get a few slaves and . . . beat them well to make them work hard" might make a good living in South Carolina. The colony's Barbadian immigrant elite enforced their dominion with a harsh slave code modeled on that of their sugar island home.

While early Carolina planters experimented their way toward the cultivation of rice and indigo that would eventually become the colony's eighteenth-century staples, greedy Carolina traders ranged west as far as the Mississippi in search of deerskins and Indian captives (see Chapter 8). By 1700 they were shipping to London an average of 54,000 deerskins per year, a figure that would rise rapidly in the following decades. Indian slaves were harder to obtain but far more profitable to Carolinians and their native allies. In 1708, a Chickasaw hunter could collect "a Gun, ammunition, horse, hatchet, and a suit of Cloathes" for each slave sold to Carolina traders, a deal whose worth the historian James Axtell has estimated at "a whole year's worth of deerskins."

The Carolinian lust for Indian slaves cost the colony dearly when hostilities broke out in 1711 between Tuscaroras and colonists living in the northern part of Carolina. Appalled by reports of Tuscarora atrocities, the Carolina legislature dispatched Colonel John Barnwell with a force of over one thousand English, Yamassee, Wateree, Congaree, Waxhaw, and Pee Dee troops. Carolina law permitted Barnwell and his army to sell as slaves any Tuscaroras captured, but circumstances initially thwarted their quest for profit. When Tuscarora defenses proved more formidable than anticipated, nearly half of Barnwell's force deserted. The colonel salvaged his campaign by capturing a Tuscarora fort and forcing its inhabitants to flee, a victory that persuaded the Tuscaroras to come to terms with the Carolinians. On the return trip to Charles Town the remnants of Barnwell's army managed to score a profit by inviting an unsuspecting company of Tuscaroras to meet for discussions, then capturing them for sale on the slave market. Barnwell and his allies claimed that they had acted before the conclusion of peace, but news of his treachery nevertheless sparked a new round of brutal frontier warfare that lasted more than a year. The conflict ended with most Tuscarora survivors migrating north to settle as "little brothers" of the Iroquois. In the meantime, Virginia's lieutenant governor Alexander Spotswood declared that Barnwell's greed had left North Carolina "in a worse condition than he found" it.

Only three years after the Tuscarora War, South Carolina experienced its own frontier conflict when the Yamassee broke their alliance and attacked, killing 90 of the colony's 100 traders and attacking border settlements. Other Indian nations—including Choctaws, Cherokees, Apalachees, Shawnees, and Santees—joined the Yamassees to settle old scores with the Carolinians or seize portions of their trading system. This powerful Indian alliance drove Carolina colonists back toward Charles Town, closing off the western routes by which the colony's traders had devastated the Southeast in vicious trade wars with Indian, Spanish, and French competitors. Warfare subsided only after Carolina diplomats managed to pry the Cherokees away from other Indian nations. Besides the loss of life and property, the war cost South Carolina much of its western commerce as Virginia traders moved in. Carolina proprietors also lost their charter for South Carolina, which was made a royal colony in the aftermath of the Yamassee War.

NATIVE BORDERLANDS

The conflicts in the Carolinas reveal the eighteenth-century transformation of North America as involving far more than an imperial contest among English, French, and Spanish. It also embroiled native participants in a complex, constantly shifting struggle with Europeans and each other for advantages in trade, territory, and military alliance. Whole new peoples such as the Catawba and the Cherokee were emerging in the first decades of the eighteenth century, as disparate survivors of wars and epidemics forged new identities from the remnants of cultural traditions or were absorbed into larger groups that had escaped the devastation. Stronger nations or leagues such as the Iroquois incorporated weaker ones such as the Tuscarora as tributaries or lesser members. Skillful Indian diplomats often managed to wrest advantages not only by playing one European power against another, but also by negotiating tacit cooperation among rival European groups, even in wartime. Indeed, Indians could often pit representatives of rival English colonies against one another, as traders and government officials jockeyed for control of trade in skins and furs.

The impact of this contest extended far beyond the direct reach of the Europeans. Indians who had never seen a European traded avidly with native middlemen for European knives, hatchets, mirrors, and guns. Some goods made their way along native trade routes to sites thousands of miles from the place where they were originally traded. Archaeological evidence suggests, for instance, that Spanish goods first traded in central Mexico could pass overland through many different exchanges among native peoples to Cherokee towns in what is now western North Carolina. By the early 1700s, native middlemen were also carrying French goods from western Lake Superior or newly founded settlements on the Mississippi Delta to peoples of the Great Plains.

Covenant Chains and Middle Grounds: From the Hudson to the Great Lakes

At the opening of the eighteenth century the Iroquois held sway over a great swath of territory from Lake Ontario south, often deploying war parties that ranged into western Virginia and North Carolina in search of captives for adoption. The Covenant Chain forged during the 1680s continued to link the Iroquois in trading alliances with New Englanders, New Yorkers, Pennsylvanians, and Virginians as well as with various Indian nations to the west (see Chapter 7). Yet in the Grand Settlement of 1701, an Iroquois Confederacy exhausted by more than a decade of war had gained respite by negotiating a position of formal neutrality in conflicts between their French and English neighbors (see Chapter 9). Historian Daniel Richter has called the settlement a "precarious framework for an elusive new system of intercultural relationships," yet it did provide the Iroquois time to rebuild their population and gave them new commercial opportunities to exploit. French and English, equally eager to court Iroquois favor and gain influence in tribal councils, sent missionaries and interpreters as well as resident black-

Conflicting Claims in Eighteenth-Century North America

Competition for territory and influence intensified throughout the first half of the eighteenth century as the French and English pressed claims against each other, the Spanish, and the various native inhabitants of North America.

smiths and gunsmiths who supplied village residents with cheap iron tools and kept their guns in good repair. Peace with New France also gave the Iroquois a chance to cultivate commercial relations with Mississaugas, Ottawas, Wyandots, and Miamis, diverting their supplies of furs from the St. Lawrence to the Hudson in exchange for cheaper, more plentiful English goods.

The Algonquian peoples to the west of Iroquoia remained allied to the French through a complex set of formal and informal arrangements, often involving intermarriage as well as exchange of gifts and military aid. Historian Richard White has termed this system of Franco-Indian relations a "middle ground," a conceptual as well as a geographical space where Indians and French could "adjust their differences through . . . creative, often expedient misunderstandings," producing new meanings and practices which enabled both sides to work together for overlapping goals. The Algonquians no more intended to isolate themselves from European contact than did any other native group. They relied on French traders to provide essential metal goods and weapons. The goal of nations such the Ojibwa, Ottawa, Potawatomi, and the Miami was rather to maintain a strong independent voice in these commercial exchanges. So long as they had sufficient military strength—that is, large numbers of healthy armed warriors—they compelled everyone who came to negotiate in the "middle ground" to give them proper respect. Western Algonquians took advantage of French, Iroquois, and English rivals when possible; they compromised when necessary. It is best to imagine the middle ground as an open, dynamic process of creative interaction.

Between Empires: Indians of the Southeast

Around 1700, the Southeast was emerging as a new site of intense and creative contact among Europeans and Indians. This territory bounded by the Mississippi River, the Gulf Coast, and the Carolina coast was home to many large Indian nations with complex societies that stretched back in many cases to Mississippian origins (see Chapter 1). Many were the remnants of Native American groups who had lost so many people to warfare and epidemic disease that they could no longer sustain an independent cultural identity. These survivors joined with other Indians to establish new multiethnic communities. In this respect, Native American villages may not have seemed all that different from the mixed European settlements of the backcountry.

Stronger groups of Indians generally welcomed the refugees. Strangers were formally adopted to take the places of family members killed in battle or overcome by sickness, and many seemingly traditional Indian villages of the eighteenth century actually represented innovative responses to rapidly shifting external conditions. As historian Peter Wood explains, "Physically and linguistically diverse groups moved to form loosely organized confederacies, unions of mutual convenience, that effectively restrained interethnic hostilities."

Like their native neighbors to the north and east, native peoples of the Southeast pursued diplomacy and trade with Europeans when they could, yet these dealings often unfolded in a climate of conflict and danger that differed from the middle-ground experience of the Great Lakes Algonquians. Their relatively large numbers and control of strategic territory gave many southeastern Indians considerable leverage in their dealings with Europeans. Yet the Indian nations were too divided and the competition among rival European trading partners too intense for Great Lakes–style "creative misunderstandings" to foster widespread intercultural cooperation.

Instead, each nation exercised its bargaining power pragmatically in pursuit of its own ends. The diverse peoples of the Catawba River valley in the Carolina Piedmont shrewdly played rival Virginia and South Carolina traders against each other to get the best price for their deerskins. The Chickasaws on the eastern banks of the Mississippi allied with Carolinians against their Choctaw rivals, using English firearms to capture Choctaws for sale on the slave market. Choctaws responded by seeking arms from the French and using them to disrupt Chickasaw-Carolinian trade caravans. The Creek towns of what is now southeastern Alabama and southwestern Georgia divided their loyalties between English, Spanish, and French. The trading preferences of the eastern allies of the English in Georgia enriched Creeks of the Lower Towns, but eventually they were embroiled in a devastating civil war with the western Upper Town allies of the French in Mobile. The Cherokee capitalized on their position at the southern Appalachian crossroads of early eighteenth-century leather-trading routes to act as powerful middlemen between English and western nations in the deerskin trade.

Yet southeastern Indians understood all too well when their own uses of exchange to augment their spiritual power and cultural well-being clashed with French or English desires for profit in skins, land, or slaves. When such conflicts came to light, natives resisted as specific circumstances demanded. Individual Indian trappers and hunters might make an unscrupulous trader pay for his duplicity by capturing his goods or taking his life, a warning for other traders to follow more honorable codes of conduct. European demands sometimes pushed rival Indian nations into alliance against the aggressors, and the resulting wars produced sudden shifts in European-Indian relations. Cherokees and Choctaws joined the Yamassees in their war against Carolinians in 1715, killing the traders and driving the colonists back toward Charles Town (see p. 261).

Just as often, conflicting aims among different Indian nations led one nation to ally with a European power against another. Southeastern Westoes, Shawnees, and Yamassees forged a succession of alliances with South Carolinians against Apalachee neighbors that eventually forced Apalachee survivors to forsake their traditional homelands for refuge towns near St. Augustine and Pensacola. In the Yamassee War of 1715, the Cherokees eventually forsook their native allies and came to occupy the Yamassees' former place in the Carolina leather trade. Differing political and religious aims prevented some nations such as the Natchez from ever establishing stable relations with Europeans. Franco-Natchez relations eventually degenerated into a war of conquest that wiped out the Natchez as a distinct nation. Like an environmental ecotone, or zone of transition between two different habitats, the Indians' new south represented a constantly shifting borderland of opportunity and danger.

THE BORDER CONFLICTS OF QUEEN ANNE'S WAR

By the first decade of the eighteenth century, a complex tangle of interethnic and imperial conflict and cooperation laced across eastern North America, linking some rivals into unlikely partnerships while setting natural allies against one another. Nowhere was this dynamic more evident than in the imperial contest English colonists called Queen Anne's War, known in Europe as the War of the Spanish Succession (1702–1713). The conflict pitted Spain and France against England, Holland, and Austria after Spain's last Hapsburg monarch, Charles II, designated as his heir Philippe d'Anjou, grandson of France's Louis XIV. A little more than a year after war broke out in Europe, a Canadian force of French soldiers and their Indian allies opened a North American front by attacking English frontier settlements in Maine. Queen Anne's War plunged North American

A Century of Conflict: Major Wars, 1689–1763

Dates	European Name	American Name	Major Allies
1689–1697	War of the League of Augsburg	King William's War	Britain, Holland, Spain, their colonies, and Native American allies against France, its colonies, and Native American allies
1702–1713	War of the Spanish Succession	Queen Anne's War	Britain, Holland, their colonies, and Native American allies against France, Spain, their colonies, and Native American allies
1743–1748	War of the Austrian Succession (War of Jenkins's Ear)	King George's War	Britain, its colonies, and Native American allies, and Austria against France, Spain, their Native American allies, and Prussia
1756–1763	Seven Years War	French and Indian War	Britain, its colonies, and Native American allies against France, its colonies, and Native American allies

Indians and colonists into a ten-year turmoil of border conflicts and informal, often illegal alliances that brought windfall profits to some participants and devastation to many others.

New England Captives and Iroquois Neutrals

Canada's blow against Maine in August, 1703 was just the first in a long string of raids that ravaged communities all along the New England frontier. Only a few months later on March 1, 1704, a detachment of Abenaki warriors left their French allies in camp and crossed the frozen Connecticut River to strike the frontier town of Deerfield, Massachusetts, the most famous raid of the war. Nearly fifty settlers—many of them women and young children deemed unable to survive a long winter's march—lost their lives in the "Sack of Deerfield." The Abenaki rounded up 112 survivors and marched them through the deep snow to Canada. Once arrived, the surviving captives were adopted into Abenaki bands or redeemed by the French for prisoner exchanges. The chief prize of the raid, Deerfield's minister John Williams, spent three years negotiating for his captive congregation's return to New England. Canadian authorities eventually agreed to exchange Williams and other English captives for French captives being held in Boston. Williams memorialized his peoples' ordeal in a popular narrative, *The Redeemed Captive, Returning to Zion* (1707). Yet Williams's own daughter, Eunice, remained unredeemed in New France, where she converted to Roman Catholicism and married an Abenaki man with whom she spent the rest of her life.

Issues	Major American Battle	Treaty
Opposition to French bid for control of Europe	New England troops assault Quebec under Sir William Phips (1690)	Treaty of Ryswick (1697)
Austria and France hold rival claims to Spanish throne	Attack on Deerfield (1704)	Treaty of Utrech (1713)
Struggle among Britain, Spain, and France for control of New World territory; among France, Prussia, and Austria for control of central Europe	New England forces capture Louisbourg under William Pepperrell (1745)	Treaty of Aix-la-Chapelle (1748)
Struggle among Britain, Spain, and France for worldwide control of colonial markets and raw materials	British and Continental forces capture Quebec under Major General James Wolfe (1759)	Peace of Paris (1763)

Throughout Queen Anne's War, many other New England settlers lost their lives or were taken captive to Canada in similar raids. Massachusetts authorities responded by granting tax relief to frontier communities hard hit by wartime damage to crops and property and by reinforcing the towns with small garrisons of militia. Many colonists, especially those in Maine and New Hampshire, retreated to more densely populated areas near the coast. The English retaliated against the French from the sea by raiding settlements along the Acadian coast and the mouth of the St. Lawrence.

Not all inhabitants of the Northeast suffered equally. While New England frontier settlements and French coastal communities bore the brunt of imperial conflict, the Five Nations struggled to preserve their hard-won neutrality between England and France for the first several years of the war. Neutrality served not only Iroquois interests but also the interests of New France, New York, and the Great Lakes Algonquians, all of whom profited from wartime commerce. Quebec merchants carried on a lucrative clandestine trade with their counterparts in Albany, exchanging beaver pelts for the English woolen cloth preferred by Abenaki trading partners for their superior quality at a lower price. Meanwhile, the Iroquois capitalized on their peace with New France by diverting the Great Lakes fur trade from Canada to Albany. Neutrality allowed the Five Nations to negotiate peace with France's Algonquian allies, then guide them on safe passage through Iroquoia to the Hudson. Iroquois guides gained from employment by western Algonquians, and Iroquois villages collected from each trading party appropriate ceremonial gifts as it passed through, yet the Algonquians still netted higher profits in Albany than they could earn from Quebec.

These good times did not last forever. In 1709, New York authorities persuaded Mohawk warriors to join a major military expedition against Canada. The expedition fizzled out on the shores of Lake Champlain, but in 1711 the English tried again to launch a combined land and naval assault against Quebec. This campaign likewise ended in disaster when the English naval commander, Sir Hovenden Walker, ran part of the fleet aground on an island in the St. Lawrence with a loss of over seven hundred lives.

The 1711 campaign against Quebec was not a total loss, however. On its way up the coast to the St. Lawrence, the English fleet had captured the Acadian town of Port Royal. Their ability to hold the port for the remainder of the war gave British diplomats leverage to claim Acadia during peace negotiations. In 1713 France ceded the region to Great Britain in the Treaty of Utrecht, and Acadia became Nova Scotia.

War and Exchange in the Southeast

In the Southeast, the presence of a Bourbon on the Spanish throne prompted French and Spanish colonists to suppress their historic rivalry and unite against their common English enemy. The English, however, in 1702 struck the first blow of Queen Anne's War when South Carolina's Governor James Moore personally led a force of 50 colonists and 1,500 Yamassees to attack Spanish Florida by sea. Moore's troops devastated the Spanish district of Guale en route to St. Augustine and burned the town to the ground once they arrived. Moore lacked the mortars or scaling ladders needed to take the fort, however, so after an eight-week siege he gave up the fight and retreated overland to Charles Town. Two years later, Moore led another force on a path of death and destruction across northern Florida, laying waste to all remaining Apalachee missions and forcing the Spanish to abandon the district. In 1707, Carolinians burned the town of Pensacola but failed to take the fort. The Spanish managed to fend off a second English assault on Pensacola in 1711. By then, however, the remaining Indians of northern Florida had allied firmly with the English, reducing Spanish influence to tattered refugee settlements near St. Augustine and Pensacola Bay.

Spanish officials in Florida did not leave English aggression wholly unanswered. French allies from Louisiana had provided vital aid in the defense of Pensacola, and the Spanish turned again to them for help in launching an offensive against South Carolina. In 1706, a combined force of French and Spanish privateers sailed from Havana, Cuba, to attack Charles Town but failed to take the city.

While Queen Anne's War put Spanish Florida on the defensive, Franco-Spanish cooperation gave Louisiana colonists and traders breathing room to establish their presence firmly in the Southeast. Spanish officials permitted French traders to extend their influence among Gulf Coast Indians as far eastward as Pensacola. Other French traders made their way west up the Red River to cultivate contacts with the Caddo Indians, whose friendship and trade the Spanish had earlier worked so hard to keep for themselves. Louisiana traders could not capitalize fully on these new contacts, however. The war diverted resources away from colonial development and made trade goods scarce and expensive. The ability of English traders to offer greater variety and quantity for better rates enabled them to win more Indian allies and slowed French expansion into the interior.

The second colonial war ended in 1713 when Great Britain and France signed the Treaty of Utrecht. During the conflict, the English Crown and Parliament had consolidated rule in the British Isles by the Act of Union with Scotland in 1707. Diplomats of this newly-created Great Britain scored significant territorial gains on the peripheries of North America, acquiring Nova Scotia, Newfoundland, and Hudson Bay. The negotiators showed much less interest in the New World's military situation. Their major concern was preserving a balance of power among the European states. A decade of intense fighting had taken a heavy toll in North America, but neither French nor English colonists had much to show for their sacrifice.

The Stakes of Conflict

After George I succeeded to the British throne in 1714, parliamentary leaders were determined to preserve peace—mainly because of the rising cost of war. Yet on the American frontier, the hostilities continued with raids and reprisals. As people on both sides of this conflict now realized, the stakes of the war for North American empire were very high; they were fighting for control over the entire West, including the Mississippi Valley.

Both sides viewed this great contest in conspiratorial terms. From South Carolina to Massachusetts Bay, colonists believed the French planned to "encircle" the English settlements and to confine the English to a narrow strip of land along the Atlantic coast. The English noted that in 1682, La Salle had claimed for the King of France a territory—Louisiana—that included all the people and resources located on "streams and Rivers" flowing into the Mississippi River. To make good on their claim, the French constructed forts on the Chicago and Illinois Rivers. In 1717, they established a military post two hundred miles up the Alabama River, well within striking distance of the Carolina frontier, and in 1718, they settled New Orleans. One New Yorker declared in 1715 that "it is impossible that we and the French can both inhabit this Continent in peace but that one nation must at last give way to the other."

On their part, the French suspected that their English rivals intended to seize all of North America. Anglo-American land speculators and frontier traders pushed aggressively into territory claimed by the French and owned by the Native Americans. In 1716, one Frenchman urged his government to hasten the development of Louisiana, since "it is not difficult to guess that their [the British] purpose is to drive us entirely out . . . of North America."

To their great sorrow and eventual destruction, the original inhabitants of the frontier, the Native Americans, became swept up in this undeclared war. The Indians maneuvered to hold their own in the steadily shrinking zone between the European colonial powers. In the Northeast, the Iroquois favored the British; the Algonquian peoples generally supported the French. Indians of the Southeast played English colonists against each other as well as the French for advantage in trade and warfare. But regardless of the groups to which they belonged, Indian warriors—acting independently and for their own strategic reasons—found themselves enmeshed in imperial policies set by distant European kings.

CHRONOLOGY

1694	Vargas initiates campaign to reconquer Pueblos.
1700	Iberville founds Fort Mississippi, first settlement of French Louisiana.
1701	Cadillac founds Detroit.
1702	War of the Spanish Succession (Queen Anne's War) begins.
1704	French and Indians sack Deerfield, Massachusetts.
1706	Spanish and French assault Charles Town.
1707	Carolinians sack Pensacola.
1711	English capture Port Royal, Acadia; Tuscarora War breaks out in North Carolina.
1713	Peace of Utrecht ends War of the Spanish Succession.
1714	Yamassee War in South Carolina.
1716	Spotswood opens Shenandoah Valley to settlement.
1718	San Antonio founded by Spanish; New Orleans founded by French.
1769	California missions founded at San Diego, Monterey, San Francisco, and Santa Barbara.

RECOMMENDED READING

A good general discussion of the varieties of European colonization in eighteenth-century America may be found in D. W. Meinig's *The Shaping of America: A Geographical Perspective on 500 Years of History: Volume 1, Atlantic America, 1492–1800* (New Haven, 1986). For the French in America, an essential starting point is W. J. Eccles, *The French in North America, 1500–1783* rev. ed. (East Lansing, 1998). Eccles's earlier work, *The Canadian Frontier, 1534–1760* (Albuquerque, 1969) provides a closer look at the development of New France in the region that became Canada and the Great Lakes states of the United States. For French fur trading west of the Great Lakes, see W. Raymond Wood and Thomas D. Thiessen, eds., *Early Fur Trade on the Northern Plains: Canadian Traders Among the Mandan and Hidatsa Indians, 1738–1818* (Norman, 1985). Daniel Usner, *Indians, Settlers, and Slaves in a Frontier Exchange Economy: The Lower Mississippi Valley Before 1783* (Chapel Hill, 1992) provides an analysis of the economic and cultural life of French Louisiana during the eighteenth century. Winstanley Briggs, "Le Pays des Illinois," *William and Mary Quarterly*, 3rd ser., 47 (1990): 30–56, provides an analysis of French settlement in the Illinois country.

The best survey of the eighteenth-century Spanish borderlands remains David J. Weber, *The Spanish Frontier in North America* (New Haven, 1992). For the eighteenth-century culture of Spanish and Indians in New Mexico, see Ramón Gutiérrez, *When*

Jesus Came, the Corn Mothers Went Away: Marriage, Sexuality, and Power in New Mexico, 1500–1846 (Stanford, 1991). For the Spanish search for La Salle in Texas, see Robert S. Weddle, *Wilderness Manhunt: The Spanish Search for La Salle* (Austin, 1973). Henry Folmer, *Franco-Spanish Rivalry in North America, 1524–1763* (Glendale, Calif., 1953), explores the imperial contest between France and Spain along the Gulf Coast.

The cultural zone among Indians, colonists, and in many cases, slaves has become the focus of a growing number of studies. In addition to Usner's book on the lower Mississippi, Richard White has analyzed the succession of European and Indian interactions in the Great Lakes in his influential study, *The Middle Ground: Indians, Empires, and Republics in the Great Lakes Region, 1650–1815* (Cambridge, 1991), while Michael McConnell examines the Ohio Valley in his *A Country Between: The Upper Ohio Valley and Its Peoples, 1725–1774* (Lincoln, 1992). Andrew R. L. Cayton and Fredrika J. Teute, *Contact Points: American Frontiers from the Mohawk Valley to the Mississippi, 1750–1830* (Chapel Hill, 1998) treats a somewhat later period but contains essays that critique and offer alternatives to the "middle ground" as an analytical concept. For the bloody history of interaction between Carolinians and Indians see Alan Gallay, *The Indian Slave Trade: The Rise of English Empire in the American South, 1670–1717* (New Haven, 2002).

Queen Anne's War is treated in Howard H. Peckham, *The Colonial Wars, 1689–1762* (Chicago, 1964), and Douglas Edward Leach, *The Northern Colonial Frontier, 1607–1763* (New York, 1966). For the "Sack of Deerfield" and its aftermath, see Richard I. Melvoin, *New England Outpost: War and Society in Colonial Deerfield* (New York, 1989), and John Demos, *The Unredeemed Captive: A Family Story from Early America* (New York, 1994).

Chapter 11

Shifting Borderlands

Population Growth, Immigration, and the Movement of Peoples in Eighteenth-Century America

On August 1, 1740, a party of Delawares and Mingoes, or western Iroquois, made their way through the streets of Philadelphia. A large crowd of curious Philadelphians clustered around the Indians as they passed. The travelers had crossed the mountains from Kittanning on the banks of the Allegheny River, carrying to Pennsylvania proprietor Thomas Penn 160 buckskins "to make you Gloves." When they arrived at the city's Quaker Meetinghouse, Penn welcomed them inside to sit in Council with him and a delegation of colonial officials. The townspeople filed in after the Indians, packing the seats with "as many of the Inhabitants of Philadelphia as the House could conveniently hold."

The Delaware spokesman Sassoonan opened the meeting by laying a belt of wampum upon the table between the Indians and the colonists, assuring Penn and the Pennsylvania delegation as he did so that his people had not "forgot[ten] this place." Sassoonan, also known as Alumapees, had led his band of Delawares sixteen years earlier from the banks of the Schuylkill River near Philadelphia to "Allegheny a Long way off" after selling much of their eastern lands to English newcomers. His people "loved to hunt" at Allegheny, Sassoonan declared, "because we there meet with some of our Brethren your Indian Traders who furnish us with Powder and Shot and other things." This commerce, he said, had helped sustain his people's affection for the English despite the distance between Kittanning and Philadelphia. The Delaware leader assured Pennsylvania officials that "we do not listen to any Idle Tales or Lies which we may have heard" from hostile natives or French who constantly attempted to draw his people away from alliance with the English. "We know where our Brethren dwell."

Yet the road between Allegheny and Philadelphia had recently begun bringing not only the traders whose commerce secured the bonds of loyalty, but also unwelcome English hunters who competed directly with the Delawares and western Iroquois for game. "Your young Men have killed so many Deer, Beavers, Bears, and Game of all sorts," Sassoonan complained, "that we can hardly find any for our selves." He therefore asked Thomas Penn to prevent further European hunting in Allegheny. "God has made us Hunters," Sassoonan declared, but the "white people have other Ways of living without that."

The 1740 meeting between Sassoonan and Thomas Penn provides a revealing glimpse at a central dynamic of eighteenth-century colonial development. Fifteen years earlier, the pressure of incoming European settlers had pushed Sassoonan's band off their ancestors' land. Now an advance guard of English hunters and trappers were knocking on the Delaware door in faraway Allegheny. Indeed, the European demand for North American land was rising exponentially as the coastal population burgeoned and unprecedented numbers of immigrants poured in from across the Atlantic.

But the backcountry coveted by European settlers was not a vast empty territory awaiting their arrival, as historical maps often suggest. West of Atlantic coastal cities, towns, farms, and plantations lay much more than a huge blank area with no mark of civilization. Indeed, Sassoonan and his people would not have understood such maps. They had made some of the empty space on the maps their home. The Allegheny Delawares knew the area as a populous, contested, rapidly shifting border zone stretching far beyond the horizon of the Delawares' experience—from New England and New France to the Spanish borderlands of the far Southwest.

The pace of change in those borderlands accelerated dramatically after the 1713 Treaty of Utrecht, which brought Queen Anne's War to an end. The period of peace that followed made the Atlantic relatively safe for passenger vessels and slave ships, while the older Atlantic settlements provided a staging ground for colonization of the interior. No longer did colonists have to look to European investors and suppliers for crucial aid in occupying and settling the land. The hold of colonial governments may have seemed tenuous to contemporaries, but Europeans were in North America to stay. Furthermore, they had put in place the military, diplomatic, economic, and legal structures needed to support those eager to settle on the frontier.

Faced with the consequent intrusion of Europeans into the interior, native peoples adapted in a variety of ways to seize new opportunities while maintaining their independence. Most eagerly tapped into expanding trade networks. Many pushed further west to avoid being surrounded by foreigners. Others played rival European powers against one another to gain concessions that preserved and even augmented native power. When all else failed, Native Americans fought. Cooperation, exchange, and conflict in the borderlands produced ripples of change far beyond the direct influence of Europeans, across the Great Plains and to the Rocky Mountains.

"AN INCREASE WITHOUT PARALLEL": GROWTH AND MIGRATION

The phenomenal growth of British America during the eighteenth century amazed Benjamin Franklin, one of the first persons to bring scientific rigor to the study of demography. The population of the English colonies doubled approximately every twenty-five years. Franklin calculated in 1751 that, if the expansion continued at such an extraordinary rate for another century or so, "the greatest Number of Englishmen will be on this Side [of] the water." Not only was the total population increasing at a very rapid rate; it also was becoming more dispersed and heterogeneous. Each year witnessed the arrival of thousands of non-English Europeans, most of whom soon moved to the backcountry of Pennsylvania and the southern colonies.

Accurate population data from the colonial period are extremely difficult to find. The first national census did not occur until 1790. Still, various sources surviving from pre-Revolutionary times indicate quite clearly that the total white population of Britain's thirteen mainland colonies rose from about 250,000 in 1700 to 2,150,000 in 1770, an annual growth rate of 3 percent.

Few societies in recorded history have expanded so rapidly, and if the growth rate had not dropped substantially during the nineteenth and twentieth centuries, the current population of the United States would stand at well over one billion people. Natural reproduction was responsible for most of the growth. More families bore children who in turn lived long enough to have children of their own. Because of this sudden expansion, the population of the late colonial period was strikingly young; approximately one-half of the populace at any given time was under age 16.

In New England and the Chesapeake, the regions of oldest English settlement, natural increase contributed heavily to frontier expansion. Heirs of the first settlers used established institutions and forms to extend familiar patterns of life and labor into new territory. This made for a great deal of homogeneity among the population of New England. In colonies further south, settlers from families long established in America shared territory with newcomers from the British Isles and the European continent.

Families, Land, and Movement in New England

In New England, the generous parcels of land granted to first-generation townspeople enabled most children and grandchildren to marry and raise families in the same communities as their parents. As many as three generations of fathers in towns such as Andover, Massachusetts could divide family lands equally among sons while remaining confident that each would have enough to support his own family. Young people in New England often moved soon after marriage, but only a short distance away. They might remain within the same town, supporting their families on parcels that had earlier been set aside for future use, or move to a neighboring town where a father had managed to purchase additional lands. Ties of kinship and friendship kept most of these yeomen farming families close to their ancestral homes. So did the expectation of hardship in frontier settlements, where recurring outbreaks of warfare reminded colonists how dangerous the "howling wilderness" remained (see Chapters 9 and 10).

These patterns gradually changed during the eighteenth century as family parcels became too small to subdivide further and successive generations came to occupy the towns' reserve lands. A growing minority of young men found it necessary to move north to frontier lands along the Connecticut River or east to the forests of Maine. These frontier settlers usually carried with them a cash inheritance sufficient to purchase cheap frontier parcels large enough to sustain their own families in the same kind of landed independence that their parents had

This engraving from the mid-eighteenth century depicts a vast clearing of trees whose stumps would either be pulled out or cultivated around. Rivers formed the colonists' and Indians' best means of travel and communication.

Rare Book Division, New York Public Library, Astor, Lenox and Tilden Collections

enjoyed. The governments of Massachusetts, Connecticut, and New Hampshire continued to regulate frontier settlement much as they had in the seventeenth century. Settlers were required to cluster on home lots of 3 to 4 acres near twenty to thirty other families, forming communities for mutual support and protection. Once established, these communities could attract additional migrants as inhabitants wrote home to inform relatives about the progress of settlement and the availability of land. Indeed, such patterns of chain migration made many frontier towns virtual colonies of older communities near the coast.

Eighteenth-century expansion produced another kind of mobility in New England as a growing number of laboring poor began traveling the countryside in search of work. These mostly young people lacked the funds needed to obtain and cultivate frontier lands. They relied for support on temporary agricultural employment during planting and harvest times, or on unskilled jobs in nearby towns. Some made their way to port towns such as Boston, Massachusetts; New London, Connecticut; or Newport, Rhode Island, where they found work on the docks or in warehouses and workshops. Some became sailors. Others with a farming background found themselves recruited by the proprietors of great estates along the Hudson River, who sought to develop their holdings by renting parcels to capable New England farmers on favorable terms.

Diversity and Growth in the Middle Colonies

The multiethnic population that had settled the Hudson and Delaware Valleys during the seventeenth century was multiplying rapidly in the early decades of the eighteenth century. In 1700, New York's 19,000 people remained the most ethnically diverse in British America, yet the colony's numbers were soon surpassed by more recently settled Pennsylvania, the fastest-growing English colony of the century.

The population of the Middle Colonies was also extraordinarily mobile. In the first decades of the eighteenth century, modest Dutch farmers began migrating from the Hudson River valley to New Jersey. Many had supported Jacob Leisler in the upheavals of the early 1690s (see Chapter 9) and were now fleeing what they saw as the corrupting influence of the increasingly Anglicized Dutch merchants of Albany and New York City. They were also responding to demographic pressures similar to those in coastal New England. The Dutch practice of dividing land inheritances equally among all children of a deceased father gradually reduced average land parcels to sizes that could not sustain all heirs. Cheap New Jersey lands enabled Dutch migrants to recreate the rural, highly separate communities that had evolved in New York during the seventeenth century.

The Dutch farming families of the Hackensack River valley in New Jersey established what the historian A. G. Roeber has described as a "domestically oriented hybrid adaptation to North American conditions." They built gambrel-roofed barns and houses different from those of either English or older Dutch settlers. Unlike English custom, a Dutch widow retained control of property when her husband died and inherited half the family estate, while Dutch daughters received inheritance portions equal to sons. Dutch American children put wooden shoes outside their doors on the feast of St. Nicholas for Sinter Claes to fill with presents. Dutch mothers taught their children to speak the Dutch language, read the Dutch Bible, sing Dutch hymns, and listen to Dutch Reformed sermons preached in the language of their homeland. New Jersey Dutch women and men soon drifted toward a radical brand of pietism that emphasized informal worship, simple singing of psalms, spontaneous prayer, and fiery preaching from charismatic ministers like the Dutch immigrant Theodore Frelinguysen.

Pennsylvania Quakers also developed a distinctive, child-centered pattern of domestic life on what one historian has described as "the most economically successful" family farms in colonial North America. Profits gleaned from the cultivation and sale of wheat on the Atlantic market enabled Quaker mothers and fathers to raise large families, rearing each child in an affectionate atmosphere of "holy conversation." By the early 1730s, the Quaker practice of bequeathing equal shares to each heir was reducing farm sizes, and this, combined with rising property values, was prompting a few third-generation Quaker sons and daughters to migrate south and west in search of cheaper, more abundant land. Others followed to escape the growing eighteenth-century consumer economy whose temptations they feared would entice their children from lives of holy conversation.

Quaker migrants moved farther from their place of origin than migrants in New England. In the late 1720s a small stream of Pennsylvania Quakers began exiting eastern Pennsylvania to establish new communities in North Carolina's Cape Fear region. One of those migrants was young Benjamin Franklin's first partner, Hugh Meredith, who left Philadelphia and the printing business in 1730 to return to farming in Cape Fear, "where land is cheap." The next year Franklin published in the *Pennsylvania Gazette* two letters written by Meredith to entice even more Quaker farmers to join the Cape Fear settlement. Similar unpublished correspondence from migrant Quaker communities in the Virginia Piedmont attracted single people and young families to leave Pennsylvania via the Great Wagon Road, which ran west and south along the Blue Ridge Mountains. Quaker migrants who arrived at these frontier destinations recreated the landed domesticity they had known in Pennsylvania.

The tobacco colonies of Virginia and Maryland expanded rapidly in the eighteenth century as the population grew and demand for tobacco rose. The skewed sex ratio of the seventeenth century had evened out considerably among Anglo-Americans, increasing the rate of marriages and births to a level comparable with that of New England. Eighteenth-century Virginia already boasted a total population greater than that of New England, and its rapid birthrate ensured that it would remain the most populous colony in British North America until well after the American Revolution. The children and grandchildren of small landholders, most of whom had come to the Chesapeake as servants, attempted like their New England counterparts to establish households near the place of their birth. By the early 1700s, however, the price of Tidewater land was prompting small landholders to sell out and move west toward the mountains or south toward the Carolinas, leaving the bulk of coastal plantations in the hands of some of the wealthiest Virginians.

From Tidewater to Piedmont: Expansion of the Chesapeake Colonies

Virginia's gentry also established the pattern for settlement of the Piedmont. Small planters who attempted to settle this region between the coast and the Blue Ridge Mountains often found that leading planters had beaten them to the choicest soil. During the late seventeenth century, families such as the Byrds and the Randolphs carved out vast western estates beyond the falls of the James River. They developed the best tracts into tobacco plantations; the rest they set aside for future development or sold to newcomers at a profit. Some great planters such as William Byrd II managed their western lands from Tidewater mansions, while others such as Thomas and Isham Randolph built imposing Piedmont estates. Other gentry families moved into the upper James River valley and intermarried with the Randolph clan, establishing in the process a powerful kinship network that maintained an unbreakable hold on the region.

The Randolph clan's grip on the upper James River was so tight that even royal officials had to look elsewhere for land. Lieutenant Governor Alexander Spotswood, one of eighteenth-century Virginia's most enterprising Crown appointees, sought his landholding fortune in the more remote Rappahannock River valley. As the penniless heir of an ancient but declining British family, Spotswood had to rely on his wits and the favor of well-placed English patrons to amass wealth commensurate with his aspirations. He exercised actual power in Virginia for twenty-seven years, thanks to the absentee governorship of George Hamilton, Earl of Orkney, who never visited the colony. Spotswood used his position as acting governor to acquire more than 83,000 acres—nearly 130 square miles—of land in the Piedmont and Shenandoah Valley, which he organized as Spotswood County in 1720. He also worked with allies in the Virginia government to secure passage of a law exempting settlers in new counties from taxes for ten years, while requiring all property holders to cultivate 3 acres out of every 50 in their possession or forfeit their claim.

Thanks to Spotswood, Virginia law promoted rapid settlement of the Piedmont while discouraging absentee speculators from buying up vast tracts but leaving them untouched for long periods. Those who acquired large patents of land either settled on them or parceled them out and sold them to small planters willing to move west for cheap lands. Even before 1730, some gentry families were establishing tobacco plantations of 1,000 to 15,000 acres near the Blue Ridge Mountains. Small planters also moved onto less desirable parcels of 100 to 500 acres, which they gradually cleared and planted in tobacco and grain. Lieutenant Governor Spotswood himself took a leading role in settling the region. He recruited miners to establish the fortified community of Germanna in the Shenandoah Valley, where they developed mines and ironworks for the governor. During his tenure, Spotswood also carved fifty-seven plantations out of his Piedmont and Shenandoah lands.

Slavery and Settlement

The larger Piedmont plantations could not have operated without the labor of African slaves. Planters brought many of the slaves on their western plantations from the Tidewater and supplemented them from time to time with "outlandish" slaves brought directly from Africa. The planters sought to maintain a roughly equal ratio of male to female slaves and usually permitted slaves to supplement their diet by cultivating their own garden plots. The favorable sex ratio and relatively good nutrition helped to promote slave marriages and child rearing, contributing to a steady growth in the African American population.

The population growth among African Americans on the Piedmont mirrored development in the Tidewater itself, where since as early as 1710 a relative parity between male and female slaves had made it possible for Chesapeake planters to meet at least some of their need for labor through the natural increase of the existing slave population. Early in the century, planters nevertheless imported large numbers of African slaves—almost 35,000 between 1700 and 1740. Yet already in 1724 the Virginia clergyman Hugh Jones could comment that "the Negroes are not only encreased by fresh supplies from Africa and the West Indian Islands but also are very prolific among themselves." By 1750, the number of African slaves had grown to comprise about 40 percent of Virginia and Maryland's total population, and four-fifths of them were Creoles, persons born in the colony. Another 26,700 Africans arrived between 1740 and 1775, but after that date, Virginia planters relied almost entirely on natural increase to supply their need for slave labor. The highest concentration of slaves remained in the Tidewater, with a smaller percentage in the Piedmont.

Important though the slaves were to the development of a distinctive Virginian slaveholding society, the majority of eighteenth-century freeholding inhabitants of the Piedmont did not own slaves. Indeed, even the great majority of slaveholders owned no more than one or two slaves who helped to cultivate staple crops, tend livestock, clear land, and perform domestic chores. The largest landholders tended to distribute their slave workforce among several plantations, so that few estates held more than thirty-five slaves.

The Lower South's Black Majority

The population of South Carolina lagged well behind that of the Chesapeake and northern colonies during the first third of the eighteenth century. It also constituted the only colony in mainland British North America where the majority population was of African rather than European descent. Indeed, in 1721, one year after South Carolina became a royal colony, census figures pegged the black population at nearly 12,000, 84 percent more than the 6,500 whites who inhabited the colony. Nearly a third of the slaves counted in that census were born in South Carolina. During the following two decades the proportion of white colonists in the population gradually rose to about 40 percent of the total. Nevertheless, Africans remained in the majority throughout the colonial period.

South Carolina's black majority grew mainly by the forced immigration of slaves from Africa and the Caribbean. For a short time between 1690 and 1710 the population sustained itself through natural increase. As rice became the colony's staple, however, imports of African slaves rose dramatically. Between 1700 and 1740 nearly 35,000 slaves arrived in the colony. More than half of that number— 17,700—arrived in the 1730s alone. Slave imports dropped off dramatically in the next decade to only 1,580, but shot up again after 1750. Between 1750 and 1775 slave ships brought to South Carolina almost 45,000 black men and women in chains.

The predominance of African and Creole slaves in the population left a permanent mark on all aspects of South Carolina's growth, including its westward expansion. One observer noted in the 1730s that "if one wishes to plant anything" on newly distributed western lands, "especially in the beginning when it must be cleared, it requires strong hand-work." Slaves and masters labored side by side in South Carolina forests, clearing fields, digging irrigation ditches, planting rice, tending livestock, cutting pine masts for ships, and rendering pine tar, pitch, rosin, and turpentine for naval stores. White settlers relied on slave boatmen to transport goods and passengers from inland settlements to the coasts and to guide migrants to new plantations on the frontier. Slave militiamen also served as comrades in arms with their white masters during the frontier wars of the early eighteenth century, but rising concern about internal security eventually prompted masters to disarm their slaves.

Bondage and Death in the British West Indies

The ability of the North American slave population to become self-sustaining was especially remarkable when compared with slavery in the British West Indies and elsewhere in the Americas. Nowhere else in the New World did the slave population begin growing through natural increase until the first third of the nineteenth century. To be sure, West Indian slave women and men formed temporary or enduring unions and produced offspring. But the fertility rate was low, and poor nutrition and tropical diseases took a heavy toll in infant mortality. Hard labor in often hazardous working conditions killed many slaves within seven years of their arrival on the islands. Consequently, the Caribbean slave population experienced not an increase, but a *depletion* rate of 2 to 4 percent annually.

Nevertheless, the British West Indian slave population grew dramatically during the eighteenth century, even as European Caribbean numbers stagnated. Between 1700 and 1748, the total white population of all British Caribbean possessions rose from 31,000 to 43,900. At the same time, the total black population rose from 114,300 to 258,500. The distribution of the population throughout the British West Indies, already uneven at the beginning of the century, became even more skewed by 1750. While Barbados maintained a fairly steady ratio of one white to every three black slaves, the ratio in the Leeward Islands rose from one white to three blacks in 1700 to nearly one white to eight blacks by 1748. In Jamaica, the shift in the ratio of whites to blacks was evident to Lieutenant Governor Thomas Handasyd as early as 1703. "Our number of Slaves Augments dayly," he wrote to the Board of Trade, "but to my great grief the Number of white men dayly decrease." Indeed, by 1748 the proportion of whites in Jamaica's population had decreased to less than one for every eleven blacks.

Of all the British sugar islands, Jamaica grew most dramatically during the eighteenth century. Barbados reached the practical limits of its growth during the first third of the century. The Leeward Islands took several years to recover from the ravages of the turn-of-the-century wars for empire (see Chapter 9), but by the 1750s they too were approaching the limits of their growth. Jamaica's much larger size enabled more planters to build sugar estates, enlarge them, and staff them with more slaves every year throughout the eighteenth century. By 1748 Jamaica hosted a total population of 128,000—almost 42 percent of the entire British

West Indian population—and produced 17,399 tons of sugar, about 42 percent of the sugar islands' total output. By the end of the century, Jamaica boasted a population of 402,700, well over twice that of Barbados and the Leewards combined, and produced 73,849 tons of sugar, almost 58 percent more than the other sugar islands.

The dramatic rise in the eighteenth-century slave population masked the terrible human cost of British West Indian slavery, because planters boosted their slave labor forces only by importing massive numbers to replace those who died. In Barbados between 1712 and 1734, for instance, only one slave baby was born for every six adult slaves who died. Other West Indian islands repeated the pattern to some degree. By century's end, British sugar planters had imported 1.6 million slaves to the Caribbean, yet the slave population of the sugar islands remained less than 600,000.

Convicts, Debtors, and a Buffer Colony

The African slaves were not the only large group of people brought to the New World in bonds. During the eighteenth century, thousands of British convicts were transported to America. Still others signed contracts of indenture, choosing a term of servitude in the colonies to escape debtors' prison in England. By the early 1730s, the problem of indebtedness and bankruptcy was inspiring various proposals for reform. James Oglethorpe, an enterprising general and member of Parliament, managed to join this reforming impulse to an ambitious plan for grabbing additional territory from Spain. Parliament embraced Oglethorpe's scheme, and the colony of Georgia was born.

Convicts for America

In 1718, Parliament passed the Transportation Act, allowing judges in England, Scotland, and Ireland to send convicted felons to the American colonies. Between 1718 and 1775, the courts shipped approximately 50,000 convicts across the Atlantic. Some of these men and women may actually have been dangerous criminals, but the majority seem to have committed minor crimes against property. Although transported convicts—almost 75 percent of whom were young males— escaped the hangman, they found life difficult in the colonies. Eighty percent of them were sold in the Chesapeake colonies as indentured servants. At best they faced an uncertain future, and it is probably not surprising that few former convicts prospered in America.

British authorities lavished praise on this system. According to one writer, transportation drained "the Nation of its offensive Rubbish, without taking away their Lives." Although Americans purchased the convict servants, they expressed fear that these men and women would create a dangerous criminal class. In one irate essay, Benjamin Franklin asked his readers to consider just how the colonists might repay the leaders of Great Britain for shipping so many felons to America. He suggested that rattlesnakes might be the appropriate gift. "I would propose to have them carefully distributed . . . ," Franklin wrote, "in the Gardens of all the Nobility and Gentry throughout the Nation; but particularly in the Gardens of the

Prime Ministers, the Lords of Trade and Members of Parliament." The Revolution forced the British courts to redirect the flow of convicts to another part of the world; an indirect result of American independence was the founding of Australia by transported felons.

Fledgling Colony—The Founding of Georgia

The early history of Georgia was strikingly different from that of Britain's other mainland colonies. Its settlement was really an act of aggression against the Spanish, who had as good a claim to this area as did the English. During the eighteenth century, the two nations were often at war, and South Carolinians worried that the Spaniards moving up from bases in Florida would occupy the disputed territory between Florida and the Carolina grant.

Georgia owed its existence primarily to James Oglethorpe, who believed that he could thwart Spanish designs on the area south of Charles Town while at the same time providing a fresh start for London's worthy poor, saving them from debtors' prison. Although Oglethorpe envisioned Georgia as an asylum as well as a garrison, the military aspects of his proposal were especially appealing to the leaders of the British government. In 1732, the king granted Oglethorpe and a board of trustees a charter for a new colony to be located between the Savannah and Altamaha Rivers and from "sea to sea." The trustees living in Britain were given complete control over Georgia politics. They ruled through a system of regulations which were not subject to royal oversight as laws were. They appointed their own petty officials and did not call an elected assembly until the very last years of the board's existence. They doled out land in 50-acre plots. They prohibited the importation of slaves and rum. Settlers soon found this constitutional situation intolerable.

During the first years of colonization, Georgia fared no better than had earlier utopian experiments. The poor people of England showed little desire to move to an inclement frontier, and the trustees, in their turn, provided little incentive for emigration. Each colonist received only 50 acres. Another 50 acres could be added for each servant transported to Georgia, but in no case could a settler amass more than 500 acres. Moreover, land could be passed only to an eldest son, and if a planter had no sons at the time of his death, the holding reverted to the trustees. Slavery was prohibited. So too was rum.

Almost as soon as they arrived in Georgia, the settlers complained. The colonists demanded slaves, pointing out to the trustees that unless the new planters possessed an unfree labor force, they could not compete economically with their South Carolina neighbors. The settlers also wanted a voice in local government. In 1738, 121 people living in Savannah petitioned for fundamental reforms in the colony's constitution. Oglethorpe responded angrily, "The idle ones are indeed for Negroes. If the petition is countenanced, the province is ruined." The settlers did not give up. In 1741, they again petitioned Oglethorpe, this time addressing him as "our Perpetual Dictator."

While the colonists grumbled about various restrictions, in 1740 Oglethorpe tried and failed to capture the Spanish fortress at St. Augustine. This personal disappointment coupled with the growing popular unrest destroyed his interest in

Georgia. The trustees were forced to compromise their principles. In 1738, they eliminated all restrictions on the amount of land a man could own and allowed women to inherit land. In 1750, they permitted the settlers to import slaves. Soon Georgians could drink rum. In 1751, the trustees returned Georgia to the king, undoubtedly relieved to be free of what had become a hard-drinking, slave-owning plantation society much like that in South Carolina. The king authorized an assembly in 1751, but even with these social and political changes, Georgia attracted very few new settlers.

"Bettering Their Condition": Eighteenth-Century Immigration

Between 1700 and 1775, more than 250,000 immigrants arrived from the European continent and the British Isles. The flow of immigrants ebbed and surged periodically as events prompted people to look beyond the localities of their birth for opportunities to improve their prospects. All over western Europe and the British Isles, warfare and economic change were prompting people to move from the countryside to growing coastal cities or to farming and grazing lands in central and eastern Europe. Those who crossed the Atlantic represented only a fraction of this vast movement of people. Yet their decision to embark for British America prompted important shifts in the character of Atlantic shipping and increased the ethnic diversity of Great Britain's North American colonies.

A person or family considering a voyage to the New World had to confront legal, financial, and psychological obstacles. A decision to embark for America carried migrants and their families across thousands of miles of ocean, far from familiar networks of kinship and community. Migrants from continental Europe had to transfer their loyalty to a new sovereign. Those from the Continent and Ireland alike often faced opposition at home from local rulers and landlords whose wealth depended heavily on their ability to retain people who would work the land and pay the required dues, taxes, or rents. The high price of passage posed yet another obstacle. Fares to North America ranged from £5 to £8—a sum well beyond the means of many who wanted to go. Merchants and shippers extended credit to those who could not pay in advance, but on terms that required payment soon after arrival at their destinations. Such people often became redemptioners, indentured servants whose American masters paid their passage in exchange for four to seven years' labor. Many redemptioners initially took passage on credit in hopes that friends or relatives in America would help them pay but were sold when their American contacts failed to come through for them.

The North Atlantic Passage

Prospective immigrants braved these daunting obstacles for a variety of reasons. Some were refugees of war or famine. In 1709–1710, for instance, thousands of "Palatines" from the region of the upper Rhine River migrated downriver to escape wartime devastation and crop failures. British officials eventually sent 2,500 of them on to New York and the Carolinas. During the 1720s, severe famines in Ireland prompted more than 5,000 Scots-Irish to flee to British North America. Similar outbreaks of war and famine sent additional surges to America in every decade after 1730.

Dim economic prospects in Europe and the British Isles, coupled with reports of cheap land and generous wages in America, prompted many others to take the trip. Promotional literature often exaggerated North America's promise, but migrants could often verify the reports for themselves against firsthand accounts from relatives who had gone before. German farmers and artisans who labored under heavy taxes and hidebound local regulations took hope in letters from family members painting America as a place where they could "buy, settle and borrow without restrictions" and "all trades and professions are free." Scots-Irish tenant weavers, though not as strapped as many Germans, found appealing the prospect of becoming freeholders themselves. Reports of Anglo-American religious toleration further encouraged immigrants.

The volume of European migrants seeking passage to America prompted eighteenth-century merchants and shippers to adapt to the demand. They refitted vessels to accommodate more passengers and provisions, hoping to reap profits greater than they could expect by shipping trade goods alone. Many shipowners employed agents—often successful migrants or "newlanders" who received free return passage from America in exchange for their service—to travel the countryside recruiting migrants to sail for America on their employers' vessels. Owners' preoccupation with the bottom line often prompted them to crowd on too many passengers and to stock the ship with provisions of poor quality or insufficient quantity for the voyage.

Cramped quarters and spoiled provisions often made the voyage to America difficult to endure, especially when compounded with rough weather conditions. Passengers crowded into tiny compartments whose bunks or hammocks measured no larger than 6 feet by 18 inches, piling all their chests and baggage around them to prevent theft. Those located between decks had to stoop constantly to avoid hitting their heads on the low ceilings. Parents squeezed together in the small bunks with any children under five years of age, while older children shared half a bunk with a sibling or another passenger close in age. Single passengers were assigned berths with no consistent effort to segregate them by sex. In good weather, passengers could go up to the main deck and exercise, socialize, and take their meals. During a storm, however, all had to remain below with the hatches and portholes battened down.

Overcrowding remained a constant feature of transatlantic voyages, but other conditions on board vessels could vary widely. A harsh captain or a rough voyage could make life miserable even on a well-fitted and provisioned vessel, whereas a smooth, quick passage could at least mitigate the misery on a poorly fitted one. The sour-tempered German observer Gottfried Mittelberger complained that his ship to America was "full of pitiful signs of distress—smells, fumes, horrors, vomiting, various kinds of sea sickness, fever, dysentery" and worse, all caused by the "age and highly salted state of the food" and the "very bad and filthy water." A Huguenot immigrant remembered a much happier voyage during which "the women, the young girls, and the young children gathered on deck almost every day for diversion."

Arrival in an American port brought relief to the passengers and excitement onshore. Crowds of prospective masters gathered to bid for immigrants "exposed for redemption sale." Fellow countryfolk already settled in America came on board to refresh expected relatives and friends with bread, fruit, and beer or to glean news and collect letters from home. Paying passengers settled accounts and gathered belongings, whereas those sailing on credit tried to arrange for payment or prepared themselves for terms of servitude. Customs collectors checked the cargo for smuggled goods, while health officials inspected the passengers for signs of infectious disease or scurvy. Non-British passengers then made their way to the courthouse, where English officials required them to take the oath of allegiance to the King and his successors, renounce any allegiance to the Pope, and abide by the laws of the colony where they were settling. Afterward, immigrants could complete whatever arrangements they needed to begin a new life in America.

Newly arrived immigrants had come to America in the hope of obtaining their own property and setting up as independent farmers. They found land abundantly available in the backcountry, a region stretching approximately 800 miles from western Pennsylvania to Georgia. Although they planned to follow customs they had known in Europe, they found the challenge of surviving on the British frontier far more demanding than they had anticipated. They plunged into a complex, fluid, often violent society that included large numbers of Native Americans and African Americans as well as other Europeans.

Ethnic Diversity in the Backcountry

The largest group of newcomers consisted of Scots-Irish. The experiences of these people in Great Britain influenced not only their decision to move to the New World but also their behavior once they arrived. During the seventeenth century, English rulers thought they could thoroughly dominate Catholic Ireland by transporting thousands of lowland Scottish Presbyterians to northern Ireland. The plan failed. English officials who were members of the Anglican church discriminated against the Presbyterians. They passed laws that placed the Scots-Irish at a severe disadvantage when they traded in England; they taxed them at exorbitant rates. After several poor harvests, many of the Scots-Irish elected to emigrate to America, where they hoped to find the freedom and prosperity that had been denied them in Ireland. "I have seen some of their letters to their friends here [Ireland]," one British agent reported in 1729, ". . . in which after they set forth and recommend the fruitfulness and commodities of the country [America], they tell them, that if they will but carry over a little money with them, they may for a small sum purchase considerable tracts of land." It is estimated that 150,000 Scots-Irish migrated to the colonies before the Revolution.

Most Scots-Irish immigrants landed initially in Philadelphia, but instead of remaining in that city, they carved out farms on Pennsylvania's western frontier. The colony's proprietors welcomed the influx of new settlers, for it seemed that they would form an ideal barrier between the Indians and the older, coastal communities. The Penn family soon had second thoughts, however. The Scots-Irish squatted on whatever land looked best, and when colonial officials pointed out that large tracts had already been reserved, the immigrants retorted that "it was against the laws of God and nature that so much land should be idle when so many Christians wanted it to labour on and to raise their bread." Wherever they located, the Scots-Irish challenged established authority.

A second large body of non-English settlers, more than 100,000 people, came from the upper Rhine Valley, the German Palatinate. Some of the migrants, especially those who relocated to America around the turn of the century, belonged to small pietistic Protestant sects whose religious views were somewhat similar to those of the Quakers. These Germans moved to the New World primarily in the hope of finding religious toleration. Under the guidance of Francis Daniel Pastorius (1651–1720), a group of Mennonites established in Pennsylvania a prosperous community known as Germantown.

By mid-century, however, the characteristics of the German migration had begun to change. Large numbers of Lutherans transferred to the Middle Colonies. Unlike members of the pietistic sects, these men and women were not in search of religious freedom. Rather, they traveled to the New World looking to better their material lives. The Lutheran church in Germany initially tried to maintain control over the distant congregations, but even though the migrants themselves fiercely preserved many aspects of traditional German culture, they were eventually forced to accommodate to new social conditions. Henry Melchior Mühlenberg (1711–1787), a tireless leader, helped German Lutherans through a difficult cultural adjustment. In 1748, Mühlenberg organized a meeting of local pastors and lay delegates that ordained ministers of their own choosing, an act of spiritual independence that has been called "the most important single event in American Lutheran history."

The German migrants—mistakenly called Pennsylvania Dutch because the English confused deutsch (meaning "German") with Dutch ("a person from Holland")—began reaching Philadelphia in large numbers after 1717. By 1766, persons of German stock accounted for more than one-third of Pennsylvania's total population. Even their most vocal detractors admitted the Germans were the best farmers in the colony.

Ethnic differences in Pennsylvania bred disputes. The Scots-Irish as well as the Germans preferred to live with people of their own background, and they sometimes fought to keep members of the other nationality out of their neighborhoods. The English were suspicious of both groups. They could not comprehend why the Germans insisted on speaking German in America. In 1753, for example, Franklin described these settlers as "the most stupid of their nation." He warned that "unless the stream of [German] importation could be turned from this to other colonies . . . they will soon outnumber us . . . [and] all the advantages we have, will in my opinion, be not able to preserve our language, and even our government will become precarious."

Such prejudice may have persuaded members of both groups to search for new homes. After 1730, Germans and Scots-Irish pushed south from western Pennsylvania into the Shenandoah Valley, thousands of them settling in the backcountry of Virginia and the Carolinas. The Germans usually remained wherever they found unclaimed fertile land. By contrast, the Scots-Irish often moved two or three times, acquiring a reputation as a rootless people.

Wherever the newcomers settled, they often found themselves living beyond the effective authority of the various colonial governments. To be sure, backcountry residents petitioned for assistance during wars against the Indians, but most of the time they preferred to be left alone. These conditions heightened the importance of religious institutions within the small ethnic communities. Although the original stimulus for coming to America may have been a desire for economic independence and prosperity, backcountry families—especially the Scots-Irish—flocked to evangelical Protestant preachers, to Presbyterian, Baptist, and, later, Methodist ministers who not only fulfilled the settlers' spiritual needs but also gave these scattered backcountry communities a pronounced moral character that survived long after the colonial period.

MIGRATION AND ADAPTATION IN INDIAN COUNTRY

The rapid westward movement of Europeans after Queen Anne's War brought dramatic changes to eighteenth-century native peoples. The permanent presence of conflicting, expansive European empires shaped the terms of encounter far more decisively than they had done in the seventeenth century. Native Americans had to adapt flexibly and quickly to a constantly shifting situation. They had to develop new strategies of trade, diplomacy, and warfare to cope with an expanding European population, to stem the decline of their own numbers, and to maintain their self-determination. Some accomplished this demanding task superbly, not only recovering from earlier losses but even strengthening their position in the contest for land and influence. Those who failed became absorbed into stronger groups or wound up on tiny reservations in a now-alien land.

During the 1720s and 1730s, the site of the most intense and creative contact between Europeans and Indians shifted to the cis-Mississippian west, that is, to the huge territory between the Appalachian Mountains and the Mississippi River, where thousands of Native Americans made their homes. As in the previous century, contact brought unintended consequences. Contagious disease, for instance, continued to take a fearful toll. In the southern backcountry between 1685 and 1790, the Indian population dropped an astounding 72 percent. In the Ohio Valley, the numbers suggest similar rates of decline. Intermittent conflict between natives and Europeans only exacerbated the losses.

Yet Indians experienced more than dispossession and decline. Many formed new communities from the remnants of old. Some relocated to take advantage of more abundant game and more fertile farmland. Their new homelands, between competing British and French empires, gave many groups new leverage in negotiating favorable terms for trade and protection. As the century progressed, similar experiences of European encroachment and imperial conflict prompted leaders of various bands and nations to overcome ancient divisions and forge new kinds of unities, the beginnings of a self-conscious awareness of a shared set of interests and identity across traditional ethnic lines.

Indian Pioneers

The experience of migration was nothing new to Native Americans. Members of many nations could recite legends of mass relocation from distant homelands to the territories they occupied when Europeans arrived, and linguistic analysis has confirmed the essential truth of many such traditions. De Soto's exploration of the Southeast in the sixteenth century set in motion cycles of depopulation, reconstitution of new groups, and movement from place to place that only intensified after the English arrived in 1607. Iroquois expansion in the seventeenth and early eighteenth century had cleared areas such as the Susquehanna River valley, the Carolina Piedmont, and the Allegheny Plateau of long-time inhabitants.

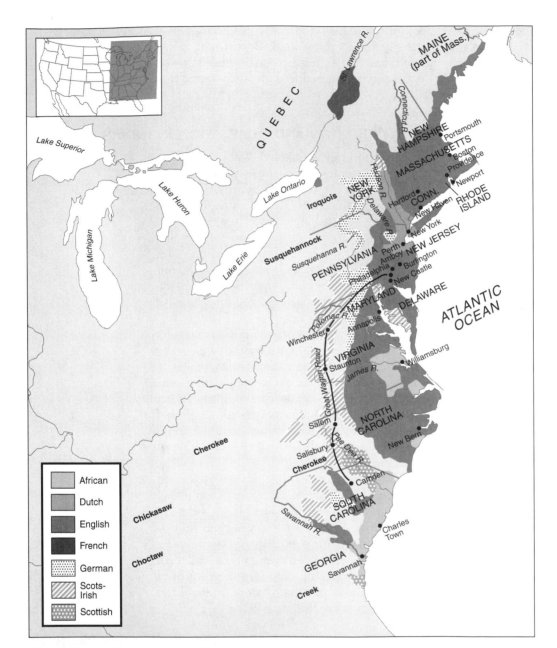

Ethnic Groups in North America, 1750

A flood of non-English immigrants swept the British colonies between 1700 and 1750, pressing native peoples further inland and prompting groups such as the Cherokees and Creeks of the Southeast to rise to greater prominence.

Shawnees and Delawares moved in to settle the Susquehanna Valley in the late seventeenth century. By the 1720s, they were on the move again, even as the newly formed Catawba nation of western North Carolina took possession of former Tuscarora land.

The first substantial Delaware trek beyond the Appalachians took place in 1724, when the headman Sassoonan led his people to found Kittanning on the banks of the Allegheny River in what is now western Pennsylvania. Sassoonan's people took this momentous step to escape European encroachments that were thinning out their game and chipping away at their lands on the Schuylkill River near Philadelphia. Sassoonan's band finally sold their remaining eastern lands to the Pennsylvania agent James Logan and settled permanently on the Allegheny Plateau. Shawnees from the Susquehanna Valley soon followed, while crop failures and shortages of game pushed Senecas from their homelands near western Lake Ontario southwest into the region.

The rapid influx of European settlers into Pennsylvania pressed additional Delaware bands to sell out and move west. Because the Delawares possessed no centralized leadership or confederacy, each headman conducted independent negotiations with Pennsylvania agents. Agents often took advantage of individual headmen's greed, styling them "kings of the Delaware" and enticing them to trade their people's farming and hunting grounds for goods, rum, and status. Shawnee and Iroquois observers soon complained that Delaware leaders were allowing their land to "pass through their guts" in the form of rum.

Agents also capitalized on ambiguities in the terms of exchange. In the infamous "Walking Purchase" of 1737, for instance, James Logan gained title to a huge tract of Delaware territory in the Lehigh Valley through a clause that specified one boundary as extending as far north from a point near Trenton as a man could walk in a day and a half. To the Delawares, the expression denoted a journey of that length at a normal traveling pace, perhaps 15 miles on foot. Logan, however, cleared a path through the woods and hired three tall and specially trained walkers to pace off a 60-mile northward boundary. A second line from the termination point eastward to the Delaware River, fully 65 miles away, completed a triangle that encompassed all Delaware villages in the area. Logan set aside a paltry 10 square miles of the land for a Delaware reservation and began selling the rest to incoming English and German settlers. The original inhabitants protested the landgrab repeatedly until 1762, when they finally relinquished all claims in exchange for additional concessions from Pennsylvania.

Although the Delawares and Shawnees possessed insufficient strength or unity to resist European encroachment onto their eastern lands, they did manage to carry familiar forms of social organization and cultural practice to their new homes in the Ohio country. They quickly established patterns of community life as familiar to them as were the barns, fences, and crops to the Europeans who built and farmed on former native land. Delaware towns such as Kittanning consisted of multiple clustered settlements, each identified with a prominent headman, an arrangement much like that of eastern Delaware communities. Shawnee settlements such as Sewikaley's Town and Seneca communities such as Aliquippa's Town similarly reflected traditional forms of organization. Town inhabitants plied traditional farming and hunting practices, trading skins and furs for European goods, which they incorporated into traditional patterns of use.

During the next several decades the towns of the Allegheny Plateau attracted additional migrants who shared connections of kinship and ethnicity. Other Indian refugees also drifted to the region, often joining multiethnic communities of farmers, hunters, and traders such as Shamokin and Logg's Town. The various groups forged webs of formal and informal relations among one another and nearby Indian nations that contributed to a common regional identity. The resources controlled by these Ohio Indians made them coveted trading partners of English from Pennsylvania as well as French from Quebec. As long as they remained united, the Ohio Indians could play the two European powers against each other to maintain their own independence.

Persisting Indian Power

Through migration, the native peoples of the Ohio country managed to gain a degree of power similar to that enjoyed by their Indian neighbors to the north and south. Increasingly during the eighteenth century, the key to maintaining influence and self-determination lay in native groups' access to French as well as English resources and their ability to play the interests of one against the other. The possibility that a powerful Indian nation could join the French to drive back British settlement made officials in London and the colonies more solicitous of Indian interests. "The prosperity of our Colonies on the Continent," the British official Edmund Atkin observed in 1755, "will stand or fall with our Interest and favour among [the Indians]. While they are our Friends, they are the Cheapest and strongest Barrier for the Protection of our Settlements; when Enemies, they are capable . . . to render those Possessions almost useless."

The Iroquois capitalized on this dynamic to replenish numbers lost in the devastating imperial wars under the William III and Anne as well as to compensate for loss of influence in the west (see Chapters 9 and 10). The Iroquois Confederacy turned south, where the presence of weaker nations presented an opportunity for them to capture adoptees through a fresh round of mourning wars. Even if they had been inclined to do so, British colonial officials could seldom have intervened in these wars. The Iroquois wielded substantial military might, and the English could not afford to risk action that might drive the Indians into the arms of the French governor at Quebec. Furthermore, the extension of Iroquois authority over other frontier Indians served British interests by reducing the number of native political entities with which they had to negotiate.

Eighteenth-century Iroquois expansion often proceeded with the nervous blessing of British officials. One of the century's earliest examples was the incorporation of the Tuscaroras after 1713 (see Chapter 10), a move that enlarged the Iroquois Confederacy to Six Nations and augmented Iroquois fighting strength with warriors who possessed detailed knowledge of the southern terrain. Other acts of expansion soon followed. Pennsylvania officials made the Iroquois overlords of all other native peoples within the colony's boundaries by a peculiar interpretation of the Anglo-Iroquois Albany Treaty of 1722. "The Five Nations . . . have included you" in the treaty, James Logan declared to Pennsylvania's Delaware and Conoy people, "and have obliged you to observe it as well as themselves."

The Iroquois did not hesitate to exert this newfound influence over additional tributary peoples when it suited their interests. They also took advantage of access to markets in Philadelphia to negotiate more favorable terms of trade with competing merchants in New York and Quebec.

British colonial competition for Iroquois trade proved advantageous to the Six Nations as well, because it gave them leverage to negotiate better terms for their goods. Iroquois spokespersons made it their business to know the relative value of trade items in various markets, and cited prices offered by a rival colony's traders in an effort to obtain the same price nearby. Other nations within the Six Nations' orbit followed suit. When the Delawares from Kittanning visited Philadelphia in 1740, for instance, they expressed concern about competitive pricing for furs as well as for interloping white hunters (see Vignette at the beginning of the chapter). "Our Brethren the Mingoes [western Iroquois] got so great a price for their Skins" at Albany "that I am ashamed to tell them how small a price the Delawares get from you," the Delaware headman Sassoonan declared. "We hope you will Allow Us something of a better price for the future."

The Iroquois reach extended further south during the eighteenth century than ever before, but they reached their limit at the edge of Catawba territory in the Carolina Piedmont. This powerful, warlike nation had emerged in the first decades of the eighteenth century as a disparate core of remnant peoples absorbed other refugees of the period's vicious warfare (see Chapter 10). By the early 1730s, the Catawbas had even managed to absorb whole bands of neighboring weaker peoples through cajoling and veiled threats. In the process they acquired a reputation as fearsome fighters among the English and other Indian nations alike. The Catawbas earned implacable hatred from the Iroquois as "disorderly . . . Irregular . . . false . . . and deceitful People" so treacherous they had even murdered Iroquois peace envoys in cold blood.

South Carolinians anxiously courted Catawba cooperation to serve as a "Bulwark at our Backs" as well as a barrier to slave escape. Indeed, one South Carolina official argued that without the Catawbas, runaway slaves might well "get to a head in the Woods and prove as mischevious a thorn in our sides as the fugitive Slaves in Jamaica did in theirs." Catawbas could not stop the flow of runaways completely, and reports of runaway "maroon communities" in the Carolina forests persisted throughout the eighteenth century. Nevertheless, South Carolinians' need for native allies ensured a constant stream of diplomatic traffic between Catawba towns and Charles Town to maintain good relations. Catawbas held their own in these exchanges, extracting important concessions from South Carolina officials that enabled them to preserve their independence into the 1760s.

The "Five Civilized Tribes" Take Shape

Native peoples to the south and west of the Catawbas were also struggling during the eighteenth century to cope with loss of population and encroachment of European settlers. Like the Iroquois, these groups occupied a territory between competing European imperial powers and were able to use that position to some advantage in their quest for continuing self-determination. In contrast to the Six Nations, however, native peoples of the Southeast began to coalesce into multiple confederacies that often clashed with one another as well as with French and

English colonists. In the decades after Queen Anne's War, the largest and most influential of these groups began a process of economic, social, and political adaptation to their new situation. These adaptations gradually gave shape to powerful native nations that, by the early nineteenth century, European Americans were calling the "Five Civilized Tribes"—the Cherokees, Chickasaws, Choctaws, Creeks, and Seminoles.

In the 1730s and 1740s, the balance of power in the southeastern backcountry shifted increasingly to the towns of the Cherokees, as Catawba strength began to ebb while the French pressed north and east from the Gulf of Mexico and the Mississippi River valley. Cherokees themselves struggled to maintain their strength in the face of intermittent warfare and epidemic disease. A smallpox epidemic in 1739 caused "a most depopulating shock" among the Cherokee villages, and their numbers continued to decline until the Revolution. The changing demographics, combined with pressure from the competing Creek Confederacy to their southwest, prompted some Cherokee bands to relocate northward into areas where Europeans were also settling. The intersection of Cherokee and European migration gave rise to intercultural environments such as the Long Cane settlement of western South Carolina, where white settlers farmed and raised cattle while Cherokees continued to hunt in nearby forests. Yet the Cherokees' grip on the strategic Upper Towns of the western Carolinas and Georgia—a territory South Carolina's mid-eighteenth-century governor James Glen regarded as "the Key of Carolina"—gave them the power to inflict costly casualties in times of war and to extract generous concessions in exchange for peace.

Increasing contact with Europeans prompted Cherokee people to adapt in a variety of ways. The power Cherokee women enjoyed within their villages enabled them to play a decisive role in the process of adaptation. Cherokee women often decided whether or not to go to war and usually determined the fate of wartime captives. As warfare and disease reduced Cherokee numbers, village matrons increasingly chose to adopt the newcomers. This contributed greater ethnic diversity as villages incorporated fugitive groups of Natchez and Creeks as well as European and African captives. Women's control of village trade sometimes prompted them to marry French or English traders to strengthen their competitive advantage in the market for European goods. These marriages introduced conflict between European patriarchy and Cherokee matriarchy. Over time, women's influence gradually eroded in some aspects of domestic and social life, but Cherokee women continued to exercise political authority throughout the colonial period. The *métis* offspring of Cherokee-white unions often possessed intense loyalty to their Cherokee clans and villages as well as an intimate knowledge of European ways. Some *métis* took advantage of their dual identity to become powerful brokers in Anglo-Cherokee trade and diplomacy, whereas others repudiated their European identity and took leading roles in resisting further colonization.

To the west of the Cherokee towns the Chickasaws still thrived in a region they had occupied since well before de Soto's expedition in the 1540s (see Chapter 2). This powerful group's position near the Mississippi River, within easy striking distance of both New Orleans and the Illinois country, made them critical allies of the English. One English observer called them the "Spartans" of southeastern

Indian peoples because they made "martial virtue, and not riches" their "only standard of preferment." The Chickasaws proved their military prowess by dealing repeated, often humiliating losses to French forces and their Indian allies between 1720 and 1763. South Carolina governors labored to keep these powerful allies well supplied with cheap British arms and trade goods. English horses supplemented stock acquired from trans-Mississippi Indian tribes to give the Chickasaws a mounted force of raiders who could strike French and Indian targets from north of the Ohio to the Gulf Coast. English-supplied African slaves became dependent laborers for Chickasaw patrons, bearing burdens and working fields. Over time, enslaved African laborers became a permanent element of Chickasaw society.

The Chickasaws' enemies to the south, the Choctaws, also depended on horses to wage warfare, carry trade goods, and herd the cattle that by the 1730s had become a part of the Choctaw economy. Like the Chickasaw, the Choctaw received some of their first horses from trans-Mississippi Indian traders who had captured or traded them from the Spanish or had domesticated them from wild herds descended from Spanish stock. Choctaw cattle also derived from Spanish stock that since de Soto's expeditions had roamed rich southeastern river bottoms along with deer and buffalo. Both horses and cattle took on increasing importance in Choctaw life during the eighteenth century. Indeed, Choctaws imparted a sacred significance to horses in funeral rituals by sacrificing and feasting on the horses of a deceased village member.

The French relied on this ancient and numerous people—at 20,000 members the largest unified group in the region—to counter English influence in the Southeast. French officials kept Choctaw warriors well supplied with arms and encouraged them to raid Chickasaw villages. Yet the enticement of cheap English goods drew an increasing number of Choctaw bands into an Anglo-Chickasaw orbit toward the middle of the eighteenth century despite the unscrupulous practices of many English traders. Only by preserving a reputation for "good faith in trading" were the French able to keep most of their Choctaw allies "attach[ed] to our side."

East of the Choctaws, the powerful Creek Confederacy was taking shape, but its position between empires was proving a mixed blessing. In contrast to other southeastern groups, the Creek Confederacy grew in numbers during the eighteenth century by uniting several surrounding bands into a loose, consensual coalition, adopting native refugees and incorporating runaway slaves from South Carolina and Georgia. This confederacy embraced the Creek name, which the English had habitually applied to all the tribes of the lower Southeast. The common name, however, belied deep internal divisions. English-leaning factions enjoyed access to better trade goods at cheaper prices than did factions favoring the French. The only exception was in firearms, whose weight made them more difficult for English traders to transport. French control of the waterways enabled them to transport firearms to Creek and other native trading partners. As a result, French weapons helped fuel a conflict among Creek factions until the 1750s, when native leaders finally secured peace.

Like other groups, the Creeks had to adjust to rapid westward migration of Europeans. By the 1750s, Georgia ranchers had begun moving into Creek hunting grounds with domestic cattle that drove off the bear and displaced the deer. Creeks initially protested, but soon began adjusting both their approach to property and their way of life. Some Creeks began acquiring and herding cattle themselves, a practice which prompted them to begin incorporating European ideas of property. Leading Creek cattlemen were often children of a mixed European and Creek marriage such as the famous Revolutionary-era headman Alexander McGillivray, who understood both worlds but remained loyal to his native kin. These and other Creek ranchers incorporated progressively more European ways of life, soon building plantations and acquiring slaves.

Successive groups of Creeks also migrated south during the eighteenth century into the depopulated lands of Florida, where they herded wild cattle introduced by Spanish missionaries of the previous century. Over time, these bands of people whom the Spanish called *cimarrónes*, or wild men, developed a distinct identity as Seminoles. The Seminoles obtained their living as cattlemen, fishermen, and hunters. They also developed a significant trade with Cuba, lading large cypress canoes with deerskins, dried fish, and honey, then crossing the Gulf of Mexico to trade in Havana for Spanish consumer goods.

Horses, Raiders, and Traders: Native Mobility on the Great Plains

The dramatic changes overtaking the world between the Appalachians and the Mississippi were not confined to the great river's eastern banks. The peoples who occupied the hills and plains beyond were also experiencing a transformation in their ways of life. Native pioneers were pushing west across the Mississippi River into Great Plains hunting grounds as eastern game became scarce and European settlers occupied traditional lands. Mounted native raiders from the Rocky Mountains were sweeping east and south into present-day Kansas, Oklahoma, and Texas in search of captives and game.

Even in the Great Lakes region, where pressure from European colonists was remote, overhunting of deer and fur-bearing animals prompted groups like the Ojibwas and Crees to range further west into the Cheyenne and Lakota Sioux hunting grounds of what is now Minnesota. French weapons gave the Ojibwa sufficient military advantage to drive their enemies west, where the Sioux began hunting buffalo in what is now the Dakotas and Nebraska. The Cheyenne followed buffalo herds even further west to present-day eastern Wyoming and Colorado. Mounted Comanche raiders rode out from traditional homelands in the foothills of the Colorado Rockies to harass not only Cheyenne hunters but also groups as far south as Texas. Shoshones also moved east on horseback from traditional homelands in the Great Basin, but moved back to the Rockies later in the eighteenth century as more eastern groups arrived on the Great Plains. A large group of Hidatsas migrated westward from the Big Bend of the Missouri River to form a new life as the Crow people of what is now northern Montana.

In the Southwest, competition between the French and the Spanish for native trade intensified as outposts established in the aftermath of Queen Anne's War began to thrive. In Texas, San Antonio began drawing Apache farmers to settle nearby where they could gain access to Spanish goods and military defense against Comanche raiders. El Paso, Santa Fe, and Taos provided similar havens for Pueblo farmers, many of whom, ironically, were seeking defense against mounted Apache raiders who celebrated the horses on which they rode as gifts of Apache gods. The Red River trading village of Natchitoches in French Louisiana attracted native migrants such as the Caddoes and the Wichitas from plains homelands hundreds of miles to the west. Other French outposts along the Arkansas and Missouri Rivers enticed similar migrant communities to gain advantages in European trade against native competitors.

The peoples of the trans-Mississippi West were experiencing a burst of migratory activity almost unprecedented in its speed and scope, one that transformed the landscape and settlement patterns of the entire Great Plains in less than one hundred years. The world Lewis and Clark encountered in their famous expedition of 1804 was not the pristine result of thousands of years of natural development, as people continued to believe until well into the twentieth century. Rather, it was a product of the very recent past, an environment shaped by creative human adaptations to often wrenching eighteenth-century events and conditions.

WORLDS OF MOTION

In 1761, the Quaker itinerant John Woolman paid a visit to a Delaware band who lived "on the east branch of the river Susquehanna." As he journeyed, Woolman meditated on the change in circumstances native peoples had experienced since the coming of Europeans. In some places natives had sold fertile, well-watered lands with easy river access "for trifling considerations," Woolman mused, while in other places they had been "driven back by superior force." Many now lived so far away that they had to "pass over mountains, swamps, and barren deserts, where travelling is very troublesome in bringing their furs and skins to trade with us." The expansion of European settlements and hunting had also produced drastic ecological change, reducing the numbers of "wild beasts which the natives chiefly depend on for subsistence." Indeed, Woolman lamented, "people too often, for the sake of gain," induced the natives to "waste their skins and furs in purchasing a liquor which tends to the ruin of them and their families."

Woolman observed only a portion of the many far-reaching effects of eighteenth-century expansion. Not all Indians allowed their lands to "pass through their guts" in the form of liquor. Intense imperial conflict enabled many native groups to consolidate their hold on territory and power. But Europeans did keep pressing westward across the Atlantic to North America's eastern shores and from those shores into the Appalachian Mountains, transforming the continent into a world of swirling motion stirred by interrelated currents of growth and migration.

The variety of eighteenth-century North American experience defies easy generalization. The striking differences that had developed among Anglo-American colonies during the seventeenth century were now complemented by increasing ethnic and racial diversity within. Yet as European observers surveyed North America's rapid growth, they could not help recognizing its commercial and political significance. Its diverse population could secure crucial territory in the great contest for empire. It also offered European merchants and manufacturers a market for consumer goods that had become too big to ignore.

CHRONOLOGY

1700	British colonial mainland population at 250,000.
1710	Palatines arrive in New York.
1718	Transportation Act authorizing transport of convicts in America passed.
1720	Pennsylvania Quaker migrants establish settlements in Cape Fear region of North Carolina; Spotswood County organized in Shenandoah Valley.
1721	South Carolina's black population at 12,000; whites at 6,500.
1724	Sassoonan founds Kittanning on Allegheny River.
1728	Famine pushes Scots-Irish immigrants to America.
1732	James Oglethorpe founds Georgia.
1737	"Walking Purchase" sparks tension between Pennsylvania English and Delawares.
1748	American Lutheran ministers ordained in Philadelphia.
1750	Slavery permitted in Georgia.
1770	British colonial mainland population at 2,150,000.

RECOMMENDED READING

The growth and migration of the colonial population, and the impact of colonial expansion on the lands between empires and Native American nations, have generated a growing body of illuminating historiography. The rapid population growth of England's thirteen mainland colonies is summarized in James T. Lemon, "Colonial America in the Eighteenth Century," in *North America: The Historical Geography of a Changing Continent*, ed. Robert D. Mitchell and Paul A. Groves (Totowa, N.J., 1987), 121–48. Alan Kulikoff's *The Agrarian Origins of American Capitalism* (Charlottesville and London, 1992) includes extensive discussion of migration patterns in colonial America. David Hackett Fisher's *Albion's Seed: Four British Folkways in America* (New York and Oxford, 1989) offers the provocative, if controversial, argument that patterns of the colonial era transferred enduring folkways to various parts of North America from English regions where the immigrants predominantly originated.

Internal migration to northern New England is discussed at length in Charles E. Clark, *The Eastern Frontier: The Settlement of Northern New England, 1610–1763* (New York, 1970). Barry Levy discusses the development of Pennsylvania Quaker society in *Quakers and the American Family: British Settlement in the Delaware Valley* (New York, 1988), and Larry Dale Gragg explores Quaker migration from Pennsylvania to Virginia and North Carolina in *Migration in Early America: The Virginia Quaker Experience* (Ann Arbor, 1980). David Hacket Fischer and James C. Kelly discuss Virginia migration in *Bound Away: Virginia and the Westward Movement* (Charlottesville and London, 2000), while Richard R. Beeman examines in detail the development of one Virginia Piedmont county in *The Evolution of the Southern Backcountry: A Case Study of Lunenburg County, Virginia, 1746–1832* (Philadelphia, 1984). For the settlement of Georgia, see Harold E. Davis, *The Fledgling Province: Social and Cultural Life in Colonial Georgia, 1733–1776* (Chapel Hill, 1976). Bernard Bailyn and Philip D. Morgan, ed., *Strangers within the Realm: Cultural Margins of the First British Empire* (Chapel Hill, 1991) provide a valuable review of migration literature. A. G. Roeber provides an impressively original interpretation of the transfer of German culture in *Palatines, Liberty, and Property: German Lutherans in Colonial British America* (Baltimore, 1993). For the Scots see Ned Landsman, *Scotland and Its First American Colony, 1683–1765* (Princeton, 1985), and for the Scots-Irish see Patrick Griffin, *The People with No Name: Ireland's Ulster Scots, America's Scots Irish, and the Creation of a British Atlantic World, 1689–1764* (Princeton, 2001). Marianne S. Wokeck argues that eighteenth-century immigration to North America from Germany and Ireland inaugurated a distinctly modern form of mass migration in her *Trade in Strangers: The Beginnings of Mass Migration to North America* (University Park, Pa., 1999). Roger A. Ekirch offers a thorough analysis of the convict trade in *Bound for America: The Transportation of British Convicts to the Colonies, 1718–1775* (Oxford, 1987).

Some of the most exciting recent historical literature deals with the formation of a multicultural backcountry, especially that of Native American societies. Richard S. White's concept of the middle ground remains very influential: see *The Middle Ground: Indians, Empires, and Republics in the Great Lakes Region, 1650–1815* (Cambridge, 1991). Michael N. McConnell explores the migration to and interaction of native groups in the eighteenth-century Ohio country in *A Country Between: The Upper Ohio Valley and Its Peoples, 1724–1774* (Lincoln and London, 1992). James H. Merrell's *The Indians' New World: Catawbas and Their Neighbors from European Contact Through the Era of Removal* (New York, 1989) offers an innovative account of the formation and persistence of the Catawba nation in western North Carolina through the eighteenth century. Merrell's *Into the American Woods: Negotiators on the Pennsylvania Frontier* (New York, 1999) explores eighteenth-century Indian-European relations in Pennsylvania through the experience of Indian and Anglo-American interpreters and go-betweens. For native peoples of the Southeast, see James Axtell's *The Indians' New South: Cultural Change in the Colonial Southeast* (Baton Rouge, 1997); Tom Hatley's *The Dividing Paths: Cherokees and South Carolinians Through the Revolutionary Era* (New York, 1995); and Claudio Saunt, *A New Order of Things: Property, Power, and the Transformation of the Creek Indians, 1733–1816* (Cambridge, 1999). Colin G. Calloway surveys eighteenth-century trans-Mississippi Indian migration in his *New Worlds for All: Indians, Europeans, and the Remaking of Early America* (Baltimore, 1997).

Chapter 12

The Anglicization of Provincial America

In the summer of 1744, the physician Alexander Hamilton set out from his home in Annapolis, Maryland to tour the colonies for his "health and recreation." This genteel Scottish immigrant carried with him an appetite for "polite conversation" and the finest English luxuries, a set of cosmopolitan tastes by which he measured everyone he met. Few colonists mentioned in Hamilton's journal of the 1600-mile trip fared well against such exacting standards. Most dressed poorly, smelled badly, ate barbarously, sprinkled their English with regional colloquialisms, or spoke with heavy accents.

Hamilton found it especially humorous that so many of those he met on his tour committed their offenses while attempting to emulate the British gentility in which he had himself been groomed. In every tavern Hamilton visited, he found the customers eager to discuss news from the latest weekly journals concerning English politics, fashionable London gossip, and the imminent "French war." One "rough-spun, forward, clownish blade" who traveled a short distance with Hamilton attempted to establish his credentials as an informed British American gentleman by "damning the late Sir R[obert] W[alpole] for a rascal." When Hamilton challenged the man's impertinence in cursing the former British prime minister, the would-be gentleman offered additional evidence that he was much more than the "plain, homely fellow" he seemed. He declared that his bags contained "good linen . . . a pair of silver buckles, silver clasps, and gold sleeve buttons, two Holland shirts and some neat nightcaps." Furthermore, "his little woman at home drank tea twice a day."

Most colonists Hamilton encountered—even the poorest—displayed similar aspirations to British fashion and sophistication. Village philosophers discoursed about the theories of English physicist Sir Isaac Newton. Rustic country doctors feigned knowledge of the latest European medical theories. Nearly everyone possessed some British imported goods. A brief visit ashore during a voyage up the Hudson brought Hamilton to the house of a family so poor that fresh-picked blackberries formed "the greatest present they could make us." Even so, they "showed an inclination to finery" by displaying such "superfluous things" as a "looking-glass with a painted frame, half a dozen pewter spoons, and as many plates" as well as a "set of stone tea dishes and a teapot." In Rhode Island, the physician visited an "Indian King named George"—the Niantic leader Ninigret—who ironically managed to live "after the English mode" more successfully than many colonists. Ninigret lived in a great house surrounded by over 20,000 acres of prime land on which he kept "a good stock of horses and other cattle." The king's wife, Hamilton recorded, "goes in a high modish dress in her silks, hoops, stays, and dresses," and his children learned "the *belles lettres*." This "very complaisant, mannerly man" treated Hamilton and his traveling companions with a "glass of good wine" before they took their leave.

Alexander Hamilton's journal reveals a mid-eighteenth-century Anglo-American world where the growth of population, communication, and commerce had brought colonists much closer to one another than had been the case even thirty years before. Although the physician encountered a great deal of mutual suspicion among inhabitants of different colonies, his entries also reveal that colonists everywhere were scrambling to become part of a larger Anglo-American world. The change was striking. Colonists whose parents or grandparents had come to the New World to confront a "howling wilderness" now purchased imported European manufactures, read English journals, participated in imperial wars, and sought favors from a growing number of resident royal officials. No one— not even the inhabitants of the distant frontiers—could escape the influence of Great Britain. The cultural, economic, and political links connecting the colonists to the imperial center in London grew stronger with time.

This surprising development raises a difficult question for the modern historian. If the eighteenth-century colonists were so powerfully attracted to Great Britain, then why did they ever declare independence? The answer may well be that as the colonists became more British, they inevitably became more American as well. This was a development of major significance, for it helps to explain the appearance after mid-century of genuine nationalist sentiment. Colonists sought to fulfill their aspirations in ways adapted to the particular social and physical environments that they and their forebears had built over the previous century. In doing so, the commercial and cultural links that brought them into more frequent contact with Great Britain also made them more aware of other colonists. It was within an expanding, prosperous empire that they first began seriously to consider what it meant to be American.

BONDS OF EMPIRE

The rapid growth of transatlantic commerce excited many eighteenth-century colonial observers. In 1741, an essayist writing in Philadelphia's gentleman's periodical, the *American Magazine*, celebrated commercial policies "unknown to the ancient *Romans*" which were enabling England to surpass that renowned empire in its quest for greatness. Year by year, the American colonies were contributing to British greatness by channeling their own trade "like rivulets . . . into the great *British* Stream, which will swell and rise in the same Proportion as those Rivulets do." The growing market for American staples also brought an expanding range of British imported goods to colonial shopkeepers' shelves. Communication became more frequent as a growing number of ships crossed the Atlantic and plied American coastal waters. The influx of vessels into colonial ports gradually made cities such as Boston more cosmopolitan, more sinful, and, in Alexander Hamilton's words, "more civilized."

Economic Transformation

The British American economy kept pace with the rapid growth of the colonial population. During the first three-quarters of the eighteenth century, the population increased at least tenfold (see Chapter 11), and yet even with so many additional people to feed and clothe, the per capita income did not decline. Indeed, with the exception of poor urban dwellers, such as sailors whose employment varied with the season, white Americans did quite well. An abundance of land and the extensive growth of agriculture accounted for their economic success. New farmers were able not only to provide for their families' well-being but also to sell their crops in European and West Indian markets. Each year, more Americans produced more tobacco, wheat, or rice—to cite just the major export crops—and by this means, they maintained a high level of individual prosperity without developing an industrial base.

At mid-century, colonial exports flowed along well-established routes. More than half of American goods produced for export went to Great Britain. The Navigation Acts (see Chapter 7) were still in effect, and "enumerated" items such as tobacco had to be landed first at a British port. Furs were added to the restricted list in 1722. The White Pines Acts passed in 1711, 1722, and 1729 forbade Americans from cutting white pine trees without a license. The purpose of this legislation was to reserve the best trees for the use of the Royal Navy. The Molasses Act of 1733—also called the Sugar Act—placed a heavy duty on molasses imported from foreign ports; the Hat and Felt Act of 1732 and the Iron Act of 1750 attempted to limit the production of colonial goods that competed with British exports.

These statutes might have created tensions between the colonists and Great Britain had they been rigorously enforced. Crown officials, however, generally ignored the new laws. New England merchants imported molasses from French Caribbean islands without paying the full customs; ironmasters in the Middle Colonies continued to produce iron. Even without the Navigation Acts, however, a majority of colonial exports would have been sold on the English market. The emerging consumer society in Great Britain was beginning to create a new generation of buyers who possessed enough income to purchase American goods, especially sugar and tobacco. This rising demand was the major market force shaping the colonial economy.

The transatlantic demand not only stimulated production of colonial staples, it also sparked the growth of a significant colonial shipping industry. Shipyards had existed in Massachusetts since the early 1630s, and during the seventeenth century others were established in Connecticut, Rhode Island, New York, Pennsylvania, the Chesapeake, and South Carolina. Most concentrated on building modest vessels for the coastal and West Indian trade until the early decades of the eighteenth century, when they began building larger ships for the ocean trade. By the 1760s, colonial shipyards were selling as many as half their annual total of new vessels to overseas buyers, usually sending them on their maiden voyages packed with cargoes of colonial staples for sale in the ship's European home. In 1784, American-built ships comprised as much as 30 percent of the total British merchant fleet.

Most vessels remaining in the colonies entered the fleets of great colonial merchant families such as the Hancocks of Boston, the Browns of Newport, the Livingstons of New York, or the Whartons of Philadelphia. Colonial merchants cultivated far-flung trading connections, and the goods they imported kept great numbers of small shopkeepers and craftsmen in business from year to year.

The West Indian Connection

Colonial merchants operating out of Boston, Newport, and Philadelphia also carried substantial tonnage to the West Indies. In 1768, this market accounted for 27 percent of all American exports. The West Indies played a vital role in preserving American credit in Europe. Without this source of income, colonists would not have been able to pay for the manufactured items they purchased from Britain. To be sure, they exported American products in great quantity to Great Britain, but the value of the exports seldom equaled the cost of British goods shipped back to the colonists. To cover this small but recurrent deficit, colonial merchants relied on profits made in the West Indies.

The West Indian planters' efforts to maximize sugar production ensured that mainland colonists would find a ready market for their agricultural staples. By the mid-eighteenth century, planters on Barbados and the Leeward Islands had cleared the vast majority of productive land and placed it into sugar cultivation. To feed their large slave labor force, these planters relied almost entirely on imports of corn, salted pork, beef, and fish produced in mainland colonies from Virginia north to New England. Indeed, a few wealthy Caribbean planters even attempted to reduce their expenses by purchasing grain plantations on the mainland, staffing them with slaves, and shipping the yearly harvests at cost to their island holdings. Eighteenth-century West Indian planters also imported lumber, iron, tar, and building materials from the mainland, because their own forests had disappeared long before. Among Britain's sugar colonies, only Jamaica retained enough land and forests to supply local demand for lumber and foodstuffs.

In return for agricultural goods from the mainland, the West Indian planters exported sugar and molasses in growing quantities. Sugar rose in popularity as a sweetener for three other tropical goods—tea, coffee, and chocolate—and consumption of all four commodities rose as their prices fell steadily to within reach of more colonial buyers. Colonists quickly learned to bake sugar and molasses into a growing range of custards, cakes, pastries, sweet breads, and creams. Molasses also supplied New England distillers with the raw material for making very high-proof rum, which sold more cheaply than West Indian varieties and became an important regional commodity for export.

This traffic in New England rum also created a small triangular trade with West Africa, but it was not very significant for the overall balance of colonial commerce. Some merchant vessels did carry rum across the Atlantic to trade for slaves, whom they sold in the West Indies before bringing molasses back to New England. Most colonial ships, however, sailed directly for the Caribbean with agricultural and forestry goods, then returned immediately to the mainland colonies with their cargoes of sugar products. Recent research indicates, contrary to the beliefs of earlier generations of historians, that eighteenth-century trade with Africa involved less than 1 percent of all American exports. Slaves were transported directly to West Indian and mainland colonial ports where they were sold for cash or credit.

Birth of a Consumer Society

Even with the West Indian connection, the balance of trade turned dramatically against the colonists after mid-century. The reasons for this change were complex, but, in simplest terms, Americans began buying more English goods than had their parents or grandparents. Between 1740 and 1770, English exports to the American colonies increased by an astounding 360 percent.

In part, this shift reflected a fundamental transformation in the British economy. Although the Industrial Revolution was still far in the future, the pace of the British economy picked up dramatically after 1690. Small factories produced certain goods more efficiently and more cheaply than the colonists could. The availability of these products altered the lives of most Americans, even those with modest incomes. Staffordshire china replaced crude earthenware; imported cloth replaced homespun. Benjamin Franklin noted in his *Autobiography* how changing consumer habits affected his life. For years, he had eaten his breakfast in an earthenware bowl with a pewter spoon, but one morning it was served "in a china bowl, with a spoon of silver." Franklin observed that "this was the first appearance of plate and china in our house which afterwards in the course of years, as our wealth increased, augmented gradually to several hundred pounds in value." In this manner, British industrialization undercut American handicraft and folk art.

To help Americans purchase manufactured goods, British merchants offered generous credit. Colonists deferred settlement by agreeing to pay interest on their debts. The temptation to acquire English finery blinded many people to hard economic realities. They gambled on the future, hoping bumper farm crops would reduce their dependence on the large merchant houses of London and Glasgow. Obviously, some persons lived within their means, but the aggregate American debt continued to grow. Colonial leaders tried various expedients to remain solvent—issuing paper money, for example—and while these efforts delayed a crisis, the balance-of-payments problem was clearly very serious.

The eighteenth century also saw a substantial increase in intercoastal trade. Southern planters sent tobacco and rice to New England and the Middle Colonies, where these staples were exchanged for meat and wheat as well as goods imported from Great Britain. By 1760, approximately 30 percent of the colonists' total tonnage capacity was involved in this extensive "coastwise" commerce. In addition, backcountry farmers in western Pennsylvania and the Shenandoah Valley carried their grain to market along an old Iroquois trail that became known as the Great Wagon Road, a rough, hilly highway that by the time of the Revolution stretched 735 miles along the Blue Ridge Mountains to Camden, South Carolina. Most of their produce was carried in long, gracefully designed Conestoga wagons. These vehicles—sometimes called the "wagons of empire"— had been invented by German immigrants living in the Conestoga River valley in Lancaster County, Pennsylvania.

The shifting patterns of trade had significant effects on the development of an American culture. First, the flood of British imports eroded local and regional identities. Commerce helped to "Anglicize" American culture by exposing colonial consumers to a common range of British manufactured goods. Deep sectional differences remained, of course, but Americans from New Hampshire to Georgia were increasingly drawn into a sophisticated economic network centered in London. Second, the expanding coastal and overland trade brought colonists of different backgrounds into more frequent contact. Ships that sailed between New England and South Carolina, and between Virginia and Pennsylvania, provided dispersed Americans with a means to exchange ideas and experiences on a more regular basis.

Communication and the "Public Prints"

Correspondence and print enhanced the intercolonial and transatlantic exchange of ideas even further. An increasing number of colonists had commercial dealings or ties of kinship and friendship with people across the Atlantic, in neighboring colonies, or along the colonial frontier. Migrants linked old localities with new through emotional and familial bonds, maintained by correspondence and occasional visits (see Chapter 11). News from one community could spread throughout an entire region through the agency of family visitors or traveling peddlers.

Letters among distant family members augmented an existing network of intercolonial and transatlantic correspondence and spurred the organization of an empirewide postal system. The increase of commercial shipping aided the growth of this correspondence network and the speed of communication during the eighteenth century. An increase in the number and range of travelers, who often carried letters from one place to another, supplemented the postal system. As the century progressed, these two means of corresponding drew formerly isolated communities steadily closer to one another.

The most important development in communication, however, came with the extension of what the historian Benedict Anderson has termed "print capitalism" across the Atlantic and into an increasing number of locales. The production of books, sermons, pamphlets, broadsides, chapbooks, and almanacs for sale to the empire's literate populace became a means for colonists to learn about and adopt a common way of speaking and thinking about issues that affected their everyday lives.

The rise of weekly newspapers multiplied this effect a thousandfold. Under the Licensing Act of 1662, the Crown had restricted publication to only one newspaper, the *London Gazette*. When Boston printers attempted to produce news sheets during the 1680s, Crown officials moved swiftly to enforce the law in America as well. In 1695, however, the Crown and Parliament allowed the Licensing Act to expire. Presses responded quickly, pouring forth a flood of competing periodicals in London, the English provinces, and the colonies.

The first American newspaper with a sustained circulation, the *Boston Weekly News-Letter*, made its debut in 1704. By 1740 Boston had four newspapers, New York two, Philadelphia two, Williamsburg one, and Charles Town one. In these and a number of lesser colonial journals, colonists could read reports from correspondents in other colonies, London, the various English provinces, and the Continent. In addition, colonial publishers regularly reprinted news items, essays, and poetry from other colonial journals, London newspapers, and gentlemen's magazines. This vast increase in the volume and relative currency of information began to give people in the various locales of the British Atlantic a greater sense of kinship with distant, anonymous people who were now sharing common news and forming similar opinions about it.

Newspapers constituted a special type of consumer good. Colonists who could afford subscriptions bought them not only for information of important events but also for learning about the availability of other types of goods. Even those who could not purchase or read the paper for themselves could often browse a copy or hear it read at the local tavern. Merchants quickly learned to use newspapers in sophisticated ways to hawk the "latest English fashions" to inhabitants of the British Atlantic. The popularity of newspapers and imported English goods complemented each other in transforming colonial tastes and fostering greater awareness of colonial commonalities.

Provincial Cities

The colonial port cities provided crucial links between colonial Americans and the eighteenth-century British Atlantic, despite the small percentage of colonists who lived in them. Boston, Newport, New York, Philadelphia, and Charles Town—the five largest cities—contained only about 5 percent of the colonial population. In 1775, no colonial city had a population greater than 40,000. Their highly specialized commercial character explains both the relatively slow development of colonial American cities and the extent of their influence. Colonial port towns served as entrepôts, intermediary trade and shipping centers where bulk cargoes were broken up for inland distribution and where agricultural products were gathered for export. These ports did not support large-scale manufacturing. Indeed, the pool of free urban laborers was quite small, because the type of person who was forced to work for wages in Europe usually became a farmer in America.

Yet despite the limited urban population, cities profoundly influenced colonial culture. It was in the cities that Americans were exposed to and welcomed the latest European ideas. Wealthy colonists—merchants and lawyers—tried to emulate British culture. They sponsored concerts and plays. They learned to dance. They rehearsed the posture, manners, pronunciation, and conversational habits of the English gentry. Women as well as men picked up the new fashions quickly, and even though most of them had never been outside the colony of their birth, they sometimes appeared to be the products of London's best families.

It was in the cities, also, that wealthy merchants transformed commercial profits into architectural splendor. In their desire to outdo one another, they built grand homes of enduring beauty. Most of these buildings are described as Georgian because they were constructed during the reign of Britain's early Hanoverian kings, who all happened to be named George. Actually these homes were provincial copies of grand country houses of Great Britain. They drew their inspiration from the great Italian Renaissance architect Andrea Palladio (1508–1580), who had incorporated classical themes into a rigidly symmetrical form. Palladio's ideas were popularized in the colonies by James Gibbs, an Englishman whose *Book of Architecture* (1728) provided blueprints for the most spectacular homes of mid-eighteenth-century America.

Their owners filled the houses with fine furniture. Each city patronized certain skilled craftsmen, but the artisans of Philadelphia were known for producing magnificent copies of the works of Thomas Chippendale, Great Britain's most famous furniture designer. These developments gave American cities an elegance they had not possessed in the previous century. One foreign visitor noted of Philadelphia in 1748 that "its natural advantages, trade, riches and power, are by no means inferior to any, even of the most ancient towns of Europe." As this traveler understood, the cultural impact of the cities went far beyond the number of people who actually lived there.

Families and Farms in the Colonial Countryside

Life outside the major port centers varied significantly according to the density of the regional population and the distance from the coast and major port cities. Most free white families farmed for a living, forming rural communities where they could buy and sell goods, labor, and specialized services such as carpentry and smithing in regional exchange economies. Most aspired to what the historian Daniel Vickers has termed "competency" in their standard of living—a modest prosperity that ensured adequate housing, apparel, food, possessions sufficient to maintain a community standard of comfort and decency, and an inheritance that could assist children to achieve a competency in the next generation. Ownership of land unencumbered by too much debt secured the independence needed to achieve this goal.

Historians continue to debate the extent to which eighteenth-century farming families sought to enter the growing market economy. Some argue that families resisted the influx of the market, with its pressure to compete and to compromise independence by staking too much on a single cash crop. Indeed, studies of colonial farming habits do show that families often diversified production in ways consistent with a regional exchange economy.

Nevertheless, recent research also suggests that the standard of competency was gradually shifting in eighteenth-century America. The increasing quantity and affordability of British imported goods attracted more rural buyers, growing cities increased demand and opened new opportunities for farmers to enter the market, and transportation steadily improved to connect more rural communities

Westover, the huge Virginia estate of William Byrd II, shows the influence of the architectural style of Andrea Palladio on eighteenth-century Georgian buildings.
From the Collection of Tazwell Ellet

with coastal cities and the Atlantic market beyond. Examinations of estate inventories in eighteenth-century New England reveal that families there were filling their homes with an increasing quantity and variety of British imported goods. By the 1740s, ordinary farmers in New England and the Middle Colonies were demanding new issues of paper money so that they could participate in the burgeoning market economy. And in southeastern Pennsylvania, German and Quaker farmers plunged into the grain export market with both feet, fueling a rapid rise to a standard of living they could scarcely have imagined in Europe.

The entry of rural families into the Atlantic market stimulated a gradual shift in the pattern of household production, transforming the experience of colonial women. During the eighteenth century, a growing number of wives and daughters began working in nonfarm occupations to gain the extra income needed to participate in the consumer economy. Women followed a variety of pursuits, including midwifery and shopkeeping, but the most common nonfarm occupation for women was in textile production. Many families purchased carding equipment, spinning wheels, and looms so that the women of the household could produce yarn, thread, and cloth for sale on a regional market. Textile work was tedious and repetitive, but it gave a growing number of rural women the opportunity to earn money and conduct business at the local shop. The historian Laurel Thatcher Ulrich has observed that this experience, coupled with evidence that more "country girls were attending school and learning how to write" suggests that eighteenth-century women were beginning to gain "greater control over their own lives."

The market and its attendant changes extended only gradually into inland settlements. Visitors to the backcountry commented frequently on the poverty they observed among the settlers. Yet even on the frontier, British imported goods found a market among recent white arrivals, who competed with native hunters for hides and furs to sell to incoming traders. The reach of the Atlantic markets was very long, and nowhere did colonists offer much resistance to its allure so long as they could find some way to pay for the "baubles of Britain."

A Transatlantic Community of Letters

The expansion of trade, the rising consumption of British manufactured goods, the proliferation of print and correspondence, the growth of small but influential urban centers—all contributed to an emerging culture of what the literary historian David S. Shields has termed "civil discourse and private society" in eighteenth-century America. In every colonial city, literate colonists who aspired to polite standards of learning and civility converged in settings where they could engage and challenge one another through witty conversation on various fashionable topics. In doing so, participants shaped the rules of entry into local circles of power and influence while enforcing polite standards of fashion and conduct upon members of those circles. They also transmitted new European ideas to America and stimulated gifted colonists to contribute theories and inventions of their own to the intellectual revolution that was sweeping across eighteenth-century Europe.

Taverns, Salons, and "Private Societies"

Eighteenth-century colonists who aspired to European standards of fashion and civility sought to transform the culture of some traditional gathering places, while at the same time introducing new forms already fashionable in Europe. Taverns, for instance, were traditionally considered places of drunkenness, loitering, and brawling. Nevertheless, they provided convenient public places for men of "substance and parts" to gather and conduct business, discuss important political matters, and exchange ideas on topics ranging from agriculture to philosophy and religion. Not every tavern-keeper was willing to discourage the patronage of paying customers whose conduct fell short of genteel. By mid-century, however, every colonial city boasted taverns such as Philadelphia's Indian King, which catered to a polished clientele of leading merchants and professionals.

Similar sites for civil exchange formed around popular imported beverages such as coffee and tea. Coffeehouses provided aspiring gentlemen with an alternative to the taverns. There they could meet to sip sweetened coffee or chocolate and share pipefuls of tobacco while discussing important affairs of the day or reading to each other from unpublished manuscript literature. Tea tables provided women with similar settings for exchanging local news and commenting on fashion, topics of conversation whose influence extended beyond the parlor or drawing room to shape social conduct and expectations in the larger community. Over time, prominent women in many communities transformed the ladies' tea tables into mixed-gender salons where women could exert more direct influence in public affairs by challenging men to cultivate "sense"—a more tempered, humane perspective—concerning important issues of the day. The colonial poet Elizabeth

Graeme, for instance, expressed the belief that a sensible woman (represented in the following passage by "Rossela") could exercise a civilizing effect on a man:

> His Passions should be guided
>   By Reason's ruling Hand;
> And with Good Sense provided,
>   *Rossela* to Command.

Rising Anglo-American gentlemen also established social clubs where they could engage in table games and free conversation on topics of the day. Clubs often met in semiprivate rooms set aside for the purpose in taverns and coffeehouses. There the local gentry would enjoy dinners together, often capped with toasts to various persons of affairs in state and society. These toasts, which ranged from sincere to boldly satirical and irreverent, served as a vehicle for displaying wit as well as perception about matters of economy, governmental policy, international affairs, religious life, or scientific investigation. Conversation often centered on manuscript literature produced by one of the club's own number or circulated from club to club along an expanding intercolonial gentleman's network. These literary performances honed the skills of writer and critic alike in the rhetorical strategies most prized for debating, selecting, and expressing the powerful ideas that could shape official public action taken by members of the ruling class.

American Enlightenment

The various forms of private society provided fertile ground for the spread in British America of new ideas from Europe. European historians often refer to the eighteenth century as an Age of Reason. During this period, a body of new, often radical, ideas swept through the salons and universities, altering the way that educated Europeans thought about God, nature, and society. This intellectual revolution, called the Enlightenment, involved the work of Europe's greatest minds, Sir Isaac Newton, John Locke, Voltaire, David Hume, and others like them. The writings of these thinkers eventually reached the colonies, where they received a mixed reception. On the whole, the American Enlightenment was a rather tame affair compared to its European counterpart, for while the colonists welcomed experimental science, they defended the tenets of traditional Christianity.

Enlightenment thinkers shared basic assumptions. Philosophers of the Enlightenment replaced the concept of original sin with a much more optimistic view of human nature. A benevolent God, having set the universe in motion, gave human beings the power of reason to enable them to comprehend the orderly workings of his creation. Everything, even human society, operated according to these mechanical rules. The responsibility of right-thinking men and women, therefore, was to make certain that institutions such as church and state conformed to self-evident natural laws. It was possible—or so some of the *philosophes* claimed—to achieve perfection in this world. In fact, human suffering had come about only because people had lost touch with the fundamental insights of reason.

For many Americans, the appeal of the Enlightenment was its focus on a search for useful knowledge, ideas, and inventions that would improve the quality of human life. What mattered was practical experimentation. A speech delivered in 1767 before the members of the American Society in Philadelphia reflected the new utilitarian spirit: "Knowledge is of little Use when confined to mere Speculation," the colonist explained, "But when speculative Truths are reduced to Practice, when Theories grounded upon Experiments . . . and the Arts of Living made more easy and comfortable . . . Knowledge then becomes really useful." The Enlightenment spawned scores of earnest scientific tinkerers, people who dutifully recorded changes in temperature, the appearance of strange plants and animals, and the details of astronomic phenomena. Although these eighteenth-century Americans made few earth-shattering discoveries, they did encourage their countrymen, especially those who attended college, to apply reason to the solution of social and political problems.

Benjamin Franklin (1706–1790) absorbed the new cosmopolitan culture. European thinkers regarded him as a genuine *philosophe*, a person of reason and science, a role that he self-consciously cultivated when he visited England and France in later life. Franklin had little formal education, but as a young man working in his brother's print shop, he managed to keep up with the latest intellectual currents. In his *Autobiography*, Franklin described the excitement of discovering a new British journal. It was like a breath of fresh air to a boy growing up in Puritan New England. "I met with an odd volume of *The Spectator*," Franklin recounted; ". . . I had never before seen any of them. I bought it, read it over and over, and was much delighted with it. I thought the writing excellent, and wished if possible to imitate it."

Benjamin Franklin

Franklin's opportunity came in August 1721 when he and his brother founded the *New England Courant*, a weekly newspaper that satirized Boston's political and religious leaders in the manner of the contemporary British press. Writing under the name Silence Dogood, young Franklin asked his readers "Whether a Commonwealth suffers more by hypocritical Pretenders to Religion, or by the openly Profane?" Proper Bostonians were not prepared for a journal that one minister described as "full freighted with Nonesense, Unmannerliness, Railery, Prophaneness, Immorality, Arrogance, Calumnies, Lyes, Contradictions, and what not, all tending to Quarrels and Divisions and to Debauch and Corrupt the Minds and Manners of New England." Franklin got the point; he left Massachusetts in 1723 in search of a less hostile intellectual environment.

After he had moved to Philadelphia, leaving behind an irritable brother as well as New England Puritanism, Franklin devoted himself to the pursuit of useful knowledge, ideas that would increase the happiness of his fellow Americans. Franklin never denied the existence of God. Rather, he pushed the Lord aside, making room for the free exercise of human reason. Franklin tinkered, experimented, and reformed. Almost everything he encountered in his daily life aroused his curiosity. His investigation of electricity brought him world fame, but Franklin was never satisfied with his work in this field until it yielded practical application. In 1756, he invented the lightning rod. He also designed a marvelously efficient stove that is still used today. In modern America, Franklin has become exactly what he would have wanted to be, a symbol of material progress through human ingenuity.

Franklin energetically promoted the spread of reason. In Philadelphia, he organized groups that discussed the latest European literature, philosophy, and science. In 1727, for example, he "form'd most of my ingenious Acquaintances into a Club for mutual Improvement, which we call'd the Junto." Four years later Franklin took a leading part in the formation of the Library Company, a voluntary association that for the first time allowed people like him to pursue "useful knowledge." The members of these societies communicated with Americans living in other colonies, providing them not only with new information but also with models for their own clubs and associations.

RELIGIOUS REVIVALS IN PROVINCIAL SOCIETIES

Although clubs like Franklin's Junto occupied the interest of a small, largely urban Anglo-American elite, most colonists continued to pursue their daily lives in a spiritual environment shaped by popular Protestantism. In the 1730s, the contours of their social world began shifting rapidly under the impact of a spontaneous series of Protestant revivals known as the Great Awakening. This unprecedented evangelical outpouring altered the course of American history. In our own time, of course, the force of religious revivals has been witnessed in different regions throughout the world. It is no exaggeration to claim that a similar populist movement took place in mid-eighteenth-century America, and the new, highly personal appeal to a "new birth" in Christ caused men and women of all backgrounds to rethink basic assumptions about church and state, institutions and society.

The Great Awakening

Only with hindsight does the Great Awakening seem a unified religious movement. Revivals occurred in different places at different times; the intensity of the events varied from region to region. The first signs of a spiritual awakening appeared in New England during the 1730s, but within a decade the revivals in this area had burned themselves out. It was not until the 1750s and 1760s that the Great Awakening made more than a superficial impact on the people of Virginia. The revivals were most important in Massachusetts, Connecticut, Rhode Island, Pennsylvania, New Jersey, and Virginia. Their effect on religion in New York, Delaware, and the Carolinas was marginal. No single religious denomination or sect monopolized the Awakening. In New England, revivals shattered Congregational churches, and in the South, especially in Virginia, they had an impact on Presbyterians, Methodists, and Baptists. Moreover, there was nothing peculiarly American about the Great Awakening. Mid-eighteenth-century Europe experienced a similar burst of religious emotionalism.

Regardless of their origins, the seeds of revival were generally sown on fertile ground. In the early decades of the century, many Americans—but especially New Englanders—complained that organized religion had lost vitality. They looked back at Winthrop's founding generation of Puritans with nostalgia, assuming that common people at that time must have possessed greater piety than did later, more worldly colonists. Congregational ministers seemed obsessed with dull, scholastic matters; their preaching no longer touched the heart. And in the southern colonies, there were simply too few ordained ministers to tend to the religious needs of the population.

The Great Awakening arrived unexpectedly in Northampton, a small farm community in western Massachusetts, sparked by Jonathan Edwards, the local Congregational minister. Edwards accepted the traditional teachings of Calvinism (see Chapter 5), reminding his parishioners that their eternal fate had been determined by an omnipotent God, that there was nothing they could do to save themselves, and that they were totally dependent on the Lord's will. He thought his fellow ministers had grown soft. They left men and women with the mistaken impression that sinners might somehow avoid eternal damnation simply by performing good works. "How dismal will it be," Edwards told his complacent congregation, "when you are under these racking torments, to know assuredly that you never, never shall be delivered from them." Edwards was not exaggerating his message in an attempt to be dramatic. He spoke of God's omnipotence with such self-assurance that even people who had not thought deeply about religious matters were shaken by his words.

Why this uncompromising message set off several religious revivals during the mid-1730s is not known. Whatever the explanation for the popular response to Edwards's preaching, young people began flocking to the church. They experienced a searing conversion, a sense of "new birth" and utter dependence on God. "Surely," Edwards pronounced, "this is the Lord's doing, and it is marvelous in our eyes." The excitement spread, and evangelical ministers concluded that God must be preparing Americans, his chosen people, for the millennium. "What is now seen in America and especially in New England," Edwards explained, "may prove the dawn of that glorious day."

The Voice of Popular Religion

News of the Northampton revivals under Edwards spread throughout New England and traveled across the Atlantic to London and Scotland through a correspondence network of Calvinistic ministers. The reports sparked outbreaks of revival in other New England towns, and the dissenting minister and hymn writer Isaac Watts saw to it that Edwards's *Faithful Narrative of the Surprising Work of God in . . . Northampton* was printed in England. Yet Edwards, brilliant theologian though he was, did not possess the dynamic personality required to sustain the revival. That responsibility fell to a gifted young Anglican preacher named George Whitefield.

Whitefield made his first great preaching tour of the Anglo-American mainland in 1739 and 1740. A young associate of the Methodist leaders John and Charles Wesley, he had already achieved fame in England for his stirring messages. Although Whitefield was not an original thinker, he was an extraordinarily effective public speaker as well as an innovative promoter. Like his friend Benjamin Franklin, Whitefield came to symbolize the powerful cultural forces that were transforming the Atlantic world. According to Edwards's wife, Sarah, it was wonderful to witness what a spell Whitefield "casts over an audience . . . I have seen upwards of a thousand people hang on his words with breathless silence, broken only by an occasional half-suppressed sob."

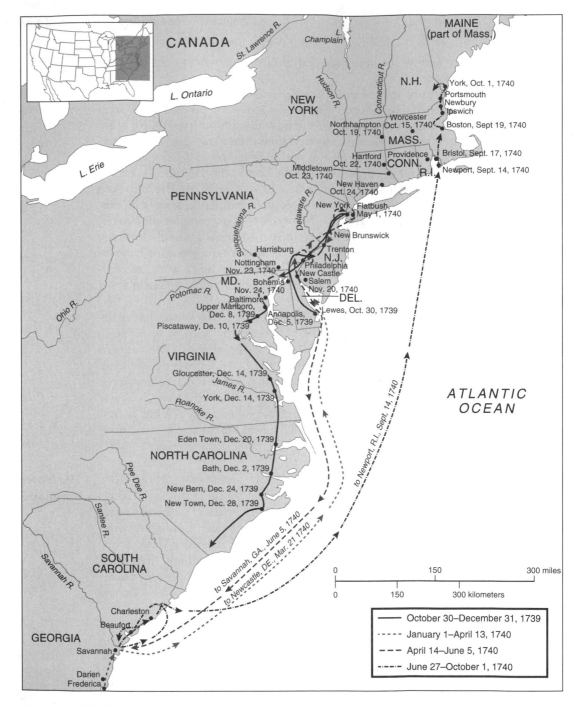

George Whitefield in America, 1739-1740

The Anglican itinerant minister George Whitefield followed increasingly well traveled intercolonial roads and water routes with his message of the New Birth. People throughout the colonies shared the experience of Whitefield's powerful preaching, making the revivals of the 1740s some of the first intercolonial events.

Whitefield's audiences came from all groups of American society: rich and poor, young and old, rural and urban. While Whitefield described himself as a Calvinist, he welcomed all Protestants. He spoke from any pulpit that was available. "Don't tell me you are a Baptist, an Independent, a Presbyterian, a dissenter," he thundered, "tell me you are a Christian, that is all I want."

Whitefield was a brilliant entrepreneur. Like Franklin, with whom he published many popular volumes, the itinerant minister possessed an almost intuitive sense of how this burgeoning consumer society could be turned to his own advantage, and he embraced the latest merchandising techniques. He appreciated, for example, the power of the press in selling the revival, and he regularly promoted his own work in advertisements placed in British and American newspapers. The crowds flocked to hear Whitefield, while his critics grumbled about the commercialization of religion. One anonymous writer in Massachusetts noted that there was "a very wholesome law of the province to discourage Pedlars in Trade" and it seemed high time "to enact something for the discouragement of Pedlars in Divinity also."

Other, American-born itinerant preachers followed Whitefield's example. The most famous was Gilbert Tennent, a Presbyterian of Scots-Irish background who had been educated in the Middle Colonies. His sermon "On the Danger of an Unconverted Ministry," printed in 1741, set off a storm of protest from established ministers who were understandably insulted. Lesser known revivalists traveled from town to town, colony to colony, challenging local clergymen who seemed hostile to evangelical religion. Men and women who thronged to hear the itinerants were called "New Lights," and during the 1740s and 1750s, many congregations split between defenders of the new emotional preaching and those who regarded the entire movement as dangerous nonsense.

Despite Whitefield's successes, many ministers remained suspicious of the itinerants and their methods. These more critical ministers became known as "Old Lights." Some complaints may have amounted to little more than sour grapes. One Old Light spokesman labeled Tennent "a monster! impudent and noisy." He claimed Tennent told anxious Christians that "they were damned! damned! damned! This charmed them; and, in the most dreadful winter I ever saw, people wallowed in snow, night and day, for the benefit of his beastly brayings; and many ended their days under these fatigues." Charles Chauncy, minister of the prestigious First Church of Boston, raised much more troubling issues. How could the revivalists be certain God had sparked the Great Awakening? Perhaps the itinerants had relied too much on emotion? "Let us esteem those as friends of religion," Chauncy advised, ". . . who warn us of the danger of enthusiasm, and would put us on our guard, that we may not be led aside by it."

Although Tennent did not condone the excesses of the Great Awakening, his attacks on formal learning invited the crude anti-intellectualism of such fanatics as James Davenport. This deranged revivalist traveled along the Connecticut coast in 1742 playing upon popular emotion. At night, under the light of smoky torches, he danced and stripped, shrieked and laughed. He also urged people to burn books written by authors who had not experienced the New Light as defined by Davenport. Like so many fanatics throughout history who have claimed a special knowledge of the "Truth," Davenport later recanted and begged pardon for his disruptive behavior.

To concentrate on the bizarre activities of Davenport—as many critics of the Great Awakening have done—is to obscure the positive ways in which this vast revival changed American society. First, despite occasional anti-intellectual outbursts, the New Lights founded several important centers of higher learning. They wanted to train young men who would carry on the good works of Edwards, Whitefield, and Tennent. In 1746, New Light Presbyterians established the College of New Jersey, which later became Princeton University. Just before his death, Edwards was appointed its president. The evangelical minister Eleazar Wheelock launched Dartmouth (1769); other revivalists founded Brown (1764) and Rutgers (1766) colleges.

The Great Awakening also encouraged men and women who had been taught to remain silent before traditional figures of authority to speak up, to take an active role in their salvation. They could no longer rely on ministers or institutions. The individual alone stood before God. Knowing this, New Lights made religious choices that shattered the old harmony among Protestant sects, and in its place, they introduced a noisy, often bitterly fought competition. As one New Jersey Presbyterian explained, "There are so many particular sects and Parties among professed Christians . . . that we know not . . . in which of these different paths, to steer our course for Heaven."

The itinerancy introduced by Whitefield also provided an extraordinarily effective means for his followers to carry Whitefield's message of the new birth to parts of Anglo-America where few churches yet existed. The new evangelical style of preaching found substantial support among New England's Congregational clergy and the Middle Colonies' Presbyterian and Pietistic Dutch Reformed groups. Yet its most explosive growth occurred outside these older traditions, where it could flourish unhindered by clerical attempts to control it. New Light Baptist and Methodist preachers honed their message and methods to resonate powerfully with the experiences of ordinary people. These itinerants were usually simple lay preachers whose only claim to the ministry was an overpowering sense that God had called them. Unencumbered by the requirements of long, formal preparation in ministry, they spread a simple, Bible-centered form of Protestant Christianity among the mobile backcountry population. By the 1760s, the influence of such people was prompting the Anglican missionary Charles Woodmason to complain that his mission field in the backcountry of South Carolina was "eaten up by Itinerant Teachers, Preachers, and Impostors from New England and Pennsylvania—Baptists, New Lights, Presbyterians, Independents, and an hundred other Sects."

The Great Awakening also opened opportunities in many communities for women to express themselves and assert leadership in the religious sphere. Women were at the forefront of many praying societies that sprang up during the Awakening. A number of women joined men in exhorting and took leadership in local revivals. A few even preached from colonial pulpits. Opponents attacked such practices as evidence of the revivalists' mad "enthusiasm," and many "friends of revival" attempted to suppress women's activities. Other New Lights defended female leadership, searching the Bible for evidence that the Lord would bless the gracious words of women who spoke out in "publick assembly." During their earliest years, revivalist Separate Baptists permitted women to vote on matters of policy and discipline. The radical practices of female exhortation, preaching, and voting disappeared as the revival fires subsided. Even so, evangelical religion gave women a new sense of their own worth in the eyes of God and of their importance in sustaining the spiritual fervor of their congregations and homes through prayer and pious example.

Expressive evangelicalism struck a particularly responsive chord among African Americans. Itinerant ministers frequently preached to large sympathetic audiences of slaves. Richard Allen (1760–1831), founder of the African Methodist Episcopal Church, reported that he owed his freedom in part to a traveling Methodist minister who persuaded Allen's master of the sinfulness of slavery. Allen himself was converted, as were thousands of other black colonists. According to the historian Mechal Sobel, evangelical preaching "shared enough with traditional African styles and beliefs such as spirit possession and ecstatic expression . . . to allow for an interpenetration of African and Christian religious beliefs."

With religious contention came an awareness of a larger community, a union of fellow believers that extended beyond the boundaries of town and colony. In fact, evangelical religion was one of several forces at work during the mid-eighteenth century that brought scattered colonists into contact with one another for the first time. In this sense, the Great Awakening was a "national" event long before a nation actually existed.

People who had been touched by the Great Awakening shared an optimism about the future of America. With God's help, social and political progress was possible, and from this perspective, of course, the New Lights did not sound much different than the mildly rationalist American spokesmen of the Enlightenment. Both groups prepared the way for the development of a revolutionary mentality in colonial America.

Indian Awakenings in Eighteenth-Century America

North America's native peoples also felt the impact of eighteenth-century colonial cultural and economic developments. To be sure, American Indians had been experiencing the transforming effects of a "consumer revolution" in European manufactured goods for well over a hundred years. They had also been contending with massive influxes of epidemic disease, increasing dislocation, dramatic reductions in game, and chronic warfare. Even so, a growing number of native leaders discerned new features in the situation confronting them by the early 1740s. Those who remained as postcolonial minorities behind the line of European settlement experienced directly the same forces of change as their white neighbors, but they responded to those changes in their own way and for their own purposes. Native leaders in the borderlands of the Ohio country and the Southeast discerned new challenges and opportunities in the accelerating expansion of the Anglo-American population, the pace of change in native communities themselves, and the extension of native networks of travel, communication, and exchange across a widening territorial expanse.

Living Like "Our Christian English Neighbors"

The encounter of Dr. Hamilton with the Niantic leader Ninigret (see vignette at the beginning of the chapter) reveals how some native peoples responded to the growing availability of British consumer goods in ways that, superficially at least, resembled the responses of Anglo-Americans themselves. Indians had always selectively incorporated some European goods and methods into the way they lived. By the mid-eighteenth century, however, a growing number were beginning to appear less distinct from their English neighbors than they had fifty years earlier.

Ninigret's adoption of large-scale ranching to support his heavily Anglicized way of life was reproduced among many native communities, even those far from the coast such as the Creeks of the colonial Southeast. The overhunting of deer and the loss of habitat for wildlife made herding of cattle increasingly necessary for those who wished to retain access to meat and skins. The value of horses for transportation and farming made them a natural choice to add to the livestock on the farm or ranch. To be sure, native ranching could increase occasions for conflicts with neighboring European Americans, who were prone to accuse Indian ranchers of stealing livestock. As long as the disputants remained calm enough to undertake a legal investigation, however, native ranchers could often prove their ownership of the horses or cattle in question.

The poverty of most eighteenth-century Indians prevented the bulk of native dwellings from attaining the relative grandeur of Ninigret's great house. Nevertheless, by the mid-eighteenth century a growing number of native peoples were adopting European house styles. Iroquois families, for instance, gradually moved out of the communal, clan-based longhouses their ancestors had known into single-family log homes. Eighteenth-century Iroquois villages were more often comprised of scattered single-family dwellings than of the compact, palisaded communities that seventeenth-century visitors had observed. The Swedish visitor Peter Kalm recorded that mid-eighteenth-century Hurons of Quebec had abandoned their bark dwellings for houses built "after the French fashion." Houses in the Indian Praying Towns of New England tended to look like the clapboard-sided saltboxes of white colonists nearby, though eighteenth-century visitors often commented on the number of bark dwellings still visible in towns such as those of the Narragansetts and Mohegans. Creeks, Choctaws, and Cherokees of the Southeast adopted the log home styles introduced by nearby Scots-Irish, German, or French settlers. The move to single-family dwellings often weakened traditional clan ties. The historian Colin Calloway has observed that many native children "grew up in what, in the context of their societies, constituted 'broken homes.'"

Like Ninigret's wife who dressed in English-style "silks, hoops and stays," a growing number of Indians also dressed in English fashions at least some of the time. The clothing made from European cloth often proved more comfortable and convenient than that made from hides. To be sure, Indians often wore their clothing in non-European ways—leaving shirttails hanging, cutting off pants to make leggings, wearing shirts but no "breeches"—often to the ridicule or chagrin of European observers. Yet many Indians wore complete outfits of English clothing, shoes, and hats, frequently causing Anglo-American observers to "mistake them for English." Moreover, Ninigret's taste for English fashion was far from exceptional. English observers at eighteenth-century diplomatic or treaty councils frequently noted that Indian participants wore laced hats, laced matchcoats, and ruffled shirts.

The donning of European clothing served a variety of Indian purposes. English clothes could often smooth the way for various dealings with European neighbors. Indian interpreters and brokers often signified their status and skills by the mixing of English and Indian articles of dress. The most observant and successful English brokers, people such as the eighteenth-century Indian agent Sir William Johnson, recognized the value of cultural cross-dressing and followed suit themselves. Johnson knew how to cut a very grand figure among his Mohawk allies by dressing and painting himself "after the manner of an *Indian* War Captain."

Ninigret's determination to give his children an education in the *belles lettres* was also becoming more common among eighteenth-century Indians. Colonists attempted to accommodate this desire on their own terms, establishing boarding schools and seats at colonial colleges where Indian children could be educated away from the "pernicious influence of their Parents' Example," as the New England minister Eleazar Wheelock put it. Such efforts often met with resistance from Indians who, like the Onondaga leader Canasatego, observed that Indian alumni who returned home from English schools often proved worthless, unable to find their way around in the woods or to string a bow and shoot an arrow. They also objected to the harsh treatment Indian pupils received from English teachers, who were notorious for speaking roughly, flogging their charges "for every little mistake," and working their students at household and farm chores more than at their academic subjects.

Despite these obstacles, some Indian leaders did send their children to English schools. Those who survived the experience often acquired skills that proved valuable in achieving native objectives. Proficiency in speaking, reading, and writing English gave those who wielded it significant advantages in trade and diplomatic negotiations. An understanding of Anglo-American politics, history, and international affairs enhanced those advantages further still. The Mohawk Joseph Brant, a graduate of Eleazar Wheelock's school, returned to his home in New York to translate the four Gospels of the New Testament into his native language. During the American Revolution he put his considerable talents to use in diplomacy and military service, leading many of the Mohawks into alliance with Great Britain.

The Great Awakening in Indian Country

Joseph Brant exemplifies a small but growing number of eighteenth-century American Indians who not only embraced Protestant Christianity themselves, but sought to foster its spread in their communities. The religious revivals of the 1740s contributed to this growth in part by stimulating a fresh surge of missionary zeal among colonists. The Moravians, a German-speaking Pietist sect associated with the Wesleys, introduced a variety of Protestantism that appealed to native groups in the Appalachians and Ohio country. The lay-oriented style of the Moravians and other evangelicals appears to have been especially attractive to native converts, because it allowed Indians to take greater initiative in adapting Christianity to their own interests and aims.

Indians in New England frequently participated in the Great Awakening, and some took an active role in spreading it to new communities. In Westerly, Rhode Island, for instance, the Congregational minister Joseph Park wrote that the "Power of GOD . . . began to be most remarkable among *the Body of the Indians*" in his parish only when a group of New Light Indians brought the message of new birth from neighboring Stonington, Connecticut. Park himself could make only a small contribution to the local Awakening, a prayer that God's "Kingdom might be seen coming with Power." When he attempted to preach or do anything more, the "*Outcry*" of native souls in distress became so loud he had to "give it up." The Indians from Stonington took over, leading a "wonderful Time of God's Power" which continued for two days. "*From that Time,*" Park declared, "the *Indians* were generally stirred up to seek after eternal Life."

Anglo-American missionaries who felt the Spirit's call to carry the Awakening to native peoples did not often enjoy such a fervent response. David Brainerd, the most famous eighteenth-century missionary to the Indians, encountered varying degrees of resistance as he preached among the Lenni-Lenape (or Delawares) of Pennsylvania. The scattered, demoralized bands who remained living near European communities behind the line of settlement proved more receptive to Brainerd's message of new birth than those beyond, who preferred to "live as their fathers lived and go where their fathers were when they died." The emotionally fragile evangelist slipped into despair when the Lenni-Lenape bands at the forks of the Delaware River repeatedly "refused to believe the truth" of what Brainerd taught them. He regained hope, however, when his ministry among "Settlement Indians" in well-colonized New Jersey sparked a modest number of conversions. Yet even there, Brainerd discovered that he had to adapt his message to native tastes if he hoped to win a sympathetic hearing. His Delaware converts responded poorly to "harangues of [Hell's] terror," preferring instead "the free offers of divine Grace to needy and distressed Sinners."

Many native groups preferred Moravian Pietism—newly imported in the 1740s from German-speaking Saxony—to the Calvinism of Brainerd and other New Light missionaries. Where evangelical Calvinists held native converts to stringent doctrinal standards for baptism, Moravians simply required that they express a "love and Desire" to believe in Jesus. The Moravians' mystical approach to dreams and visions resembled natives' own belief that these phenomena could provide access to the spiritual world. By helping their converts interpret dreams, Moravian missionaries stepped into roles similar to those of traditional shamans. Moravians also supplemented their preaching with visual images of the wounded, bleeding Jesus enduring the tortures of the Cross, a practice Calvinists regarded as idolatrous. The historian Jane T. Merritt has suggested that the strong emphasis on the blood of Christ in Moravian art, hymns, and preaching transformed Jesus into the ultimate warrior captive, making Christianity powerfully attractive to young Delaware and Shawnee males who aspired to a similar stoicism. As a result,

Moravian missionaries won several hundred converts among the Delaware, Shawnee, and Mingo people of western Pennsylvania and the Ohio country. The Moravians' peaceful ways also earned them friendship with many non-Christian Indians who distrusted other white settlers.

The Great Awakening also inspired native converts such as the Mohegan Samson Occom to become ordained ministers and missionaries themselves. Occom became the most famous of these Indian preachers by partnering with the revivalist minister Eleazar Wheelock to promote what eventually became Dartmouth College. Wheelock initially billed the college as an extension of Moore's Indian Charity School, which he had been operating for several years. Occom was a natural publicist for the new college, having put his own learning under Wheelock to effective use as an ordained minister and missionary to the Montauk Indians of Long Island. In 1765 Occom agreed to undertake a two-year preaching tour in England on behalf of Wheelock's new venture, anticipating that it would benefit mostly young native men. The tour, which Occom and his companions modeled on Whitefield's market-savvy methods, made the Mohegan itinerant a celebrity in England and raised the enormous sum of £12,000 for the New Hampshire college. Dartmouth, however, trained few native youth, becoming instead another center of higher learning for aspiring Anglo-American gentry and clergy. Deeply disillusioned, Occom broke with Wheelock to found the Brother-town community, a haven for New England's Christian Indians in the Oneida country of central New York.

Samson Occom's bitter experience demonstrates that even the most sincere native converts to evangelical Christianity saw no inconsistency in using their newfound faith to pursue advantages for their own people. The new religious ways could help families and communities survive dislocation and social strain. Christian faith could give young men access to an education that could make them more effective in protecting native legal and commercial interests. Conversion to Christianity could give new force to native demands for equal treatment under the law. Even if such demands did not often succeed, they could provide temporary respite while Anglo-American officials scrambled to find new justifications for discriminatory policies. Similarities between certain strands of Protestant and native belief also allowed Indian Christians to preserve important cultural practices such as seeking spiritual guidance through dreams and visions. Even those Indians who refused conversion incorporated select elements of Christianity into traditional belief systems, sometimes producing compelling new forms of challenge and resistance to Anglo-American advance.

The sweeping cultural changes that made evangelical Christianity attractive to some native groups prompted others to call for total repudiation of all things European. By the 1740s it had become evident to all perceptive observers that the balance of power in Anglo-Indian relations had shifted drastically in favor of the English. Multiethnic Indian towns such as Logstown also (Logg's Town) and Sonioto on the Ohio River were choked with refugees who had been displaced by English migrants or had seen their home villages decimated by European disease (see Chapter 11). Native dependence on European imported goods had taken a

Prophets of Resistance in the Borderlands

heavy toll in the loss of traditional crafts and the overhunting of game. Rum, one of the most abundantly traded eighteenth-century commodities, was wreaking havoc among native families and clans through addiction and abuse. Indeed, native leaders commonly blamed the rapid loss of tribal lands on the weakness for rum among individual Indians and lesser chiefs.

The experience of dislocation and distress made many borderlands Indians especially receptive to the message of a new group of prophets who began appearing in the late 1730s among Indian towns from Pennsylvania's Wyoming Valley to the French Illinois country. The earliest of these visionaries preached simple separation from white society. The Pennsylvania agent Conrad Weiser reported in 1737 that one such seer had warned starving Shawnee and Delaware inhabitants of the Susquehanna Valley to stop trading skins for English rum. God had "driven all the wild animals out of the country" as a punishment for this practice, he declared, and if they refused to listen he would wipe them "from the earth." A decade later, a Naticoke appeared in the same region to warn that God "was not at peace" with either whites or Indians. If Indians did not stop associating with whites, he warned, "the white people would devour all of them." In the Wyoming Valley, a Delaware woman preached that God had originally made "three men and three women, the indians, the negro, and the white man." He intended each group to live and worship separately, with whites alone following the Bible.

Prophets sought to restore Indian spiritual power by revitalizing traditional religious practices through ritual, dance, and song, but these forms could also include new elements borrowed from Christianity. In the early 1760s, for instance, the Delaware prophet Neolin traveled the Ohio country teaching followers to dance, sing, kneel, and pray to a "little God" whose function of carrying "petitions & present[ing] them to a Great Being" resembled certain Christian teachings about Jesus. Neolin also urged Indians to "learn to live without any Trade or Connections with the White people, Clothing & Supporting themselves as their forefathers did." Like most prophets, Neolin preached against the use of rum, substituting a herbal emetic known as the "black drink," whose repeated use over a seven-year period would purge his followers of the "White people's Ways and Nature." Ritual drinking and vomiting of the tea spread throughout the Ohio Valley, becoming so common in the Shawnee town of Wakatomica that English traders began calling it "vomit town."

Like the itinerancy of George Whitefield among Anglo-American settlements, the travels of prophets like Neolin served to make Indians of the Ohio and Southeastern borderlands aware of each other and of the common challenges they faced. Indian hearers of native preachers and prophets shared the experience of cultural change through participation in Atlantic trade, one parallel in some ways to the experience of English colonists. Yet English manufactured goods often failed to raise native standards of living. Rather, they did quite the reverse, reducing Indian consumers to chronic dependency, addiction, dislocation, and death.

Prophets of revitalization offered a cure for the common Indian affliction of dependence on European trade. They reached intentionally across ancient divisions of geography and ethnicity, inviting their listeners to unite in a nativist movement that could restore Indian power to resist the advance of European trade and settlement.

The nativist message exerted an especially powerful appeal as Franco-British imperial conflict over North America intensified between 1745 and 1763. Yet the prophets of those decades could not overcome the competing alliances, conflicts of interest, and ongoing reliance on trade that would set native peoples and their French or English allies against one another in the looming war for North American empire.

CHRONOLOGY

1704	*Boston News-letter* begins publication.
1706	Benjamin Franklin born.
1714	George I, first of Hanoverian line, becomes monarch of Great Britain.
1721	*New England Courant* begins publication.
1728	James Gibbs's *Book of Architecture* published.
1732	George Washington born; *Poor Richard's Almanac* begins publication.
1737	Jonathan Edwards's *Faithful Narrative of the Surprising Work of God* published; nativist prophet Neolin warns Shawnee and Delaware to stop trading skins for rum.
1739	George Whitefield begins first American tour.
1741	David Brainerd becomes missionary to the Lenni-Lenape.
1746	College of New Jersey (Princeton University) founded.
1764	Rhode Island College (Brown University) founded.
1760	Richard Allen, founder of African Methodist Episcopal church, born.
1765	Mohegan minister Samson Occom embarks on preaching tour of England.
1766	Queens College (Rutgers) founded.
1769	Dartmouth College founded.

RECOMMENDED READING

Jon Butler provides a general introduction to many topics addressed in this chapter in *Becoming America: The Revolution Before 1776* (Cambridge, Mass., 2000), but Richard Hoftsader's *America at 1750: A Social Portrait* (New York, 1971) remains a brilliant and often disturbing treatment of the period. A detailed, comprehensive overview of colonial economic growth is John J. McCusker and Russell R. Menard, *The Economy of*

British America, 1607–1789 (Chapel Hill, 1991). For a superb biography of Benjamin Franklin, see Edmund S. Morgan, *Benjamin Franklin* (New Haven, 2002).

On the Great Awakening, see Jon Butler, *Awash in a Sea of Faith: Christianizing the American People* (Cambridge, Mass., 1990), and a recent challenge to Butler's interpretation in Frank Lambert, *Inventing the Great Awakening* (Princeton, 1999). See also Timothy D. Hall, *Contested Boundaries: Itinerancy and the Reshaping of the Colonial American Religious World* (Durham, 1994), and Christine L. Heyrman, *The Southern Cross: The Beginnings of the Bible Belt* (Chapel Hill, 1997). Two excellent treatments of women's experience in the revivals are Susan Juster, *Disorderly Women: Sexual Politics and Evangelicalism in Revolutionary New England* (Ithaca, 1994), and Catherine A. Brekus, *Strangers and Pilgrims: Female Preaching in America 1740–1845* (Chapel Hill, 1998).

On consumption and the cultural concerns of a rising middle class on the eighteenth-century colonial mainland, see Carol Shammas, *The Preindustrial Consumer in England and America* (Oxford, 1990); Cary Carson, Ronald Hoffman, and Peter J. Albert, eds., *Of Consuming Interests: The Style of Life in the Eighteenth Century* (Charlottesville, 1994); Richard L. Bushman, *The Refinement of America: Persons, Houses, Cities* (New York, 1992); and T. H. Breen, *Revolutionary Marketplace: The Consumer Origins of American Independence* (New York, 2004).

Several recent studies explore the growth and cultural significance of communication and print culture in eighteenth-century America. Ian K. Steele traces the Atlantic context of these developments in *The English Atlantic 1675–1740: An Exploration of Communication and Community* (New York, 1986). Richard D. Brown explores various developments in colonial communication in *Knowledge Is Power: The Diffusion of Information in Early America, 1700–1865* (New York, 1989), while print culture is explored in David S. Shields, *Civil Tongues and Polite Letters in British America* (Chapel Hill, 1997); Christopher Clark, *The Public Prints: The Newspaper in Anglo-American Culture, 1665–1740* (New York, 1994); and David D. Hall and Hugh Amory, eds., *The Colonial Book in the Atlantic World* (Cambridge, 2000).

James A. Henretta advanced the classic argument for familial resistance to the growth of the market in his "Families and Farms: *Mentalité* in Pre-Industrial America," *William and Mary Quarterly*, 3rd ser., 35 (1978): 3–32, while James T. Lemon's *The Best Poor Man's Country: A Geographical Study of Early Southeastern Pennsylvania* (Baltimore, 1972) remains an excellent study of one agricultural region's robust participation in the Atlantic economy. More recent studies include Daniel Vickers, "Competency and Competition: Economic Culture in Early America," *William and Mary Quarterly* 3rd ser., 47 (1990): 3–29; Allan Kulikoff, *The Agrarian Origins of American Capitalism* (Charlottesville, 1992); and Richard Lyman Bushman, "Markets and Composite Farms in Early America," *William and Mary Quarterly*, 3rd ser., 55 (1998): 351–74. The shifting place of women's work in the household is treated in Gloria L. Main, "Gender, Work, and Wages in Colonial New England," *William and Mary Quarterly*, 3rd ser., 51 (1994), and Laurel Thatcher Ulrich, "Wheels, Looms, and the Gender Division of Labor in Eighteenth-Century New England," *William and Mary Quarterly*, 3rd ser., 55 (1998): 3–38. Barry Levy, *Quakers and the American Family: British Settlement in the Delaware Valley* (New York, 1988), treats the impact of prosperous farming on Quaker family life.

The impact of eighteenth-century cultural transformations on native cultures is explored in Gregory Evans Dowd, *A Spirited Resistance: The North American Indian*

Struggle for Unity, 1745–1815 (Baltimore, 1992); James Axtell, *Natives and Newcomers: The Cultural Origins of North America* (New York, 2001); and Colin G. Calloway, *New Worlds for All: Indians, Europeans, and the Remaking of Early America* (Baltimore, 1997). On Indians and missions in the Great Awakening, see Richard W. Pointer, "'Poor Indians' and the 'Poor in Spirit': The Indian Impact on David Brainerd," *New England Quarterly* 67 (1994): 403–26, and Jane T. Merritt, "Dreaming of the Savior's Blood: Moravians and the Indian Great Awakening in Pennsylvania," *William and Mary Quarterly*, 3rd ser., 54 (1997): 723–68. On Indians and alcohol see Peter C. Mancall, *Deadly Medicine: Indians and Alcohol in Early America* (Ithaca, 1995).

Chapter 13

Slavery and African American Cultures in the Colonial British Atlantic

In December 1738, a group of "settlers, freeholders, and inhabitants of the province of Georgia" petitioned the colony's trustees to lift their ban on the importation and use of African slave labor. These petitioners from Savannah complained that well-intentioned efforts to found a colony without slaves had doomed Georgia to economic failure. Neighboring South Carolina planters could use slaves to prepare and ship timber, "the only thing . . . we might export," for "one half of the price we can do." The petitioners expressed confidence that "in time, silk and wine may be produced here" for export, but not at competitive prices so long as the ban on slaves remained. Neighboring Carolinians could "raise every thing this colony can," the colonists reminded the trustees, "and they having their labor so much cheaper will always ruin our market." Permitting the "use of negroes," they concluded, would "both occasion great numbers of white people to come here, and also render us capable to subsist ourselves . . . until we could make some produce fit for export."

Not all Georgians supported the Remonstrance of 1738, but the petition helps illuminate the central role of eighteenth-century slavery in the economics of empire. By 1740, slave-based plantations had become the engines that drove the British Atlantic economy. The most lucrative colonial staples—tobacco, dyes, rice, and above all, sugar products—were cultivated overwhelmingly by slave labor at relatively low cost for handsome profits to planters and merchants alike. Ownership of slaves had become the key to success throughout much of British America. Planters like Virginia's William Byrd II derived their entire fortunes—complete with great, elegantly furnished country houses, luxury goods, fashionable clothing, and English educations—from the backbreaking labor of slaves who cultivated their fields. Slavery also extended economic opportunity to Anglo-Americans without slaves by generating a plantation-based market for agricultural surpluses, shipping, and building materials. Many northern farm families purchased their first sip of tea or coffee with profits from grain sold on the Caribbean market.

In such an environment, the Savannah petitioners could legitimately wonder "what should induce persons to bring ships here" to purchase commodities when they could obtain the same goods at "one half the expense" in a nearby slave colony. Governor James Oglethorpe might retort that a few wealthy landowners stood to gain most by slavery's introduction to Georgia, but the fact remained that the colonial slave economy elsewhere was making it increasingly difficult for the fledgling colony to prosper as many inhabitants desired without the competitive advantage that slavery would bring. Georgia's sagging fortunes over the next twelve years made proslavery arguments increasingly difficult to resist, and in 1750 the trustees finally lifted the ban. Within a decade, the colony became as dependent on slave labor as neighboring South Carolina.

Georgia planters, like Anglo-Americans elsewhere, came to enjoy the growth of the eighteenth-century consumer economy at exorbitant human cost. The Atlantic slave trade coincided with the eighteenth-century "consumer revolution," reaching a peak of 5.1 million souls between 1700 and 1800. Most enslaved Africans ended up on sugar plantations in Brazil or the Caribbean. Around 4 percent of the total number—some 200,000 persons—found themselves in North America.

As eighteenth-century European immigrants struggled to improve Anglo-American holdings—for many the first real property they had ever owned—African newcomers faced the wrenching challenge of adjusting to colonial life as an article of human property. Indeed, slaves comprised one of the most important commodities of British Atlantic trade, valuable chattel acquired and distributed throughout the empire on the basis of supply and demand. Yet slaves never forgot that they were far more than mere chattel, nor did they let their masters forget.

Wherever they found themselves, slaves strenuously resisted European efforts to reduce them to mere property as "human tools." Each New World destination confronted Africans newcomers with a different environment, a different set of demands, and a different range of resources that they could employ to influence the conditions of life in slavery. During the eighteenth century, African slaves and their descendants—the African Diaspora of the

British Atlantic—created a rich range of cultures as they struggled daily with specific local processes of adaptation to unfamiliar persons, novel surroundings, and unaccustomed tasks.

PLANTATIONS, COMMERCE, AND SLAVERY

Eighteenth-century British Atlantic commerce rested squarely on a foundation of trade in plantation staples. Like the automobile industry in twentieth-century America, the colonial-era plantation system generated a range of high-demand goods as well as many more enterprises linked in some way to the primary staple market. By the 1690s, British observers could plainly see the plantation system's importance to the English Atlantic economy. The Bristol merchant John Cary celebrated the circuit of Atlantic trade which carried from Africa the workers "whereby our Plantations are improved, and 'tis by their Labours such great Quantities of *Sugar, Tobacco, Cotton, Ginger,* and *Indigo* are raised, which being bulky Commodities imploy great Numbers of our Ships for their transporting hither, and the greater number of Ships imploys the greater number of Handecraft Trades at home, spends more of our Product and Manufactures, and makes more Saylors, who are maintained by the separate Imploy." By 1700, the labor demands of large-scale plantation production had prompted Anglo-American planters to follow the lead of their West Indian counterparts in relying on African slaves rather than English or Irish indentured servants (see Chapters 6 and 8). Consumption of the goods produced by these slaves fueled eighteenth-century commercial growth.

An Empire of Sugar and Slaves

In the mid-eighteenth century, West Indian sugar constituted Great Britain's most important colonial staple. The value of sugar imported to the British Isles rose from £630,000 between 1699 and 1701 to over £2,362,000 between 1772 and 1774. By the latter period, North American colonists imported £2,168,000 worth of sugar, almost as much as Britain itself. The breathtaking growth of sugar production reflects the commodity's transformation from a luxury item consumed mainly by the wealthy to a "decency" consumed by all but the poorest members of eighteenth-century British society. By 1750, sugar's incorporation into the daily diet of ordinary people assured its dominance over all other plantation staples. The volume of capital at stake in the sugar trade gave West Indian planters access to the highest levels of power and prestige in London. The price of the sugar barons' power was borne by their African slaves, most of whom were doomed to comparatively short lives of cultivating and processing this most grueling of plantation crops.

The end of the War of the Spanish Succession in 1713 (see Chapter 10) established the conditions for a shift in the balance of production on the British sugar islands, with a consequent shift in the number of slaves destined for each. In 1714, Barbados still outstripped Jamaica and the Leeward Islands—St. Christopher, Nevis, Antigua, and Montserrat—in total output, producing nearly 50 percent of all sugar exported from the British West Indies. Over the next few decades, how-ever, production in the Leewards and Jamaica both surpassed that of Barbados, Britain's oldest sugar island, which slipped to less than one-fifth of the total by 1750. During the same period, the number of slave laborers on Barbados increased from 50,000 to 69,000, while those on the Leewards nearly tripled to just under 63,000 and those on Jamaica almost quadrupled to 118,000. Only the massive im-portation of new slaves could have supported such phenomenal population growth. Indeed, because death rates on the sugar islands remained higher than birthrates until well after 1750, the numbers of slaves transported from Africa greatly exceeded the number of those who survived to be counted at mid-century.

This rapidly expanding circuit of sugar, slaves, and capital placed the British West Indies at the vortex of the empire's economic growth. The rising demand for labor employed more than a hundred slaving vessels each year in bringing thou-sands of men and women from West Africa to the islands. Between 1720 and 1729, for instance, slavers brought over 72,000 slaves to Jamaica alone, an annual average of 7,200 persons. The West Indian demand for fish, livestock, agricultural products, building materials, and barrel staves attracted a steady stream of ships each year from North America. By the end of the colonial period, the annual value of Anglo-American goods shipped to the British West Indies was approach-ing £850,000, nearly three-fifths of the value of North American goods shipped to England and Scotland.

While West Indian sugar plantations dominated the British Atlantic economy, the tobacco and rice plantations of the Chesapeake and the low-country South domi-nated the Anglo-American export market. Indeed, Chesapeake tobacco ranked second in importance only to sugar until the 1760s, when it was surpassed by tea. Exports to Europe from eighteenth-century mainland southern colonies—Maryland, Virginia, and South Carolina—outstripped those from the northern colonies by almost two to one. By far the largest percentage of these products were produced by slaves laboring on tobacco and rice plantations. Chesapeake and low-country slaves also produced much of the wheat, corn, boards, and barrel staves shipped from southern ports to the Caribbean.

Chesapeake Tobacco and Low-Country Rice

Tobacco planters' dependence on slavery grew rapidly after 1700. The crop was labor-intensive but required little initial investment beyond land, a tobacco shed, and a few hand tools. Thus, yeomen farmers could continue to grow the crop on small, single-family plots of less than 200 acres even as larger planters began amassing land and slaves. Indeed, most plantations employed fewer than eleven slaves until mid-century, and the majority of bondpeople lived on plantations of less than twenty slaves throughout the colonial period. By the 1730s, however, the great Tidewater planters living along the James, York, and Rappahannock estuar-ies had begun building large estates staffed with twenty or more slaves. Many wealthy planters also established plantations for their children in the Virginia Piedmont and staffed each with eleven or more slaves, even as ordinary freehold-ers began purchasing additional land along with one or two slaves to increase their own production.

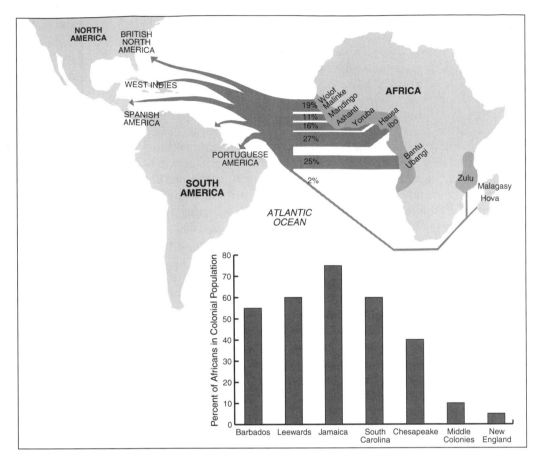

Africans in America

This map shows the relative percentages of slaves brought from each major region in Africa to various destinations in the New World. Only 4 percent of captured Africans arrived in North America. The graph depicts the percentage of Africans within the total population of each major British colonial region.

The corresponding demand for slave laborers prompted white Virginians to import more than 62,000 Africans between 1700 and 1775. Unlike the slave population in the British West Indies, however, the existing slave population in Virginia and Maryland always contributed to overall population growth. Even in the first decade of the century, when imports nearly doubled the number of slaves in Virginia, births contributed 0.2 percent to the total black population growth. Natural increase peaked at 4.7 percent between 1740 and 1750, and averaged 2.6 percent over the entire period.

In contrast to Virginia tobacco, the production of South Carolina rice depended on slave labor from the very beginning. Planters who began cultivating the crop after 1695 quickly came to believe that a rice plantation had to start out as a large-scale operation to achieve profitability. The planter Thomas Nairne estimated an initial outlay of at least £1,000 to purchase equipment and a minimum of thirty slaves for clearing, draining, damming, and ditching the land as well as planting and tending the crop. Despite the daunting expense, Carolina rice plantations multiplied, and imports to England surged from a negligible amount in 1700 to a value of over £340,000 between 1772 and 1774. The rapid growth in rice production stimulated a demand for slaves that made Africans the majority population in South Carolina as early as 1708. Between 1700 and 1770, the number of slaves increased from 2,400 to 82,000, with most growth coming by importation from Africa.

The development of new crops and slave-based plantation enterprises brought about a dramatic shift in the distribution of blacks throughout Great Britain's eighteenth-century New World empire. In 1700, most of the empire's blacks—nearly 200,000—resided in the Caribbean, more than a quarter of them on Barbados. Less than 20,000 lived in North America. By 1750, however, the combination of importations and natural increase had boosted the proportion of blacks living on the mainland to four in ten. In the Caribbean, Jamaica's black population had far outstripped that of Barbados, and a much greater proportion of West Indian blacks labored on sugar plantations in the Leewards. By 1774, mainland blacks comprised a majority of the empire's black population, outnumbering the black population on the islands by more than 30,000. The processes of migration, adaptation, birth, growth, and death took place within a wide variety of New World environments. The empire's black Diaspora encountered an extraordinary range of experience, which nevertheless remained unified by a number of common elements.

COMMON THREADS OF AFRICAN EXPERIENCE

The eighteenth-century Atlantic slave trade wrenched millions of sub-Saharan Africans from exceedingly diverse cultural settings and thrust them into a harrowing process of bondage, forced migration, and resettlement an ocean away from their homes. Passage on the cramped, reeking vessels that carried these slaves to various New World destinations also confronted them with the first of several common threads that ran through the divergent experiences of bondage (see Chapter 3). No matter where they were sold, new arrivals faced other common challenges. The effort to communicate with one another, to learn the ropes of work and survival, and to forge new patterns of community and family life from the remembered fragments of disparate languages and traditions posed a series of difficulties that engaged the highest creative energies of the Africans who survived the Middle Passage.

No matter where slavery took root or what justifications its practitioners offered, the institution remained violent at its very core. It began in violence through war or capture and was sustained in violence through the process of sale and transatlantic transport. In the New World, violence continued to lurk just beneath the

Coercion, Resistance, Negotiation

surface of the slave-master relationship. Slaves and masters always worked at cross-purposes: the master seeking to extract as much labor as possible from his slave property, the slave constantly seizing on opportunities for even a moment's freedom from forced toil. Masters used all means at their disposal to gain their objectives, but when all else failed, the final resort remained the whip, maiming, torture, even death.

Eighteenth-century mainland slaves faced much harsher regimes of discipline and punishment than had their seventeenth-century predecessors. The smaller numbers of slaves, coupled with the frequent need for seventeenth-century masters and slaves to live and work side by side, had required different patterns of accommodation. But as the slave numbers grew, the harsh measures that had been instituted earlier in British West Indian slave societies took hold in the Chesapeake and the low-country South as well. Planters lived in constant fear of slave uprisings and used brutal measures to nip any resistance in the bud. Slaves endured vicious lashings for infractions such as working too slowly or balking at orders. Masters made humiliating examples of recalcitrant slaves who failed to meet their expectations or resisted their orders. The Virginia planter William Byrd II punished his house-slave Eugene for bed-wetting by forcing him to "drink a pint of piss." Byrd and South Carolina planter Joseph Ball fitted metal bits into the mouths of slaves who persistently ran away. The Virginia planter Robert "King" Carter preferred to chop off the toes of "Incorrigible" runaways. Masters throughout colonial America bound offending slaves to pillories, lashed them mercilessly at whipping posts, subjected some to torture, and hung others on a gallows. Despite such inhuman tortures, many slaves continued to resist—even unto death—rather than endure a lifetime of unrelieved bondage.

To be sure, masters did not rely on violence alone to bring their slaves into line. They recognized the usefulness of leniency and reward, and most defined their own role within an ideology which made them a *pater familias*, the benevolent, if sometimes necessarily strict, head of a household that extended beyond his wife and children to all the slaves residing on his plantation. William Byrd compared himself to one of the biblical patriarchs with a "large family" that included "my flocks and my herds, my bond-men and bond-women." Planters expressed their benevolence through such practices as granting midday breaks, setting aside Sundays as days of rest, allowing slaves to visit spouses or gather for merrymaking off the plantation, and granting occasional holidays—usually Christmas, Easter, and Whitsuntide, a church holiday falling in late May or early June. Many delegated the harshest duties of daily discipline to the plantation overseer and positioned themselves as stern but fair authorities who might occasionally intervene to adjudicate disputes between slaves and overseers, reducing or suspending punishments as the situation warranted.

Slaves resisted the plantation regime of work and discipline through a variety of measures ranging from feigning illness or stupidity to outright rebellion. Newly arrived slaves pretended ignorance of the language to avoid work. As one visitor to Maryland observed, "Let an hundred Men shew" a new slave "how to hoe, or drive a Wheelbarrow, he'll still take one by the bottom, and the Other by the Wheel."

Slaves on rice plantations often escaped into the surrounding swamps during harvest season to avoid the punishing task of threshing and processing the crop. Slaves on tobacco or sugar plantations might break hoes or feign illness to get out of work. Running away was a constant problem, and planters salted the advertising sections of colonial newspapers with notices detailing missing slaves' appearance, attire, habits, and manners of speech or behavior. Where terrain such as Jamaica's Cockpit Country or South Carolina swamps permitted, runaways formed maroon communities where members could evade capture for months or years. Indeed, Jamaican maroons became a permanent presence on the island, feared for their fierce, well-organized raids and tenacious defense of territory that eventually forced planters to recognize their independence.

Occasionally, slaves protested their debasement through organized revolt. The most serious slave rebellion on the colonial mainland was the Stono Uprising, which took place in September 1739. One hundred fifty South Carolina blacks rose up and, seizing guns and ammunition, murdered several white planters. "With Colours displayed, and two Drums beating," they marched toward Spanish Florida, where they had been promised freedom. The local militia soon overtook the rebellious slaves and killed most of them. Jamaican slaves mounted many such rebellions throughout the eighteenth century. In 1760, for instance, Tacky's Rebellion embroiled several parishes around Kingston in a conflict that lasted for several weeks and took an alliance of regular British troops and local militia to suppress. Although no slave revolt succeeded until the 1790s, recurrent outbreaks of rebellion persuaded whites everywhere that their own blacks might secretly be planning bloody revolt. Fear bred paranoia. When an unstable white servant woman in New York City announced in 1741 that blacks intended to burn the town, frightened authorities executed 34 suspected arsonists (30 blacks and 4 whites) and dispatched 72 others either to the West Indies or to Madeira off the north coast of Africa. Although interracial violence remained sporadic and comparatively low, everyone recognized that the blacks—in the words of one Virginia governor— longed "to Shake off the fetters of Slavery."

Most slaves recognized the improbability of successful revolt and chose instead to win concessions from the planters that could ameliorate the conditions of slavery. The eighteenth-century master-slave relationship thus involved an incessant, if often clandestine, struggle that pitted the planter's demand for labor against the slave's desire for liberty. The balance of power and coercion remained with the masters, who did not hesitate to employ whatever method seemed most effective. Yet the slaves possessed their own means of prosecuting the struggle, and their resources increased with new knowledge and new skill. Experienced field hands on tobacco plantations knew how to ruin the crop by hoeing in the wrong places or cutting the leaves at the wrong time. Slaves on a sugar estate could sabotage the mill during the critical harvest season, decimating production as the cane dried in the fields while the equipment was being repaired. A strategic swipe of a hoe in an irrigation ditch might flood a rice field prematurely or drain it to let the plants bake dry in the midsummer sun. A toxin extracted from a local herb and slipped into a hated planter's food might leave the victim doubled over with abdominal pains or put him into an early grave. As the slaves' ability to undertake such actions grew, so did their masters' willingness to extend them limited concessions—longer breaks, additional time off, monetary compensation for overwork, the right to sell produce from provision plots—in order to avoid costly mishaps or the trouble and expense of tracking down runaways.

Race and Freedom

Africans who disembarked from eighteenth-century slave ships stepped into a world in which their place had become more sharply bounded by evolving European notions of immutable racial difference. In this respect their situation differed markedly from that of the seventeenth century, when blacks had lived in a comparatively fluid social environment governed more by categories of status and ethnicity than race. To be sure, Caribbean and Anglo-American masters of the earlier period had often justified the practice of slavery in racist terms. English writers had frequently associated blacks in Africa with heathen religion, barbarous behavior, sexual promiscuity—in fact, with evil itself. From such a perspective, the enslavement of Africans had seemed unobjectionable. The planters maintained that if black slaves converted to Christianity, shedding their supposedly savage ways, they would benefit from their loss of freedom. Yet practice had not yet fully conformed with this rhetoric of race. In the seventeenth century, not all unfree blacks were enslaved for life, and those who gained their freedom after a time of servitude could gain entry into colonial society as property holders and masters themselves.

By the first decade of the eighteenth century, however, the legal status of the empire's unfree black people was no longer in doubt. Nearly every plantation colony had on its books a set of black codes which, among many other things, designated unfree persons of African descent as slaves for life, along with their children after them. This transformation reached British North America somewhat later than the West Indies because of the lag in African American population growth on the mainland. Yet as the black population expanded, lawmakers in colonies from the Carolinas to New England drew up increasingly strict slave statues that codified the racism always latent in New World societies. Slavery came to be based unequivocally on the color of a person's skin. Blacks fell into this status simply because they were black.

A vicious pattern of discrimination had been set in motion. Even conversion to Christianity could not free an African from bondage. Associations between blacks and poor whites diminished as African slaves displaced white servants. Increasingly discriminatory laws made it difficult for free blacks to remain in plantation colonies. Similar statutes pushed free blacks to the margins of life in New England and the Middle Colonies. The new racial code permitted white planters to deal with their black property as they alone saw fit. One Virginia statute excused a master who had killed a slave on the grounds that no rational person would purposely "destroy his own estate." Children born to a slave woman became slaves regardless of the father's race. Unlike the Spanish colonies, where persons of lighter color enjoyed greater legal privileges in society, the English colonies tolerated no mixing of the races. Mulattoes and those of pure African descent fell under the same legal designation as slaves for life.

The legal codification of racism prevented neither whites nor blacks from recognizing a wide range of actual differences and acting on them. One of the primary tensions confronting slaves throughout the eighteenth-century British empire was that between newly arrived "outlandish" Africans and Creoles who had been born and reared within colonial society. The continuing large-scale importation of Africans made this distinction a constant dynamic within slave communities everywhere, one that altered as the balance shifted from African to Creole predominance. A growing minority of Mulattos—offspring of sexual unions between white and black parents—produced further complications. Where Africans formed the majority population—as they did in the Caribbean for much of the eighteenth century and in the Carolina low country for many years—Creoles often suffered derision, mockery, and exclusion from community life. Newly arrived men and women from Africa were far more likely to run away, assault their masters, and organize rebellion than were Creole slaves. The people described in colonial newspaper advertisements as "New Negroes" tried desperately to regain control over their lives. Most resisted their masters' attempts to subdue them. Many ran away repeatedly. In 1770—just to cite one poignant example—two young Africans, both recently sold in Virginia, "went off with several others, being persuaded that they could find their way back to their own Country."

As Creoles became the majority, they often began looking down on Africans as "Guineabirds" or "Salt-water Negroes" and sometimes took advantage of the newcomers' lack of experience. Caribbean Creoles might take a new arrival into their household and force him or her to work their garden plots. The Creole community could make life very difficult for Africans who held themselves aloof or who resisted adaptation to local custom. Yet Creoles could also be very helpful, assisting new arrivals to perfect the language, teaching them how to master their tasks, showing them how to evade punishment, and helping them survive the hardships of slave life.

As slaves adapted to their environment and began rearing children, a second tension emerged between slaves of fully African descent and mulatto slaves. Colonial law may have distinguished between black and white, and various colonial legislatures attempted to enforce the separation by prohibiting miscegenation, or the fathering of mixed-race children. Nevertheless, interracial sexual liaisons frequently occurred, producing mulatto offspring who inherited their mother's legal status. Caribbean planters thought of mulattoes as a distinct group of "coloureds" between blacks and whites. Mainland planters seldom made such distinctions in speech or writing, but they often followed their island counterparts in extending relatively privileged treatment to mulatto slaves. Caribbean planters never assigned mulattoes to field work, as often happened in the Chesapeake and the low country. Yet in all regions, lighter-skinned mulattoes tended to receive preference for places of domestic service and for training in crafts such as carpentry, masonry, and smithing. These distinctions alone created divisions of rank within local African American communities, often fostering a sense of superiority among the lighter-skinned domestics and skilled laborers and resentment among the common field hands.

African, Creole, Mulatto

Mulattoes were also more likely to receive their freedom than other slaves, a fact that further complicated their place within the empire's larger African American communities. To be sure, manumission remained rare throughout the eighteenth century. In 1770, freedmen and freed women comprised a mere 2 percent of the black population in Jamaica and Virginia, and less than 1 percent in South Carolina and Barbados. Yet when masters did consent to free a slave, the favor most often went to lighter-skinned mulattoes. Because of their training in craft work, mulattoes also frequently enjoyed additional trade skills needed to meet conditions of manumission, which often included the earning and payment of their value on the slave market.

Once they gained liberty, however, freed mulattoes occupied a tenuous place in plantation society. Their practical situation often differed little from the legal status they had so recently escaped. Freed blacks usually continued to associate most closely with slaves. Ties of kinship or financial need often kept them working at the same tasks for the same employers they had formerly served in bondage.

Family and Community

Historians of an earlier generation believed that eighteenth-century slaves had little opportunity to marry or raise families, and in truth, slaves did face formidable obstacles in this area of life. British American slave codes recognized only the mother-child tie, primarily to determine the legal status of the child. The law neither recognized nor protected slave marriages. The preponderance of males among new arrivals—more than two-thirds throughout the eighteenth century—made it impossible for many men to find wives. Ethnic differences and linguistic barriers among new arrivals also deterred slaves from marrying. Masters often housed new arrivals from Africa in sex-segregated barracks as a means of controlling their labor force. Slave women, married or not, remained vulnerable to the unwanted sexual attention and assault of their masters. Masters intervened constantly in the parent-child relationship, conferring names of their own choice on children as they did on African parents, sending mothers back into field work while consigning care of their children to others, determining the age at which children could be assigned tasks, and overruling parental discipline and protection to impose the master's own regime of punishment and reward. Slave sales could separate children, parents, and spouses from one another at any time.

Yet historians now recognize that many slaves exercised extraordinary resourcefulness in overcoming these barriers to establish resilient networks of family and kin. Even where families proved most difficult to form and maintain—places such as the mainland northern colonies and the rapidly expanding Leeward Islands of the 1720s and 1730s—slaves practiced "fictive kinship" in which they faithfully cared for each others' children as their own. First-generation Africans who married tended to establish nuclear family units, and married couples lived together wherever possible in a dwelling that also housed the woman's children.

Despite the absence of legal protections, marriage among slaves became commonplace as the population became established in a region. Slaves wedded "after their own way" in rites that took various forms throughout the British American mainland and Caribbean colonies. Most remained simple ceremonies in which the proposing groom offered a gift—a "*Brass Ring* or some other Toy" in the tobacco country, roasted peanuts in South Carolina—whose acceptance by the prospective bride sealed the marriage. European observers considered such unions remarkably casual, believing that a wife could dissolve a marriage simply by returning the husband's gift. Europeans also commented frequently on the persistence of the African custom of polygyny—the union between a man and more than one woman—which the Anglican minister Francis Le Jau described as "a General Sin" among South Carolina slaves. Although such comments reflected a great deal of misunderstanding about the cultural significance of marriage among Africans, they do demonstrate the slaves' resourcefulness in reconstructing one of the central institutions of their social life.

As plantations became established and marriages more common, slaves developed extended kinship networks across several different holdings. Slave couples frequently lived on different estates. Guy, a slave carpenter who lived on the Sabine Hall estate of Virginia planter Landon Carter, left frequently to spend the night with his wife on a neighboring plantation. Like many other planters throughout the British Atlantic, Carter usually granted permission for Guy to visit, but the carpenter harbored no scruples about leaving even without his master's permission. Like other planters, Carter usually conceded what he could not prevent. Planters living on adjoining estates might allow slave couples multiple visits each week, while those living more than 10 miles apart might allow visits only once per month or less. Such circumstances strained the nuclear family arrangement of husband, wife, and children which Creole slaves attempted to construct, demanding the creation of larger networks of kin, both real and fictive. Through these networks, the center of family life shifted from households and couples to more extensive units involving one or more grandparents, uncles, aunts, and cousins as well as spouses.

The extension of kinship networks across several plantations facilitated the growth of slave communities over time. As with the development of family life, slaves had to confront various legal and practical barriers to the formation of community. Black codes typically prohibited unauthorized travel or gathering of slaves or the observance of secret rituals. They also proscribed certain activities such as the beating of drums and the blowing of horns, means by which slaves might signal a revolt. In addition to these legal restrictions, new arrivals confronted barriers of language and custom, and often of distance as well. Yet slaves managed to overcome these barriers to community life, sometimes with their masters' permission and at other times behind the masters' backs.

Visitors to the southern mainland colonies and the Caribbean alike commented frequently on the community life they observed among the slaves. The arrangements of slave houses afforded the first evidence of community formation. Where slaves were given the latitude to build housing after their own design, they arranged dwellings in patterns that supported communal living. Quarters constructed by West African slaves frequently resembled the clustered compounds of small shelters that they had known in Africa. Even when European-style construction and layout was used, archaeological evidence reveals that slaves conducted most daily activities such as cooking, eating, and washing in the common outdoor space around their quarters. This practice fostered frequent opportunities to socialize and forge community. Aspects of building construction and layout changed in various ways over time depending on local circumstances, but the communal features of life in the slave quarters persisted into the nineteenth century.

Slaves throughout the British empire took many other opportunities to socialize. Field laborers in Virginia and the Carolinas frequently followed backpaths between plantations to open meadows or forest clearings where they would meet to socialize and dance at the end of the day. The evangelist George Whitefield encountered one such group "dancing round the fire" as he traveled through rural South Carolina in the winter of 1739. Thomas Jefferson marveled at the stamina his own slaves displayed as they congregated in back meadows to dance and sing until midnight after completing a full day's work in his tobacco fields. In South Carolina and the Caribbean islands, slaves also developed thriving internal markets for the sale and exchange of produce they grew on their own plots. The Scottish traveler Janet Schaw observed during her visit to Antigua in the mid-1770s that slaves were "the only market people. Nobody else dreams of selling provisions."

In colonial New York, where their employment as domestics and farmhands impeded the communal life that emerged on the plantations, blacks found other ways to come together. New York slaves, for instance, transformed the traditional Dutch festival of Pinkster, or Pentecost, into an opportunity for celebration, dance, and song that reflected strong African influences. They adapted traditional Dutch songs and rituals of role reversal to satirize their masters. They played African music on traditional instruments such as bangars, rattles, and drums as well as adapting fiddles to their own percussive style. African modes of dance rounded out a celebration strongly reminiscent of festivals in their African homelands.

Marriages and funerals also became occasions for communal celebration. Though marriage rites were simple and private, the news of a slave marriage brought celebrants together from surrounding plantations for dancing and feasting. Masters permitted the celebrations at night after the day's work had been completed, and sometimes contributed a hog to the festivities. Funerals drew slaves together to mourn the loss of a friend or kin. Visitors to the British West Indies remarked upon slaves' highly structured funerals. Rites on Montserrat, according to the 1760s traveler John Singleton, included long processions attended with mourning dances, chants sung in "full chorus," and graveside rituals performed by a religious leader to "compose the spirit of the dead."

Slave Religion

Slave funerals and burial customs reveal the persistence of African religious beliefs and practices that imparted deep spiritual significance to the lives of eighteenth-century slaves. West African slaves clung to their native religious traditions with a tenacity that frustrated Christian missionaries and prompted frequent comment from masters and visitors to the plantations. Slaves seemed determined to remain "as much under the influence of Pagan darkness, idolatry, and superstition, as they were at their first arrival from Africa." Such comments provide a record of African beliefs too fragmentary for historians to reconstruct into a coherent system, although they do suggest that African religion remained a powerful element in the slaves' lives.

The religious beliefs that Africans brought to the New World varied according to the region from which they came. Some, especially those shipped from the region of Gambia, were Muslims or familiar with Islam, and a select few were literate in Arabic. Another smaller group came from regions such as the Kingdom of Kongo where Christianity was practiced. The vast majority, however, observed neither Christianity nor Islam, but belonged to various "overlapping networks of religious relationship," in the words of the historian John Thornton. Many venerated their ancestors and believed in various benevolent and malevolent spirits whose power they might harness for good or ill. Others had likely belonged to hunters' guilds or were initiates into spirit possession cults. Some brought sufficient knowledge to act as conjurors or healers, and at least a few of these may have served as herbalists, witch doctors, or diviners in their African homelands.

Africans called on whatever spiritual resources they had brought with them to help them survive in the New World. Caribbean slaves fused together certain religious practices and offices into a form which European visitors referred to as "Obeah," an Anglicized term combining two different West African words: *ubio*, a charm that caused sickness or death, and *o-bayifo*, a sorcerer. Practitioners of Obeah reputedly possessed the power to diagnose and treat diseases, to detect witches and cure the bewitched, and to predict the future. Though British American mainland observers never mentioned Obeah directly, similar practices of conjuring were everywhere known and feared. Conjurers brought with them a font of herbal lore and quickly found or discovered New World plants from which they could extract a variety of poisons and remedies. Planters throughout the British empire took precautions to protect themselves against poisoning by their slaves. Slaves likewise feared being poisoned by a vengeful conjuror. Indeed, the historian Philip D. Morgan has asserted that slavery brought about a decisive shift away from "benevolent lesser spirits" to "those spirits deemed useful in injuring other people." Still, slaves and masters alike could benefit from herbal remedies concocted by experienced conjurors. Over time, European planters and physicians learned to respect and ask—or force—African conjurors to divulge the secret properties of various medicinal herbs.

Blacks expressed enduring African beliefs through customs ranging from dance and music to the way they buried their dead. European observers were convinced that the "great activity and strength of Body" exerted in dance, coupled with its apparent eroticism and the wearing of adornments such as masks and animal skins or tails, possessed religious significance for Africans. Archaeological evidence from Maryland to Barbados reveals that slaves buried their dead with talismans, beads, and pots of food and drink which Europeans thought were intended to assist the departed on their journey to the place of the dead.

Most first-generation African Americans took refuge in their traditional beliefs and strenuously resisted the religion of their masters, but by the mid-eighteenth century the British empire's emerging Creole population began turning to Christianity. Their manner of adopting the new faith suggests that converts sought in it an alternative set of spiritual resources that could help them adapt to their circumstances, even though many of their kin continued to find African religion sufficient for this purpose. A comparative few submitted to Anglican baptism and presented their infants for baptism as well. Most, however, were repelled by eighteenth-century Anglicanism's stiff, creedal forms, the racial condescension of its clergy, and the blatant racism of Anglo-American church members. The evangelical Christianity of the Great Awakening, by contrast, proved much more congenial to the needs and aspirations of black converts.

Early evangelical leaders demonstrated much greater sympathy for the slaves and a far greater readiness to present the message of Christian conversion in terms they could readily embrace. Indeed, John Wesley, the founder of the Methodist movement and an Anglican missionary to Georgia during the 1730s, was highly critical of slavery and of planter opposition to converting the slaves. Wesley's concern struck a powerful chord among many slaves who heard him, as did the preaching of his successor, George Whitefield. During Whitefield's first great tour of the mainland colonies in 1739 and 1740 (see Chapter 12), the itinerant minister criticized slavery frequently and invited blacks to respond to his message of new birth on terms no different than those he extended to white hearers. His South Carolina followers Hugh and Jonathan Bryan encouraged their slaves to convert to evangelical Christianity. Later evangelists such as the Presbyterian Samuel Davies also devoted special attention to converting blacks. Davies held meetings especially for "poor Negroes" at his home in Hanover County, Virginia. To be sure, few of these early evangelical leaders opposed slavery completely, and Whitefield eventually joined in lobbying the Georgia trustees to lift their ban on slavery. Nevertheless, the evangelicals' open, sympathetic preaching of the new birth resonated with black listeners.

Blacks embraced evangelical Christianity for its emphasis on experience, its potent themes of salvation and deliverance, and the opportunity it offered for converts to take the initiative in church participation as well as leadership. Historian Mechal Sobel has suggested that evangelicalism—especially in its Baptist form—shared with West African religion a similar emphasis on sudden conversion accompanied by a ritual bath signifying death and rebirth. Evangelical Baptists and Methodists expressed their devotion in boisterous meetings accompanied by exuberant singing, dancing, skipping, and falling, physical demonstrations of faith that invited black participation on familiar terms. Early evangelicals also welcomed black converts into church membership on an equal basis with whites. In so doing they gave concrete expression to hopes for Christ's return to deliver his oppressed people and establish a millennial kingdom of righteousness, justice, liberty, and peace. Evangelicals also stressed the Holy Spirit's readiness to empower blacks as well as whites to preach and exhort, opening the way for many black laypersons to assume places of leadership in evangelical circles. Black lay preachers soon began establishing their own congregations on southern plantations, and many became itinerants, preaching to blacks in neighboring locales. Runaway slave ads of the period reveal that some black lay preachers used their itinerancy as a path to freedom.

Because evangelicalism emerged late in the colonial period, the number of black converts in British America remained small before the 1770s. Evangelicalism proved more popular among the Creole population of the Chesapeake and the northern mainland colonies than in the African-dominated low country and the British West Indies. South Carolina slaves did not turn to Christianity in large numbers until after the American Revolution. Evangelical Methodism began attracting a few converts on Antigua and Jamaica in the 1760s. Obeah, however, remained popular in the Caribbean well into the nineteenth century. In Jamaica the new African-derived Myalism, with its initiation ceremony of public burial and resurrection, also appeared in the 1760s to offer a compelling alternative to evangelicalism.

The efforts to reconstruct viable family, community, and religious lives engaged African and Creole slaves in an imaginative reshaping of African and European customs. As first-generation Africans married spouses from different ethnic groups, the partners worked to learn a new language and to meld remembered traditions into new cultural forms that could facilitate their life together. Fictive kinships and communal living arrangements required similar adjustments, as did the development of larger networks of kin and community. Blacks transformed Christianity into an expression of religious feeling with vibrant African ingredients. In music and folk art, they gave voice to a cultural identity that even the most degrading conditions could not eradicate. Out of these daily patterns of interaction and experience, blacks forged a series of truly African American cultures.

CONSTRUCTING AFRICAN AMERICAN IDENTITIES

Despite the common strands that ran through eighteenth-century African experience, no single colonial African American culture emerged. The circumstances of black slavery and freedom simply varied too much, making daily life quite different for a black person in South Carolina or Jamaica than for an African American who happened to live in Pennsylvania or Massachusetts Bay.

The single most important factor in shaping experience among the empire's slaves was the rate of natural increase. Where deaths exceeded births, as they did throughout the British West Indies until well after mid-century, high import rates impeded the development of stable family and community life. Where birthrates exceeded death rates, as occurred on the British American colonial mainland by 1720, slave communities began gaining greater stability and coherence.

Other factors also influenced the development of particular black cultures. The proportion of slaves in the local population, the climate of the region, the crops most often cultivated, the differences between rural and urban settings—all influenced profoundly how blacks experienced and adapted to life in the New World.

West Indian Slaves

The great majority of slaves transported from Africa to the British colonies ended up laboring and dying on a Caribbean sugar plantation. Sugar was a brutal taskmaster that kept nearly 90 percent of the plantation's slaves at hard labor in the cane fields from sunup to sundown while the crop was maturing. Harvest season kept them busy round the clock (see Chapter 6). Planters exempted from fieldwork only children under the age of six and the few who managed to outlive their effective laboring years. The rigors of field work coupled with inadequate diet suppressed the fertility of slave women, who bore far fewer children than their counterparts on the mainland. The sugar barons took few measures to ameliorate

Old Plantation, *a watercolor by an unknown artist (about 1800) shows that African customs survived plantation slavery. The man and women in the center dance to the music of drum and banjo, possibly to celebrate a wedding. Instruments, turbans, and scarves reflect a distinctive African American culture in the New World.*
Abby Aldrich Rockefeller Folk Art Museum, Colonial Williamsburg Foundation, Williamsburg, VA.

working conditions or encourage childbearing until after mid-century, when rising prices prompted them to reassess the widely held notion that it cost less to buy a new laborer than to raise one.

The resulting predominance of newly arrived West African slaves in this harsh West Indian environment ensured both the survival of African cultural forms and a chronic instability of family and community life. The sex ratio in the Caribbean remained unbalanced throughout much of the eighteenth century. More than half of the new arrivals lived with friends rather than spouses or relatives. Caribbean planters were much less reluctant than those on the mainland to cohabit with slave women, and their habit of keeping concubines further reduced opportunities to establish black families. The tendency to associate by ethnic groups divided slaves into separate and sometimes conflicting communities such as Ashanti, Yoruba, and Igbo while dividing all the newcomers from the Creole minority.

On the other hand, the existence of black majorities on all the sugar islands, coupled with high rates of absentee ownership among the planters, permitted slaves to recreate African cultural forms with far fewer European influences. The Creole languages that emerged on various sugar islands incorporated English vocabularies into African grammatical forms. Music and dance on the islands combined elements from various African sources into rich new forms that owed little to European structures of tonality and rhythm. Religion, too, remained strongly African in content and form. Slaves carved out time to grow produce on their provision grounds and sold it in African-style markets on Sundays. The markets provided a setting where slaves could not only engage in commerce, but also socialize, make music and dance, and share food and drink.

Although sugar production consumed the lives and labor of most Caribbean slaves, blacks also served in many other roles. A growing minority worked on coffee plantations after 1750 as the beverage's increasing popularity stimulated demand. Cocoa, cotton, and spice production occupied other Caribbean slaves. The work on such plantations was less arduous than that on sugar estates, as was labor in trades, domestic service, fishing, and ranching. Slaves who worked in areas other than sugar production could squeeze more personal time out of their daily schedules. In some settings, such as coffee plantations, that gain was somewhat offset by the smaller size and relative isolation of the planters' holdings, which constricted opportunities for social interaction and family life. Slave artisans gradually won from their masters concessions such as limited hours, the right to work for pay on their own time, the right to trade on their own account, and a limited right to property. Some gained permission to set up separate households for themselves.

Jamaica also hosted the British Empire's largest enduring Maroon society. During the early eighteenth century, the Maroons grew from a few score runaways to a population of nearly 1,000, with its own coherent structures of leadership and cultural life. English planters tried repeatedly to suppress them, but the tenacity of Maroon warriors and the inaccessibility of their Cockpit Country homeland defeated such efforts. In 1739, the planters finally settled for peace on terms that bound the Maroons to return future runaways and to assist the English in maintaining order on the island. Maroons agreed to these terms, in part to prevent their own numbers from rising too rapidly to sustain and to keep out potential troublemakers. By 1760, relations had become so stable that when the Jamaican slave Tacky led a large uprising, Maroons readily allied with planters to suppress it. A Maroon's bullet ended Tacky's life.

Rice and Slaves

Of all the eighteenth-century mainland colonies, South Carolina most resembled the Caribbean in the structure of its plantation society. Rice proved nearly as punishing to produce as sugar, and disease and malnutrition killed low-country slaves almost as rapidly as those in the West Indies. Like Caribbean sugar barons, low-country planters had to rely on the Atlantic slave trade to meet their labor demands. The colony's black majority, like its Caribbean counterpart, did not begin reproducing itself until the 1760s.

African men and women who arrived in eighteenth-century South Carolina found themselves on large, isolated rice plantations, where their contact with whites was nearly as limited as that of slaves on Caribbean sugar plantations. Most planters spent the summer months in Charles Town to escape the sultry low-country heat and malarial mosquitoes. They left overseers and trusted black drivers to supervise the slaves in the heavy work of weeding rice, clearing and draining swamps, and digging mazes of irrigation ditches through the sticky clay soil.

During harvest the slaves worked late into the nights gathering the crop and beating the rice kernels in large mortars. The Anglo-American painter Benjamin West regarded this "excessive hard labor" fatal to many slaves, "carrying off great numbers every winter." Desperately overtaxed, slaves sometimes burned down the threshing barns to escape the hated mortars. The cycle of rice production occupied the entire year, and slaves often found themselves planting a new crop while still threshing the previous year's harvest.

Other low-country slaves produced indigo, a weed that yielded a brilliant blue dye used in Britain's textile industry. The crop required less field work, but the process of rendering the harvested plants kept slaves sweating for weeks over steaming vats of fermenting vegetation. The putrid reek drew hordes of flies, which tormented the slaves as they worked. They had to stir the mixture constantly while pouring it through a series of containers, setting its color with lime at the critical moment, then draining and drying the blue sediment into blocks for shipping. Dye making demanded great skill, and the slaves who endured the process to learn its secrets gained power to bargain concessions from masters whose profits depended on the dye-makers' expertise.

These circumstances of low-country plantation work—a majority black population, limited contact with whites, and some slave control over production—permitted slaves to preserve many African elements within their culture. The process of creating a culture remained slow and uneven, however, hindered by factors similar to those in the Caribbean. Although planters desired to create a relatively homogeneous labor force by acquiring African slaves from the rice-producing regions of Gambia and Senegal, limited supply forced them to accept less desirable slaves from regions such as Angola. The resulting divisions among new arrivals, as well as between salt-water slaves and Creoles, took time to overcome. So too did the sexual imbalance which slowed the development of slave families. The size of plantations—averaging well over 500 acres with a resident labor force of thirty or more slaves—made contact among groups from different plantations more difficult and tended to foster insular plantation communities.

Over time, however, a distinctive low-country culture did emerge among South Carolina blacks. Creole languages mixed the basic vocabulary of English with words borrowed from various African tongues. Until the end of the nineteenth century, one Creole language, Gullah, was spoken on some of the Sea Islands along the Georgia–South Carolina coast. Slaves also established elaborate and enduring kinship networks. They created an extensive internal market in provisions and crafted goods such as ceramic pots. The practice of using black slaves as drivers created opportunities to negotiate concessions, the most important of which was the task system of labor management. By persuading planters to agree to a specified quota of work per slave per day, drivers and field slaves managed to limit the number of hours spent working on the master's crop and preserved some time for cultivating provisions, raising families, and socializing. The life of an eighteenth-century field slave remained difficult, but such developments may have helped reduce the more dehumanizing aspects of bondage on South Carolina's rice and indigo plantations.

The hardening of racial lines that attended rice and indigo cultivation propelled divergent changes on the Carolina frontier and in Charleston. Slaves, free blacks, and mulattoes, all of whom had experienced a more fluid environment on the seventeenth-century frontier, responded to shifts in race relations by fleeing to Indian country or to Spanish Florida. Groups of runaway slaves also found hiding places in the low-country swamps where they could form mobile Maroon communities and evade capture for long periods. Maroon communities remained small— rarely more than two or three dozen—and no one knows how many slaves became Maroons. Blacks who reached Cherokee, Chickasaw, or Choctaw villages were often able to exchange an African for an Indian identity through adoption into the local community (see Chapter 11). Those who reached St. Augustine could join a growing black community whose freedom was guaranteed by the Spanish Crown and defended by the guns of the San Marcos *castillo*. The governor of Florida continued extending sanctuary to runaway slaves until 1748 as a means of destabilizing South Carolina and Georgia.

In Charleston, African American women and men created a distinctive urban culture. Mulattos who had gained their freedom by the early eighteenth century sought to protect their hard-won status by avoiding contact with slaves and passing wherever possible into white society. By the 1750s, Charleston's slaves managed to accumulate a range of concessions that gave them significant, though still limited, autonomy. The demand for skilled labor permitted male slave artisans to earn money for themselves after satisfying their daily obligations to the master. As in the Caribbean, some artisans gained permission to set up their own households, and a tiny minority earned enough to purchase their freedom.

Many of Charleston's slave women also found opportunities for employment and profit outside their masters' households. Some made tidy sums as cooks, seamstresses, or weavers. Many others became prosperous hawkers of consumer goods, which they marketed from street carts. Still others opened shops and taverns that catered to an African American clientele. Groups of younger slave women developed thriving clandestine markets in prostitution, organizing balls for entertaining sailors, merchants, and planters alike. This choice of profession registered the terrible constraints that confronted African women in Charleston, yet those who followed it often found themselves able, like the hawkers, cooks, and seamstresses, to dress fashionably, adorn themselves with watches or jewelry, and gain a measure of control over their lives. Even so, the visitor Benjamin West observed that these "genteelly dressed" slaves had to endure "their full share of floggings."

White South Carolinians found the relative liberty and prosperity of Charles Town's slaves unsettling. Critics decried the slaves' appetite for luxury in the *South Carolina Gazette*. Legislators tried to curtail slave spending through sumptuary laws that prohibited slaves from wearing finery considered appropriate only for free white gentry. Yet white buyers continued to generate profits for African American consumers by hiring slave tradesmen and patronizing slave-run enterprises. Slaves simply ignored the sumptuary laws and continued to adorn themselves with the scraps of self-assertion they had managed to wrest from the masters' grudging grasp.

A significantly different pattern emerged in the tobacco-producing regions of the Chesapeake and Virginia Piedmont. There the black population, though large, never reached more than 40 percent of the total. Most slaves lived in groups of twenty or less on moderately sized plantations with a resident white master or

Slave Life on the Tobacco Plantations

overseer, his wife, and children. Several great planter families held well over a hundred slaves, and the largest held over three hundred. But even these planters tended to divide their workforce into smaller units that they scattered throughout the Chesapeake and Piedmont on multiple holdings of a few hundred acres each. These factors established an environment of frequent contact among Europeans and Africans and regular communication among white and black residents on neighboring plantations.

Tobacco cultivation was not so onerous as labor in a rice field, but it kept slaves busy throughout the year at tedious, time-consuming tasks. The season began with sowing seed into small, protected seedbeds "as early after Christmas as the weather will permit." During the next few months as the seedlings grew, slaves hoed the main fields into rows of small tobacco hills in preparation for transplanting. During the anxious months of April, May, and early June, the entire workforce, children included, awaited downpours that would loosen the soil and permit the wet labor of transplanting the seedlings without damage. The summer occupied the slaves in daily tasks of weeding, "topping"—removing the flowering portion of the plant—and pruning each plant of suckers to encourage maximum growth in the leaves. September brought the cutting season, a critical time when the ripe plants were gathered and hung in barns for curing. Once plants had dried to exactly the right point—a condition known as "case"—slaves began to "prize" them into hogsheads (barrels) for shipping. Planters who received the highest returns also put skilled slaves to work before packing in "stemming," or removing all stem fibers from the leaves, a delicate and boring process that kept those involved working deep into the nights. If everything went perfectly, the heavy hogsheads were ready for shipping by Christmas, leaving just a few days to celebrate the holiday before the cycle began once again.

This work regimen, along with other factors, hindered Chesapeake slaves from creating the African patterns of economy and agricultural life that emerged in the rice country. Masters organized their laborers into gangs which worked long days in the fields, leaving less time for discretionary activities. Slaves cultivated small gardens and raised a few barnyard fowl, but rarely produced enough for sale on a larger market. Masters rationed out staples of corn and meat while providing their slaves specified allotments of fabric or clothing each year. The predominance of Creole over African slaves in the Chesapeake tended to inhibit the survival of African customs. Creole blacks learned to cope with whites on a daily basis and looked with contempt on slaves who had just arrived from Africa. "Outlandish" Negroes were forced by blacks as well as whites to accept elements of English culture. It was especially important for newcomers to speak English. Consider, for example, the pain of twelve-year-old Olaudah Equiano, an African sold in Virginia in 1757. "I was now exceedingly miserable," Equiano later recalled, "and thought myself worse off than any . . . of my companions; for they could talk to each other [in English], but I had no person to speak to that I could understand. In this state I was constantly grieving and pining, and wishing for death."

If the presence of a large percentage of Creoles made life difficult for salt-water slaves, it also facilitated the growth of family life. Masters took an active interest in promoting slave families as well, if only to encourage the growth of a self-reproducing labor force. Chesapeake slaves parlayed this interest into a series of concessions that achieved some security for family life. In addition to granting visitation privileges to spouses living on separate plantations, masters sometimes agreed to purchase spouses so that couples could live together. Women demanded a period of respite from field work to breast-feed their infants. Husbands saw to it that their pregnant wives and young families received food beyond the daily ration. A new area of negotiation and resistance emerged as parents contested with planters for greater control over their children's upbringing and work patterns. Masters who refused to grant such concessions often found themselves paying for their reluctance as aggrieved slaves ran away, refused to work, or sabotaged tools or crops. Eventually, most masters chose to endure the inconvenience of concessions.

By the 1750s, the maturation of Chesapeake tobacco culture had brought a measure of stability to plantation life, while previous years' prosperity combined with the decline of tobacco production motivated planters to diversify. Many planters sought to create relatively self-sufficient estates where skilled slaves provided most essential trades and produced most of the food consumed on the plantation. Some planters began producing wheat and other small grains for export as well. Grain required much less attention than tobacco, and slaves who cultivated it gained time for other economic activities. Some began tending draft animals and livestock; others moved into related trades as wagoners, tanners, and leather workers. The growth of modest urban centers such as Williamsburg and Baltimore opened opportunities for more slaves to move into domestic service and trades in the towns. Like those in other urban areas, Chesapeake slave artisans often hired themselves out on their own time to gain a modest source of independent income. A few slave artisans in the Chesapeake as in South Carolina managed to save enough to purchase their freedom.

These developments broadened the range of African American experience and opened new fields of struggle between slaves and masters for control of time, labor, and resources. Yet masters always commanded by far the greatest share of power in this contest. All aspects of slave life—family, customary privileges, discretionary time and earnings—remained fragile, their continuation always subject to the master's pleasure.

Slaves and Free Blacks in the North

In the New England and Middle Colonies, African Americans made up a far smaller percentage of the population. A combination of natural increase and significant importation boosted the mid-eighteenth-century slave population to 8 percent of the total in Pennsylvania, 10 percent in New Jersey, 16 percent in the five southernmost counties of New York, and 3 percent in Massachusetts. In such environments, contact between blacks and whites became even more frequent than in the Chesapeake. Slaves worked at a far greater variety of tasks, often side by side with white servants, laborers, or masters. Those working outside of the cities most often served as field hands on a family farm, though Pennsylvania's nascent iron industry brought groups of slaves together to labor in mines and foundries. In northern cities, most slaves worked as domestics or artisans and lived in the houses of their masters. Urban slaves saw other blacks more frequently than did those living on family farms, but they had far less opportunity than southern blacks to develop Creole languages or reaffirm a common African past.

Family life among northern slaves proved very hard to sustain. Few masters maintained more than one or two domestics or artisans, which meant that most slave couples lived in separate households. Masters discouraged childbearing among their female slaves because of the expense and loss of labor it entailed, and many sold slave women at the first sign of pregnancy. Masters frequently failed or refused to provide enough food for slave families, producing high infant mortality rates among northern blacks. Nevertheless, many slaves defied the odds, marrying and doing their best to sustain the relationship despite living in households several miles apart.

Northern slaves had to adopt more European cultural forms in order to survive. First-generation Africans arriving in the north soon learned to speak English proficiently, and those working for Dutch masters learned that language as well. An increasing number learned to read and write. Literacy enabled black slaves to participate in a greater range of activities as well as to bid for freedom by forging passes and documents. A few eventually applied their writing skills to poetry and prose. Colonial African American poets Phillis Wheatley and Jupiter Hammond gained enduring fame through such literary efforts. Black musicians learned to play the fiddle, combining African and European elements into ballads and dance tunes that became popular throughout the north. Many northern blacks embraced Christianity during the Great Awakening of the 1740s and became sought-after lay preachers who followed their calling in itinerant ministries. Just as blacks in New York and New Jersey made Pinkster their own, so those in New England adapted Election Day to a similar role. On Negro Election Day, black people dressed in their finest and traveled from the surrounding countryside to a central town such as Boston or Newport. There, amid raucous celebration that mingled African music and dance with Anglo-American elements, participants elected a state of black kings, governors, and judges. Both Pinkster and Negro Election Day offered one of the few times during the year in which slaves could share remembered traditions using African musical instruments, dance, and song. Both also provided slaves an opportunity to assert a separate identity in ritual role reversals that mocked white society.

The northern colonies also hosted a small population of free blacks, but it began to dwindle in the eighteenth century as slavery took greater hold. Many who remained free were descendants of black slaves who had been brought to a northern colony in the seventeenth century and later gained freedom there. Others were descendants of free blacks who migrated north as hardening racial lines closed opportunities for them in the Chesapeake. An unknown percentage were fugitive slaves who escaped detection to build new lives for themselves as free people, and a small number were slaves manumitted by northern masters, often through a will after the owner's death. Such candidates for manumission often continued languishing in slavery for years while the estate was being settled.

Free blacks found themselves occupying an increasingly marginal status in the eighteenth-century North. They pursued many of the same occupations as did slaves. A small number owned farms. Augustine and Rachel Van Donck, for instance, operated a small cattle farm near Tappan, New Jersey from the late 1720s until the 1770s, when they parceled it out to their three children. Yet the prosperity and status of free blacks slipped as northern colonial law strengthened the structural links between race and slavery. Free blacks were often barred from voting and serving on juries. Some colonies or localities required them to carry a pass when traveling and to obtain special licenses to trade or carry a firearm. Colonies such as Pennsylvania established special courts for trying free blacks as well as slaves, and made some offenses committed by free blacks punishable by enslavement.

Recent scholarship has discovered that during the eighteenth century many black men gained a degree of personal freedom by working as boatmen, fishermen, or mariners. Many first-generation slaves brought considerable skills from their homelands along African rivers and coasts. Masters were quick to put these skills to use in an expanding commercial environment that relied heavily on water transport. South Carolina slaves constructed large dugout canoes known as "pettiaugers" and painted them in bright colors reminiscent of styles familiar in their homeland. They poled, paddled, or rowed these canoes through the labyrinth of low-country waterways, becoming intimately familiar with them. North Carolina boatmen became similarly familiar with the numerous inlets and waterways along that coast. The largest of the pettiaugers frequently sported a mast and sail that could carry its navigator and cargo out into open water.

Coastal Blacks— Boatmen, Fishermen, Sailors

Slaves became proficient fishermen as well, another skill they brought from Africa and adapted to North American conditions. African slaves knew how to obtain large catches by drugging the fish in a stream or using special seines and weirs to capture them. They also possessed considerable skill in coastal fishing, which masters often exploited to supplement provisions for their labor force. Slaves and free blacks exploited the skill as well, plying an independent trade that gained them considerable profit.

Many eighteenth-century blacks also set out to sea. It is now estimated that by 1803, African Americans held at least 18 percent of all jobs open to American seamen, and although the number of positions may have been fewer before the Revolution, black colonial sailors—many of them slaves—sought work on sailing vessels to escape the drudgery of life on rice or tobacco plantations. Knowledge of sailing could provide runaways an avenue to freedom, and many notices cautioned "all masters of vessels" not to carry runaway sailors out of a colony. These African American seamen connected black communities scattered throughout the Caribbean and along the mainland coast, bringing news about distant rebellions and spreading radical political ideologies to slaves who might otherwise not have known much about the transforming events of the eighteenth century.

A WORLD WITHIN A WORLD

Eighteenth-century masters and slaves alike lived amid a swirl of expanding horizons, burgeoning growth, and rapid change. Planters had to remain constantly attentive and diligent in managing their affairs if they hoped to thrive in this unforgiving environment, where so many factors lay beyond anyone's control. The South Carolina overseer Josiah Smith, Jr. reminded his absentee employer, George

Austin, that to turn a profit, a rice planter had to keep a steady eye on the fluctuations of the market, seizing opportunities to sell on favorable terms without fixating too rigidly on the exact price he would consider acceptable. He had to remain attentive to seasonal shipping patterns, the price of storage, and the effects of long-term storage on the quality of his crop. He had to remain abreast of transatlantic events in politics and international relations that could affect trade. In short, an "able Planter" must remain "ever employ'd in the contriving every thing that can make for their Advantage, save every Expence that can possibly be avoided, & often by hard-driving, save a Crop from Destruction." Such persons, Smith declared, "have enrich'd themselves very much, especially of late years by the hard Labour & Sweat of wretched Slaves."

Smith's observations remind us that, from the masters' perspective, the slaves' primary place in this colonial commercial world was to provide the "hard Labour & Sweat" that produced their profits. All other contributions they made to that world—the thriving Sunday markets, the colorful pettiaugers, the production of "country cloth," the lively music, the herbal remedies, the nursing and tending of the masters' children—remained subordinate to their role as laborers in the staples that maintained the circulation of people and goods in the British Atlantic.

By choosing to fill that role with enslaved Africans, Europeans had created a world that by the first third of the eighteenth century was explicitly divided by race and power. The master-slave relationship was permeated with calculation. No other relationship in eighteenth-century America matched it. Every conversation between master and slave, every show of affection, every outburst of anger, every stroke of the whip, marked an exchange between owner and owned. Very few transactions remained free of the calculus of exploitation, negotiation, resistance, and concession between profoundly unequal parties. Masters took all they could and rarely conceded anything to their slaves without a fight. Slaves gave what the balance of power prevented them from keeping—their labor, their bodies, often their very lives.

This contradiction of owning a person as property rested at the heart of the eighteenth-century British Empire. Its dynamic framed the conditions for the emergence of an African American world that was both an indispensable element of the larger British Atlantic world and inaccessibly other. Slaves like the Virginia runaway Peter Deadfoot exhibited intelligence and resourcefulness that their masters could not help admiring. Deadfoot became "an indifferent shoemaker, a good butcher, ploughman, and carter; an excellent sawyer, and waterman, understands breaking oxen well, and is one of the best scythemen, either with or without a cradle, in *America*: in short, he is so ingenious a fellow, that he can turn his hand to any thing."

The African Diaspora in the British Atlantic was replete with men and women who employed their collective ingenuity in adapting to the harsh economic and social environments where they found themselves so violently thrust. They contributed their labor to the products others consumed, the prosperity others enjoyed, the fashions others displayed, the houses in which others lived. They built their own worlds from resources others considered stolen—fragments of time, material, and human relationships that others grudgingly conceded because of the slaves' desperate persistence. Out of this patchwork of suffering and pain, of worn remnants, broken tools, broken bodies, broken families, broken lives, they created cultures of enduring beauty and sustaining power.

CHRONOLOGY

1696	South Carolina passes colony's first slave code.
1700	Black population of British Caribbean and colonial American mainland at 200,000; less than 20,000 blacks on mainland.
1701	Annual imports of West Indian sugar to Great Britain total £210,000; imports of Chesapeake tobacco to Great Britain total £83,000; imports of south Carolina rice to Great Britain are negligible.
1705	Virginia slave code passed.
1729	Average slave imports to Jamaica reach 7,200 yearly.
1739	Stono Uprising breaks out in South Carolina.
1741	Rumored slave plot to burn New York City prompts execution of 34 suspected arsonists.
1750	Black population of British Caribbean and colonial American mainland at 542,000; 247,000 on mainland.
1760	Tacky's Rebellion breaks out in Jamaica.
1774	Annual value of West Indian sugar imported to Great Britain totals £787,000; annual value of West Indian sugar to colonial American mainland, £723,000; annual value of Chesapeake tobacco imported to Great Britain totals £173,000; annual value of Carolina rice imported to Great Britain totals £340,000.

RECOMMENDED READING

A vast body of rich and highly sophisticated scholarship on slavery and early African American culture has emerged in the past thirty years. A good comparative analysis of African experience on the colonial American mainland and the British West Indies is Michael Mullin, *Africa in America: Slave Acculturation and Resistance in the American South and the British Caribbean, 1736–1831* (Urbana, 1992), while Ira Berlin and Philip D. Morgan have edited an excellent collection of comparative essays on New World slavery, *Cultivation and Culture: Labor and the Shaping of Slave Life in the Americas* (Charlottesville, 1993). The most comprehensive analysis of the slave experience in colonial North America is Ira Berlin, *Many Thousands Gone: The First Two Centuries of Slavery in North America* (Cambridge, Mass., 1998), while the richest comparative study of slavery in the Chesapeake and the Lower South is Philip D. Morgan, *Slave Counterpoint: Black Culture in the Eighteenth-Century Chesapeake and Lowcountry* (Chapel Hill, 1998). For a survey of Caribbean slavery, see Herbert S. Klein, *African Slavery in Latin America and the Caribbean* (New York, 1986).

For the economic background of slavery in the British Atlantic, see Jacob M. Price, *Capital and Credit in the British Overseas Trade* (Cambridge, 1980), as well as John J. McCusker and Russell R. Menard, *The Economy of British America, 1607–1789* (Chapel Hill, 1985). David Eltis explores the relationship between Atlantic economic developments and the slave trade in *The Rise of African Slavery in the Americas* (Cambridge, 2000). For a provocative analysis of the role of sugar in the Atlantic economy, see Sidney W. Mintz, *Sweetness and Power: The Place of Sugar in Modern History* (New York, 1985).

Additional studies of African American culture in the eighteenth-century Chesapeake include Alan Kulikoff, *Tobacco and Slaves: The Development of Southern Cultures in the Chesapeake, 1680–1800* (Chapel Hill, 1986), and Mechal Sobel, *The World They Made Together: Black and White Values in Eighteenth-Century Virginia* (Princeton, 1987). Peter Wood's *Black Majority: Negroes in Colonial South Carolina from 1670 Through the Stono Rebellion* (New York, 1974) remains a pathbreaking study of the emergence of slavery and the development of African American culture in the low-country South. Leland Ferguson's *Uncommon Ground: Archaeology and Early African America, 1650–1800* (Washington, 1992) explores the material culture of North American slaves. Graham Russell Hodges explores one facet of northern black experience in *Root and Branch: African Americans in New York and East Jersey, 1613–1863* (Chapel Hill, 1998), while Gary B. Nash analyzes the development of African American community life in Philadelphia in his *Forging Freedom: The Formation of Philadelphia's Black Community, 1720–1840* (Cambridge, Mass., 1988).

Studies of specific island societies include David Barry Gaspar, *Bondmen and Rebels: A Study of Master-Slave Relations in Antigua with Implications for North America* (Baltimore, 1985); Jerome S. Handler and Frederick W. Lange, *Plantation Slavery in Barbados: An Archaeological and Historical Investigation* (Cambridge, Mass., 1978); and Douglas Hall, *In Miserable Slavery: Thomas Thistlewood in Jamaica, 1750–86* (London, 1989).

Several recent studies explore specific themes in colonial black experience and culture. Two excellent collections of essays discuss aspects of sex, gender, family life, and women's experience in colonial African American communities: David Barry Gaspar and Darlene Clark Hine, eds., *More than Chattel: Black Women and Slavery in the Americas* (Bloomington, Ind., 1996), and Catherine Clinton and Michele Gillespie, eds., *The Devil's Lane: Sex and Race in the Early South* (New York, 1997). Sylvia R. Frey and Betty Wood explore the incorporation of Protestant Christianity into Atlantic African American culture in *Come Shouting to Zion: African American Protestantism in the American South and British Caribbean to 1830* (Chapel Hill, 1998). W. Jeffrey Bolster analyzes the experience of African American seamen in his *Black Jacks: African American Seamen in the Age of Sail* (Cambridge, Mass., 1998).

Chapter 14

Contesting Rule in a Commercial Empire

I n the summer of 1749, Captain Pierre-Joseph Céloron de Blainville led
an armed flotilla of canoes down the Allegheny and Ohio Rivers to reassert France's claims to the region's territory and trade. The French envoy
well knew he was entering lands controlled by native peoples who were determined to preserve their independence and to trade wherever they could
obtain the best prices. All along his route, Céloron found depressing evidence that the English were winning the contest for Ohio country markets.

Céloron did what he could to discourage the natives' trade with the
English. At one village where he found a newly constructed English trading
post, the captain made the inhabitants promise to turn away the traders and
leave the unfinished building "only . . . to amuse the youth." At several others Céloron caught up with English traders themselves. He sent them back to
their home governments with letters warning the English to stay away from
the "Belle Rivière." At the Western Iroquois or Mingo town, Chiningue,
which the English called Logstown, Céloron noted that the "cheap market
which the English offered" had drawn Indians from areas within New France
itself: "some Iroquois from Sault St. Louis, from the Lake of Two Mountains
[both near Montreal]; some Nepassingues, Abanakes, Ottowas and other nations." Despite his efforts to dissuade them, Céloron recognized that
Logstown's inhabitants remained committed to trade with the English. So
too did the people of the Shawnee town of Sonioto further down the Ohio.

With many of the Ohio country Indians "drawn into a very bad disposition for" the French, Céloron had to act with extreme caution. Indeed, the
inhabitants of Logstown and Sonioto signaled their defiance by firing

English-supplied musket balls into the air over the heads of Céloron's soldiers. Despite such moments of tension, the captain managed to avoid bloodshed in his quest to "reassure the natives of these countries" and "treat with them of good things." In councils with local leaders Céloron expressed surprise at their disloyalty to "their father Onontio," the governor of Canada, and warned that the English harbored intentions for their "entire ruin." "They will make themselves masters of this whole country and drive you away if I would let them do so," the French envoy cautioned. To mark the Ohio as French territory, Céloron's men also buried several lead plates at various points in the riverbank, each accompanied by a French royal coat of arms nailed to a nearby tree.

Céloron's mission to the Ohio offers a glimpse of how the contest for North American empire was intensifying at mid-century. Although the balance of trade occupied the captain's immediate attention, his speeches to native leaders reveal the French conviction that the land itself was at stake. By 1749 the pattern had become clear. Where commercial exchange remained the focus of Franco-Indian relations, English traders formed but the advance guard of a swarming population intent on transforming the entire Ohio landscape, clearing the countryside of trees and game to make room for European crops and livestock.

Yet even though the Ohio country Indians recognized the truth of Céloron's warnings, the enticement of cheap British goods proved hard to resist (see Chapter 12). In this great contest for North American empire, the advantage was shifting to the English. Céloron doubted whether "the nations of these places . . . can be reclaimed." Military force could not easily bring the Ohio Country Indians to terms because the Indians could readily flee to "a grand refuge in the flat plains from which they are not far." Moreover, the French traders could "never give our merchandise at the price the English do." Indeed, Céloron mused, Canadian traders earned most of their own profits through clandestine trade, exchanging beaver pelts to the English for other "peltry, cats, otters, and skins" which fetched higher prices on the French market. This experienced military man could see only one solution: to "make a strong defense," fortifying strategic locations in the Ohio country.

The eighteenth-century contest for empire lay behind many of the period's most important political developments. The French threat pushed Anglo-American colonists to adapt political and military institutions that could raise the increasing amounts of funds and troops needed for defense. In the process, a distinctive imperial relationship emerged between colonial governments and the administration in London, one defined by a mutual need for accommodation and compromise to maintain the bonds of empire. As Anglo-French conflict intensified toward mid-century, leaders of various English colonies also began seeking ways to overcome mutual suspicions and devise unprecedented measures for intercolonial military and political cooperation.

Native Americans remained crucial participants in these efforts, situated as they were between these great imperial rivals who competed for native trade and military alliance. Indeed, native peoples found it difficult to avoid entanglement in the intensifying contest for empire. They responded by adapting their own institutions of leadership and interethnic cooperation to preserve native independence against European encroachment. As the century progressed, however, their efforts increasingly took on the character of rearguard actions, responses to imperial policies set by distant European kings.

POLITICS AND EMPIRE

The political history of eighteenth-century North America illuminates the growing tensions of empire. The colonial administrations of North America's European rivals mirrored in many respects the forms of rule known in the parent countries. Yet varying economic conditions, local circumstances, and imperial pressures produced differences that set the colonial political cultures apart.

Anglo-Americans of all regions repeatedly stated their desire to replicate British political institutions. Parliament, they claimed, provided a model for the American assemblies. They revered the English constitution. However, the more that the colonists studied British political theory and practice—in other words, the more that they attempted to become British—the more aware they became of major differences. By trying to copy Great Britain, they unwittingly discovered something about being American.

Eighteenth-century French and Spanish colonial government possessed a more sharply military cast. Colonial governors were always experienced officers who exercised supreme authority over both military and civil affairs, frequently combining the two. Indeed, the entire government of New France reflected a military chain of command under the governor-general, who oversaw all colonial administration, and the intendants, who oversaw military supply as well as civil matters. Yet to visitors, the *habitants* of New France seemed remarkably unburdened by taxes or regulations, proud, and independent.

The English Constitution

During the eighteenth century, Anglo-American political discussion began with the British constitution. It was the object of universal admiration among leaders of Europe's Enlightenment. Unlike the U.S. Constitution of 1787, the British constitution was not a formal written document. It was something much more elusive. The English constitution found expression in a growing body of law, court decisions, and statutes, a sense of traditional political arrangements that people of all classes believed had evolved from the past, preserving life, liberty, and property. Eighteenth-century political commentators reluctantly admitted that the English constitution had in fact changed. Historic confrontations between king and Parliament had generated new understandings about what the constitution did or did not allow. Nevertheless, almost everyone regarded change as dangerous and destabilizing, a threat to the political tradition that seemed to explain Britain's greatness.

In theory, the English constitution contained three distinct parts. The monarch was at the top, advised by handpicked court favorites. Next came the House of Lords, a body of 180 aristocrats who served with 26 Anglican bishops as the upper house of Parliament. And third was the House of Commons, composed of 558 members elected by various constituencies scattered throughout the realm.

Political theorists waxed eloquent on the workings of the British constitution. Each of the three parts of England's "mixed government," it seemed, represented a separate socioeconomic interest: king, nobility, and common people. Acting alone, each body would run to excess, even tyranny, but operating within a mixed system, they automatically checked one another's ambitions for the greater common good. "Herein consists the excellence of the English government," explained the famed eighteenth-century jurist Sir William Blackstone, "that all parts of it form a mutual check upon each other." Unlike the delegates who wrote the Constitution of the United States, eighteenth-century Englishmen did not perceive their constitution as a balance of executive, legislative, and judicial branches.

The Reality of British Politics

The reality of daily political life in Great Britain, however, bore little relation to theory. The three elements of the constitution did not, in fact, represent distinct socioeconomic groups. Men elected to the House of Commons often came from the same social background as those who served in the House of Lords. All represented the interests of Britain's landed elite. Moreover, there was no attempt to maintain strict constitutional separation. The king, for example, organized parliamentary associations, loose groups of political followers who sat in the House of Commons and who openly supported the monarch's policies in exchange for patronage or pension.

The claim that the members of the House of Commons represented all the people of England also seemed far-fetched. As of 1715, no more than 20 percent of Britain's adult males had the right to vote. Property qualifications or other restrictions often greatly reduced the number of eligible voters. In addition, the size of the electoral districts varied throughout the kingdom. In some boroughs—towns that could elect a member of Parliament—representatives were chosen by several thousand voters. In many districts, however, a handful of electors controlled the result. These tiny, or "rotten," boroughs were an embarrassment. The Methodist leader John Wesley complained that Old Sarum, an almost uninhabited borough, "in spite of common sense, without house or inhabitant, still sends two members to the parliament." Because these districts were so small, a wealthy lord or ambitious politician could easily bribe or otherwise "influence" the entire constituency, a regular practice throughout the century.

Before 1760, few people spoke out against these constitutional abuses. The main exception was a group of radical publicists whom historians have labeled the Commonwealthmen. These writers decried the corruption of political life, noting that a nation that compromised civic virtue, that failed to stand vigilant against fawning courtiers and would-be despots, deserved to lose its liberty and property. The most famous Commonwealthmen were John Trenchard and Thomas Gordon, who between 1720 and 1723 penned a series of essays titled *Cato's Letters*. If England's rulers were corrupt, they warned, then the people could not expect the balanced constitution to save them from tyranny. In one typical article, Trenchard and Gordon observed, "The Appitites . . . of Men, especially of Great Men, are carefully to be observed and stayed, or else they will never stay themselves. The Experience of every Age convinces us, that we must not judge of Men by what they ought to do, but by what they will do."

But however shrilly these writers protested, they won little support for political reforms. Most eighteenth-century Englishmen admitted that there was more than a grain of truth in the commonwealth critique, but they were not willing to tamper with a system of government that had so recently survived a civil war and a Glorious Revolution. Americans, however, took Trenchard and Gordon to heart.

The American mainland colonists assumed—perhaps naively—that their own governments were modeled on the balanced constitution of Great Britain. They argued that within their political systems, the governor corresponded to the king and the governor's council to the House of Lords. The colonial assemblies were perceived as American reproductions of the House of Commons and were expected to preserve the interests of the people against those of the monarch and aristocracy. As the colonists discovered, however, general theories about a mixed constitution were even less relevant in America than they were in Britain.

Governing England's Colonies: The North American Experience

By mid-century a majority of the American mainland colonies had royal governors appointed by the crown. Many were career army officers who through luck, charm, or family connection had gained the ear of someone close to the king. These patronage posts did not generate income sufficient to interest the most powerful or talented personalities of the period, but they did draw middle-level bureaucrats who were ambitious, desperate, or both. It is perhaps not surprising that most governors decided simply not to "consider any Thing further than how to sit easy."

George Clinton, who served as New York's governor from 1743 to 1753, was probably typical of the men who hoped to "sit easy." Before coming to the colonies, Clinton had compiled an extraordinary record of ineptitude as a naval officer. He gained the governorship more as a means to get him out of England than as a sign of respect. When he arrived in New York City, Clinton ignored the colonists. "In a province given to hospitality" wrote one critic, "he [Clinton] erred by immuring himself in the fort, or retiring to a grotto in the country, where his time was spent with his bottle and a little trifling circle."

Whatever their demerits, royal governors in America possessed enormous powers. In fact, royal governors could do certain things in America that a king could not do in eighteenth-century Great Britain. Among these powers were the rights to veto legislation and dismiss judges. The governors also served as military commanders in each colony.

Political practice in America differed from the British model in another crucial respect. Royal governors were advised by a council, usually a body of about twelve wealthy colonists selected by the Board of Trade in London upon the recommendation of the governor. During the seventeenth century, the council had played an important role in colonial government, but its ability to exercise independent authority declined steadily over the course of the eighteenth century. Its members certainly did not represent a distinct aristocracy within American society.

If royal governors did not look like kings, nor American councils like the House of Lords, colonial assemblies bore little resemblance to the eighteenth-century House of Commons. The major difference was the size of the American electorate. In most colonies, adult white males who owned a small amount of land could vote in colonywide elections. One historian estimates that in Massachusetts 95 percent of adult white male property owners were eligible to participate in elections. The number in Virginia was about 85 percent. These figures—much higher than those in Great Britain during the same period—have led some scholars to view the colonies as "middle-class democracies," societies run by moderately prosperous yeomen farmers who—in politics at least—exercised independent judgment. There were too many of them to bribe, no "rotten" boroughs, and when these people moved west, colonial assemblies usually created new electoral districts.

Colonial governments were not democracies in the modern sense of that term, however. Possessing the right to vote was one thing, exercising it quite another. Colonial Americans participated in elections when major issues were at stake—the formation of banks in mid-eighteenth-century Massachusetts, for example—but most of the time they were content to let members of the rural and urban gentry represent them in the assemblies. To be sure, colonial governments excluded women and nonwhites from voting. The point to remember, however, is that the power to expel legislative rascals was always present in America, and it was this political reality that kept autocratic gentlemen from straying too far from the will of the people.

Anglo-American Assemblies

Elected members of the colonial assemblies believed that they had a special obligation to preserve colonial liberties. They perceived any attack on the legislature as an assault on the rights of British Americans. Elected representatives brooked no criticism, and several colonial printers landed in jail because they criticized actions taken by a lower house.

So aggressive were these bodies in seizing privileges, determining procedures, and controlling money bills that some historians have described the political development of eighteenth-century America as "the rise of the assemblies." No doubt this is exaggerated, but the long series of imperial wars against the French, demanding large public expenditures, transformed the small, amateurish assemblies of the seventeenth century into the more professional, vigilant legislatures of the eighteenth century.

This political system seemed designed to generate hostility. There was simply no reason for colonial legislators to cooperate with appointed royal governors. Alexander Spotswood, Virginia's acting governor from 1710 to 1722, for example, attempted to institute a bold new land program backed by the Crown. He tried persuasion and gifts and, when these failed, chicanery. But the members of

Virginia's House of Burgesses refused to support a plan that did not suit their own interests. Before leaving office, Spotswood gave up trying to carry out royal policy in America. Instead, he allied himself with the local Virginia gentry who controlled the House as well as the Council, and because they awarded their new friend with large tracts of land, he became a wealthy man.

A few governors managed briefly to recreate in America the political culture of patronage, the system that eighteenth-century Englishmen took for granted. Most successful in this endeavor was William Shirley, who held office in Massachusetts from 1741 to 1757. The secret to his political successes in America was connection to people who held high office in Great Britain. But Shirley's practices—and those of men like him—clashed with colonial perceptions of politics. The colonists really believed in the purity of the balanced constitution. They insisted on complete separation of executive and legislative authority. Therefore, when Americans suspected a governor, or even some of their own representatives, of employing patronage to influence government decisions, their protests seem to have been lifted directly from the pages of *Cato's Letters*.

Weekly journals and newspapers offered a major source of shared political information as well as a forum for vigorous public debate on issues of the day (see Chapter 12). In New York and Massachusetts especially, weekly newspapers urged readers to preserve civic virtue and to exercise extreme vigilance against the spread of privileged power. In the first issue of the *Independent Reflector*, published in New York (November 30, 1752), the editor announced defiantly that no discouragement shall "deter me from vindicating the civil and religious RIGHTS of my Fellow-Creatures: From exposing the peculiar Deformity of publick Vice, and Corruption; and displaying the amiable Charms of Liberty, with the detestable Nature of Slavery and Oppression." Through such journals, a pattern of political rhetoric that in Great Britain had gained only marginal respectability became after 1765 America's normal form of political discourse.

The rise of the assemblies shaped American culture in other, subtler ways. Over the course of the century, the language of the law became increasingly Anglicized. The Board of Trade, the Privy Council, and Parliament scrutinized court decisions and legislative actions from all thirteen American mainland colonies. As a result, varying local legal practices that had been widespread during the seventeenth century became standardized. Indeed, according to one historian, the colonial legal system by 1750 "was substantially that of the mother country." Not surprisingly, many men who served in colonial assemblies were either lawyers or persons who had received legal training. When Americans from different regions met—as they frequently did in the years before the Revolution—they discovered that they shared a commitment to the preservation of the English common law.

As eighteenth-century political developments drew the colonists closer to England, they also brought Americans a greater awareness of each other. As their horizons widened, they learned they operated within the same general imperial system, and the problems confronting the Massachusetts House of Representatives were not too different from those facing Virginia's House of Burgesses or South Carolina's Commons House. Like the revivalists and merchants—people who crossed old boundaries—colonial legislators laid the foundation for a larger cultural identity.

Nevertheless, no real political unity emerged in the colonies prior to the 1760s. Colonial assemblies remained intensely focused on internal provincial concerns. In nearly every colony factions in which "court" politicians representing Crown or proprietary interests vied with "country" elements made up of coalitions representing various agricultural and commercial interests characterized political life. Some divisions, such as the one between New York's De Lancey and Livingston factions, pitted powerful merchant and landowning families against each other for influence and control of patronage. Competition for western land and Indian trade also sparked intercolonial rivalries that only intensified as the century wore on. By the early 1750s, for example, Pennsylvania was locked in a fierce struggle with Virginia over Ohio country lands while simultaneously laboring to fend off a bid by Connecticut agents for rights to the Wyoming Valley in eastern Pennsylvania along the Susquehanna River. Disputes over land and trade also pitted Virginia officials against South Carolina counterparts and New York agents against rivals from New Hampshire. Colonial agents in London lobbied for the interests of the colony or faction that employed them while working to undermine the influence of opponents. Such practices drew colonies closer to London even as they perpetuated intercolonial divisions.

Sugar and Politics in the British West Indies

The political history of the British West Indies mirrored that of the mainland British colonies in many respects. The legislatures of these wealthy plantation colonies proved if anything even more truculent in defending their rights against royal encroachment. Indeed, as early as 1651 the Barbados assembly had taken a stand which mainland assemblies would not dare until 1774 by denying parliamentary authority to legislate for them (see Chapter 6). Well into the 1750s, the Jamaican assembly remained unique among Anglo-American colonies in its refusal to insert into any law a clause allowing the Board of Trade to suspend its implementation until the law could be reviewed. West Indian colonists shared with their mainland counterparts the constitutional ideals of eighteenth-century Commonwealthmen such as Trenchard and Gordon.

Yet important differences marked the British West Indian political experience. The transience of the British population on most islands, coupled with the presence of black slave majorities on all, produced at least two distinctive features of politics in the British sugar islands. The first was the white minority's reliance on British regular army forces to control the volatile slave population. The British minority simply lacked the numbers to police their slaves. Absentee plantation owners and a large proportion of first-generation Africans exacerbated the problem. British West Indians lived in constant fear of slave resistance, escape, and rebellion. Indeed, before the British abolition of slavery in 1837, the sugar islands experienced 75 incidents of slave revolt (see Chapter 13). As a result, all British West Indian legislatures except Barbados voted large annual subsidies to maintain garrisons of British Redcoats on the islands. To be sure, the assemblies jealously guarded their exclusive rights to levy the local taxes from which these subsidies were paid. Nevertheless, their willing reliance on the British professional military for security contrasted sharply with mainland colonial opposition to a standing army.

The transience of the white West Indian population also contributed to much stronger ties of patronage and political influence in England. West Indian planter elites commonly viewed their residence on the islands as temporary and planned to return to England with fortunes sufficient to retire on a magnificent country estate. Planters built few schools and colleges, instead sending their sons to England to be educated. In England, planters' sons could establish friendships and connections with members of the English ruling and mercantile elites, strengthening networks of credit and influence that could benefit them if they returned to the islands. They could also hire others to manage their island plantations and remain in England, joining the growing community of West Indian returnees who dominated parts of London, Bath, and Bristol.

Members of the absentee West Indian planter community formed an important element of the most powerful colonial lobby in London. They helped shape English colonial policy in effective collaboration with the islands' official agents, powerful English merchants in the West Indies trade, and members of Parliament with West Indian connections. Mainland colonial agents resented the influence of the West Indian lobby, which often favored measures prejudicial to North American interests. While serving as agent for Pennsylvania in the 1760s, Benjamin Franklin complained that "the West Indies vastly outweigh us of the Northern Colonies" in Parliamentary influence.

The West Indian political experience drew the British inhabitants of the sugar islands far closer to England than to the mainland North American colonies. While commercial ties stimulated increasing interaction between the islands and the mainland, London exerted a far greater cultural and political pull. Few West Indian absentee families settled in British North America, and West Indian planters spurned colonial colleges, preferring to send their children to British universities which boasted "the ablest Teachers in every Branch." Many returning planters gained entry into the British ruling elite for themselves or their children through marriage, patronage, and reception of minor titles such as baronetcies. The frequent clash of mainland and West Indian interests in matters of policy also drove a wedge between the two parts of Britain's American empire.

Spanish Garrisons and the French River Empire

In the decades following the War of the Spanish Succession (see Chapter 10), British views concerning their imperial rivals underwent a gradual transformation as Spain's hold on North America slipped while France's seemed to grow stronger. Until the 1740s, officials in South Carolina and Georgia worried as much about the threat of Spanish Florida as did northern officials about the French in Canada. By the later 1740s, however, concerns about the Spanish waned as British officials everywhere became increasingly convinced of French designs to seize control of all North America.

Contrasting patterns of rule between French and Spanish North America help to account for this shift in Anglo-American anxieties. After 1713, Spanish colonial officials found themselves increasingly occupied with rearguard actions designed to preserve their tenuous hold on a few remaining northern outposts of its tottering empire. The Spanish presence in the Southeast consisted almost exclusively of three military garrisons, the Atlantic fortress of St. Augustine, the small Gulf coast Fort San Marcos de Apalachee near present-day Tallahassee, and the presidio of San Carlos de Austria on Pensacola Bay (see Chapter 10). St. Augustine remained a formidable bastion protecting the northernmost edge of Spain's Caribbean empire, one never conquered despite repeated attacks by the English. Yet its military governors lacked the resources to preserve order more than 50 miles beyond the fortress walls. Spanish officials chose to invest a greater proportion of their meager resources to securing Texas against French encroachment, but chronic lack of security and insufficient numbers of colonists hampered their efforts.

New France's river empire, on the other hand, drew grudging admiration from English observers who marveled at its leaders' ability to influence "an extent of country larger perhaps than all Europe . . . only with a few woods-men and Indians." English analysts credited this achievement to the combined effects of French colonial administration and shrewd Franco-native diplomacy. French rule in North America appeared highly centralized, with most colonial authority concentrated in the hands of the governor-general and the intendant. As the principal representative of the Crown, the Canadian governor-general maintained obedience to the monarchy and possessed exclusive jurisdiction over military affairs and diplomacy. Always a professional soldier, the governor-general exercised authority through a clear chain of command that included two lieutenant governors, one at Montreal and another at Trois-Rivières, as well as a militia captain in each parish who could muster all able-bodied men from sixteen to sixty years old.

The colonial intendant, though second to the governor-general in authority, wielded almost independent control over taxes, economic policy, and judicial matters. A Superior Council aided the intendant in meting out justice over New France by serving as a court of appeal from lower courts. The captains of parish militia also served the intendant by acting as local agents of civil administration and law enforcement. In practice, militia captains exercised this authority loosely. As *habitants*, they shared the peasant status of most of their neighbors, a factor that made them much more sympathetic in the administration of local justice than a member of the colonial nobility might have been. The absence of taxation, coupled with modest prosperity and a low crime rate, also made their jobs much easier. Indeed, visitors to New France frequently commented on how lightly the Canadians were governed. As Colonel Louis-Antoine de Bougainville remarked in 1757, "The ordinary habitants . . . pay no taxes . . . have the right to hunt and fish, and . . . live in a sort of independence."

However lightly it rested on the *habitants*, New France's government remained military in form. Indeed, the governor-general's authority extended beyond the militia to include a permanent army of *troupes de la marine*, whose officers by the eighteenth century had come to form a significant element of a true colonial aristocracy. Leading Canadian families avidly lobbied the governor and intendant to recommend their sons for commissions in the *troupes de la marine*. The governor-general's role in securing these commissions prompted the colonial aristocracy to curry his favor. The King's minister in France retained the exclusive right to grant these commissions, a policy that bound the loyalties of aspiring Canadians closely to the French Crown. English advocates of colonial reform admired this method of fostering a loyal Canadian aristocracy. Some urged the English ministry to adapt a similar system to Anglo-American colonies as a means of weaning the gentry from their annoying attachment to provincial charters and assemblies.

Canadians complemented the military organization of their settlements with an extensive network of alliances that usually treated native peoples as equal partners in trade and warfare. English official Thomas Pownall perceptively described the Franco-native treaties as founded and maintained "according to the true Spirit of the Indian Laws of Nations." Although French officials may have wanted to exercise full dominion over North American territory and its native inhabitants, they recognized that French numbers remained far too small for any such attempt. Indeed, their dependence on native partners required Canadians to continue accommodating native interests as they had since the early seventeenth century. By 1757, this policy of middle-ground accommodation, in Pownall's estimation, had won the French full access to the North American interior, where they could acquire a strategic "Knowledge of all the Waters, Passes, Portages, and Posts that may hold Command" of the continental waterways. French officials had used that knowledge to place a system of forts at strategic locations along the great interior waterways. Pownall rightly recognized that without the cooperation of native allies, "all the Power of France" could not support such an extensive military presence. "'Tis the Indian Interest alone," he observed, "that does maintain these Forts."

Power, Leadership, and Empire in Indian America

The constant flux of eighteenth-century diplomatic relations among French, Indians, and English reflected shifting balances of power within Native American communities. Since the close of the seventeenth century, native peoples had found it necessary to adjust their patterns of leadership, diplomacy, trade, and warfare to the permanent presence of competing European imperial powers. Some groups managed to respond more effectively than others.

Groups who remained loosely structured in semiautonomous bands under a multiplicity of local leaders often found themselves unable to hold on to power or land in the face of European encroachments. Delaware bands in Pennsylvania, for instance, steadily lost ground as English agents and settlers cut separate deals with various local headmen for rights to land and trade. Such headmen constantly resisted European efforts to make them subjects, guarding as best they could their power to act on their own initiative and manage their own affairs. Yet as Indians grew more dependent on imported goods, headmen often found themselves caught in a bind between a desire for autonomy and a need to hold on to prestige and power by maintaining the flow of trade. The dilemma proved almost impossible to escape, and many groups found themselves having to choose between abandoning tribal homelands for new hunting grounds further west or remaining in a condition of chronic poverty and dependence among a dominant English population. The Delawares, like several other eighteenth-century tribes within the Iroquois sphere of influence, faced a third alternative. They could escape subjugation to the English Crown by becoming clients of the Six Nations (see Chapter 11). Yet such groups resented client status and looked for opportunities to reassert their autonomy, often under new leaders who criticized the older headmen and called on native people to renounce European ways.

The Iroquois' strategic position between two great European imperial rivals continued to provide important advantages in trade and diplomacy during the first half of the eighteenth century. Iroquois leaders used their leverage well to preserve their status as the dominant native power in the Northeast. The creation of an Iroquois Confederacy in the 1690s to complement the older Iroquois League proved a very effective political adjustment to new economic and diplomatic realities, one that coincided with the emergence of new Anglo-American political practices in the aftermath of the Glorious Revolution. The Confederacy's flexible

This certificate issued by William Johnson, superintendent of Indian affairs, signifies an alliance between the English settlers and the Native Americans in the "middle ground." Calumets (ceremonial pipes), wampum belts, and medals were other tokens used to mark alliances.

Collection of The New York Historical Society, (Neg #27844)

system of alliances enabled Iroquois headmen to respond to new opportunities and challenges in a comparatively unified manner. Its framework allowed them to incorporate the Tuscaroras as the sixth nation of the Iroquois in 1712 (see Chapter 10), as well as augment their strength by making clients of neighboring groups.

The inner workings of the Confederacy also permitted individual Iroquois leaders to use intercolonial rivalries to their own advantage as well as that of the Six Nations as a whole. Iroquois participation in Pennsylvania's infamous Walking Purchase of 1737 illuminates this dynamic. Although the transaction was a tragedy for the Delawares, who were defrauded of their lands (see Chapter 12), it increased the regional influence of the Oneida leader Shikellamy and the Seneca leader Hetaquantagechty by enabling them to assert authority over new Delaware clients. The prestige of the two rose even further when the Confederacy confirmed both the Walking Purchase and Delaware clientage on terms that Shikellamy, Hetaquantagechty, and three other leaders had at first negotiated on their own initiative. Other Iroquois headmen did not object to such independent action when its benefits to the Six Nations were so readily apparent. The Walking Purchase presented a golden opportunity not only to gain important new clients, but also to stir up rivalries among Pennsylvania, New York, and Maryland. In playing the three colonial governments against each other, the Confederacy shrewdly undercut their ability to act in concert against Iroquois interests.

Despite the Confederacy's flexibility and its leaders' formidable diplomatic skill, Iroquois power gradually eroded. By the late 1740s, the steady westward advance of traders from Pennsylvania and Virginia undercut Iroquois control over commerce in trans-Appalachian hunting grounds. It also enabled clients like the western Delawares and Shawnees, who had always resented Iroquois interference, to make fresh bids for self-determination in trade and communal affairs. Renewed French interest in the Ohio country after 1749 opened further opportunities for the western Indians to assert their independence by taking a page from Iroquois diplomacy itself, playing French, Six Nations', and rival Anglo-American colonial interests against one another.

The Ohio Indians' bid for power entailed enormous risk in the heightened imperial tensions of the mid-eighteenth century. The advancing line of English settlement, the renewed French effort to control commerce along the continent's great interior waterways, and the Indians' own chronic dependence on European imported goods all worked together increasingly to constrain the political and diplomatic options of all native groups east of the Mississippi River. The time was rapidly approaching when the options of most would be reduced to one decision: whether to side with England or France in a great war for North American empire.

THE CONTEST FOR EMPIRE

For nearly three decades after the close of Queen Anne's War in 1713, the great European rivals for North American empire remained officially at peace. Even so, English colonists frequently clashed with their French and Spanish counterparts over trade, territory, and shipping rights. Everyone involved recognized that a transatlantic contest for empire lay behind even the most seemingly minor inter-cultural dispute. Yet only gradually would the latent threat to security force people in different British colonies to overcome their mutual suspicion and begin devising measures for military and political cooperation.

On paper, at least, the British colonies enjoyed military superiority over their imperial rivals for North America. The small, demoralized border outposts of New Spain posed only a minor threat to the southernmost colonies, though St. Augustine's harbor did shelter Spanish privateers who could harass British vessels engaged in transatlantic or Caribbean trade. New France possessed a more exten-sive American empire, yet its population remained tiny in comparison to that of British America. In 1754, New France contained only 75,000 inhabitants as com-pared to 1.2 million people living in Britain's mainland colonies. Despite its mili-tary organization and the permanent presence of French *troupes de la marine*, the challenge of defending Canada's far-flung river empire seemed almost impossible for such small numbers.

For most of the century, the theoretical advantages enjoyed by the English colonists did them little good. Although the British settlements possessed a larger and more prosperous population, they were divided into separate governments that sometimes seemed more suspicious of one another than of the French. When war came, French officers and Indian allies exploited these jealousies with consid-erable skill. Moreover, although the population of New France was comparatively small, it was concentrated along the St. Lawrence River, so that although the French found it difficult to mount effective offensive operations against the English, they could easily mass the forces needed to defend Montreal and Quebec. Smaller outposts on the Mississippi at New Orleans and in Illinois were protected by their sheer remoteness from the English colonies.

Most importantly, the French colonists constantly cultivated the support of Native American allies in the regions they claimed. The propensity to overlook this factor led officials in eighteenth-century London—as well as many historians since—to underestimate the actual strength of France's American empire. Canadian military officers from the governor-general on down understood and ac-commodated to native ways of warfare. Canadian militiamen adopted native ways of fighting. They also acknowledged the right of native allies to engage in military action on their own terms, including the taking of captives for ritual torture or adoption and the taking of scalps as trophies of valor in battle. Such practices led not only the English, but also visiting French officers themselves, to view Canadian warriors as barbaric. Yet these practices gave the Canadians an advan-tage in terror and tactics in backcountry campaigns and helped secure the loyalty of native allies so long as the Indians could participate on their own terms.

During the 1720s and 1730s, the full strength of the three European rivals for empire remained untested even though an eighteenth-century version of cold war generated a string of skirmishes on the frontier and high seas. Parliamentary lead-ers in England were determined to preserve official peace, mainly so that they could hold the line on military expenditures. Yet the tensions could not remain suppressed forever either in America or in Europe. In the late 1730s a running feud between Anglo-American smugglers and Spanish privateers widened into open conflict between Spain and England. Once begun, the war took on a life of its own.

The fresh outbreak of transatlantic war originated in Anglo-Spanish disputes over trade and shipping rights. Throughout the first third of the eighteenth century, British and Anglo-American smugglers had been tapping into lucrative Spanish American markets. The clandestine trade brought manufactured goods to New Spain's ports in quantities far larger and at prices far lower than overregulated Spanish merchants could supply them. Smugglers returned with plantation goods and the Spanish "pieces of eight" that supplemented colonists' scarce supply of hard currency. To suppress this illicit trade, Spanish officials deployed often privately owned patrol vessels known as *guardacostas*, which possessed authority to stop and search suspected smugglers. The *guardacostas* became notorious for the harsh treatment they meted out to captured English sailors as well as for the questionable practice of seizing rival nations' ships in international waters.

Jenkins's Ear and War

The seamen's cause became a rallying point for English nationalism, and leaders of the parliamentary opposition to Sir Robert Walpole's ministry seized the moment to call for war on Spain to secure the "Freedom of the seas." The opposition's poster-boy for Spanish villainy was an obscure one-eared mariner named Robert Jenkins, who testified before Parliament in 1738 that Spanish *guardacostas* had cut off his ear without provocation after waylaying and plundering his ship. Captain Jenkins punctuated his testimony by displaying the severed member as tangible evidence of Spanish brutality. The captain's testimony helped pressure Walpole's ministry into issuing a declaration of war against Spain in 1739 that became known as the War of Jenkins's Ear.

In America, the war against Spain recapitulated exploits of the famed sixteenth-century Sea Dogs and the seventeenth-century English buccaneers. British Vice Admiral Edward Vernon led a small fleet to Jamaica, where he planned to stage a series of raids on Spanish targets. His first victory came at Portobelo on the coast of Panama, which Sir Henry Morgan had also raided in 1670. Vernon's booty of 10,000 Spanish dollars fell disappointingly short of Morgan's earlier £70,000 prize, but the admiral managed to disable a notorious haven for *guardacostas* and capture three of the hated vessels. Vernon's success encouraged an even more ambitious effort to capture the Spanish port of Cartagena on the coast of what is now Columbia, the starting point of the fabled treasure convoys of the *Carrera de Indias*. This campaign, which involved approximately 3,600 Anglo-American recruits, ended in miserable failure. The troops died like flies in the fever-ridden lowlands outside the fortress, and the tragic remnant who returned to their colonial homes became heroes merely for surviving the ordeal of Cartagena. One Virginia survivor, Lawrence Washington, commemorated the event by naming his family estate Mount Vernon after the commander of the Cartagena campaign.

In North America itself the war initially pitted a force from James Oglethorpe of Georgia against the Spanish fortress of San Marcos at St. Augustine. In 1740, Oglethorpe invaded with a combined force of 2,000 English, Creeks, Cherokees, and Chickasaws. The allies captured several outlying posts and laid siege to San Marcos for 38 days before a Spanish relief force from Cuba forced Oglethorpe's force to withdraw. The Spanish attempted to retaliate against Frederica, Georgia, in 1742, but withdrew after suffering defeat at the Battle of Bloody Marsh. The hostilities dragged on until 1748 in a series of inconclusive raids along the Georgia-Florida frontier, but the war soon widened and its main theater shifted north.

In 1743, France and England declared war on one another, dragging the Americans into a much wider imperial conflict. During King George's War (1743–1748), known in Europe as the War of the Austrian Succession, the colonists scored a magnificent victory over the French. Louisbourg, a gigantic fortress on Cape Breton Island, the easternmost promontory of Canada, guarded the approaches to the Gulf of St. Lawrence and Quebec. It was described as the Gibraltar of the New World. An army of New England troops under the command of William Pepperrell captured Louisbourg in June 1745, a feat which demonstrated that the British colonists were able to fight and to mount effective joint operations.

The Americans, however, were in for a shock. When the war ended with the signing of the Treaty of Aix-la-Chapelle in 1748, the British government handed Louisbourg back to the French in exchange for concessions elsewhere. Such decisions exposed the deep and continuing ambivalence the colonists felt about participation in imperial wars. They were proud to support Great Britain, of course, but the Americans seldom fully understood why the wars were being fought, why certain tactics had been adopted, and why the British accepted treaty terms that so blatantly ignored colonial interests.

Unstable Interlude

Officials of the exhausted Spanish empire welcomed the return of peace, and Anglo-Spanish relations improved after 1748. The French, on the other hand, were not prepared to surrender an inch of their vast American empire to the English. But they recognized that time was running out for them. Not only were the English colonies growing more populous, but they also possessed a seemingly inexhaustible supply of manufactured goods to trade with the Indians. The French decided in the early 1750s, therefore, to seize the Ohio Valley before the Virginians could do so. They established forts throughout the region, the most formidable being Fort Duquesne, located at the strategic fork in the Ohio River and later renamed Pittsburgh.

The French entertained no illusions about their ability to maintain their new line of forts without the cooperation of nearby native peoples. Officials in Quebec sent large quantities of gifts and trade goods, which the forts' commanders could use to forge alliances. The agreements, they hoped, would yield new bundles of pelts and food supplies for the garrisons as well as assistance in arms against the English. The French found many Ohio Delawares and Shawnees eager to cooperate. An alliance with the French would give them a chance to throw off the Iroquois yoke and push back the tide of English settlement.

Although France and England had not officially declared war, British officials advised the governor of Virginia to "repell force by force." The Virginians needed little encouragement. They were eager to make good their claim to the Ohio Valley, and in 1754, militia companies under the command of an ambitious young officer, George Washington, constructed Fort Necessity not far from Fort Duquesne. The plan failed. A joint force of French and Indians—including many newly allied Delaware and Shawnee warriors—overran the badly exposed outpost (July 3, 1754). Among other things, the humiliating setback revealed that a single colony could not defeat the French.

In addition to this setback in the Ohio country, colonial officials also confronted a serious rift in Anglo-Iroquois relations in 1754. The Mohawk leader Hendrick, exasperated with the corruption and fraudulent dealing of Albany merchants and traders, declared broken the Covenant Chain system of alliances that had sustained peace and trade since the previous century (see Chapter 9). "Brother," he declared to New York's Governor Clinton, "you are not to expect to hear of me any more, and Brother we desire to hear no more of you."

The twin crises of renewed French aggression and Anglo-Iroquois tension prompted British colonial leaders to advance an unprecedented proposal for intercolonial cooperation in the summer of 1754. Representatives from the northern colonies met at Albany that June to discuss how to mend relations with the Iroquois. Benjamin Franklin, who traveled to the Albany Congress as Pennsylvania's representative, used the occasion to present a bold blueprint for colonial union. His so-called Albany Plan envisioned the formation of a Grand Council, made up of elected delegates from the various colonies, to oversee matters of common defense, western expansion, and Indian affairs. A President General appointed by the king would preside. Franklin's most daring suggestion involved taxation. He insisted the council be authorized to collect taxes to cover military expenditures.

Albany Congress and Braddock's Defeat

The first reaction to the Albany Plan was enthusiastic. To take effect, however, it required the support of the separate colonial assemblies as well as Parliament. It received neither. Each assembly jealously guarded its own fiscal authority, and the English thought the scheme undermined the crown's power over American affairs.

In 1755, the Ohio Valley again became the scene of fierce fighting. Even though there was still no formal declaration of war, the British resolved to destroy Fort Duquesne, and to that end, they dispatched units of the regular army to America. In command was Major General Edward Braddock, an obese, humorless veteran who inspired neither fear nor respect. One colonist described Braddock as "very indolent, Slave to his passions, women & wine, as great an Epicure as could be in his eating, tho a brave man."

That summer, Braddock led a joint force of 2,500 British Redcoats and colonists to humiliating defeat. For more than a month, Indian scouts had tracked the British as they cut noisily through "an hundred and ten Miles [of] . . . uninhabited Wilderness" toward the new French post. On July 9, a force of French and Indians opened fire as Braddock's army waded across the Monongahela River, about 8 miles from Fort Duquesne. Along a freshly cut road already congested with heavy wagons and confused men, Braddock ordered a counterattack, described by one of his officers as "without any form or order but that of a parcell of school boys coming out of s[c]hool." Nearly 70 percent of Braddock's troops were killed or wounded in western Pennsylvania. The general himself died in battle. The attackers, including many Delaware and Shawnee warriors, suffered only light casualties. The French remained in firm control of the Ohio Valley.

The entire affair profoundly angered Washington, who fumed, "We have been most scandalously beaten by a trifling body of men." The British thought their Iroquois allies might desert them after the embarrassing defeat. The Indians, however, took the news in stride, observing that "they were not at all surprised to hear it, as they [Braddock's Redcoats] were men who had crossed the Great Water and were unacquainted with the arts of war among the Americans."

Seven Years of War

Braddock's defeat shocked British officials on both sides of the Atlantic, yet for the next two years no one in England or America seemed to possess the leadership necessary to respond effectively. French and Indian war parties raided the Pennsylvania and Virginia backcountry at will, devastating frontier communities and pushing back the line of Anglo-American settlement more than 100 miles to the east. Despite this escalating colonial conflict, Great Britain did not issue the declaration that formally began the Seven Years' War until May, 1756.

Braddock's successor in the supreme command, Massachusetts governor William Shirley, prepared for open war with New France by sending two New England battalions and a detachment of regulars to secure the strategic province of Nova Scotia. After capturing the French post of Beauséjour, New Englanders began rounding up and deporting the French-speaking Acadians who had been living there under British rule since 1713 (see Chapter 10). In doing so, Anglo-Americans hoped to defuse a threat to their northern borders as well as to take over rich Acadian farmsteads for resettlement by New Englanders. The "Great Upheaval" proceeded with a brutal efficiency that eventually left Nova Scotia virtually depopulated. Most Acadians found themselves refugees, dispersed to England or the mainland British colonies. Some escaped to the Canadian mainland or Île-St.-Jean (now Prince Edward Island), where they joined forces with Abenakis and Micmacs in an attempt to recapture their homeland. The deportees faced terrible hardship among a hostile Anglo-American population. Many eventually emigrated once again to New Orleans, where they formed the core of Louisiana's Cajun people.

French officials responded to unfolding events in America by sending a detachment of several hundred regular troops under the capable command of Louis-Joseph, Marquis de Montcalm-Gozon de Saint-Véran early in 1756. The cabinet of England's George II (r. 1727–1760) moved more slowly, its members lacking the will to organize and finance a sustained military campaign in the New World. Governor William Shirley fell victim to cabinet intrigues and intercolonial rivalry and was recalled to London in the summer of 1756. Shirley's replacement, John Campbell, Earl of Loudon, quickly learned that even a formal declaration of war, which came on May 18, 1756, was not sufficient to secure colonial cooperation. Indeed, Loudon's high-handed demands for men and money alienated colonial assemblies, impeding his efforts to prosecute the conflict.

Imperial lack of direction coupled with increasing colonial disunity cost Anglo-Americans dearly in the early phase of the Seven Years' War—known to colonists as the French and Indian War. In 1756, the French commander

Montcalm led a combined force of French regulars, Canadian militiamen and *troupes de la marine*, and allied Indians to his first American victory with the capture of Fort Oswego near Lake Ontario.

The magnitude of the French victory over Oswego persuaded an army of 2,000 western Algonquians—representing more than 30 nations from as far away as Lake Superior—to join Montcalm's force of 6,000 French and Canadians for the 1757 campaign against New York. Montcalm led the bulk of this force in a siege of Fort William Henry, which guarded the upper Hudson River valley from its location at the south end of Lake George. On August 9, the fort's commander completed negotiations with Montcalm to surrender the fort with the "honors of war." Defenders would receive safe passage to another British fort, carrying with them their possessions, arms, and colors. The French would care for the wounded until they could be transported home.

Montcalm, however, had made a fatal mistake for the future of Franco-Indian cooperation. His own disdain for allies whom he regarded as barbarians had prompted the French commander to break with historic Canadian policy, excluding Indian leaders from the negotiations over the terms of the fort's surrender. When the victorious Montcalm issued a peremptory order not to take captives, plunder, or trophy scalps, the Algonquians simply ignored this ally who had presumed to act as their overlord. As the British began departing the next day, Algonquian warriors surrounded the provincials near the rear of the retreating column. They seized captives; plundered food, clothing, and weapons; and took scalps from the wounded as battle trophies. The killing and plunder ended within minutes, and the Algonquians departed abruptly for home with what they regarded as just compensation for their part in the campaign.

The "massacre of Fort William Henry" incensed the British, who resolved never again to give the French the honors of war in any future terms of surrender. The incident also confirmed Montcalm in his opinion of Indians as bloodthirsty barbarians and left him determined to avoid further joint campaigns with them. He need not have worried. After experiencing what they regarded as Montcalm's betrayal of their interests, many Algonquians refused to cooperate any further in the war effort. The campaign of 1757 marked the high point of Franco-Indian alliance. From then on, Indian numbers dwindled steadily, leaving the French ever more alone to defend their river empire.

Pitt and Victory

Had it not been for William Pitt, the most powerful minister in George II's cabinet, the Anglo-French contest for empire might have ground down to a stalemate. This supremely self-confident Englishman believed he was the only person capable of saving the British empire, an opinion he publicly expressed. When he became effective head of the ministry in December 1756, Pitt had an opportunity to demonstrate his talents.

In the past, warfare on the European continent had worked mainly to France's advantage. Pitt saw no point in continuing to concentrate on Europe. Even as Fort William Henry fell in 1757, Pitt was advancing a bold new imperial policy based on commercial assumptions. In Pitt's judgment, the critical confrontation would take place in North America, where Britain and France were struggling to control colonial markets and raw materials. Indeed, according to Pitt, America was "where

England and Europe are to be fought for." He was determined, therefore, to expel the French from North America, however great the cost.

To effect this ambitious scheme, Pitt took personal command of the army and navy. He mapped strategy. He even promoted young promising officers over the heads of their superiors. He also recognized that the success of the war effort could not depend on the generosity of the colonial assemblies. Great Britain would have to foot most of the bill. Pitt's military expenditures, of course, created an enormous national debt that would soon haunt both Britain and its colonies, but at the time, no one foresaw the fiscal consequences of victory in America.

To implement his grand campaign, Pitt moved late in 1757 to replace the imperious Lord Loudon with two relatively obscure officers, Jeffrey Amherst and James Wolfe. It was a masterful choice, one that a less self-assured man than Pitt would never have risked. Both officers were young, talented, and ambitious. On July 26, 1758, forces under their direction captured Louisbourg, the same fortress the colonists had taken a decade earlier!

This victory helped cut the Canadians' main supply line with France. The small population of New France could no longer meet the military demands placed on it. As the situation became increasingly desperate, the French forts of the Ohio Valley and the Great Lakes began to fall. Duquesne was simply abandoned late in 1758 as French and Indian troops under the Marquis de Montcalm retreated toward Quebec and Montreal. During the summer of 1759, the French surrendered key forts at Ticonderoga, Crown Point, and Niagara. Their remaining native allies quietly abandoned them to return to their Great Lakes homes or to make peace with the English who now held a permanent presence in the Ohio country.

The climax to a century of war came dramatically in September 1759. Wolfe, now a major general, assaulted Quebec with 9,000 men. But it was not simply force of arms that brought victory. Wolfe proceeded as if he were preparing to attack the city directly, but under cover of darkness, his troops scaled a cliff to dominate a less well defended position. At dawn on September 13, 1759, they took the French from the rear by surprise. The decisive action occurred on the Plains of Abraham, atop a bluff high above the St. Lawrence River. Both Wolfe and Montcalm were mortally wounded. When an aide informed Wolfe the French had been routed, he sighed, "Now, God be praised, I will die in peace."

Bereft of their Indian allies, prevented from reinforcement and supply by the destruction of the French fleet in Europe, New France tottered and fell. An effort to retake Quebec failed in May 1760. During the summer, Amherst sailed up the St. Lawrence with a fleet of troop transports, encountering little effective resistance along the way. On September 8, 1760, Amherst accepted the final surrender of the French army at Montreal.

TROUBLED TRIUMPH

Even as Amherst and Wolf were converging on Quebec in the summer of 1759, British naval and amphibious forces had captured two jewels of France's Caribbean empire, the rich sugar islands of Guadeloupe and Marie-Galante. Another campaign in 1761 secured the island of Martinique. And in 1762, Spain belatedly entered the war as an ally of France only to lose Havana, the key of its Caribbean possessions. The immediate extension of liberal terms to French and Spanish West Indian planters increased British Atlantic commerce by literally millions of pounds sterling during the early 1760s. Yet even as these new Caribbean acquisitions began generating profits and payments on Britain's burgeoning war debt, fresh challenges emerged in the trans-Appalachian West that would reveal the high cost of managing a vast New World empire.

The Cherokee War

The first indication of future trouble in Anglo-Indian relations emerged in the Southeast as Jeffrey Amherst was savoring the fall of Quebec and preparing his final campaign to Montreal. Late in 1759, border strife between Carolina settlers and the Cherokees, up to this point one of South Carolina's most reliable allies, escalated into a full-scale war. Western Carolina settlers had been encroaching on Cherokee hunting grounds and cornfields for several years. In the fall of 1758, however, thirty Cherokee warriors lost their lives to colonial militia as they traveled home from a joint campaign with British forces. Warriors from the Cherokee Lower Towns arrived home to find that colonists from the nearby Long Canes settlement had invaded their hunting grounds. The poaching had cut deeply into supplies of game that the Cherokees needed to survive the winter.

Throughout the summer of 1759, the Cherokees debated what to do as border incidents continued. Finally that fall, nativist warriors conducted retaliatory raids, which claimed the lives of thirty backcountry settlers, a number equal to the number of Cherokees killed the year before. South Carolina governor William Henry Lyttelton responded with an embargo on all gunpowder shipments. The Cherokees, who desperately needed the gunpowder for winter hunts, sent a delegation of chiefs to negotiate with Lyttelton. The governor promptly imprisoned them as hostages until their kinsmen surrendered the warriors who had participated in the raids.

Lyttelton accomplished precisely the opposite of his intention. Rather than cowing the Cherokees into submission, he had managed to remove the moderate chiefs from Cherokee councils. The remaining nativist leaders launched an offensive that by October 1760 pushed the line of colonial settlement back eastward more than 100 miles. It took a combined force of 2,800 British regulars, colonial rangers, and Catawba and Chickasaw warriors to "chastise the Cherokees" during the summer of 1761. Only after months of fighting in the rugged Carolina mountains did the Cherokees submit, compelled by the prospect of a winter without corn to eat, gunpowder for the hunt, or shelter sufficient for a population largely burned out of house and home.

Pontiac's War

Scarcely had the Cherokee War subsided when a fresh threat to British rule appeared in the Ohio country. In 1762, the Delaware prophet Neolin called for a pan-Indian movement dedicated to renouncing European goods and returning to ancient ways of worship, hunting, and cultivation. The prophet's message found a growing audience among western Indians of the Ohio country and the Great Lakes, who had observed the establishment of permanent British garrisons in the region with increasing alarm. They knew from experience that permanent garrisons meant an eventual influx of settlers. Indeed, the new military road to Fort

Pitt was bringing more settlers to western Pennsylvania every year, filling up the region with European competitors for land and game. General Jeffrey Amherst's recent reforms in Indian policy fueled discontent even further. Amherst had known that he would provoke some unrest by instituting new trade regulations and sharply curtailing gifts to native allies but had persuaded himself that the British could no longer afford the expense of lubricating Anglo-Indian relations by the tradition of gift-giving. In any case, Amherst reasoned, the defeat of the French would leave the Indians no choice but to accept the new policy. The British commander-in-chief therefore dismissed as "Meer Bugbears" the rumors of Indian war that filtered toward him in the fall of 1762.

The pan-Indian uprising of 1763 thus took the British high command almost completely by surprise. It began on May 9, when the Ottawa leader Pontiac led a combined force of Ottawa, Potawatomi, Wyandot, and Chippewa warriors to besiege the small British garrison at Fort Detroit. Pontiac had invoked Neolin's teachings in his call for war against the English. Within a month, a vast alliance of Great Lakes peoples had seized thinly manned British garrisons throughout the region—Fort Michilimackinac on the Lake Michigan–Lake Huron straits; Fort St. Joseph near present-day Niles, Michigan; Fort Miami (now Fort Wayne, Indiana); Fort Ouiatenon near present-day Lafayette, Indiana; and Fort Sandusky on the west end of Lake Erie. The garrison commander and troops of the remote Fort Edward Augustus on Green Bay handed over the post to the local Sioux and began an overland trek to British-controlled territory, only to be captured by Ottawa and Chippewa warriors who carried them to Montreal for ransom.

Pontiac kept the British bottled up in Fort Detroit throughout the summer of 1763. Meanwhile, an alliance of Ottawa, Chippewa, and Seneca warriors captured all posts between Fort Niagara and Fort Pitt, while Shawnee, Delaware, and Mingo warriors severed communications between Fort Pitt and eastern Pennsylvania. While the British fumbled to respond, Indians raided almost at will throughout the Pennsylvania and Virginia backcountry. Finally in mid-July, Captain James Dalyell led a 260-man relief convoy to Fort Detroit while Colonel Henry Bouquet marched with 460 troops to relieve Fort Pitt and "extirpate" the native "vermin." Both commanders discovered, however, that their Indian foes would not be pushovers. On July 31, Dalyell lost his life at the Battle of Bloody Run when he led a sortie from Fort Detroit straight into Pontiac's ambush. Bouquet's force narrowly escaped being extirpated itself in a similar ambush at the Battle of Bushy Run Creek. Only brilliant, desperate maneuvering saved his force.

Pontiac finally lifted the siege of Detroit on October 15, after the French commandant in Illinois refused to support the campaign. Realization that the French had relinquished their North American claims prompted some Indian nations to advocate accommodating the English. As divisions among their leaders grew, many Indians slipped homeward to begin the winter hunt. The Ottawa leader's inability to maintain unity or force the English to terms damaged his credibility irreparably. He faded into obscurity and was eventually murdered by a Peoria warrior in April 1769.

The lifting of Pontiac's siege saved Fort Detroit, but Anglo-Indian hostilities dragged on into 1765 before finally coming to an end in a practical victory for the

Indians. The British mistook several lightly opposed operations in 1764 and 1765 as military victories, but the treaties they forged conceded to the Indians all the major issues of Pontiac's war. Anglo-American officials resumed diplomatic gift-giving, ended limitations on trade in arms and ammunition, and reopened the rum trade. The British also established the Proclamation Line of 1763 along the Appalachian fall line to keep white settlers from encroaching further on Indian lands. As normal trade resumed, both sides chose to ignore for the time being the renewed rush of European settlers into the Ohio country.

The Peace of Paris, signed on February 10, 1763, almost fulfilled William Pitt's **Peace** grandiose dreams. Great Britain took possession of an empire that stretched around the globe. Only Guadeloupe and Martinique, the Caribbean sugar islands, were given back to the French. After a century-long struggle, the French had been driven from the mainland of North America. Even Louisiana passed out of France's control into Spanish hands. The treaty gave Great Britain title to Canada, Florida, and all the land east of the Mississippi River. Moreover, with the stroke of a diplomat's pen, 80,000 French-speaking Canadians, most of them Catholics, became British subjects.

The Americans were overjoyed. It was a time of good feelings and national pride. Together, the English and their colonial allies had thwarted the "Gallic peril." Samuel Davies, a Presbyterian who had brought the Great Awakening to Virginia, announced confidently that the long-awaited victory would inaugurate "a new heaven and a new earth."

The Seven Years' War made a deep impression on American society. Even though **Perceptions of** Franklin's Albany Plan had failed, the military struggle had forced the colonists to **War** cooperate on an unprecedented scale. It also drew them into closer contact with Great Britain. They became aware of being part of a great empire, military and commercial, but in the very process of waging war, they acquired a more intimate sense of an America that lay beyond the plantation and the village. Conflict had carried thousands of young men across colonial boundaries, exposing them to a vast territory full of opportunities for a booming population. Moreover, the war trained a corps of American officers, men like George Washington, who learned from firsthand experience that the British were not invincible.

British officials later accused the Americans of ingratitude. England, they claimed, had sent troops and provided funds to liberate the colonists from the threat of French attack. The Americans, appreciative of the aid from England, cheered on the British but dragged their feet at every stage, refusing to pay the bills. These charges were later incorporated into a general argument justifying parliamentary taxation in America.

The British had a point. The colonists were, in fact, slow in providing the men and materials needed to fight the French. Nevertheless, they did make a significant contribution to the war effort, and it was perfectly reasonable for Americans to regard themselves at the very least as junior partners in the empire. After all, they had supplied almost 20,000 soldiers and spent well over £2 million.

North America After 1763

The Peace of Paris (1763) redrew the map of North America. Great Britain received all the French holdings except a few islands in the Atlantic and some sugar-producing islands in the Caribbean.

In a single year, in fact, Massachusetts enlisted 5,000 men out of an adult male population of about 50,000, a commitment that, in the words of the military historian Fred Anderson, meant "the war was being waged on a scale comparable to the great wars of modern times." After making such a sacrifice—indeed, after demonstrating their loyalty to the mother country—the colonists would surely have been disturbed to learn that General James Wolfe, the hero of Quebec, had stated, "The Americans are in general the dirtiest, the most contemptible, cowardly dogs that you can conceive. There is no depending upon them in action. They fall down in their own dirt and desert in battalions, officers and all."

RULE BRITANNIA?

James Thomson, an Englishman, understood the hold of empire on the popular imagination of the eighteenth century. In 1740, he composed words that British patriots have proudly sung for more than two centuries:

> Rule Britannia, rule the waves,
> Britons never will be slaves.

Colonial Americans—at least, those of British background—joined the chorus. By mid-century they took their political and cultural cues from Great Britain. They fought its wars, purchased its consumer goods, flocked to hear its evangelical preachers, and read its many publications. Without question, the empire provided American colonists with a compelling source of identity.

An editor justified the establishment of New Hampshire's first newspaper in precisely these terms. "By this Means," the publisher observed, "the spirited Englishman, the mountainous Welshman, the brave Scotchman, and Irishman, and the loyal American, may be firmly united and mutually RESOLVED to guard the glorious Throne of BRITANNIA . . . as British Brothers, in defending the Common Cause." Even new immigrants, the Germans, Scots-Irish, and Africans, who felt no political loyalty to Great Britain and no affinity to English culture, had to assimilate to some degree to the dominant English culture of the colonies.

Americans hailed Britannia. In 1763, the colonists were the victors, the conquerors of the backcountry. In their moment of glory, the colonists assumed that Britain's rulers saw the Americans as "Brothers," as equal partners in the business of empire. Only slowly would they learn that the British had a different perception. For them, "American" was a way of saying "not quite English."

CHRONOLOGY

1739	War of Jenkins's Ear begins.
1741	British-led siege of Cartagena fails.
1742	Battle of Bloody Marsh halts Spanish campaign against Frederica, Georgia.
1743	War of the Austrian Succession (King George's War) begins.
1745	British American colonial troops capture Louisbourg.
1748	Treaty of Aix-la-Chapelle concludes King George's War.
1754	Albany Congress meets; Virginians under George Washington defeated at Fort Necessity in Pennsylvania.
1755	Braddock defeated by French and Indians in western Pennsylvania.
1756	Seven Years' War formally declared.

1757	Fort William Henry falls to the French.
1759	British victorious at Quebec, Wolfe and Montcalm killed in battle; Cherokee War breaks out in the Carolinas.
1760	George III becomes king of Great Britain.
1762	British forces capture Havana.
1763	Peace of Paris ends French and Indian War; Pontiac's Uprising in Great Lakes, cis-Mississippi West.

RECOMMENDED READING

Eighteenth-century Atlantic political culture, in theory and practice, is the subject of an increasingly sophisticated literature. A thoughtful comparative study of European empires in the New World is available in Anthony Pagden's *Lords of All the World: Ideologies of Empire in Spain, Britain, and France* (New Haven, 1995). On eighteenth-century Britain, see Linda Colley, *Britons: Forging the Nation, 1707–1837* (New Haven, 1992); Lawrence Stone, ed., *An Imperial State at War: Britain from 1689 to 1815* (1994); John Brewer, *The Sinews of Power: War, Money, and the English State* (New York, 1989); and Colin Kidd, *British Identities Before Nationalism: Ethnicity and Nationhood in the Atlantic World, 1600–1800* (Cambridge, 1999). The relationship between Parliament and the colonial governments of the eighteenth-century British empire is explored in Philip Lawson, ed., *Parliament and the Atlantic Empire* (Edinburgh, 1995).

How colonial British Americans perceived politics, both in their own assemblies and in Parliament, is discussed in Bernard Bailyn, *The Origins of American Politics* (1968); and Jack P. Green, *Quest for Power: The Lower Houses of Assembly in the Southern Royal Colonies, 1689–1776* (New York, 1983) and *Peripheries and Center: Constitutional Development in the Extended Politics of the British Empire and the United States, 1607–1788* (Athens, 1986). The best study of how Indians and British colonists negotiated power within the empire is Timothy Shannon, *Indians and Colonists at the Crossroads of Empire: The Albany Congress of 1754* (Ithaca, 2000).

The impact of the contest for empire on Native American leadership is discussed in a growing number of excellent studies. Richard White's *The Middle Ground: Indians, Empires, and Republics in the Great Lakes Region, 1650–1815* (Cambridge, 1991) explores the impact of imperial contest on the Algonquians of the Great Lakes, while Michael N. McConnell, *A Country Between: The Upper Ohio Valley and Its Peoples, 1724–1774* (Lincoln, 1992) examines shifting power and alliances in the Ohio country. Gregory Evans Dowd, *A Spirited Resistance: The North American Indian Struggle for Unity, 1745–1815* (Baltimore, 1992), examines successive eighteenth-century efforts to form pan-Indian alliances in the Great Lakes and Ohio country. Discussions of political change within individual confederations include Daniel K. Richter, *The Ordeal of the Longhouse: The Peoples of the Iroquois League in the Era of European Colonization* (Chapel Hill, 1992); Tom Hatley, *The Dividing Paths: Cherokees and South Carolinians through the Revolutionary Era* (New York, 1995); and Claudio Saunt, *A New Order of*

Things: Property, Power, and the Transformation of the Creek Indians, 1733–1816 (Cambridge, 1999). For Pontiac's War see Gregory Evans Dowd, *War Under Heaven: Pontiac, Indian Nations, and the British Empire* (Baltimore, 2002).

Fred Anderson offers the most complete treatment of war and empire in *Crucible of War: The Seven Years' War and the Fate of Empire in British North America, 1754–1766* (New York, 2000). For the removal of the Acadians, see Carl Brasseaux, *Scattered to the Wind: Dispersal and Wanderings of the Acadians, 1755–1809* (Lafayette, La., 1991). For war in the eighteenth-century Caribbean, see Richard Harding, *Amphibious Warfare in the Eighteenth Century: The British Expeditions to the West Indies, 1740–42* (Woodbridge, Conn., 1991), and Richard Pares, *War and Trade in the West Indies, 1739–1763* (Oxford, 1936). For an analysis of Pontiac's uprising from the British perspective, see William R. Nester, *"Haughty Conquerors": Amherst and the Great Indian Uprising of 1763* (Westport, Conn., 2000).

Index